INTRODUCTORY
ALGEBRA

Custom Edition for
Mercer County Community College

Taken from:

Introductory Algebra through Applications
by Geoffrey Akst and Sadie Bragg

PEARSON
Custom
Publishing

PEARSON
Addison
Wesley

Cover Art: *Riverdance*, by Angela Sciaraffa

Taken from:

Introductory Algebra through Applications
by Geoffrey Akst and Sadie Bragg
Copyright © 2005 by Pearson Education, Inc.
Published by Addison Wesley
Boston, Massachusetts 02116

This special edition published in cooperation with Pearson Custom Publishing.

Printed in the United States of America

10 9 8 7 6 5 4 3 2 1

ISBN 0-536-96605-2

2005360487

TW

Please visit our web site at *www.pearsoncustom.com*

PEARSON CUSTOM PUBLISHING
75 Arlington Street, Suite 300, Boston, MA 02116
A Pearson Education Company

Contents

Preface

From the Authors

Our goal in writing *Introductory Algebra through Applications* was to help motivate students and to establish a strong foundation for their success in a developmental mathematics program. The text, in addition to a review of arithmetic, deals with the major topics in a college elementary algebra course: real numbers and algebraic expressions, solving linear equations and inequalities both algebraically and by graphing, systems of linear equations, exponents and polynomials, factoring, quadratic equations, rational expressions and equations, and radical expressions and equations. In contrast to many other texts, graphing is not relegated to a late chapter, a recognition of the value of visualizing mathematical relationships in fostering understanding.

For all these topics, we have carefully selected interdisciplinary applications that we believe are relevant, interesting, and motivating. This thoroughly integrated emphasis on applications reflects our view that college students need to master the mathematics in a developmental mathematics program not so much for its own sake but rather to be able to apply this understanding to their everyday lives and to the demands of subsequent college courses.

Our goal throughout the text has been to address many of the issues raised by the American Mathematical Association of Two-Year Colleges and the National Council of Teachers of Mathematics by writing a flexible, approachable, and readable text that reflects

- an emphasis on applications that model real-world situations;
- explanations that foster conceptual understanding;
- exercises with connections to other disciplines;
- the use of real data in charts, tables, and graphs to help develop quantitative literacy;
- the appropriate use of technology;
- the integration of geometric visualization with concepts and applications; and
- exercises in student writing and groupwork that encourage interactive and collaborative learning.

The following key content and key features stem from our strong belief that mathematics is logical, useful, and fun.

Key Content

Applications One of the main reasons to study mathematics is its application to a wide range of disciplines, to a variety of occupations, and to everyday situations. Each chapter begins with a real-world application to show the usefulness of the topic under discussion and to motivate student interest. These opening applications vary widely, and include getting rich with graphing, layoffs and polynomials, and rational expressions and grapes (see pages 31, 375, and 529). Also, applications are highlighted in section exercise sets with an Applications heading (see pages 54, 128, and 413).

Concepts Explanations in each section foster intuition by promoting student understanding of underlying concepts. To stress these concepts, we included discovery-type exercises on reasoning and pattern recognition that encourage students to be logical in their problem-solving techniques, promote self-confidence, and allow students with varying learning styles to be successful (see pages 64, 226, and 414–5).

Skills Practice is necessary to reinforce and maintain skills. In addition to comprehensive chapter problem sets, chapter review exercises include mixed applications, requiring students to use skills learned in previous sections and chapters (see pages 116, 307, and 463).

Writing Writing both enhances and demonstrates students' understanding of concepts and skills. In addition to the user-friendly worktext format, open-ended questions throughout the text give students the opportunity to explain their answers in full sentences. Students can build on these questions by keeping individual journals (see pages 33, 271, and 355).

Use of Geometry Students need to develop their abilities to visualize and compare objects. Throughout this text, students have opportunities to use geometric concepts and drawings to solve problems (see pages 121, 180, and 423).

 Use of Technology Each student should be familiar with a range of problem-solving techniques—mental, paper-and-pencil, and calculator-based—depending on the problem and the student's level of mathematical preparation. This text includes optional calculator inserts (see pages 271, 327, and 401), which provide explanations for calculator techniques. These inserts also feature paired side-by-side examples and practice exercises (see pages 52, 398, and 461). At the end of the text is an Introduction to Calculators that combines and extends the calculator inserts.

Key Features

Side-by-Side Example/Practice Format A distinctive side-by-side format pairs each numbered example with a corresponding practice exercise, encouraging students to get actively involved in the mathematical content from the start. Examples are immediately followed by solutions so that students can have a ready guide to follow as they work (see pages 58, 145, and 326).

Cultural Notes To show how mathematics has evolved over the centuries—in many cultures and throughout the world—each chapter features a compelling Cultural Note that investigates and illustrates the origins of mathematical concepts. Cultural notes give students further evidence that mathematics grew out of a universal need to find efficient solutions to everyday problems. Diverse topics include the use of the letter x to represent something mysterious, the discovery of the coordinate plane by the Frenchman Descartes, and the early work done by al-Khwarizmi in developing algebra (see pages 216, 363, and 416).

Mindstretchers   For every appropriate section in the text, exercises on related investigations, critical thinking, mathematical reasoning, pattern recognition, Web-based research, and writing—along with corresponding groupwork and historical connections—are incorporated into one broad-ranged problem set called Mindstretchers. Mindstretchers target different levels and types of student understanding and can be used for enrichment, homework, or extra credit (see pages 72, 213, and 414–5).

Tips   Throughout the text, students will find these helpful suggestions for understanding certain concepts, skills, or rules, and advice on avoiding common mistakes (see pages 74, 176, and 345).

Pretests and Posttests   To promote individualized learning—particularly in a self-paced or lab environment—pretests and posttests help students gauge their level of understanding of chapter topics both at the beginning and at the end of each chapter. The pretests and posttests also allow students to assess their own strengths and weaknesses, targeting topics for which they may need to do extra work to achieve mastery. All answers to pretests and posttests are given in the answer section of the student edition.

Section Objectives   At the beginning of each section, clearly stated learning objectives help students and instructors identify and organize individual competencies covered in the upcoming content.

For Extra Help   Several valuable study aids accompany this text. Located at the top of the first page of every section exercise set are references to the appropriate videotape and CD, the tutorial software, the Addison-Wesley Math Tutor Center, and the *Student's Solutions Manual,* to make it easy for students to find the correct support materials.

Key Concepts and Skills   At the end of each chapter, a comprehensive chart organized by section relates the key concepts and skills to a corresponding description and example, giving students a unique tool to help them review and translate the main points of the chapter.

Chapter Review Exercises   Following the Key Concepts and Skills at the end of each chapter, a variety of relevant exercises organized by section helps students test their comprehension of the chapter content. As mentioned earlier, included in these exercises are mixed applications, which give students an opportunity to practice their reasoning skills by requiring them to choose and apply an appropriate problem-solving method (see pages 113, 303, and 460).

Cumulative Review Exercises   At the end of Chapter 2, and for every chapter thereafter, Cumulative Review Exercises help students maintain and build on the skills learned in previous chapters.

Supplements for the Student

Student's Solutions Manual (ISBN 0-201-66229-9)
This useful manual contains solutions to all odd-numbered exercises in each exercise set and solutions to all chapter pretests and posttests, practice exercises, review exercises, and cumulative review exercises.

Videotapes (ISBN 0-201-70727-6)

The videotapes feature an engaging team of mathematics instructors who present comprehensive coverage of each section of the text. The lecturers' presentations include examples and exercises from the text and support an approach that emphasizes visualization and problem solving. The videos include a stop-the-tape feature that encourages students to pause the video, work through the example presented on their own, and then resume play to watch the lecturer explain the solution.

Digital Video Tutor (ISBN 0-321-23715-3)

The video lectures for this text are also available on CD-ROM, making it easy and convenient for students to watch the videos from a computer at home or on campus. The complete, digitized video set, affordable and portable for students, is ideal for distance learning or supplemental instruction.

MathXL® Tutorials on CD-ROM (ISBN 0-201-70722-5)

This interactive tutorial CD-ROM provides algorithmically generated practice exercises that are correlated at the objective level to the exercises in the textbook. Every practice exercise is accompanied by an example and a guided solution designed to involve students in the solution process. Selected problems may also include a video clip to help students visualize concepts. The software tracks student activity and scores and can generate printed summaries of students' progress.

Addison-Wesley Math Tutor Center

The Addison-Wesley Math Tutor Center is staffed by qualified mathematics and statistics instructors who provide students with tutoring on examples and odd-numbered exercises from the textbook. Tutoring is available via toll-free telephone, toll-free fax, e-mail, and the Internet. Interactive, Web-based technology allows tutors and students to view and work through problems together in real time over the Internet. For more information, please visit our Web site at www.aw-bc.com/tutorcenter or call us at 1-888-777-0463.

MathXL®: www.mathxl.com

MathXL® is a powerful, online homework, tutorial, and assessment system that accompanies your Addison-Wesley textbook in mathematics or statistics. With MathXL, instructors can create, edit, and assign online homework and tests using algorithmically generated exercises correlated at the objective level to your textbook. All student work is tracked in MathXL's online gradebook. Students can take chapter tests in MathXL and receive personalized study plans based on their test results. The study plan diagnoses weaknesses and links students directly to tutorial exercises for the objectives they need to study and retest. Students can also access supplemental animations and video clips directly from selected exercises. For more information, visit our Web site at www.mathxl.com.

MyMathLab®

MyMathLab® is a complete online course designed to help you succeed in learning and understanding mathematics. MyMathLab contains an online version of your textbook with links to multimedia resources—such as video clips, practice exercises, and animations—that are correlated to the examples and exercises in the text. MyMathLab also provides you with online homework and tests and generates a personalized study plan based on your test results. Your study plan links directly to unlimited practice exercises for the areas you need to study and retest, so you can practice until you have mastered the skills and concepts in your textbook. All of the online homework, tests, and practice work you do is tracked in your MyMathLab gradebook. For more information, visit our Web site at www.mymathlab.com.

For more information on these and other helpful supplements published by Addison-Wesley, please contact your bookstore.

Supplements for the Instructor (available to qualifying adopters)

Annotated Instructor's Edition (ISBN 0-201-66225-6)
The annotated version of the student text includes answers to all exercises printed in blue on the same page as those exercises. Teaching tips in each chapter provide instructors with alternative explanations and approaches, typical student misconceptions, and connections to previous and future topics to consider conveying to their students, including annotations for suggested student journal entries (see pages 33, 86, and 203).

Instructor's Solutions Manual (ISBN 0-201-70726-8)
This manual contains worked-out solutions to every even-numbered text exercise as well as solutions to Mindstretcher exercises.

Printed Test Bank/Instructor's Resource Guide (ISBN 0-201-70725-X)
This supplement includes four different versions of chapter tests for every chapter, and two final exams.

Adjunct Support Manual (ISBN 0-321-27793-7)
This manual includes resources designed to help both new and adjunct faculty with course preparation and classroom management, and offers helpful teaching tips.

TestGen with QuizMaster dual-platform CD-ROM (ISBN 0-201-70724-1)
TestGen enables instructors to build, edit, print, and administer tests using a computerized bank of questions developed to cover all the objectives of the test. TestGen is algorithmically based, allowing instructors to create multiple, but equivalent, versions of the same question or test with the click of a button. Instructors can also modify test bank questions or add new questions by using the built-in question editor, which allows users to create graphs, import graphics, and insert math notation, variable numbers, or text. Tests can be printed or administered online via the Internet or another network. TestGen comes packaged with QuizMaster, which allows students to take tests on a local area network. The software is available on a dual-platform Windows/Macintosh CD-ROM.

MyMathLab®
MyMathLab® is a series of text-specific, easily customizable online courses for Addison-Wesley textbooks in mathematics and statistics. MyMathLab is powered by CourseCompass®—Pearson Education's online teaching and learning environment—and by MathXL®—our online homework, tutorial, and assessment system. MyMathLab gives you the tools you need to deliver all or a portion of your course online, whether your students are in a lab setting or working from home. MyMathLab provides a rich and flexible set of course materials, featuring free-response exercises that are algorithmically generated for unlimited practice and mastery. Students can also use online tools, such as video lectures, animations, and a multimedia textbook, to

independently improve their understanding and performance. Instructors can use MyMathLab's homework and test managers to select and assign online exercises correlated directly to the textbook, and they can import TestGen tests into MyMathLab for added flexibility. MyMathLab's online gradebook—designed specifically for mathematics and statistics—automatically tracks students' homework and test results and gives the instructor control over how to calculate final grades. Instructors can also add offline (paper-and-pencil) grades to the MathXL gradebook. MyMathLab is available to qualified adopters. For more information, visit our Web site at www.mymathlab.com or contact your Addison-Wesley sales representative for a live demonstration.

Acknowledgments

We are grateful to everyone who has helped to shape this textbook by responding to questionnaires and by reviewing the manuscript. We wish to thank all of you, especially the following reviewers:

Sheila Anderson, Housatonic Community College
James J. Ball, Indiana State University
Mike Benningfield, Paris Junior College
Amanda Bertagnolli-Comstock, Bishop State Community College
Donald M. Carr, College of the Desert
Alison Carter, California State University, Hayward
Karla Childs, Pittsburgh State University
O. Pauline Chow, Harrisburg Area Community College
Susi Curl, McCook Community College
Karena Curtis, Labette Community College
Lucy Edwards, Las Positas College
Gene Forster, Southeastern Illinois College
Naomi Gibbs, Pitt Community College
Tim Hagopian, Worcester State College
Anthony Hearn, Community College of Philadelphia
Lori Holdren, Manatee Community College
Marlene Ignacio, Pierce College-Puyallup
Marilyn Jacobi, Gateway Community College
John Jacobs, Mass Bay Community College
Mary Ann Klicka, Bucks County Community College
Sandy Lanoue, Tulsa Community College
Ken Mead, Genesee Community College
Kimberly McHale, Columbia College
Debbie Moran, Greenville Technical College
Carol Phillips-Bey, Cleveland State University
Nancy Ressler, Oakton Community College
Richard Sturgeon, University of Southern Maine
Marcia Swope, Nova Southeastern University
Jane Tanner, Onondaga Community College
Betty Vix Weinberger, Delgado Community College
Cora S. West, Florida Community College at Jacksonville
Mary Wolyniak, Broome Community College

Writing a textbook requires the contributions of many individuals. Special thanks go to Greg Tobin, our publisher at Addison-Wesley, for encouraging and supporting us throughout the entire process. We are very grateful to Elka Block and Laura Wheel, our developmental editors, who assisted us in more ways than one could imagine and whose unwavering support made our work more manageable. We thank Maureen O'Connor, Editor in Chief, for her constant support and advice; Kari Heen, Executive Project Manager, for her patience and tact in gently reminding us of deadlines; Jennifer Crum, Acquisitions Editor, for believing in us from the beginning; Lauren Morse, Project Editor, and Katie Nopper, Assistant Editor, for attending to the endless details connected with the project; Ron Hampton, Managing Editor, for his support throughout the production process; Dennis Schaefer, Designer, for the text and cover design; Dona Kenly and Jay Jenkins, marketing managers, for their marketing expertise; and the entire Addison-Wesley developmental mathematics team for helping to make this text one of which we are very proud.

Geoffrey Akst   Sadie Bragg
gakst@bmcc.cuny.edu   sbragg@bmcc.cuny.edu

*This book is dedicated to our sisters,
Harriet Young and Maxine Jefferson.*

Walk-Through

Chapter 2
Solving Linear Equations and Inequalities

Cell Phones and Algebra

Today's generation takes wireless communication for granted. The cellular telephone, one of the more important wireless devices, was first introduced to the public in the mid-1980s. Since then, cell phones have shrunk both in size and in price.

Using a cell phone generally entails choosing a calling plan with a monthly service charge. As a rule, this charge consists of two parts: a specified flat monthly fee and a per-minute usage charge varying with the number of minutes of airtime used.

The choice among calling plans can be confusing, especially with the lure of promotional incentives. One nationally advertised calling plan requires a monthly charge of $34.99 for 300 minutes of free local calls and 79 cents per minute for additional local calls. A competing plan is for $29.99 a month for 200 minutes of free local calls plus 49 cents a minute for additional local calls. Under what circumstances is one deal better than the other? The key to answering this question is solving inequalities such as

$$34.99 + 0.79(x - 300) < 29.99 + 0.49(x - 200).$$

119

Chapter Openers:

The focus of this textbook is applications, and you will find them everywhere—in the chapter openers, in the explanation of the material, in the examples, and in the exercise sets. Each chapter opener introduces students to the material that lies ahead through an interesting and real career application, in an effort to grab students' attention and help them understand the relevance of mathematics to their lives and different careers. (p. 119)

Chapter 2 Pretest

To see if you have already mastered the topics in this chapter, take this test.

1. Is 4 is a solution of the equation $7 - 2x = 3x - 11$?

2. Solve and check: $n + 2 = -6$

3. Solve and check: $\frac{y}{-5} = 1$

4. Solve and check: $-n = 8$

5. Solve and check: $\frac{2}{3}x - 3 = -9$

6. Solve and check: $4x - 8 = -10$

7. Solve and check: $6 - y = -5$

8. Solve and check: $9x + 13 = 7x + 19$

9. Solve and check: $-2(3n - 1) = -7n$

10. Solve and check: $14x - (8x - 13) = 12x + 3$

11. Solve $v - 5u = w$ for v in terms of u and w.

12. 9 is what percent of 36?

13. 60% of what number is 12?

14. Draw the graph of $x \le 2$.

$$\xleftarrow{\quad}\!\!\!\underset{-3\,-2\,-1\ \ 0\ \ 1\ \ 2\ \ 3}{+\!+\!+\!+\!+\!+\!+}\!\!\!\xrightarrow{\quad}$$

15. Solve and graph: $x + 3 > 3$

$$\xleftarrow{\quad}\!\!\!\underset{-3\,-2\,-1\ \ 0\ \ 1\ \ 2\ \ 3}{+\!+\!+\!+\!+\!+\!+}\!\!\!\xrightarrow{\quad}$$

16. An office photocopier makes 30 copies per minute. How long will it take to copy a 360-page document?

17. A florist charges a flat fee of $100 plus $70 for each centerpiece for a wedding. If the total bill for the centerpieces was $1500, how many centerpieces did the florist make?

18. The formula for finding the amount of kinetic energy used is $E = \frac{1}{2}mv^2$. Solve this equation for m in terms of E and v.

19. A certain amount of money was invested in two different accounts. The amount invested at 8% simple interest was twice the amount invested at 5% simple interest. If the total interest earned on the investments was $420, how much was invested at each rate?

20. A gym offers two membership options: Option A is $55 per month for unlimited use of the gym and Option B is $10 per month plus $3 for each hour you use the gym. For how many hours of use per month will Option A be a better deal?

● *Check your answers on page A-4.*

120

Pretests:

Pretests, found at the beginning of each chapter, help students to gauge their understanding of the chapter ahead. Answers can be found in the back of the book. (p. 120)

Student Tips:

These insightful tips help students avoid common errors and provide other helpful suggestions to foster understanding of the material at hand. (p. 74)

Geometry:

The authors integrate this important topic, where appropriate, throughout the text so students can see its relevance to their surroundings.

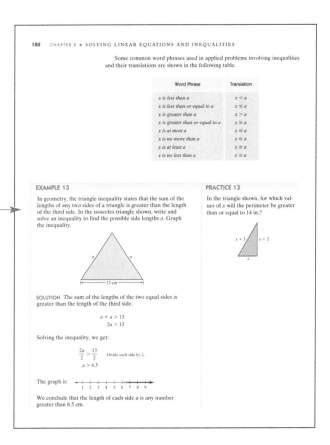

Teaching Tips:

These tips, found only in the Annotated Instructor's Edition, help instructors with explanations, reminders of previously covered material, and tips on encouraging students to write in a journal.

Side-by-Side Format:

A unique side-by-side format pairs examples with corresponding practice exercises, encouraging active learning from the start. Students use this format for solving skill exercises, application problems, and technology exercises throughout the text.

Writing Exercises:

Students understand a concept better if they have to explain it in their own words. Journal assignments (provided in the Teaching Tips) give students an opportunity to improve their mathematical vocabulary and communication skills, thus improving their understanding of mathematical concepts.

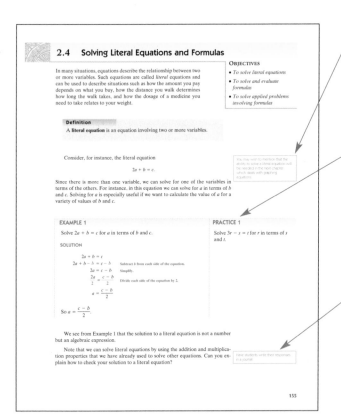

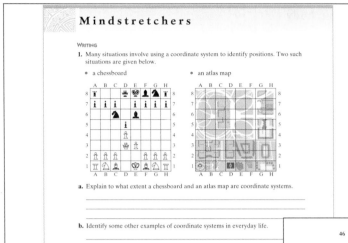

Mindstretchers:

At the end of almost every section, students find these engaging activities that incorporate related investigation, critical thinking, mathematical reasoning, pattern recognition, and writing exercises along with corresponding groupwork and historical connections in one comprehensive problem set. These problem sets target different levels and types of student understanding. (p. 213)

Cultural Notes:

In an effort to get students to realize that mathematics was created out of a need to solve problems in everyday life, Cultural Notes investigate the origins of mathematical concepts, discussing and illustrating the evolution of mathematics over the centuries, in many cultures, and throughout the world. (p. 46)

Technology Inserts:

In order to familiarize students with a range of problem-solving methods—mental, paper-and-pencil, and calculator arithmetic—the authors include optional technology inserts that instruct students on how to use the scientific calculator to perform arithmetic operations. Note that even in these inserts, the authors use their side-by-side format to provide consistency in the students' learning environment. (p. 398)

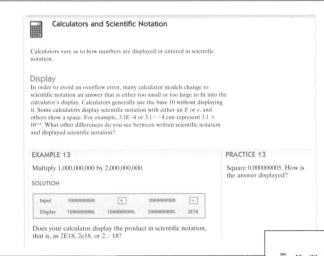

Calculator Exercises:

These optional exercises can be found in the exercise sets, giving students the opportunity to use a calculator to solve a variety of real-life applications. (p. 414)

49. The number of U.S. radio stations with a rock music format is approximated by the polynomial $1.68x^3 + 9.95x^2 - 11.6x + 730$, where x represents the number of years since 1999. To the nearest whole number, estimate the number of U.S. radio stations with a rock music format in 2003. (*Source:* M Street Corporation)

50. The number (in thousands) of U.S. households with cable television can be approximated by the expression $24.5t^3 - 253t^2 + 2043t + 60{,}920$, where t represents the number of years since 1995. According to this model, how many U.S. households were there with cable television in 2004? (*Source: Statistical Abstract of the United States*)

For Extra Help:

These boxes, found at the top of the first page of every section excercise set, direct students to helpful resources to aid in their study of the material.

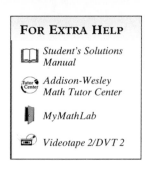

End-of-Chapter Material:

In order to reinforce the concepts presented in current and previous chapters, the authors provide a wealth of end-of-chapter material designed to help students retain the concepts they have learned.

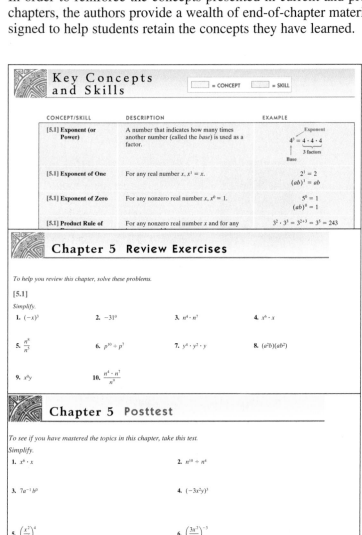

Key Concepts and Skills

☐ = CONCEPT ☐ = SKILL

CONCEPT/SKILL	DESCRIPTION	EXAMPLE
[5.1] **Exponent (or Power)**	A number that indicates how many times another number (called the *base*) is used as a factor.	$4^3 = 4 \cdot 4 \cdot 4$
[5.1] **Exponent of One**	For any real number x, $x^1 = x$.	$2^1 = 2$ $(ab)^1 = ab$
[5.1] **Exponent of Zero**	For any nonzero real number x, $x^0 = 1$.	$5^0 = 1$ $(ab)^0 = 1$
[5.1] **Product Rule of**	For any nonzero real number x and for any	$3^2 \cdot 3^3 = 3^{2+3} = 3^5 = 243$

Chapter 5   Review Exercises

To help you review this chapter, solve these problems.

[5.1]

Simplify.

1. $(-x)^3$
2. -31^0
3. $n^4 \cdot n^7$
4. $x^6 \cdot x$
5. $\dfrac{n^8}{n^5}$
6. $p^{10} \div p^7$
7. $y^4 \cdot y^2 \cdot y$
8. $(a^2 b)(ab^2)$
9. $x^0 y$
10. $\dfrac{n^4 \cdot n^7}{n^9}$

Chapter 5   Posttest

To see if you have mastered the topics in this chapter, take this test.

Simplify.

1. $x^6 \cdot x$
2. $n^{10} \div n^4$
3. $7a^{-1} b^0$
4. $(-3x^2 y)^3$
5. $\left(\dfrac{x^2}{y^3}\right)^4$
6. $\left(\dfrac{3x^2}{y}\right)^{-3}$

Cumulative Review Exercises

To help you review, solve the following.

1. Solve $y = mx + b$ for m.
2. Evaluate $3a^2 - 5ab + b^2$ for $a = -3$ and $b = 2$.
3. Solve for x: $2x + 12 - 9x = 5(4 - 3x) + 6x$
4. Find the slope and y-intercept of the line $2x - 3y = 6$.
5. Graph the inequality: $y < 2x + 1$.
6. Solve by elimination:
$$3x - 2y = 10$$
$$2x + 3y = -2$$

Key Concepts and Skills:

These give students a quick overview of what they have learned in the chapter. Each concept/skill is keyed to the section in which it was introduced, and a brief description and example are provided for a one-stop quick review of the chapter material.

Chapter Review Exercises:

These exercises are keyed to the corresponding sections for easy student reference. Numerous mixed application problems complete each of these exercise sets, always keeping the focus on the applicability of what students are learning.

Chapter Posttest:

Just as every chapter begins with a Pretest to gauge student understanding BEFORE attempting the material, every chapter ends with a Posttest to measure student understanding AFTER completing the chapter material. Answers to these tests are provided in the back of the book.

Cumulative Review Exercises:

Beginning with the end of Chapter 2, students have the opportunity to maintain their skills by completing the Cumulative Review Exercises. These exercises are invaluable, especially when students need to recall a previously learned concept or skill before beginning the next chapter, or when studying for midterm and final examinations.

Introductory Algebra
through Applications

Chapter R

Prealgebra Review

Why a Review of Prealgebra Topics Is Important

This chapter is a brief review of the major procedures, concepts, and vocabulary in basic mathematics that you will need to succeed in working through this text. The results of the pretest that you have just taken will help you to pinpoint topics that you need to review. For these topics, study the explanations and worked-out examples and then solve the related practice problems and exercises until you have mastered the material.

Knowledge of basic mathematics is important to the study of algebra not only for calculating the value of arithmetic expressions but also for understanding algebraic procedures that are based on arithmetic procedures. For instance, familiarity with adding numerical fractions puts you one step ahead when learning how to add algebraic fractions.

In this chapter, we assume that you are proficient in whole-number arithmetic. Accordingly, we begin with a discussion of exponents and order of operations. Then we consider factors, primes, and least common multiples. These topics are needed for working with fractions—the focus of the following section. Next comes a brief review of decimals and finally percent conversions.

If you find that you need to delve more deeply into any particular arithmetic topic, take the initiative of exploring what resources—books, print material, tutoring, computer software, or videos—are available at your college to support your personal arithmetic review. You will benefit from doing this sooner rather than later.

OBJECTIVES

- *To review exponents and order of operations*
- *To review factors, primes, and least common multiples*
- *To review fractions*
- *To review decimals*
- *To review percent conversions*
- *To review applications of basic mathematics*

Chapter R Pretest

To see if you have already mastered the topics in this chapter, take this test.

1. Rewrite $7 \cdot 7 \cdot 7$ as a power of 7.

2. Compute: $2^4 \cdot 5^2$

3. Simplify: $16 - 2^3$

4. Find the value of $20 - 2(3 - 1^2)$.

5. What are the factors of 12?

6. Rewrite 20 as a product of prime factors.

7. Write $\frac{16}{24}$ in simplest form.

8. Find the sum: $\dfrac{3}{10} + \dfrac{1}{10}$

9. Subtract: $10\frac{1}{3} - 2\frac{5}{6}$

10. Find the product of $\frac{2}{9}$ and $\frac{2}{3}$.

11. Calculate: $4 \div 1\frac{1}{2}$

12. Write 9.013 in words.

13. Round 3.072 to the nearest tenth.

14. Find the sum: $7 + 4.01 + 9.3003$

15. Find the difference: $8 - 2.34$

16. What is the product of 9.23 and 4.1?

17. Evaluate: 0.235×100

18. What is 0.045 divided by 0.25?

19. Compute: $\dfrac{3.1}{1000}$

20. What is the decimal equivalent of 7%?

21. A university launched a campaign to collect \$3 million to build a new dormitory. If \$1.316 million has been collected so far, how much more money, to the nearest million dollars, is needed?

22. Yesterday, you swam $\frac{2}{3}$ of a mile. This morning, you swam $\frac{1}{2}$ that distance. How far did you swim this morning?

23. A doctor increases your daily dosage of thyroxin from 0.05 mg to 0.1 mg. The new dosage is how many times as great as the previous dosage?

24. Snow weighs 0.1 as much as water. Express this decimal as a percent.

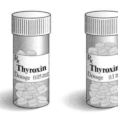

25. About 95% of all animal species on Earth are insects. Express this percent as a decimal.

• Check your answers on page A-1.

R.1 Exponents and Order of Operations

Exponents

There are many mathematical situations in which we multiply a number by itself repeatedly. Writing such expressions using *exponents* (or *powers*) provides a short-hand method for representing this repeated multiplication of the same factor:

$$\underbrace{5 \cdot 5 \cdot 5 \cdot 5}_{4 \text{ factors of } 5} = 5^{\text{←exponent}}_{\text{└base}}$$

The expression 5^4 is read "5 to the fourth power" or simply "5 to the fourth."

To evaluate 5^4, we multiply 4 factors of 5:

$$5^4 = \underbrace{5 \cdot 5} \cdot 5 \cdot 5$$
$$= \underbrace{25 \cdot 5} \cdot 5$$
$$= \underbrace{125 \cdot 5}$$
$$= 625$$

So $5^4 = 625$.

Sometimes we prefer to shorten expressions by using exponents. For instance,

$$\underbrace{3 \cdot 3}_{2 \text{ factors of } 3} \cdot \underbrace{4 \cdot 4 \cdot 4}_{3 \text{ factors of } 4} = 3^2 \cdot 4^3$$

EXAMPLE 1	PRACTICE 1
Rewrite $6 \cdot 6 \cdot 6$ using exponents.	Write $2 \cdot 2 \cdot 2 \cdot 2 \cdot 2$ as a power of 2.
SOLUTION $\quad \underbrace{6 \cdot 6 \cdot 6}_{3 \text{ factors of } 6} = 6^3$	

EXAMPLE 2	PRACTICE 2
Calculate $4^3 \cdot 5^3$.	Compute $7^2 \cdot 2^4$.
SOLUTION $\quad 4^3 \cdot 5^3 = (4 \cdot 4 \cdot 4) \cdot (5 \cdot 5 \cdot 5)$ $= 64 \cdot 125$ $= 8000$	

It is especially easy to compute powers of 10:

$$10^2 = \underbrace{10 \cdot 10}_{\text{2 factors}} = \underbrace{100}_{\text{2 zeros}}$$

$$10^3 = \underbrace{10 \cdot 10 \cdot 10}_{\text{3 factors}} = \underbrace{1000}_{\text{3 zeros}}$$

and so on.

EXAMPLE 3	PRACTICE 3
The distance from the Sun to the star Alpha-one Crucis is about 1,000,000,000,000,000 miles. Express this number as a power of 10.	In 1850, the world population was approximately 1,000,000,000. Represent this number as a power of 10. (**Source:** *World Almanac and Book of Facts 2000*)

SOLUTION $\underbrace{1,000,000,000,000,000}_{\text{15 zeros}} = 10^{15}$ (miles)

Order of Operations

Some mathematical expressions involve more than one mathematical operation. For instance, consider the expression $5 + 3 \cdot 2$. This expression seems to have two different values, depending on the order in which we perform the given operations.

Add first	**Multiply first**
$5 + 3 \cdot 2$	$5 + 3 \cdot 2$
$= 8 \cdot 2$	$= 5 + 6$
$= 16$	$= 11$

How do we know which operation to carry out first? By consensus we agree to follow the rule called the **order of operations** so that everyone always gets the same value as the answer.

Order of Operations Rule

To evaluate mathematical expressions, carry out the operations *in the following order:*

1. First, perform the operations within any grouping symbols, such as parentheses ( ) or brackets [ ].

2. Then raise any number to its power.

3. Next, perform all multiplications and divisions as they appear from left to right.

4. Finally, do all additions and subtractions as they appear from left to right.

Applying the order of operations rule to the previous example gives us the following result.

$$5 + \underbrace{3 \cdot 2} \qquad \text{Multiply first.}$$
$$= \underbrace{5 + 6} \qquad \text{Then add.}$$
$$= 11$$

So 11 is the correct answer.

EXAMPLE 4

Simplify: $20 - 18 \div 9 \cdot 8$

SOLUTION The order of operations rule gives us

$$20 - 18 \div 9 \cdot 8 = 20 - 2 \cdot 8 \qquad \text{Divide first.}$$
$$= 20 - 16 \qquad \text{Then multiply.}$$
$$= 4 \qquad \text{Finally subtract.}$$

PRACTICE 4

Evaluate: $8 \div 2 + 4 \cdot 3$

EXAMPLE 5

Find the value of $3 + 2 \cdot (8 + 3^2)$.

SOLUTION

$$3 + 2 \cdot (8 + 3^2) = 3 + 2 \cdot \underbrace{(8 + 9)} \qquad \text{Perform operations in parentheses: square the 3.}$$
$$= 3 + \underbrace{2 \cdot \quad 17} \qquad \text{Add 8 and 9.}$$
$$= \underbrace{3 + \quad 34} \qquad \text{Multiply 2 and 17.}$$
$$= 37 \qquad \text{Add 3 and 34.}$$

PRACTICE 5

Simplify: $(4 + 1)^2 - 4 \cdot 6$

TIP When a division problem is written as a fraction, parentheses are understood to be around both the numerator and the denominator. For instance,

$$\frac{10 - 2}{3 - 1} \qquad \text{means} \qquad (10 - 2) \div (3 - 1).$$

EXAMPLE 6

A student's test scores in a class were 85, 94, 93, 86, and 92. If the average of these scores was 90 or above, she earned an A. Did the student earn an A?

SOLUTION

$$\text{Average} = \frac{\text{The sum of the scores}}{\text{The number of scores}}$$

$$= \frac{85 + 94 + 93 + 86 + 92}{5}$$

$$= (85 + 94 + 93 + 86 + 92) \div 5$$

$$= 450 \div 5$$

$$= 90$$

Therefore, the student did earn an A.

PRACTICE 6

Last year, your average monthly electricity bill was $110. This year, these bills amounted to $84, $85, $88, $92, $80, $96, $150, $175, $100, $95, $75, and $80. On average, were your monthly bills higher this year?

R.2 Factors, Primes, and Least Common Multiples

Recall that in a multiplication problem involving two or more whole numbers, the whole numbers that are multiplied are called **factors**. For example, since $2 \cdot 4 = 8$, we say that 2 is a factor of 8, or that 8 is divisible by 2. The factors of 8 are 1, 2, 4, and 8.

Now let's discuss the difference between prime numbers and composite numbers. A **prime number** is a whole number that has exactly two factors, namely, itself and 1. A **composite number** is a whole number that has more than two factors. For instance, 5 is prime because its only factors are 1 and 5. However, 9 is a composite because it has more than two factors, namely, 1, 3, and 9. Note that 1 is considered neither prime nor composite.

Every composite number can be written as the product of prime factors, called its **prime factorization**. For instance, the prime factorization of 12 is $2 \cdot 2 \cdot 3$, or $2^2 \cdot 3$.

The **multiples** of a number are the products of that number and the whole numbers. For instance some of the multiples of 5 are

$$\underset{0 \times 5}{0} \quad \underset{1 \times 5}{5} \quad \underset{2 \times 5}{10} \quad \underset{3 \times 5}{15}$$

A number that is a multiple of two or more numbers is called a **common multiple** of these numbers. Some of the common multiples of 6 and 8 are 24, 48, and 72.

The **least common multiple** (LCM) of two or more numbers is the smallest nonzero number that is a multiple of each number. For example, the LCM of 6 and 8 is 24.

A good way to find the LCM involves prime factorization.

EXAMPLE 1

Find the LCM of 8 and 12.

SOLUTION We first find the prime factorization of each number.

$$8 = 2 \cdot 2 \cdot 2 = 2^3 \qquad 12 = 2 \cdot 2 \cdot 3 = 2^2 \cdot 3$$

Since 2 appears *three* times in the factorization of 8 and *twice* in the factorization of 12, it must be included three times in forming the least common multiple. So we use 2^3 (the highest power of 2 in the factorizations). The factor of 3 must also be included. Therefore, the LCM of 8 and 12 is

$$\text{LCM} = 2^3 \cdot 3 = 8 \cdot 3 = 24$$

PRACTICE 1

What is the LCM of 10 and 25?

Example 1 suggests the following procedure:

To Compute the Least Common Multiple (LCM) of Two or More Numbers
- Find the prime factorization of each number.
- Identify the prime factors that appear in each factorization.
- Then multiply these prime factors, using each factor the greatest number of times that it occurs in any of the factorizations.

EXAMPLE 2

What is the LCM of 18, 30, and 45?

SOLUTION We first find the prime factorization of each number.

$$18 = 2 \cdot 3 \cdot 3 = 2 \cdot 3^2 \qquad 30 = 2 \cdot 3 \cdot 5 \qquad 45 = 3 \cdot 3 \cdot 5 = 3^2 \cdot 5$$

The prime factors that appear in the prime factorizations are 2, 3, and 5. Since 2 and 5 occur at most one time and 3 occurs at most two times in any of the factorizations, we get

$$\text{LCM} = 2 \cdot 3^2 \cdot 5 = 2 \cdot 9 \cdot 5 = 90$$

PRACTICE 2

Find the LCM of 20, 36, and 60.

EXAMPLE 3

A gym that is open every day of the week offers aerobic classes every third day and yoga classes every fourth day. If both classes were offered today, in how many days will the gym again offer both classes on the same day?

SOLUTION To answer this question, we find the LCM of 3 and 4. As usual, we begin by finding prime factorizations.

$$3 = 3 \qquad 4 = 2 \cdot 2 = 2^2$$

To find the LCM, we multiply 3 by 2^2.

$$\text{LCM} = 2^2 \cdot 3 = 12$$

So both classes will be offered again on the same day 12 days from today.

PRACTICE 3

A patient gets two medications while in the hospital. One medication is given every 6 hours and the other is given every 8 hours. If the patient is given both medications now, in how many hours will both medications again be given at the same time?

R.3 Fractions

A **fraction** can mean a part of a whole. For example, $\frac{2}{3}$ of a class means two of every three students. A fraction can also mean the quotient of two whole numbers.

A fraction has three components:

- the **denominator** (on the bottom), that stands for the number of parts into which the whole is divided,

- the **numerator** (on top) that tells us how many parts of the whole the fraction contains,

- the **fraction line** (or **fraction bar**) that separates the numerator from the denominator and stands for the phrase *out of* or *divided by*.

Note that the denominator of a fraction cannot be zero.

A fraction whose numerator is smaller than its denominator is a **proper fraction**. A **mixed number** consists of a whole number and a proper fraction. A mixed number can also be expressed as an **improper fraction**, which is a fraction whose numerator is larger than or equal to its denominator. For example, the mixed number $1\frac{1}{2}$ can be written as the improper fraction $\frac{3}{2}$.

To Change a Mixed Number to an Improper Fraction

- Multiply the denominator of the fraction by the whole number part of the mixed number.

- Add the numerator of the fraction to this product.

- Then write this sum over the original denominator to form the improper fraction.

EXAMPLE 1

Write $12\frac{1}{4}$ as an improper fraction.

SOLUTION
$$12\frac{1}{4} = \frac{(4 \times 12) + 1}{4}$$
$$= \frac{48 + 1}{4} = \frac{49}{4}$$

PRACTICE 1

Express $3\frac{2}{9}$ as an improper fraction.

To Change an Improper Fraction to a Mixed Number

- Divide the numerator by the denominator.

- Then if there is a remainder, write it over the denominator.

EXAMPLE 2

Write $\frac{11}{2}$ as a mixed number.

SOLUTION

$$\frac{11}{2} = 2\overline{)\begin{array}{c} 5 \\ 11 \end{array}}$$ Divide the numerator by the denominator.

$$\underline{10}$$

$$1 \longleftarrow \text{Remainder}$$

$$\frac{11}{2} = 5\frac{1}{2}$$ Write the remainder over the denominator.

PRACTICE 2

Express $\frac{8}{3}$ as a mixed number.

Two fractions are **equivalent** if they represent the same value. To generate fractions equivalent to a given fraction, say $\frac{1}{3}$, multiply both its numerator and denominator by the same nonzero whole number. For instance,

$$\frac{1}{3} = \frac{1 \cdot 2}{3 \cdot 2} = \frac{2}{6}$$

$$\frac{1}{3} = \frac{1 \cdot 3}{3 \cdot 3} = \frac{3}{9}$$

A fraction is said to be in **simplest form** (or **reduced to lowest terms**) when the only common factor of its numerator and its denominator is 1. To simplify a fraction, we divide its numerator and denominator by the same number, or common factor. To find these common factors, it is often helpful to express both the numerator and denominator as the product of prime factors. We can then divide out (or cancel) all common factors.

EXAMPLE 3

Write $\frac{42}{28}$ in lowest terms.

SOLUTION

$$\frac{42}{28} = \frac{2 \cdot 3 \cdot 7}{2 \cdot 2 \cdot 7}$$ Express the numerator and denominator as the product of primes.

$$= \frac{\overset{1}{\cancel{2}} \cdot 3 \cdot \overset{1}{\cancel{7}}}{\underset{1}{\cancel{2}} \cdot 2 \cdot \underset{1}{\cancel{7}}}$$ Divide out common factors.

$$= \frac{3}{2}$$ Multiply the remaining factors.

PRACTICE 3

Reduce $\frac{24}{30}$ to lowest terms.

Fractions with the same denominator are said to be **like**; those with different denominators are called **unlike**.

To Add (or Subtract) Like Fractions
● First add (or subtract) the numerators.
● Use the given denominator.
● Then write the answer in simplest form.

EXAMPLE 4

Find the sum of $\frac{7}{12}$ and $\frac{2}{12}$.

SOLUTION Using the rule for adding like fractions, we get:

$$\frac{7}{12} + \frac{2}{12} = \frac{\overbrace{7+2}^{\text{Add numerators.}}}{\underbrace{12}_{\text{Keep same denominator.}}} = \frac{9}{12}, \quad \text{or } \underset{\underset{\text{Simplest form}}{\uparrow}}{\frac{3}{4}}$$

PRACTICE 4

Add: $\dfrac{7}{15} + \dfrac{3}{15}$

EXAMPLE 5

Find the difference between $\frac{11}{12}$ and $\frac{7}{12}$.

SOLUTION

$$\frac{11}{12} - \frac{7}{12} = \frac{\overbrace{11-7}^{\text{Subtract numerators.}}}{\underbrace{12}_{\text{Keep same denominator.}}} = \frac{4}{12}, \quad \text{or } \underset{\underset{\text{Simplest form}}{\uparrow}}{\frac{1}{3}}$$

PRACTICE 5

Subtract: $\dfrac{19}{20} - \dfrac{11}{20}$

Unlike fractions are more complicated to add (or subtract) than like fractions because we must first change the unlike fractions to equivalent like fractions. Typically, we use their **least common denominator** (**LCD**), that is, the least common multiple of their denominators, to find equivalent fractions.

To Add (or Subtract) Unlike Fractions

- Rewrite the fractions as equivalent fractions with a common denominator, usually the LCD.
- Add (or subtract) the numerators, keeping the same denominator.
- Then write the answer in simplest form.

EXAMPLE 6

Add: $\dfrac{5}{12} + \dfrac{5}{16}$

SOLUTION First find the LCD, which is 48.

$$\frac{5}{12} + \frac{5}{16} = \frac{20}{48} + \frac{15}{48} \qquad \text{Find equivalent fractions.}$$

$$= \frac{35}{48} \qquad \text{Add the numerators, keeping the same denominator.}$$

The fraction $\frac{35}{48}$ is already in lowest terms because 35 and 48 have no common factors other than 1.

PRACTICE 6

Add: $\dfrac{11}{12} + \dfrac{3}{4}$

EXAMPLE 7

Subtract $\frac{1}{12}$ from $\frac{1}{3}$.

SOLUTION First find the LCD, which is 12.

$\frac{1}{3} - \frac{1}{12} = \frac{4}{12} - \frac{1}{12}$ Write equivalent fractions with a common denominator.

$= \frac{3}{12}$ Subtract the numerators, keeping the same denominator.

$= \frac{1}{4}$ Reduce $\frac{3}{12}$ to lowest terms.

PRACTICE 7

Calculate: $\frac{4}{5} - \frac{1}{2}$

To Add (or Subtract) Mixed Numbers

- Rewrite the fractions as equivalent fractions with a common denominator, usually the LCD.
- When subtracting, rename (or borrow from) the whole number on top if the fraction on the bottom is larger than the fraction on top.
- Add (or subtract) the fractions.
- Add (or subtract) the whole numbers.
- Then write the answer in simplest form.

EXAMPLE 8

Find the sum of $3\frac{3}{5}$ and $7\frac{2}{3}$.

SOLUTION Since the denominators have no common factor other than 1, the least common denominator is the product of 5 and 3, which is 15.

$$3\frac{3}{5} = 3\frac{9}{15}$$
$$+7\frac{2}{3} = +7\frac{10}{15}$$

Now we use the rule for adding mixed numbers with same denominator.

$$3\frac{3}{5} = 3\frac{9}{15}$$ Add the fractions.
$$+7\frac{2}{3} = +7\frac{10}{15}$$ Add the whole numbers.
$$10\frac{19}{15}$$

Because $\frac{19}{15}$ is an improper fraction, we need to rewrite $10\frac{19}{15}$:

$$10\frac{19}{15} = 10 + \frac{19}{15} = 10 + 1\frac{4}{15} = 11\frac{4}{15}$$

$$\frac{19}{15} = 1\frac{4}{15}$$

So the sum of $3\frac{3}{5}$ and $7\frac{2}{3}$ is $11\frac{4}{15}$.

PRACTICE 8

Add $4\frac{5}{8}$ to $3\frac{1}{2}$.

EXAMPLE 9

Compute: $13\frac{2}{9} - 7\frac{8}{9}$

SOLUTION First, write the problem, $13\frac{2}{9} - 7\frac{8}{9}$, in a vertical format.

$$13\frac{2}{9}$$
$$-7\frac{8}{9}$$

Since $\frac{8}{9}$ is larger than $\frac{2}{9}$, we need to rename $13\frac{2}{9}$:

$$13\frac{2}{9} = 12 + 1 + \frac{2}{9} = 12 + \frac{9}{9} + \frac{2}{9} = 12\frac{11}{9}$$

$$13 = 12 + 1$$

The problem now becomes

$$13\frac{2}{9} = 12\frac{11}{9}$$
$$-7\frac{8}{9} = -7\frac{8}{9}$$

Finally, we subtract and then write the answer in simplest form.

$$13\frac{2}{9} = 12\frac{11}{9}$$
$$-7\frac{8}{9} = -7\frac{8}{9}$$
$$5\frac{3}{9} = 5\frac{1}{3}$$

PRACTICE 9

Find the difference between $15\frac{1}{12}$ and $9\frac{11}{12}$.

Now let's look at how we multiply fractions.

To Multiply Fractions
- First multiply the numerators.
- Multiply the denominators.
- Then write the answer in simplest form.

EXAMPLE 10

Multiply: $\frac{2}{3} \cdot \frac{4}{5}$

SOLUTION

$$\frac{2}{3} \cdot \frac{4}{5} = \frac{2 \cdot 4}{3 \cdot 5} = \frac{8}{15}$$

PRACTICE 10

Compute: $\frac{1}{2} \cdot \frac{3}{4}$

In multiplying some fractions, we can first simplify (or cancel) by dividing *any* numerator and *any* denominator by a common factor. Simplifying before multiplying allows us to work with smaller numbers and still gives us the same answer.

EXAMPLE 11

Find the product of $\frac{4}{9}$ and $\frac{5}{8}$.

SOLUTION

Divide the numerator (4) and the denominator (8) by the same number (4). Then multiply.

$$\frac{4}{9} \cdot \frac{5}{8} = \frac{\overset{1}{\cancel{4}} \cdot 5}{9 \cdot \underset{2}{\cancel{8}}} = \frac{5}{18}$$

PRACTICE 11

Multiply $\frac{7}{10}$ by $\frac{5}{11}$.

To Multiply Mixed Numbers
- Change each mixed number to its equivalent improper fraction.
- Follow the steps for multiplying fractions.
- Then write the answer in simplest form.

EXAMPLE 12

Compute: $2\frac{1}{2} \cdot 1\frac{1}{4}$

SOLUTION

$$2\frac{1}{2} \cdot 1\frac{1}{4} = \frac{5}{2} \cdot \frac{5}{4} \qquad \text{Change each mixed number to an improper fraction.}$$

$$= \frac{5 \cdot 5}{2 \cdot 4} \qquad \text{Multiply the fractions.}$$

$$= \frac{25}{8}, \text{ or } 3\frac{1}{8} \qquad \text{Simplify.}$$

PRACTICE 12

Find the product of $3\frac{3}{4}$ and $2\frac{1}{10}$.

Dividing fractions is equivalent to multiplying by the *reciprocal* of the divisor. The reciprocal is found by *inverting*—switching the position of the numerator and denominator of the divisor.

To Divide Fractions
- Change the divisor to its reciprocal.
- Multiply the resulting fractions.
- Then simplify the answer.

EXAMPLE 13

Divide: $\frac{4}{5} \div \frac{3}{10}$

SOLUTION

$$\frac{4}{5} \div \frac{3}{10} = \frac{4}{\underset{1}{\cancel{5}}} \times \frac{\overset{2}{\cancel{10}}}{3} = \frac{4 \times 2}{1 \times 3} = \frac{8}{3}, \text{ or } 2\frac{2}{3}$$

$\frac{3}{10}$ and $\frac{10}{3}$ are reciprocals.

PRACTICE 13

Divide: $\frac{3}{4} \div \frac{1}{8}$

To Divide Mixed Numbers

• Change each mixed number to its equivalent improper fraction.

• Follow the steps for dividing fractions.

• Then simplify the answer.

EXAMPLE 14

Calculate: $9 \div 2\frac{7}{10}$

SOLUTION

$$9 \div 2\frac{7}{10} = \frac{9}{1} \div \frac{27}{10}$$ Change all mixed numbers to improper fractions.

$$= \frac{\overset{1}{\cancel{9}}}{1} \times \frac{10}{\underset{3}{\cancel{27}}}$$ Invert the divisor and multiply.

$$= \frac{10}{3}, \text{ or } 3\frac{1}{3}$$ Simplify.

PRACTICE 14

Divide: $6 \div 3\frac{3}{4}$

EXAMPLE 15

Suppose that you spend $\frac{3}{8}$ of your monthly salary on rent. If that salary is $960, how much money do you have left after paying the rent?

SOLUTION Let's break up the question into two parts:

1. First find $\frac{3}{8}$ of 960.

$$\frac{3}{\underset{1}{\cancel{8}}} \times \frac{\overset{120}{\cancel{960}}}{1} = 360$$

2. Then subtract that result from 960.

$$960 - 360 = 600$$

So you have $600 left after paying for rent.

PRACTICE 15

At a college with 1000 students, $\frac{3}{5}$ of the students take a math course. How many students in the college are not taking a math course?

R.4 Decimals

A number written as a *decimal* has

- a whole number part, which precedes the decimal point, and
- a fractional part, which follows the decimal point.

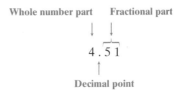

A decimal without a decimal point shown is understood to have one at the end of the last digit and is the same as a whole number. For instance, 32 and 32. are the same number.

Each digit in a decimal has a place value. The place value system for decimals is an extension of the place value system for whole numbers.

The places to the right of the decimal point are called *decimal places*. For instance, the number 64.149 is said to have three decimal places.

For a whole number, the place values are 1, 10, 100, and other powers of 10. By contrast, the place values for the fractional part of a decimal are $\frac{1}{10}$, $\frac{1}{100}$, $\frac{1}{1000}$, and the reciprocals of other powers of 10.

The first decimal place after the decimal point is the ten**ths** place. Working to the right, the next decimal places are the hundred**ths** place, the thousand**ths** place, the ten-thousand**ths**, and so forth.

The following chart shows the place values in the numbers 0.54 and 513.285.

... thousands	hundreds	tens	ones	.	tenths	hundredths	thousandths ...
			0	.	5	4	
	5	1	3	.	2	8	5

Knowing the place value system is the key to changing a decimal to its equivalent fraction and to reading the decimal. For a given decimal, the place value of the rightmost digit is the denominator of the equivalent fraction.

$$0.9 = \frac{9}{10}$$

read "nine tenths"

$$0.21 = \frac{21}{100}$$

read "twenty-one hundredths"

Let's look at how to rewrite any decimal as a fraction or mixed number.

To Change a Decimal to the Equivalent Fraction or Mixed Number

- Copy the nonzero whole number part of the decimal and drop the decimal point.
- Place the fractional part of the decimal in the numerator of the equivalent fraction.
- Then make the denominator of the equivalent fraction the same as the place value of the rightmost digit.

EXAMPLE 1

Write each decimal as a fraction or mixed number.

a. 0.25

b. 1.398

SOLUTION

a. Write 0.25 as $\dfrac{25}{100}$, which simplifies to $\dfrac{1}{4}$. So $0.25 = \dfrac{1}{4}$.

b. The decimal 1.398 is equivalent to a mixed number. The whole number part is 1. The fractional part (.398) of the decimal (without the decimal point) is the numerator of the equivalent fraction. Since the decimal has three decimal places, the denominator of the fraction is 1000. So $1.398 = 1\frac{398}{1000} = 1\frac{199}{500}$.

PRACTICE 1

Express each decimal in fractional form.

a. 0.5

b. 2.073

EXAMPLE 2

Write 2.019 in words.

SOLUTION The fractional part of 2.019 is .019, which is equivalent to $\frac{19}{1000}$. We read the original decimal as "two and nineteen thousandths," keeping the whole number unchanged. Note that we use the word *and* to separate the whole number and the fractional part.

PRACTICE 2

Write 4.003 in words.

In computations with decimals, we sometimes *round* the decimal to a certain number of decimal places.

To Round a Decimal to a Given Decimal Place

- Underline the place to which you are rounding.
- Look at the digit to the right of the underlined digit—*the critical digit*. If this digit is 5 or more, add 1 to the underlined digit; if it is less than 5, leave the underlined digit unchanged.
- Then drop all places to the right of the underlined digit.

EXAMPLE 3

Round 94.735 to the nearest tenth.

SOLUTION First we underline the digit 7 in the tenths place: 94.735. Since the critical digit 3 is less than 5, we do not add 1 to the underlined digit. Dropping all digits to the right of the 7, we get 94.7. So 94.735 ≈ 94.7 (the symbol ≈ is read "is approximately equal to"). Note that our answer has only one decimal place because we are rounding to the nearest tenth.

PRACTICE 3

Round 748.0772 to the nearest hundredth.

To Add Decimals
- Rewrite the numbers vertically, lining up the decimal points.
- Add.
- Then insert a decimal point in the answer below the other decimal points.

EXAMPLE 4

Add: $2.7 + 80.13 + 5.036$

SOLUTION Rewrite the numbers with decimal points lined up vertically so that digits with the same place value are in the same column. Then add.

$$
\begin{array}{r}
2.7 \\
80.13 \\
+\ 5.036 \\
\hline
87.866
\end{array}
$$

Insert the decimal point in the answer.

PRACTICE 4

Add: $5.92 + 35.872 + 0.3$

To Subtract Decimals
- First rewrite the numbers vertically, lining up the decimal points.
- Subtract, inserting extra zeros if necessary for borrowing.
- Then insert a decimal point in the answer below the other decimal points.

EXAMPLE 5

Subtract: $5 - 2.14$

SOLUTION

$$
\begin{array}{r}
5.00 \\
-\ 2.14 \\
\hline
2.86
\end{array}
$$

Rewrite 5 as 5.00 and line up decimal points vertically.

Subtract.

Insert the decimal point in the answer.

PRACTICE 5

Find the difference: $3.8 - 2.621$

To Multiply Decimals

- Multiply the factors as if they were whole numbers.
- Find the total number of decimal places in the factors.
- Then count that many places from the right end of the product and insert a decimal point.

EXAMPLE 6	PRACTICE 6
Multiply: 6.1×3.7	Find the product of 2.81 and 3.5.

SOLUTION First multiply: $61 \times 37 = 2257$

$$
\begin{array}{r}
6\,1 \\
\times\ 3\,7 \\
\hline
4\,2\,7 \\
1\,8\,3\ \ \\
\hline
2\,2\,5\,7
\end{array}
$$

Then count the total number of decimal places.

$$
\begin{array}{r}
6.1 \\
\times\ 3.7 \\
\hline
4\,2\,7 \\
1\,8\,3\ \ \\
\hline
2\,2.5\,7
\end{array}
$$

←One decimal place (tenths)
←One decimal place (tenths)

← Two decimal places (hundredths) in the product

So the answer is 22.57.

A shortcut for multiplying a decimal by a power of 10 is to *move the decimal point to the right the same number of places as the power of 10 has zeros.*

EXAMPLE 7	PRACTICE 7
Find the product: $(1000)(2.89)$	Multiply 32.7 by 10,000.

SOLUTION We notice that 1000 is a power of 10 and has three zeros. To multiply 1000 by 2.89, we move the decimal point in 2.89 to the right three places.

$$(1000)\,(2.890) = 2\,8\,9\,0. = 2890$$

Need to insert a 0 to move three places.

The product is 2890.

> **To Divide Decimals**
> • If the divisor is not a whole number, move the decimal point in the divisor to the right end of the number.
> • Move the decimal point in the dividend the same number of places to the right as we did in the divisor.
> • Insert a decimal point in the quotient directly above the decimal point in the dividend.
> • Then divide the new dividend by the new divisor, inserting zeros at the right end of the dividend as necessary.

EXAMPLE 8

Divide 0.035 by 0.25.

SOLUTION

Move the decimal point to the right end, making the divisor a whole number.

$$0.25 \overline{)0.035} \quad \Rightarrow \quad 0.25 \, \overline{)0.035}$$

Move the decimal point in the dividend the same number of places.

Finally, we divide 3.5 by 25, which gives us 0.14.

$$
\begin{array}{r}
0.14 \\
25\overline{)3.50} \\
25 \\
\hline
100 \\
100 \\
\hline
\end{array}
$$

PRACTICE 8

Divide: $2.706 \div 0.15$

A shortcut for dividing a decimal by a power of 10 is to *move the decimal point to the left the same number of places as the power of 10 has zeros.*

EXAMPLE 9

Compute: $\dfrac{7.2}{100}$

SOLUTION Since we are dividing by the power of 10 with two zeros, we can find this quotient simply by moving the decimal point in 7.2 to the left two places:

Need to insert a 0 to move two places.

$$0 7 . 2 = .072, \quad \text{or } 0.072$$

The quotient is 0.072.

PRACTICE 9

Calculate: $0.86 \div 1000$

EXAMPLE 10

Suppose you raise chickens using organic feed. Four of them weigh 3.2 lb, 3.5 lb, 2.9 lb, and 3.6 lb. How much less than the average weight of the four chickens is the weight of the lightest chicken?

SOLUTION This question falls into two parts:

What is the average weight of the chickens? The average weight is the sum of the weights divided by the number of weights.

$$\frac{3.2 + 3.5 + 2.9 + 3.6}{4} = \frac{13.2}{4} = 3.3$$

The average weight is 3.3 lb.

How much less than the average weight (3.3 lb) *is the weight of the lightest chicken* (2.9 lb)?

$$3.3 - 2.9 = 0.4$$

The weight of the lightest chicken is 0.4 lb less than the average weight.

PRACTICE 10

In a diving competition, five judges scored each diver. To compute a diver's overall score, the judges averaged the diver's scores after first dropping the highest and lowest scores. What is the overall score of a diver who earns scores of 6.2, 6.7, 6.3, 6.4, and 6.5?

Chapter 1

Introduction to Real Numbers and Algebraic Expressions

Osteoporosis and Real Numbers

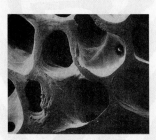

Normal bone

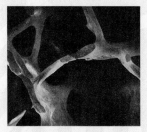

Osteoporotic bone

Of the approximately 10 million Americans who have osteoporosis, a disease in which bones become weak and are likely to break, 8 million are women. Although men develop the disease, women are much more likely to suffer from osteoporosis. Some risk factors for developing the disease are family history of osteoporosis, advanced age, and low calcium intake.

To diagnose osteoporosis, doctors commonly employ a bone mineral density (BMD) test. A person's BMD score is compared to a norm based on the optimal density of a healthy 30-year-old adult. Scores below the norm are indicated in negative numbers. For instance, a score of -2 indicates a low bone mass and a score of -2.5 or less is diagnosed as osteoporosis. Generally, a score of -1 is equivalent to a 10% loss of bone density.

The National Osteoporosis Foundation recommends treatment if you have a result that is

- less than -1.5 with risk factors, or
- less than -2 with no risk factors

The results of many medical tests are reported in terms of positive and negative numbers.

Source: Dempster, D. W. et al., *Journal of Bone and Mineral Research* 1:15–21, 1986.

31

To see if you have already mastered the topics in this chapter, take this test.

1. Express as a real number: a profit of $2000

2. Is 0 a rational number?

3. Graph the number -0.5 on the following number line.

4. What is the opposite of -5?

5. Evaluate $\left| -\dfrac{2}{3} \right|$.

6. Use $>$ or $<$ to fill in the box to make a true statement: $-31 \;\boxed{}\; -1$

7. Subtract: $-6 - 7$

8. Add: $9 + (-4) + 2 + (-9)$

9. Simplify: $3(-7) - 5$

10. What is the reciprocal of $\dfrac{1}{4}$?

11. Divide: $(-72) \div (-8)$

12. Translate the algebraic expression to words: $3n - 10$

13. Express in exponential form: $-6 \cdot 6 \cdot 6 \cdot 6$

14. Evaluate: $2x - 4y + 8$, if $x = -2$ and $y = 3$

15. Combine like terms: $3n - 7 + n$

16. Simplify: $-5(2 - x) + 9x$

17. Mount Kilimanjaro, Africa's highest point, is 5895 meters (m) above sea level. Lake Assal, its lowest point, is 156 m below sea level. What is the difference in the elevations of these two points?
(**Source:** *National Geographic Family Reference Atlas of the World*, 2002)

18. A wire of length L is to be cut into three pieces of equal length. Write an expression that represents the length of each piece of wire.

19. The formula for the perimeter of a rectangle is $P = 2l + 2w$. Calculate the perimeter of the following rectangle.

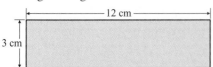

20. Each month a student writes a check for $200 to repay a loan. What is the net debit to the checking account from the checks after 4 months?

• *Check your answers on page A-1.*

1.1 Integers, Rational Numbers, and the Real-Number Line

OBJECTIVES

- *To identify integers, rational numbers, and real numbers*
- *To graph rational numbers on the real-number line*
- *To find the opposite and the absolute value of real numbers*
- *To compare real numbers*
- *To solve applied problems involving the comparison of real numbers*

What Algebra Is and Why It Is Important

Algebra is a language that allows us to express the patterns and rules of arithmetic. Consider, for instance, the rule for finding the product of two fractions: Multiply the numerators to get the numerator of the product and multiply the denominators to get the denominator of the product.

$$\frac{3}{4} \cdot \frac{1}{2} = \frac{3 \cdot 1}{4 \cdot 2} = \frac{3}{8}$$

In the language of algebra, we can write the general rule using letters to represent numbers:

$$\frac{a}{b} \cdot \frac{c}{d} = \frac{a \cdot c}{b \cdot d} = \frac{ac}{bd}$$

Can you think of another arithmetic rule that can be expressed algebraically?

Algebra allows us not only to communicate rules like the preceding one but also to solve problems. These problems arise in a variety of disciplines such as chemistry, economics, and medicine.

In this chapter, we focus on two key elements of algebra: real numbers and algebraic expressions.

The Real Numbers

Real numbers are numbers that can be represented as points on a number line. They extend the numbers used in arithmetic and allow us to solve problems that we could not otherwise solve.

Let's begin our discussion by looking at different kinds of real numbers.

Integers

In arithmetic, we use *natural numbers* for counting. The natural numbers are 1, 2, 3, 4, 5, 6, 7, 8, 9, ... The three dots mean that these numbers go on forever in the same pattern. The *whole numbers* consist of 0 and the natural numbers: 0, 1, 2, 3, 4, 5, 6, 7, 8, 9 ... .

We can represent the whole numbers on a number line. A number to the right of another on the number line is the larger number, as shown on the following number line.

```
        ┌─────────────┬──────────────┐
        │ Smaller than 5 │ Larger than 5 │
◄───────┴──┬──┬──┬──┬──┴──┬──┬──┬──┬──┴──────►
        0  1  2  3  4  5  6  7  8  9···
```

Sometimes we need to consider numbers that are to the left of 0, that is, numbers that are smaller than 0. For instance, we may want to express 2 degrees below zero, as shown on the thermometer to the left.

Numbers to the left of 0 on the number line are said to be *negative*. We write $-1, -2, -3, -4$, and so on. By contrast, the whole numbers 1, 2, 3, 4, and so on are said to be *positive* and can also be written as $+1, +2, +3, +4$, and so on. The numbers $-1, -2, -3$, and so on, together with the whole numbers are called *integers*, as shown on the following number line. Note that the number line extends continuously to the right and to the left as the arrows indicate.

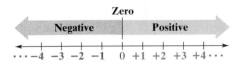

Zero

Negative   **Positive**

$\cdots -4 \quad -3 \quad -2 \quad -1 \quad 0 \quad +1 \quad +2 \quad +3 \quad +4 \cdots$

Definition

The **integers** are the numbers

$$\ldots, -4, -3, -2, -1, 0, +1, +2, +3, +4, \ldots,$$

continuing indefinitely in both directions.

EXAMPLE 1

The Dow Jones Industrial Average on the stock market declined 4 points today. Express this situation as an integer.

SOLUTION The number in question represents a decline (or loss), so we write a negative integer, namely, -4.

TIMES

Dow Jones
Industrial Average
Falls 4 Points

PRACTICE 1

Represent as an integer: A carnation plant freezes and dies at a temperature of 5° below 0° Fahrenheit (°F).

Rational Numbers

Suppose that we want to represent the following situation: *The New York Giants lost one-half yard on a play.* To express a loss of one-half yard, we need a kind of number other than whole numbers or integers. We need a *rational number*—a number that can be written as the quotient of two integers, where the denominator is not equal to zero.

Some examples of rational numbers are

$$\frac{2}{5}, -\frac{1}{2}, 4, 0, 7\frac{1}{4}, -0.03$$

This number represents negative one-half.
We can express a loss of one-half yard as $-\frac{1}{2}$ yd.

> **Definition**
>
> **Rational numbers** are numbers that can be written in the form $\frac{a}{b}$, where a and b are integers and $b \neq 0$.

A rational number can be expressed in several ways. For instance, we can write $-\frac{1}{2}$ as either $\frac{-1}{2}$ or $\frac{1}{-2}$. The numbers 4 and 0 can also be written as $\frac{4}{1}$ and $\frac{0}{1}$, respectively. And we can write $7\frac{1}{4}$ as $\frac{29}{4}$ and -0.03 as $-\frac{3}{100}$. It is important to note that all rational numbers have corresponding decimal representations that either *terminate* or *repeat*. Here are some examples.

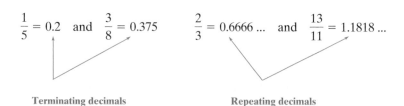

$$\frac{1}{5} = 0.2 \quad \text{and} \quad \frac{3}{8} = 0.375 \qquad \frac{2}{3} = 0.6666\ldots \quad \text{and} \quad \frac{13}{11} = 1.1818\ldots$$

Terminating decimals   Repeating decimals

Just as with integers, we can picture rational numbers as points on a number line. To *graph* a rational number, we locate the point on the number line and mark it as shown.

On the preceding number line, note that

- the point at 0 is called the *origin*,
- numbers to the right of 0 are positive, and numbers to the left of 0 are negative,
- the number 0 is neither positive nor negative.

In this text, we will work mostly with rational numbers until Chapter 8.

EXAMPLE 2

Graph each number on the same number line.

a. $-\dfrac{7}{2}$ **b.** 2.1

SOLUTION

a. Because $-\dfrac{7}{2}$ can be expressed as $-3\frac{1}{2}$, the point $-\dfrac{7}{2}$ is graphed halfway between -3 and -4.

b. The number 2.1, or $2\frac{1}{10}$, is between 2 and 3 but is closer to 2.

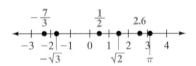

PRACTICE 2

Graph each number on the number line.

a. -1.7 **b.** $\dfrac{5}{4}$

More Real Numbers

Recall that any rational number can be written as the quotient of two integers. However, there are other real numbers that cannot be written in this form. Such numbers are called *irrational numbers*, and their corresponding decimal representations neither terminate or repeat. Examples of irrational numbers are

$$\sqrt{2} = 1.4142 \dots$$ **The square root of 2**

$$-\sqrt{3} = -1.7320 \dots$$ **The negative square root of 3**

$$\pi = 3.14159 \dots$$ **Pi, the ratio of the circumference of a circle to its diameter**

In many computations with irrational numbers, we use decimal approximations that are rounded to a certain number of decimal places, for instance:

$$\sqrt{2} \approx 1.41 \qquad -\sqrt{3} \approx -1.73 \qquad \pi \approx 3.14$$

Recall that the symbol $\approx$ is read "is approximately equal to."

Irrational numbers, like rational numbers, can be graphed on the number line. The rational numbers and the irrational numbers together make up the *real numbers*.

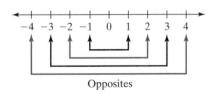

Absolute Value

On the number line, the numbers -3 and $+3$ (that is, 3) are opposites of each other. Similarly, $-\frac{1}{2}$ and $+\frac{1}{2}$ are opposites. What is the opposite of 0?

Opposites

Definition

Two real numbers that are the same distance from 0 on the number line but on opposite sides of 0 are called **opposites**. For any real number n, its opposite is $-n$.

EXAMPLE 6

Find the opposite of each number in the table.

Number	Opposite
a. 10	
b. $-\dfrac{1}{3}$	
c. $10\frac{1}{2}$	
d. -0.3	

SOLUTION

Number	Opposite
a. 10	-10
b. $-\dfrac{1}{3}$	$\dfrac{1}{3}$
c. $10\frac{1}{2}$	$-10\frac{1}{2}$
d. -0.3	0.3

PRACTICE 3

Find the opposite of each number.

Number	Opposite
a. -41	
b. $-\dfrac{8}{9}$	$\dfrac{8}{9}$
c. 1.7	
d. $-\dfrac{2}{5}$	$\dfrac{2}{5}$

Because the number -3 is negative, it lies 3 units to the left of 0. The number 3 is positive and lies 3 units to the right of 0.

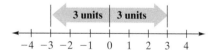

When we locate a number on the number line, the distance that number is from 0 is called its *absolute value*. Thus, the absolute value of $+3$, which we write as $|3|$, is 3. Similarly, the absolute value of -3, or $|-3|$, is 3.

Definition

The **absolute value** of a number is its distance from 0 on the number line. The absolute value of the number n is written as $|n|$.

The following properties help us to compute the absolute value of any number:

- The absolute value of a positive number is the number itself.
- The absolute value of 0 is 0.
- The absolute value of a number is always positive or 0.
- Opposites have the same absolute value.

EXAMPLE 4

Evaluate.

a. $|-6|$ **b.** $|4.6|$

c. $\left|-\dfrac{1}{3}\right|$ **d.** $-|-2|$

SOLUTION

a. $|-6| = 6$ Because the absolute value of a negative number is its opposite, the absolute value of −6 is 6.

b. $|4.6| = 4.6$ Because the absolute value of a positive number is the number itself, the absolute value of 4.6 is 4.6.

c. $\left|-\dfrac{1}{3}\right| = \dfrac{1}{3}$ Because $-\frac{1}{3}$ is negative, its absolute value is its opposite, namely, $\frac{1}{3}$.

d. $-|-2| = -(2) = -2$ Because $|-2| = 2$, we get $-|-2| = -2$.

PRACTICE 4

Find the value.

a. $\left|\dfrac{1}{2}\right|$

b. $|0|$

c. $|-9|$

d. $-|-3|$

Comparing Real Numbers

The number line helps us to compare two real numbers, that is, to determine which number is larger.

Given two numbers on the number line, *the number to the right is larger than the number to the left.* Similarly, *the number to the left is smaller than the number to the right.* The *equals sign* (=) and the *inequality symbols* (≠, <, ≤, >, and ≥) are used to compare numbers.

=	means *is equal to*	$\frac{5}{2} = 2\frac{1}{2}$ is read "$\frac{5}{2}$ is equal to $2\frac{1}{2}$."
≠	means *is not equal to*	$3 \neq -3$ is read "3 is not equal to −3."
<	means *is less than*	$-1 < 0$ is read "−1 is less than 0."
≤	means *is less than or equal to*	$4 \leq 7$ is read "4 is less than or equal to 7."
>	means *is greater than*	$-2 > -5$ is read "−2 is greater than −5."
≥	means *is greater than or equal to*	$3 \geq 1$ is read "3 is greater than or equal to 1."

The statements $3 \neq -3$, $-1 < 0$, $4 \leq 7$, $-2 > -5$, and $3 \geq 1$ are *inequalities*.

When comparing real numbers, it is important to remember the following:

- Zero is greater than any negative number because all negative numbers on the number line lie to the left of 0. For example, $0 > -5$.

- Zero is less than any positive number because all positive numbers lie to the right of 0 on the number line. For example, $0 < 3$.

- Any positive number is greater than any negative number because on the number line all positive numbers lie to the right of all negative numbers. For example, $4 > -1$.

EXAMPLE 5

Indicate whether each inequality is true or false.

a. $0 > -1$

b. $0 \geq \dfrac{1}{2}$

c. $-3.5 < 1.5$

d. $-10 \leq -10$

e. $-4 > -2$

SOLUTION

a. $0 > -1$ True, because 0 is to the right of -1.

b. $0 \geq \dfrac{1}{2}$ False, because 0 is to the left of $\frac{1}{2}$.

c. $-3.5 < 1.5$ True, because -3.5 is to the left of 1.5.

d. $-10 \leq -10$ True, because -10 is equal to -10.

e. $-4 > -2$ False, because -4 is to the left of -2.

PRACTICE 5

Determine whether each inequality is true or false.

a. $-2 < -1$

b. $0 \leq -5$

c. $\dfrac{10}{4} \geq \dfrac{5}{2}$

d. $0.3 > 0$

e. $-2.4 > 1.6$

We noted in Example 5(a) that $0 > -1$. Is $-1 < 0$? Explain why.

EXAMPLE 6

Graph the numbers $-2, \dfrac{1}{2}, -1$, and $-\dfrac{1}{4}$. Then list them in order from least to greatest.

SOLUTION

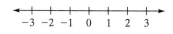

Reading the graph, we see that the numbers in order from the least to the greatest are $-2, -1, -\dfrac{1}{4}$, and $\dfrac{1}{2}$.

PRACTICE 6

Graph the numbers $-2.4, 3, -\dfrac{1}{2}$, and -1.6. Then write them in order from largest to smallest.

EXAMPLE 7

The average temperature in Fairbanks, Alaska, in the month of December is $-7°F$. The average temperature in Barrow, Alaska, in the same month is $-11°F$. Which place is warmer in December? How do you know? (*Source: World Almanac and Book of Facts*, 2000)

SOLUTION We need to compare -7 with -11. Because $-7 > -11$, it is warmer in Fairbanks in December.

PRACTICE 7

Your college is located 10 ft below sea level. Your house is 15 ft below sea level. Which is lower, your house or your college? How do you know?

EXAMPLE 8

Historians use number lines, called *timelines*, to show dates of historical events. On a timeline, the years before the birth of Christ are denoted as B.C., and after the birth of Christ as A.D. The B.C. dates are considered to be negative numbers on the timeline.

a. Locate on the following timeline the world history events before A.D. 1600 shown in the table.

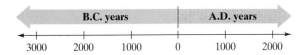

Event	Date
(A) Hieroglyphic writing developed in Egypt.	3200 B.C.
(B) Charlemagne (Charles the Great) was crowned emperor by Pope Leo III in Rome.	A.D. 800
(C) Hun invaders from Asia entered Europe.	A.D. 372
(D) Mayan civilization began to develop in Central America.	1500 B.C.
(E) Sweden seceded from the Scandinavian Union.	A.D. 1523
(F) In Greece, the Parthenon was built.	438 B.C.
(G) The city of Rome was founded, according to legend, by Romulus.	753 B.C.
(H) The evolution of England's unique political institutions began with the *Magna Carta*.	A.D. 1215

(*Source: The World Almanac Book of Facts*, 2000)

b. Order the events from the most recent to the earliest event.

SOLUTION B.C. dates are considered to be negative numbers, and A.D. dates positive numbers. So we graph on a timeline similar to the way we graph on a number line. That is, we locate each year on the timeline and mark it as shown on the next page.

a.

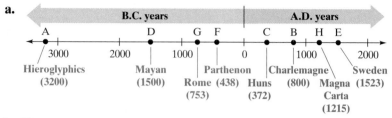

b. The events from the most recent to the earliest: E, H, B, C, F, G, D, and A.

PRACTICE 8

Consider the following table that shows the highlights in the development of algebra.

Event	Date
(A) Babylonian algebra found on cuneiform clay tablets dates back to the reign of King Hammurabi.	1700 B.C.
(B) Greek algebra (as formulated by the Pythagoreans) was geometric.	500 B.C.
(C) The Greek mathematician Diophantus introduced a style of writing equations.	A.D. 250
(D) Greek algebra (as formulated by Euclid) was geometric.	300 B.C.
(E) Bhaskara was one of the most prominent Hindu mathematicians in algebra.	A.D. 1100
(F) Mohammed ibn-Musa al-Khowarizmi wrote the book *Al-jabr* (translated as "algebra" in Latin).	A.D. 825
(G) Modern symbols and notation in algebra emerged.	A.D. 1500

(*Source:* NCTM, *Historical Topics for the Mathematics Classroom*, 1969)

a. Locate on the timeline below the events listed in the table.

b. Then order these highlights from the earliest to the most recent event.

Exercises 1.1

FOR EXTRA HELP

📖 *Student's Solutions Manual*

📞 *Addison-Wesley Math Tutor Center*

🚪 *MyMathLab*

📼 *Videotape 2/DVT 2*

Express each quantity as a positive or negative number.

1. 5 km below sea level

2. A profit of $1000

3. A temperature drop of 22.5°C

4. A gain of $6\frac{1}{2}$ lb

5. A withdrawal of $160 from an account

6. A debt of $1500.45

Graph each number on the number line.

7. -3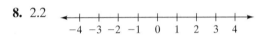
$$-4 \;-3 \;-2 \;-1 \;\; 0 \;\; 1 \;\; 2 \;\; 3 \;\; 4$$

8. 2.2
$$-4 \;-3 \;-2 \;-1 \;\; 0 \;\; 1 \;\; 2 \;\; 3 \;\; 4$$

9. $-\dfrac{1}{2}$
$$-4 \;-3 \;-2 \;-1 \;\; 0 \;\; 1 \;\; 2 \;\; 3 \;\; 4$$

10. 0
$$-4 \;-3 \;-2 \;-1 \;\; 0 \;\; 1 \;\; 2 \;\; 3 \;\; 4$$

11. $-\dfrac{3}{8}$
$$-4 \;-3 \;-2 \;-1 \;\; 0 \;\; 1 \;\; 2 \;\; 3 \;\; 4$$

12. $2\dfrac{9}{10}$
$$-4 \;-3 \;-2 \;-1 \;\; 0 \;\; 1 \;\; 2 \;\; 3 \;\; 4$$

13. -2.9
$$-4 \;-3 \;-2 \;-1 \;\; 0 \;\; 1 \;\; 2 \;\; 3 \;\; 4$$

14. $-\dfrac{1}{4}$
$$-4 \;-3 \;-2 \;-1 \;\; 0 \;\; 1 \;\; 2 \;\; 3 \;\; 4$$

Classify each number by writing a check in the appropriate boxes.

	Whole Numbers	Integers	Rational Numbers	Real Numbers
15. -7				
16. $3\frac{1}{6}$				
17. -1.9				
18. 0				
19. 10				
20. $\dfrac{2}{5}$				

Find the opposite of each number.

21. -3

22. 21

23. 0

24. $\dfrac{2}{3}$

25. -3.5

26. $1\frac{1}{2}$

Evaluate.

27. $|-4|$

28. $\left|-\dfrac{2}{3}\right|$

29. $|0|$

30. $|-15|$

31. $|-4.6|$

32. $|2.6|$

33. $-\left|\dfrac{1}{2}\right|$

34. $-\left|-\dfrac{6}{5}\right|$

Solve. If impossible, explain why.

35. Name all numbers that have an absolute value of 4.

36. Name all numbers that have an absolute value of 0.4.

37. Name a number whose absolute value is -2.

38. Name three different numbers that have the same absolute value.

Indicate whether each inequality is true or false.

39. $-7 < -5$

40. $-1 > 3$

41. $-1 < 2.5$

42. $-3.2 > -3$

43. $0 \geq -1\frac{1}{4}$

44. $-6 \leq -6$

Replace each ▧ *with* $<, >,$ *or* $=$ *to make a true statement.*

45. 0 ▧ -1

46. -7 ▧ 4

47. -1.5 ▧ -2

48. -1 ▧ -1.6

49. $|-4|$ ▧ $|4|$

50. $-|5|$ ▧ $|-5|$

51. 6.2 ▧ $|-7.1|$

52. $-\left|\dfrac{1}{4}\right|$ ▧ $-\dfrac{2}{3}$

Graph the numbers in each group on the number line. Then, write the numbers from largest to smallest.

53. $3\frac{1}{2}, -1\frac{1}{2}, -\dfrac{1}{2}, 0$

$\longleftarrow \!\!\! \overset{\displaystyle +\ +\ +\ +\ +\ +\ +\ +\ +}{\underset{-4\ \ -3\ \ -2\ \ -1\ \ \ 0\ \ \ 1\ \ \ 2\ \ \ 3\ \ \ 4}{}} \!\!\! \longrightarrow$

54. $-1, 2, -2, -3, 1$

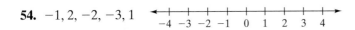

55. $-3, 3, -3.5, 3.5$

56. $2\frac{1}{2}, -4, 3, -2.5$

Applications

Solve.

57. Today you owe $200. Last week, you owed $2000. Were you better off finan-cially last week, or are you better off today?

58. Will you weigh more if you lose 6 lb or gain 2 lb?

59. Three of the coldest temperature readings ever recorded on Earth were $-64.8\,°C$, $-64.3\,°C$, and $-54.5\,°C$. Of these three temperatures, which was the coldest?

60. Each liquid has its own boiling point—the temperature at which it changes to a gas. Liquid chlorine, for example, boils at $-35\,°C$, whereas liquid fluorine boils at $-188\,°C$. Which liquid has the higher boiling point? (*Source: Handbook of Chemistry and Physics*)

61. Astronomers use the term *apparent magnitude* to indicate the brightness of a star as seen from Earth. The following number line shows the apparent magnitude of various stars and other objects. For historical reasons, the brighter a star or object is, the farther to the left it is graphed on the number line.

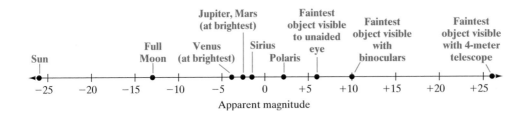

a. Which star is brighter as seen from Earth—Polaris or Sirius?

b. Use this number line to estimate the apparent magnitude of the full Moon.

c. The giant star Beta Sagittae lies hundreds of light-years from Earth, with an apparent magnitude of 4.4. Plot this star's apparent magnitude on the number line.

62. The following timeline shows the year of some major technological innovations.

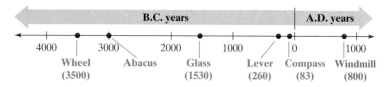

(*Source:* Bill Yenne, *100 Inventions That Shaped World History,* 1993)

a. Which was invented earlier—the lever or the compass?

b. According to the timeline, what was invented between 2000 B.C. and A.D. 1000?

c. The mechanical clock was invented around A.D. 950. Plot a point on the time-line to represent this invention.

• *Check your answers on page A-2.*

Mindstretchers

GROUPWORK

1. Working with a partner, develop a diagram to show the relationship among the real numbers, the rational numbers, the irrational numbers, the integers, the non-integer rational numbers, the whole numbers, the negative integers, the natural numbers, and zero.

MATHEMATICAL REASONING

2. Is there a largest number less than 5 that is

a. an integer? _____

b. a rational number? _____

_____

RESEARCH

3. Using your college library or the Web, investigate the role the Pythagoreans played in discovering irrational numbers. Write a few sentences to summarize your findings. _____

Cultural Note

Sources:
Lancelot Hogben, *Mathematics in the Making* (London: Galahad Books, 1960).

Henri Michel, *Scientific Instruments in Art and History* (New York: Viking Press, 1966).

Calvin C. Clawson, *The Mathematical Traveler* (New York and London: Plenum Press, 1994).

U p until the work of sixteenth-century Italian physicists, no one was able to measure temperature. Liquid-in-glass thermometers were invented around 1650, when glass blowers in Florence were able to create the intricate shapes that thermometers require. Thermometers from the seventeenth and eighteenth centuries provided a model for working with negative numbers that led to their wider acceptance in the mathematical and scientific communities. Numbers above and below 0 represented temperatures above and below the freezing point of water, just as they do on the Centigrade scale today. Before the introduction of these thermometers, a number such as −1 was difficult to interpret for those who believed that the purpose of numbers is to count or to measure.

By contrast, the early Greek mathematicians had rejected negative numbers, calling them absurd. A thousand years later in the seventeenth century A.D., the Indian mathematician Brahmagupta argued for accepting negative numbers and wrote the first comprehensive rules for computing with them.

1.2 Addition of Real Numbers

OBJECTIVES

- *To add real numbers*
- *To solve applied problems involving the addition of real numbers*

In Chapter R, computations were restricted to zero and positive numbers—whether those positive numbers happened to be whole numbers, fractions, or decimals. Now we consider computations involving negative numbers as well. Let's start with addition.

Suppose that we want to add two negative numbers: -2 and -3. It is helpful to look at this problem using a real-world situation. If you have a debt of \$2 and another debt of \$3, altogether you owe \$5.

$$-2 + (-3) = -5$$

The number line gives us a picture of adding real numbers. To add -2 and -3, we start at the point corresponding to the first number, -2. The second number, -3, is negative, so we move 3 units to the *left*. We end at -5.

Move 3 units to the *left*.

$$\begin{array}{ccccccccccccc}
\leftarrow & + & + & + & + & + & + & + & + & + & + & + & + & \rightarrow \\
-6 & -5 & -4 & -3 & -2 & -1 & 0 & 1 & 2 & 3 & 4 & 5 & 6
\end{array}$$
End Start

Note that both -2 and -3 are negative and their sum is negative.

To Add Real Numbers, *a* and *b*, on a Number Line

- Start at *a*.
- Then move according to *b* as follows:

  If *b* is positive, move to the right.

  If *b* is negative, move to the left.

  If *b* is zero, remain at *a*.

Consider these examples.

EXAMPLE 1

Add -1 and 3 on the number line.

SOLUTION

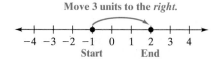

Move 3 units to the *right*.

So $-1 + 3 = 2$.

PRACTICE 1

Add 2 and -3 on the number line.

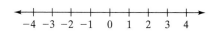

EXAMPLE 2

Add 2 and −2 on the number line.

SOLUTION

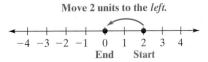

So $2 + (-2) = 0$. Note that 2 and (-2) are opposites, and their sum is 0.

PRACTICE 2

Add −5 and 5 on the number line.

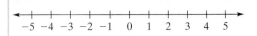

Example 2 suggests that when adding two numbers that are opposites, such as 2 and −2, the sum is 0. We call such numbers **additive inverses**. Every real number has an opposite, or additive inverse, as stated in the following property.

Additive Inverse Property

For any real number a, there is exactly one real number $-a$ such that

$$a + (-a) = 0 \quad \text{and} \quad (-a) + a = 0.$$

EXAMPLE 3

Using a number line, add $-1\frac{1}{2}$ and 0.

SOLUTION

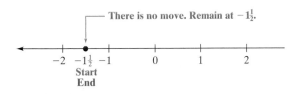

So $-1\frac{1}{2} + 0 = -1\frac{1}{2}$. Note that adding 0 to $-1\frac{1}{2}$ gives us $-1\frac{1}{2}$, the same number we started with.

PRACTICE 3

Add 0 and 0.5 on the following number line.

Example 3 illustrates another important property in adding real numbers—the *additive identity property*, also called the *identity property of 0*.

Additive Identity Property

For any real number a,

$$a + 0 = a \quad \text{and} \quad 0 + a = a.$$

The previous examples illustrated how to add real numbers on a number line. However, this method is not very efficient, especially for adding large numbers. Instead, let's look at a *rule* for the addition of real numbers.

To Add Real Numbers

- If the numbers have the same sign, add their absolute values and keep their sign.
- If the numbers have different signs, find the difference between the larger absolute value and the smaller one and take the sign of the number with the larger absolute value.

Now let's consider some examples of applying this rule for adding real numbers.

EXAMPLE 4	**PRACTICE 4**

Add −8 and −19.

Find the sum: −13 + (−18)

SOLUTION Because both numbers are negative, we find their absolute values and then add:

$$|-8| + |-19| = 8 + 19 = 27$$

The sum of two negative numbers is negative.

$$-8 + (-19) = -27$$

Negative numbers ⎯⎯⎯⎮⎯⎯⎯⎮   ⎮⎯⎯ Negative sum

TIP When adding numbers with the same sign, the sum has that sign.

EXAMPLE 5	**PRACTICE 5**

Find the sum of −6.7 and 5.2.

Add: 10.1 + (−6.6)

SOLUTION Here we are adding numbers with *different* signs. First, we find the absolute values:

$$|-6.7| = 6.7 \quad \text{and} \quad |5.2| = 5.2$$

Then we find the difference between the larger absolute value and the smaller one:

$$6.7 - 5.2 = 1.5$$

Because −6.7 has the larger absolute value and its sign is negative, the sum is also negative. So

$$-6.7 + (+5.2) = -6.7 + 5.2 = -1.5$$

Negative ⎯⎮   ⎮⎯ Positive   ⎮⎯ The sum takes the sign
number   number   of the number with the
                                             larger absolute value.

Can you use the number line to explain why the sum in Example 5 is negative?

EXAMPLE 6

Combine: $-\dfrac{2}{9} + \dfrac{2}{9}$

SOLUTION

$$-\dfrac{2}{9} + \dfrac{2}{9} = 0$$

Note that $-\dfrac{2}{9}$ and $\dfrac{2}{9}$ are additive inverses. So their sum is 0.

PRACTICE 6

Combine: $-\dfrac{1}{3} + \dfrac{1}{3}$

The *commutative property of addition* allows us to add two numbers in any order, getting the same sum. For example, $2 + 6 = 8$ and $6 + 2 = 8$.

Commutative Property of Addition

For any two real numbers a and b,

$$a + b = b + a.$$

By contrast, the *associative property of addition* lets us regroup numbers that are added without affecting the sum. For example, $(2 + 6) + 3 = 8 + 3 = 11$ and $2 + (6 + 3) = 2 + 9 = 11$.

Associative Property of Addition

For any three real numbers, a, b, and c,

$$(a + b) + c = a + (b + c).$$

When adding three or more real numbers, it is usually easier to add the positives separately from the negatives. This rearrangement does not affect the sum because of the commutative and associative properties.

EXAMPLE 7	PRACTICE 7

EXAMPLE 7

Find the sum: $5 + (-6) + (-9) + 3 + (-5)$

SOLUTION Let's rearrange the numbers by sign.

$$\underbrace{5 + 3}_{\text{Positives}} \quad + \quad \underbrace{(-6) + (-9) + (-5)}_{\text{Negatives}}$$

$5 + 3 = 8$ Add the positives.

$(-6) + (-9) + (-5) = -20$ Add the negatives.

$8 + (-20) = -12$ Find the sum of the positive and the negative sums.

So $5 + (-6) + (-9) + 3 + (-5) = -12$.

Can you think of another way to get the sum in Example 7?

PRACTICE 7

Find the sum:
$-8 + (-4) + 7 + (-8) + 3$

EXAMPLE 8

In a chemistry class, you study the properties of atomic particles, including protons and electrons. You learn that a proton has an electric charge of $+1$, whereas an electron has an electric charge of -1. The charge of a proton cancels out that of an electron. If a charged particle of magnesium has 12 protons and 10 electrons, what is its total charge?

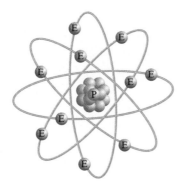

SOLUTION We can represent the 12 protons and 10 electrons by $+12$ and -10, respectively. To find the total charge of the particle, we add $+12$ and -10.

$$+12 + (-10) = +2$$

So the total charge of the particle of magnesium is $+2$.

PRACTICE 8

The price of a certain stock on Monday was $37.50 per share. On Tuesday, the price of a share went up $2; on Wednesday, it went down $1; and on Thursday, it went down another $2. What was the share price of the stock on Thursday?

Calculators and Real Numbers

To enter a negative number, we need to hit the key that indicates that the sign of the number is negative. Some calculators have a *change-of-sign key*, $+/-$. Others have a negative sign key, $(-)$. Do not confuse either of these keys with the subtraction key, $-$. When entering a negative number, the order in which the change-of-sign key or the negative key must be pressed will depend on the calculator being used. The $+/-$ key is usually pressed *after* the number is entered, whereas the $(-)$ key is usually pressed *before* the number is entered.

EXAMPLE 9	PRACTICE 9
Calculate: $-1.3 + (-5.891) + 4.713$	Add: $6.002 + (-9.37) + (-0.22)$

SOLUTION Using the $+/-$ key:

Input	1.3	$+/-$	$+$	5.891	$+/-$		$+$	4.713	$=$
Display	1.3	-1.3	-1.3	5.891	-5.891	-7.191		4.713	-2.478

So $-1.3 + (-5.891) + 4.713 = -2.478$.

If your calculator has the $(-)$ key, check to see that you get the same answer.

Exercises 1.2

FOR EXTRA HELP

📖 Student's Solutions Manual

📞 Addison-Wesley Math Tutor Center

🚪 MyMathLab

📼 Videotape 2/DVT 2

Find the sum of each pair of numbers using the number line.

1. $4 + (-3)$

2. $-8 + 7$

3. $8 + (-8)$

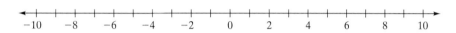

4. $-3 + (-4)$

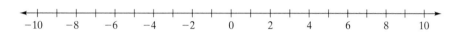

5. $-5 + 10$

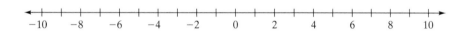

6. $-1.5 + 2$

Name the property of addition illustrated.

7. $3 + (-3) = 0$

8. $(-4) + 0 = -4$

9. $5 + (-6) = (-6) + 5$

10. $(2 + 3) + 6 = 2 + (3 + 6)$

11. $(-100) + 100 = 0$

12. $0 + 2\frac{1}{2} = 2\frac{1}{2}$

13. $-1.8 + 2.4 = 2.4 + (-1.8)$

14. $(5 + 6) + (-1) = 5 + [6 + (-1)]$

15. $-a + 0 = -a$

16. $-a + (-b) = -b + (-a)$

Find the sum.

17. $24 + (-1)$

18. $-12 + 5$

19. $-10 + 5$

20. $-6 + (-6)$

21. $10 + (-6)$

22. $60 + (-90)$

23. $-50 + (-30)$

24. $-9 + (-4)$

25. $-10 + 2$

26. $2 + (-10)$

27. $-18 + 18$

28. $(-18) + (-18)$

29. $5.2 + (-0.9)$

30. $-0.6 + 2$

31. $-0.2 + 0.8$

32. $-10.5 + 0$

33. $0 + (-0.3)$

34. $(-0.1) + 0.1$

35. $-9.6 + 3.9$

36. $6.1 + (-5.9)$

37. $(-9.8) + (-6.5)$

38. $-0.8 + (-0.9)$

39. $-\dfrac{1}{2} + \left(-\dfrac{1}{2}\right)$

40. $\left(-\dfrac{1}{4}\right) + \left(-\dfrac{3}{4}\right)$

41. $-1\frac{3}{5} + 2$

42. $-10 + 3\frac{1}{2}$

43. $-24 + (25) + (-89)$ **44.** $36 + (-17) + (-28)$

45. $15 + (-9) + (-15) + 9$

46. $45 + (-27) + 0 + (-18)$

47. $-0.4 + (-2.6) + (-4)$

48. $(-6.25) + (-0.4) + 3$

49. $(-58) + 10.48 + 58$

50. $-3.7 + 3.7 + (-1.88)$

51. $107 + (-97) + (-45) + 23$

52. $-64 + 7 + (-10) + (-19)$

▦ **53.** $-2.001 + (0.59) + (-8.1) + 10.756$

▦ **54.** $-10 + 6.17 + (-10.005) + (-4.519)$

Applications

Solve. Express your answer as a real number.

55. The temperature on the top of a mountain was 2° below 0°. If it then got 7° warmer, what was the temperature?

56. An elevator goes up 2 floors, down 3 floors, up 1 floor, and finally up 1 floor. What is the overall change in position of the elevator?

57. Last year, a corporation took in $132,000 with expenses of $148,000. How much money did the corporation make or lose?

58. In order to conduct an experiment, a chemist cooled a substance down to −5°C. In the course of this experiment, a chemical reaction took place that raised the temperature of the substance by 15°. What was the final temperature?

59. Cleopatra became queen of Egypt in the year 51 B.C. She left the throne 21 years later. In what year was that?

60. In the last 4 months, a dieter lost 2 lbs, gained 3 lbs, lost 1 lb, and maintained her weight, respectively. What was the dieter's overall change in weight?

61. With $371.25 in your checking account, you write checks for $71.33 and $51.66. You also deposit $35. After the two checks clear and your deposit is credited, will you still have enough money to cover a check of $250?

62. Estimate the total annual profits for Dot.com Corporation according to the following chart. (Note that a red number written in parentheses is negative.)

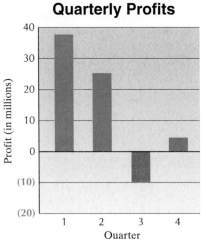

63. A plane cruising at an altitude of 32,000 ft hit an air pocket and dropped 700 ft. What was its new altitude?

64. The balance on a customer's credit card account at the start of this month was $782.48. This month, purchases of $72.99, $125.00, and $271.88 were charged to her account. There was also a credit of $250 for items returned. What was the account balance at the end of the month?

● *Check your answers on page A-2.*

Mindstretchers

GROUPWORK

1. Working with a partner, consider the following addition table.

a. Complete the table.

+	4	−3	−1
6			
−2			
−4			

b. Explain why the nine numbers that you entered add up to 0.

MATHEMATICAL REASONING

2. Consider the following addition table.

+	x	y	z
x	y	z	x
y	z	x	y
z	x	y	z

a. Use the table to find $x + y$. _____

b. What is the additive identity element in the addition table? Explain how you know. _____

_____

c. What is the opposite of x in this table? Explain how you know.

_____

WRITING

3. Do you prefer to add real numbers using the number line or using the rule method? Explain why. _____

1.3 Subtraction of Real Numbers

OBJECTIVES

• *To subtract real numbers*

• *To solve applied problems involving the subtraction of real numbers*

The subtraction of real numbers is based on two topics that we have previously covered—adding real numbers and finding the opposite of a number.

We already know how to compute the difference between two positive numbers, for instance, $10 - 2$:

$$10 - (+2) = 8$$

In the previous section, we learned how to add a positive number and a negative number, for example, $10 + (-2)$:

$$10 + (-2) = 8$$

Note that the answers to these two computations are the same. So,

$$10 - (+2) = 10 + (-2)$$

More generally, for any real numbers a and b,

$$a - b = a + (-b)$$

In other words, we can change a subtraction problem to an equivalent addition problem by adding the *opposite* of the number being subtracted.

To Subtract Real Numbers
- Change the operation of subtraction to addition and change the number being subtracted to its opposite.
- Then follow the rule for adding real numbers.

Consider these examples.

EXAMPLE 1

Find the difference: $2 - (-5)$

SOLUTION

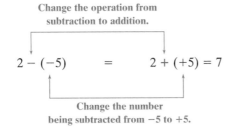

PRACTICE 1

Find the difference: $4 - (-1)$

EXAMPLE 2

Subtract: $-3 - (-9)$

SOLUTION

$$-3 - (-9) = -3 + (+9) = 6$$

Negative 9 → Positive 9 →

↑ Subtract   ↑ Add

PRACTICE 2

Subtract: $-12 - (-15)$

EXAMPLE 3

Find the difference: $2 - 5$

SOLUTION

$$2 - 5 = 2 - (+5) = 2 + (-5) = -3$$

PRACTICE 3

Find the difference: $8 - 12$

EXAMPLE 4

Subtract: $9 - (-13.2)$

SOLUTION

$$9 - (-13.2) = 9 + (+13.2) = 22.2$$

PRACTICE 4

Subtract: $-8.1 - 7.6$

In Chapter R, we discussed the order of operations rule, which states that when a problem involves addition and subtraction, we work from left to right. Let's look at how this rule works with positive and negative numbers.

EXAMPLE 5

Simplify: $-2 - (-6) - (-11)$

SOLUTION

$$
\begin{aligned}
-2 - (-6) - (-11) &= \underbrace{-2 + (+6)} - (-11) && \text{Subtract } -6 \text{ from } -2. \\
&= \quad\; 4 \quad\; - (-11) && \text{Add } -2 \text{ and } +6. \\
&= 4 + 11 && \text{Subtract } -11 \text{ from } 4. \\
&= 15 && \text{Add } 4 \text{ and } 11.
\end{aligned}
$$

PRACTICE 5

Simplify: $5 - (-8) - (-15)$

EXAMPLE 6

Evaluate: $-7 - (-1) + 5 + (-3)$

SOLUTION

$-7 - (-1) + 5 + (-3)$

$$= \underbrace{-7 + (+1)} + 5 + (-3) \qquad \text{Subtract } -1 \text{ from } -7.$$

$$= \underbrace{-6 + 5} + (-3) \qquad \text{Add } -7 \text{ and } +1.$$

$$= \underbrace{-1 + (-3)} \qquad \text{Add } -6 \text{ and } 5.$$

$$= -4 \qquad \text{Add } -1 \text{ and } -3.$$

PRACTICE 6

Simplify: $4 + (-6) - (-11) + 8$

EXAMPLE 7

Egypt emerged as a nation in about 3100 B.C. and Ethiopia in about 3000 B.C. How much older is Egypt than Ethiopia?
(*Source: The World Book Encyclopedia*)

SOLUTION Recall that a B.C. year corresponds to a negative integer. So 3100 B.C. and 3000 B.C. are represented by -3100 and -3000, respectively. Because $-3000 > -3100$, we write -3000 first:

$$-3000 - (-3100) = -3000 + (+3100)$$
$$= 100$$

So Egypt is 100 years older than Ethiopia.

PRACTICE 7

Paper was invented in China in about 100 B.C., and wood block printing in about A.D. 770. How much older is the invention of paper than that of wood block printing? (*Source: The World Book Encyclopedia*)

Exercises 1.3

FOR EXTRA HELP

📖 *Student's Solutions Manual*

Addison-Wesley Math Tutor Center

MyMathLab

Videotape 2/DVT 2

Find the difference.

1. $25 - 8$

2. $8 - 25$

3. $-24 - 7$

4. $-6 - 9$

5. $(-19) - 25$

6. $-49 - 2$

7. $52 - (-19)$

8. $24 - (-31)$

9. $60 - 95$

10. $95 - 60$

11. $-34 - (-2)$

12. $-30 - (-1)$

13. $16 - (-16)$

14. $(-16) - 16$

15. $0 - 45$

16. $45 - 0$

17. $-31 - 31$

18. $31 - 31$

19. $22 - (-22)$

20. $8 - (-19)$

21. $200 - (-800)$

22. $30 - (-10)$

23. $6 - 7.42$

24. $10.1 - 11.84$

25. $-7.3 - (0.5)$

26. $-3 - (-0.1)$

27. $(-5.6) - (-5.6)$

28. $0.4 - (-0.4)$

29. $8.6 - (-1.7)$

30. $-1.7 - 8.6$

31. $-\dfrac{1}{3} - \dfrac{5}{6}$

32. $\dfrac{4}{5} - \left(-\dfrac{7}{8}\right)$

33. $-12 - \dfrac{1}{4}$

34. $-12 - \left(-\dfrac{1}{4}\right)$

35. $4\frac{3}{5} - \left(-1\frac{1}{2}\right)$

36. $-6\frac{1}{2} - \left(-1\frac{1}{4}\right)$

Simplify.

37. $3 + (-6) - (-15)$

38. $-12 - (-4) + 9$

39. $8 - 10 + (-5)$

40. $12 + (-16) - (-5)$

41. $-9 + (-4) - 9 + 4$

42. $-6 - (-1) + 5 + (-8)$

43. $9 - 12 - 18$

44. $-7 - (-4) - 2$

▦ **45.** $-10.722 + (-3.913) - 8.36 - 3.492$

▦ **46.** $1.884 - 0.889 + (-6.12) - (-4.001)$

Applications

Solve. Express your answer as a real number.

47. The first Olympic Games occurred in 776 B.C. Approximately how many centuries were there between the first Olympic games and the Olympic games held in A.D. 2002?

48. Going into your last round of a golf tournament, your score was 4 strokes over par. At the end of the tournament, it was 2 strokes under par. During the last round, what was your score relative to par?

49. Two airplanes take off from the same airport. One flies north and the other flies south, as pictured. How far apart are the airplanes? (*Hint:* Consider north to be positive and south to be negative.)

50. Two friends get on different elevators at the same floor. One of the friends goes up 2 floors, and the other goes down 3 floors. How many floors are the two friends apart?

51. A company reported a loss of $281,330 last year and a loss of $5291 this year. By how much money were the losses reduced?

52. The value of a computer company's stock rose by $\frac{1}{2}$ of a dollar per share and then dropped by $\frac{3}{4}$ of a dollar. What was the overall change in value?

53. The U.S. city with the greatest elevation is Leadville, Colorado. The U.S. city with the lowest elevation is Calipatria, California. If their respective elevations are 10,152 ft above sea level and 184 ft below sea level, what is the difference in the elevations of these cities?

54. The following chart shows the record high and low temperatures (in degrees Fahrenheit) for a number of U.S. states.

State	Record High (°F)	Record Low (°F)
Alabama	112	−27
California	134	−45
Louisiana	114	−16
Minnesota	114	−60
New York	108	−52
Virginia	110	−30

Which state had the greatest difference in record extreme temperatures?

55. Matter is liquid when its temperature is between its melting point and its boiling point. The following table shows the melting and boiling points (in degrees Celsius) of various elements.

Element	Melting Point (°C)	Boiling Point (°C)
Radon	−71	−61.8
Neon	−248.7	−246
Bromine	−7.2	58.8

(*Source: The New York Times Almanac,* 2000)

a. For each of these elements, find the difference between its boiling and melting points.

b. Which of the elements is liquid in the widest range of temperatures?

c. Which of the elements is liquid at 0°C?

56. Superconductors allow for very efficient passage of electric currents. For practical use, a superconductor must work above −196°C, which is the boiling point of nitrogen.

a. In 1986, the first high-temperature superconductor that was able to conduct electricity without resistance at a temperature of −238°C was discovered. How many degrees below the boiling point of nitrogen did this first high-temperature superconductor work?

b. In 1987, the researcher Paul Chu discovered a new class of materials that conduct electricity at −178°C. How many degrees above the boiling point of nitrogen did the new materials conduct electricity?

c. In 1990, other researchers created a miniature transistor that conducts electricity at a temperature that is 48°C above the boiling point of nitrogen. What is this temperature?

(*Sources: World Book Encyclopedia* and *Webster's New World Book of Facts,* 1999)

● *Check your answers on page A-2.*

Mindstretchers

CRITICAL THINKING

1. Rearrange the numbers in the square on the left so that it becomes a magic square in which the sum of every row, column, and diagonal is −6.

−3	2	−2
−5	−4	−6
0	−1	1

MATHEMATICAL REASONING

2. Consider the following two problems:

$$8 - (-2) = 8 + 2 = 10$$

$$8 \div \frac{4}{7} = 8 \times \frac{7}{4} = 14$$

a. Explain in what way the two problems are *similar*. _____

_____

b. Explain in what way the two problems are *different*. _____

_____

_____

_____

WRITING

3. Explain whether it is always true that the difference between two numbers is smaller than either of the numbers. Give an example to justify your answer.

_____

_____

1.4 Multiplication of Real Numbers

OBJECTIVES

- *To multiply real numbers*
- *To solve applied problems involving the multiplication of real numbers.*

In this section we deal with the multiplication of real numbers. From arithmetic, we know that when multiplying two positive numbers, we get a positive number. Now let's look at multiplying a positive number by a negative number.

Consider, for example, finding the product of 3 and -2. Looking at multiplication as repeated addition, we know that multiplying a number by 3 means the same as adding that number to itself three times.

$$3(-2) = -2 + (-2) + (-2)$$
$$= -6$$

Note that when multiplying a positive number by a negative number, we get a negative answer.

What about multiplying two negative numbers? Let's consider the following pattern:

This number is **decreasing**   The product is **increasing**
by **1** each time.   by **2** each time.

$$3\,(-2) = -6$$
$$2\,(-2) = -4$$
$$1\,(-2) = -2$$
$$0\,(-2) = 0$$
$$-1\,(-2) = +2 \quad \longleftarrow \text{ The pattern continues.}$$
$$-2\,(-2) = +4$$
$$-3\,(-2) = +6$$

Note that when we multiply two negative numbers, the product is positive. This suggests the following rule.

To Multiply Real Numbers

- Multiply their absolute values.
- If the numbers have the same sign, their product is positive; if they have different signs, their product is negative.

EXAMPLE 1	PRACTICE 1
Multiply -2 by -9.	Find the product of -1 and -100.
SOLUTION	

$$|-2| = 2 \quad \text{and} \quad |-9| = 9 \qquad \text{Find the absolute values.}$$
$$2 \cdot 9 = 18 \qquad \text{Multiply the absolute values.}$$
$$-2(-9) = 18 \qquad \text{The product of two negatives is positive.}$$

TIP

Same Sign

Positive · Positive = Positive   Negative · Negative = Positive

Different Signs

Positive · Negative = Negative   Negative · Positive = Negative

---

EXAMPLE 2

Multiply: $3(-5)$

SOLUTION

$|3| = 3$ and $|-5| = 5$ Find the absolute values.

$3 \cdot 5 = 15$ Multiply the absolute values.

$3(-5) = -15$ The product of a positive and a negative is negative.

PRACTICE 2

Calculate: $-5 \cdot 3$

Comparing Example 2 and Practice 2, we see that $3(-5) = -5 \cdot 3$, which suggests another property of real numbers—the *commutative property of multiplication*.

Commutative Property of Multiplication

For any two real numbers a and b,

$$a \cdot b = b \cdot a.$$

This property states that when we multiply two numbers in either order, we get the same product.

Other properties involving the multiplication of real numbers are the *multiplicative identity property* (multiplying by 1) and the *multiplication property of zero*.

Multiplicative Identity Property

For any real number a,

$$a \cdot 1 = a   \text{ and }   1 \cdot a = a.$$

This property states that the product of any number and 1 is the original number. The next property states that the product of any number and zero is zero.

Multiplication Property of Zero

For any real number a,

$$a \cdot 0 = 0   \text{ and }   0 \cdot a = 0.$$

EXAMPLE 3

Find the product.

a. $-9\left(\dfrac{1}{3}\right)$ **b.** $-\dfrac{1}{5}(-25)$ **c.** $-4(0)$

d. $-1.5(-1.5)$ **e.** $0.4(-6)$ **f.** $-7(1)$

SOLUTION

a. $-9\left(\dfrac{1}{3}\right) = \dfrac{-\overset{3}{\cancel{9}}}{1}\cdot\dfrac{1}{\underset{1}{\cancel{3}}} = -3$ Negative · Positive = Negative

b. $-\dfrac{1}{5}(-25) = -\dfrac{1}{\underset{1}{\cancel{5}}}\cdot\dfrac{-\overset{5}{\cancel{25}}}{1} = 5$ Negative · Negative = Positive

c. $-4(0) = 0$ Multiplication property of zero

d. $-1.5(-1.5) = 2.25$ Negative · Negative = Positive

e. $0.4(-6) = -2.4$ Positive · Negative = Negative

f. $-7(1) = -7$ Multiplicative identity property

PRACTICE 3

Multiply.

a. $\left(-\dfrac{2}{3}\right)(-12)$

b. $\left(-\dfrac{1}{3}\right)\left(\dfrac{5}{9}\right)$

c. $(-0.4)(-0.3)$

d. $2.5(-1.9)$

e. $0 \cdot (-2.8)$

f. $1 \cdot \dfrac{2}{3}$

The next property of real numbers—the *associative property of multiplication*—allows us to *regroup* the product of three numbers.

Associative Property of Multiplication

For any three real numbers, *a*, *b*, and *c*,

$$(a \cdot b)\, c = a\, (b \cdot c).$$

When multiplying three or more real numbers, their product is the same regardless of how they are grouped. For example, $(2 \cdot 3) \cdot 5 = 6 \cdot 5 = 30$ and $2 \cdot (3 \cdot 5) = 2 \cdot 15 = 30$.

EXAMPLE 4

Calculate: $-3(-2)(9)$

SOLUTION

$$-3(-2)(9) = 6(9)$$ Multiply -3 by -2.
$$= 54$$ Multiply 6 by 9.

So $(-3)(-2)(9) = 54$.

PRACTICE 4

Multiply: $-8(4)(-2)$

EXAMPLE 5

Multiply: $5(-2)(-1)(3)(-2)$

SOLUTION A good way to calculate this product is to rearrange the numbers by sign.

$$\underbrace{5(3)}_{\text{Positives}} \qquad \underbrace{-2(-1)(-2)}_{\text{Negatives}}$$

$5(3) = 15$	Multiply the positives.
$-2(-1)(-2) = 2(-2) = -4$	Multiply the negatives.
$15(-4) = -60$	Find the product of the positive and the negative products.

So $5(-2)(-1)(3)(-2) = -60$.

PRACTICE 5

Find the product:
$(-6)(-1)(4)(2)(-5)$

In Example 4, the product was positive because there were *two* negative factors. By contrast, in Example 5 the answer was negative because there were *three* negative factors. Can you explain why a product is positive if it has an even number of negative factors, whereas a product is negative if it has an odd number of negative factors?

According to the order of operations rule given in Chapter R, multiplication is performed before either addition or subtraction, working from left to right.

Order of Operations Rule

To evaluate mathematical expressions, carry out the operations *in the following order*:

1. First, perform the operations within any grouping symbols, such as parentheses ( ) or brackets [ ].
2. Then raise any number to its power.
3. Next, perform all multiplications and divisions as they appear from left to right.
4. Finally, do all additions and subtractions as they appear from left to right.

EXAMPLE 6

Simplify: $-2(24) - 5(-6)$

SOLUTION We use the order of operations rule.

$-2(24) - 5(-6) = -48 - (-30)$	Multiply first.
$= -48 + 30$	Subtract -30 from -48.
$= -18$	Add -48 and 30.

So $-2(24) - 5(-6) = -18$.

PRACTICE 6

Calculate: $4(-25) - (-2)(36)$

Following the order of operation rule, we simplify mathematical expressions by first performing the operations within any grouping symbols such as parentheses ( ) or brackets [ ].

EXAMPLE 7

Simplify: $-3(6 - 10)$

SOLUTION

$$-3(6 - 10) = -3(-4)$$ Subtract within parentheses.
$$= 12$$ Multiply.

So $-3(6 - 10) = 12$.

PRACTICE 7

Calculate: $-5(-9 + 15)$

EXAMPLE 8

Temperatures can be measured in both the Fahrenheit and Celsius systems. To find the Celsius equivalent of the temperature $-4°F$, we need to compute $\frac{5}{9}(-4 - 32)$. Simplify this expression.

SOLUTION

$$\frac{5}{9}(-4 - 32) = \frac{5}{9}(-36)$$ Subtract within parentheses.

$$= -20$$ Multiply.

So $-4°F$ is equivalent to $-20°C$.

PRACTICE 8

If an object is thrown upward with an initial velocity of 5 ft/sec, the object's velocity after 2 sec will be $5 + (-32)(2)$ ft/sec. Simplify this expression and interpret the result. (*Note:* Objects moving upward have positive velocity and objects moving downward have negative velocity.)

Exercises 1.4

FOR EXTRA HELP

📖 Student's Solutions Manual

Addison-Wesley Math Tutor Center

🚪 MyMathLab

📼 Videotape 2/DVT 2

Name the property of multiplication illustrated.

1. $2(5) = 5(2)$

2. $0 \cdot \frac{1}{2} = 0$

3. $(-4 \cdot 6) \cdot 3 = -4 \cdot (6 \cdot 3)$

4. $1.7(-3) = -3(1.7)$

5. $-9 \cdot 1 = -9$

6. $(-8 \cdot 5) \cdot 4 = -8 \cdot (5 \cdot 4)$

7. $-8 \cdot 0 = 0$

8. $1 \cdot (-10) = -10$

Find the product.

9. $6(-2)$

10. $-10 \cdot 300$

11. $-7(-3)$

12. $-5(-5)$

13. $-12\left(\frac{1}{4}\right)$

14. $-\frac{1}{3} \cdot \frac{4}{9}$

15. $\left(-\frac{5}{6}\right)\left(-\frac{2}{7}\right)$

16. $\left(1\frac{1}{3}\right)\left(-\frac{4}{9}\right)$

17. $-1.5(-0.6)$

18. $0.7(0.4)$

19. $1.2(-50)$

20. $-1.7(-4.6)$

21. $3(-2)(-20)$

22. $-9(-12)(2)$

23. $-15(-3)(0)$

24. $-8.5(0)(2.6)$

25. $-6(1)(-2)(-3)(-4)$

26. $6(-1)(-2)(3)(-4)$

27. $-4(5)(-6)(1)$

28. $10(1)(-10)(-1)$

29. $\left(-\frac{1}{3}\right)\left(-\frac{1}{3}\right)\left(-\frac{1}{3}\right)$

30. $\left(-\frac{1}{2}\right)\left(-\frac{1}{2}\right)\left(-\frac{1}{2}\right)$

Multiply and round to the nearest hundredth.

31. $-6.24(0.08)(-1.97)$

32. $-5.42(-0.19)(-4.8)$

Simplify.

33. $-7 + 3(-2) - 10$

34. $4 - 2(-5) - (-3)$

35. $4(-3) + (-2)(-6)$

36. $7(-2) + 4(-10)$

37. $-3 - 5(-6)$

38. $10 - 2(-8)$

39. $\left(\frac{3}{5}\right)(-15) - 6$

40. $\left(\frac{3}{4}\right)(-16) + 20$

41. $-5 \cdot (-3 + 4)$

42. $(-10 + 7) \cdot (-3)$

Complete each table.

43.

Input	Output
a. -2	$-4(-2) - 3 = ?$
b. -1	$-4(-1) - 3 = ?$
c. 0	$-4(0) - 3 = ?$
d. 1	$-4(1) - 3 = ?$
e. 2	$-4(2) - 3 = ?$

44.

Input	Output
a. 2	$-6(2) + 2 = ?$
b. 1	$-6(1) + 2 = ?$
c. 0	$-6(0) + 2 = ?$
d. -1	$-6(-1) + 2 = ?$
e. -2	$-6(-2) + 2 = ?$

Applications

Solve.

45. On a double-or-nothing wager, a gambler bets $5 and loses. Express as a real number the amount of money he lost.

46. On January 31, the high temperature in Chicago was 40°F. The high temperature then dropped 3°F per day for 3 days. If 32°F is freezing on the Fahrenheit scale, was it below freezing on February 3?

47. In the 10 games played this season, a team won 3 games by 4 points, won 2 games by 1 point, lost 4 games by 3 points, and tied in the final game. In these games, did the team score more or fewer points than its opposing teams?

48. On the stock market, the Dow Jones Industrial Average lost $1\frac{3}{8}$ point on each of five consecutive days. Express the overall change as a real number.

49. During a drought, the water level in a reservoir dropped 3 in. each week for 5 straight weeks. Express the overall change in water level as a real number.

50. The submarine shown dives to 3 times its current depth of 150 ft below sea level. What is its new depth?

150 ft

51. The following tables show the number of calories in servings of various foods and the number of calories burned by various activities.

Food	Number of Calories Per Serving
Apple	80
Banana	105
Pretzel, stick	30
Ginger ale, can	125
Donut	210

(**Source:** *The World Almanac and Book of Facts*, 2000)

Activity (1 hr)	Number of Calories Burned*
Swimming	−288
Bicycling	−612
Football	−498
Basketball	−450
Scrubbing floors	−440

*For a 150-lb person.

(*Source: Exercise & Weight Control*, President's Council on Physical Fitness and Sports, 1986)

Find the net calories in each situation.

a. Suppose that you eat 3 servings of pretzel sticks and then play basketball for $\frac{1}{2}$ hr.

b. Suppose that you swim for 30 min and drink 2 cans of ginger ale.

c. Suppose that you eat 3 servings of apples and 2 servings of donuts. Later you go bicycling for 2 hr and then swim for 1 hr.

52. To discourage guessing on a test, an instructor takes off for wrong answers, grading according to the following scheme:

Performance on a Test Item	Score
Correct	5
Incorrect	−2
Blank	0

What score would the instructor give to each of the following tests?

	Number of Items Correct	Number of Items Incorrect	Number of Items Blank	Test Grade
a.	17	1	2	
b.	19	1	0	
c.	12	7	1	

• Check your answers on page A-2.

Mindstretchers

MATHEMATICAL REASONING

1. Explain how the number line can be used to find the product of two integers.

_____

_____

_____

HISTORICAL

2. At a very early age, the eighteenth-century mathematician Carl Friedrich Gauss found the sum of the first 100 positive integers within a few minutes by using the following method. First he wrote the sum both forward and backward.

$$1 + \ 2 + \ 3 + \cdots + 98 + 99 + 100$$
$$100 + 99 + 98 + \cdots + \ 3 + \ 2 + \ 1$$

Then he added the 100 vertical pairs, getting a sum of 101 for each pair. He concluded that the product 100(101) was twice the correct answer, which turns out to be $\frac{100(101)}{2} = 50(101) = 5050$. Show how to find the sum of the first 1000 *negative* integers using Gauss's method. Explain your work.

_____

_____

WRITING

3. A salesman says that he loses a little money on each item sold but makes it up in volume. Explain if this is possible.

_____

_____

_____

_____

1.5 Division of Real Numbers

OBJECTIVES

- *To divide real numbers*
- *To solve applied problems involving the division of real numbers*

We now consider division—the last of the four basic operations on real numbers. From arithmetic, we know that every division problem has a related multiplication problem.

$$8 \div 2 = 4 \qquad \text{because} \qquad 2 \cdot 4 = 8$$

Division   Related multiplication

Now suppose that the division problem involves a negative number, for instance, $-8 \div 2$. From the previous section we know that $(-4) \cdot 2 = -8$. So $(-8) \div 2 = -4$. This problem suggests that when we divide a negative number by a positive number, we get a negative quotient.

Similarly, suppose that we want to calculate $(-8) \div (-2)$. Since $4 \cdot (-2) = -8$, it follows that $(-8) \div (-2) = 4$. This example suggests that the quotient of two negative numbers is a positive number.

We can use the following rule for dividing real numbers.

To Divide Real Numbers

- Divide their absolute values.
- If the numbers have the same sign, their quotient is positive; if the numbers have different signs, their quotient is negative.

EXAMPLE 1	PRACTICE 1
Find the quotient.	Divide.
a. $(-16) \div (-2)$	**a.** $40 \div (-5)$
b. $\dfrac{-24}{6}$	**b.** $\dfrac{-42}{-6}$
c. $\dfrac{9.4}{-2}$	**c.** $\dfrac{-6.3}{9}$
d. $\dfrac{-15}{-0.3}$	**d.** $\dfrac{-24}{-0.4}$

SOLUTION In each problem, first find the absolute values. Next, divide them. Then attach the appropriate sign to this quotient.

a. $(-16) \div (-2)$

$|-16| = 16$ and $|-2| = 2$

$16 \div 2 = 8$

Since the numbers have the *same sign*, their quotient is positive. So $(-16) \div (-2) = 8$.

b. $\dfrac{-24}{6}$ $\qquad$ $|-24| = 24$ and $|6| = 6$

$$\dfrac{24}{6} = 4$$

Since the numbers have *different* signs, the quotient is

negative. So $\dfrac{-24}{6} = -4$.

c. $\dfrac{9.4}{-2}$ $\qquad$ $|-9.4| = 9.4$ and $|-2| = 2$

$$\dfrac{9.4}{2} = 4.7$$

Since the numbers have different signs, the quotient is

negative. So $\dfrac{9.4}{-2} = -4.7$.

d. $\dfrac{-15}{-0.3}$ $\qquad$ $|-15| = 15$ and $|-0.3| = 0.3$

$$\dfrac{15}{0.3} = \dfrac{15\underset{\smile}{.0}}{0\underset{\smile}{.3}} = \dfrac{150}{3} = 50$$

Since the numbers have the same signs, the quotient is

positive. So $\dfrac{-15}{-0.3} = 50$.

TIP

Same Sign

$$\dfrac{\text{Positive}}{\text{Positive}} = \text{Positive} \qquad \dfrac{\text{Negative}}{\text{Negative}} = \text{Positive}$$

Different Signs

$$\dfrac{\text{Positive}}{\text{Negative}} = \text{Negative} \qquad \dfrac{\text{Negative}}{\text{Positive}} = \text{Negative}$$

Some division problems involve 0. For instance, $0 \div (-5) = 0$ because $(-5) \cdot 0 = 0$. On the other hand, $(-5) \div 0$ is *undefined* because there is no real number that when multiplied by 0 gives -5.

These two examples lead us to the following conclusion.

Division Involving Zero

For any nonzero real number a,

$$0 \div a = 0.$$

For any real number a,

$$a \div 0 \text{ is undefined.}$$

Recall that in Chapter R we expressed the rule for dividing fractions in terms of the *reciprocal* of a number. In algebra, we also refer to the reciprocal of a number as its *multiplicative inverse.*

Multiplicative Inverse Property

For any nonzero real number a,

$$a \cdot \frac{1}{a} = 1 \quad \text{and} \quad \frac{1}{a} \cdot a = 1,$$

where a and $\frac{1}{a}$ are **multiplicative inverses** (or **reciprocals**) of each other.

This property says that the product of a number and its multiplicative inverse is 1. For example,

- $\frac{1}{3}$ and 3 are multiplicative inverses because $\frac{1}{3} \cdot 3 = 1$

- $\frac{5}{-6}$ and $\frac{-6}{5}$ are multiplicative inverses because $\frac{5}{-6} \cdot \frac{-6}{5} = 1$

TIP A number and its reciprocal have the same sign.

EXAMPLE 2

Complete the following table.

SOLUTION

	Number	Reciprocal
a.	4	$\frac{1}{4}$ is the reciprocal of 4 because $4 \cdot \frac{1}{4} = 1$
b.	$-\frac{3}{4}$	$-\frac{4}{3}$ is the reciprocal of $-\frac{3}{4}$ because $-\frac{3}{4} \cdot \left(-\frac{4}{3}\right) = 1$
c.	-10	$\frac{1}{-10}$ or $-\frac{1}{10}$ is the reciprocal of -10 because $-10\left(\frac{1}{-10}\right) = 1$
d.	$1\frac{1}{2}$	$\frac{2}{3}$ is the reciprocal of $1\frac{1}{2}$ because $1\frac{1}{2} \cdot \frac{2}{3} = \frac{3}{2} \cdot \frac{2}{3} = 1$

PRACTICE 2

Fill in the following table.

	Number	Reciprocal
a.	-5	
b.	$\frac{1}{-8}$	
c.	$1\frac{1}{3}$	
d.	$-\frac{8}{5}$	

TIP We can rewrite a fraction such as $\frac{1}{-10}$ or $\frac{-1}{10}$ as $-\frac{1}{10}$. That is,

$$\frac{1}{-10} = \frac{-1}{10} = -\frac{1}{10}.$$

Now let's consider division of real numbers by using reciprocals. Recall that we subtract by adding an opposite. Similarly, we can divide by multiplying by a reciprocal.

Division of Real Numbers

For any real numbers a and b, where b is nonzero,

$$a \div b = \frac{a}{b} = a \cdot \frac{1}{b}.$$

This rule states that to divide two real numbers, multiply by the reciprocal of the divisor.

EXAMPLE 3

Divide.

a. $-\dfrac{1}{3} \div \dfrac{5}{6}$

b. $-\dfrac{1}{2} \div 4$

SOLUTION

a. $-\dfrac{1}{3} \div \dfrac{5}{6} = -\dfrac{1}{3} \cdot \dfrac{6}{5} = -\dfrac{1}{\overset{}{\underset{1}{\cancel{3}}}} \cdot \dfrac{\overset{2}{\cancel{6}}}{5} = -\dfrac{2}{5}$

b. $-\dfrac{1}{2} \div 4 = -\dfrac{1}{2} \div \dfrac{4}{1} = -\dfrac{1}{2} \cdot \dfrac{1}{4} = -\dfrac{1}{8}$

PRACTICE 3

Divide.

a. $-\dfrac{8}{9} \div \dfrac{2}{3}$

b. $-10 \div \left(-\dfrac{2}{5}\right)$

We use the order of operations rule to simplify the following expressions.

EXAMPLE 4

Simplify.

a. $-8 \div (-2)(-2)$

b. $\dfrac{-5 + (-7)}{2}$

SOLUTION

a. $-8 \div (-2)(-2) = 4(-2)$ **Perform multiplications and divisions as they occur from left to right. Divide −8 by −2.**

$= -8$ **Multiply.**

b. $\dfrac{-5 + (-7)}{2} = \dfrac{-12}{2}$ **Parentheses are understood to be around the numerator. Add −5 and −7.**

$= -6$ **Divide.**

PRACTICE 4

Simplify.

a. $(-3)(-4) \div (2)(-2)$

b. $\dfrac{-9 - (-3)}{2}$

EXAMPLE 5

During clinical practice, a student nurse took care of a patient with a fever. He recorded the patient's temperature at the same time every day for five days. The following table shows the change in the patient's temperature each day.

Day	Temperature Change
Monday	Up 2.5°
Tuesday	Down 2°
Wednesday	Down 1.5°
Thursday	Up 1°
Friday	Down 3°

What was the average daily change in the patient's temperature?

SOLUTION To compute the average daily change, we add the five temperature changes and divide the sum by 5—the number of days the temperature was recorded.

$$\frac{2.5 + (-2) + (-1.5) + 1 + (-3)}{5}$$

Since parentheses are understood to be around both the numerator and the denominator, we find the sum in the numerator before dividing by the denominator.

$$\frac{2.5 + (-2) + (-1.5) + 1 + (-3)}{5} = \frac{-3}{5} = -0.6$$

Therefore, the average daily change during the five days was $-0.6°$.

PRACTICE 5

During the past four weeks, the value of a particular stock market investment changed as follows.

Week	Change
1	Down $300
2	Up $200
3	Down $500
4	Up $100

What was the average weekly change in the value of the investment?

Exercises 1.5

FOR EXTRA HELP

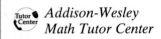 *Student's Solutions Manual*

 *Addison-Wesley Math Tutor Center*

MyMathLab

Videotape 2/DVT 2

Complete each table.

1.

Number	Reciprocal
a. $-\dfrac{1}{2}$	
b. 5	
c. $-\dfrac{3}{4}$	
d. $3\frac{1}{5}$	
e. -1	

2.

Number	Reciprocal
a. -12	
b. $\dfrac{1}{4}$	
c. 7	
d. $-2\frac{1}{3}$	
e. $-\dfrac{5}{6}$	

Divide.

3. $-8 \div (-1)$

4. $0 \div (-10)$

5. $-63 \div 7$

6. $16 \div (-4)$

7. $\dfrac{0}{-9}$

8. $\dfrac{-12}{3}$

9. $-2500 \div 100$

10. $-300 \div (-10)$

11. $-200 \div (-8)$

12. $400 \div (-5)$

13. $-64 \div (-16)$

14. $81 \div (-9)$

15. $\dfrac{-25}{-5}$

16. $\dfrac{-125}{5}$

17. $\dfrac{-2}{16}$

18. $\dfrac{2}{-10}$

19. $\dfrac{10}{-20}$

20. $\dfrac{-35}{-40}$

21. $\dfrac{4}{5} \div \left(-\dfrac{2}{3}\right)$

22. $-\dfrac{7}{12} \div \left(-\dfrac{1}{6}\right)$

23. $8 \div \left(-\dfrac{1}{4}\right)$

24. $(-5) \div \left(-\dfrac{1}{6}\right)$

25. $2\frac{1}{2} \div (-20)$

26. $\dfrac{4}{5} \div (-1\frac{1}{15})$

27. $(-3.5) \div 7$ **28.** $(-0.56) \div (-8)$ **29.** $10 \div (-0.5)$ **30.** $4.5 \div -3$

31. $\dfrac{-7.2}{0.9}$ **32.** $\dfrac{-2.5}{5}$ **33.** $\dfrac{-3}{-0.3}$ **34.** $\dfrac{1.8}{-0.6}$

Divide and round to the nearest hundredth.

35. $(-15.5484) \div (-6.13)$ **36.** $6.4516 \div (-3.54)$ **37.** $-0.8385 \div (0.715)$ **38.** $0.3102 \div (-0.129)$

Simplify.

39. $-16 \div (-2)(-2)$ **40.** $-3(-8) \div (-2)$ **41.** $(3 - 7) \div (-4)$ **42.** $[10 - (-8)] \div (-9)$

43. $\dfrac{2 + (-6)}{-2}$ **44.** $\dfrac{-10 - (-4)}{3}$ **45.** $(4 - 6) \div (1 - 5)$ **46.** $(-15 - 3) \div (-2 - 4)$

47. $-56 \div 7 - 4 \cdot (-3)$ **48.** $32 \div (-8) + (-5) \cdot 6$

Applications

Solve. Express your answer as a real number.

49. The change in a stock market index over a 5-day period was -130. What was the average daily change?

50. Two investors bought an equal number of shares of stock in a company. The value of their stock fell by $7000. How much did each of the investors lose?

51. The population of a city decreased by 47,355 people in 10 years. Find the average annual change in population.

52. The federal deficit in 1940 was about $3 billion. Five years later at the end of World War II, it was about $48 billion. How many times the deficit of 1940 was that of 1945? (**Source:** *Budget of the United States Government, Fiscal Year 2000,* 1999)

53. A football running back lost a total of 24 yd in 6 plays. What was the average number of yards he lost on each play?

54. A client at a weight-loss clinic lost 20 lb in 15 weeks. What was the client's average weekly change in weight?

55. A small company's business expenses for the year totaled $72,000. What were the company's average monthly expenses?

56. Over a 5-year period, the height of a cliff eroded by 4.5 ft. By how many feet did the cliff erode per year?

57. A meteorologist predicted an average daily high temperature of $-3°F$ for a five-day period. During this period, the daily high temperatures (in Fahrenheit degrees) were 2°, 0°, $-7°$ $-11°$, and 1°. Was the meteorologist's prediction correct?

58. The value of a house decreased from $183,000 to $174,000 during a decade. What was the average amount of depreciation per year?

• *Check your answers on page A-3.*

Mindstretchers

PATTERNS

1. Find the missing numbers in the following:

$+1296, +648, -216, -108, +36, +18, -6, \_\_, \_\_, \_\_$

GROUPWORK

2. Consider the following five integers: $-2, 6, -9, 18, -36$. Working with a partner, explain which two of the five integers you would choose

a. to find the smallest quotient.

b. to find the largest quotient.

WRITING

3. Explain the difference between the *opposite* of a number and the *reciprocal* of a number. _____

_____

1.6 Algebraic Expressions, Translations, and Exponents

Algebraic Expressions

Suppose that each week, you spend $\frac{2}{5}$ of your time on campus working in the student activities area. If the *variable n* represents the total number of hours that you spend during a particular week on campus, then the *algebraic expression* $\frac{2}{5} \cdot n$ stands for the amount of time you worked in the student activities area that week.

In algebra, a variable is used in two ways—as an unknown quantity or as a quantity that can change in value. We can use any letter or symbol to represent a variable. By contrast, a *constant* is a known quantity whose value does not change. So n is a variable, whereas $\frac{2}{5}$ is a constant. An algebraic expression is an expression in which constants and variables are combined using standard arithmetic operations. So $\frac{2}{5} \cdot n$ is an example of an algebraic expression. When writing an algebraic expression involving a product, we usually omit any multiplication symbol. For instance, we would write $\frac{2}{5} n$ rather than $\frac{2}{5} \cdot n$.

Algebraic expressions consist of one or more *terms*, separated by addition signs. If there are subtraction signs, we can rewrite the expression in an equivalent form using addition. For instance, we can think of the algebraic expression

$$2x + \frac{y}{3} - 4 \quad \text{as} \quad 2x + \frac{y}{3} + (-4).$$

This algebraic expression is made up of three terms.

$$\underset{\text{Terms}}{2x + \frac{y}{3} + (-4)}$$

Definition

A **term** is a number, a variable, or the product or quotient of numbers and variables.

EXAMPLE 1

Find the number of terms in each expression.

a. $3y + 1$ **b.** $\frac{a}{b}$

SOLUTION

a. The expression $3y + 1$ has two terms.

b. The expression $\frac{a}{b}$ has one term.

PRACTICE 1

Determine how many terms are in each expression.

a. $2a + 3 - b$ **b.** $-4xy$

Translating Algebraic Expressions to Word Phrases and Word Phrases to Algebraic Expressions

In solving word problems, we may need to translate algebraic expressions to word phrases and vice versa. First, let's consider the many ways we can translate algebraic expressions to words.

$x + 5$ translates to
• x plus 5
• x increased by 5
• the sum of x and 5
• 5 more than x

$y - 4$ translates to
• y minus 4
• y decreased by 4
• the difference between y and 4
• 4 less than y

$\frac{2}{5}n$, $\frac{2}{5} \cdot n$, or $\left(\frac{2}{5}\right)(n)$ translates to
• $\frac{2}{5}$ times n
• the product of $\frac{2}{5}$ and n
• $\frac{2}{5}$ of n

$z \div 3$ or $\frac{z}{3}$ translates to
• z divided by 3
• the quotient of z and 3
• the ratio of z and 3
• z over 3

Note that there are other possible translations as well.

EXAMPLE 2	**PRACTICE 2**
Translate each algebraic expression to words.	Translate each algebraic expression to words.
SOLUTION	

Alegraic Expression	Translation
a. $5x$	5 times x
b. $y - (-2)$	the difference between y and -2
c. $-3 + z$	the sum of -3 and z
d. $\frac{m}{-4}$	m divided by -4
e. $\frac{3}{5}n$	three-fifths of n

Algebraic Expression	Translation
a. $\frac{1}{3}p$	
b. $9 - x$	
c. $s \div (-8)$	
d. $n + (-6)$	
e. $\frac{3}{8}m$	

Note that in Example 2 other translations are also correct.

EXAMPLE 3

Translate each algebraic expression to words.

SOLUTION

Algebraic Expression	Translation
a. $2m + 5$	five more than twice m
b. $1 - 3y$	the difference between 1 and $3y$
c. $4(x + y)$	four times the sum of x and y
d. $\dfrac{a + b}{a - b}$	the sum of a and b divided by the difference between a and b

PRACTICE 3

Translate each algebraic expression to words.

Algebraic Expression	Translation
a. $2x - 3y$	
b. $4 + 3m$	
c. $5(a - b)$	
d. $\dfrac{r - s}{r + s}$	

Note that in Example 3(c) the sum $x + y$ is considered to be a single quantity, because it is enclosed in parentheses. Similarly in Example 3(d), the numerator $a + b$ and the denominator $a - b$ are each viewed as a single quantity.

In the previous examples, we discussed translating algebraic expressions to word phrases. Now let's look at some examples of translating word phrases to algebraic expressions.

EXAMPLE 4

Translate each word phrase to an algebraic expression.

SOLUTION

Word Phrase	Translation
a. twice x	$2x$
b. n decreased by -7	$n - (-7)$
c. the quotient of -6 and z	$(-6) \div z$ or $\dfrac{-6}{z}$
d. one-half of n	$\dfrac{1}{2}n$
e. ten more than y	$y + 10$

PRACTICE 4

Express each word phrase as an algebraic expression.

Word Phrase	Translation
a. one-sixth of n	
b. n increased by -5	
c. the difference between m and -4	
d. the ratio of 100 and x	
e. the product of -2 and y	

EXAMPLE 5

Translate each word phrase to an algebraic expression.

SOLUTION

Word Phrase	Translation
a. the difference between x and the product of three and y	$x - 3y$
b. six more than four times z	$4z + 6$
c. ten times the quantity r minus s	$10(r - s)$
d. twice q divided by the sum of p and q	$\dfrac{2q}{p + q}$

PRACTICE 5

Express each word phrase as an algebraic expression.

Word Phrase	Translation
a. the sum of m and $-n$	
b. eleven less than the product of five and y	
c. the sum of m and n divided by the product of m and n	
d. negative six times	

EXAMPLE 6

If a polygon has n sides, the sum of the measures of its interior angles, in degrees, is 180 times the quantity n minus 2. Write this expression symbolically.

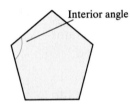

Interior angle

SOLUTION We translate the word phrase into an algebraic expression as follows:

180	times	the quantity n minus 2
↓	↓	↓
180	·	$(n - 2)$

So the algebraic expression is $180(n - 2)$, which is in degrees.

PRACTICE 6

In a keyboarding class, you type 60 words per minute. How many words do you type in $(m + 1)$ minutes?

Exponents

As discussed in Chapter R, we can use *exponential notation* as a shorthand method for representing repeated multiplication of the same factor. For instance, we can write $5 \cdot 5 \cdot 5 \cdot 5$ in *exponential form* as

This expression is read "5 to the fourth power."

Definition

For any real number x and any positive integer a,

$$x^a = \underbrace{x \cdot x \cdots x \cdot x}_{a \text{ factors}},$$

where x is called the **base** and a is called the **exponent** (or **power**).

In exponential notation, the exponent indicates how many times the base is used as a factor.

The expression x^a is read "x to the ath power," or "x to the a"; however, the exponents 2 and 3 are usually read in a special way. For instance, we generally read 5^2 as "5 *squared*" rather than "5 to the second power." Similarly, we read 5^3 as "5 *cubed*" instead of "5 to the third power."

In Chapter R, we evaluated 2^4. Now let's consider the expression $(-2)^4$. To evaluate this expression, we multiply 4 factors of -2:

$$(-2)^4 = \underbrace{(-2)(-2)(-2)(-2)}_{4 \text{ factors of } -2}$$

Base ⟶ | Exponent

$$(-2)^4 = \underbrace{(-2)(-2)}(-2)(-2)$$
$$= \underbrace{4(-2)}(-2)$$
$$= \underbrace{(-8)(-2)}$$
$$= 16$$

In short, $(-2)^4 = 16$.

Next let's consider the expression -2^4. To evaluate this expression, we multiply 4 factors of 2. Then we take the opposite:

$$-2^4 = -\underbrace{(2)(2)(2)(2)}_{4 \text{ factors of } 2}$$

Base ⟶ | Exponent

$$= -16$$

Note that in $(-2)^4$ the base is -2, whereas in -2^4 the base is 2.

EXAMPLE 7

Evaluate.

a. $(-3)^4$

b. $-3^4 \cdot (-2)^2$

SOLUTION

a. $(-3)^4 = (-3)(-3)(-3)(-3) = 81$

b. $-3^4 \cdot (-2)^2 = -(3)(3)(3)(3)(-2)(-2)$
$$= -(81)(4)$$
$$= -324$$

PRACTICE 7

Evaluate.

a. -6^2

b. $(-6)^2 \cdot (-3)^2$

Sometimes we put an expression into exponential form. Such expressions may involve more than one base. For instance, the expression $-4(-4)(-4)(-3)(-3)$ can be rewritten in terms of powers of -4 and -3:

$$\underbrace{-4(-4)(-4)}_{\substack{3 \text{ factors} \\ \text{of } -4}}\underbrace{(-3)(-3)}_{\substack{2 \text{ factors} \\ \text{of } -3}} = (-4)^3(-3)^2$$

Consider the following examples.

EXAMPLE 8

Express $6(6)(-10)(-10)(-10)(-10)$ in exponential form.

SOLUTION

$$\underbrace{6(6)}_{\substack{2 \text{ factors} \\ \text{of } 6}}\underbrace{(-10)(-10)(-10)(-10)}_{4 \text{ factors of } -10} = 6^2(-10)^4$$

PRACTICE 8

Write $2(2)(2)(2)(-5)(-5)$ using exponents.

EXAMPLE 9

Rewrite each expression using exponents.

a. $-2n \cdot n$

b. $-3x \cdot x \cdot y \cdot y \cdot y \cdot y$

SOLUTION

a. $-2n \cdot n = -2n^2$

b. $-3x \cdot x \cdot y \cdot y \cdot y \cdot y = -3x^2 \cdot y^4$

Can you explain the difference between the expressions $2n$ and n^2?

PRACTICE 9

Express in exponential form.

a. $-x \cdot x \cdot x \cdot x \cdot x$

b. $2m \cdot m \cdot m \cdot n \cdot n \cdot n \cdot n$

EXAMPLE 10

The population of a small town doubles every 5 years. If the town's population started with n people, what is its population after 20 years?

SOLUTION We know that the town's population started with n people and doubles every 5 years. To find the population after 20 years, consider the following table.

Time (in years)	Number of 5-Year Time Periods	Pattern	Population of the Town
Initial	0	$2^0 \cdot n$	$1n$
5	1	$2^1 \cdot n$	$2n$
10	2	$2^2 \cdot n$	$4n$
15	3	$2^3 \cdot n$	$8n$
20	4	$2^4 \cdot n$	$16n$

↑
Each time period,
the population is doubled,
that is, multiplied by 2.

So the population after 20 years is $16n$, or $2^4 \cdot n$ in exponential form.

PRACTICE 10

A bacteriologist observes that the population of a bacteria growing in a petri dish triples in size every 2 hr. If x cells were present in the initial population, what was the population after 10 hr? Write the answer using exponents.

Exercises 1.6

FOR EXTRA HELP

📖 *Student's Solutions Manual*

📞 *Addison-Wesley Math Tutor Center*

🚪 *MyMathLab*

📼 *Videotape 2/DVT 2*

Determine the number of terms in each expression.

1. $-5x$

2. $a + b$

3. $xy + \dfrac{x}{y} - z$

4. $\dfrac{m}{n}$

5. $10 + 2y$

6. $x - y + z$

Translate each algebraic expression to a word phrase.

7. $3 + t$

8. $r + 2$

9. $x - 4$

10. $y - 10$

11. $7r$

12. $-4x$

13. $\dfrac{a}{4}$

14. $x \div 3$

15. $\dfrac{4}{5}w$

16. $\dfrac{1}{2}y$

17. $-3 + z$

18. $m - (-5)$

19. $2n + 1$

20. $-3c + 4$

21. $4(x - y)$

22. $2(m + n)$

23. $1 - 3x$

24. $5x - 2$

25. $\dfrac{ab}{a + b}$

26. $\dfrac{x + y}{x - y}$

27. $2x - 5y$

28. $4a + 7b$

Translate each word phrase to an algebraic expression.

29. five more than x

30. y increased by 10

31. d minus 4

32. twelve less than n

33. the product of -6 and a

34. negative seven times x

35. the sum of y and -15

36. the difference of 2 and z

37. one-eighth of k

38. one-half of m **39.** the quotient of m and n **40.** n divided by y

41. the difference between a and twice b **42.** ten less than three times x

43. five more than four times z **44.** the sum of twice n and three times m

45. twelve times the quantity x minus y **46.** twice the sum of three times m and n

47. b divided by the difference between a and b **48.** x times y divided by the quantity x minus y

Evaluate.

49. -3^2 **50.** $(-4)^2$ **51.** $(-3)^3 \cdot (-4)^2$ **52.** $-4^2 \cdot (-3)^2$

Write using exponents.

53. $-2(-2)(-2)(4)(4)$ **54.** $-5(-5)(-5)(-5)(2)(2)$ **55.** $6(6)(-3)(-3)(-3)$

56. $-2(-2)(4)(4)(4)(4)$ **57.** $3(n)(n)(n)$ **58.** $-2x \cdot x$

59. $-4a \cdot a \cdot a \cdot b \cdot b$ **60.** $5r \cdot s \cdot s \cdot s \cdot s$ **61.** $-y \cdot y \cdot y$

62. $(-y)(-y)(-y)$ **63.** $10a \cdot a \cdot a \cdot b \cdot b \cdot c$ **64.** $-5x \cdot y \cdot y \cdot z$

65. $-x \cdot x \cdot y \cdot y \cdot y$ **66.** $(-x)(-x)(-x)(-y)(-y)$

Applications

Solve.

67. In the triangle shown, write an expression for the sum of the measures of the three angles.

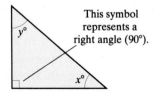

This symbol represents a right angle (90°).

68. Write an expression for the sum of the lengths of the sides in the figure shown.

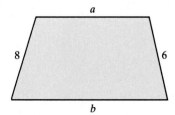

69. Suppose that p partners share equally in the profits of an e-business. What is each partner's share, if the profits were $30,000?

70. An investment of a dollars doubles in value. What is the new value of this investment?

71. A plane ticket costs t dollars before taxes. If the taxes on the plane ticket were x dollars, what was the total cost of the ticket?

72. Tonight's attendance at a concert was 100 more than double the attendance last night. If p people attended the concert last night, how many people attended the concert tonight?

73. An initial investment of 5000 dollars doubles every 10 years. Write in exponential form the value of the investment after 30 years.

74. A colony of bacteria *E. coli* doubles in size every 20 min when grown in a rich medium. If the colony started with m bacteria, how many bacteria were in the colony 2 hr later? Express the answer using exponents.

75. The area of a square can be found by squaring the length of a side. Write an expression in exponential form to represent the area of the following square.

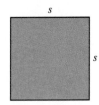

76. The volume of a cube can be found by cubing the length of an edge. Write an expression in exponential form to represent the volume of this cube.

77. A company buys a copier for $10,000. After n years, the Internal Revenue Service values the copier at $10,000 times $\frac{1}{20}$ times the quantity 20 minus n. Write this value as an algebraic expression.

78. In a math lab, a tutors were assisting b students each, and c tutors were assisting d students each. There were an additional e students in the lab. How many students were there in the lab altogether?

79. An area rug is placed on the wood floor shown. Find the area of the floor not covered by the rug.

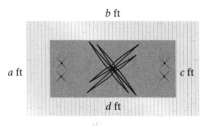

b ft

a ft   *c* ft

d ft

80. In a baseball game, a team scored 2 runs in each of *x* innings and 1 run in each of *y* innings. How many runs did the team score?

● *Check your answers on page A-3.*

Mindstretchers

WRITING

1. Algebra is used in all countries of the world regardless of the language spoken. If you know how to speak a language other than English, translate each of the following algebraic expressions to that language as well as to English.

a. $\dfrac{x}{2}$ _____

b. $2 - x$ _____

c. $6 + x$ _____

d. $3x$ _____

MATHEMATICAL REASONING

2. Can there be two different numbers *a* and *b* for which $a^b = b^a$? Justify your answer.

_____

GROUPWORK

3. The *algebra tiles* shown below represent the expressions $3x - 2$ and $x^2 + 1$, respectively.

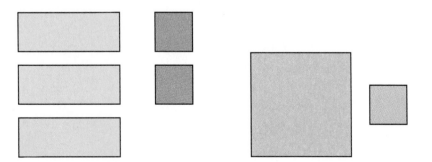

continued

Working with a partner, represent each of the following expressions by algebra tiles.

a. $x - 4$

b. $2x + 3$

c. $x^2 + x + 1$

1.7 Evaluating Algebraic Expressions and Formulas

OBJECTIVES

- *To evaluate algebraic expressions*
- *To translate rules to formulas*
- *To evaluate formulas*
- *To solve applied word problems involving algebraic expressions and formulas*

In the previous section, we discussed translations involving algebraic expressions. For these expressions to be useful, however, we need to be able to *evaluate* them.

Consider the following example. Suppose that you had a temporary job that lasted 75 days. If you were absent from work for d days, then it follows that you were at work for $75 - d$ days. To evaluate the expression $75 - d$ for a particular value of d, replace d with that number. For instance if you were not at work for 4 days, replace d in this expression with 4:

$$75 - d = 75 - 4 = 71$$

Replace d with 4.

We can conclude that you were at work 71 days.

The following method is helpful for evaluating expressions.

To Evaluate an Algebraic Expression
- Replace each variable with the given number.
- Then carry out the computation using the order of operations rule.

EXAMPLE 1

Evaluate each algebraic expression.

SOLUTION

Algebraic Expression	Value
a. $9 - z$, if $z = -2$	$9 - z = 9 - (-2) = 9 + 2 = 11$
b. $-2cd$, if $c = -1$ and $d = 2$	$-2cd = -2(-1)(2) = 4$

PRACTICE 1

Find the value of each algebraic expression.

Algebraic Expression	Value
a. $25 + m$, if $m = -10$	
b. $-3xy$, if $x = -2$ and $y = 5$	

In evaluating some algebraic expressions, we need to use the order of operations rule.

EXAMPLE 2

Find the value of each expression for $x = -3$, $y = 2$, $w = -5$, and $z = 4$.

a. $2x + 5y$

b. $4x^2$

c. $3(w + z)$

d. $2w^2 - 3y^3$

PRACTICE 2

Evaluate each expression for $a = 2$, $b = -3$, $c = -4$, and $d = 5$.

a. $5a - 2c$

b. $2(d - b)$

c. $3cd^2$

d. $2a^3 + 4b^2$

continued

93

SOLUTION

a. $2x + 5y = 2(-3) + 5(2)$ Replace x with -3 and y with 2.
Then multiply.

$\qquad\qquad = -6 + 10$ Add.

$\qquad\qquad = 4$

b. $4x^2 = 4(-3)^2$ Replace x with -3.

$\qquad = 4 \cdot 9$ Square -3.

$\qquad = 36$

c. $3(w + z) = 3(-5 + 4) = 3(-1) = -3$

d. $2w^2 - 3y^3 = 2(-5)^2 - 3(2)^3 = 2(25) - 3(8) = 50 - 24 = 26$

Consider the expression in Practice 2(c). Are $3cd^2$ and $3(cd)^2$ the same? If not, explain the difference between them.

EXAMPLE 3

Evaluate each expression if $a = 3$, $b = 4$, and $c = -2$.

a. $\dfrac{c}{5 - a}$ **b.** $\dfrac{b + c}{b - c}$

c. $(-b)^2$ **d.** $-b^2$

SOLUTION

a. $\dfrac{c}{5 - a} = \dfrac{-2}{5 - 3} = \dfrac{-2}{2} = -1$

b. $\dfrac{b + c}{b - c} = \dfrac{4 + (-2)}{4 - (-2)} = \dfrac{2}{6} = \dfrac{1}{3}$

c. $(-b)^2 = (-4)^2 = (-4)(-4) = 16$

d. $-b^2 = -4^2 = -(4)(4) = -16$

PRACTICE 3

Find the value of each expression when $x = -5$, $y = -3$, and $z = 1$.

a. $\dfrac{x - 2z}{y}$

b. $\dfrac{x - z}{x + y}$

c. $(-y)^4$

d. $-y^4$

Note the difference between the answers in Examples 3(c) and 3(d). In $(-4)^2$ the exponent applies to -4, that is, the base is -4. By contrast, in -4^2 the exponent applies to 4 only, because the base is 4.

EXAMPLE 4

Physicists have shown that if an object is shot straight upward at a speed of 100 ft/sec, its location after t sec will be

$$-16t^2 + 100t$$

feet above the point of release. How far above or below the point of release will the object be after 5 sec?

PRACTICE 4

In a statistics course, you need to evaluate the expression

$$\dfrac{a^2 + b^2 + c^2}{3}$$

Find the value of the expression for $a = -0.5$, $b = 0.3$, and $c = 0.2$, rounded to the nearest tenth.

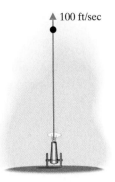

100 ft/sec

SOLUTION To determine the position of the object after 5 sec, we must substitute 5 for t in the expression $-16t^2 + 100t$.

$$-16t^2 + 100t = -16(5)^2 + 100(5)$$
$$= -16(25) + 100(5)$$
$$= -400 + 500$$
$$= 100$$

So after 5 sec, the object will be 100 ft above the point of release. Note that a position above the point of release is positive, whereas a position below the point of release is negative.

Formulas

A *formula* is an equation that provides a symbolic description of a real-world situation. Some formulas express geometric relationships; others express physical laws. Just as with algebraic expressions, the letters and mathematical symbols in a formula represent numbers and words.

EXAMPLE 5	PRACTICE 5
To predict the temperature T at a particular altitude a, meteorologists subtract $\frac{1}{200}$ of the altitude from the temperature g on the ground. Here, T and g are in degrees Fahrenheit and a is in feet. Translate this rule to a formula.	To convert a temperature C expressed in Celsius degrees to the temperature F expressed in Fahrenheit degrees, we multiply the Celsius temperature by $\frac{9}{5}$ and then add 32. Write a formula that expresses this relationship.

SOLUTION Stating the rule briefly in words, the temperature at a particular altitude equals the difference between the temperature on the ground and $\frac{1}{200}$ times the altitude. Now we translate this rule to mathematical symbols.

$$T = g - \frac{1}{200}a,$$

which is the desired formula.

The method of evaluating formulas is similar to that of evaluating algebraic expressions. We substitute all the given numbers for the variables and then carry out the computations using the order of operations rule.

EXAMPLE 6

The formula for finding simple interest is $I = Prt$, where I is the interest in dollars, P is the principal (the amount invested) in dollars, r is the annual rate of interest, and t is the time in years that the principal has been on deposit. Find the amount of interest on a principal of $3000 that has been on deposit for 2 years at a 6% annual rate of interest.

SOLUTION We know that $P = 3000$, $r = 6\%$, and $t = 2$. Converting 6% to its decimal form, we get 0.06. Substituting into the formula gives us

$$I = Prt$$
$$= 3000(0.06)(2)$$
$$= 360$$

So the interest earned is $360.

PRACTICE 6

Given the distance formula $d = rt$, find the value of d if the rate r is 50 mph and the time t is 1.6 hr.

EXAMPLE 7

The markup m on an item is its selling price s minus its cost c.

a. Express this relationship as a formula.

b. If a digital camera cost a retailer $399.95 and was then sold for $559, how much was the markup on the camera?

SOLUTION

a. We write the formula $m = s - c$.

b. To find the markup, we substitute for s and c.

$$m = s - c$$
$$= 559 - 399.95$$
$$= 159.05$$

So the markup was $159.05.

PRACTICE 7

Kelvin and Celsius temperature scales are commonly used in science. To convert a temperature expressed in Celsius degrees C to Kelvins K, add 273 to the Celsius temperature.

a. Write this relationship as a formula.

b. Suppose that in a chemistry experiment, C equals −6. What is the value of K?

Exercises 1.7

FOR EXTRA HELP

📖 Student's Solutions Manual

Addison-Wesley Math Tutor Center

MyMathLab

Videotape 2/DVT 2

Evaluate each algebraic expression, if a = 4, b = 3, and c = −2.

1. $b - 5$

2. $-6 + a$

3. $-2ac$

4. $4cb$

5. $-2a^2$

6. $-b^2$

7. $2a - 15$

8. $5 + 3c$

9. $a + 2c$

10. $4b - 3a$

11. $2(a - c)$

12. $-3(a + b)$

13. $-a + b^2$

14. $-b + c^2$

15. $3a^2 - c^3$

16. $c^3 - 2a^2$

17. $\dfrac{a + b}{b - a}$

18. $\dfrac{a - c}{c + a}$

19. $\dfrac{3}{5}(a + b + c)^2$

20. $\dfrac{5}{9}(a - b - c)^2$

Evaluate each algebraic expression if w = −0.5, x = 2, y = −3, and z = 1.5.

21. $2w^2 - 3x + y - 4z$

22. $2x - 3w - y^2 + z$

23. $w - 7z - \dfrac{1}{4}(x - 6y)$

24. $5x - \dfrac{2}{5}(8w + 2y) - 4z$

25. $\dfrac{-10xy}{(w - z)^2}$

26. $\dfrac{-(2z - y)^2}{9wx}$

Complete each table.

27.

x	2x + 5
0	
1	
2	
−1	
−2	

28.

x	−3x + 1
0	
1	
2	
−1	
−2	

29.

y	y − 0.5
0	
1	
2	
3	
4	

30.

y	y + 2.8
0	
1	
2	
3	
4	

31.

x	$-\dfrac{1}{2}x$
0	
2	
4	
−2	
−4	

32.

x	$\dfrac{3}{5}x$
0	
5	
10	
−5	
−10	

33.

n	$\frac{n}{2}$
2	
4	
6	
-2	
-4	

34.

n	$-\frac{n}{5}$
5	
10	
-5	
-10	
-15	

35.

g	$-g^2$
0	
1	
2	
-1	
-2	

36.

g	g^2
0	
1	
2	
-1	
-2	

37.

a	$a^2 + 2a - 2$
0	
1	
2	
-1	
-2	

38.

a	$-a^2 - 2a + 2$
0	
1	
2	
-1	
-2	

Evaluate each formula for the given quantity.

Formula	Given	Find
39. $C = \frac{5}{9}(F - 32)$	$F = -4°$	C
40. $A = P(1 + rt)$	$P = \$2000$, $r = 5\%$, and $t = 2$ yr	A
41. $P = 2l + 2w$	$l = 2\frac{1}{2}$ ft and $w = 1\frac{1}{4}$ ft	P
42. $A = \dfrac{a + b + c + d}{4}$	$a = -8$, $b = -6$, $c = 4$, and $d = -2$	A
43. $C = \pi d$	$\pi \approx 3.14$ and $d = 100$ m	C
44. $C = A \cdot \dfrac{W}{150 \text{ lb}}$	$A = 100$ mg and $W = 30$ lb	C
45. $A = 6e^2$	e $= 1.5$ cm	A
46. $V = \pi r^2 h$	$\pi \approx 3.14$, $r = 10$ in., and $h = 10$ in.	V

Applications

Write each relationship as a formula.

47. The average A of three numbers a, b, and c is the sum of the numbers divided by 3.

48. For every right triangle, the sum of the squares of the two legs *a* and *b* equals the square of the hypotenuse *c*.

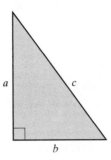

49. The perimeter *P* of a rectangle is twice the sum of the length *l* and the width *w*.

50. The *aspect ratio* of a hang glider is a measure of how well it can glide and soar. The aspect ratio *R* is the square of the glider's wingspan *s* divided by the wing area *A*.

51. The equivalent energy *E* of a mass equals the product of the mass *m* and the square of the speed of light *c*.

52. The weight of an object depends on the gravitational pull of the planet or moon it is on. For instance, the weight *E* of an astronaut on Earth is 6 times the astronaut's weight *m* on the moon.

53. The length *l* of a certain spring in centimeters is 25 more than 0.4 times the weight *w* in grams of the object hanging from it.

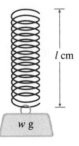

54. In electronics, when two resistors R_1 and R_2 are connected in parallel, the total resistance *R* between the points *X* and *Y* can be founded by dividing the product of the resistances by the sum of the resistances.

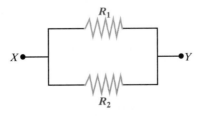

Solve.

55. The distance that a free-falling object drops, ignoring friction, is given by the formula

$$S = \frac{1}{2}gt^2,$$

where S is the distance in feet, g is the acceleration due to gravity, and t is time in seconds. Find the distance that an object falls if $g = 32$ ft/sec^2 and $t = 2$ sec.

56. The volume of a right circular cylinder is given by the formula

$$V = \pi r^2 h,$$

where r is the radius of the base of the cylinder and h is the height of the cylinder. For the cylinder shown, find the volume in cubic centimeters.

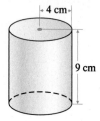

57. The percent markup m of an item is equal to 100 times the difference of the selling price s of the item and its cost c, divided by the cost.

a. Express this relationship as a formula.

b. If the selling price of a bottle of vitamin E is $8.75 and the cost is $6.25, what is the percent markup on the vitamin E?

58. To calculate the speed f of an object in feet per second, we multiply its speed m in miles per hour by $\frac{22}{15}$.

a. Write this relationship as a formula.

b. If an object is moving at 60 mph, what is its speed in feet per second?

• *Check your answers on page A-3.*

Mindstretchers

MATHEMATICAL REASONING

1. Complete the first three rows of the following table. Make up your own values of *a* and *b* in the 4th and 5th rows, and complete the table.

a	*b*	*a* + *b*	|*a*|	|*b*|	|*a*| + |*b*|	|*a* + *b*|	T or F, |*a*| + |*b*| = |*a* + *b*|	T or F, |*a*| + |*b*| ≥ |*a* + *b*|
−3	4							
1	−2							
−5	−4							

What general relationship do these examples suggest? Explain why this relationship is true. _____

_____

PATTERNS

2. Consider the following table.

Odd number, *n*	1	3	5	7	...	1999
Counting number, *C*	1	2	3	4	...	1000

Write a formula that expresses *C* in terms of *n*.

GROUPWORK

3. Some expressions that appear to be different are, in fact, equivalent.

a. Confirm that the expressions $\dfrac{x^2 - 9}{x + 3}$ and $x - 3$ are equal for various values of *x*.

_____

b. Determine if there are any values of *x* for which the expressions are not equal.

_____

_____

1.8 Simplifying Algebraic Expressions

OBJECTIVES

- *To combine like terms*
- *To simplify algebraic expressions involving parentheses*
- *To solve applied problems involving algebraic expressions*

Each variable term of an algebraic expression is said to have a *numerical coefficient* or, simply, a *coefficient*. For instance, the term $3y$ has coefficient 3 and the term $-4y$ has coefficient -4. Note that the coefficient of y is 1, because $y = 1y$. Likewise, the coefficient of $-y$ is -1, because $-y = -1y$.

The terms $3y$, $-4y$, and y are said to be *like* terms.

> **Definition**
>
> **Like** terms are terms that have the same variables with the same exponents. Terms that are not like are called **unlike** terms.

EXAMPLE 1

For each algebraic expression, identify the terms and indicate whether they are like or unlike.

a. $3a + 5b$ **b.** $n - 6n$

c. $4x^2 + 2x$ **d.** $2a^2b - 3a^2b$

SOLUTION

a. $3a + 5b$ has terms $3a$ and $5b$. Unlike

different variables

b. $n - 6n$ has terms n and $-6n$. Like

same variable

c. $4x^2 + 2x$ has terms $4x^2$ and $2x$. Unlike

same variable
but different exponents

d. $2a^2b - 3a^2b$ has terms $2a^2b$ and $-3a^2b$. Like

same variables
with same exponents

PRACTICE 1

Identify the terms of each algebraic expression and state whether they are like or unlike.

a. $m - 3m$

b. $5x + 7$

c. $2x^2y - 3xy^2$

d. $m + 2m - 4m$

Combining Like Terms

An important property used to simplify algebraic expressions is the *distributive property*. This property allows us to multiply a number by the sum of two numbers.

> **The Distributive Property**
>
> For any real numbers a, b, and c,
>
> $$a \cdot (b + c) = a \cdot b + a \cdot c.$$

Another way to express the distributive property is $(b + c)\,a = ba + ca$. Can you explain why?

The distributive property also holds for $a\,(b - c)$. Since $b - c = b + (-c)$, it follows that $a\,(b - c) = ab - ac$ and $(b - c)\,a = ba - ca$.

EXAMPLE 2	PRACTICE 2

EXAMPLE 2

Use the distributive property.

a. $2(x + y)$

b. $(3 + 7) \cdot n$

c. $(-5)(a - 2b)$

d. $0.6(x - 5)$

SOLUTION

a. $2(x + y) = 2 \cdot x + 2 \cdot y = 2x + 2y$

b. $(3 + 7) \cdot n = 3 \cdot n + 7 \cdot n = 3n + 7n$

c. $(-5)(a - 2b) = (-5) \cdot a + (-5) \cdot (-2b) = -5a + 10b$

d. $0.6(x - 5) = 0.6(x) - 0.6(5) = 0.6x - 3$

PRACTICE 2

Rewrite using the distributive property.

a. $(-10)(4r + s)$

b. $(5 + 1) \cdot w$

c. $3(g - 3h)$

d. $1.5(y + 2)$

We can use the distributive property to simplify algebraic expressions involving like terms. Adding or subtracting like terms using the distributive property is called *combining like terms*. Unlike terms, such as $4x^2$ and $2x$, cannot be combined.

EXAMPLE 3

Simplify.

a. $2x + 6x$

b. $a - 8a$

c. $6y - y + 5$

d. $3b + 2b - 5b$

SOLUTION

a. $2x + 6x = (2 + 6)x$ Use the distributive property.

       $= 8x$ Add 2 and 6.

b. $a - 8a = (1 - 8)a$ Recall that the coefficient of a is 1.
       Use the distributive property.

       $= -7a$

c. $6y - y + 5 = (6 - 1)\,y + 5$ Recall that the coefficient of $-y$ is
       -1. Use the distributive property.

       $= 5y + 5$

d. $3b + 2b - 5b = (3 + 2 - 5)b$ Use the distributive property.
       Recall that $0 \cdot b = 0$.

       $= 0 \cdot b$

       $= 0$

PRACTICE 3

Simplify.

a. $5x + x$

b. $-5y - y$

c. $a - 3a + b$

d. $-9t + 3t + 6t$

EXAMPLE 4

Combine like terms if possible.

a. $2x^2 + x$ **b.** $8m^2n^2 + 2m^2n^2$ **c.** $-6a^2b + 5a^2b$

SOLUTION

a. $\underbrace{2x^2 + x}_{\text{Unlike terms}}$ This algebraic expression cannot be simplified because the terms are unlike.

b. $\underbrace{8m^2n^2 + 2m^2n^2}_{\text{Like terms}} = (8 + 2)\,m^2n^2 = 10m^2n^2$

c. $\underbrace{-6a^2b + 5a^2b}_{\text{Like terms}} = (-6 + 5)a^2b = -1a^2b = -a^2b$

PRACTICE 4

Combine like terms if possible.

a. $y^2 - 3y^2$

b. $7a^2b + 3ab^2$

c. $4xy^2 - xy^2$

Simplifying Algebraic Expressions Involving Parentheses

Some algebraic expressions involve parentheses. We can use the distributive property to remove the parentheses in order to simplify these expressions.

EXAMPLE 5

Simplify: $\dfrac{1}{2}(x + 6) - 4$

SOLUTION

$$\dfrac{1}{2}(x + 6) - 4 = \dfrac{1}{2}x + 3 - 4 \quad \text{Use the distributive property.}$$

$$= \dfrac{1}{2}x - 1 \quad \text{Combine like terms.}$$

PRACTICE 5

Simplify: $3(y - 4) + 2$

Let's consider simplifying algebraic expressions such as $-(4y - 6)$ in which a negative sign precedes an expression in parentheses.

EXAMPLE 6

Simplify: $-(4y - 6)$

SOLUTION

$$-(4y - 6) = -1(4y - 6) \quad \text{The coefficient of } -(4y - 6) \text{ is } -1.$$
$$= -1 \cdot 4y + (-1)(-6) \quad \text{Use the distributive property.}$$
$$= -4y + 6$$

Because the terms in the expression $-4y + 6$ are unlike, it is not possible to simplify the expression further.

PRACTICE 6

Simplify: $-(2a - 3b)$

EXAMPLE 7

Simplify: $2x - 3 - (x + 4)$

SOLUTION

$$2x - 3 - (x + 4) = 2x - 3 - 1(x + 4)$$ The coefficient of $-(x - 4)$ is -1.
$$= 2x - 3 - x - 4$$ Use the distributive property.
$$= 2x - x - 3 - 4$$
$$= x - 7$$ Combine like terms.

PRACTICE 7

Simplify: $5y - 6 - (y - 5)$

TIP

- When removing parentheses preceded by a *minus sign,* all the terms in parentheses change to the opposite sign.
- When removing parentheses preceded by a *plus sign,* all the terms in parentheses keep the same sign.

EXAMPLE 8

Simplify: $(14a - 9) - 2(3a + 4)$

SOLUTION

$$(14a - 9) - 2(3a + 4) = 14a - 9 - 6a - 8$$
$$= 8a - 17$$

PRACTICE 8

Simplify: $(y + 3) - 3(y + 7)$

Some algebraic expressions contain not only parentheses but also brackets. When simplifying expressions containing both grouping symbols, first remove the innermost grouping symbols by using the distributive property and then continue to work outward.

EXAMPLE 9

Simplify: $5 + 2[-4(x - 3) + 8x]$

SOLUTION

$$5 + 2[-4(x - 3) + 8x] = 5 + 2[-4x + 12 + 8x]$$ Use the distributive property inside the brackets.

$$= 5 + 2[4x + 12]$$ Combine like terms inside the brackets.

$$= 5 + 8x + 24$$ Use the distributive property.

$$= 8x + 29$$ Combine like terms.

PRACTICE 9

Simplify: $10 - [4y + 3(2y - 1)]$

Now we consider applied problems that involve simplifying expressions. To solve these problems, first we translate word phrases to algebraic expressions, and then simplify.

EXAMPLE 10

When a hospital is filled to capacity, it has p patients in private rooms and 20 more patients in semiprivate rooms than in private rooms. The daily rate for a patient in a private room is $300, and in a semiprivate room, the daily rate is $200. Write an algebraic expression to represent the total amount of money that the hospital takes in per day when all of the rooms are full. Then simplify the expression.

SOLUTION We know that p represents the number of patients in private rooms. Since the hospital has 20 more patients in semiprivate rooms than in private rooms, $p + 20$ represents the number of patients in semiprivate rooms. A patient in a private room pays $300 per day, and a patient in a semiprivate room pays $200 per day.

Organizing the information into a table can help us to clarify the relationship between the key quantities in the problem.

Type of Room	Cost per Patient	Number of Patients in Rooms	Total Amount of Money
Private	$300	p	$300\,p$
Semiprivate	$200	$p + 20$	$200(p + 20)$

So when the hospital is full, the total amount of money that the hospital takes in per day is represented by the algebraic expression $300p + 200(p + 20)$.

Simplifying $300p + 200(p + 20)$, we get:

$$300p + 200(p + 20) = 300p + 200p + 4000$$
$$= 500p + 4000$$

So the total amount of money that the hospital receives per day is $(500p + 4000)$ dollars.

PRACTICE 10

For a concert, a local performing arts center sold c tickets for children and 40 fewer tickets for adults. Write an algebraic expression to represent the total income received by the center if the cost of a ticket is $12 for adults and $5 for children. Then simplify the expression.

Exercises 1.8

Name the coefficient in each term.

1. $7x$ **2.** $-5y$ **3.** ab

4. $-x^2$ **5.** $-0.1n$ **6.** m

Identify the terms, and indicate whether they are like or unlike.

7. $2a - a$ **8.** $10r + r$

9. $5p + 3$ **10.** $30 - 2A$

11. $4x^2 - 6x^2$ **12.** $-20n - 3n$

13. $x^2 + 7x^3$ **14.** $-2x^2 + 3x$

Use the distributive property.

15. $-7(x - y)$ **16.** $3(4x + 2y)$ **17.** $(1 - 10) \cdot a$

18. $(3 - 12) \cdot x$ **19.** $-0.5(r + 3)$ **20.** $-3(p + 2.2)$

Simplify, if possible, by combining like terms.

21. $3x + 7x$ **22.** $8p + 3p$ **23.** $-10n - n$

24. $-y - 5y$ **25.** $20a - 10a + 4a$ **26.** $2r - 5r - r$

27. $3y - y + 2$ **28.** $7y - 2y - 1$ **29.** $8b^3 + b^3 - 9b^3$

30. $6x^2 + 2x^2 - 14x^2$ **31.** $-b^2 + ab^2$ **32.** $-3x^2 - 5x$

33. $3r^2t^2 + r^2t^2$ **34.** $m^2n^2 + 2m^2n^2$

35. $3x^2y - 5xy^2$ **36.** $10ab^2 + a^2b$

Simplify.

37. $2(x + 3) - 4$ **38.** $3(a - 5) - 1$ **39.** $(7x + 1) + (2x - 1)$

40. $(3x - 4) + 2(2x - 18)$ **41.** $-(3y - 10)$ **42.** $-(2x + 5)$

43. $5x - 3 - (x + 6)$

44. $5x - 9 - 2(x + 4)$

45. $-4(n - 9) + 3(n + 1)$

46. $5(2b - 1) - 4(c + b)$

47. $x - 4 - 2(x - 1) + 3(2x + 1)$

48. $a + 1 - 3(a + 1) + 8(4a + 5)$

49. $7 + 3[x - 2(x - 1)]$

50. $2 - [n - 4(n + 5)]$

51. $10 - 3[4(a + 2) - 3a]$

52. $5 + 2[-(z + 7) + 4z]$

Applications

Write an algebraic expression. Then simplify.

53. What is the sum of the angles in the triangle shown?

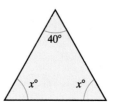

54. According to a will, an estate is to be divided among 2 children and 2 grandchildren. Each grandchild is to receive one-half the amount c that each child receives from the estate. What is the total value of the estate?

55. A baseball fan buys a ticket for a game for d dollars. Two of his friends decide to go to the game at the last minute and purchase tickets for $4 more per ticket. What is the total cost of the 3 tickets?

56. The shape of Colorado is almost a rectangle. Its length is 100 mi more than the width, w. What is the approximate perimeter of Colorado?

57. If n is the first of 3 consecutive integers, what is the sum of the 3 consecutive integers? (*Hint:* Consecutive integers are integers that differ by 1 unit.)

58. On Tuesday, a company's stock fell by 6% from its value the day before. If v represents the value of the stock on Monday, what was its value on Tuesday?

59. Find the total annual interest on $1000 where x dollars is invested at an interest rate of 5% per year and the remainder is invested at 4% per year.

60. An apartment house contains 100 apartments. Of these, y are 3-room apartments, and the others are 4-room apartments. How many rooms are there in the apartment house?

● *Check your answers on page A-3.*

Mindstretchers

GROUPWORK

1. Parentheses have different meanings in different situations. Working with a partner, explain the meaning of parentheses in each context.

a. $(-2)(-3)$

_____

b. $5(x + 2)$

_____

c.

Income	$713,014
Expenditures	$961,882
Profit	($248,868)

_____

d. I am studying algebra (my favorite subject!).

_____

RESEARCH

2. By searching the Web or checking in your college's math learning center, investigate how *algebra tiles* can be used to combine like terms. Summarize your findings.

_____

_____

WRITING

3. Explain the meaning of *combining like terms* in the following examples.

a. 5 ft 3 in. + 7 ft 6 in.

_____

_____

b. $16\frac{2}{3} - 5\frac{1}{3}$

_____

_____

_____

c. $10x - 1 + 4 + 2x$

_____

_____

CONCEPT/SKILL	DESCRIPTION	EXAMPLE
[1.1] Real Numbers	Numbers that can be represented as points on a number line	$\frac{2}{3}, -\frac{1}{2}, 5, 7.4$, and $\sqrt{2}$
[1.1] Integers	The numbers ... ,$-4, -3, -2, -1, 0, +1, +2, +3, +4, ...$ continuing indefinitely in both directions.	$-20, -7, 0, +5$, and $+17$
[1.1] Rational Numbers	Numbers that can be written in the form $\frac{a}{b}$, where a and b are integers and $b \neq 0$.	$-1.6, \frac{2}{3}, -\frac{1}{2}, 5$, and 0.04
[1.1] Opposites	Two real numbers that are the same distance from 0 on a number line but on opposite sides. For any real number n, its oppostie is $-n$.	3 and -3
[1.1] Absolute Value	A given number's distance from 0 on a number line. The absolute value of a number n is written as $\lvert n \rvert$.	$\lvert 8 \rvert = 8$ $\lvert -8 \rvert = 8$
[1.2] To Add Real Numbers, _a_ and _b_, on a Number Line	• Start at a. • Then move according to b as follows: 　If b is positive, move to the right. 　If b is negative, move to the left. 　If b is zero, remain at a.	Add -1 and 3 on a number line: Start at -1 then move 3 units to the right. $-1 + 3 = 2$
[1.2] Additive Inverse Property	For any real number a, there is exactly one real number $-a$, such that $$a + (-a) = 0 \quad \text{and} \quad -a + a = 0,$$ where a and $-a$ are **additive inverses (opposites)** of each other.	$7 + (-7) = 0$ and $-7 + 7 = 0$
[1.2] Additive Identity Property	For any real number a, $$a + 0 = a \text{ and } 0 + a = a.$$	$7 + 0 = 7$ and $0 + 7 = 7$
[1.2] To Add Real Numbers	• If the numbers have the same sign, add the absolute values and keep the sign. • If the numbers have different signs, find the difference between the larger absolute value and the smaller one and take the sign of the number with the larger absolute value.	$-5 + (-2) = -7$ $+5 + (+2) = +7$, or 7 $-5 + (+2) = -3$ $+5 + (-2) = +3$, or 3
[1.2] Commutative Property of Addition	For any two real numbers a and b, $$a + b = b + a.$$	$6 + 2 = 2 + 6$
[1.2] Associative Property of Addition	For any three real numbers, a, b, and c, $$(a + b) + c = a + (b + c).$$	$(8 + 4) + 1 = 8 + (4 + 1)$

continued

= CONCEPT	= SKILL

CONCEPT/SKILL	DESCRIPTION	EXAMPLE
[1.3] To Subtract Real Numbers	• Change the operation of subtraction to addition and change the number being subtracted to its opposite. • Then follow the rule for adding real numbers.	$2 - (-5)$ $= 2 + (+5) = 7$
[1.4] To Multiply Real Numbers	• Multiply their absolute values. • If the numbers have the same sign, their product is positive; if they have different signs, their product is negative.	$(-3)(-8) = 24$ $3(-8) = -24$
[1.4] Commutative Property of Multiplication	For any two real numbers a and b, $$a \cdot b = b \cdot a.$$	$(-2)(-7) = (-7)(-2)$
[1.4] Multiplicative Identity Property	For any real number a, $$a \cdot 1 = a \quad \text{and} \quad 1 \cdot a = a.$$	$3 \cdot 1 = 3$ and $1 \cdot 3 = 3$
[1.4] Multiplication Property of Zero	For any real number a, $$a \cdot 0 = 0 \quad \text{and} \quad 0 \cdot a = 0.$$	$2 \cdot 0 = 0$ and $0 \cdot 2 = 0$
[1.4] Associative Property of Multiplication	For any three real numbers, a, b, and c, $$(a \cdot b)\, c = a\, (b \cdot c).$$	$(-1 \cdot 2)\, 3 = -1(2 \cdot 3)$
[1.5] To Divide Real Numbers	• Divide their absolute values. • If the numbers have the same sign, their quotient is positive; if they have different signs, their quotient is **e.**	negative. $-16 \div (-2) = 8$ $-24 \div 3 = -8$
[1.5] Division Involving Zero	For any nonzero real number a, $$0 \div a = 0.$$ For any real number a, $$a \div 0 \text{ is undefined.}$$	$0 \div 5 = 0$ and $5 \div 0$ is undefined.
[1.5] Division of Real Numbers	For any real numbers a and b where b is nonzero, $$a \div b = \frac{a}{b} = a \cdot \frac{1}{b}.$$	$-\dfrac{3}{5} \div 6 = -\dfrac{3}{5} \div \dfrac{6}{1}$ $= -\dfrac{\overset{1}{\cancel{3}}}{5} \cdot \dfrac{1}{\underset{2}{\cancel{6}}} = -\dfrac{1}{10}$
[1.5] Multiplicative Inverse Property	For any nonzero real number a, $$a \cdot \frac{1}{a} = 1 \text{ and } \frac{1}{a} \cdot a = 1,$$ where a and $\dfrac{1}{a}$ are **multiplicative inverses (reciprocals)** of each other.	$-\dfrac{3}{4}$ and $-\dfrac{4}{3}$ are multiplicative inverses because $-\dfrac{3}{4} \cdot \left(-\dfrac{4}{3}\right) = 1.$
[1.6] Variable	A letter that represents an unknown quantity or one that can change in value.	x, n
[1.6] Constant	A known quantity.	$5, -3.2$

continued

[░░░░░] = CONCEPT   [░░░░░] = SKILL

CONCEPT/SKILL	DESCRIPTIONE	EXAMPLE
[1.6] Algebraic Expression	An expression in which constants and variables are combined using standard arithmetic operations.	$\frac{2}{5}n + 9$
[1.6] Term	A number, a variable, or the product or quotient of numbers and variables.	$-11, 3x, \frac{n}{4}$
[1.6] Exponential Notation	For any real number x and any positive integer a, $$x^a = \underbrace{x \cdot x \cdots x \cdot x}_{a \text{ factors}},$$ where x is called the **base** and a is called the **exponent** (or **power**).	$\overset{\text{Exponent}}{(-2)^3} = (-2)(-2)(-2)$ $= -8$ Base
[1.7] To Evaluate an Algebraic Expression	• Replace each variable with the given number. • Then carry out the computation using the order of operations rule.	If $c = -1$ and $d = 2$, then $-2cd = (-2)(-1)(2) = 4.$
[1.8] Like Terms	Terms that have the same variable and the same exponent.	n and $6n$ $5x^3$ and $-2x^3$
[1.8] Unlike Terms	Terms that are not like. x and $3y$	a^2 and a
[1.8] Distributive Property	For any real numbers a, b, and c, $$a \cdot (b + c) = a \cdot b + a \cdot c$$ and $$(b + c) \cdot a = b \cdot a + c \cdot a.$$	$2(x + y) = 2x + 2y$ and $(3 + 7) \cdot n = 3 \cdot n + 7 \cdot n$
[1.8] To Combine Like Terms	• Use the distributive property. • Add or subtract.	$2x + 6x = (2 + 6)x$ $= 8x$

Chapter 1 Review Exercises

[1.1]

Express each quantity as a signed number.

1. 3 mi above sea level

2. A withdrawal of $160 from an account

Graph each number on the number line.

3. −1

4. $2\frac{9}{10}$

5. 0.5

6. −3.75

Find the opposite of each number.

7. −4

8. 6.5

9. $\frac{2}{3}$

10. −0.7

Compute.

11. $|-4|$

12. $|0|$

13. $|2.6|$

14. $\left|-\frac{5}{9}\right|$

Indicate whether each inequality is true or false.

15. $-7 < -5$

16. $-1 > 3$

[1.2]

Find the sum of each pair of numbers using the number line.

17. $-4 + (-1)$

18. $3 + (-7)$

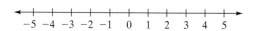

Name a property of addition illustrated by each statement.

19. $5 + (-6) = (-6) + 5$

20. $0 + 25 = 25$

21. $(1 + 3) + 6 = 1 + (3 + 6)$

22. $-10 + 10 = 0$

Find the sum.

23. $9 + (-9)$

24. $4 + (-2)$

25. $-3 + 5$

26. $0 + (-15)$

27. $-3 + (-2)$

28. $-3 + 7 + (-89)$

29. $-0.5 + (-3.6) + (-4)$

30. $-2 + 5.3 + 12$

[1.3]

Find the difference.

31. $12 - 3$

32. $36 - 47$

33. $-52 - 3$

34. $2 - 5$

35. $-19 - 8$

36. $24 - (-3)$

37. $8 - (-8)$

38. $0 - 5$

39. $6 - 7.42$

40. $-9 - \left(-\dfrac{3}{8}\right)$

Combine.

41. $2 + (-4) - (-7)$

42. $-3 - (-1) + 12$

[1.4]

Name the property of multiplication illustrated by each statement.

43. $-3(5) = 5(-3)$

44. $(-8 \cdot 6) \cdot 2 = -8 \cdot (6 \cdot 2)$

45. $-9 \cdot 1 = -9$

46. $-7 \cdot 0 = 0$

Find the product.

47. $2(-5)$

48. $-3 \cdot 7$

49. $-60 \cdot 90$

50. $-8(-300)$

51. $(-2.7)(-10)$

52. $\left(\dfrac{3}{4}\right)\left(-\dfrac{1}{3}\right)$

53. $5(-4)(-300)$

54. $(-1)(-12)(3)$

Simplify.

55. $-8 + 3(-2) - 9$

56. $3 - 2(-3) - (-5)$

57. $-9 - 5(-7)$

58. $20 - 3(-6)$

59. $-4(-2 + 5)$

60. $(-12 + 6)(-1)$

[1.5]

Find the reciprocal.

61. $-\dfrac{2}{3}$

62. 8

Find the quotient. Simplify.

63. $-30 \div (-10)$

64. $6 \div (-1)$

65. $-\dfrac{11}{5}$

66. $\dfrac{4}{5} \div \left(-\dfrac{2}{3}\right)$

Simplify.

67. $-16 \div 2(-4)$

68. $(9 - 23) \div (-13 + 6)$

69. $\dfrac{3 + (-1)}{-2}$

70. $\dfrac{5(7 - 3)}{-8 - 2}$

71. $(-3) + 8 - 2 \cdot (-4)$

72. $10 \div (-2) + (-3) \cdot 5$

[1.6]

Determine the number of terms in each expression.

73. $-x + y - 3z$

74. $\dfrac{m}{n} + 4$

75. $-9t$

76. $3a - 1 + 7b + c$

Translate each algebraic expression to a word phrase.

77. $-6 + w$

78. $-\dfrac{1}{3}x$

79. $-3n + 6$

80. $5(p - q)$

Translate each word phrase to an algebraic expression.

81. ten less than x

82. one-half of s

83. the quotient of p and q

84. the difference between R and twice V

85. six times the quantity two less than four times n

86. the quantity negative four times *a* divided by the quantity five times *b* plus *c*.

Write each using exponents.

87. $-3(-3)(-3)(-3)$

88. $-5(-5)(-5)(3)(3)$

89. $4(x)(x)(x)$

90. $-5a \cdot a \cdot b \cdot b \cdot b \cdot c$

[1.7]

Evaluate each algebraic expression if a = 2, b = 5, and c = −1.

91. $30 + c$

92. $-\dfrac{4}{9}b$

93. $-5a^2$

94. $10(b - c)$

95. $\dfrac{1 - a}{c}$

96. $4a^2 - 4ab + b^2$

[1.8]

97. Apply the distributive property: $-5(x - y)$

98. Combine like terms: $4x + 10x - 2y$

99. Simplify: $3x^2 - x^2 - 4x^2$

100. Combine: $2r^2t^2 - r^2t^2$

101. Simplify: $2(a - 5) + 1$

102. Simplify: $-(3x + 2)$

103. Combine like terms: $-3x - 5 - (x + 10)$

104. Simplify: $(2a - 4) + 2(a - 5) - 3(a + 1)$

Mixed Applications

Solve.

105. Express as a real number: a gain of $700

106. A company lost $7000 last year. Express this situation as a real number.

107. The price of a share of stock fell by $\dfrac{1}{2}$ a dollar each week for 4 weeks in a row. What was the overall change in the price?

108. In exothermic chemical reactions, the surrounding temperature rises; in endothermic chemical reactions, the surrounding temperature drops. If a chemical reaction causes the surrounding temperature to change from $-7°C$ to $-4°C$, was it exothermic or endothermic?

109. A patient's temperature drops by 0.5 degrees per hour. If the initial temperature was I degrees, write an algebraic expression for the temperature after h hours.

110. Use the formula $F = \dfrac{9}{5}C + 32$ to determine the Fahrenheit temperature F that corresponds to the Celsius temperature C if $C = -10°$.

111. The length of a rectangle is double its width w. Find the rectangle's perimeter.

112. Which is warmer, $-4°$ or $-7°$?

113. The boiling point of the element radon is $-61.8°C$, whereas its melting point is $-71°C$. How much higher is the boiling point?

114. The price of a stock on Monday was $12.34 per share. On Tuesday, the price per share was down $0.43 from the price on Monday. What was the price per share on Tuesday?

115. A colony of bacteria triples in size every 6 hours. At one point there are 10 bacteria in the colony. Write in exponential form the number of bacteria in the colony 18 hours later.

116. Firefighters use the formula $S = 0.5N + 26$ to compute the maximum horizontal range S in feet of water from a particular hose, where N is the hose's nozzle pressure in pounds. Calculate S if $N = 90$ lb.

117. The playwright Sophocles was born in 496 B.C. and died approximately 90 years later. In what year did he die?

118. One year, a company's loss was $60,000. The next year, it was only $20,000. How many times the second loss is the first loss?

119. A homeowner needs to have sufficient current to operate the electrical appliances in the home. Electricians use the formula $I = \dfrac{P}{E}$ to compute the current I in amperes needed in terms of the power P in watts and the energy E in volts. Find I if $P = 2300$ watts and $E = 115$ volts.

120. A checking account has a balance of $410. If $900 is deposited, a check for $720 is written, and two withdrawals of $300 each are made through an ATM, by how much money is the account overdrawn?

121. In addition to a monthly flat fee of x dollars, you are charged y dollars for each hour over 20 that you surf the Web. What do you pay in a month in which you surf the Web for 32 hours?

122. The first day of the term, f students attended the computer lab. As the term went on, attendance increased by s students per day. What was the attendance on the fifth day of the term?

● *Check your answers on page A-4.*

Chapter 1 Posttest

To see if you have mastered the topics in this chapter, take this test.

1. Express as a real number: a loss of 10,000 jobs

2. Is the number $\dfrac{2}{5}$ rational?

3. Graph the number -2 on the following number line.

$$\begin{array}{c} \xleftarrow{\quad|\quad|\quad|\quad|\quad|\quad|\quad|\quad} \\ \;-3\;-2\;-1\;\;\;0\;\;\;1\;\;\;2\;\;\;3 \end{array}$$

4. Find the additive inverse of 7.

5. Compute: $|-3.5|$

6. True or false? $1 > -4$

7. Add: $10 + (-3)$

8. Combine: $2 + (-3) + (-1) + 5$

9. Simplify: $4 + (-1)(-6)$

10. What is the reciprocal of 12?

11. Divide: $-15 \div 0.3$

12. Translate to an algebraic expression: the sum of x and twice y

13. Write in exponential form: $-6(-6)(-6)$

14. Evaluate $3a + b - c$ if $a = -1$, $b = 0$, and $c = 2$.

15. Simplify: $4y + 3 - 7y + 10y + 1$

16. Combine: $8t + 1 - 2(3t - 1)$

17. Which is warmer, a temperature of $2°$ or a temperature of $-3°$?

18. The balance in a checking account was d dollars. Some time later, the balance was 5% higher. What was the new balance?

19. Last year, a company suffered a loss of $20,000. This year, it showed a profit of $50,000. How big an improvement was this?

20. Find the annual interest earned on an investment of $500 if x dollars is invested at an interest rate of 6% per year and the remainder is invested at a rate of 8% per year.

• *Check your answers on page A-4.*

Chapter 2
Solving Linear Equations and Inequalities

Cell Phones and Algebra

Today's generation takes wireless communication for granted. The cellular telephone, one of the more important wireless devices, was first introduced to the public in the mid-1980s. Since then, cell phones have shrunk both in size and in price.

Using a cell phone generally entails choosing a calling plan with a monthly service charge. As a rule, this charge consists of two parts: a specified flat monthly fee and a per-minute usage charge varying with the number of minutes of airtime used.

The choice among calling plans can be confusing, especially with the lure of promotional incentives. One nationally advertised calling plan requires a monthly charge of $34.99 for 300 minutes of free local calls and 79 cents per minute for additional local calls. A competing plan is for $29.99 a month for 200 minutes of free local calls plus 49 cents a minute for additional local calls. Under what circumstances is one deal better than the other? The key to answering this question is solving inequalities such as

$$34.99 + 0.79(x - 300) < 29.99 + 0.49(x - 200).$$

To see if you have already mastered the topics in this chapter, take this test.

1. Is 4 is a solution of the equation $7 - 2x = 3x - 11$?

2. Solve and check: $n + 2 = -6$

3. Solve and check: $\dfrac{y}{-5} = 1$

4. Solve and check: $-n = 8$

5. Solve and check: $\dfrac{2}{3}x - 3 = -9$

6. Solve and check: $4x - 8 = -10$

7. Solve and check: $6 - y = -5$

8. Solve and check: $9x + 13 = 7x + 19$

9. Solve and check: $-2(3n - 1) = -7n$

10. Solve and check: $14x - (8x - 13) = 12x + 3$

11. Solve $v - 5u = w$ for v in terms of u and w.

12. 9 is what percent of 36?

13. 60% of what number is 12?

14. Draw the graph of $x \le 2$.

$$\begin{array}{ccccccc} -3 & -2 & -1 & 0 & 1 & 2 & 3 \end{array}$$

15. Solve and graph: $x + 3 > 3$

$$\begin{array}{ccccccc} -3 & -2 & -1 & 0 & 1 & 2 & 3 \end{array}$$

16. An office photocopier makes 30 copies per minute. How long will it take to copy a 360-page document?

17. A florist charges a flat fee of $100 plus $70 for each centerpiece for a wedding. If the total bill for the centerpieces was $1500, how many centerpieces did the florist make?

18. The formula for finding the amount of kinetic energy used is $E = \dfrac{1}{2}mv^2$. Solve this equation for m in terms of E and v.

19. A certain amount of money was invested in two different accounts. The amount invested at 8% simple interest was twice the amount invested at 5% simple interest. If the total interest earned on the investments was $420, how much was invested at each rate?

20. A gym offers two membership options: Option A is $55 per month for unlimited use of the gym and Option B is $10 per month plus $3 for each hour you use the gym. For how many hours of use per month will Option A be a better deal?

• Check your answers on page A-4.

2.1 Solving Linear Equations: The Addition Property

What Equations Are and Why They Are Important

OBJECTIVES

- *To determine whether a given number is a solution of a given equation*
- *To solve linear equations using the addition property*
- *To solve applied problems using the addition property*

In this chapter, we work with one of the most important concepts in algebra, the *equation*. Equations are important because they help us to solve a wide variety of problems.

For instance, suppose that we want to find the measure of $\angle B$ (read "angle B") in triangle ABC.

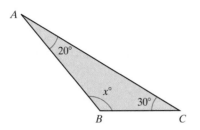

We know from geometry that for any triangle, the sum of the measures of the angles is $180°$. To solve this problem, we can write the following equation, where x represents the measure of $\angle B$.

$$20 + 30 + x = 180$$

An equation has two algebraic expressions—one on the left side of the equals sign and one on the right side of the equals sign.

Equals sign

$$\underbrace{20 + 30 + x}_{\text{Left side}} = \underbrace{180}_{\text{Right side}}$$

Definition

An **equation** is a mathematical statement that two expressions are equal.

Some examples of equations are:

$$1 + 3 + 2 = 6 \qquad y - 6 = 9 \qquad y + 4 = -8 \qquad -5x = 10$$

Solving Equations

An equation may be either true or false. The equation $x + 4 = 9$ is true if 5 is substituted for the variable x.

$$x + 4 = 9$$
$$5 + 4 = 9 \qquad \text{True.}$$

However, this equation is false if 6 is substituted for the variable x.

$$x + 4 = 9$$
$$6 + 4 = 9 \qquad \text{False.}$$

How many values of x will make $x + 4 = 9$ a true equation? How many values of x will make this equation false?

The number 5 is called a *solution* of the equation $x + 4 = 9$ because we get a true statement when we substitute 5 for x.

> **Definition**
>
> A **solution of an equation** is a value of the variable that makes the equation a true statement.

EXAMPLE 1

Is 2 a solution of the equation $3x + 1 = 11 - 2x$?

SOLUTION

$$3x + 1 = 11 - 2x$$
$$3(2) + 1 \stackrel{?}{=} 11 - 2(2) \qquad \text{Substitute 2 for } x.$$
$$6 + 1 \stackrel{?}{=} 11 - 4 \qquad \text{Evaluate each side of the equation.}$$
$$7 = 7 \qquad \text{True.}$$

Since $7 = 7$ is a true statement, 2 is a solution of $3x + 1 = 11 - 2x$.

PRACTICE 1

Determine whether 4 is a solution of the equation $5x - 4 = 2x + 5$.

EXAMPLE 2

Determine whether -1 is a solution of the equation $2x - 4 = 6(x + 2)$.

SOLUTION

$$2x - 4 = 6(x + 2)$$
$$2(-1) - 4 \stackrel{?}{=} 6(-1 + 2) \qquad \text{Substitute } -1 \text{ for } x.$$
$$-2 - 4 \stackrel{?}{=} 6(1) \qquad \text{Evaluate each side of the equation.}$$
$$-6 = 6 \qquad \text{False.}$$

Since $-6 = 6$ is a false statement, -1 is *not* a solution of the equation.

PRACTICE 2

Is -8 a solution of the equation $5(x + 3) = 3x - 1$?

In this chapter, we will work mainly with equations in one variable that have one solution. These equations are called *linear equations* or *first-degree equations* because the exponent of the variable is 1.

> **Definition**
>
> A **linear equation in one variable** is an equation that can be written in the form
>
> $$ax + b = c,$$
>
> where a, b, and c are real numbers and $a \neq 0$.

Some linear equations have a special relationship. Consider the equations $x = 2$ and $x + 1 = 3$:

$x = 2$ The solution is 2.

$x + 1 = 3$ By inspection, we see the solution is 2.
$2 + 1 \overset{?}{=} 3$
$3 = 3$ True.

The equations $x = 2$ and $x + 1 = 3$ have the same solution and so are *equivalent*.

> **Definition**
>
> **Equivalent equations** are equations that have the same solution.

To solve an equation means to find the number or constant that, when substituted for the variable, makes the equation a true statement. This solution is found by changing the equation to an equivalent equation of the form

$$x = \boxed{}$$

The variable is isolated (alone on one side with coefficient 1).   The number or constant is isolated on the other side.

Using the Addition Property to Solve Linear Equations

One of the properties that we use in solving equations involves adding. Suppose we have the equation $\frac{6}{3} = 2$. If we were to add 4 to each side of the equation, we would get $\frac{6}{3} + 4 = 2 + 4$. Using mental arithmetic, we see that $\frac{6}{3} + 4 = 2 + 4$ is also a true statement. This example leads us to the following property.

> **Addition Property of Equality**
>
> For any real numbers a, b, and c, if $a = b$, then $a + c = b + c$.

This property allows us to add any real number to each side of an equation, resulting in an equivalent equation.

EXAMPLE 3

Solve and check: $x - 5 = -11$

SOLUTION To solve this equation, we isolate the variable by adding 5, which is the additive inverse of -5, to each side of the equation.

$$x - 5 = -11$$
$$x - 5 + 5 = -11 + 5 \qquad \text{Add 5 to each side of the equation.}$$
$$x + 0 = -6$$
$$x = -6 \qquad \text{Recall that } x + 0 = x.$$

We can check if -6 is the solution to the original equation by substituting for x.

CHECK $x - 5 = -11$
$$-6 - 5 \stackrel{?}{=} -11 \qquad \text{Substitute } -6 \text{ for } x \text{ in the original equation.}$$
$$-11 = -11 \qquad \text{True.}$$

So the solution is -6.

PRACTICE 3

Solve and check: $y - 12 = -7$

Can you explain why checking a solution is important?

EXAMPLE 4

Solve and check: $-9 = a + 6$

SOLUTION

$$-9 = a + 6$$
$$-9 + (-6) = a + 6 + (-6) \qquad \text{Add } -6 \text{ to each side of the equation.}$$
$$-15 = a + 0$$
$$-15 = a$$
or $\qquad a = -15$

CHECK $-9 = a + 6$
$$-9 \stackrel{?}{=} (-15) + 6 \qquad \text{Substitute } -15 \text{ for } a.$$
$$-9 = -9 \qquad \text{True.}$$

So the solution is -15.

PRACTICE 4

Solve and check: $-2 = n + 15$

Are the solutions to the equations $-9 = a + 6$ and $a + 6 = -9$ the same? Explain.

Because subtracting a number is the same as adding its opposite, the addition property allows us to subtract the same value from each side of an equation. For instance, suppose $a = b$. Subtracting c from each side gives us $a - c = b - c$. So an alternative approach to solving Example 4 is to subtract the same number, namely 6, from each side of the equation as shown.

$$-9 = a + 6$$
$$-9 - 6 = a + 6 - 6$$
$$-15 = a, \quad \text{or } a = -15$$

EXAMPLE 5

Solve and check: $m - (-26.1) = 32$

SOLUTION

$$m - (-26.1) = 32$$
$$m + 26.1 = 32$$
$$m + 26.1 - \mathbf{26.1} = 32 - \mathbf{26.1} \qquad \text{Subtract 26.1 from each side of the equation.}$$
$$m = 5.9$$

CHECK
$$m - (-26.1) = 32$$
$$\mathbf{5.9} - (-26.1) \stackrel{?}{=} 32 \qquad \text{Substitute 5.9 for } m.$$
$$5.9 + 26.1 \stackrel{?}{=} 32$$
$$32 = 32 \qquad \text{True.}$$

So the solution is 5.9.

PRACTICE 5

Solve and check: $5 = 4.9 - (-x)$

Equations are often useful *mathematical models* that represent real-world situations. Although there is no magic formula for solving applied problems in algebra, it is a good idea to keep the following problem-solving steps in mind.

To Solve a Word Problem in Algebra

- Read the problem carefully.
- Translate the word problem to an equation.
- Solve the equation.
- Check the solution in the original equation.
- State the conclusion.

We have discussed how to translate word phrases to algebraic expressions. Now let's look at some examples of translating word sentences to equations, namely those involving addition or subtraction.

Word sentence: A number increased by 1.1 equals 8.6.

Equation: $n + 1.1 = 8.6$

Word sentence: A number minus one-half equals five.

Equation: $y - \dfrac{1}{2} = 5$

Note that in both examples we used a variable to represent the unknown number.

In solving applied problems, first we translate the given word sentences to equations, and then we solve the equations.

EXAMPLE 6

The mean distance between the planet Venus and the Sun is 31.2 million miles more than the mean distance between the planet Mercury and the Sun. (**Source:** *Time Almanac 2000*)

a. Using the following diagram, write an equation to find Mercury's mean distance from the Sun.

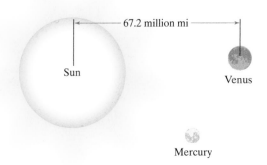

— 67.2 million mi —

Sun

Venus

Mercury

Not to scale

b. Solve this equation.

SOLUTION

a. Let x represent Mercury's mean (or average) distance from the Sun. Reading from the diagram, we see that the mean distance between Venus and the Sun is 67.2 million miles. This distance is 31.2 million miles more than Mercury's mean distance to the Sun. So we translate this sentence to an equation:

Word sentence: 67.2 is 31.2 plus x

Equation: $67.2 = 31.2 + x$

b. Solve the equation:

$$67.2 = x + 31.2$$
$$67.2 - 31.2 = x + 31.2 - 31.2 \qquad \text{Subtract 31.2 from each side of the equation.}$$
$$36.0 = x$$

CHECK

$$67.2 = x + 31.2$$
$$67.2 \overset{?}{=} 36.0 + 31.2 \qquad \text{Substitute 36.0 for } x \text{ in the original equation.}$$
$$67.2 = 67.2 \qquad \text{True.}$$

So we conclude that Mercury's mean distance from the Sun is 36.0 million miles.

PRACTICE 6

A chemistry experiment requires you to find the mass of the solution in a plastic bottle. If the mass of the bottle with the solution is 24.56 g and the mass of the empty bottle is 9.68 g, what is the mass of the solution?

Exercises 2.1

FOR EXTRA HELP

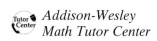 *Student's Solutions Manual*

 *Addison-Wesley Math Tutor Center*

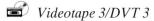 *MyMathLab*

Videotape 3/DVT 3

Indicate whether the value of x shown is a solution to the given equation by answering true or false.

1.

Value of x	Equation	True or False
a. -8	$3x + 13 = -11$	
b. 7	$28 - x = 7 - 4x$	
c. 9	$2(x - 3) = 12$	
d. $\frac{2}{3}$	$12x - 2 = 6x + 2$	

2.

Value of x	Equation	True or False
a. -2	$3x - 2 = 10$	
b. 4	$2x + 3 = 5x - 9$	
c. 1	$3(5 - x) = 18$	
d. $-\frac{1}{2}$	$6 - 5x = 5x + 11$	

Indicate what must be done to each side of the equation in order to isolate the variable.

3. $x + 4 = -6$ **4.** $x - 3 = -3$ **5.** $-2 = -1 + x$

6. $x - (-15) = 10$ **7.** $z - (-3.5) = 5$ **8.** $x - 3.4 = 9.6$

9. $9 = x - 2\frac{1}{5}$ **10.** $m + \frac{1}{3} = 2$

Solve and check.

11. $y + 9 = -14$ **12.** $x + 2 = -10$ **13.** $t - 4 = -4$ **14.** $m - 6 = 1$

15. $9 + a = -3$ **16.** $10 + x = -4$ **17.** $z - 4 = -10$ **18.** $n - 4 = -1$

19. $12 = x + 12$ **20.** $-25 = y + 21$ **21.** $-6 = t - 12$ **22.** $-19 = r - 19$

23. $-4 = -10 + r$ **24.** $-7 = -2 + m$ **25.** $-15 + n = -2$ **26.** $-14 + c = 33$

27. $x + \dfrac{2}{3} = -\dfrac{1}{3}$

28. $z - \dfrac{1}{8} = \dfrac{3}{8}$

29. $8 + y = 4\dfrac{1}{2}$

30. $2 = z - 1\dfrac{1}{4}$

31. $m + 2.4 = 5.3$

32. $13.9 = n - 12.5$

33. $-2.3 + t = -5.9$

34. $-3.4 + r = -9.5$

35. $a - (-35) = 30$

36. $x - (-25) = 24$

37. $m - \left(-\dfrac{1}{4}\right) = -\dfrac{1}{4}$

38. $a - (-1.5) = 2$

Solve and round to the nearest hundredth.

39. $y + 2.932 = 4.811$

40. $x + 3.0245 = 9$

Translate each sentence to an equation. Then solve and check.

41. Two more than a number is 12.

42. The sum of a number and 3.2 is the same as 20.

43. If 4 is subtracted from a number, the result is 21.

44. A number minus $2\dfrac{1}{7}$ is the same as $1\dfrac{1}{2}$.

45. If -3 is added to a number, the result is -1.

46. 5.2 less than a number equals 12.

47. A number plus 7 equals 11.

48. The difference between a number and 1 is 9.

Applications

Choose the equation that best describes the situation.

49. After dieting and exercising, a featherweight boxer lost 6 lb. If the boxer now weighs 127 lb, what was his original weight?

    a. $x - 127 = -6$ **b.** $x + 6 = 127$

    c. $x + 127 = 6$ **d.** $x - 6 = 127$

50. After paying a bill of \$5.25, a customer has \$2.75 left. How much money did she have prior to paying the bill?

    a. $d - 5.25 = 2.75$ **b.** $d + 2.75 = 5.25$

    c. $d + 5.25 = 2.75$ **d.** $d - 2.75 = -5.25$

51. A digital picture that takes up 4.7 megabytes (Mb) of memory is saved on a computer. If 250 Mb of memory are left after the picture is saved, how many megabytes of free memory did the computer have before the picture was saved?

    a. $x - 4.7 = 250$ **b.** $x - 250 = -4.7$

    c. $x + 4.7 = 250$ **d.** $x + 250 = 4.7$

52. At a college, tuition costs students \$3000 a semester. If a student received \$2250 in financial aid, how much more money does the student need to pay the balance of the semester's tuition?

    a. $m - 2250 = 3000$ **b.** $m + 2250 = 3000$

    c. $m + 3000 = 2250$ **d.** $m - 3000 = 2250$

Write an equation. Solve and check.

53. If the speed of a car is increased by 10 mph, the speed will be 44 mph. What is the speed of the car now?

54. The difference between the boiling point of aluminum and the boiling point of gold is 340°C. If aluminum boils at 2467°C, the lower temperature of the two metals, what is the boiling point of gold? (***Source:*** *2001 World Book Almanac*)

55. A student uses about 220 calories after 1 hour of gardening. This is 130 calories less than is used after 1 hour of roller-skating. How many calories does the student use in an hour of roller-skating?

56. A patient's temperature dropped by 2.4°F to 98.6°F. What had the patient's temperature been?

57. What was the original altitude of the traffic helicopter shown in the following diagram?

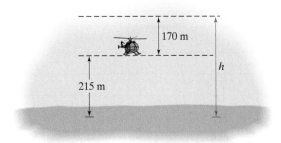

58. In the following diagram, $\angle ABC$ and $\angle CBD$ are complementary angles because the sum of their measures is 90°. Find the number of degrees in $\angle CBD$.

• *Check your answers on page A-4.*

59. In the diagram shown, angles x and y are supplementary angles because the sum of their measures is 180°. Find the measure of $\angle x$ if the measure of $\angle y$ is 118.5°.

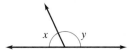

60. At the close of business today, the price per share of a stock was $21.63. This was down $0.31 from the closing price per share yesterday. What was the closing price per share of the stock yesterday?

Mindstretchers

MATHEMATICAL REASONING

1. Suppose that $x - a = b$.

a. What happens to x if a decreases and b remains the same?

_____

b. What happens to x if a remains the same and b decreases?

_____

CRITICAL THINKING

2. In the magic square to the right, the sum of each row, column, and diagonal is the same. Calculate that sum. Then write and solve equations to find $v, w, x, y,$ and z.

v	6	11
w	10	y
x	14	z

RESEARCH

3. In your college library or on the Web, investigate the origin of the word *algebra*. Write a few sentences to show what you have learned.

_____

_____

_____

Cultural Note

Source: O. A. W. Dilke, *Mathematics and Measurement* (Berkeley: University of California Press/British Museum, 1987).

Just as we solve an equation to identify an un known number, we use a balance scale to determine an unknown weight. In this picture, an image from 3400 years ago shows an Egyptian weighing gold rings against a counterbalance in the form of a bull's head.

The balance scale is an ancient measuring device. These scales were used by Sumarians for weighing precious metals and gems at least 9000 years ago.

2.2 Solving Linear Equations: The Multiplication Property

In the previous section we used the addition property of equality to solve equations. Another property that is useful in solving equations involves multiplication. Consider the equation $\frac{6}{3} = 2$. If we were to multiply each side of this equation by 9, we would get $\frac{6}{3} \cdot 9 = 2 \cdot 9$. Note that each side of the equation equals 18. In general, multiplying each side of a true equation by the same number results in another true equation.

OBJECTIVES

- *To solve linear equations using the multiplication property*
- *To solve applied problems using the multiplication property*

Multiplication Property of Equality

For any real numbers a, b, and c, if $a = b$, then $a \cdot c = b \cdot c$.

This property allows us to multiply each side of an equation by any real number to get an equivalent equation.

EXAMPLE 1

Solve and check: $\dfrac{x}{4} = 11$

SOLUTION In this equation, note that $\dfrac{x}{4}$ is the same as $\dfrac{1}{4} \cdot x$. To solve this equation, we isolate the variable by multiplying each side of the equation by 4, the reciprocal of $\dfrac{1}{4}$.

$$\frac{x}{4} = 11$$

$$4 \cdot \frac{x}{4} = 4 \cdot 11 \qquad \text{Multiply each side of the equation by 4.}$$

$$1x = 44 \qquad 4 \cdot \frac{x}{4} = 4 \cdot \frac{1}{4}x = 1x$$

$$x = 44 \qquad 1x = x$$

CHECK

$$\frac{x}{4} = 11$$

$$\frac{44}{4} \stackrel{?}{=} 11 \qquad \text{Substitute 44 for } x \text{ in the original equation.}$$

$$11 = 11 \qquad \text{True.}$$

So the solution is 44.

PRACTICE 1

Solve and check: $\dfrac{y}{3} = 21$

EXAMPLE 2

Solve and check: $9x = -72$

SOLUTION

$$9x = -72$$

$$\left(\frac{1}{9}\right)9x = \left(\frac{1}{9}\right)(-72) \qquad \text{Multiply each side of the equation by } \tfrac{1}{9}.$$

$$1x = -8 \qquad \frac{1}{9} \cdot 9 = 1$$

$$x = -8$$

CHECK
$$9x = -72$$
$$9(-8) \stackrel{?}{=} -72$$
$$-72 = -72 \qquad \text{True.}$$

So the solution is -8.

PRACTICE 2

Solve and check: $7y = 63$

Because dividing by a number is the same as multiplying by its reciprocal, the multiplication property allows us to divide each side of an equation by a nonzero number. For instance, suppose $a = b$. Multiplying each side by $\dfrac{1}{c}$ gives us $a \cdot \dfrac{1}{c} = b \cdot \dfrac{1}{c}$, for $c \neq 0$. This equation is equivalent to $\dfrac{a}{c} = \dfrac{b}{c}$. So an alternative approach to solving Example 2 is to divide each side of the equation by the same number, namely 9, as shown.

$$9x = -72$$
$$\frac{9x}{9} = \frac{-72}{9}$$
$$x = -8$$

Note that this approach gives us the same solution, -8, that we got using the approach in Example 2.

EXAMPLE 3

Solve and check: $-y = -15$

SOLUTION

$$-y = -15$$
$$-1y = -15 \qquad \text{The coefficient of } -y \text{ is } -1.$$
$$\frac{-1y}{-1} = \frac{-15}{-1} \qquad \text{Divide each side of the equation by } -1.$$
$$y = 15$$

CHECK
$$-y = -15$$
$$-1(15) \stackrel{?}{=} -15 \qquad \text{Substitute 15 for } y \text{ in the original equation.}$$
$$-15 = -15 \qquad \text{True.}$$

So the solution is 15.

PRACTICE 3

Solve and check: $-x = 10$

EXAMPLE 4

Solve and check: $46 = -4.6n$

SOLUTION

$$46 = -4.6n$$

$$\frac{46}{-4.6} = \frac{-4.6n}{-4.6} \qquad \text{Divide each side of the equation by } -4.6.$$

$$-10 = n \quad \text{or}$$

$$n = -10$$

CHECK

$$46 = -4.6n$$

$$46 \stackrel{?}{=} -4.6\,(-10) \qquad \text{Substitute } -10 \text{ for } n \text{ in the original equation.}$$

$$46 = 46 \qquad \text{True.}$$

So the solution is -10.

PRACTICE 4

Solve and check: $-11.7 = -0.9z$

EXAMPLE 5

Solve and check: $\dfrac{2w}{3} = 8$

SOLUTION

$$\frac{2w}{3} = 8$$

$$\frac{2}{3}w = 8$$

$$\frac{3}{2} \cdot \frac{2}{3}w = \frac{3}{2} \cdot 8 \qquad \text{Multiply each side of the equation by } \tfrac{3}{2}.$$

$$w = 12 \qquad \frac{3}{2} \cdot \frac{2}{3} = 1 \text{ and } 1w = w.$$

CHECK

$$\frac{2}{3}w = 8$$

$$\frac{2}{3}(12) \stackrel{?}{=} 8 \qquad \text{Substitute 12 for } w \text{ in the original equation.}$$

$$2 \cdot 4 \stackrel{?}{=} 8 \qquad \text{Simplify.}$$

$$8 = 8 \qquad \text{True.}$$

So the solution is 12.

PRACTICE 5

Solve and check: $\dfrac{6}{7}y = -12$

Can you show another way to solve Example 5? Explain.

Let's now consider applied problems involving the multiplication property. To solve these problems, we translate word sentences to equations involving multiplication or division as follows:

Word sentence: Three times a number x equals -12.

$$3 \quad \cdot \quad x \quad = \quad -12$$

Equation: $\qquad\qquad\qquad 3x \quad = \quad -12$

Word sentence: A number d divided by -2 equals 8.

Equation: $\qquad d \qquad \div \qquad -2 \quad = \quad 8$

$$\frac{d}{-2} = 8$$

EXAMPLE 6	PRACTICE 6

EXAMPLE 6

Suppose you apply for a job that pays an hourly overtime wage of $15.90. The overtime wage is 1.5 times the regular hourly wage. What is the regular hourly wage for the job?

SOLUTION Letting w represent the regular hourly wage, we write the word sentence and then translate it to an equation.

Word sentence:

The overtime wage $15.90 is **1.5 times** the regular hourly wage.

Equation: $15.90 = 1.5 \quad \cdot \qquad\qquad w$

$\qquad\qquad 15.90 = 1.5w$

Next we solve the equation for w.

$$15.9 = 1.5w$$
$$\frac{15.9}{1.5} = \frac{1.5}{1.5}w$$
$$10.6 = w, \quad \text{or}$$
$$w = 10.6$$

CHECK

$$15.90 = 1.5w$$
$$15.90 \stackrel{?}{=} 1.5\,(10.6)$$
$$15.90 = 15.90 \qquad \text{True.}$$

So the regular wage is $10.60.

PRACTICE 6

A mechanic billed you $189.50 for labor to repair your car. If one-fourth of the bill was for labor, how much was the total bill?

Let's now turn to a particular kind of word problem—a problem involving motion. To solve such problems, we need to use the equation $d = rt$, where d is distance, r is the average rate or speed, and t is time.

EXAMPLE 7

One of the fastest pitchers in the history of Japanese baseball was Hideki Irabu, whose pitches were clocked at about 140 ft/sec. If the distance from the pitcher's mound to home plate is 60.5 ft, approximate the time it took Irabu's pitches to reach home plate, to the nearest hundredth of a second.
(*Source:* *The Toronto Sun*, June 9, 1998, p. 12)

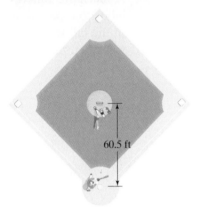

60.5 ft

SOLUTION The distance between the pitcher's mound and home plate is 60.5 ft and the rate of the ball thrown is 140 ft/sec. Using the equation $d = rt$, we can find the time.

$$d = rt$$
$$60.5 = 140t \qquad \text{Substitute 60.5 for } d \text{ and 140 for } r.$$
$$\frac{60.5}{140} = \frac{140t}{140} \qquad \text{Divide each side of the equation by 140.}$$
$$0.43 \approx t, \quad \text{or}$$
$$t \approx 0.43$$

CHECK Since the solution of the original equation is a rounded value, the check will not result in an exact equality. To verify the solution, check that the expressions on each side of the equation are approximately equal to one another.

$$60.5 = 140t$$
$$60.5 \overset{?}{\approx} 140 \cdot \mathbf{0.43} \qquad \text{Substitute 0.43 for } t \text{ in the original equation.}$$
$$60.5 \approx 60.2 \qquad \text{True.}$$

So Irabu's pitches took approximately 0.43 sec.

PRACTICE 7

A driver makes a trip from Washington, D.C., the U.S. capital, to Philadelphia, Pennsylvania, the home of Independence Hall, a distance of 130 mi, as shown. If she averages 60 mph, how long, to the nearest tenth of an hour, will it take her to get to Philadelphia? (*Source: 2001 World Almanac*)

130 mi • Philadelphia

Washington, D.C.

Exercises 2.2

FOR EXTRA HELP

📖 *Student's Solutions Manual*

Tutor Center *Addison-Wesley Math Tutor Center*

🚪 *MyMathLab*

📼 *Videotape 3/DVT 3*

Indicate what must be done to each side of the equation in order to isolate the variable.

1. $\dfrac{x}{3} = -4$ **2.** $\dfrac{a}{-6} = 1$ **3.** $-5x = 20$

4. $6x = 30$ **5.** $-2.2n = 4$ **6.** $1.5x = -6$

7. $\dfrac{3}{4}x = 12$ **8.** $\dfrac{2}{3}x = -6$

Solve and check.

9. $6x = -30$ **10.** $-8y = 8$ **11.** $\dfrac{n}{2} = 9$ **12.** $\dfrac{w}{10} = -21$

13. $\dfrac{a}{4} = 1.2$ **14.** $\dfrac{n}{7} = -1.3$ **15.** $-5x = 2.5$ **16.** $2y = 0.08$

17. $42 = -6c$ **18.** $50 = 2x$ **19.** $11 = -\dfrac{r}{2}$ **20.** $4 = \dfrac{-m}{3}$

21. $\dfrac{5}{6}x = 10$ **22.** $\dfrac{3}{4}d = -3$ **23.** $-\dfrac{2}{5}y = 1$ **24.** $\dfrac{2}{3}r = -8$

25. $\dfrac{3n}{4} = 6$ **26.** $\dfrac{5a}{6} = 5$ **27.** $\dfrac{4c}{3} = -4$ **28.** $-\dfrac{2z}{7} = 8$

29. $\dfrac{x}{2.4} = -1.2$ **30.** $-\dfrac{n}{0.5} = -1.3$ **31.** $-2.5a = 5$ **32.** $-2.25 = -1.5t$

33. $\dfrac{2}{3}y = \dfrac{4}{9}$ **34.** $\dfrac{5}{6}c = \dfrac{2}{3}$

Solve. Round to the nearest hundredth.

35. $\dfrac{x}{-1.515} = 1.515$ **36.** $\dfrac{n}{-2.968} = -3.85$ **37.** $-3.14x = 21.4148$ **38.** $2.54z = 6.4516$

Translate each sentence to an equation. Then solve and check.

39. The product of -4 and a number is 56.

40. Three-fourths of a number is equal to 12.

41. A number divided by 0.2 is 1.1.

42. Twice a number is equal to 15.

43. A number divided by -3 is 20.

44. The quotient of a number and 2.5 is 40.

45. A sixth of a number is $2\frac{4}{5}$.

46. Five-eighths of a number is 20.

Applications

Choose the equation that best describes the situation.

47. Suppose that a shopper used half his money to buy a backpack. If the backpack cost $20, how much money did he have prior to this purchase?

    a. $20 = 2m$ **b.** $20m = \dfrac{1}{2}$

    c. $20 = \dfrac{m}{2}$ **d.** $\dfrac{m}{20} = \dfrac{1}{2}$

48. A child's infant brother weighs 12 lb. If this is $\frac{1}{4}$ of her weight, how much does she weigh?

    a. $4w = 12$ **b.** $\dfrac{w}{4} = 12$

    c. $12w = \dfrac{1}{4}$ **d.** $\dfrac{w}{12} = \dfrac{1}{4}$

49. A student plans to buy a DVD player 6 weeks from now. If the DVD player costs $150, how much money must she save per week in order to buy it?

    a. $6p = 150$ **b.** $150p = 6$

    c. $\dfrac{p}{6} = 500$ **d.** $\dfrac{p}{500} = 6$

50. The student government at a college sold tickets to a play. From ticket sales, it collected $800, which was twice the cost of the play. How much did the play cost?

    a. $\dfrac{c}{800} = 2$ **b.** $800c = 2$

    c. $\dfrac{c}{2} = 800$ **d.** $2c = 800$

Write an equation that best describes the situation. Then solve and check.

51. According to a geologist, sediment at the bottom of a local lake accumulated at the rate of 0.02 cm per year. How long did it take to create a layer of sediment 10.5 cm thick?

52. Because of evaporation, the water level in an aquarium drops at a rate of $\frac{1}{10}$ in. per hour. In how many hours will the level drop 2 in.?

53. The bus trip from Miami to San Francisco, a driving distance of 3348 mi, takes 70 hr. What is the average speed of the bus rounded to the nearest mile per hour? (*Source: Greyhound*)

54. A double-trailer truck is driven at an average speed of 54 mph from Atlanta to Cincinnati, a driving distance of 440 mi. To the nearest tenth of an hour, how long did the trip take?
(*Source: The World Almanac and Book of Facts*, 2000)

55. A customer has only $20 to spend at a local print shop that charges $0.05 per copy. At this rate, how many copies can she afford to make?

56. Consider the two parcels of land shown—one a rectangle and the other a square. For which value of x do the two parcels have the same area?

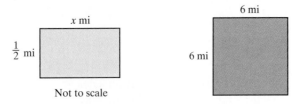

x mi

$\frac{1}{2}$ mi

Not to scale

6 mi

6 mi

57. A city offers to pay a disposal company $40 per ton to bury 20,000 tons of toxic waste. If this deal represents $\frac{2}{3}$ of the disposal company's projected income, what is that income?

58. The diameter of a tree trunk increases as the tree ages and adds rings. Suppose a trunk's diameter increases by 0.2 in. per year. How many years will it take the tree to increase in diameter from 4 in. to 12 in.?

59. The maximum depth of the Caspian Sea is 1000 m. If this depth is about $\frac{1}{5}$ the maximum depth of the Mediterranean Sea, what is the maximum depth of the Mediterranean Sea? (*Source: The 2000 New York Times Almanac*)

60. A top-secret plane flew 3000 miles in $1\frac{1}{2}$ hr. What was the average speed of this plane?

61. A student takes a job in the college's student center so that she can buy books that cost $187.50. How many hours must she work to make this amount if she earns $7.50/hr?

62. The coat in the ad shown is selling at $\frac{1}{4}$ the regular price. What was the original price?

★ Late Edition   City New

Coat Sale

$199.99

63. Last year, a young couple paid a total of $10,020 in rent for their apartment. How much money did they pay per month in rent?

64. An equilateral triangle is a triangle that has three sides equal in length. If the perimeter of an equilateral triangle is $10\frac{1}{2}$ ft, how long is each side?

• Check your answers on page A-4.

Mindstretchers

MATHEMATICAL REASONING

1. Suppose that in the course of solving a linear equation, you reach the step

$$5x = 3x$$

If you then divide both sides by x, you get $5 = 3$, which is impossible. Did you make an error? Explain.

_____

_____

_____

_____

_____

CRITICAL THINKING

2. If you multiply each side of the equation $0.24r = -12.48$ by 100, the result is an equivalent equation. Explain why it is helpful to carry out this multiplication in solving the equation.

_____

_____

WRITING

3. Write two different word problems that are applications of each equation.

a. $6x = 18$

- _____

  _____

- _____

  _____

b. $\dfrac{x}{3} = 10$

- _____

  _____

- _____

  _____

2.3 Solving Linear Equations by Combining Properties

OBJECTIVES

- *To solve linear equations using both the addition and multiplication properties*
- *To solve linear equations involving parentheses and combining like terms*
- *To solve applied problems using the addition and multiplication properties, parentheses, and combining like terms*

In the previous sections we solved simple equations involving either the addition property or the multiplication property. We now turn our attention to solving equations that involve both properties.

Solving Equations Using Both the Addition and Multiplication Properties

We need to use both the addition property and the multiplication property to solve equations such as

$$3x + 4 = 7 \quad \text{and} \quad \frac{r}{2} - 5 = 9$$

To solve these equations, we first use the addition property to get the variable term alone on one side. Then we use the multiplication property to isolate the variable.

EXAMPLE 1

Solve and check: $3x + 4 = 7$

SOLUTION

$$3x + 4 = 7$$
$$3x + 4 - 4 = 7 - 4 \qquad \text{Subtract 4 from each side of the equation.}$$
$$3x = 3$$
$$\frac{3x}{3} = \frac{3}{3} \qquad \text{Divide each side of the equation by 3.}$$
$$x = 1$$

CHECK

$$3x + 4 = 7$$
$$3(1) + 4 \overset{?}{=} 7 \qquad \text{Substitute 1 for } x \text{ in the original equation.}$$
$$3 + 4 \overset{?}{=} 7$$
$$7 = 7 \qquad \text{True.}$$

So the solution is 1.

PRACTICE 1

Solve and check: $2y + 1 = 9$

In solving Example 1, would we get the same solution if we divide before subtracting? Explain.

EXAMPLE 2

Solve and check: $\dfrac{r}{2} - 5 = 9$

SOLUTION

$$\dfrac{r}{2} - 5 = 9$$

$$\dfrac{r}{2} - 5 + 5 = 9 + 5 \qquad \text{Add 5 to each side of the equation.}$$

$$\dfrac{r}{2} = 14$$

$$2 \cdot \dfrac{r}{2} = 2 \cdot 14 \qquad \text{Multiply each side of the equation by 2.}$$

$$r = 28$$

CHECK

$$\dfrac{r}{2} - 5 = 9$$

$$\dfrac{28}{2} - 5 \stackrel{?}{=} 9 \qquad \text{Substitute 28 for } r \text{ in the original equation.}$$

$$14 - 5 \stackrel{?}{=} 9$$

$$9 = 9 \qquad \text{True.}$$

So the solution is 28.

PRACTICE 2

Solve and check: $\dfrac{c}{5} - 1 = 8$

EXAMPLE 3

Solve: $-4s + 7 = 3$

SOLUTION

$$-4s + 7 = 3$$

$$-4s + 7 - 7 = 3 - 7 \qquad \text{Subtract 7 from each side of the equation.}$$

$$-4s = -4$$

$$\dfrac{-4s}{-4} = \dfrac{-4}{-4} \qquad \text{Divide each side by } -4.$$

$$s = 1$$

So the solution is 1.

PRACTICE 3

Solve: $-6b - 5 = 13$

Solving Equations by Combining Like Terms

Now let's consider an equation that has like terms on the same side of the equation. In order to solve this kind of equation, we combine all like terms before using the addition and multiplication properties.

EXAMPLE 4

Solve and check: $7x - 3x - 6 = 6$

SOLUTION

$$7x - 3x - 6 = 6$$

$$4x - 6 \quad = 6 \qquad \text{Combine like terms.}$$

$$4x - 6 + 6 = 6 + 6 \qquad \text{Add 6 to each side of the equation.}$$

$$4x = 12$$

$$\frac{4x}{4} = \frac{12}{4} \qquad \text{Divide each side of the equation by 4.}$$

$$x = 3$$

CHECK
$$7x - 3x - 6 = 6$$
$$7(3) - 3(3) - 6 \stackrel{?}{=} 6 \qquad \text{Substitute 3 for } x.$$
$$21 - 9 - 6 \stackrel{?}{=} 6$$
$$6 = 6 \qquad \text{True.}$$

So the solution is 3.

PRACTICE 4

Solve and check: $5 - t - t = -1$

Suppose an equation has like terms that are on opposite sides of the equation. To solve, we use the addition property to get the like terms together on the same side so that they can be combined.

EXAMPLE 5

Solve: $13z + 5 = -z + 12$

SOLUTION

$$13z + 5 = -z + 12$$

$$z + 13z + 5 = z + (-z) + 12 \qquad \text{Add } z \text{ to each side of the equation.}$$

$$14z + 5 = 12 \qquad \text{Combine like terms.}$$

$$14z + 5 - 5 = 12 - 5 \qquad \text{Subtract 5 from each side of the equation.}$$

$$14z = 7$$

$$\frac{14z}{14} = \frac{7}{14} \qquad \text{Divide each side of the equation by 14.}$$

$$z = \frac{1}{2}$$

So the solution is $\frac{1}{2}$.

PRACTICE 5

Solve: $3f - 12 = -f - 15$

Solving Equations Containing Parentheses

Some equations contain parentheses. To solve these equations, we first remove the parentheses using the distributive property. Then we proceed as in previous examples.

EXAMPLE 6

Solve and check: $2c = -3(c - 5)$

SOLUTION

$$2c = -3(c - 5)$$
$$2c = -3c + 15 \qquad \text{Use the distributive property.}$$
$$3c + 2c = 3c - 3c + 15 \qquad \text{Add } 3c \text{ to each side of the equation.}$$
$$5c = 15 \qquad \text{Combine like terms.}$$
$$\frac{5c}{5} = \frac{15}{5} \qquad \text{Divide each side of the equation by 5.}$$
$$c = 3$$

CHECK

$$2c = -3(c - 5)$$
$$2(3) \overset{?}{=} -3(3 - 5) \qquad \text{Substitute 3 for } c \text{ in the original equation.}$$
$$6 \overset{?}{=} -3(-2)$$
$$6 = 6 \qquad \text{True.}$$

So the solution is 3.

PRACTICE 6

Solve and check: $-5(z + 6) = z$

In general, to solve linear equations, we use the following procedure:

To Solve Linear Equations
- Use the distributive property to clear the equation of parentheses, if necessary.
- Combine like terms where appropriate.
- Use the addition property to isolate the variable term.
- Use the multiplication property to isolate the variable.
- Check by substituting the solution in the original equation.

Let's apply this procedure in the next example. Recall from Section 1.8 that when removing parentheses preceded by a minus sign, all the terms in the parentheses change to the opposite sign.

EXAMPLE 7

Solve: $2(x + 5) - (x - 2) = 4x + 6$

SOLUTION

$$2(x + 5) - (x - 2) = 4x + 6$$
$$2x + 10 - x + 2 = 4x + 6 \qquad \text{Use the distributive property.}$$
$$x + 12 = 4x + 6 \qquad \text{Combine like terms.}$$
$$x - 4x + 12 = 4x - 4x + 6 \qquad \text{Subtract } 4x \text{ from each side of the equation.}$$
$$-3x + 12 = 6 \qquad \text{Combine like terms.}$$
$$-3x + 12 - 12 = 6 - 12 \qquad \text{Subtract 12 from each side of the equation.}$$
$$-3x = -6$$
$$\frac{-3x}{-3} = \frac{-6}{-3} \qquad \text{Divide each side of the equation by –3.}$$
$$x = 2$$

So the solution is 2.

PRACTICE 7

Solve: $2(t - 3) - 3(t - 2) = t + 8$

EXAMPLE 8

Solve: $13 - [4 + 2(x - 1)] = 3(x + 2)$

SOLUTION

$$13 - [4 + 2(x - 1)] = 3(x + 2)$$
$$13 - [4 + 2x - 2] = 3(x + 2)$$
$$13 - [2 + 2x] = 3(x + 2)$$
$$13 - 2 - 2x = 3x + 6$$
$$11 - 2x = 3x + 6$$
$$11 - 2x - 3x = 3x - 3x + 6$$
$$11 - 5x = 6$$
$$11 - 11 - 5x = 6 - 11$$
$$-5x = -5$$
$$\frac{-5x}{-5} = \frac{-5}{-5}$$
$$x = 1$$

So the solution is 1.

PRACTICE 8

Solve: $4[5y - (y - 1)] = 7(y - 2)$

Now let's consider applications that lead to equations like those that we have discussed in this section.

EXAMPLE 9

An insurance company settles a claim by multiplying the claim by a certain factor and then subtracting the deductible. A payment of $3500 is made on a claim filed for $5000. If the company has a $500 deductible, what factor was used to settle the claim?

SOLUTION Let x represent the factor used to settle a claim. Then write the equation:

The claim times the factor less the deductible is the payment.

$$5000 \quad \cdot \quad x \quad - \quad 500 \quad = \quad 3500$$

Next we solve for x.

$$5000x - 500 = 3500$$
$$5000x - 500 + 500 = 3500 + 500 \qquad \text{Add 500 to each side of the equation.}$$
$$5000x = 4000$$
$$\frac{5000x}{5000} = \frac{4000}{5000} \qquad \text{Divide each side of the equation by 5000.}$$
$$x = \frac{4}{5}, \quad \text{or } 0.8$$

So the factor used to compute the $5000 claim is $\frac{4}{5}$, or 0.8.

PRACTICE 9

A car is purchased for $12,000. The car's value depreciates $1100 in value per year for each of the first 6 years of ownership. At what point will the car have a value of $6500?

Many motion problems lead to equations of the type that we have discussed in this section, in particular, to equations containing parentheses. Some of these problems involve one or more objects traveling the same distance, at different rates and for different lengths of time.

EXAMPLE 10	PRACTICE 10

EXAMPLE 10

A bus leaves St. Petersburg traveling at 45 mph. An hour later, a second bus leaves the same city traveling at 55 mph in the same direction. In how many hours will the second bus overtake the first bus?

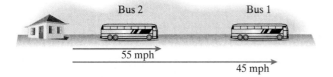

Bus 2   Bus 1

55 mph

45 mph

SOLUTION Let t represent the number of hours traveled by the second bus. Since the first bus left an hour earlier than the second, $t + 1$ represents the number of hours traveled by the first bus.

Recall from Section 2.2 that when an object travels at a constant speed, the distance that it travels is the product of its rate of travel (speed) and the time that it has traveled. Putting these quantities in a table clarifies their relationship.

	Rate	·	Time	=	Distance
First bus	45		$t + 1$		$45(t + 1)$
Second bus	55		t		$55t$

Since the two buses travel the same distance to the point where they meet, we can write the following equation and then solve:

$$45(t + 1) = 55t$$
$$45t + 45 = 55t$$
$$45t - 45t + 45 = 55t - 45t$$
$$45 = 10t$$
$$\frac{45}{10} = \frac{10}{10}t$$
$$4.5 = t, \quad \text{or}$$
$$t = 4.5$$

So the second bus will overtake the first bus in 4.5 hr, or $4\frac{1}{2}$ hr.

PRACTICE 10

Two friends plan to meet in Boston. A half an hour after one friend took a local train, the other friend takes an Amtrak express train on a parallel track. If both friends leave from the same station, how long will it take the express train to catch up with the local train if their speeds are 60 and 50 mph respectively?

EXAMPLE 11

A shopper walks from home to the market at a rate of 3 mph. After shopping, he returns home following the same route walking at 2 mph. If the walk back from the market takes 10 min more than the walk to the market, how far away is the market?

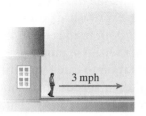 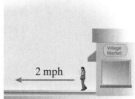

SOLUTION Let t represent the time of the walk to the market. Since the rates are given in miles per hour, we express the time in hours. The return trip takes 10 min more time. We change 10 min to $\frac{10}{60}$ hr, or $\frac{1}{6}$ hr, getting $t + \frac{1}{6}$ for the time of the return trip.

	Rate	·	Time	=	Distance
Going	3		t		$3t$
Returning	2		$t + \dfrac{1}{6}$		$2\left(t + \dfrac{1}{6}\right)$

Since the walk to and from the market followed the same route, the distances each way are equal.

$$3t = 2\left(t + \frac{1}{6}\right)$$
$$3t = 2t + \frac{1}{3}$$
$$3t - 2t = 2t - 2t + \frac{1}{3}$$
$$t = \frac{1}{3}$$

It takes $\frac{1}{3}$ hr to walk to the market. So the market is $3 \cdot \frac{1}{3}$, or 1 mi away from home.

PRACTICE 11

On a round-trip over the same roads, a car averaged 25 mph going and 30 mph returning. If the entire trip took 5 hr 30 min, what is the distance each way?

In some motion problems, an object travels at different speeds for different parts of the trip. The total distance traveled is the sum of the partial distances.

EXAMPLE 12

A car is driven for 3 hr in a rainstorm. After the weather clears, the car is driven 10 mph faster for 2 more hours, completing a 250-mi trip. How fast was the car driven during the storm?

SOLUTION Let x represent the speed of the car during the storm. The speed of the car after the storm passes can be represented by $x + 10$. Drawing a diagram helps us to visualize the problem and to see that the total distance driven is the sum of the two partial distances.

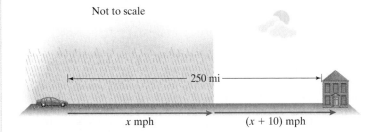

Not to scale

250 mi

x mph $(x + 10)$ mph

Next let's complete a table in order to organize the relevant information. Recall that distance is the product of rate and time.

	Rate ·	Time	=	Distance
Storm	x	3		$3x$
Clear	$x + 10$	2		$2(x + 10)$

We are told that the sum of the two partial distances is 250 mi, giving us an equation to solve.

$$3x + 2(x + 10) = 250$$
$$3x + 2x + 20 = 250$$
$$5x + 20 = 250$$
$$5x = 230$$
$$x = \frac{230}{5} = 46$$

Therefore, the car was driven at a speed of 46 mph during the storm.

PRACTICE 12

A cyclist pedals uphill for 2 hr. She then continues downhill 10 mph faster for another hour. If the entire trip was 40 mi in length, what was her downhill speed?

Exercises 2.3

FOR EXTRA HELP

📖 *Student's Solutions Manual*

Addison-Wesley Math Tutor Center

🚪 *MyMathLab*

📼 *Videotape 3/DVT 3*

Solve and check.

1. $3x - 1 = 8$

2. $7r - 8 = 13$

3. $9t + 17 = -1$

4. $2y + 1 = 9$

5. $20 - 5m = 45$

6. $25 - 3c = 34$

7. $\dfrac{n}{2} - 1 = 5$

8. $\dfrac{s}{3} - 2 = -4$

9. $\dfrac{x}{5} + 15 = 0$

10. $\dfrac{y}{3} + 3 = 42$

11. $3 - t = 1$

12. $2 - x = 2$

13. $-8 - b = 11$

14. $5 - y = 8$

15. $\dfrac{2}{3}x - 9 = 17$

16. $\dfrac{4}{5}d - 3 = 13$

17. $\dfrac{4}{5}r + 20 = -20$

18. $\dfrac{3y}{8} + 14 = -10$

19. $3y + y = -8$

20. $4a + 3a = -21$

21. $7z - 2z = -30$

22. $4x - x = 18$

23. $28 - a + 4a = 7$

24. $5 - 8x - 2x = -25$

25. $1 = 1 - 6t - 4t$

26. $-1 = 5 - z - z$

27. $3y + 2 = -y - 2$

28. $3n + 6 = -n - 6$

29. $5r - 4 = 2r + 6$

30. $7 - m = 5 + 3m$

31. $4(x + 7) = 7 + x$

32. $3t - 2 = 4(t - 2)$

33. $5(y - 1) = 2y + 1$

34. $5a - 4 = 7(a + 2)$

35. $3a - 2(a - 9) = 4 + 2a$

36. $5 - 2(3x - 4) = 3 - x$

37. $5(2 - t) - (1 - 3t) = 6$

38. $\dfrac{3}{5}(15y + 10) - 3(4y + 3) = 0$

39. $2y - 3(y + 1) = -(5y + 3) + y$

40. $9n + 5(n + 3) = -(n + 13) - 2$

41. $2[3z - 5(2z - 3)] = 3z - 4$

42. $5[2 - (2n - 4)] = 2(5 - 3n)$

43. $-8m - [2(11 - 2m) + 4] = 9m$

44. $7 - [4 + 2(a - 3)] = 11(a + 2)$

Solve. Round to the nearest hundredth.

45. $\dfrac{y}{0.87} + 2.51 = 4.03$

46. $7.02x - 3.64 = 8.29$

47. $7.37n + 4.06 = -1.98n + 6.55$

48. $10.13p = 3.14(p - 7.82)$

Applications

Choose the equation that best describes the situation.

49. A car leaves Seattle traveling at a rate of 45 mph. One hour later, a second car leaves from the same place, along the same road at 54 mph. If the first car travels for t hours, in how many hours will the second car overtake the first car?

   a. $54(t - 1) = 45t$ **b.** $45(t + 1) = 54t$

   c. $54(t + 1) = 45t$ **d.** $45(t - 1) = 54t$

50. A company budgets $600,000 for an advertising campaign. It must pay $4000 for each television commercial and $1000 per radio commercial. If the company plans to air 50 fewer radio commercials than television commercials, find the number of television commercials t that will be in the advertising campaign.

   a. $4000t + 1000(t + 50) = 600,000$ **b.** $4000t + 1000(t - 50) = 600,000$

   c. $4000t + 1000t - 50 = 600,000$ **d.** $1000t + 4000(t - 50) = 600,000$

51. A taxi fare is $1.50 for the first mile and $1.25 for each additional mile. If a passenger's total cost was $4.25, how far did she travel in the taxi?

   a. $1.50x + 1.25 = 4.25$ **b.** $1.50 + 1.25x = 4.25$

   c. $1.5 + 1.25(x + 1) = 4.25$ **d.** $1.50 + 1.25(x - 1) = 4.25$

52. A family's budget allows $\frac{1}{3}$ of the family's monthly income for housing and $\frac{1}{4}$ of its monthly income for food. If a total of $1050 a month is budgeted for housing and food, what is the family's monthly income?

   a. $\frac{1}{3}x = 1050 + \frac{1}{4}x$ **b.** $\frac{1}{3}x - \frac{1}{4}x = 1050$

   c. $\frac{1}{3}x + \frac{1}{4}x = 1050$ **d.** $\frac{1}{4}x - \frac{1}{3}x = 1050$

Write an equation and solve.

53. A part-time student at a college pays a student fee of $50 plus $120 per credit. How many credits is a part-time student carrying who pays $1010 in all?

54. A health club charges members $10 per month plus $5 per hour to use the facilities. If a member was charged $55 this month, how many hours did she use the facilities?

55. In a local election, a newspaper reported that one candidate received twice as many votes as the other. Altogether, they received a total of 3690 votes. How many votes did each candidate receive?

56. Calcium carbonate (chalk) consists of 10 parts of calcium for each 3 parts of carbon and 12 parts of oxygen by weight. Find the amount of calcium in 75 lb of chalk.

57. A parking garage charges $3 for the first hour and $2 for each additional hour or fraction thereof. If $9 was paid for parking, how many hours was the car parked in the garage?

58. A machinist earns $11.50 an hour for the first 35 hours and $15.30 for each hour over 35 per week. How many hours did he work this week if he earned $555.50?

59. The office manager of an election campaign office needs to print 5000 postcards. Suppose that it costs 2 cents to print a large postcard and 1 cent to print a small postcard. If $85 is allocated for printing postcards, how many of each type of postcard can be printed?

60. The owner of a factory has 8 employees. Some of the employees make $10 per hour, whereas the others make $15 per hour. If the total payroll is $105 per hour, how many employees make the higher rate of pay?

61. Twenty minutes after your brother left for work on the bus, you noticed that he had left his briefcase at home. You leave home, driving at 36 mph, to catch the bus that is traveling at 24 mph. How long will it take you to catch the bus?

62. In the rush hour, a commuter drives to work at 30 mph. Returning home off-peak, she takes $\frac{1}{4}$ hr less time driving at 40 mph. What is the distance between the commuter's work and her home?

63. The two snails shown to the right crawl toward each other at rates that differ by 2 cm/min. If it takes the snails 27 min to meet, how fast is each snail crawling?

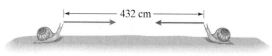

64. Suppose that a signal is sent from a station on the ground to a satellite. The signal bounces off the satellite and then is received at a second ground station. If the signal traveled 2400 mi in all, at what speed was the signal traveling?

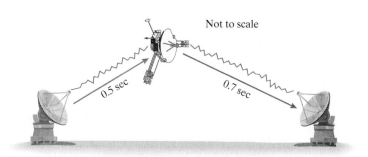

65. Two trucks leave a depot at the same time, traveling in opposite directions. One truck goes 4 mph faster than the other. After 2 hr, the trucks are 212 mi apart. What is the speed of the slower truck?

66. If a student drives from college to home at 40 mph, then he is 15 min late. However if he makes the same trip at 50 mph, he is 12 min early. What is the distance between his college and his home?

• *Check your answers on page A-5.*

Mindstretchers

MATHEMATICAL REASONING

1. Give an example of an equation that involves combining like terms and that has

a. no solution.

_____

_____

b. an infinite number of solutions.

_____

_____

PATTERNS

2. Tables can be useful in solving equations.

a. Complete the following table. After examining your results, identify the solution to the following equation: $3(x - 2) = 2(x + 1)$

x	$3(x - 2)$	$2(x + 1)$
0		
2		
4		
6		
8		
10		
12		

continued

b. Try a similar approach to solving the equation $7x = 5x + 11$. What conclusion can you draw about the solution?

x	$7x$	$5x + 11$
0		
2		
4		
6		
8		
10		
12		

_____

_____

_____

GROUPWORK

3. Working with a partner, choose a month on a calendar.

a. Ask your partner to secretly select four days of the month that form a square, but only to tell you the sum of the four days. Determine the four days.

b. Reverse roles with your partner, and repeat part (a).

c. Compare how you and your partner responded to part (a).

_____

_____

_____

2.4 Solving Literal Equations and Formulas

In many situations, equations describe the relationship between two or more variables. Such equations are called *literal* equations and can be used to describe situations such as how the amount you pay depends on what you buy, how the distance you walk determines how long the walk takes, and how the dosage of a medicine you need to take relates to your weight.

OBJECTIVES

- *To solve literal equations*
- *To solve and evaluate formulas*
- *To solve applied problems involving formulas*

Definition

A **literal equation** is an equation involving two or more variables.

Consider, for instance, the literal equation

$$2a + b = c.$$

Since there is more than one variable, we can solve for one of the variables in terms of the others. For instance, in this equation we can solve for a in terms of b and c. Solving for a is especially useful if we want to calculate the value of a for a variety of values of b and c.

EXAMPLE 1	PRACTICE 1
Solve $2a + b = c$ for a in terms of b and c.	Solve $3r - s = t$ for r in terms of s and t.

SOLUTION

$$2a + b = c$$
$$2a + b - b = c - b \quad \text{Subtract } b \text{ from each side of the equation.}$$
$$2a = c - b \quad \text{Simplify.}$$
$$\frac{2a}{2} = \frac{c - b}{2} \quad \text{Divide each side of the equation by 2.}$$
$$a = \frac{c - b}{2}$$

So $a = \dfrac{c - b}{2}$.

We see from Example 1 that the solution to a literal equation is not a number but an algebraic expression.

Note that we can solve literal equations by using the addition and multiplication properties that we have already used to solve other equations. Can you explain how to check your solution to a literal equation?

EXAMPLE 2

Solve $\dfrac{2K}{3m} = n$ for K.

SOLUTION

$$\dfrac{2K}{3m} = n$$

$$3m \cdot \dfrac{2K}{3m} = 3m \cdot n \qquad \text{Multiply each side of the equation by } 3m.$$

$$2K = 3mn$$

$$\dfrac{2K}{} = \dfrac{3mn}{} \qquad \text{Divide each side of the equation by 2.}$$

$$K = \dfrac{3mn}{2}$$

So $K = \dfrac{3mn}{2}$.

PRACTICE 2

Solve $\dfrac{4x}{5a} = c$ for x.

EXAMPLE 3

Consider the equation $Ax + By = C$.

a. Solve for y in terms of A, B, C, and x.

b. Using the equation found in part (a), find the value of y if $A = 4$, $B = 2$, $C = 2$, and $x = 5$.

SOLUTION

a. $Ax + By = C$

$$Ax - Ax + By = C - Ax \qquad \text{Subtract } Ax \text{ from each side of the equation.}$$

$$By = C - Ax \qquad \text{Simplify.}$$

$$\dfrac{By}{B} = \dfrac{C - Ax}{B} \qquad \text{Divide each side of the equation by } B.$$

$$y = \dfrac{C - Ax}{B}$$

So $y = \dfrac{C - Ax}{B}$.

b. To find the value of y, we substitute $A = 4$, $B = 2$, $C = 2$ and $x = 5$ in the equation $y = \dfrac{C - Ax}{B}$.

$$y = \dfrac{C - Ax}{B} = \dfrac{2 - 4 \cdot \mathbf{5}}{\mathbf{2}} = \dfrac{2 - 20}{2} = \dfrac{-18}{2} = -9$$

The value of y is -9.

PRACTICE 3

Consider the equation $y = mx + b$.

a. Solve for x in terms of y, m, and b.

b. Using the equation found in part (a), find the value of x if $y = 10$, $m = -3$, and $b = 7$.

Recall that in Chapter 1, we discussed formulas—a special type of literal equation. Here we focus on solving a formula for one variable in terms of the other variables. When we need to repeatedly find the value of a particular variable, the computation can be simplified by first solving for that variable in the formula.

EXAMPLE 4

$P = 2(l + w)$ is the formula for the perimeter P of a rectangle in terms of its length l and width w.

a. Solve for l in terms of P and w.

b. Using the formula found in part (a), find the length of a rectangle with a perimeter of 20 cm and a width of 6 cm.

SOLUTION

a.
$$P = 2(l + w)$$

$$P = 2l + 2w \qquad \text{Use the distributive property.}$$

$$P - 2w = 2l + 2w - 2w \qquad \text{Subtract } 2w \text{ from each side of the equation.}$$

$$P - 2w = 2l$$

$$\frac{P - 2w}{2} = \frac{2l}{2} \qquad \text{Divide each side of the equation by 2.}$$

$$\frac{P - 2w}{2} = l,$$

or $\qquad l = \dfrac{P - 2w}{2}$

So $l = \dfrac{P - 2w}{2}$.

b. $P = 20$ cm and $w = 6$ cm. We substitute in the formula $l = \dfrac{P - 2w}{2}$ to find the value of l.

$$l = \frac{P - 2w}{2} = \frac{20 - 2 \cdot 6}{2} = \frac{20 - 12}{2} = \frac{8}{2} = 4$$

So the length of the rectangle is 4 cm.

PRACTICE 4

$A = P(1 + rt)$ is the formula for computing the amount in an account earning simple interest. In the formula, A stands for the amount, P for the original principal, r for the annual rate of interest, and t for time.

a. Find a formula for r in terms of A, P, and t.

b. Using the equation found in part (a), evaluate r if $A = \$2100$, $P = \$2000$, and $t = 2$ years.

EXAMPLE 5

$V = lwh$ is the formula for finding the volume of a rectangular solid, where l represents the length of the solid, w the width, and h the height.

a. Solve the formula for h.

b. Using the equation found in part (a), find the value of h for $V = 48$ cu ft, $l = 8$ ft, and $w = 2$ ft.

SOLUTION

a. Solving $V = lwh$ for h, we get:

$$V = lwh$$

$$\frac{V}{lw} = \frac{lwh}{lw}$$

$$\frac{V}{lw} = h$$

So $h = \dfrac{V}{lw}$.

PRACTICE 5

$A = lw$ is the formula for finding the area of a rectangle.

a. Express w in terms of A and l.

b. Using the formula found in part (a), find the value of w for $A = 63$ sq in. and $l = 9$ in.

b. To find the value of h, we substitute 48 for V, 8 for l, and 2 for w in the formula $h = \dfrac{V}{lw}$.

$$h = \frac{48}{8(2)} = 3$$

The height is 3 ft.

EXAMPLE 6	PRACTICE 6

EXAMPLE 6

To convert a temperature expressed in Fahrenheit degrees F to Celsius degrees C, a meteorologist multiplies $\frac{5}{9}$ by the difference between the Fahrenheit temperature and 32.

a. Write a formula for this relationship.

b. Solve the formula for F.

c. What Fahrenheit temperature corresponds to a Celsius temperature of 30°?

SOLUTION

a. Stating the rule in words, we get:

Celsius temperature, C, is equal to $\frac{5}{9}$ times the quantity Fahrenheit temperature, F, minus 32.

Then we translate this relationship to a formula.

$$C = \frac{5}{9}(F - 32)$$

b. Now we solve the formula found in part (a) for F.

$$C = \frac{5}{9}(F - 32)$$

$$\frac{9}{5}C = \frac{9}{5} \cdot \frac{5}{9}(F - 32)$$

$$\frac{9}{5}C = F - 32$$

$$\frac{9}{5}C + 32 = F$$

So $F = \frac{9}{5}C + 32$.

c. To find the Fahrenheit temperature that corresponds to a Celsius temperature of 30°, we substitute 30 for C in the formula.

$$F = \frac{9}{5}C + 32 = \frac{9}{5}(30) + 32 = 54 + 32 = 86$$

The corresponding Fahrenheit temperature is, therefore, 86°.

PRACTICE 6

To find the area A of a trapezoid, multiply $\frac{1}{2}$ its height h by the sum of the trapezoid's upper base b and lower base B.

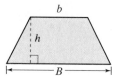

a. Translate this relationship to a formula.

b. Solve the formula for b.

c. What is the upper base of a trapezoid whose area is 32 sq cm, height is 4 cm, and lower base is 11 cm?

Exercises 2.4

FOR EXTRA HELP

📖 *Student's Solutions Manual*

📞 *Addison-Wesley Math Tutor Center*

🚪 *MyMathLab*

📼 *Videotape 3/DVT 3*

Solve each equation for the indicated variable.

1. $y + 10 = x$ for y

2. $b + 13 = a$ for b

3. $d - c = 4$ for d

4. $x - z = -5$ for x

5. $-3y = da$ for d

6. $ax = 5b$ for x

7. $\frac{1}{2}n = 2p$ for n

8. $\frac{3}{2}m = -4l$ for m

9. $a = \frac{1}{2}xyz$ for z

10. $w = \frac{2}{3}rst$ for r

11. $3x + y = 7$ for x

12. $x + 2y = 5$ for y

13. $3x + 4y = 12$ for y

14. $5a + 2b = 10$ for a

15. $y - 4t = 0$ for y

16. $6 = p - 4z$ for p

17. $-5b + p = r$ for b

18. $-7a + 3b = c$ for a

19. $h = 2(m - 2l)$ for l

20. $3(a - 2b) = c$ for b

Solve each formula for the indicated variable.

21. Simple interest: $I = prt$ for r

22. Electrical power: $P = iV$ for i

23. Uniform motion: $d = rt$ for r

24. Perimeter of square: $P = 4s$ for s

25. Perimeter of a triangle: $P = a + b + c$ for b

26. Perimeter of a rectangle: $P = 2l + 2w$ for w

27. Circumference of a circle: $C = \pi d$ for d

28. Aspect ratio of a hang glider: $R = \dfrac{s^2}{a}$ for a

29. Power: $P = I^2R$ for R

30. Centripetal force: $F = \dfrac{mv^2}{r}$ for m

31. Average of three numbers: $A = \dfrac{a + b + c}{3}$ for a

32. Distance of a free-falling object: $S = \dfrac{1}{2}gt^2$ for g

33. Arithmetic progression: $S = a + (n - 1)d$ for a

34. Simple interest: $A = P(1 + rt)$ for t

Solve for the variable shown in color. Then find the value of this variable for the given values of the other variables.

35. $3x + y = 6$ when $x = -12$

36. $2x - y = 5$ when $x = 4$

37. $3x - 7 = y$ when $y = 5$

38. $2x + 3y = -4$ when $y = -2$

39. $-\dfrac{1}{3}y = x$ when $x = \dfrac{1}{2}$

40. $\dfrac{1}{2}x = y$ when $y = -\dfrac{1}{4}$

41. $ax + by = c$ when $a = 1$, $b = 3$, $y = -4$, and $c = 2$

42. $dx - ey = f$ when $d = 5$, $x = -1$, $e = -2$, and $f = 7$

Applications

Solve.

43. In physics, Charles's Law describes the relationship between the volume of a gas and its temperature. The law states that the volume V divided by the temperature T is equal to a constant K.

   a. Write an equation to express this relationship.

   b. Solve the relationship for V.

44. In geometry, the volume V of a cylinder is the product of the area B of the circular base and the height h.

   a. Write a formula for this relationship.

   b. Solve the formula for h.

45. In nursing, Clark's Rule for medication expresses a relationship between the recommended dosages for a child and for an adult. The rule states that a child's dosage C equals the product of the weight W of the child in pounds divided by 150 and the adult's dosage A.

   a. Write a formula for this relationship.

   b. Solve the formula for A.

46. A toy rocket is launched upward with an initial velocity of 96 ft/sec. After t sec its velocity v is $96 - 32t$ ft/sec.

   a. Solve for t in terms of v.

   b. How long after launching will the rocket take to reach its highest point, that is, when is the velocity 0 ft/sec?

47. During a storm, you can estimate the number m of miles away a bolt of lightning strikes by first counting the number t of seconds between the bolt of lightning and the associated clap of thunder, and then dividing by 5.

   a. Translate this relationship to a formula.

   b. Solve for t in terms of m.

   c. If lightning strikes 2.5 mi away, how many seconds will elapse before you hear the thunder?

48. To estimate a man's shoe size S, triple his foot length l (expressed in inches) and subtract 22.

   a. Express this relationship as a formula.

   b. Estimate the shoe size of a man with a 12-in. foot.

   c. Estimate the foot length of a man with shoe size 12.

49. The circumference C of a circle can be found by doubling the product of the constant π and the circle's radius r.

   a. Express this relationship as a formula.

   b. Solve this formula for r in terms of C and π.

   c. Find the value of r rounded to the nearest tenth if C is 5 ft and π is approximately 3.14.

50. According to Newton's second law of motion, the force F (in newtons) applied to an object equals the product of the object's mass m (in kilograms) and its acceleration a (in m/sec^2).

   a. Translate this relationship to a formula.

   b. Solve for a in terms of m and F.

   c. Find a (in m/sec^2) if m is 3 kg and F is 10 newtons.

• *Check your answers on page A-5.*

Mindstretchers

RESEARCH

1. By examining books in your college library or Web sites, find several examples of literal equations that relate two or more variables. Explain what the variables represent, and write the equation that relates them.

_____

_____

_____

GROUPWORK

2. Working with a partner, give an example of a situation that the following formula might describe.

$$y = mx + b$$

Explain what each variable represents in your example.

_____

_____

_____

PATTERNS

3. Consider the following table.

x	0	1	2	3	4	$\cdots$	10
y	1	3	5	7	9	$\cdots$	21

Write an equation for y in terms of x.

2.6 Solving Inequalities

In Section 1.1, we used the symbols $<$, $\leq$, $>$, $\geq$, $=$, and $\neq$ to compare two real numbers. For example, with the real numbers -5 and 4, we can write the following statements:

$$-5 < 4 \qquad 4 > -5 \qquad -5 \neq 4$$

OBJECTIVES

- *To determine if a number is a solution of an inequality*

- *To graph the solutions of linear inequalities on the number line*

- *To solve linear inequalities using the addition and multiplication properties of inequalities*

- *To solve applied problems involving linear inequalities*

Definition

An **inequality** is any mathematical statement containing $<$, $\leq$, $>$, $\geq$, or $\neq$.

Solutions of Inequalities

Now consider an inequality that involves a variable, say $x < 2$. Let's look at the values of x that make this inequality true.

	Values for x	$x < 2$	True or False?
Values for x that are less than 2	1	$1 < 2$	True
	$\dfrac{1}{2}$	$\dfrac{1}{2} < 2$	True
	0	$0 < 2$	True
	-1	$-1 < 2$	True
Values for x that are not less than 2	2	$2 < 2$	False
	3	$3 < 2$	False
	$3\frac{1}{2}$	$3\frac{1}{2} < 2$	False
	4	$4 < 2$	False

Note that there are many values for x that make $x < 2$ true. Can you name them all? Explain.

Definition

A **solution of an inequality** is any value of the variable that makes the inequality true. To **solve an inequality** is to find all of its solutions.

EXAMPLE 1

Determine whether -3 is a solution of the inequality $2x + 5 \geq -3$.

SOLUTION To determine if -3 is a solution of the inequality, we substitute -3 for x and simplify.

$$2x + 5 \geq -3$$
$$2(-3) + 5 \overset{?}{\geq} -3 \qquad \text{Substitute } -3 \text{ for } x.$$
$$-6 + 5 \overset{?}{\geq} -3 \qquad \text{Multiply.}$$
$$-1 \geq -3 \qquad \text{True.}$$

Because $-1 \geq -3$ is a true statement, -3 is a solution of the inequality.

PRACTICE 1

Is 4 a solution of the inequality

$$\frac{1}{2}x - 2 < -1?$$

For any inequality, we can draw on the number line a picture of its solutions—the *graph* of the inequality. Graphing the solutions of an inequality can be clearer than describing the solutions in symbols or words.

EXAMPLE 2

Draw the graph of $x < 2$.

SOLUTION The graph of $x < 2$ includes all points on the number line to the left of 2. The open circle on the graph shows that 2 is *not* a solution.

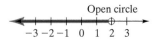

PRACTICE 2

Draw the graph of $x > 1$.

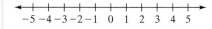

Note that solving an inequality generally results in a range of numbers rather than in a single number.

EXAMPLE 3

Draw the graph of $x \geq -\dfrac{1}{2}$.

SOLUTION The graph of $x \geq -\dfrac{1}{2}$ includes all points on the

number line to the right of $-\dfrac{1}{2}$ and also $-\dfrac{1}{2}$. The *closed circle*

shows that $-\dfrac{1}{2}$ is a solution of $x \geq -\dfrac{1}{2}$.

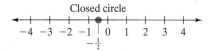

PRACTICE 3

Draw the graph of $x \leq -1\frac{1}{2}$.

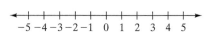

EXAMPLE 4

Draw the graph of $-1 \leq x < 2$.

SOLUTION This inequality is read either " -1 is less than or equal to x *and* x is less than 2" or "x is greater than or equal to -1 *and* x is less than 2." The solutions of this inequality are all values of x that satisfy both $-1 \leq x$ and $x < 2$ and its graph is the overlap of the graphs of $-1 \leq x$ and $x < 2$.

Graph of $-1 \leq x$:

Graph of $x < 2$:

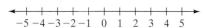

Graph of $-1 \leq x < 2$:

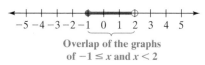

Overlap of the graphs
of $-1 \leq x$ and $x < 2$

Note that the graph includes -1 and all points *between* -1 and 2 on the number line. A closed circle at -1 means that -1 is a solution of the inequality, whereas an open circle at 2 means that 2 is not a solution of the inequality.

PRACTICE 4

Draw the graph of $-3 < x < 4$.

-5 -4 -3 -2 -1 0 1 2 3 4 5

Solving Inequalities Using the Addition Property

Now let's consider what happens when we perform the same operation on each side of an inequality. In the following inequality, we add 4 to each side of the inequality $5 < 12$.

$$5 < 12 \qquad \text{True.}$$
$$5 + 4 \overset{?}{<} 12 + 4 \qquad \text{Add 4 to each side of the inequality.}$$
$$9 < 16 \qquad \text{True.}$$

Note that $5 < 12$ and $5 + 4 < 12 + 4$ are both true, and so are equivalent.

This example suggests the addition property of inequalities.

Addition Property of Inequalities

For any real numbers a, b, and c, the following is true.

- If $a < b$, then $a + c < b + c$.
- If $a > b$, then $a + c > b + c$.

Similar statements hold for $\leq$ and $\geq$.

Alternatively, suppose we subtract 4 from each side of the original inequality:

$$5 < 12 \qquad \text{True.}$$
$$5 - 4 \overset{?}{<} 12 - 4 \qquad \text{Subtract 4 from each side of the inequality.}$$
$$1 < 8 \qquad \text{True.}$$

Note that $5 < 12$ and $5 - 4 < 12 - 4$ are both true, and so are equivalent. This suggests that subtracting the same number from both sides of an inequality also results in an equivalent inequality.

> **TIP** When the same number is added to or subtracted from each side of an inequality, the *direction* of the inequality is unchanged.

The way we solve inequalities is similar to the way we solve equations.

Equation	Inequality
$x + 3 = 5$	$x + 3 < 5$
$x + 3 - 3 = 5 - 3$	$x + 3 - 3 < 5 - 3$
$x = 2$ **Solution**	$x < 2$ **Solution**
$x + 3 = 5$ is equivalent to $x = 2$	$x + 3 < 5$ is equivalent to $x < 2$.

We solve inequalities by expressing them as equivalent inequalities in which the variable term is isolated on one side.

EXAMPLE 5

Solve and graph: $y + 5 > 9$

SOLUTION $\quad y + 5 > 9$

$\qquad y + 5 - 5 > 9 - 5$ Subtract 5 from each side of the inequality.

$\qquad\qquad y > 4$

The graph of $y > 4$ is:

$$\xleftarrow{\;\;|\;\;|\;\;|\;\;|\;\;|\;\;|\;\;|\;\;|\;\;|\;\;}\rightarrow$$
$$-1 \;\; 0 \;\; 1 \;\; 2 \;\; 3 \;\; 4 \;\; 5 \;\; 6 \;\; 7$$

Note that an open circle is drawn at 4 to show that 4 is not a solution.

Because an inequality has many solutions, we cannot check all of the solutions as we did with an equation. However, we can do a partial check of the solutions of an inequality by substituting points on the graph in the original inequality. For instance, to check that all values for y greater than 4 are the solutions of $y + 5 > 9$, we replace y in the original inequality with some points on the graph and some points not on the graph.

Values for y	$y + 5 > 9$	True or False
6	$6 + 5 > 9$	True
5	$5 + 5 > 9$	True
4	$4 + 5 > 9$	False
3	$3 + 5 > 9$	False

The table confirms that the solution of $y + 5 > 9$ is $y > 4$. That is to say, any number greater than but not equal to 4 is a solution.

PRACTICE 5

Solve and graph: $n + 5 > 4$

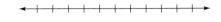

EXAMPLE 6

Solve and graph: $z - 2 \leq -3\frac{1}{2}$

SOLUTION $z - 2 \leq -3\frac{1}{2}$

$z - 2 + 2 \leq -3\frac{1}{2} + 2$ Add 2 to each side of the inequality.

$z \leq -1\frac{1}{2}$

So all numbers less than or equal to $-1\frac{1}{2}$ are solutions. The graph of $z \leq -1\frac{1}{2}$ is

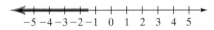

PRACTICE 6

Solve and graph: $x - 4 \leq 1\frac{1}{2}$

EXAMPLE 7

Solve and graph: $6y - 3 \leq 5y + 4$

SOLUTION $6y - 3 \leq 5y + 4$

$6y - 5y - 3 \leq 5y - 5y + 4$ Subtract 5y from each side of the inequality.

$y - 3 \leq 4$

$y - 3 + 3 \leq 4 + 3$ Add 3 to each side of the inequality.

$y \leq 7$

So all numbers less than or equal to 7 are solutions of $6y - 3 \leq 5y + 4$. The graph of $y \leq 7$ is

PRACTICE 7

Solve and graph: $4x + 5 \geq 3x - 2$

Solving Inequalities Using the Multiplication Property

Consider the inequality $12 < 15$. Let's look at what happens when we multiply this inequality by a *positive* number:

$12 < 15$

$12 \cdot 3 \overset{?}{<} 15 \cdot 3$ Multiply each side of the inequality by 3.

$36 < 45$ True.

Now consider multiplying each side of the original inequality by a *negative* number:

$12 < 15$

$12(-3) \overset{?}{<} 15(-3)$ Multiply each side of the inequality by –3.

$-36 \overset{?}{<} -45$ False, unless the direction of the inequality sign is reversed.

$-36 > -45$ True.

These examples suggest the *multiplication property of inequalities.*

Multiplication Property of Inequalities

For any real numbers a, b, and c, the following is true.

- If $a < b$ and c is positive, then $ac < bc$.
- If $a < b$ and c is negative, then $ac > bc$.

Similar statements hold for $>$, $\leq$ and $\geq$.

We can demonstrate a similar property for division.

$$12 < 15$$

$$\frac{12}{3} \overset{?}{<} \frac{15}{3} \qquad \text{Divide each side of the inequality by 3.}$$

$$4 < 5 \qquad \text{True.}$$

$$12 < 15$$

$$\frac{12}{-3} \overset{?}{<} \frac{15}{-3} \qquad \text{Divide each side of the inequality by } -3.$$

$$-4 \overset{?}{<} -5 \qquad \text{False, so we need to reverse the direction of the inequality sign.}$$

$$-4 > -5 \qquad \text{True.}$$

Note that when we multiply or divide each side of an inequality by a positive number, the direction of the inequality remains the same. But when we multiply or divide each side of an inequality by a negative number, the direction of the inequality is *reversed*.

EXAMPLE 8

Solve and graph: $\dfrac{x}{2} < 3$

SOLUTION

$$\frac{x}{2} < 3$$

$$2 \cdot \frac{x}{2} < 2 \cdot 3 \qquad \text{Multiply each side of the inequality by 2.}$$

$$x < 6$$

So any number less than 6 is a solution. The graph of $x < 6$ is

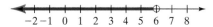

PRACTICE 8

Solve and graph: $\dfrac{x}{3} \leq 1$

EXAMPLE 9

Solve and graph: $-4z \leq 12$

SOLUTION

$$-4z \leq 12$$

$$\frac{-4z}{-4} \geq \frac{12}{-4} \qquad \text{Divide each side of the inequality by } -4 \text{ and reverse the direction of the inequality.}$$

$$z \geq -3$$

The solution of $-4z \leq 12$ is $z \geq -3$, so all numbers greater than or equal to -3 are solutions. The graph of $z \geq -3$ is

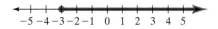

PRACTICE 9

Solve and graph: $-3x > 15$

EXAMPLE 10

Solve and graph: $-21 < 6y - 9y$

SOLUTION

$$-21 < 6y - 9y$$
$$-21 < -3y \qquad \text{Combine like terms.}$$
$$\frac{-21}{-3} > \frac{-3y}{-3} \qquad \begin{array}{l}\text{Divide each side of the inequality by } -3\\ \text{and reverse the direction of the inequality.}\end{array}$$
$$7 > y, \quad \text{or } y < 7$$

So all numbers less than 7 are solutions. The graph is:

PRACTICE 10

Solve and graph: $10 > 5x - 7x$

As in solving equations, we may need to use more than one property of inequalities to solve some inequalities.

EXAMPLE 11

Solve: $5y - 4 - 6y \le -8$

SOLUTION

$$5y - 4 - 6y \le -8$$
$$-y - 4 \le -8 \qquad \text{Combine like terms.}$$
$$-y - 4 + 4 \le -8 + 4 \qquad \text{Add 4 to each side of the inequality.}$$
$$-y \le -4 \qquad \text{Simplify.}$$
$$\frac{-y}{-1} \ge \frac{-4}{-1} \qquad \begin{array}{l}\text{Divide each side of the inequality by } -1\\ \text{and reverse the direction of the inequality.}\end{array}$$
$$y \ge 4$$

So all numbers greater than or equal to 4 are solutions.

PRACTICE 11

Solve: $-6 \ge 3z + 4 - z$

EXAMPLE 12

Solve: $3n - 2(n + 3) < 14$

SOLUTION

$$3n - 2(n + 3) < 14$$
$$3n - 2n - 6 < 14 \qquad \text{Use the distributive property.}$$
$$n - 6 < 14 \qquad \text{Combine like terms.}$$
$$n - 6 + 6 < 14 + 6 \qquad \text{Add 6 to each side of the inequality.}$$
$$n < 20$$

So all numbers less than 20 are solutions.

PRACTICE 12

Solve: $7x - (9x + 1) > -5$

Some common word phrases used in applied problems involving inequalities and their translations are shown in the following table.

Word Phrase	Translation
x is less than a	$x < a$
x is less than or equal to a	$x \leq a$
x is greater than a	$x > a$
x is greater than or equal to a	$x \geq a$
x is at most a	$x \leq a$
x is no more than a	$x \leq a$
x is at least a	$x \geq a$
x is no less than a	$x \geq a$

EXAMPLE 13

In geometry, the triangle inequality states that the sum of the lengths of any two sides of a triangle is greater than the length of the third side. In the isosceles triangle shown, write and solve an inequality to find the possible side lengths *a*. Graph the inequality.

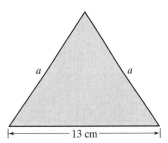

SOLUTION The sum of the lengths of the two equal sides is greater than the length of the third side.

$$a + a > 13$$
$$2a > 13$$

Solving the inequality, we get:

$$\frac{2a}{2} > \frac{13}{2} \qquad \text{Divide each side by 2.}$$
$$a > 6.5$$

The graph is:

We conclude that the length of each side *a* is any number greater than 6.5 cm.

PRACTICE 13

In the triangle shown, for which values of *x* will the perimeter be greater than or equal to 14 in.?

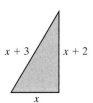

EXAMPLE 14

A factory's quality-control department randomly selects a sample of 5 lightbulbs to test. In order to meet quality control standards, the lightbulbs in the sample must last an average of at least 950 hr. Four of the selected lightbulbs lasted 925 hr, 1000 hr, 950 hr, and 900 hr. How many hours must the fifth lightbulb last if the sample is to meet quality-control standards?

SOLUTION The average number of hours that the 5 lightbulbs must last is the sum of the hours each lightbulb lasts divided by the number of lightbulbs in the sample, which is 5.

$$\text{Average number of hours} = \frac{925 + 1000 + 950 + 900 + x}{5},$$

where x represents the number of hours the fifth bulb lasted. In order for the average to be *at least* 950, it must be greater than or equal to 950. So we write and solve the inequality.

$$\frac{925 + 1000 + 950 + 900 + x}{5} \geq 950$$

$$5\left(\frac{925 + 1000 + 950 + 900 + x}{5}\right) \geq 950 \cdot 5$$

$$925 + 1000 + 950 + 900 + x \geq 4750$$

$$3775 + x \geq 4750$$

$$3775 - 3775 + x \geq 4750 - 3775$$

$$x \geq 975$$

So the fifth lightbulb in the sample must last at least 975 hr for the sample to meet quality-control standards.

PRACTICE 14

Suppose that you have two part-time jobs. On the first job, you work 15 hr a week at $8.50 an hour. The second job pays only $7.50 an hour, but you can work as many hours as you want. To make at least $300, how many hours should you work on the second job?

Exercises 2.6

FOR EXTRA HELP

 Student's Solutions Manual

 Addison-Wesley Math Tutor Center

 MyMathLab

Videotape 3/DVT 3

Indicate whether the value of x shown is a solution of the given inequality by answering true or false.

1.

Value of x	Inequality	True or False
a. 1	$8 - 3x > 5$	
b. 4	$4x - 7 \le 2x + 1$	
c. -7	$6(x + 6) < -9$	
d. $-\dfrac{3}{4}$	$8x + 10 \ge 12x + 15$	

2.

Value of x	Inequality	True or False
a. 3	$2x + 1 < -10$	
b. -5	$1 - 3x > 5x + 12$	
c. -2	$-(4x + 8) \ge 0$	
d. $\dfrac{1}{3}$	$9x - 7 \le 6x - 11$	

Graph on the number line.

3. $x > 3$

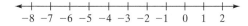

4. $x \le -1$

5. $x \ge -5$

6. $x < 1$

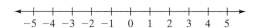

7. $x > 0$

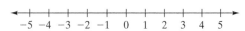

8. $x \le 0$

9. $x \le 0.5$

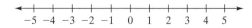

10. $x < -1.5$

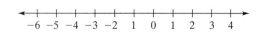

11. $x > -2\frac{1}{2}$

12. $x \ge 4\frac{1}{2}$

13. $-3 < x < 1$

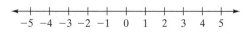

14. $0 < x \le 4$

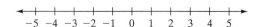

15. $-\dfrac{1}{2} \le x < 2$

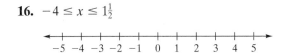

16. $-4 \le x \le 1\dfrac{1}{2}$

Solve and graph.

17. $v + 2 < -5$

18. $x - 5 > -1$

19. $y - 5 > -5$

20. $s + 1 \le 1$

21. $y + 2 \le 5.5$

22. $t - 1.5 > 1$

23. $v - 17 \le -15$

24. $n - 25 > -30$

25. $-2 \ge x - 4$

26. $4 < a - 3$

27. $\dfrac{1}{3}a < -1$

28. $\dfrac{1}{2}x \le 3$

29. $-5y > 10$

30. $-7t \le -21$

31. $2x \ge 0$

32. $-3.5m < 0$

33. $-\dfrac{3}{4}a \ge 3$

34. $\dfrac{-x}{3} > -2$

35. $6 \le \dfrac{-2}{3}n$ **36.** $4 \ge \dfrac{-y}{2}$

Solve.

37. $\dfrac{n}{3} + 2 > 3$ **38.** $\dfrac{1}{2}y + 4 \ge -1$ **39.** $3x - 12 \le 6$

40. $2v - 9 > -7$ **41.** $-21 - 3y > 0$ **42.** $7y + 4 - 2y \ge 39$

43. $5n - 11 \ge 2n + 28$ **44.** $24 - 9s < -13s + 8$ **45.** $-4m + 8 \le -3m + 1$

46. $-6y + 13 > y + 6$ **47.** $-7x + 4x + 23 < 2$ **48.** $5t - 7 + 2t \le 8t - 2$

49. $-3(z + 5) > -15$ **50.** $2(8 + w) < 22$ **51.** $0.5(2x + 1) \ge 3x$

52. $-0.2(10d - 5) > 9$ **53.** $2(x - 2) - 3x \ge -1$ **54.** $2(4z - 3) < 3(z + 4)$

55. $7y - (9y + 1) < 5$ **56.** $-(6m - 2) \le 0$ **57.** $0.4(5x + 1) \ge 3x$

58. $0.2(y - 3) > 8$ **59.** $5x + 1 < 3x - 2(4x - 3)$ **60.** $-2(0.5 - 4t) > -3(4 - 3.5t)$

61. $3 + 5n \le 6(n - 1) + n$ **62.** $3(4 - 2m) \ge 2(3m - 6)$ **63.** $-\dfrac{4}{3}x - 16 > x + \dfrac{1}{3}x$

64. $\dfrac{2}{3}z - 4 < z + \dfrac{1}{3} + \dfrac{1}{3}z$ **65.** $0.2y > 1500 + 2.6y$ **66.** $x + 1.6x \le 52$

Applications

Choose the inequality that best describes the situation.

67. To vote in the United States, a citizen must be at least 18 years old.

    a. $a < 18$ **b.** $a > 18$

    c. $a \le 18$ **d.** $a \ge 18$

68. The number of people seated in the theater is at most 650.

    a. $n < 650$ **b.** $n \le 650$

    c. $n > 650$ **d.** $n \ge 650$

69. It is generally accepted that a person has a fever if the person's temperature is above 98.6°F. To convert a Celsius temperature to its Fahrenheit equivalent, we use the formula $F = \frac{9}{5}C + 32$. For which Celsius temperatures C does the person have a fever?

a. $\frac{9}{5}C + 32 \geq 98.6$ **b.** $\frac{9}{5}C + 32 \leq 98.6$

c. $\frac{9}{5}C + 32 < 98.6$ **d.** $\frac{9}{5}C + 32 > 98.6$

70. You have $2 in change in your left pocket. How many quarters would you need to have in your right pocket to have enough money to pay for the laundry, which costs $4.25?

a. $0.25q + 2 > 4.25$ **b.** $0.25q + 2 < 4.25$

c. $0.25q + 2 \geq 4.25$ **d.** $0.25q + 2 \leq 4.25$

Write and solve an inequality.

71. On the last three chemistry exams a student scored 81, 85, and 91. What score must the student earn on the next exam to have an average above 85?

72. A rectangular deck that is 14 ft long is to be built onto the back of a house. What would be the area of the deck if it is at least 12 ft wide?

73. A novelty store, open Monday through Saturday, must sell at least $200 worth of merchandise per day to break even on expenses. The following table shows sales for one week.

Day	Amount of Sales
Monday	$250
Tuesday	$250
Wednesday	$150
Thursday	$130
Friday	$180

How much must the store make in sales on Saturday to at least break even for the week?

74. Molina's car rental company advertises two deals in the daily paper.

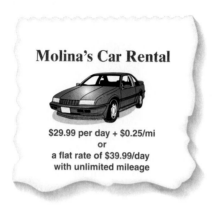

Molina's Car Rental

$29.99 per day + $0.25/mi
or
a flat rate of $39.99/day
with unlimited mileage

For which mileage is the flat rate a better deal?

75. A telemarketer claims that every call made to a customer costs at least $2. If a call costs $0.50 plus $0.10 for each minute, how long does each call last?

76. One side of a triangular garden is 2 ft longer than another side. The third side is 4 ft long. What are the maximum lengths of the other two sides if the perimeter of the garden can be no longer than 12 ft?

77. A real estate broker receives a monthly salary of $1500 plus $1200 for every house he sells during the month. His supervisor offers an alternative monthly salary: $1000 plus $1500 for each house sold. Should he accept the deal? Under what circumstances?

78. A parking garage offers two payment options: a $20 flat fee for the whole day, or $5 plus $2 per hour for each hour or part thereof that a customer parks. Which is the better option for the customer? Explain why?

79. A person weighing 200 lb volunteers for a clinical trial of a new diet pill. If he loses 2.5 lb per month using the diet pill combined with regular exercise, when will he weigh less than 180 lb?

80. A diver scored 9.2, 9.6, 9.7, 9.4, and 9.3 in the first 5 dives in a diving competition, where all scores are given in tenths. To win first place, she must beat a total score of 56.6. What is the lowest score she can get on her last dive to win the competition?

• *Check your answers on page A-5.*

Mindstretchers

MATHEMATICAL REASONING

1. Explain for which values of x the following inequality holds: $x + 5 > x + 2$.

GROUPWORK

2. Working with a partner, explore whether each of the following statements is always, sometimes, or never true. Give examples.

a. If $a < b$ and $c < d$, then $ac < bd$.

_____

_____

b. $a - b \leq a + b$

_____

_____

WRITING

3. Clearly identifying the variables, give examples of inequalities that

a. you wish were true. _____

_____

_____

b. you wish were false. _____

_____

_____

| | = CONCEPT | | = SKILL |

CONCEPT/SKILL	DESCRIPTION	EXAMPLE
[2.1] Equation	A mathematical statement that two expressions are equal.	$y - 6 = 9$
[2.1] Solution of an equation	A value of the variable that makes the equation a true statement.	2 is a solution of the equation $3x + 1 = 11 - 2x$.
[2.1] Linear equation in one variable	An equation that can be written in the form $ax + b = c$, where a, b, and c are real numbers and $a \neq 0$.	$x + 1 = 3$
[2.1] Equivalent equations	Equations that have the same solution.	$x = 2$ and $x + 1 = 3$
[2.1] Addition property of equality	For any real numbers a, b, and c, if $a = b$, then $a + c = b + c$.	If $x - 3 = 5$, then $(x - 3) + 3 = 5 + 3$.
[2.1] To solve word problems in algebra	• Read the problem carefully. • Translate the word problem into an equation. • Solve the equation. • Check the solution in the original equation. • State the conclusion.	
[2.2] Multiplication property of equality	For any real numbers a, b, and c, if $a = b$, then $a \cdot c = b \cdot c$.	If $\dfrac{n}{2} = 8$, then $\dfrac{n}{2} \cdot 2 = 8 \cdot 2$.
[2.3] To solve linear equations	• Use the distributive property to clear the equation of parentheses, if necessary. • Combine like terms where appropriate. • Use the addition property to isolate the variable term. • Use the multiplication property to isolate the variable. • Check by substituting the solution in the original equation.	$2(x + 5) = 6$ $2x + 10 = 6$ $2x + 10 - 10 = 6 - 10$ $2x = -4$ $x = -2$ CHECK $2(x + 5) = 6$ $2(-2 + 5) \overset{?}{=} 6$ $6 = 6$ True.
[2.4] Literal equation	An equation involving two or more variables.	$2t + b = c$
[2.5] To find a percent increase or decrease	• Compute the difference between the two given values. • Then compute what percent this difference is of the *original value*.	If a quantity changes from 10 to 12, the difference is 2. Since 2 is 20% of 10, the percent increase is 20%.

	= CONCEPT		= SKILL

CONCEPT/SKILL	DESCRIPTION	EXAMPLE
[2.6] Inequality	Any mathematical statement containing $<$, $\leq$, $>$, $\geq$, or $\neq$.	$x \geq -4$
[2.6] Solution of an inequality	Any value of the variable that makes the inequality true.	0 is a solution of $x < 2$.
[2.6] Addition property of inequalities	For any real numbers a, b, and c: ● If $a < b$, then $a + c < b + c$. ● If $a > b$, then $a + c > b + c$. Similar statements hold for $\leq$ and $\geq$.	If $x < 1$, then $x + 2 < 1 + 2$.
[2.6] Multiplication property of inequalities	For any real numbers a, b, and c: ● If $a < b$ and c is positive, then $ac < bc$. ● If $a < b$ and c is negative, then $ac > bc$. Similar statements hold for $>$, $\leq$, and $\geq$.	If $\frac{x}{2} > 4$, then $2 \cdot \frac{x}{2} > 2 \cdot 4$. If $-2x < 4$, then $\frac{-2x}{-2} > \frac{4}{-2}$.

Chapter 2 Review Exercises

[2.1]

1. Is 2 a solution of the equation $5x + 3 = 7 - 4x$?

2. Determine whether 0 is a solution of the equation $4x - 15 = 5(x - 3)$.

Solve and check.

3. $x - 3 = -12$

4. $t + 10 = 8$

5. $-9 = a + 5$

6. $4 = n - 7$

7. $y - (-3.1) = 11$

8. $r + 4.8 = 20$

[2.2]

Solve and check.

9. $\dfrac{x}{3} = -2$

10. $\dfrac{z}{2} = -5$

11. $2x = -20$

12. $-5d = 15$

13. $-y = -4$

14. $-x = 3$

15. $20.5 = 0.5n$

16. $30 = -0.2r$

17. $\dfrac{2t}{3} = -6$

18. $\dfrac{5y}{6} = -10$

[2.3]

Solve and check.

19. $2x + 1 = 7$

20. $-t - 4 = 5$

21. $\dfrac{a}{2} - 3 = -10$

22. $\dfrac{r}{3} - 6 = 12$

23. $-y + 7 = -2$

24. $-2t + 3 = 1$

25. $4x - 2x - 5 = 7$

26. $3y - y + 12 = 6$

27. $z + 1 = -2z + 10$

28. $n - 3 = -n + 7$

29. $c = -2(c + 1)$

30. $p = -(p - 5)$

31. $2(x + 1) - (x - 8) = -x$

32. $-(x + 2) - (x - 4) = -5x$

33. $10 - [3 + (2x - 1)] = 3x$

34. $x - [5 + (3x - 4)] = -x$

[2.4]

35. Solve $a - 5b = 2c$ for a in terms of b and c.

36. Solve $\dfrac{2a}{b} = n$ for a in terms of b and n.

37. Consider the equation $Ax + By = C$.

    a. Solve for x in terms of A, B, C, and y.

    b. Using the equation found in part (a), find the value of x if $A = 2$, $B = -1$, $C = 0$, and $y = 5$.

38. $A = \dfrac{bh}{2}$ is the formula for the area A of a triangle in terms of its base b and height h.

    a. Solve for h in terms of A and b.

    b. Using the formula found in part (a), find the height of a triangle with an area of 12 cm² and a base of 4 cm.

[2.5]

Solve.

39. 30% of what number is 12?

40. 125% of what number is 5?

41. What percent of 5 is 8?

42. What percent of 8 is 5?

43. What number is 8.5% of $300?

44. What is 3.5% of $2000?

[2.6]

Graph each inequality.

45. $x < 2$

    -4 -3 -2 -1 0 1 2 3 4

46. $x \geq -4.5$

    -6 -5 -4 -3 -2 -1 0 1 2

47. $3\frac{1}{2} \geq x$

    -2 -1 0 1 2 3 4 5 6

48. $-0.5 < x < 5$

    -2 -1 0 1 2 3 4 5 6

Solve. Then graph.

49. $y + 1 > 6$

50. $-\dfrac{1}{2}t + 3 \leq 3$

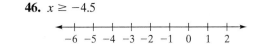

51. $8y - 2 \leq 6y + 2$

52. $\dfrac{1}{2}(8 - 12x) \leq x - 10$

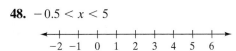

53. $0.5n - 0.3 < 0.2(2n + 1)$

Mixed Applications

Solve.

54. An air conditioner's energy efficiency ratio (EER) is the quotient of its British thermal unit (Btu) rating and its wattage. What is the Btu rating of a 2000-watt air conditioner if its EER is 8?

55. The sum of the measures of the angles in any triangle is 180°. If the three angles in an equilateral triangle are equal, what is the measure of each of these angles?

56. For a wedding, the reception costs will be $5000 plus $50 per guest. The bride and groom have budgeted $12,000 for the reception. How many guests can the bride and groom invite to the wedding?

57. A polygon is a closed geometric figure with straight sides. In any polygon with n sides, the sum of the measures of its angles is $180 (n - 2)$ degrees. If the measures of the angles of a polygon add up to 540°, how many sides does the polygon have?

58. A newspaper reported that a candidate received 15,360 more votes than her opponent, and that 39,210 votes were cast in the election. How many votes were cast for each candidate?

59. Suppose that to send a telegram it costs $2 for the first 10 words in the telegram and y cents for each additional word.

   a. Write an equation to find the cost C of a telegram 26 words long.

   b. Solve this equation for y.

60. The road connecting two factories is 380 miles long. A truck leaves one of the factories traveling toward the other factory at 45 mph, while at the same time a second truck leaves the other factory heading at 50 mph toward the first. How long after the departure will the trucks meet?

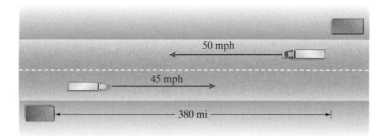

61. Two friends leave a party at 10 P.M. driving in opposite directions. One drives at a speed of 40 mph, whereas the other drives at a speed of 32 mph. At what time are the two friends 18 miles apart?

62. A plane flying between two cities at 400 mph arrives half an hour behind schedule. If the plane had flown at a speed of 500 mph, it would have been on time. Find the distance between the cities.

63. Tom Seaver received 425 out of 430 votes electing him to the Baseball Hall of Fame, surpassing the previous voting record for Ty Cobb. To the nearest whole percent, what percent of votes cast did Seaver receive? (*Source:* United Press International, Jan 7, 1992)

64. In the decade beginning with 1901, about 8.8 million immigrants entered the United States. In the following decade, this number dropped to approximately 5.7 million people. Find the percent decrease, to the nearest whole percent. (*Source: 1999 Statistical Abstract of the United States*)

65. The rarest blood type is AB⁻, which occurs in only 0.7% of people in the United States. Of the 4000 students in your college, how many would you expect to have AB⁻ blood type? (*Source: The 1995 Guinness Book of World Records*)

66. How much interest is earned in 1 year on a principal of $500 at an annual interest rate of 6%?

67. In the presidential election of 1836, Martin Van Buren earned 170 electoral votes. Four years later, Van Buren earned 60 electoral votes. To the nearest whole percent, by what percent did Van Buren's electoral vote count drop? (*Source: Time Almanac 2000*)

68. How much pure alcohol must be mixed with 6 L of a 60% alcohol solution to make a 70% alcohol solution?

69. How many pints of a 1% solution of disinfectant must be combined with 4 pt of a 10% solution to make a 5% solution?

70. To convert a weight expressed in kilograms, k, to the equivalent number of pounds, p, multiply the number of kilograms by 2.2.

   a. Write a formula for this relationship.

   b. Solve this formula for k.

71. To print b books, it costs a publisher $100,000 + 25b$ dollars. The publisher receives $50b$ in revenue for selling this number of books. For which number of books printed is the revenue equal to the cost?

72. An Internet service provider (ISP) charges a monthly fee of $5 plus $0.50 for each hour a user is surfing the Web. If you want to spend a maximum of $16 on your monthly ISP bill, how many hours can you surf the Web?

● *Check your answers on page A-6.*

To see if you have mastered the topics in this chapter, take this test.

1. Determine whether -2 is a solution of the equation $3x - 4 = 6(x + 2)$.

2. Solve and check: $x - 1 = -10$

3. Solve and check: $\dfrac{n}{2} = -3$

4. Solve and check: $-y = -11$

5. Solve and check: $\dfrac{3y}{4} = 6$

6. Solve and check: $2x + 5 = 11$

7. Solve and check: $-s + 4 = 2$

8. Solve and check: $10x + 1 = -x + 23$

9. Solve and check: $16a = -4(a - 5)$

10. Solve and check: $2(x + 5) - (x + 4) = 7x + 1$

11. Solve $5n + p = t$ for p in terms of n and t.

12. 40% of what number is 8?

13. What percent of 5 is 10?

14. Draw the graph of $-1 \le x < 3$.

$$\begin{array}{ccccccc} -3 & -2 & -1 & 0 & 1 & 2 & 3 \end{array}$$

15. Solve $-2z \le 6$. Then graph.

$$\begin{array}{ccccccc} -3 & -2 & -1 & 0 & 1 & 2 & 3 \end{array}$$

16. A taxi charges \$2.00 for the first mile plus \$1.25 for each additional mile. If the fare was \$13.25, how long was the ride?

17. A woman's shoe size S is given by the formula $S = 3L - 21$, where L is her foot length L in inches. Solve for L in terms of S.

18. In a recent year, males experienced 37%, or 8,400,000, of the operations performed in the United States. To the nearest million, how many operations were performed in all? (**Source:** *The New York Times Almanac, 2000*)

19. Two friends live 33 mi apart. They cycled from their homes, riding toward one another and meeting $1\frac{1}{2}$ hr later. If one friend cycled 2 mph faster than the other, what were their two rates?

20. A cellular phone service offers two calling plans. Plan A costs \$39.99 per month plus \$0.79 per minute (or part thereof) for calls outside the network. Plan B costs \$54.99 per month plus \$0.59 per minute (or part thereof) for calls outside the network. Under what conditions will the monthly cost of Plan A exceed the monthly cost of Plan B?

• Check your answers on page A-6.

Cumulative Review Exercises

To help you review, solve the following:

1. Express as a signed number:
a loss of 6 yd in a football play.

2. Graph the number -3 on the number line shown.

$$\xleftarrow{\hspace{0.3em}+\hspace{0.5em}+\hspace{0.5em}+\hspace{0.5em}+\hspace{0.5em}+\hspace{0.5em}+\hspace{0.5em}+\hspace{0.3em}}\rightarrow$$
$$-3\ -2\ -1\quad 0\quad 1\quad 2\quad 3$$

3. Compute $|-2|$.

4. True or false, $1 > -2$

5. Simplify: $2 + (-1) + (-4) + 4$

6. Divide: $(-10) \div (-2)$

7. Simplify: $3x + 1 - 7(2x - 5)$

8. A dieter gained 3 lb and then lost 5 lb. Express her overall change in weight as a real number.

9. An investment of $1000 triples in value every 15 years. Write in exponential form the value of this investment after 60 years.

10. A telephone technician charges $50 for the first hour of work and $25 for each additional hour of work.

    a. Write a formula that expresses the amount of money A that the technician charges in terms of the time t that the technician works.

    b. Solve this equation for t.

    c. If the repairman sent you a bill for $125, how many hours did he claim to work?

• *Check your answers on page A-6.*

Chapter 3

Graphing Linear Equations and Inequalities

Get Rich with Graphing?

If financial analysts could predict trends on Wall Street, they would know when to buy and when to sell stock in order to maximize profits. To arrive at educated predictions of future trends, analysts use the statistical tool of linear regression.

When using linear regression, an analyst plots points that show a particular stock's recent selling prices. Then the analyst sketches the straight line that is closest to passing through these points. This **regression line** provides an estimate of how much the stock is likely to increase or decrease in price, and at what pace. If the actual selling prices differ considerably from the predicted prices for a lengthy period of time, the analyst suspects a new trend and recomputes the regression line.

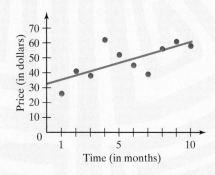

(**Sources:** "Perhaps a Little Lift," *Financial Mail,* December 1, 2000, p. 118; Mario Triola, *Elementary Statistics,* Addison-Wesley, 2000)

To see if you have already mastered the topics in this chapter, take this test.

1. On the coordinate plane below, plot the points $A(1, 4)$ and $B(-3, -6)$.

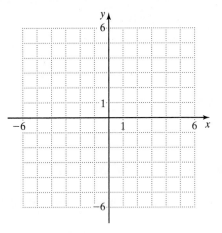

2. In which quadrant is the point $(3, -5)$ located?

3. Given two points $C(7, 5)$ and $D(1, 2)$, compute the slope of the line that passes through the points.

4. For the points $A(2, 1)$, $B(0, 5)$, $C(1, 7)$, and $D(4, 1)$, indicate whether $\overleftrightarrow{AB}$ is parallel to $\overleftrightarrow{CD}$. Explain.

5. For the points $P(-3, 3)$, $Q(1, -1)$, $R(-2, -2)$, and $S(4, 4)$, indicate whether $\overleftrightarrow{PQ}$ is perpendicular to $\overleftrightarrow{RS}$. Explain.

6. In the graph shown, find the *x*-intercept and the *y*-intercept.

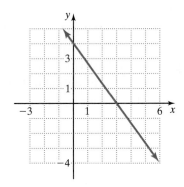

7. In the graph shown, the *y*-axis stands for the number of congressional representatives from a state and the *x*-axis stands for the state's population according to a recent U.S. census.

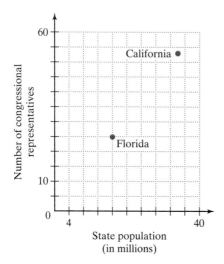

Draw the line that passes through the points. Is this line's slope positive, negative, or zero? How does state population relate to the number of representatives from that state?

8. Agriculturalists are trying to develop varieties of wheat that grow at a faster rate. The graph shown displays the growth pattern of two new varieties of wheat. Which variety grows more quickly?

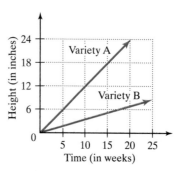

9. For the equation $y = 2x - 5$, complete the following table.

x	y
4	
7	
	0
	−1

Graph the equation indicated in questions 10–13.

10. $y = -3$

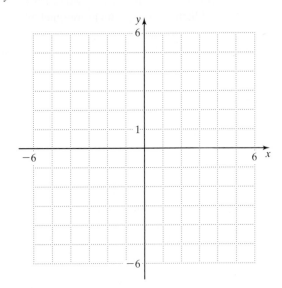

11. $x = 2$

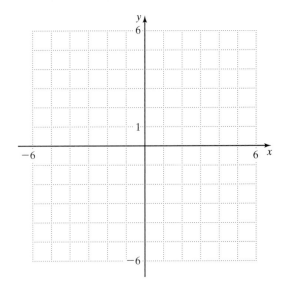

12. $y = -3x + 2$

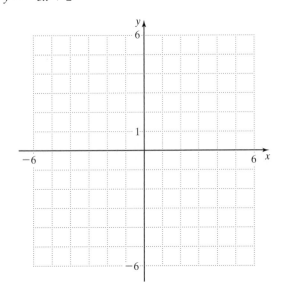

13. $2x - 3y = 6$

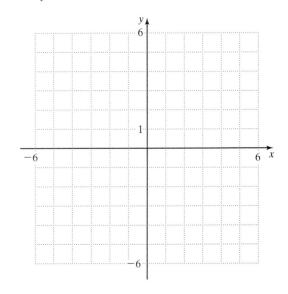

14. What are the slope and the y-intercept of the graph of $y = 2x - 5$?

15. Write the equation $5x - y = 8$ in slope-intercept form.

16. Find an equation of the line with slope 2 that passes through the point $(0, 8)$.

17. Find an equation of the line that passes through the points $(4, 1)$ and $(2, -1)$.

18. Graph: $y > 3x + 1$

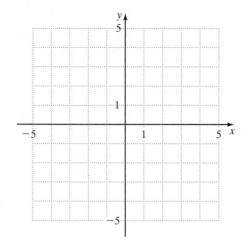

19. A local video store charges a daily rental fee of $2.50 per movie.

   a. Express the daily cost c of renting x movies.

   b. Choose an appropriate scale for the axes and graph this relationship.

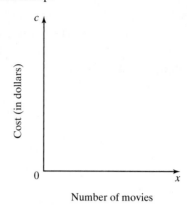

Number of movies

   c. What is the slope of the line in part (b)? Explain its significance in this context.

20. A textbook sales representative is driving to a college 200 mi away at a speed of 50 mph.

   a. Express the distance d (in miles) the sales representative travels in terms of the time t (in hours) he has been driving.

   b. Choose an appropriate scale for the axes and graph this relationship.

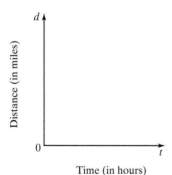

Time (in hours)

   c. What is the slope of the graph? Explain its significance in terms of the trip.

● *Check your answers on page A-6.*

3.1 Introduction to Graphing

OBJECTIVES

- *To identify and plot points on the coordinate plane*
- *To identify the quadrants of the coordinate plane*
- *To interpret graphs in applied problems*

What Graphing Is and Why It Is Important

When we graph a mathematical relationship such as an equation or an inequality, we draw a picture of it. Such a picture or graph is a geometric interpretation of the algebraic representation, providing an alternative approach to solving problems. Rather than manipulating symbols as we did in Chapter 2, graphing allows us to focus on the geometry of a problem.

Although lacking the precision of an equation, a graph can clarify at a glance patterns and trends in a relationship, helping us to understand that relationship better.

In the past, the graphing approach to problem solving was usually more time-consuming than the traditional algebraic approach. Today, the use of graphing calculators and computer software packages has made graphing easier. But to utilize these graphing tools, you must first understand the concepts and skills involved in graphing, which are discussed in this chapter.

In Chapter 3, the relationships that we graph are relatively simple. In Chapters 4 and 9, we will apply graphing techniques to more complex relationships.

Plotting Points

If you were to enter a theater or sports arena with a ticket for row 5, seat 3, you would know exactly where to sit. Such a system of *coordinates* in which we associate a pair of numbers in a given order with a corresponding location is commonplace.

The flat surface on which we draw graphs is called a *coordinate plane*. To create a coordinate plane, we first sketch two perpendicular number lines—one horizontal, the other vertical—that intersect at their zeros. The point where they intersect is called the *origin*. Each number line is called an *axis*. It is common practice to refer to the horizontal number line as the *x-axis* and the vertical number line as the *y-axis*.

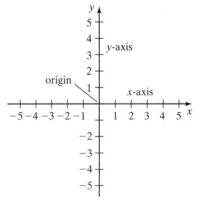

Each point in the coordinate plane is represented by a pair of numbers called an *ordered pair*. For example, the origin is the point $(0, 0)$. The first number in an ordered pair represents a horizontal distance and is called the *x-coordinate*. The second number represents a vertical distance and is called the *y-coordinate*.

To *plot* a point in the coordinate plane, we find its location represented by its ordered pair. For example, to plot (3, 1), start at the origin and go 3 units *to the right,* then go *up* 1 unit. For this point, we say that $x = 3$ and $y = 1$.

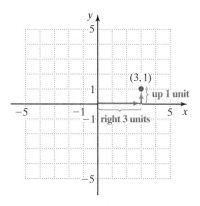

Notice that the two numbers in an ordered pair are written in parentheses, separated by a comma. Do the ordered pairs (3, 1) and (1, 3) correspond to different points? Why?

When an ordered pair has a negative *x-coordinate,* the corresponding point is to the left of the *y*-axis, as shown in the following coordinate plane. Similarly, when an ordered pair's *y-coordinate* is negative, the point is below the *x*-axis.

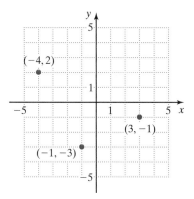

Any ordered pair whose *y-coordinate* is 0 corresponds to a point that is on the *x*-axis. For instance, the points (−4, 0), (0, 0), and (3, 0) are on the *x*-axis, as shown in the graph below on the left. Similarly, any ordered pair whose *x-coordinate* is 0 corresponds to a point that is on the *y-axis.* For instance, the points (0, 2), (0, −1), and (0, −4) are on the *y*-axis, as shown in the graph on the right.

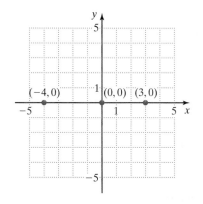 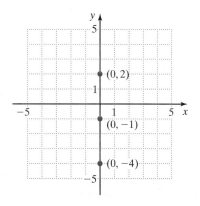

Sometimes we name points with letters. We can refer to a point as *P* or *A* or any other letter that we choose. Generally, a capital letter is used. If we want to emphasize that point *P* has coordinates (2, 8), we can write it as *P*(2, 8).

If there is a point whose coordinates we do not know, we can refer to it as (x, y) or $P(x, y)$, where x and y are the unknown coordinates.

Sometimes to distinguish one point from another, we use *subscripts* to name them. For instance, we can refer to two different points as

- P_1 and P_2 (read "P sub one" and "P sub two")
- (x_1, y_1) and (x_2, y_2)
- $P_1(x_1, y_1)$ and $P_2(x_2, y_2)$

Notice that y_1 is the *y-coordinate* that corresponds to the *x-coordinate* x_1, and y_2 corresponds to x_2.

Now let's look at plotting points.

EXAMPLE 1	PRACTICE 1
Plot the following points on a coordinate plane.	On a coordinate plane, plot the points corresponding to each ordered pair.

EXAMPLE 1

Plot the following points on a coordinate plane.

a. $(5, 2)$

b. $(3, -4)$

c. $(-1, 1)$

d. $(0, 3)$

e. $(-4, -2)$

f. $(0, 0)$

SOLUTION The points are plotted on the coordinate plane as shown.

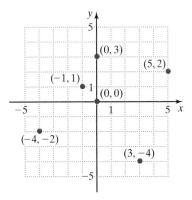

PRACTICE 1

On a coordinate plane, plot the points corresponding to each ordered pair.

a. $(0, -5)$

b. $(4, 4)$

c. $(-2, 2)$

d. $(5, 0)$

e. $(-3, -2)$

f. $(2, -4)$

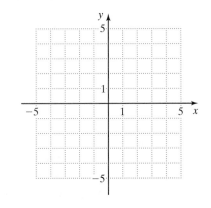

The x- and y-axes are boundaries that separate a coordinate plane into four regions called *quadrants*. These quadrants are named in counterclockwise order starting with Quadrant I, as pictured.

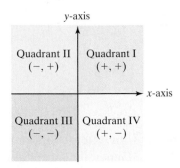

The quadrant in which a point is located tells us something about its coordinates. For instance, any point in Quadrant I is to the right of the y-axis and above the x-axis, so both its coordinates must be positive. Points in this quadrant are of particular interest in application problems in which all quantities are positive.

Any point in Quadrant II lies to the left of the y-axis and above the x-axis, so its x-coordinate must be negative and its y-coordinate positive. Points in Quadrant III are to the left of the y-axis and below the x-axis, so both coordinates are negative. And finally, any point in Quadrant IV is to the right of the y-axis and below the x-axis, so its x-coordinate must be positive and its y-coordinate negative. Points on an axis do not belong to a quadrant.

EXAMPLE 2

Determine the quadrant in which each point is located.

Point	Quadrant
$(-5, 5)$	
$(7, 20)$	
$(1.3, -4)$	
$(-4, -5)$	

SOLUTION

Point	Quadrant
$(-5, 5)$	II
$(7, 20)$	I
$(1.3, -4)$	IV
$(-4, -5)$	III

PRACTICE 2

In which quadrant is each point located?

Point	Quadrant
$\left(-\dfrac{1}{2}, 3\right)$	
$(6, -7)$	
$(-1, -4)$	
$(2, 9)$	

Often the points that we are to plot affect how we draw the axes on a coordinate plane. For instance, in the following coordinate planes we choose on each axis an appropriate *scale*—the length between adjacent tick marks—to conveniently plot all points in question.

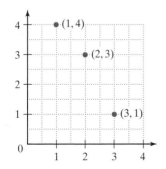   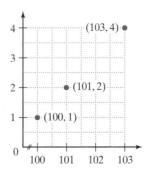

TIP Depending on the location of the points to be plotted, we can choose to show only part of a coordinate plane.

EXAMPLE 3

In its first year of business, an Internet company made a profit of $10,000. In the second year, the company's profit grew to $15,000. In the third year, however, the company lost $5000. Plot points on a coordinate plane to display this information.

SOLUTION We let x represent the year of business and y represent the company's profit in dollars that year. The three points to be plotted are:

$$(1, 10{,}000), (2, 15{,}000), \text{ and } (3, -5000)$$

Notice that in the third year, the company's loss is represented by a negative profit. Because the y-coordinates are large, we use 5000 as the scale on the y-axis. Then we plot the points on the following coordinate plane.

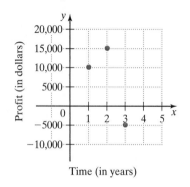

PRACTICE 3

The following table shows the average monthly temperatures for the first four months of the year (where month 1 represents January) for Chicago, Illinois. (*Source:* U.S. National Climatic Data Center)

Month	Temperature (°F)
1	21
2	25
3	37
4	49

On the coordinate plane shown, graph the information displayed in the table.

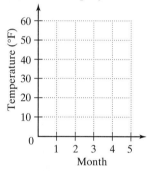

We end this discussion of plotting points with a final comment about variables. On a coordinate plane, the first coordinate of each point is a value of one quantity (or variable), and the second coordinate is a value of another quantity. For instance, in Example 3 we considered the profit that a company makes at various times. One variable represents time and the other variable the profit. Notice that the profit made by the company depends on the time rather than the other way around. So we refer to time as the *independent* variable and the profit as the *dependent* variable. It is customary when plotting points to assign the independent variable to the horizontal axis and the dependent variable to the vertical axis.

Interpreting Graphs

Points plotted on a coordinate plane are merely dots on a piece of paper. However, their significance comes to life when we understand the information that they convey.

Describing the trend on a coordinate plane tells the story of that trend. When key points are missing, as is frequently the case, the story is incomplete. In such cases, we may want to make a prediction, that is, to extend the observed pattern so as to estimate the missing data. Such predictions, while not certain, at least allow us to make decisions based on the best available evidence. We may also want to speculate about the conditions that underlie an observed pattern of plotted points.

The trend among plotted points on a coordinate plane shows a relationship between the two variables. To highlight the relationship, it is common practice either to draw a line that passes through the plotted points or to connect adjacent points with short line segments.

Consider the following examples that involve interpreting trends on a coordinate plane.

EXAMPLE 4

The graph shows the cost C of parking a car at a lot for time t hr.

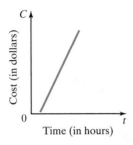

Describe the trend that you observe in terms of both the coordinate plane and the cost of parking.

SOLUTION On the graph, the larger C-values correspond to the larger t-values. In terms of parking, we see that the longer a car is parked in the lot, the more it costs to park the car.

PRACTICE 4

A new car is purchased for $20,000. The value V of the car after t years is displayed on the following graph. Describe the line graph in terms of the changing value of the car.

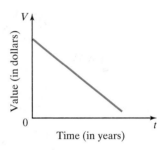

EXAMPLE 5

The following graph shows the cost that a shipping company charges to send a package, depending on the package's weight.

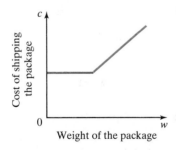

Write a brief story describing the displayed relationship. What business practice does the horizontal line segment reflect?

SOLUTION From the horizontal line segment, we see that the cost of shipping is constant (that is, a flat rate) for lighter packages up to a certain weight. The horizontal line segment indicates that the company established a minimum cost for sending lightweight packages. Since the slanted line segment goes upward to the right, the cost of shipping increases with the weight of heavier packages.

PRACTICE 5

The following graph shows the number of times per minute that a runner's heartbeats. Describe in a sentence or two the pattern you observe. Use this pattern to write a scenario as to what the runner might be doing.

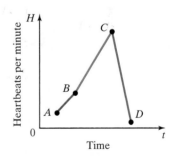

Exercises 3.1

FOR EXTRA HELP

📖 *Student's Solutions Manual*

🔘 *Addison-Wesley Math Tutor Center*

🚪 *MyMathLab*

📼 *Videotape 4/DVT 4*

On the coordinate plane to the right, plot the points with the given coordinates.

1. $A(0, 5)$ $B(-1, -5)$

$C(1, 4)$ $D(3, -3)$

$E(-4, 2)$ $F(5, 0)$

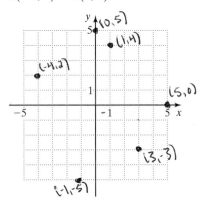

2. $A(-2, 4)$ $B(0, 0)$

$C(2, -1)$ $D(-3, 0)$

$E(3, 4)$ $F(-4, -2)$

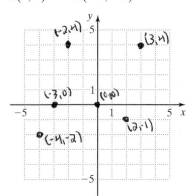

Next to each point, write its coordinates.

3.

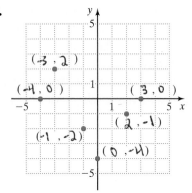

4.

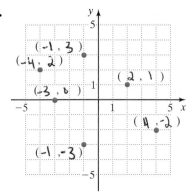

Identify the quadrant in which each point is located.

5. $(-2, -3)$ III

6. $(-9, 5)$ II

7. $(3, -\frac{1}{2})$ IV

8. $(3\frac{1}{2}, -8)$ IV

9. $(65, 11)$ I

10. $(-13, -24)$ III

11. $(-5.1, 4)$ II

12. $(8, 6.2)$ I

Applications

Solve.

13. College students coded A, B, C, and D
took placement tests in mathematics
and in English. The following coordinate
plane displays their scores.

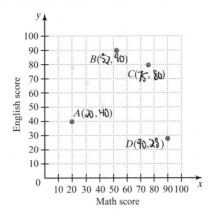

a. Estimate the coordinates of the plotted
points.

b. Which students scored higher in English
than in mathematics?

Studen A, B, & C

14. Suppose that a financier owns shares of stock in three companies—Dearborn,
Inc. (D), Ellsworth Products (E), and Fairfield Publications (F). On the following coordinate plane, the x-value of a point represents the change in value of a
share of the indicated stock from the previous day, and the y-value stands for the
number of shares of that stock.

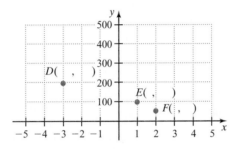

a. Name the coordinates of the plotted points.

b. For each point, explain the significance of the product of the point's
coordinates.

15. The following table gives the total enrollment in U.S. public colleges
for various years, rounded to the nearest million. (*Source:* U.S. National
Center for Education Statistics, 2001)

Year	Enrollment (in millions)
1970	6
1980	9
1990	11
2000	12

Plot this information on the following coordinate plane.

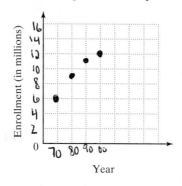

16. The number of electoral votes cast by Republicans in recent presidential elections is displayed in the following table. (*Source: Congressional Quarterly*)

Year	Republican Electoral Votes
1988	426
1992	168
1996	159
2000	271

Plot this information in the coordinate plane shown.

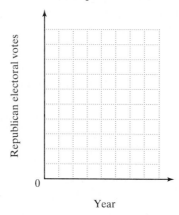

17. A chemist conducts an experiment to measure the melting and boiling points of four substances, as indicated in the following table.

Substance	Symbol	Melting Point (°C)	Boiling Point (°C)
Chlorine	Cl	−101	−35
Oxygen	O	−218	−183
Bromine	Br	−7	59
Phosphorous	P	44	280

On the following coordinate plane, an *x*-value represents a substance's melting point and a *y*-value stands for its boiling point, both in degrees Celsius.

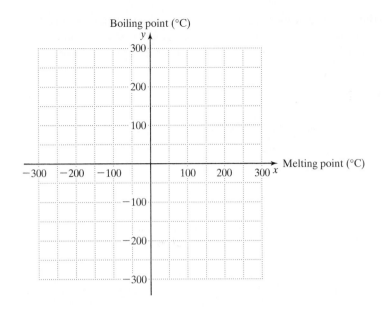

a. Plot points for the four substances. Label each point with the appropriate substance symbol.

b. For each point, which of its coordinates is larger—the x-value or the y-value? In a sentence, explain this pattern.

18. Meteorologists use the windchill index to determine the windchill temperature (how cold it feels outside) relative to the actual temperature when the wind speed is considered. The table following shows the actual temperatures and the related windchill temperatures when the wind speed is 5 mph.

Actual Temperature (°F), T	Windchill Temperature (°F), W
−10	−22
−5	−16
0	−11
5	−5
10	1
15	7

a. Plot points (T, W) on the given coordinate plane.

b. For the plotted points, describe the pattern that you observe.

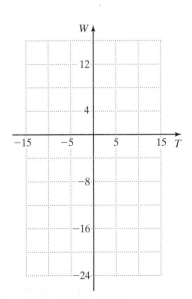

19. On the following coordinate plane, a *y*-coordinate stands for the number of senators from a state. The corresponding *x*-coordinate represents that state's population according to a recent U.S. census. Describe the pattern that you observe.

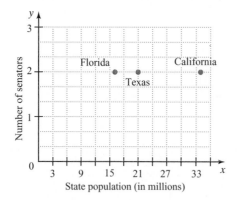

20. Last year's daily closing values (in dollars) of a share of a technology stock are plotted on the following graph. What story is this graph telling?

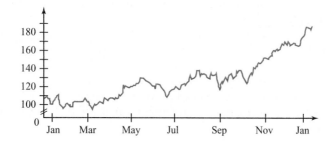

21. A child walks away from a wall, stands still, and then approaches the wall. In a couple of sentences, explain which of the following graphs could describe this motion.

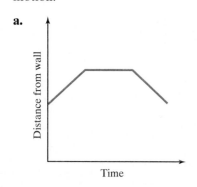

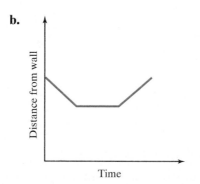

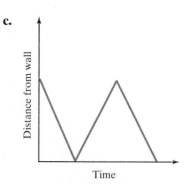

22. The following graph shows the temperature of a patient on a particular day. Describe the overall pattern you observe in the patient's temperature over the time period.

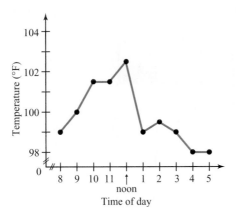

● *Check your answers on page A-8.*

Mindstretchers

1. Many situations involve using a coordinate system to identify positions. Two such situations are given below.

● a chessboard   ● an atlas map

a. Explain to what extent a chessboard and an atlas map are coordinate systems.

_____

_____

_____

b. Identify some other examples of coordinate systems in everyday life.

_____

2. The map shows a square section of a city surrounded by a wall. You want to walk along the horizontal and vertical streets from point $(-2, -2)$ to point $(2, 2)$.

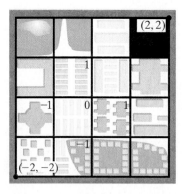

One possible route is

$(-2, -2) \rightarrow (-1, -2) \rightarrow (0, -2) \rightarrow (0, -1) \rightarrow (0, 0) \rightarrow (0, 1) \rightarrow (0, 2) \rightarrow (1, 2) \rightarrow (2, 2)$
as pictured.

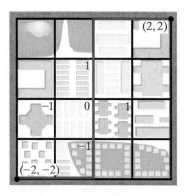

This route is 8 blocks long. List four other 8-block routes from $(-2, -2)$ to $(2, 2)$.

_____

$(-2, -2) \rightarrow (\_\_, \_\_) \rightarrow (\_\_, \_\_) \rightarrow (\_\_, \_\_) \rightarrow (\_\_, \_\_)$
$\rightarrow (\_\_, \_\_) \rightarrow (\_\_, \_\_) \rightarrow (\_\_, \_\_) \rightarrow (2, 2)$

_____

$(-2, -2) \rightarrow (\_\_, \_\_) \rightarrow (\_\_, \_\_) \rightarrow (\_\_, \_\_) \rightarrow (\_\_, \_\_)$
$\rightarrow (\_\_, \_\_) \rightarrow (\_\_, \_\_) \rightarrow (\_\_, \_\_) \rightarrow (2, 2)$

_____

$(-2, -2) \rightarrow (\_\_, \_\_) \rightarrow (\_\_, \_\_) \rightarrow (\_\_, \_\_) \rightarrow (\_\_, \_\_)$
$\rightarrow (\_\_, \_\_) \rightarrow (\_\_, \_\_) \rightarrow (\_\_, \_\_) \rightarrow (2, 2)$

_____

$(-2, -2) \rightarrow (\_\_, \_\_) \rightarrow (\_\_, \_\_) \rightarrow (\_\_, \_\_) \rightarrow (\_\_, \_\_)$
$\rightarrow (\_\_, \_\_) \rightarrow (\_\_, \_\_) \rightarrow (\_\_, \_\_) \rightarrow (2, 2)$

_____

GROUPWORK

3. For any two points with coordinates (x_1, y_1) and (x_2, y_2) on the coordinate plane, consider a third point with the average of these coordinates: $\left(\dfrac{x_1 + x_2}{2}, \dfrac{y_1 + y_2}{2}\right)$.

Experiment by choosing different values of x_1, y_1, x_2, and y_2, and then filling in the given table.

x_1	y_1	x_2	y_2	$\dfrac{x_1 + x_2}{2}$	$\dfrac{y_1 + y_2}{2}$

Plot the various points (x_1, y_1), (x_2, y_2) and $\left(\dfrac{x_1 + x_2}{2}, \dfrac{y_1 + y_2}{2}\right)$ on the following coordinate plane.

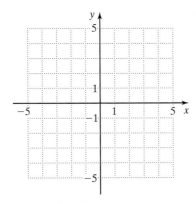

In a couple of sentences explain what you observed about the third point.

_____

_____

_____

Cultural Note

It was the seventeenth-century French mathematician and philosopher René Descartes (pronounced day-KART) who developed the concepts that underlie graphing. The story goes that one morning Descartes, who liked to stay in bed and meditate, began to eye a fly crawling on his bedroom ceiling. In a flash of insight, he realized that it was possible to express mathematically the fly's position in terms of its distance to the two adjacent walls.

3.2 Slope

OBJECTIVES

- *To find the slope of a line that passes through two given points*
- *To determine whether the slope of a given line is positive, negative, zero, or undefined*
- *To graph a line that passes through a given point and has a given slope*
- *To determine whether two given lines are parallel or perpendicular*
- *To solve applied problems involving slope*

In the previous section, we discussed points on a coordinate plane. Now let's look at lines connected by points. We know that any two points determine a unique line passing through them. For example, exactly one line passes through the points P and Q shown. We can write this line as $\overleftrightarrow{PQ}$ (read "line PQ").

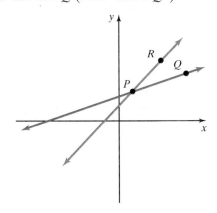

If we take P and choose another point R, we get a different line. Notice that $\overleftrightarrow{PQ}$ and $\overleftrightarrow{PR}$ have different slants.

In this section we focus on a key characteristic of lines, namely, their slopes.

Slope

On an airplane, would you rather glide downward gradually or drop like a stone? Would you rather climb a sheer cliff or stroll up a gently sloping hill? These questions relate to *slope*, the extent to which a line is slanted. In other words, slope measures a line's steepness.

Slope, also called **rate of change**, is an important concept in the study of graphing. Examining the slope of a line can tell us if the quantity being graphed increases or decreases, as well as how fast the quantity is changing. For example, in one application, the slope of a line can represent the speed of a moving object. In another application, the slope can stand for the rate at which a share of stock is changing in value.

To understand exactly what slope means, let's suppose that a straight line on a coordinate plane passes through two points with coordinates (x_1, y_1) and (x_2, y_2).

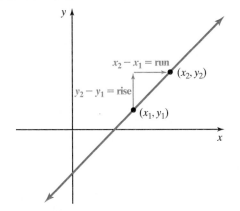

We usually represent the slope of a line by the letter m and define slope to be the ratio of the change in the y-values to the change in the x-values. Using the coordinates of the points (x_1, y_1) and (x_2, y_2), we have the formula

$$m = \frac{\text{change in } y\text{-values}}{\text{change in } x\text{-values}} = \frac{y_2 - y_1}{x_2 - x_1}, \quad \text{where } x_1 \neq x_2.$$

In this formula, the numerator of the fraction is the vertical change called the *rise* and the denominator is the horizontal change called the *run*. So another way of writing the formula for slope is $m = \dfrac{\text{rise}}{\text{run}}$.

> ### Definition
>
> The **slope** m of a line passing through the points (x_1, y_1) and (x_2, y_2) is defined to be
>
> $$m = \frac{y_2 - y_1}{x_2 - x_1}, \quad \text{where } x_1 \neq x_2.$$

Can you explain why in the definition of slope, x_1 and x_2 must not be equal?

Note that when using the formula for slope, it does not matter which point is chosen for (x_1, y_1) and which point for (x_2, y_2) as long as the order of subtraction of the coordinates is the same in both the numerator and denominator.

EXAMPLE 1

Find the slope of the line that passes through the points $(2, 1)$ and $(4, 2)$. Plot the points and then sketch the line.

SOLUTION Let $(2, 1)$ stand for (x_1, y_1) and $(4, 2)$ for (x_2, y_2). Substituting into the formula for slope, we get:

$$m = \frac{y_2 - y_1}{x_2 - x_1} = \frac{2 - 1}{4 - 2} = \frac{1}{2}$$

Now let's plot $(2, 1)$ and $(4, 2)$ and then sketch the line passing through them.

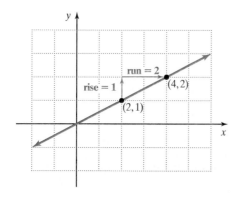

PRACTICE 1

Find the slope of a line that contains the points $(1, 2)$ and $(4, 3)$. Plot the points and then sketch the line.

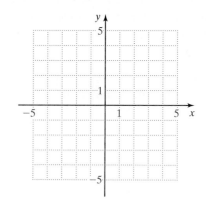

We can also find the slope of a line using its graph. From $(2, 1)$ and $(4, 2)$, we see that the change in y-values (the rise) is $2 - 1$, or 1. The change in x-values (the run) is $4 - 2$, or 2. So $m = \dfrac{\text{rise}}{\text{run}} = \dfrac{1}{2}$. Therefore, we get the same answer whether we use the formula $m = \dfrac{y_2 - y_1}{x_2 - x_1}$ or $m = \dfrac{\text{rise}}{\text{run}}$.

A line rising to the right as shown in Example 1 has a *positive* slope. We say that such a line is *increasing* because as the x-values gets larger, the corresponding y-values also get larger.

EXAMPLE 2

Sketch the line passing through the points $(-3, 1)$ and $(2, -2)$. Find the slope.

SOLUTION First, we plot the points $(-3, 1)$ and $(2, -2)$. Then we draw a line passing through them.

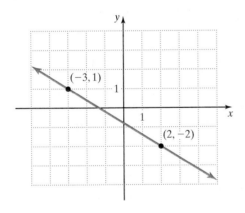

Next, find the slope.

$$\underset{\underset{x_1\ \ y_1}{\uparrow\ \uparrow}}{(-3, 1)} \qquad \underset{\underset{x_2\ \ y_2}{\uparrow\ \uparrow}}{(2, -2)}$$

$$m = \frac{y_2 - y_1}{x_2 - x_1} = \frac{-2 - 1}{2 - (-3)} = \frac{-3}{5} = -\frac{3}{5}$$

PRACTICE 2

Sketch the line that contains the points $(-2, 1)$ and $(3, -5)$. Find the slope.

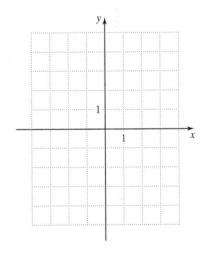

A line falling to the right as shown in Example 2 has a *negative* slope. We say that such a line is *decreasing* because as the x-values get larger, the corresponding y-values get smaller.

EXAMPLE 3

Find the slope of a line that passes through the points $(7, 5)$ and $(-1, 5)$. Plot the points and then sketch the line.

SOLUTION First, find the slope of the line.

$$
\begin{array}{cc}
(7, 5) & (-1, 5) \\
\uparrow\ \uparrow & \uparrow\ \uparrow \\
x_1\ y_1 & x_2\ y_2
\end{array}
$$

$$m = \frac{y_2 - y_1}{x_2 - x_1} = \frac{5 - 5}{-1 - 7} = \frac{0}{-8} = 0$$

So the slope of this line is 0.

Next, we plot the points and then sketch the line passing through them.

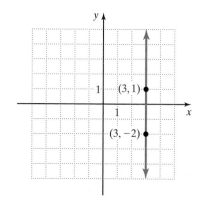

PRACTICE 3

On the following coordinate plane, plot the points $(2, -1)$ and $(6, -1)$. Sketch the line and then compute its slope.

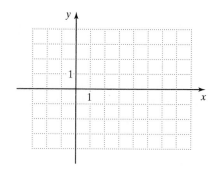

When the slope of a line is 0, its graph is a *horizontal* line as shown in Example 3. All points on a horizontal line have the same y-coordinate, that is, the y-values are constant for all x-values.

EXAMPLE 4

What is the slope of the line pictured on the following coordinate plane?

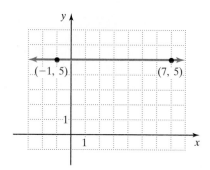

PRACTICE 4

Find the slope of the line that passes through the points $(-2, 7)$ and $(-2, 0)$.

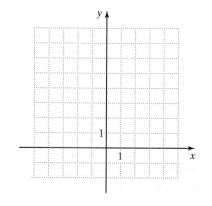

SOLUTION

$$(3, -2) \qquad (3, 1)$$
$$\uparrow \quad \uparrow \qquad \quad \uparrow \quad \uparrow$$
$$x_1 \quad y_1 \qquad \quad x_2 \quad y_2$$

$$m = \frac{y_2 - y_1}{x_2 - x_1} = \frac{1 - (-2)}{3 - 3} = \frac{3}{0}$$

Since division by 0 is undefined, the slope of this line is undefined.

When the slope of a line is undefined, its graph is a *vertical* line as shown in Example 4. All points on a vertical line have the same x-coordinate, that is, the x-values are constant for all y-values.

As we have seen in Examples 1 through 4, the sign of the slope of a line tells us a lot about the line. As we continue graphing lines, it will be helpful to keep in mind the following graphs.

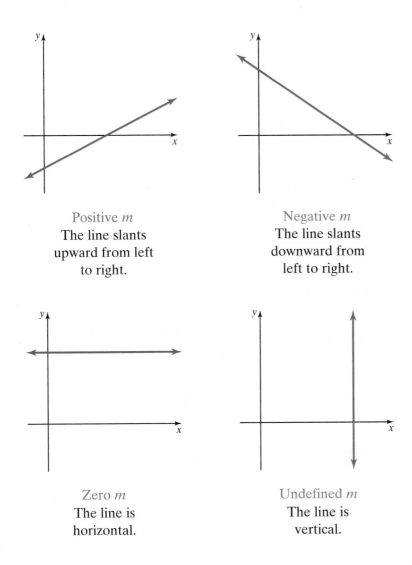

Positive m
The line slants
upward from left
to right.

Negative m
The line slants
downward from
left to right.

Zero m
The line is
horizontal.

Undefined m
The line is
vertical.

In the next example, we graph two lines on a coordinate plane.

EXAMPLE 5

Calculate the slopes for the lines shown.

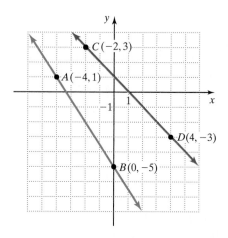

SOLUTION For $\overleftrightarrow{AB}$ passing through $A(-4, 1)$ and $B(0, -5)$, the slope is:

$$m = \frac{y_2 - y_1}{x_2 - x_1} = \frac{1 - (-5)}{(-4) - 0} = \frac{1 + 5}{-4} = \frac{6}{-4} = -\frac{3}{2}$$

For $\overleftrightarrow{CD}$ passing through $C(-2, 3)$ and $D(4, -3)$, the slope is:

$$m = \frac{y_2 - y_1}{x_2 - x_1} = \frac{3 - (-3)}{(-2) - 4} = \frac{3 + 3}{(-2) - 4} = \frac{6}{-6} = -1$$

Note that both lines have negative slopes and slant downward from left to right.

PRACTICE 5

Compute the slopes for the lines shown.

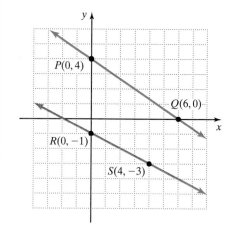

As shown in the next example, how a line slants often helps us to interpret the information given in the graph.

EXAMPLE 6

The following graph shows the amount of money that your dental insurance reimburses you, depending on the amount of your dental bill.

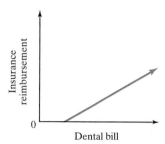

Is the slope of the graphed line positive or negative? Explain how you know. What does this mean in terms of insurance reimbursement?

PRACTICE 6

Suppose you are a doctor trying to help eliminate an epidemic. Explain, in terms of slope, which of the following four scenarios would be most desirable.

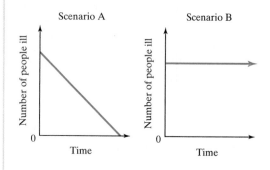

SOLUTION Since the graphed line slants upward from left to right, its slope is positive. According to this graph, larger *x*-values correspond to larger *y*-values. So, your dental insurance reimburses you more for larger dental bills.

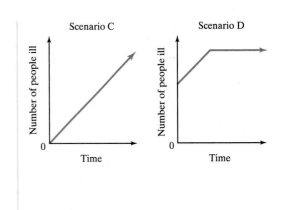

We have already graphed a line by plotting two points and drawing the line passing through them. Now let's look at graphing a line when given the slope of the line and a point on the line.

EXAMPLE 7

The slope of a line that passes through the point (2, 5) is 3. Graph the line.

SOLUTION The line in question passes through the point (2, 5). But there are many such lines—which is the right one? We use the slope 3 to find a second point through which the line also passes. Since 3 can be written as $\frac{3}{1}$, we have

$$\text{slope} = \frac{\text{rise}}{\text{run}} = \frac{3}{1}.$$

We first plot the point (2, 5). Starting at (2, 5), we move 3 units up (for a rise of 3) and then 1 unit to the right (for a run of 1). We arrive at the point (3, 8). Finally, we sketch the line passing through the points (2, 5) and (3, 8), as shown in the graph on the left on the next page.

Since $\frac{3}{1} = \frac{-3}{-1}$, we could have started at (2, 5) and moved down 3 units (for a rise of -3) and then 1 unit to the left (for a run of -1). In this case, we would arrive at (1, 2), which is another point on the same line, as shown in the graph on the right on the next page.

PRACTICE 7

Graph the line with slope 4 that passes through the point (1, -2).

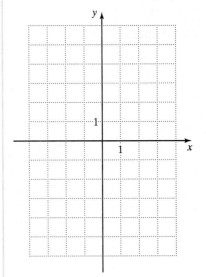

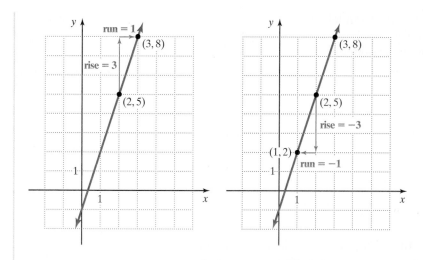

Can you find other points on this line? Explain.

EXAMPLE 8

Suppose that a family on vacation is driving out of town at a constant speed, and that at 2 o'clock they have traveled 110 mi. By 6 o'clock, they have traveled 330 mi.

a. On a coordinate plane, label the axes and then plot the appropriate points.

b. Compute the slope of the line passing through the points.

c. Interpret the meaning of the slope in this situation.

SOLUTION

a. Label the axes on the coordinate plane. Then plot the points (2, 110) and (6, 330).

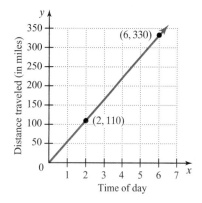

b. The slope of the line through the two points is:

$$m = \frac{y_2 - y_1}{x_2 - x_1} = \frac{330 - 110}{6 - 2} = \frac{220}{4} = 55$$

c. Here the slope is the change in distance divided by the change in time. In other words, the slope is the average speed the family traveled, which is 55 mph.

PRACTICE 8

An auto rental company advertises that a certain car rents for $80 with a weekly mileage of 100 mi and $90 when the weekly mileage is 200 mi.

a. On a coordinate plane, label the axes and then plot the appropriate points.

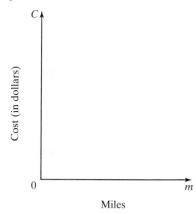

b. Compute the slope of the line that passes through the points.

c. Interpret the meaning of the slope in this situation.

Parallel and Perpendicular Lines

By examining the slopes of straight lines on a coordinate plane, we can solve problems that require us to determine if

- two given lines are parallel or
- two given lines are perpendicular.

Let's consider parallel lines first.

Since the slope of a line measures its slant, lines with equal slopes are parallel. So on the coordinate plane shown, if we knew the coordinate of points P, Q, R, and S, we could verify that $\overleftrightarrow{PQ}$ and $\overleftrightarrow{RS}$ are parallel by computing their slopes and then checking that they are equal.

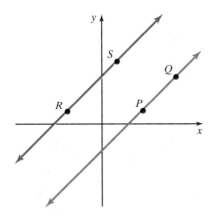

Definition

Two nonvertical lines are **parallel** if and only if their slopes are equal. That is, if the slopes are m_1 and m_2, then $m_1 = m_2$.

EXAMPLE 9

Consider points $P(0, 0)$, $Q(-2, -5)$, $R(0, 5)$, and $S(-2, 0)$. Are $\overleftrightarrow{PQ}$ and $\overleftrightarrow{RS}$ parallel?

SOLUTION Let's check if the slopes of $\overleftrightarrow{PQ}$ and $\overleftrightarrow{RS}$ are equal. The slope of $\overleftrightarrow{PQ}$ is:

$$m = \frac{y_2 - y_1}{x_2 - x_1} = \frac{0 - (-5)}{0 - (-2)} = \frac{0 + 5}{0 + 2} = \frac{5}{2}$$

The slope of $\overleftrightarrow{RS}$ is:

$$m = \frac{y_2 - y_1}{x_2 - x_1} = \frac{5 - 0}{0 - (-2)} = \frac{5}{0 + 2} = \frac{5}{2}$$

Since the slopes of $\overleftrightarrow{PQ}$ and $\overleftrightarrow{RS}$ are equal, $\overleftrightarrow{PQ}$ and $\overleftrightarrow{RS}$ are parallel.

PRACTICE 9

Decide whether $\overleftrightarrow{EF}$ and $\overleftrightarrow{GH}$ are parallel, given points $E(0, 4)$, $F(4, -1)$, $G(0, 8)$, and $H(8, -2)$.

EXAMPLE 10

A pediatric nurse kept track of the weights of two children who are twins. Use the graph to answer the following questions.

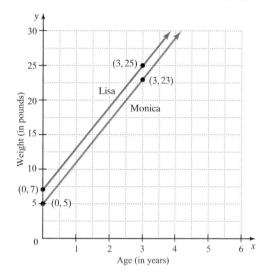

a. Which twin was heavier at birth?

b. Are the two lines parallel?

c. Which twin grew at a faster rate?

d. Could this graph be used to project the weight of the twins at age 8? Explain.

SOLUTION

a. At birth, Lisa weighed 7 lb and Monica weighed 5 lb. So Lisa was heavier.

b. To determine if the two lines are parallel, we begin by computing the slope of the line passing through the points $(0, 7)$ and $(3, 25)$.

$$m = \frac{y_2 - y_1}{x_2 - x_1} = \frac{7 - 25}{0 - 3} = \frac{-18}{-3} = 6$$

Now we compute the slope for the line passing through the $(0, 5)$ and $(3, 23)$.

$$m = \frac{y_2 - y_1}{x_2 - y_1} = \frac{5 - 23}{0 - 3} = \frac{-18}{-3} = 6$$

Since the slopes of the two lines are equal, the graphed lines are parallel.

c. Since the two lines are parallel, the twins grew at the same rate.

d. If we extend the x- and y-axes, we could determine the weight of each child at age 8 by reading the corresponding y-coordinate for x equal to 8.

PRACTICE 10

The graph shown gives the income of a computer lab technician and a Web site designer as related to the number of years that they have been employed. Use this graph to answer the following questions.

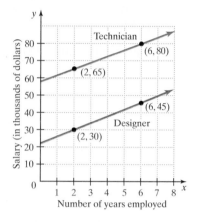

a. Are the two lines parallel?

b. Does your answer to part (a) agree with your observation of the graph? Explain.

c. Which employee's salary increased at a faster rate?

d. From the graph, estimate the starting salary of the computer lab technician.

Now let's consider the problem of determining whether two given lines are perpendicular.

On a coordinate plane, two lines are perpendicular to one another when the product of their slopes is -1. For instance, the slope of $\overleftrightarrow{PQ}$ in the following graph is:

$$m = \frac{7 - 2}{3 - 1} = \frac{5}{2}$$

The slope of $\overleftrightarrow{QR}$ is

$$m = \frac{2 - 0}{1 - 6} = \frac{2}{-5} = -\frac{2}{5}$$

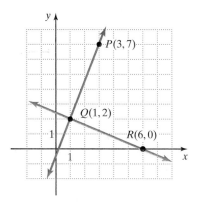

The product of these slopes is:

$$m = \left(\frac{5}{2}\right)\left(-\frac{2}{5}\right) = -1$$

We say that the slopes are *negative reciprocals* of each other. Therefore, the two lines must be perpendicular to one another.

Definition

Two nonvertical lines are **perpendicular** if and only if the product of their slopes is -1. That is, if the slopes are m_1 and m_2, then $m_1 \cdot m_2 = -1$.

EXAMPLE 11

Determine if $\overleftrightarrow{AB}$ and $\overleftrightarrow{BC}$ shown in the graph are perpendicular to one another.

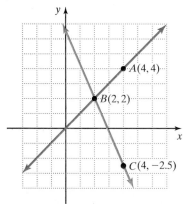

PRACTICE 11

Consider points $A(1, 3)$, $B(2, 5)$, and $C(-1, 2)$. Decide if $\overleftrightarrow{AB}$ is perpendicular to $\overleftrightarrow{AC}$.

SOLUTION First let's compute the slopes of the two lines in question. The slope of $\overleftrightarrow{AB}$ is:

$$m = \frac{y_2 - y_1}{x_2 - x_1} = \frac{4 - 2}{4 - 2} = \frac{2}{2} = 1$$

The slope of $\overleftrightarrow{BC}$ is:

$$m = \frac{y_2 - y_1}{x_2 - x_1} = \frac{2 - (-2.5)}{2 - 4} = \frac{2 + 2.5}{2 - 4} = \frac{4.5}{-2} = -2.25$$

To check if $\overleftrightarrow{AB}$ and $\overleftrightarrow{BC}$ are perpendicular, we find the product of their slopes:

$$(-2.25)(1) = -2.25$$

Since this product is not equal to -1, the lines are not perpendicular to one another.

EXAMPLE 12

On the coordinate plane shown, x-values represent streets and y-values represent avenues. Suppose that a road is to be constructed running straight from 4th Street and 3rd Avenue to 9th Street and 9th Avenue. A second road will run from 2nd Street and 10th Avenue to 8th Street and 5th Avenue. Will the roads meet at right angles?

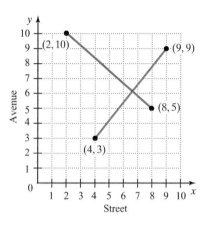

SOLUTION Let's find the slopes of the two roads. The slope of the road from 9th Street and 9th Avenue to 4th Street and 3rd Avenue is:

$$m = \frac{y_2 - y_1}{x_2 - x_1} = \frac{9 - 3}{9 - 4} = \frac{6}{5}$$

The slope of the road from 2nd Street and 10th Avenue to 8th Street and 5th Avenue is:

$$m = \frac{y_2 - y_1}{x_2 - x_1} = \frac{10 - 5}{2 - 8} = \frac{5}{-6} = -\frac{5}{6}$$

The product of these slopes is:

$$\left(\frac{6}{5}\right)\left(-\frac{5}{6}\right) = -1$$

Therefore, the roads will be perpendicular to one another.

PRACTICE 12

Consider the square 6 units on each side shown in the following diagram. By examining their slopes, determine whether the diagonals of the square are perpendicular to one another.

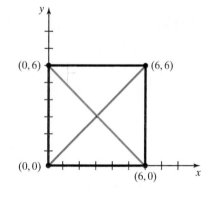

Exercises 3.2

Compute the slope m of the line that passes through the given points. Plot these points on the coordinate plane, and sketch the line that passes through them.

1. $(2, 3)$ and $(-2, 0)$, $m = \dfrac{3}{4}$

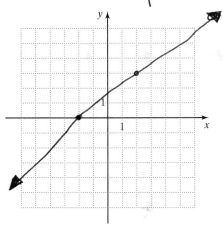

2. $(0, 0)$ and $(-2, 5)$, $m =$

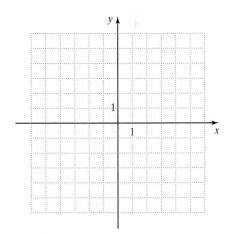

3. $(6, -4)$ and $(6, 1)$, $m = $ undefined

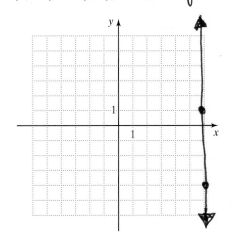

4. $(1, 1)$ and $(1, -3)$, $m =$

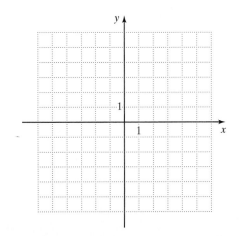

5. $(-2, 1)$ and $(3, -1)$, $m = -\dfrac{2}{5}$

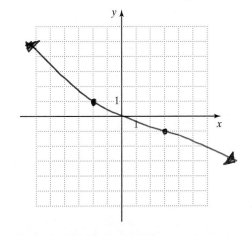

6. $(-1, 4)$ and $(0, 5)$, $m =$

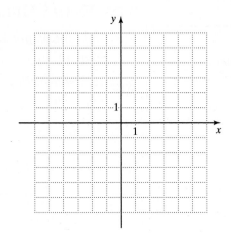

7. $(-1, -4)$ and $(3, -4)$, $m = 0$

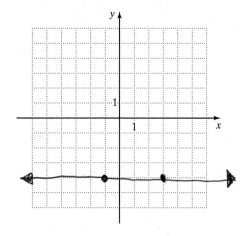

8. $(3, 0)$ and $(5, 0)$, $m =$

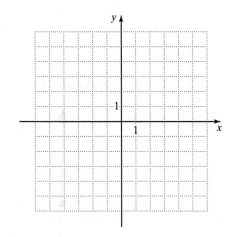

9. $(0.5, 0)$ and $(0, 3.5)$, $m = \dfrac{-7}{1}$

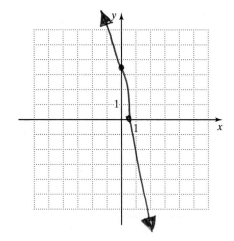

10. $(4, 4.5)$ and $(1, 2.5)$, $m =$

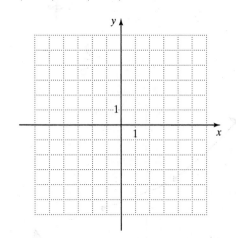

On each graph, calculate the slopes for the lines shown.

11.

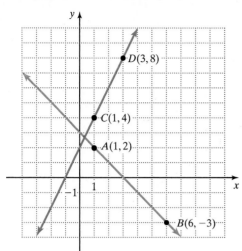

12.

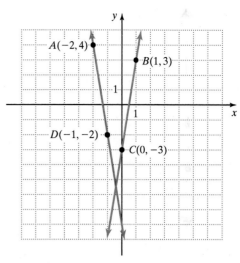

Graph the line on the coordinate plane using the given information.

13. Passes through $(2, 5)$ and $m = 4$

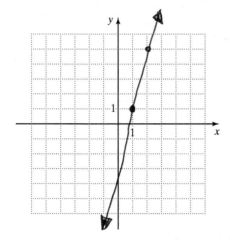

14. Passes through $(0, -6)$ and $m = 0$

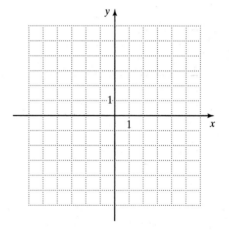

15. Passes through $(1, 5)$ and $m = -3$.

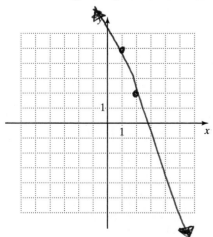

16. Passes through $(0, 0)$ and $m = 6$.

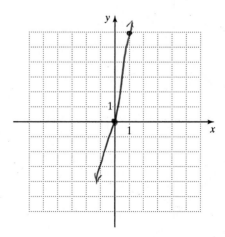

17. Passes through $(-4, 0)$ and the slope is undefined.

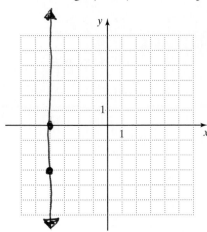

18. Passes through $(-6, 2)$ and the slope is $-\dfrac{3}{5}$.

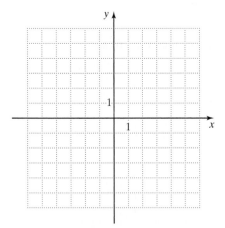

Indicate whether the slope of each graph is positive, negative, zero, or undefined. Then state whether the line is horizontal, vertical, or neither.

19.

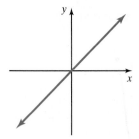

20.

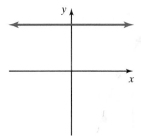

21.

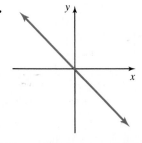

22.

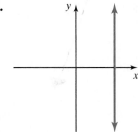

23.

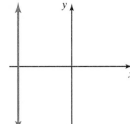

24.

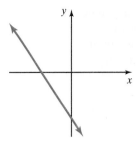

25.

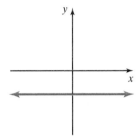

26.

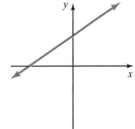

Determine whether $\overleftrightarrow{PQ}$ and $\overleftrightarrow{RS}$ are parallel or perpendicular.

27.

	P	Q	R	S
a.	$(0, -1)$	$(1, 3)$	$(5, 0)$	$(7, 8)$
b.	$(9, 1)$	$(7, 4)$	$(0, 0)$	$(6, 4)$

28.

	P	Q	R	S
a.	$(3, 3)$	$(7, 7)$	$(-5, 5)$	$(2, -2)$
b.	$(8, 0)$	$(0, 4)$	$(0, -4)$	$(-12, 2)$

Applications

Solve.

29. A chemist conducts an experiment on the gas contained in a sealed tube. The experiment is to heat the gas and then to measure the resulting pressure in the tube. In the lab manual, points are plotted and the line is sketched to show the gas pressure for various temperatures.

a. Is the slope of this line positive, negative, zero, or undefined?

b. In a sentence, explain the significance of the answer to part (a) in terms of temperature and pressure.

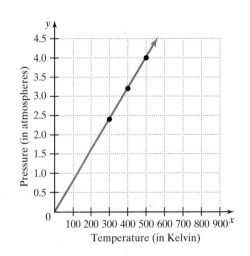

30. To reduce their taxes, many businesses use *the straight-line method of depreciation* to estimate the change in the value over time of equipment that they own. The graph shows the value of equipment owned from the time of purchase to 7 years later.

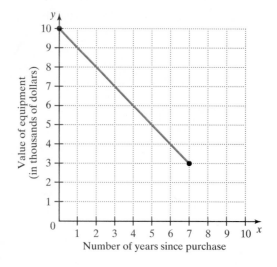

a. Is the slope of this line positive, negative, zero, or undefined?

b. In a sentence or two, explain the significance of the answer to part (a) in terms of the value of the equipment over time.

31. Two motorcyclists leave at the same time, racing down a road. Consider the lines in the graph that show the distance traveled by each motorcycle at various times.

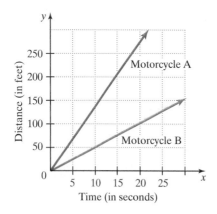

a. Which motorcycle first travels 100 ft?

b. Which motorcycle is traveling more slowly?

c. Explain what the slopes mean in this situation.

32. Most day-care centers charge parents additional fees for arriving late to pick up their children. The following graph shows the late fee for two day-care centers.

a. Which day-care center charges a higher late fee?

b. Explain what the slopes represent in this situation.

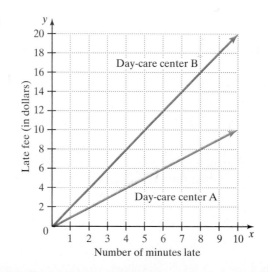

33. The following graph records the amount of garbage deposited in landfills A and B after they are opened.

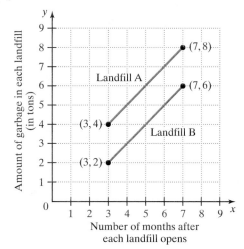

Are the garbage deposits at the two landfills growing at the same rate? Explain in a sentence or two how you know.

34. The weights of a brother and sister from age 3 years to 7 years are recorded in the graph. Did their weights increase at the same rate? Explain.

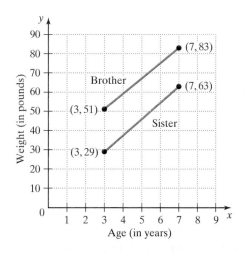

35. After a stock split, the per share value of the stock increased, as shown in the table.

Point	Number of Days After the Split	Value (in dollars)
P	2	27
Q	4	51
R	8	79

a. Choose appropriate scales and label each axis. Plot the points and then sketch $\overleftrightarrow{PQ}$ and $\overleftrightarrow{QR}$.

b. Determine whether the rate of increase changed over time. Explain.

36. The position of a dropped object for various times after the object is released is given in the table.

Point	Time After Release (in seconds)	Position (in feet)
A	1	-16
B	2	-64
C	3	-144

a. Choose appropriate scales and label each axis. Plot the points and then sketch $\overleftrightarrow{AB}$ and $\overleftrightarrow{BC}$.

b. Compute the slopes of $\overleftrightarrow{AB}$ and $\overleftrightarrow{BC}$.

c. Was the rate of fall for the dropped object constant throughout the experiment? Explain.

37. A hiker is at point A as shown in the graph and wants to take the shortest route through a field to reach a nearby road represented by $\overleftrightarrow{BC}$. The shortest route will be to walk perpendicular to the road. Is $\overleftrightarrow{AD}$ the shortest route? Explain.

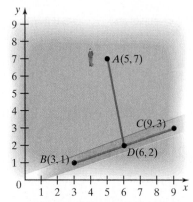

38. The coordinates of the vertices of triangle *ABC* are shown. Is triangle *ABC* a right triangle? Explain.

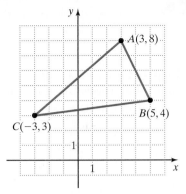

39. On a highway, a driver sets a car's cruise control for a constant speed of 55 mph.

a. Which graph shows the distance the car travels? Using the slope of the line, explain.

b. Which graph shows the speed of the car? Using the slope of the line, explain.

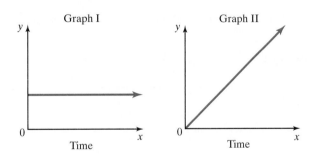

40. Suppose city leaders consider imposing an income tax on residents whose income is above a certain amount, as pictured.

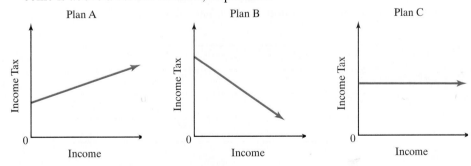

a. Using the slopes of the lines, describe each plan.

b. Which plan do you think is the fairest? Explain.

● Check your answers on page A-9.

Mindstretchers

GROUPWORK

1. A geoboard is a square flat surface with pegs forming a grid pattern. You can stretch rubber bands around the pegs to explore geometric questions. Pictured is a geoboard with rubber bands forming a stairway design.

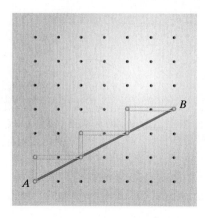

Using a geoboard or graph paper, determine whether the slope of $\overleftrightarrow{AB}$ increases or decreases if

a. the rise of each step increases by one peg.

_____

b. the run of each step increases by one peg.

_____

2. Describe a real-world situation that each of the following graphs might illustrate. Explain the significance of slope in the situation that you have described.

a.

b.

c.

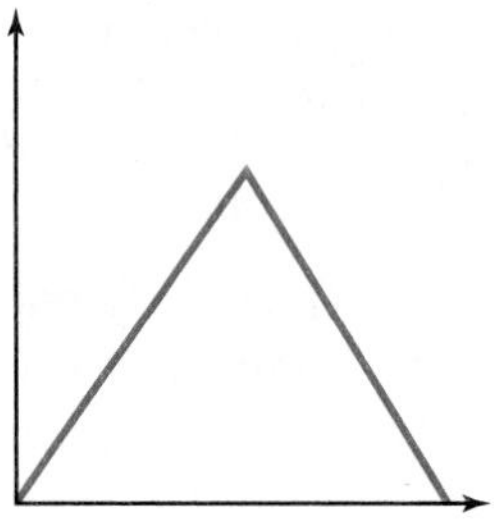

MATHEMATICAL REASONING

3. If the slope of a line is positive, explain why any line perpendicular to it must have a negative slope.

_____

_____

_____

_____

3.3 Linear Equations and Their Graphs

OBJECTIVES

- *To identify a given linear equation in general form*
- *To identify the coordinates of points that satisfy a given linear equation in two variables*
- *To graph a given linear equation in two variables*
- *To solve applied problems involving the graph of a linear equation*

In the first section of this chapter, we developed the idea of coordinates—an ordered pair of numbers associated with a point on the plane. In the second section, we shifted our attention from points to lines. In this section, we focus on Descartes' most startling idea—on a coordinate plane, lines (and indeed other graphs) correspond to equations. Line graphs and their associated equations, called *linear* equations, have important applications in the real world, allowing us to model many situations. In later chapters, we will discuss other types of graphs.

Solutions of a Linear Equation in Two Variables

Recall that linear equations in one variable generally have one and only one solution. For instance, the solution of $2x + 5 = 11$ is 3 because when we substitute 3 for x, the equation balances.

$$2x + 5 = 11$$
$$2 \cdot 3 + 5 \stackrel{?}{=} 11$$
$$11 = 11 \quad \text{True.}$$

So we say that $x = 3$.

We now consider linear equations in *two* variables, say $y = 2x + 5$. We can also express $y = 2x + 5$ as $-2x + y = 5$.

$$y = 2x + 5$$
$$-2x + y = 5 \qquad \text{Subtract } 2x \text{ from each side of the equation.}$$

> **Definition**
>
> A **linear equation in two variables**, x and y, is an equation that can be written in the *general form* $Ax + By = C$, where A, B, and C are real numbers and A and B are not both 0.

Note that in the general form of a linear equation, the two variable terms are on one side of the equation and the constant term is on the other. The equation $-2x + y = 5$, for instance, is in general form, with $A = -2$, $B = 1$, and $C = 5$.

Here are some other examples of linear equations in general form:

Equation	A	B	C
$5x + 3y = 10$	5	3	10
$x - 2y = 6 \rightarrow 1x + (-2)y = 6$	1	-2	6
$x = -4 \rightarrow 1x + 0y = -4$	1	0	-4
$y = -4 \rightarrow 0x + 1y = -4$	0	1	-4

Now let's look at what we mean by a solution of a linear equation in two variables.

Definition

A **solution** of an equation in two variables is an ordered pair of numbers that when substituted for the variables makes the equation true.

Applying this definition to the equation $-2x + y = 5$, we observe that $x = 3$ and $y = 11$ is a solution of the equation because substituting 3 for x and 11 for y makes the equation true.

$$-2x + y = 5$$
$$-2 \cdot 3 + 11 \overset{?}{=} 5$$
$$5 = 5 \quad \text{True.}$$

However, there are other solutions of this equation as well, including $x = 0$ and $y = 5$.

$$-2x + y = 5$$
$$-2 \cdot 0 + 5 \overset{?}{=} 5$$
$$5 = 5 \quad \text{True.}$$

In general, a linear equation in one variable has one and only one solution. However, linear equations in two variables have an infinite number of solutions. Can you explain why this is the case?

Now, how do we *find* solutions of a linear equation in two variables? Typically, we start with the value of one of the variables and then compute the corresponding value of the other, as the following example illustrates.

EXAMPLE 1

For the equation $4x + y = -5$, find five solutions by completing the following table.

x	y
-2	
3	
0	
	0
	1

SOLUTION In the first row of this table, we substitute -2 for x in the given equation, and then solve for y.

$$4x + y = -5$$
$$4(-2) + y = -5$$
$$-8 + y = -5$$
$$y = 3$$

To find the corresponding y in the second row, we substitute 3 for x:

$$4x + y = -5$$
$$4(3) + y = -5$$
$$12 + y = -5$$
$$y = -17$$

PRACTICE 1

For the equation $-2x + y = 1$, find the missing values in the following table:

x	y
0	
5	
-3	
	0
	-3

And in the third row, we substitute 0 for x:

$$4x + y = -5$$
$$4(\mathbf{0}) + y = -5$$
$$0 + y = -5$$
$$y = -5$$

The next two rows are different from the earlier ones: they give us y-values and require us to solve for x. First we see that in the fourth row y is 0.

$$4x + y = -5$$
$$4x + \mathbf{0} = -5 \qquad \text{Substitute 0 for } y.$$
$$4x = -5$$
$$x = -\frac{5}{4}$$

In the final row of the table, $y = 1$.

$$4x + y = -5$$
$$4x + \mathbf{1} = -5 \qquad \text{Substitute 1 for } y.$$
$$4x = -6$$
$$x = -\frac{6}{4} = -\frac{3}{2}$$

We have found the missing values, so the table reads:

x	y
-2	3
3	-17
0	-5
$-\frac{5}{4}$	0
$-\frac{3}{2}$	1

The Graph of a Linear Equation in Two Variables

The graph of an equation, more precisely the graph of the *solutions* of that equation, is a kind of picture of the equation.

> **Definition**
>
> The **graph** of a linear equation in two variables consists of all points whose coordinates satisfy the equation.

Given a linear equation, how do we find its graph? A general strategy is to first isolate one of the variables, unless it is already done. Then we identify several solutions of the equation, keeping track of the x- and y-values in a table. We plot the points and then sketch the line passing through them. That line is the graph of the given equation, as the following example illustrates.

Let's graph the equation $y = 3x + 1$. The variable y is already isolated, so we find y-values by substituting arbitrary values of x. For instance, let x equal 0. To find y, we substitute 0 for x.

$$y = 3x + 1 = 3 \cdot 0 + 1 = 0 + 1 = 1$$

So $x = 0$ and $y = 1$ is a solution of this equation. We say that the ordered pair $(0, 1)$ is a solution of $y = 3x + 1$.

Let's choose three other values of x, say -1, 1, and 2. Substituting -1 for x in the equation, we get:

$$y = 3x + 1 = 3(-1) + 1 = -2$$

Substituting 1 for x, we get:

$$y = 3x + 1 = 3 \cdot 1 + 1 = 4$$

Substituting 2 for x gives:

$$y = 3x + 1 = 3 \cdot 2 + 1 = 7$$

Next, we enter these results in a table.

x	y
-1	-2
0	1
1	4
2	7

Then we plot on a coordinate plane the four points $(-1, -2)$, $(0, 1)$, $(1, 4)$, and $(2, 7)$. If we have not made a mistake, the points will all lie on the same line. The graph of the equation $y = 3x + 1$ is the line passing through these points. So any point on this line satisfies the equation $y = 3x + 1$.

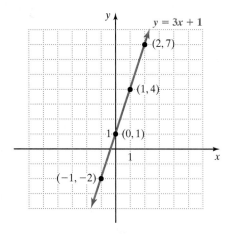

Do you think that if we had chosen three other x-values we would have gotten the same graph? Check to see that this is the case.

This example suggests the following procedure for graphing a linear equation.

To Graph a Linear Equation in Two Variables

- Isolate one of the variables—usually *y*—if it is not already done.
- Choose three *x*-values, entering them in a table.
- Complete the table by calculating the corresponding *y*-values.
- Plot the three points—two to draw the line and the third to serve as a *checkpoint*.
- Check that the points seem to lie on the same line.
- Draw the line passing through the points.

A couple of observations about the preceding example are worth making:

- The slope of the line graphed is 3. We can see this by taking any pair of points on the line, for example $(0, 1)$ and $(1, 4)$, and computing the slope of the line between them.

$$m = \frac{y_2 - y_1}{x_2 - x_1} = \frac{1 - 4}{0 - 1} = \frac{-3}{-1} = 3$$

- This slope is identical to the coefficient of *x* in the equation $y = 3x + 1$.

We also see that the point where the graph crosses the *y*-axis is $(0, 1)$. This point is called the *y-intercept*. Note that the constant term in the equation $y = 3x + 1$ is also 1.

These relationships are more than a coincidence, and we will say more about them in Section 3.4.

EXAMPLE 2

Graph the equation $y = -\frac{3}{2}x$ by choosing three points whose coordinates satisfy the equation.

SOLUTION We begin by choosing *x*-values. In this case, we choose multiples of 2 for the *x*-values. Then we find the corresponding *y*-values.

x	$y = -\frac{3}{2}x$	*(x, y)*
0	$y = -\frac{3}{2}(0) = 0$	$(0, 0)$
2	$y = -\frac{3}{2}(2) = -3$	$(2, -3)$
4	$y = -\frac{3}{2}(4) = -6$	$(4, -6)$

PRACTICE 2

Graph the equation $y = -\frac{3}{5}x$.

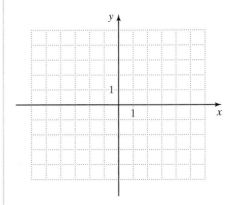

We plot the points and then draw a line passing through them to get the desired line.

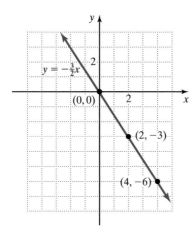

Note that in Example 2, we chose multiples of 2 for the *x*-values. Can you explain why?

EXAMPLE 3

Consider the equation $6x + 3y = 9$.

a. Graph the equation.

b. Find the slope of the line.

SOLUTION

a. We begin by solving the equation for *y*.

$$6x + 3y = 9$$
$$3y = -6x + 9 \quad \text{Subtract } 6x \text{ from each side.}$$
$$y = \frac{-6x + 9}{3} \quad \text{Divide each side by 3.}$$
$$y = -2x + 3$$

Next we choose three values for *x*, for instance, -1, 0, and 2. Then we enter them into a table and find their corresponding *y*-values as follows.

x	$y = -2x + 3$	(x, y)
-1	$y = -2(-1) + 3 = 2 + 3 = 5$	$(-1, 5)$
0	$y = -2(0) + 3 = 0 + 3 = 3$	$(0, 3)$
2	$y = -2(2) + 3 = -4 + 3 = -1$	$(2, -1)$

PRACTICE 3

Consider the equation
$-4x + 2y = -10$.

a. Graph the equation.

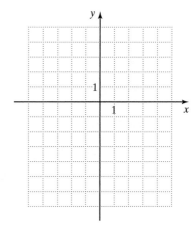

b. Find the slope of the line.

Now we plot the points on the coordinate plane. Since the points seem to lie on the same line, we draw a line passing through the points.

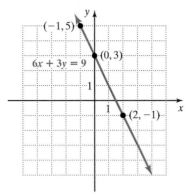

b. To find the slope of the line, we can consider the points $(0, 3)$ and $(2, -1)$.

$$m = \frac{3 - (-1)}{0 - 2} = \frac{4}{-2} = -2$$

Note that the slope is the coefficient of x in the equation $y = -2x + 3$.

We have graphed equations in general form by first isolating y and then computing y-values for arbitrary x-values. Now we graph equations in general form with a different approach using x- and y-intercepts. Note that intercepts stand out on a graph and are easy to plot. Since an x-intercept lies on the x-axis, its y-value must be 0. Similarly, since a y-intercept lies on the y-axis, the x-value of a y-intercept must be 0.

Definition

The **x-intercept** of a line is the point where the graph crosses the x-axis. The **y-intercept** is the point where the graph crosses the y-axis.

The following graph shows a line passing through two points, $(0, 4)$ and $(3, 0)$, which are both intercepts.

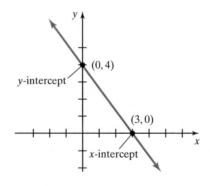

Using the x- and y-intercepts to graph equations can save work, especially when the coefficients of the two variables are factors of the constant term, as shown in the next example.

EXAMPLE 4

Consider the equation $2x + 3y = 6$. Find the x- and y-intercepts. Then graph.

SOLUTION Since the y-intercept has x-value 0, we let $x = 0$ and then solve for y.

For $x = 0$:

$$2x + 3y = 6$$
$$2 \cdot 0 + 3y = 6 \qquad \text{Substitute 0 for } x.$$
$$3y = 6$$
$$\frac{3y}{3} = \frac{6}{3}$$
$$y = 2$$

So the y-intercept is $(0, 2)$.

Similarly, the x-intercept has y-value 0. So we let $y = 0$ and then solve for x.

For $y = 0$:

$$2x + 3y = 6$$
$$2x + 3 \cdot 0 = 6 \qquad \text{Substitute 0 for } y.$$
$$2x = 6$$
$$\frac{2x}{2} = \frac{6}{2}$$
$$x = 3$$

So the x-intercept is $(3, 0)$.

   Before graphing, we choose a third point to be used as a checkpoint.

For $2x + 3y = 6$, let $x = 6$:

$$2x + 3y = 6$$
$$2 \cdot 6 + 3y = 6 \qquad \text{Substitute 6 for } x.$$
$$12 + 3y = 6$$
$$3y = -6$$
$$y = -2$$

So the checkpoint is $(6, -2)$.

   Plotting the points $(0, 2)$, $(3, 0)$, and $(6, -2)$ on a coordinate plane, we confirm that they seem to lie on the same line. Finally, we draw a line through the points, getting the desired graph.

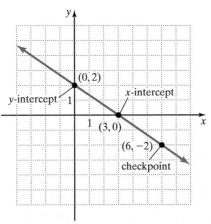

PRACTICE 4

Consider the equation $2x - 4y = 8$. Find the x- and y-intercepts. Then graph.

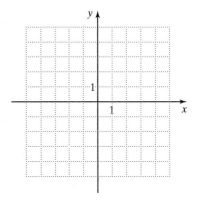

Example 4 suggests the following procedure.

To Graph a Linear Equation in Two Variables Using the *x*- and *y*-intercepts
- Let $x = 0$ and find the *y*-intercept.
- Let $y = 0$ and find the *x*-intercept.
- Find a checkpoint.
- Plot the three points.
- Check that the points seem to lie on the same line.
- Draw the line passing through the points.

We know that the general form of a linear equation in two variables is $Ax + By = C$. Sometimes in a linear equation one of the two variables is missing, that is, the coefficient of one of the two variables is zero. Consider the following equations:

$$y = 9 \quad \longrightarrow \quad 0x + y = 9$$
$$x = -5.8 \quad \longrightarrow \quad x + 0y = -5.8$$

Let's look at the graphs of these equations.

EXAMPLE 5

Graph:

a. $y = 9$

b. $x = -5.8$

SOLUTION

a. For the line $y = 9$, the coefficient of the *x*-term is 0. The *x*-value can be any real number and the *y*-value is always 9. Hence the graph is as follows.

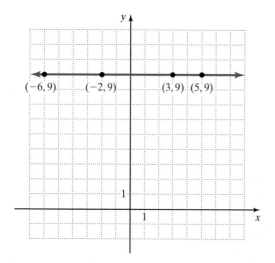

The graph of this equation is a horizontal line. Recall that the slope of a horizontal line is 0.

PRACTICE 5

On the given coordinate plane, graph:

a. $y = -1$

b. $x = 2.5$

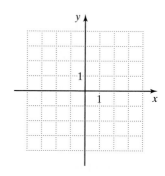

b. For the line $x = -5.8$, the coefficient of the y-term is 0. The y-value can be any real number and the x-value is always -5.8. Hence the graph is as follows.

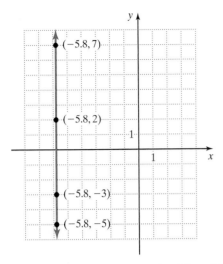

The graph of this equation is a vertical line. The slope of this line is undefined.

In general, the graph of the equation $x = a$ is a vertical line passing through the point $(a, 0)$, and the graph of the equation $y = b$ is a horizontal line passing through the point $(0, b)$.

Now let's use our knowledge of graphing linear equations to solve applied problems.

EXAMPLE 6

For cable television, a homeowner pays $30 per month plus $5 for each pay-per-view movie ordered.

a. Express as an equation the relationship between the monthly bill B and the number n of pay-per-view movies.

b. Draw the graph of this equation in Quadrant I of a coordinate plane.

c. Compute the slope of this graph. In terms of the cable TV bill, explain the significance of the slope.

d. In terms of the cable TV bill, explain the significance of the B-intercept of the graph.

e. From the graph in part (b), estimate what the cable bill would be if the homeowner had ordered 15 pay-per-view movies that month.

SOLUTION

a. The monthly bill (in dollars) amounts to the sum of 30 and 5 times the number of pay-per-view movies which the homeowner ordered, so

$$B = 5n + 30.$$

PRACTICE 6

A stockbroker charges as her commission on stock transactions $40 plus 3% of the value of the sale.

a. Write as an equation the commission C in terms of the sales s.

b. To draw the graph of this equation in Quadrant I, we enter several nonnegative *n*-values, say 0, 10, and 20, in a table and then compute the corresponding *B*-values.

n	$B = 5n + 30$	(n, B)
0	$B = 5(0) + 30 = 30$	$(0, 30)$
10	$B = 5(10) + 30 = 80$	$(10, 80)$
20	$B = 5(20) + 30 = 130$	$(20, 130)$

Since the monthly bill *B* depends on the number *n* of pay-per-view movies ordered each month, we label the horizontal axis with the independent variable *n* and the vertical axis with the dependent variable *B*. Now we choose an appropriate scale for each axis and plot (0, 30), (10, 80), and (20, 130). Then we draw the line passing through these points.

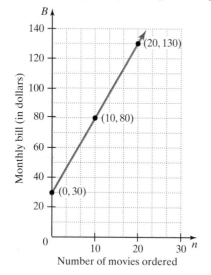

We restricted the graph to Quadrant I because the number of movies ordered *n* and the corresponding bill *B* are always positive.

c. Substituting *n* and *B* for *x* and *y*, respectively, in the slope formula, we get slope

$$m = \frac{B_2 - B_1}{n_2 - n_1} = \frac{80 - (30)}{10 - (0)} = \frac{50}{10} = 5.$$

Note that we could have predicted this answer since we know that the bill increases by $5 for every additional pay-per-view movie ordered.

d. Since the *B*-intercept is the point (0, 30), $30 would be the amount of the bill if the homeowner had watched no pay-per-view movies at all during the month.

e. From the graph, it appears that if $n = 15$, then $B = 105$.

b. Draw a graph showing this relationship on sales up to $1000. Be sure to choose an appropriate scale for each axis.

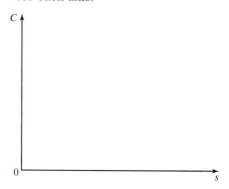

c. Compute the slope of this graph. In terms of the stock broker's commission, explain the significance of the slope.

d. If the value of a sale is $500, estimate from the graph in part (b) the broker's commission.

EXAMPLE 7

A shopper has $90 in his wallet in five-dollar and one-dollar bills.

a. If f represents the number of five-dollar bills and d the number of one-dollar bills, write an equation that relates f and d.

b. Graph this equation.

c. Explain the significance of the two intercepts in terms of the bills in the shopper's wallet.

d. Explain how we could have predicted that the slope of this graph would be negative.

SOLUTION

a. The value of the five-dollar bills is $5f$, and the value of the one-dollar bills is d. Since the total is $90, the following equation holds:

$$5f + d = 90$$

b. To graph, we identify the f- and d-intercepts, as well as a third point, say with $f = 10$.

f	d
0	90
18	0
10	40

Next we choose an appropriate scale for each axis and plot the three points, checking that the points all lie on the same line. Then we draw the line passing through them.

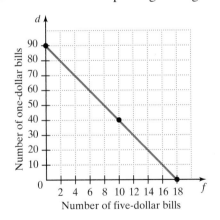

c. The d-intercept is the point corresponding to a zero value of f. At this point, the shopper has only one-dollar bills in his wallet. The f-intercept corresponds to a 0 value of d, in which case he has nothing but five-dollar bills.

d. Even without drawing this graph, we know that its slope has to be negative for the following reason: The wallet contains a fixed total dollar amount ($90). So larger values of f must correspond to smaller values of d. The line will therefore have to be decreasing, falling to the right and with a negative slope.

PRACTICE 7

Suppose an athlete has just signed a contract with a total value of $10 million. According to the terms of the contract, she earns $1 million in some years and $2 million in other years.

a. Let w stand for the number of years in which she earns $1 million and t the number of $2 million years. Write an equation that relates w and t.

b. Choose an appropriate scale for each axis on the coordinate plane. Graph the equation found in part (a).

c. Describe in terms of the contract the significance of the slope of the graph.

d. Describe in terms of the contract the significance of the t- and w-intercepts of the graph.

Exercises 3.3

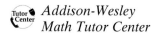
Complete each table so that the ordered pairs are solutions of the given equation.

1. $y = 3x - 8$

x	y
4	
7	
	0

2. $y = -x + 20$

x	y
0	
	3
	2

3. $y = 5x$

x	y
3.5	
6	
	$\frac{1}{2}$
	-8

4. $y = -10x$

x	y
$\frac{1}{5}$	
2.9	
	-6
	-1

5. $3x + 4y = 12$

x	y
0	
-4	
	-3
	0

6. $4x - y = 8$

x	y
5	
0	
	0
	8

7. $y = \frac{1}{3}x - 1$

x	y
3	
6	
-3	
	-1

8. $y = -\frac{3}{2}x + 2$

x	y
$\frac{4}{3}$	
6	
-2	
	2

Graph each equation by finding three points whose coordinates satisfy the equation.

9. $y = x$

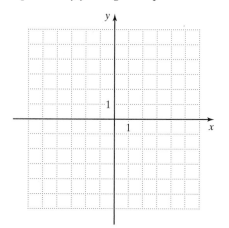

10. $y = 3x$

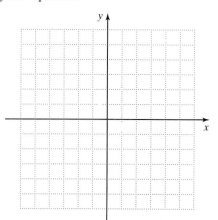

11. $y = \frac{1}{2}x$

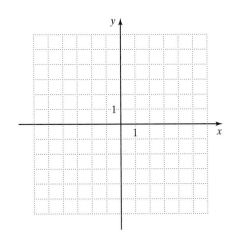

12. $y = \frac{1}{4}x$

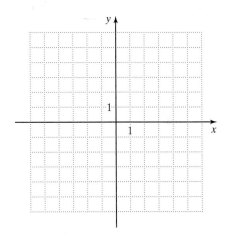

13. $y = -\frac{2}{3}x$

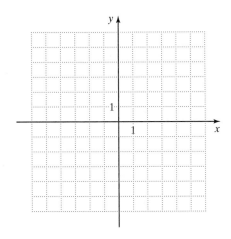

14. $y = -\frac{1}{5}x$

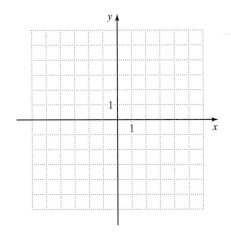

15. $y = 2x + 1$

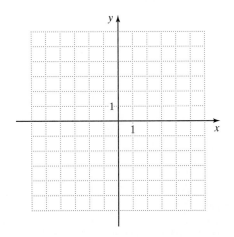

16. $y = -4x - 3$

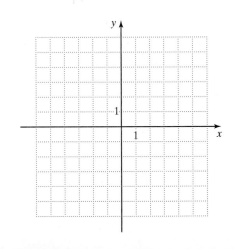

17. $y = -\frac{1}{3}x + 1$

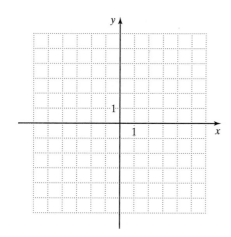

18. $y = -\frac{3}{4}x + 2$

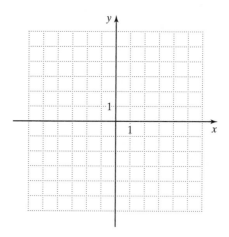

19. $y - 2x = -3$

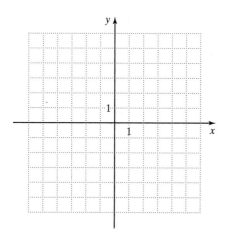

20. $y - 3x = 2$

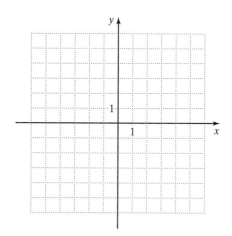

21. $x + y = 6$

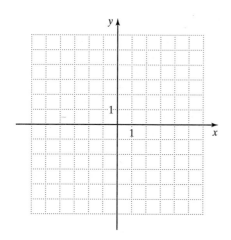

22. $3x + y = 4$

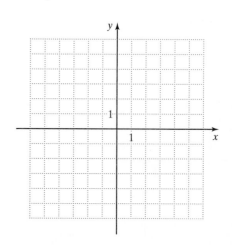

23. $x - 2y = 4$

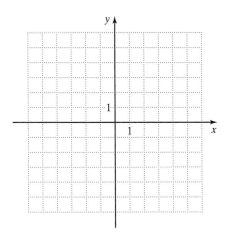

24. $x - 3y = 15$

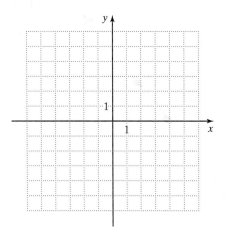

For each equation, find the x- and y-intercepts. Then use the intercepts to graph the equation.

25. $5x + 3y = 15$

X-intercept $(3,0)$
Y-intercept $(0,5)$

$Y=3$ $\dfrac{3y-15}{3}\dfrac{3}{3}$ $\dfrac{5x=15}{5}\dfrac{5}{5}$

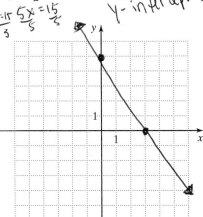

26. $4x + 5y = 20$

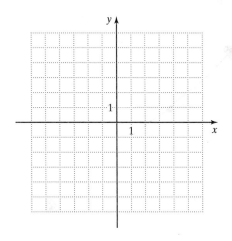

27. $3x - 6y = 18$

$Y=-3$

$\dfrac{-6y=18}{-6}\dfrac{-6}{-6}$ $\dfrac{3x=18}{3}\dfrac{3}{3}$ $x=6$

X-intercept $(6,0)$
Y-intercept $(0,-3)$

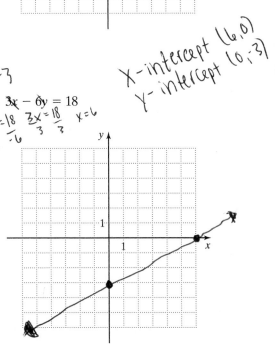

28. $3y - 2x = -6$

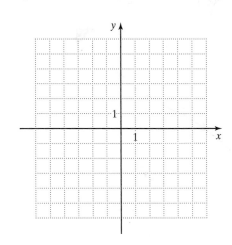

29. $4x - 5x = 10$

$x = -2$ $\frac{-5x}{-5} = \frac{-10}{-5}$ $\frac{4y}{4} = \frac{10}{4}$ $y = \frac{5}{2}$

X-intercept $(-2, 0)$
Y-intercept $(0, \frac{5}{2})$

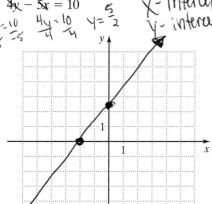

30. $7x - 2y = -7$

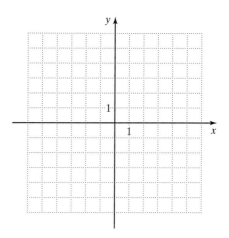

X-intercept $(\frac{3}{2}, 0)$
Y-intercept $(0, -1)$

31. $9y + 6x = -9$

$\frac{9y}{9} = \frac{-9}{9}$ $y = -1$ $\frac{6x}{6} = \frac{9}{6}$ $x = \frac{3}{2}$

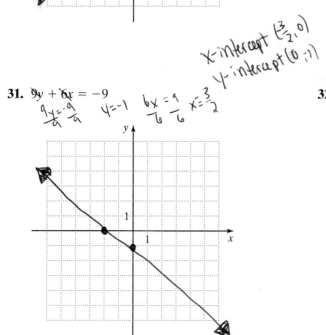

32. $4y - 8x = -4$

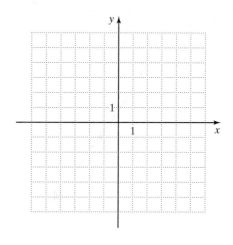

X-intercept $(-4, 0)$
Y-intercept $(0, 2)$

33. $x = \frac{1}{2}x + 2$

$y = 2$ $\frac{1}{2}y + 2$ $x = -4$

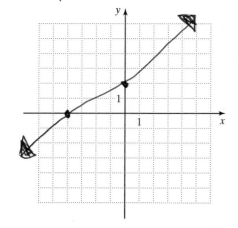

34. $y = \frac{5}{4}x - 5$

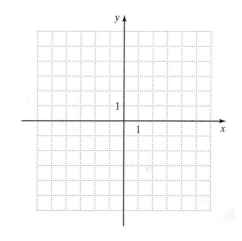

Graph.

35. $y = -2$

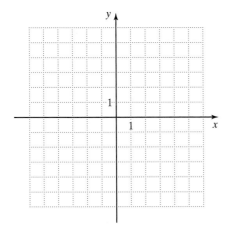

36. $x = 3$

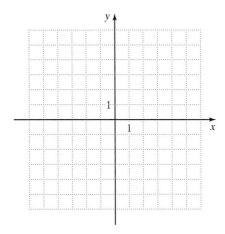

37. $x = 0$

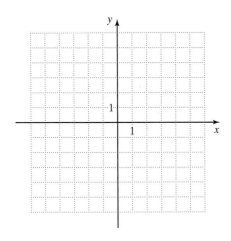

38. $y = 0$

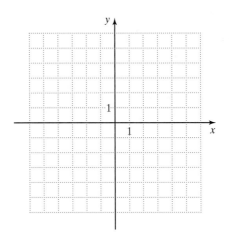

39. $x = -5.5$

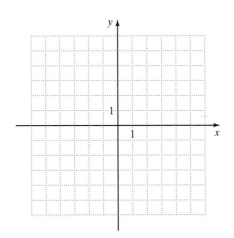

40. $y = -0.5$

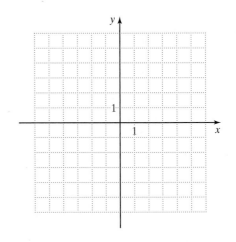

41. $y = \frac{1}{2}x + 3$

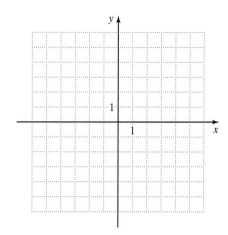

42. $y = 0.5x + 6$

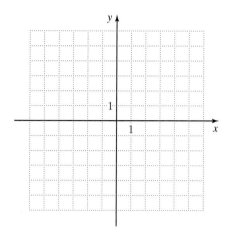

43. $3x + 5y = -15$

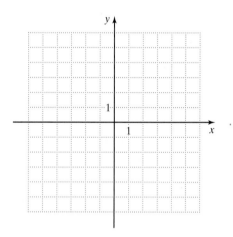

44. $3y - 5x = 15$

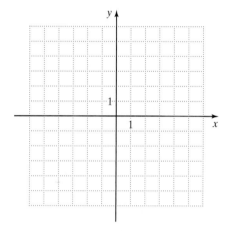

45. $y = \frac{3}{5}x + \frac{2}{5}$

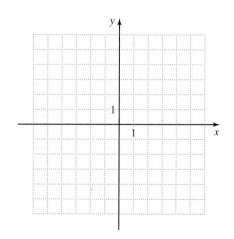

46. $y = -\frac{1}{4}x + \frac{3}{4}$

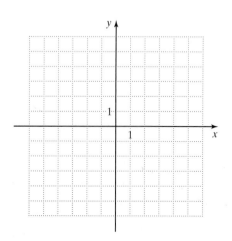

Applications

Solve.

47. In a physics lab, students study the mathematics of motion. They learn that if an object is tossed straight upward with an initial velocity of 10 ft per sec, then after t sec the object will be traveling at a velocity of v ft per sec, where

$$v = 10 - 32t.$$

a. Complete the following table.

t	v
0	
	−6
1	
1.5	
2	

Explain what a positive value of v means. What does a negative value of v mean?

b. Choose an appropriate scale for the each axis, and then graph this equation.

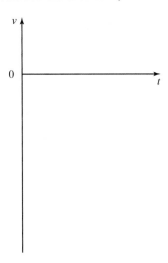

c. In terms of the object's motion, explain the significance of the v-intercept.

d. In terms of the object's motion, explain the significance of the t-intercept.

48. Each day, a local grocer varies the price p of an item in dollars and then keeps track of the number s of items sold. According to his records, the following equation describes the relationship between s and p.

$$s = -2p + 12$$

a. Complete the following table.

p	s
1	
3	
5	
	0

b. Choose appropriate scales for the axes and then graph the equation.

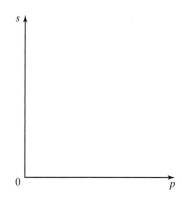

c. Explain why it makes sense to consider the graph only in Quadrant I.

d. From the graph, estimate the price required to sell 4 items.

49. A young couple buys furniture for $2000, agreeing to pay $500 down and $100 at the end of each month until the entire debt is paid off.

a. Express the amount P paid off in terms of the number m of monthly payments.

b. Complete the following table.

m	P
1	
2	
3	

c. Choose an appropriate scale for the axes and then graph this equation.

50. Students studying archaeology know that when the femur bone of an adult female is unearthed, a good estimate of her height h is 73 more than double the length l of the femur bone, where all measurements are in centimeters.

    a. Express this relationship as a formula.

    b. Complete the following table.

l	h
20	
25	
30	

    c. Choose an appropriate scale for the axes, and then graph this relationship.

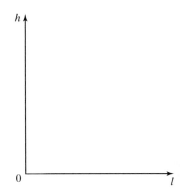

    d. Use the graph to estimate the height of a woman whose femur bone was 35 cm in length.

51. The coins in a cash register, with a total value of $2, consist of n nickels and d dimes.

    a. Represent this relationship as an equation.

    b. Graph the equation found in part (a).

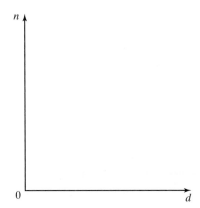

    c. Explain in a sentence or two why every point on this graph in Quadrant I is *not* a reasonable solution to the problem.

52. On the first leg of a trip, a truck driver drove for x hr at a constant speed of 50 mph. On the second leg of the trip, he drove for y hr consistently at 40 mph. In all, he drove 1000 mi.

a. Translate this information into an equation.

b. Choose appropriate scales for the axes, and then graph the equation found in part (a).

c. What are the x- and y-intercepts of this graph? Explain their significance in terms of the trip.

d. Find the slope of the line. Explain whether you would have expected the slope to be positive or negative, and why.

53. At a computer rental company, the fee F for renting a laptop is $40 plus $5 for each of the d days that the computer is rented.

a. Express this relationship as an equation.

b. Choose appropriate scales for the axes, and then graph the equation expressed in part (a).

c. Explain the significance of the F-intercept in this context.

54. At a local community center, the annual cost c to use the swimming pool includes an annual membership fee of \$75 plus \$5 per hour for h hr of pool time.

    a. Write an equation for the annual cost of swimming at the community center in terms of the number of hours of pool time.

    b. Choose appropriate scales for the axes, and then graph the equation for up to and including 150 hr.

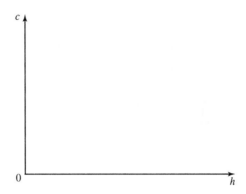

    c. Use the graph to estimate the annual cost of using the pool for 25 hr.

    d. Suppose the annual cost for swimming was \$500. Estimate the number of hours of pool time.

● *Check your answers on page A-10.*

Mindstretchers

GROUPWORK

1. Not all graphs are linear. For example, the graph of the equation $y = x^2 - 4$ is nonlinear, as the following graph illustrates.

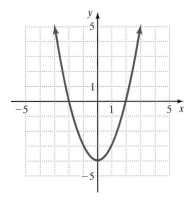

a. Identify the x- and y-intercepts for the graph shown.

_____

b. Show that the x- and y-intercepts found in part (a) satisfy the equation $y = x^2 - 4$.

_____
_____
_____

WRITING

2. Give some advantages and disadvantages of graphing a linear equation by finding three arbitrary points versus using the intercepts.

_____
_____
_____
_____

MATHEMATICAL REASONING

3. Recall that for a linear equation to be in general form, it must be written as $Ax + By = C$, where A, B, and C are real numbers and A and B are not both 0. What would the graph of this equation look like if A and B were both 0?

_____
_____

3.4 More on Linear Equations and Their Graphs

OBJECTIVES

- *To write a given linear equation in slope-intercept form*
- *To identify the slope and y-intercept of an equation written in slope-intercept form*
- *To graph a line using its slope and y-intercept*
- *To write a given linear equation in point-slope form*
- *To find the equation of a line, given two points on the line or its slope and one point*
- *To solve applied problems relating to the graph of a linear equation*

In the previous section of this chapter, we considered linear equations written in the general form and how to graph them. Now we will discuss two other forms of linear equations: the *slope-intercept form* and the *point-slope form*. Using these two forms, we will continue to show how line graphs and their corresponding equations have real-world applications.

Slope-Intercept Form

Recall from Section 3.3 that one approach to graphing an equation written in general form is to isolate y.

$$-5x + y = 2 \qquad \text{An equation in general form}$$
$$y = 5x + 2 \qquad \text{Solve for } y.$$

The linear equation $y = 5x + 2$ is said to be in slope-intercept form. The graph of this equation has slope 5, which is equal to the coefficient of x, and y-intercept $(0, 2)$, where 2 is the constant term of the equation.

Definition

A linear equation is in **slope-intercept form** if it is written as

$$y = mx + b,$$

where m and b are constants. In this form, m is the slope and $(0, b)$ is the y-intercept of the graph of the equation.

In general, we can identify the slope and y-intercept of the graph of any linear equation in slope-intercept form without drawing the graph of the equation. The coefficient of x is the slope m, and the constant term b is the y-coordinate of the y-intercept $(0, b)$.

The following table gives additional examples of equations written in slope-intercept form:

Equation	Slope, m	y-intercept $(0, b)$
$y = \frac{1}{2}x + 1$	$\frac{1}{2}$	$(0, 1)$
$y = 2x - 1$	2	$(0, -1)$
$y = -7x \rightarrow y = -7x + 0$	-7	$(0, 0)$
$y = 5 \rightarrow y = 0x + 5$	0	$(0, 5)$

EXAMPLE 1

Find the slope and y-intercept of the equation $y = 3x - 5$.

SOLUTION The equation $y = 3x - 5$ or $y = 3x + (-5)$ is already in slope-intercept form, $y = mx + b$. The slope m is 3, and the y-intercept is $(0, -5)$ since the equation has constant term -5.

PRACTICE 1

Find the slope and y-intercept of the equation $y = -2x + 3$.

EXAMPLE 2

Express $3x + 5y = 6$ in slope-intercept form.

SOLUTION Since the slope-intercept form of an equation is $y = mx + b$, we need to solve the given equation for y.

$$3x + 5y = 6$$
$$5y = -3x + 6$$
$$\frac{5y}{5} = \frac{-3}{5}x + \frac{6}{5}$$
$$y = -\frac{3}{5}x + \frac{6}{5}$$

So $y = -\frac{3}{5}x + \frac{6}{5}$ is the equation written in slope-intercept form, where m is $-\frac{3}{5}$ and b is $\frac{6}{5}$.

PRACTICE 2

Express $3x - 2y = 4$ in slope-intercept form.

EXAMPLE 3

Write $y - 1 = 5(x - 1)$ in slope-intercept form.

SOLUTION To get the equation in the form $y = mx + b$, we must solve for y.

$$y - 1 = 5(x - 1)$$
$$y - 1 = 5x - 5$$
$$y = 5x - 5 + 1$$
$$y = 5x - 4$$

So $y = 5x - 4$ is the equation written in slope-intercept form, where m is 5 and b is -4.

PRACTICE 3

Change the equation $y - 2 = 4(x + 1)$ to slope-intercept form.

EXAMPLE 4

For the graph of $y = 3x$, find the slope and y-intercept.

SOLUTION We can rewrite $y = 3x$ as $y = 3x + 0$. Now the equation $y = 3x + 0$ is in slope-intercept form, with slope $m = 3$ and $b = 0$. Since $b = 0$, the y-intercept is $(0, 0)$. That is, the graph passes through the origin.

PRACTICE 4

Find the slope and y-intercept of the graph of $y = -x$.

We have already graphed equations of the form $y = mx + b$ by finding three points whose coordinates satisfy the equation. Now let's focus on graphing such equations using the slope and the y-intercept.

Consider the equation $y = 3x - 1$, which has slope 3 and y-intercept $(0, -1)$. Since 3 is $\frac{3}{1}$, we know from the definition of slope that the *rise* is 3 and the *run* is 1. Starting at $(0, -1)$, we move up 3 units and then 1 unit to the right to find a second point $(1, 2)$ on the line. Then we draw the line through the two points $(0, -1)$ and $(1, 2)$.

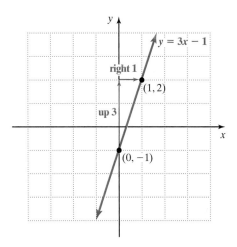

This example leads us to the following rule.

To Graph a Linear Equation in Two Variables Using the Slope and the y-intercept

- First locate the y-intercept.
- Use the slope to find a second point on the line.
- Then draw the line through the two points.

EXAMPLE 5

Graph $y = -\frac{3}{2}x + 2$ using the slope and y-intercept.

SOLUTION Since $y = -\frac{3}{2}x + 2$ is in slope-intercept form, the slope is $-\frac{3}{2}$ and the y-intercept is $(0, 2)$. First we locate the y-intercept $(0, 2)$. Since the slope $-\frac{3}{2}$ equals $\frac{-3}{2}$, from the point $(0, 2)$ we move *down* 3 units and then 2 units to the *right* to find the second point $(2, -1)$. Then we draw the line through the points $(0, 2)$ and $(2, -1)$ as shown in the graph.

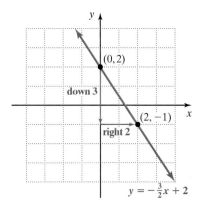

PRACTICE 5

Use the slope and y-intercept to graph $y = -\frac{1}{3}x - 4$.

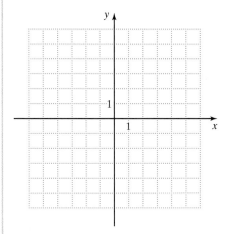

Note that since $\frac{-3}{2} = \frac{3}{-2}$, from the point $(0, 2)$ we could have moved *up* 3 units and then 2 units to the *left* to find the second point $(-2, 5)$ and then drawn the line through $(0, 2)$ and $(-2, 5)$ to obtain the same graph of the equation, as on the following coordinate plane.

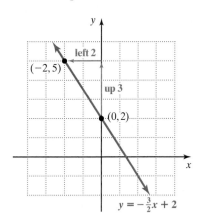

Recall that in Section 3.3 we graphed $2x + 3y = 6$ using the intercepts. We can also graph this equation using the slope and y-intercept. Which method do you prefer? Explain why.

We can use the slope-intercept form to write the equation of a line when given its slope and y-intercept.

EXAMPLE 6

Write the equation of the line with slope $-\frac{4}{5}$ and y-intercept $(0, -3)$.

SOLUTION We are given that the slope is $-\frac{4}{5}$ and the y-intercept is $(0, -3)$. So $m = -\frac{4}{5}$ and $b = -3$. We substitute these values in the slope-intercept form:

$$y = mx + b$$
$$y = -\frac{4}{5}x + (-3), \quad \text{or } y = -\frac{4}{5}x - 3$$

PRACTICE 6

A line on a coordinate plane has slope 1 and intersects the y-axis 2 units above the origin. Write its equation in slope-intercept form.

EXAMPLE 7

Find an equation of the line that is parallel to the graph of $y = 4x + 1$ and has y-intercept $(0, 3)$.

SOLUTION The line $y = 4x + 1$ is in slope-intercept form. The slope of this line is 4. Since parallel lines have the same slope, the line we want will also have slope $m = 4$. Since its y-intercept is $(0, 3)$, $b = 3$. Therefore, the desired equation is $y = 4x + 3$.

PRACTICE 7

What is the equation of the line parallel to the graph of $y = -2x + 3$ with y-intercept $(0, -1)$?

EXAMPLE 8

What is the equation of the line that is perpendicular to the graph of $y = 3x - 1$ and has y-intercept $(0, 1)$?

SOLUTION The line $y = 3x - 1$ is written in slope-intercept form. So its slope is 3. We know that the slopes of two perpendicular lines are negative reciprocals of each other. Therefore, the slope of the line we want has slope $m = -\frac{1}{3}$. Since its y-intercept is $(0, 1)$, $b = 1$. So the desired equation is $y = -\frac{1}{3}x + 1$.

PRACTICE 8

Find the equation of the line that is perpendicular to the graph of $y = 2x + 5$ and has y-intercept $(0, -2)$.

EXAMPLE 9

At her college, a student pays $75 per credit-hour plus a flat student fee of $100. Find an equation in slope-intercept form that relates the amount A that she pays to the number h of credit-hours in her program.

SOLUTION The amount A in dollars that the student pays is the sum of 100 and 75 times the number h of credit-hours in her program. So we have:

$$A = 75h + 100$$

This equation is written in slope-intercept form.

PRACTICE 9

Suppose that your bathtub, which has a capacity of 45 gal, is filled to the top with water. The tub starts to drain at a rate of 3 gal per min. Write an equation in slope-intercept form that relates the amount of water w left in the tub and the time t that the tub has been draining.

Point-Slope Form

The last form of a linear equation that we will discuss is called the point-slope form.

> **Definition**
>
> The **point-slope form** of a linear equation is written as
>
> $$y - y_1 = m(x - x_1),$$
>
> where $x_1, y_1,$ and m are constants. In this form, m is the slope and (x_1, y_1) is a point that lies on the graph of the equation.

This form, although used less frequently than other forms of a linear equation, is particularly useful for finding the equation of a line in two particular situations:

- when we know the slope of the line and a point on it, or
- when we know two points on the line.

EXAMPLE 10

A line with slope -2 passes through the point $(-1, 5)$. Find the equation of this line written in point-slope form.

SOLUTION Since we know a point on the line and the slope of the line, we can substitute directly into the point-slope formula, where $x_1 = -1$, $y_1 = 5$, and $m = -2$.

$$y - y_1 = m(x - x_1)$$
$$y - 5 = -2[x - (\mathbf{-1})]$$
$$y - 5 = -2(x + 1) \qquad \text{Point-slope form.}$$

We can leave this equation in point-slope form, or we can simplify the equation and write it in either general form

$$y - 5 = -2x - 2$$
$$2x + y = 3 \qquad \text{General form.}$$

or in slope-intercept form

$$y = -2x + 3 \qquad \text{Slope-intercept form.}$$

PRACTICE 10

A line passing through the point $(7, 0)$ has slope 2. Find its equation in point-slope form.

EXAMPLE 11

What is the equation of the line passing through the points $(3, 5)$ and $(2, 1)$?

SOLUTION Since we know the coordinates of two points on the line, we can find its slope.

$$m = \frac{y_2 - y_1}{x_2 - x_1} = \frac{5 - 1}{3 - 2} = \frac{4}{1} = 4$$

The line with slope $m = 4$ passing through the point $(3, 5)$ is:

$$y - y_1 = m(x - x_1)$$
$$y - 5 = 4(x - \mathbf{3})$$

The equation found in Example 11 is $y = 4x - 7$ in slope-intercept form. Had we substituted the point $(2, 1)$ rather than the point $(3, 5)$ into the point-slope formula, would the resulting equation be the same?

PRACTICE 11

Find the equation in point-slope form of the line passing through $(7, 7)$ and the origin.

EXAMPLE 12

An accountant's computer decreases in value by $400 a year. The computer was worth $1600 one year after he bought it. Write an equation that gives the value V of the computer in terms of the number of years t since the purchase.

SOLUTION Each year that passes, t increases by 1 and V decreases by 400. Therefore, the graph of the equation we are seeking has slope -400. Because the computer is worth $1600 one year after purchase, the graph passes through the

PRACTICE 12

The total weight of a box used for shipping baseballs increases by 5 oz for each baseball that is packed in the box. A box with 4 balls weighs 27 oz. Write an equation that relates the total weight w of the box to the number of baseballs b packed in the box.

point (1, 1600). Since we know a point on the line as well as its slope, we can find the point-slope form of the equation.

$$V - V_1 = m(t - t_1)$$
$$V - 1600 = -400(t - \mathbf{1})$$

If we like, we can simplify the equation and write it in slope-intercept form:

$$V - 1600 = -400t + 400$$
$$V = -400t + 2000$$

Can you explain why the slope of the line in Example 12 is negative?

Using a Calculator or Computer to Graph Linear Equations

Calculators with graphing capabilities and computers with graphing software allow us to graph equations at the push of a key, even those with complicated coefficients. Although they vary somewhat in terms of features and commands, these machines all graph the equation of your choice on a coordinate plane.

To graph an equation, begin by making certain that the equation is in slope-intercept form. On many graphers, pressing the $\boxed{Y =}$ key results in a screen being displayed on which you enter the equation. For instance, if you wanted to graph $2x - y = 1$, you would first solve for y, resulting in $y = 2x - 1$, and then enter $2x - 1$ to the right of $\backslash$Y1 = on the screen. Pressing the $\boxed{\text{GRAPH}}$ key displays a coordinate plane in which the graph of $y = 2x - 1$ is sketched, as we see on the following screen.

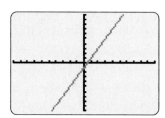

Many graphers have a **TRACE** feature that highlights a point on the graph and displays its coordinates. As you hold down an arrow key, you can see how the coordinates change as the highlighted point moves along the graph.

TIP The viewing window allows you to set the range and scales for the axes. Before you graph an equation, be sure to set the viewing window in which you would like to display the graph.

EXAMPLE 13	PRACTICE 13
Graph $y - x = 2$, and then use the **TRACE** feature to identify the y-intercept.	Graph $2y + x = 3$, and then find the y-intercept with the **TRACE** feature.

SOLUTION

First solve for y: $y = x + 2$. Next, press $\boxed{Y =}$ and enter $x + 2$ to the right of $\backslash$Y1 =. Next set the viewing window in which you want to display the graph. Then press $\boxed{\text{GRAPH}}$ to display the graph of the equation. If the graph of $y = x + 2$ does not appear, check your grapher's instruction manual.

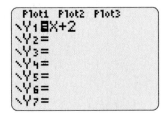 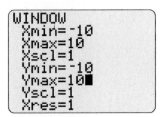

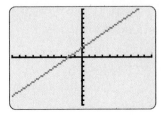

With the **TRACE** feature, run the cursor along the graph until it appears to be on the y-axis. The displayed coordinates of this y-intercept are approximately $x = 0$ and $y = 2$.

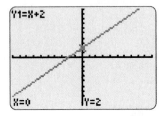

Exercises 3.4

FOR EXTRA HELP

 Student's Solutions Manual

Addison-Wesley Math Tutor Center

MyMathLab

Videotape 4/DVT 4

Complete each table.

1.

Equation	Slope, m	y-intercept (0, b)	Which Graph Type Best Describes the Line? ╱ ╲ — │	x-intercept
$y = 3x - 5$				
$y = -2x$				
$y = 0.7x + 3.5$				
$y = \frac{3}{4}x - \frac{1}{2}$				
$6x + 3y = 12$				
$y = -5$				
$x = -2$				

2.

Equation	Slope, m	y-intercept (0, b)	Which Graph Type Best Describes the Line? ╱ ╲ — │	x-intercept
$y = -3x + 5$				$(\frac{5}{3}, 0)$
$y = 2x$				
$y = 1.5x + 6$				
$y = \frac{2}{3}x + \frac{1}{2}$	$\frac{2}{3}$	$(0, \frac{1}{2})$		$(-\frac{3}{4}, 0)$
$4x + 6y = 24$	$-\frac{2}{3}$			
$y = 0.3$				
$x = 2$				

Find the slope and y-intercept of each equation.

3. $y = -x + 2$ **4.** $y = 3x - 4$

5. $y = -\frac{1}{2}x$ **6.** $y = x$

Write the following equations in slope-intercept form.

7. $x - y = 10$

8. $x + y = 7$

9. $x + 10y = 10$

10. $3x - y = 15$

11. $6x + 4y = 1$

12. $4x - 8y = 12$

13. $2x - 5y = 10$

14. $3x + 5y = 15$

15. $y + 1 = 3(x + 5)$

16. $y - 1 = 3(x - 5)$

Match the equation to its graph.

17. $4x - 2y = 6$

18. $-2x + 4y = 8$

19. $2y - x = 8$

20. $6x + 3y = -9$

a.

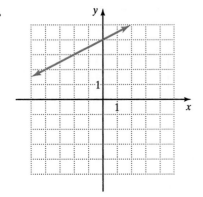

b.

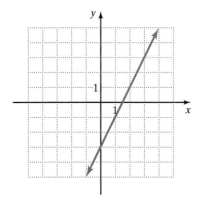

c.

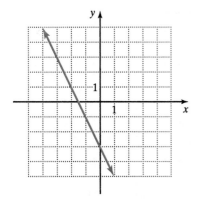

d.

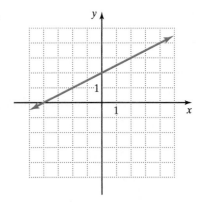

Graph the following equations using the slope and y-intercept.

21. $y = 2x + 1$

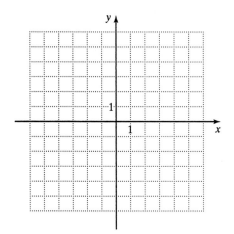

22. $y = -3x + 1$

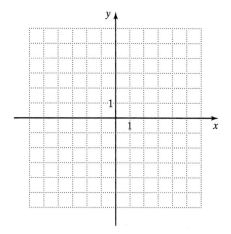

23. $y = -\frac{2}{3}x + 6$

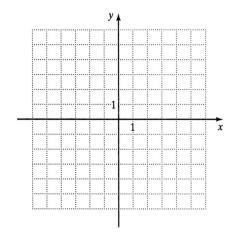

24. $y = \frac{3}{2}x - 6$

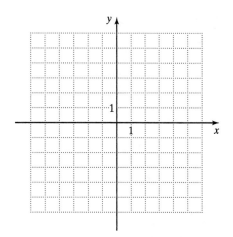

25. $x + y = 1$

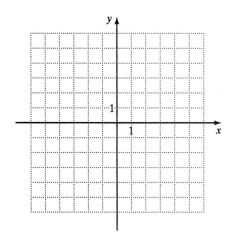

26. $x + y = -4$

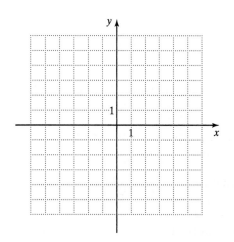

27. $y = -\frac{3}{4}x$

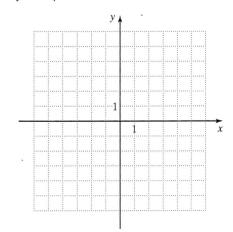

28. $y = \frac{1}{2}x$

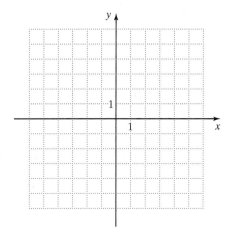

29. $x + 2y = 4$

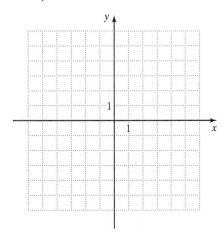

30. $-2x + 3y = 12$

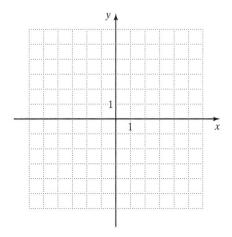

31. $y = 3.735x + 1.056$

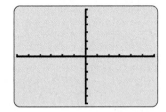

32. $y = -0.875x + 2.035$

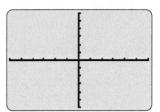

33. Find the equation of the line with slope 3 that passes through the point $(0, 7)$.

34. What is the equation of the line that has slope -1 with y-intercept $(0, -2)$?

35. Find the equation of the line that is parallel to the graph of $y = 5x - 1$ and has x-intercept $(4, 0)$.

36. What is the equation of the line that is parallel to the graph $y = \frac{1}{3}x - 1$ and has y-intercept $(0, 4)$?

37. What is the equation of the line that is perpendicular to the graph of $y = 2x$ and that passes through $(-2, 5)$?

38. Find the equation of the line that is perpendicular to the graph $y = -x$ and that passes through the point $(1, -3)$.

39. Write the equation of the vertical line that passes through the point $(-3, 5)$.

40. What is the equation of the horizontal line passing through the point $(1, -8)$?

41. What equation has the x-axis as its graph?

42. What equation has the y-axis as its graph?

43. What is the equation of the line passing through the points $(2, 1)$ and $(1, 2)$?

44. The points $(5, 1)$ and $(2, -3)$ lie on a line. Find its equation.

Find the equation of each graph.

45.

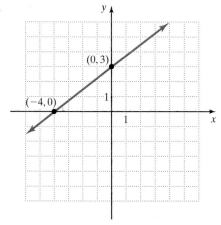

46.

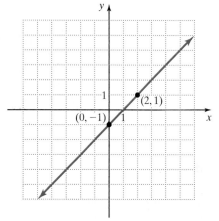

47.

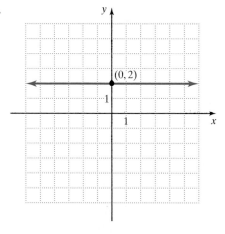

48.

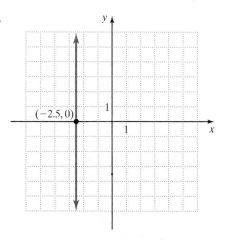

49.

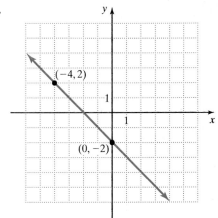

50.

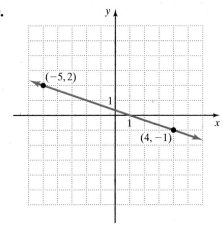

Applications

Solve.

51. The following graph describes the relationship between Fahrenheit temperature *F* and Celsius temperature *C*.

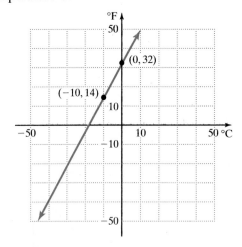

   a. Find the slope of the line.

   b. Find the equation of the line in slope-intercept form.

   c. If water boils at 212°F, use the equation found in part (b) to find the Celsius temperature at which water boils.

52. The owner of a shop buys a piece of machinery for $1500. The value *V* of the machinery declines by $150 per year.

   a. Write an equation for *V* after *t* years.

   b. Graph the equation found in part (a).

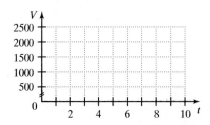

c. Explain the significance of the two intercepts in this context.

53. A utility company charges its residential customers for electricity each month a flat fee plus 4 cents per kilowatt-hour (kWh) consumed. Last month, you used 500 kWh of electricity, and your bill amounted to $35.

a. Express as an equation in point-slope form the relationship between your monthly bill y in cents and the number x of kilowatt-hours of electricity consumed.

b. Express the equation found in part (a) in slope-intercept form.

c. What does the y-intercept represent in this situation?

54. A condo unit has been appreciating in value at $5000 per year. Three years after it was purchased, it was worth $65,000.

a. Find an equation that expresses the value y of the condo in terms of the number x of years since it was purchased.

b. Graph the equation found in part (a).

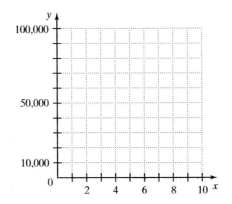

c. What is the significance of the y-intercept in this situation?

55. During a lightning storm, the relationship between the number of miles away L that lightning strikes and the number of seconds t between the flash of lightning and the sound of thunder is linear. When lightning strikes a tree 5 mi away, 1 sec passes before you hear the thunder. But when lightning strikes an old house 10 mi away, 2 sec pass between the lightning and the thunder.

a. Express the relationship between L and t as an equation in point-slope form.

b. Write the equation found in part (a) in slope-intercept form.

56. An air conditioner can reduce the temperature in a room by 8°F every 5 min. The temperature in the room was 62°F after the air conditioner had been running for 10 min.

a. Write as a linear equation the relationship between the time that the air conditioner has been running and the temperature in the room.

b. Explain how you could have predicted whether the slope of the graph of this equation is positive or negative.

57. A salesperson earns a salary of $1500 per month plus a commission of 3% of the total monthly sales.

    a. Write a linear equation giving the salesperson's total monthly income I in terms of sales S.

    b. Graph the equation found in part (a).

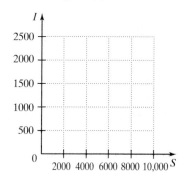

    c. Find the salesperson's income on monthly sales of $6200.

58. When the brakes on a train are applied, the speed of the train decreases by the same amount every second. Two seconds after applying the brakes, the train's speed is 88 mph. After 4 sec, its speed is 60 mph.

    a. Write an equation relating the speed s of the train and the time elapsed t seconds after applying the brakes.

    b. Graph the equation found in part (a).

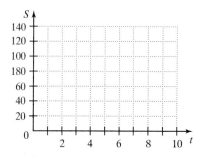

    c. What was the speed of the train when the brakes were first applied?

59. Pressure under water increases with greater depth. The pressure P on an object and the depth d below sea level are related by a linear equation. The pressure at sea level is 1 atmosphere (atm), whereas 33 ft below sea level the pressure is 2 atm. Find the equation relating P and d.

60. The length of a heated object and the temperature of the object are related by a linear equation. A rod at 0° Celsius is 10 m long, and at 25° Celsius it is 10.1 m long. Write an equation for length in terms of temperature.

61. When a force is applied to a spring, its length changes. The length L and the force F are related by a linear equation. The spring shown here was initially 10 in. long when no force was applied. What is the equation that relates length and force?

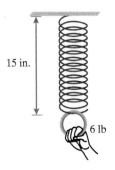

15 in.

6 lb

62. A company purchased a computer workstation for $8000. After 3 years, the estimated value of the workstation was $4400. If the value V in dollars and the age a of the workstation are related by a linear equation, find an equation that relates V and a.

● *Check your answers on page A-13.*

Mindstretchers

TECHNOLOGY

1. Consider $2x - 7 = 0$, which is a linear equation in x.

a. Solve the equation.

_____

b. On a graphing calculator or computer with graphing software, graph $y = 2x - 7$. Then find the x-intercept of the line. Explain in a sentence or two how you can use this approach to solve the equation $2x - 7 = 0$.

_____

_____

_____

_____

CRITICAL THINKING

2. Consider the equation $y = mx + b$. Explain under what circumstances its graph lies completely in Quadrants I and II.

_____

_____

MATHEMATICAL REASONING

3. What kind of line corresponds to an equation that can be written in *general form* but in neither slope-intercept form nor point-slope form?

_____

_____

_____

3.5 Linear Inequalities and Their Graphs

OBJECTIVES

- *To identify the coordinates of points that satisfy a given linear inequality in two variables*

- *To graph a linear inequality in two variables*

- *To solve applied problems relating to the graph of a linear inequality*

In Section 2.6, we showed how to graph inequalities in one variable on a number line. In such inequalities, the solutions are real numbers.

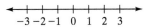

Now we consider graphing inequalities in two variables on a coordinate plane. In this case, the solutions are ordered pairs of real numbers.

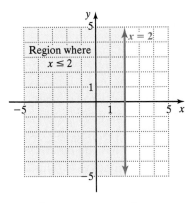

In this section, we focus our attention on graphing linear inequalities in *two* variables, such as $2x + 3y > 1$.

Definition

A **linear inequality in two variables** is an inequality that can be written in the form $Ax + By < C$, where A, B, and C are real numbers and A and B are not both 0. The inequality symbol can be $<$, $>$, $\leq$, or $\geq$.

As we will see, these inequalities have as their graphs half-planes, which are regions of the coordinate plane bounded by lines.

Consider some situations that give rise to such inequalities:

20 is the minimum number of men m and women w invited to a party. $\rightarrow$ $20 \leq m + w$

Your income i exceeds your expenses e by more than \$1000. $\rightarrow$ $i > e + 1000$

Let's look at what we mean by a *solution* in such inequalities.

Definition

A **solution to an inequality in two variables** is an ordered pair of numbers that when substituted for the variables makes the inequality a true statement.

EXAMPLE 1

Is the ordered pair $(2, 5)$ a solution to the inequality $y \geq x + 1$?

SOLUTION When we substitute 2 for x and 5 for y in the given inequality, it becomes

$$y \geq x + 1$$
$$5 \overset{?}{\geq} 2 + 1$$
$$5 \geq 3 \quad \text{True.}$$

Since $5 \geq 3$ is true, the ordered pair $(2, 5)$ is a solution to $y \geq x + 1$. Is the ordered pair $(6, 5)$ a solution to this inequality?

PRACTICE 1

Is $(1, 3)$ a solution to the inequality $y < x - 1$?

By the *graph* of an inequality in two variables, we mean the set of all points on the plane whose coordinates satisfy the inequality. To explore what such a graph looks like, let's consider $y \geq 2x$. To find the graph of this inequality, we first graph the corresponding equation $y = 2x$. Notice that the *boundary line* $y = 2x$ is drawn as a solid line since the original inequality symbol is $\geq$. This line cuts the plane into two half-planes.

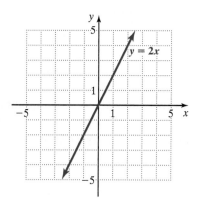

Next we take an arbitrary point on either side of the boundary line—a *test point*. If the coordinates of the test point satisfy the inequality, then the desired graph contains the half-plane in which the test point lies. Otherwise, the desired graph contains the other half-plane.

Suppose that we take $(4, 0)$ as our test point.

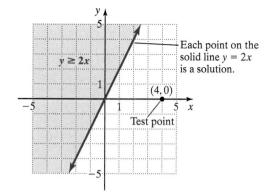

$$y \geq 2x$$
$$0 \overset{?}{\geq} 2(4)$$
$$0 \geq 8 \quad \text{False.}$$

Since the inequality does not hold for the point $(4, 0)$, the half-plane that we want is the region above the graph of $y = 2x$, so we shade this region. Therefore, the graph of $y \geq 2x$ is the boundary line and the shaded region.

If the inequality had been $y > 2x$, the boundary line would not have been part of the graph. We would have indicated the exclusion of the boundary with a broken line, as in the following diagram.

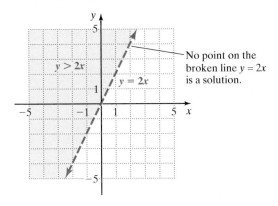

No point on the broken line $y = 2x$ is a solution.

To Graph a Linear Inequality in Two Variables

● Graph the corresponding linear equation. For an inequality with the symbol $\leq$ or $\geq$, draw a solid line; for an inequality with the symbol $<$ or $>$, draw a broken line. This line is the boundary between two half-planes.

● Choose a test point in either half-plane and substitute the coordinates of this point in the inequality. If the resulting inequality is true, then the graph of the inequality is the half-plane containing the test point. If it is not true, then the other half-plane is the graph. A solid line is part of the graph, and a broken line is not.

EXAMPLE 2

Find the graph of $y - 2x < 4$.

SOLUTION First, we graph the equation $y - 2x = 4$. Solving for y gives $y = 2x + 4$. Next we graph the line. We draw a broken line since the original inequality symbol is $<$. Then we choose in either half-plane a test point, say $(0, 0)$.

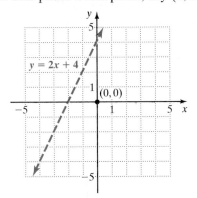

We substitute $x = 0$ and $y = 0$ into the inequality:

$$y - 2x \overset{?}{<} 4$$
$$0 - 2 \cdot 0 \overset{?}{<} 4$$
$$0 < 4 \quad \text{True.}$$

Since the inequality is true, the graph of the inequality is the half-plane containing the test point. So the half-plane below

PRACTICE 2

Graph the inequality $y + 3x \geq 6$.

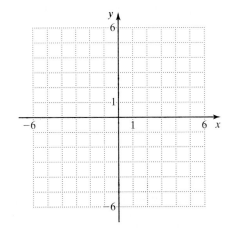

the line is our graph. Note that the graph does not include the boundary line since the original inequality symbol is $<$.

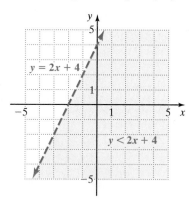

We can test any point on the graph. Why is $(0, 0)$ a good choice?

EXAMPLE 3

Graph $x < 0$.

SOLUTION The boundary line $x = 0$ is the y-axis. We need to select a test point on either side of the boundary line. Let's take the point, $(1, 0)$ as the test point, which is in the half-plane to the right of the line $x = 0$. Substituting into the inequality $x < 0$, we get $1 < 0$, which is not true. So the graph is the half-plane to the left of the line $x = 0$, but not including this line.

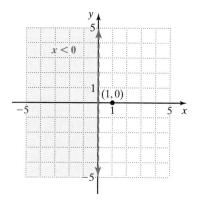

PRACTICE 3

Find the graph of $y \geq -5$.

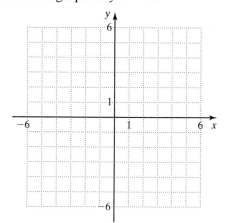

EXAMPLE 4

Graph the inequality $x - 3y < -9$ in the first quadrant.

SOLUTION The corresponding equation is $x - 3y = -9$. Solving for y gives $y = \frac{1}{3}x + 3$. Next, we graph this line, drawing a broken line since the original inequality symbol is $<$.

Taking $(0, 0)$ as the test point, we check whether $0 - 3(0) < -9$. Since this inequality does not hold, the test point is not part of the graph. So the graph in Quadrant I is the region in the quadrant above the line $y = \frac{1}{3}x + 3$, but not including it.

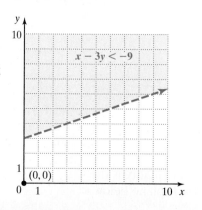

PRACTICE 4

Find the graph of $x - 2y > -6$ in Quadrant I.

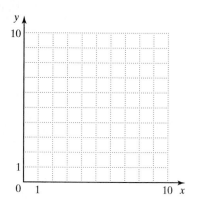

EXAMPLE 5

A clothing factory makes $50 on each coat sold and $20 on each jacket sold. To make a profit, the total amount of money made must exceed the company's overhead of $1000.

a. Express as an inequality: The amount of money made on selling c coats and j jackets is greater than the overhead.

b. Graph this inequality.

c. Use this graph to decide whether selling 10 coats and 12 jackets results in a profit.

SOLUTION

a. The factory makes $50 on each coat sold. Therefore, the factory makes $50c$ dollars on selling c coats. Similarly, the factory makes $20j$ dollars on selling j jackets. Since the total amount of money made must be greater than the overhead of $1000, the inequality is

$$50c + 20j > 1000 \quad \text{or} \quad 5c + 2j > 100.$$

Can you explain why these two inequalities are equivalent?

b. To graph the inequality $5c + 2j > 100$, we first graph the corresponding equation, $5c + 2j = 100$. The boundary line is not included since the linear inequality is $5c + 2j > 100$. Using $(0, 0)$ as a test point, we see that the inequality $5 \cdot 0 + 2 \cdot 0 > 100$ is false. So the graph of $5c + 2j > 100$ is the region in Quadrant I above the boundary line, but not including the line.

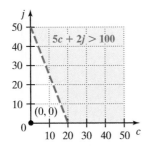

c. To decide whether there was a profit when selling 10 coats and 12 jackets, we plot the point $(10, 12)$. Since the point lies *outside* the graph of our inequality, there was no profit.

PRACTICE 5

Each day, a refinery can produce both diesel fuel and gasoline, with a total maximum output of 3000 gal.

a. Express this relationship as an inequality, where d represents the number of gallons of diesel fuel produced and g the number of gallons of gasoline produced.

b. Graph this inequality.

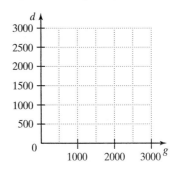

c. Explain the significance of the intercepts of this graph.

Exercises 3.5

FOR EXTRA HELP

📖 *Student's Solutions Manual*

 Addison-Wesley Math Tutor Center

🚪 *MyMathLab*

📼 *Videotape 4/DVT 4*

Decide if the given ordered pair is a solution to the inequality.

1. $y < 3x$ $(0, 0)$

2. $y > -5x$ $(-1, 4)$

3. $y \geq 2x - 1$ $(-\frac{1}{2}, -2)$

4. $y \leq -\frac{2}{3}x + 5$ $(6, 1)$

5. $2x - 3y > 10$ $(10, 8)$

6. $5x + 3y \geq 12$ $(0, -2)$

Each solid or broken line is the graph of $y = x$. Shade in the graph of the given inequality.

7. $y > x$

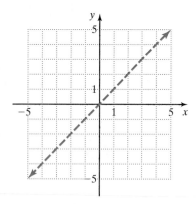

8. $y \geq x$

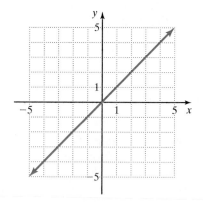

9. $x \leq y$

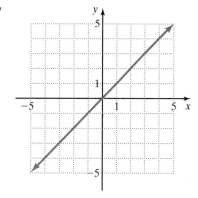

10. $x < y$

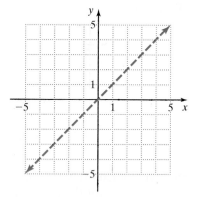

11. $y < x$

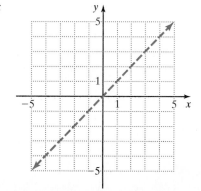

12. $y \leq x$

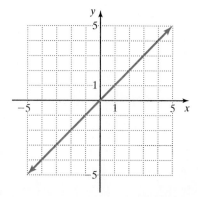

Match each inequality to its graph.

13. $y < \frac{1}{4}x - 1$

14. $y > -2x + 3$

15. $x - 4y \leq 4$

16. $4x + 2y \geq 6$

a.

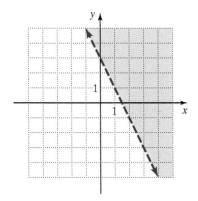

b.

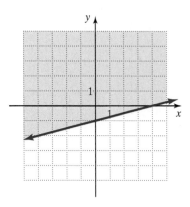

c.

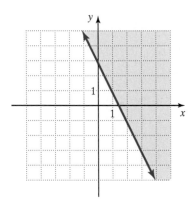

d.

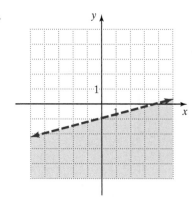

Graph the linear inequality.

17. $x > -5$

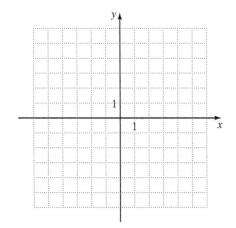

18. $x > 3$

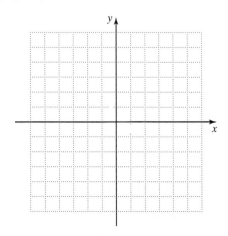

19. $y < 0$

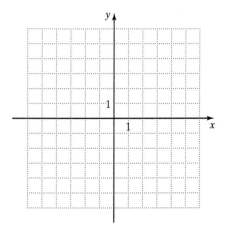

20. $y < 4$

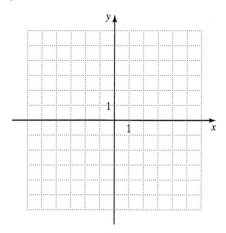

21. $y \leq 3x$

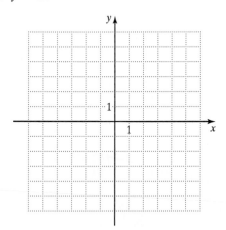

22. $y \leq -x$

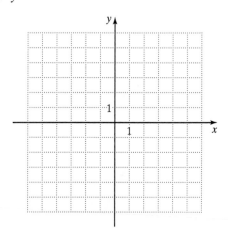

23. $y \geq -2x$

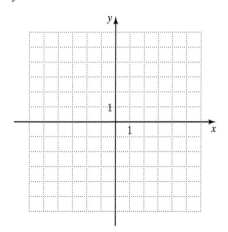

24. $y \geq 4x$

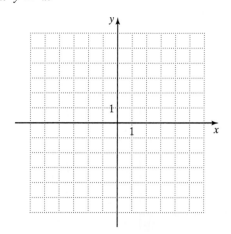

25. $y \leq \frac{1}{2}x$

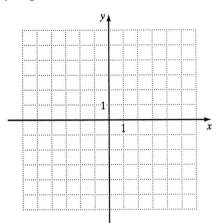

26. $y > -\frac{2}{3}x$

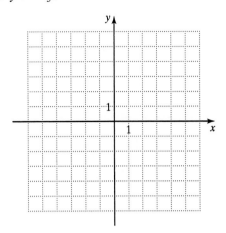

27. $y > 3x + 5$

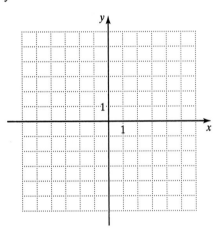

28. $y \geq -x - 1$

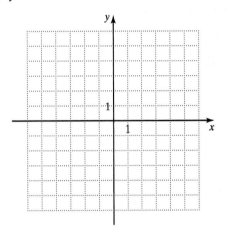

29. $5y - x > 10$

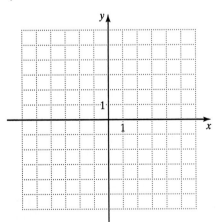

30. $4y + x < -12$

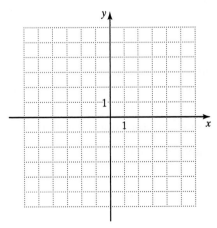

31. $2x - 3y \geq 3$

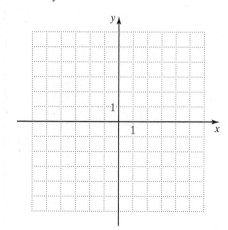

32. $6x - 4y \leq 8$

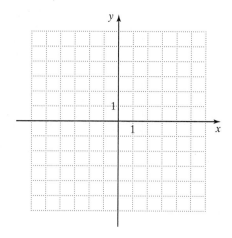

Applications

Solve.

33. According to a guideline, a family's housing expenses h should be less than $\frac{1}{4}$ of the family's combined income i.

   a. Express this guideline as an inequality.

   b. Graph this inequality.

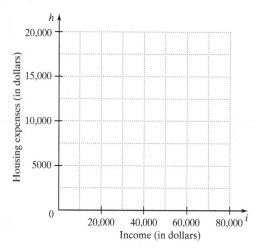

   c. Choose a point on the graph. For this point, explain why the guideline holds.

34. To purchase an apartment in a particular building, a buyer is allowed to take out a mortgage m that is at most 75% of the apartment's selling price s.

   a. Express this relationship as an inequality.

   b. Graph this inequality.

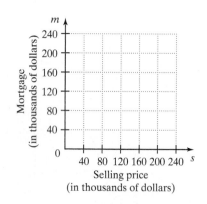

c. Plot the point (100, 90). For this point, explain in terms of the mortgage policy of the building whether the buyer will be able to buy the apartment.

35. A printing company ships x copies of a college's telephone directory to the uptown campus and y copies to the downtown campus. The company must ship a total of at least 200 copies to these two locations.

  a. Express this relationship as an inequality.

  b. Graph this inequality.

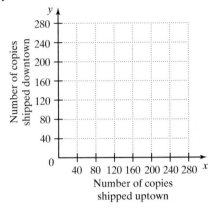

  c. Give the coordinates of a point that satisfies the inequality. Check that the coordinates satisfy the company's shipping requirement.

36. An investor has a maximum of $1000 with which to purchase stock. He purchases x shares of stock that sell for $12 apiece and y shares of stock selling for $5 apiece.

  a. Express this information as an inequality.

  b. Graph this inequality.

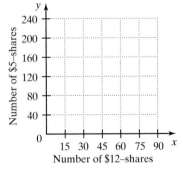

  c. Find a solution to this inequality.

37. A local gourmet coffee shop sells small and large gift baskets. A small gift basket sells for $30 and a large gift basket sells for $75. The coffee shop would like a revenue of at least $1500 per month on the sale of gift baskets.

  a. Write an inequality, where x is the number of small gift baskets sold in a month and y is the number of large gift baskets sold, to represent this situation.

b. Graph this inequality.

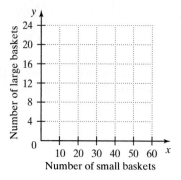

c. Use the graph to determine if selling 20 small gift baskets and 20 large gift baskets will generate the desired revenue.

38. In moving into a new apartment, a young couple needs to borrow money for both furniture and a car. The loan for furniture has a 10% annual interest rate, whereas the car loan has a 5% annual interest rate. The couple can afford at most $2000 in interest payments for the year.

a. Express the given information as an inequality, representing the car loan by c and the furniture loan by f.

b. Graph this inequality.

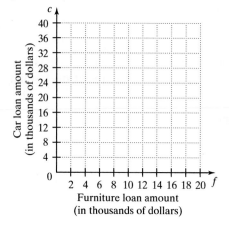

c. What is the maximum car loan that the couple can afford?

d. If the couple borrows $20,000 for the car loan, what is the most that they can afford to borrow for furniture?

39. While on a diet, a model wants to snack on fresh apples and bananas. An apple contains 60 calories and a banana contains 100 calories. If she wants to consume fewer than 300 calories, find the number of apples a and the number of bananas b that she can eat. Solve this problem graphically.

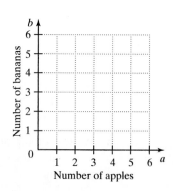

40. A student on spring break wants to drive no more than 300 mi in one day. The trip is two highways. On the first highway, the student drives at an average speed of 60 mph for x hr and on the second highway at a speed of 50 mph for y hr. What are some possible times that the student can drive? Solve this problem graphically.

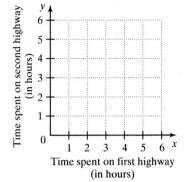

41. A plane is carrying bottled water and medicine to victims of a flood. Each bottle of water weighs 10 lb, and each container of medicine weighs 15 lb. The plane can carry a maximum of 50,000 lb of cargo.

a. Express this weight limitation of the cargo as an inequality in terms of the number of bottles of water w and the number of medicine containers m in the plane.

b. Graph this inequality.

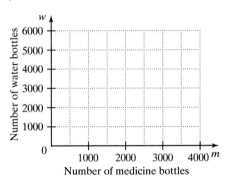

c. Identify several quantities of water and medicine that the plane can carry.

42. An elevator has a maximum capacity of 1600 lb. Suppose that the average weight of an adult is 160 lb and the average weight of a child is 40 lb.

a. Write an inequality that relates the number of adults a and the number of children c who can ride an elevator without overloading it.

b. Graph this inequality.

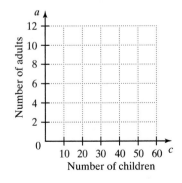

c. What is an example of a group of people who will overload the elevator?

43. A student has two part-time jobs. One pays $8 per hour, and the other $10 per hour. Between the two jobs, the student needs to earn at least $200 per week.

   a. Write an inequality that shows the number of hours that the student can work at each job.

   b. Graph this inequality.

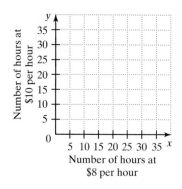

   c. Give some examples of the number of hours that the student can work at each job.

44. Scientists who study weather have developed linear models that relate a region's weather conditions to the kind of vegetation that grows in the region. One such model predicts desert conditions if $3t - 35p > 140$, where t represents the average annual temperature (in degrees Fahrenheit) and p the annual precipitation (in inches).

   a. Graph this relationship on the coordinate plane.

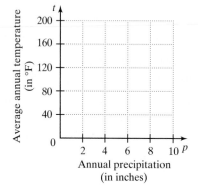

   b. Give some examples of weather conditions that this model predicts will lead to desert conditions.

● *Check your answers on page A-14.*

Mindstretchers

MATHEMATICAL REASONING

1. Consider the three graphs: $y < b$, $y = b$, and $y > b$, where b is a positive number. If you were to graph $y < b$, $y = b$, and $y > b$ on the same coordinate plane, what would you get? Would you get the same answer if b were negative?

_____

_____

GROUPWORK

2. In playing a carnival game, you roll a pair of dice—a red die and a blue die—each with six faces numbered 1, 2, 3, 4, 5, and 6. The grid below shows all the possible outcomes when you roll the two dice.

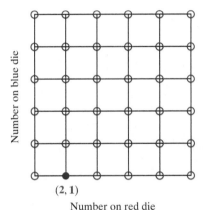

Number on blue die

(2, 1)

Number on red die

For each point on the grid, the first coordinate represents the roll on the red die and the second coordinate represents the roll on the blue die. For instance, the point (2, 1) corresponds to rolling a 2 on the red and a 1 on the blue.

a. How many points in all are there on the grid? _____

b. If the number on the blue die is greater than the number on the red die, you will win a prize. Fill in the points on the grid that correspond to winning a prize. How many points did you fill in? _____

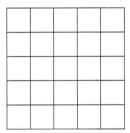

c. What fraction of the total number of points on the grid did you fill in? What does this fraction represent?

_____

3. Compare solving a linear *equation* in two variables by graphing with solving a linear *inequality* in two variables by graphing. What are the similarities? What are the differences? _____

_____

_____

_____

_____

_____

_____

_____

_____

_____

CONCEPT/SKILL	DESCRIPTION	EXAMPLE
[3.1] Coordinate Plane	A flat surface on which we draw graphs.	
[3.1] Ordered Pair	A pair of numbers that represents a point in the coordinate plane.	
[3.1] Quadrant	One of four regions of a coordinate plane separated by axes.	
[3.2] Slope	The **slope** m of a line passing through the points (x_1, y_1) and (x_2, y_2): $$m = \frac{y_2 - y_1}{x_2 - x_1}, \quad \text{where } x_1 \neq x_2$$	For $(1, 5)$ and $(-2, 6)$, $$m = \frac{6 - 5}{-2 - 1} = \frac{1}{-3} = -\frac{1}{3}$$
[3.2] Parallel Lines	Two lines are **parallel** if and only if their slopes are equal. That is, if the slopes are m_1 and m_2, then $m_1 = m_2$.	The line passing through $(0, 1)$ and $(2, 5)$ and the line passing through $(3, 6)$ and $(1, 2)$ are parallel since both lines have slope 2.
[3.2] Perpendicular Lines	Two lines are **perpendicular** if and only if the product of their slopes is -1. That is, if the slopes are m_1 and m_2, then $m_1 \cdot m_2 = -1$.	The line passing through $(0, 3)$ and $(1, 4)$ and the line passing through $(2, 8)$ and $(3, 7)$ are perpendicular since the product of their slopes, 1 and -1, is -1.

continued

CONCEPT/SKILL	DESCRIPTION	EXAMPLE
[3.3] Linear Equation in Two Variables	An equation that can be written in the general form $Ax + By = C$, where A, B, and C are real numbers and A and B are not both 0.	$3x + 5y = 7$
[3.3] Solution of an Equation in Two Variables	An ordered pair of numbers that when substituted for the variables makes the equation true.	$(1, 5)$ is a solution of the equation $y = x + 4$: $5 \overset{?}{=} 1 + 4$ $5 = 5$ True.
[3.3] Graph of a Linear Equation in Two Variables	All points whose coordinates satisfy the equation.	
[3.3] To Graph a Linear Equation in Two Variables	• Isolate one of the variables—usually y—if it is not already done. • Choose three x-values, entering them in a table. • Complete the table by calculating the corresponding y-values. • Plot the three points—two to draw the line and the third to serve as a *checkpoint*. • Check that the points seem to lie on the same line. • Draw the line passing through the points.	To graph $y - 3x = 1$: $$y = 3x + 1$$ | x	$y = 3x + 1$	(x, y)
0	$y = 3(0) + 1$	$(0, 1)$
1	$y = 3(1) + 1$	$(1, 4)$
2	$y = 3(2) + 1$	$(2, 7)$ |
[3.3] Intercepts of a Line	The x-intercept: the point where the graph crosses the x-axis. The y-intercept: the point where the graph crosses the y-axis.	

continued

▨ = CONCEPT   ▨ = SKILL

CONCEPT/SKILL	DESCRIPTION	EXAMPLE
[3.3] To Graph a Linear Equation in Two Variables Using the x- and y-intercepts	• Let $x = 0$ and find the y-intercept. • Let $y = 0$ and find the x-intercept. • Find a checkpoint. • Plot the three points. • Check that the points seem to lie on the same line. • Draw the line passing through the points.	To graph $2x + 3y = 6$: | x	$y = -\frac{2}{3}x + 2$	(x, y)
0	$y = -\frac{2}{3}(0) + 2 = 2$	$(0, 2)$
3	$y = -\frac{2}{3}(3) + 2 = 0$	$(3, 0)$
6	$y = -\frac{2}{3}(6) + 2 = -2$	$(6, -2)$ | 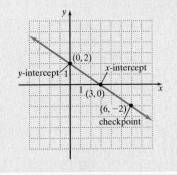
[3.4] Slope-Intercept Form	A linear equation written as $y = mx + b$, where m and b are constants. In this form, m is the slope and $(0, b)$ is the y-intercept of the graph of the equation.	The line with slope 5 and y-intercept $(0, 2)$: $$y = mx + b$$ $$y = 5x + 2$$
[3.4] To Graph a Linear Equation in Two Variables Using the Slope and y-intercept	• First locate the y-intercept. • Use the slope to find a second point on the line. • Then draw the line through the two points.	To graph $y = 3x - 1$: The y-intercept is $(0, -1)$ and the slope is 3. 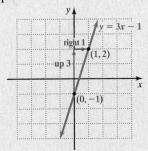
[3.4] Point-Slope Form	A linear equation written as $y - y_1 = m(x - x_1)$, where x_1, y_1, and m are constants. In this form, m is the slope and (x_1, y_1) is a point that lies on the graph of the equation.	The line with slope 5 passing through the point $(2, 1)$: $$y - y_1 = m(x - x_1)$$ $$y - 1 = 5(x - 2)$$

continued

| = CONCEPT | | = SKILL |

CONCEPT/SKILL	DESCRIPTION	EXAMPLE
[3.5] Linear Inequality in Two Variables	An inequality that can be written in the form $Ax + By < C$, where A, B, and C are real numbers and A and B are not both 0. The inequality symbol can be $<$, $>$, $\geq$, or $\leq$.	$5x + 3y < 1$
[3.5] Solution of an Inequality in Two Variables	An ordered pair of numbers that when substituted for the variables makes the inequality a true statement.	$(3, 1)$ is a solution to the inequality $x < 5y$: $3 < 5(1)$ $3 < 5$ True.
[3.5] To Graph a Linear Inequality in Two Variables	● Graph the corresponding linear equation. For an inequality with the symbol $\leq$ or $\geq$, draw a solid line; for an inequality with the symbol $<$ or $>$, draw a broken line. This line is the boundary between two half-planes. ● Choose a test point in either half-plane and substitute the coordinates of this point in the inequality. If the resulting inequality is true, then the graph of the inequality is the half-plane containing the test point. If it is not true, then the other half-plane is the graph. A solid line is part of the graph, and a broken line is not.	To graph $y > x + 1$, first graph the line $y = x + 1$. The inequality does not hold for the test point $(0, 0)$. The graph of $y > x + 1$ is the half-plane above and excluding the line $y = x + 1$.

To help you review this chapter, solve these problems.

[3.1]

1. Plot the points with the given coordinates.

$A(0, 5)$ $B(-1, -6)$ $C(3, -4)$ $D(-2, 2)$

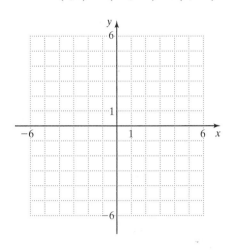

2. Fill in the coordinates of each point.

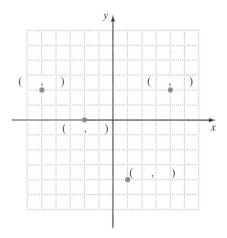

Identify the quadrant in which each point is located:

3. $(5, -1)$

4. $(-7, -2)$

[3.2]

Compute the slope m of the line that passes through the given points. Plot these points on the coordinate plane, and draw the line.

5. $(2, 0)$ and $(3, 5)$, $m =$

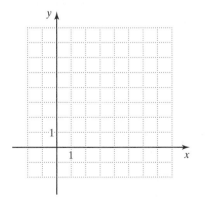

6. $(5, 7)$ and $(2, 7)$, $m =$

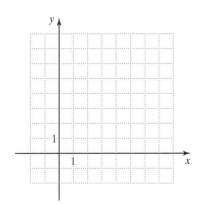

Draw the line on the coordinate plane based on the given information.

7. Passes through $(3, -1)$ and $m = 4$

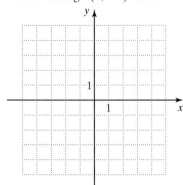

8. Passes through $(0, 0)$ and $m = -\frac{1}{2}$

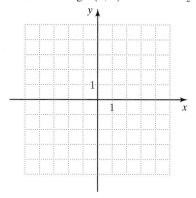

Determine whether the slope of each graph is positive, negative, zero, or undefined.

9.

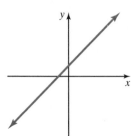

10.

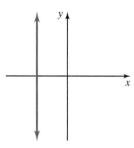

11.

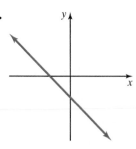

12.

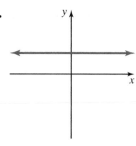

Determine whether $\overleftrightarrow{AB}$ and $\overleftrightarrow{CD}$ are parallel or perpendicular.

13. $A(5, 0)$ $B(3, 0)$ $C(-3, -2)$ $D(1, -2)$

14. $A(4, 8)$ $B(5, 9)$ $C(2, -3)$ $D(0, -1)$

For the following graphed line, find

15. the *x*-intercept.

16. the *y*-intercept.

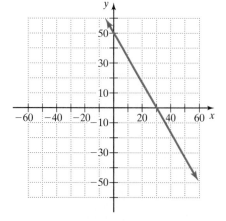

[3.3]

Complete each table of values for the given equation.

17. $y = 2x - 5$

x	y
0	
1	
	0
	1

18. $y = -x + 3$

x	y
2	
5	
	7
	-5

Graph.

19. $4x - 3y = -12$

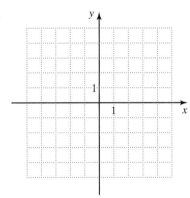

20. $x + 2y = -6$

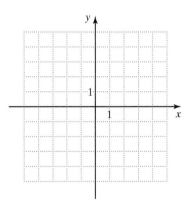

21. $y = \frac{1}{2}x$

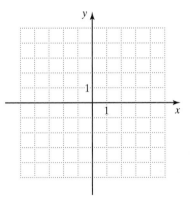

22. $y = -x + 2$

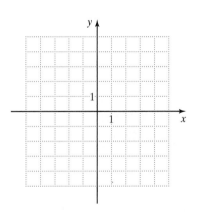

[3.4]

Write each equation in slope-intercept form.

23. $x - y = 10$

24. $x + 2y = -1$

Complete the following table.

	Equation	Slope, m	y-intercept (0, b)	Indicate Which Graph Type Best Describes the Line. ╱ ╲ —		x-intercept
25.	$y = 4x - 16$				
26.	$y = -\frac{1}{3}x$				

27. Find the slope of a line perpendicular to the line $5x - 10y = 20$.

28. Find the slope of a line parallel to the line $6x - 2y = 2$.

29. Find the equation of the line with slope -1 that passes through the point $(3, 5)$.

30. Write the equation of the horizontal line that passes through the point $(3, 0)$.

31. The points $(2, 0)$ and $(1, 5)$ lie on a line. Find its equation.

32. What is an equation of the line passing through the points $(3, 1)$ and $(-2, 0)$?

Find the equation of each graph.

33.

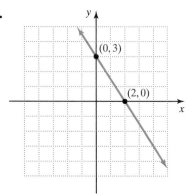

34.

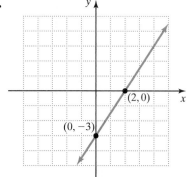

[3.5]

Decide if the ordered pair is a solution to the inequality.

35. $(-2, 7)$, $x + y < 1$

36. $(1, -4)$, $2x - 3y \geq 14$

Each line is the graph of $y = -x$. Shade in the graph of the given inequality.

37. $y > -x$

38. $y < -x$

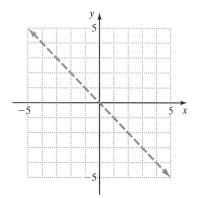

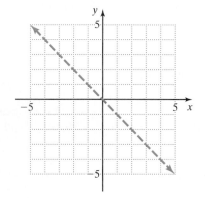

Graph the linear inequality.

39. $y \leq 2x$

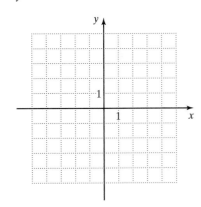

40. $y - x > -1$

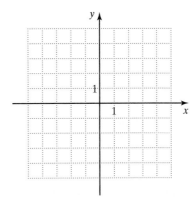

Mixed Applications

Solve.

41. A bed and breakfast charges R dollars for renting a room for d days.

Number of Days Stayed d	Cost of the Rental R
2	180
5	450

a. Graph the points given in the table. Draw a line passing through the points.

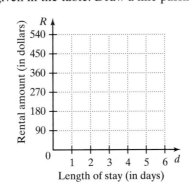

Length of stay (in days)

b. What is the R-intercept of this line? Explain its significance in terms of renting a room.

42. The following table shows the cost C in cents of duplicating q flyers at a print shop.

Quantity q	Cost C
1	4
10	40

a. Plot the points given in the table and draw the line passing through them.

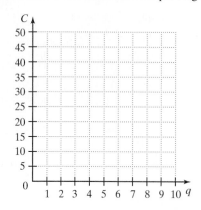

b. Calculate the slope of this line. Explain its significance in terms of the price structure at the print shop.

43. A child walks toward a wall, stands still, and then again walks toward the wall. Which of the following graphs could describe this motion? Explain your answer.

a.

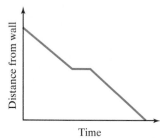

b.

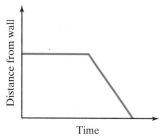

c.

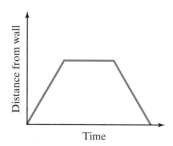

44. The graph shows the altitude of an airplane during a flight. Write a brief story describing the altitude of the plane relative to the duration of the flight.

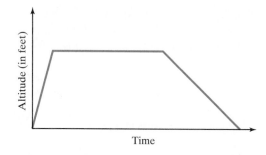

45. A novelist negotiated the following deal with her publisher: a $20,000 bonus plus 9% of book sales.

    a. Express the relationship between her income i and book sales s.

    b. Draw a graph of this equation for sales up to $500,000.

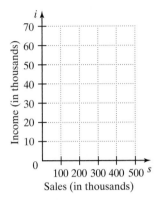

46. A bank account with an initial balance of $100 earns simple interest at an annual rate of 4%. The amount A in the account after t years is given by

$$A = 100 + 4t$$

    a. Graph this equation.

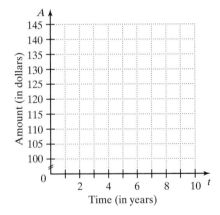

    b. What is the A-intercept of this graph? Explain its significance in terms of the bank account.

47. The width of a jewel case is $\frac{1}{4}$ of an inch for a single compact disc and $\frac{1}{2}$ of an inch for double compact discs. If there are s single jewel cases and d double jewel cases on a shelf 30 in. in length, then

$$\tfrac{1}{4}s + \tfrac{1}{2}d < 30.$$

    a. Graph this inequality.

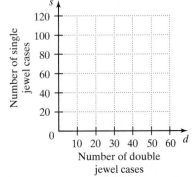

b. From this graph, identify one possible combination of single and double jewel boxes that will fit on the shelf.

48. To be able to catch up with a friend driving away at a speed of 50 mph, it is necessary to cover a distance of d miles in t hours, where

$$d > 50t$$

a. Graph this inequality.

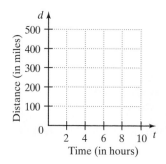

b. From this graph, choose a point in the shaded region. Explain what its coordinates mean in terms of catching up with the friend.

• Check your answers on page A-16.

Chapter 3 Posttest

To see whether you have mastered the topics in this chapter, take this test.

1. On the coordinate plane shown, plot the points $A(-2, 0)$ and $B(5, 3)$.

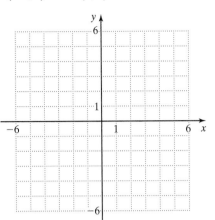

2. In which quadrant is the point $(-5, 3)$ located?

3. Given two points $C(8, 1)$ and $D(3, -4)$, compute the slope of the line that passes through the points.

4. Are the graphs of $y = 3x + 1$ and $y = 3x - 2$ parallel? Explain how you know.

5. For the points $A(0, 1)$, $B(2, 8)$, $C(0, 6)$, and $D(7, 4)$, indicate whether $\overleftrightarrow{AB}$ is perpendicular to $\overleftrightarrow{CD}$. Explain.

6. In the following graph, find the x-intercept and the y-intercept.

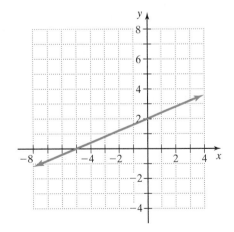

7. The graph on the following coordinate plane shows how the rental cost at a local car rental establishment relates to the number of miles that the car has been driven.

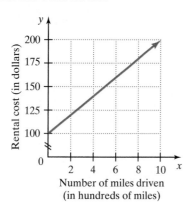

Is the slope of the graphed line positive, negative, zero, or undefined? Describe in a sentence or two the relationship between the rental cost and the number of miles driven.

8. Do the points $(0, 0)$, $(-2, -4)$, and $(1, 2)$ lie on the same line? Explain.

9. For the equation $y = -3x + 1$, complete the following table.

x	y
-3	
5	
	0
	-2

Graph the equation indicated in Exercises 10–13.

10. $y = 2$

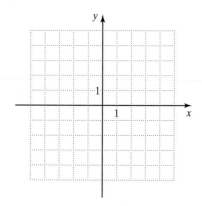

11. $x = -4$

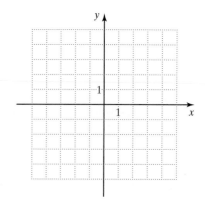

12. $y = -x - 3$

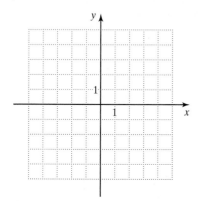

13. $3x - 2y = 6$

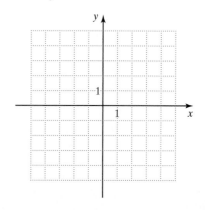

14. What are the slope and the y-intercept of the graph of $y = 3x + 1$?

15. Write the equation $2x - y = 5$ in slope-intercept form.

16. Find the equation of the line with slope -1 and that passes through the point $(0, -3)$.

17. The points $(3, 5)$ and $(-4, 2)$ lie on a line. Find its equation.

18. Graph $y \le -\frac{1}{2}x + 1$.

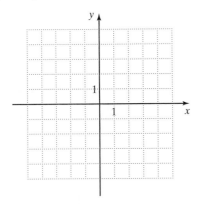

19. An entrepreneur is establishing a small business to manufacture leather bags. Her initial investment is $1000, and her unit cost to manufacture each bag is $30. Write an equation that gives the total cost C of manufacturing b bags. Plot the total cost of manufacturing 100, 200, and 300 bags.

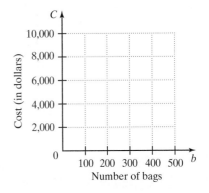

20. An investor deposits x dollars in an account that earns 4% per year and y dollars in another account earning 8% per year. His total annual earnings are at least $500. Write an inequality that describes this situation. Graph this inequality.

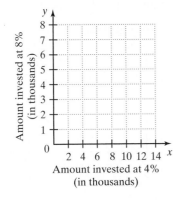

● *Check your answers on page A-17.*

Cumulative Review Exercises

To help you review, solve the following:

1. Evaluate: $2 \cdot 6 - 6^2$

2. Find the value of $x^2 - 4x + 1$ if $x = -3$.

3. Solve for x: $2x - 1 = 5x + 11$

4. Solve for x: $2x - 3(5 - x) = 4x + 2$

5. Solve for x and graph: $3x + 1 > 7$

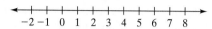

6. Graph: $2x + 5y = -12$

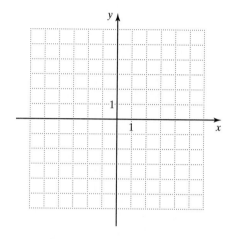

7. VA Bank and NY Bank have assets of $400 billion and $160 billion, respectively. The assets of NY Bank are what percent of those of VA Bank?

8. Lincoln's famous 1863 Gettysburg Address begins with the phrase "Four score and seven years ago." This phrase refers to 1776, the year in which the United States declared independence. How many years are there in a score of years?

9. The perimeter P of a rectangular garden is given by the formula

$$P = 2l + 2w,$$

where l is the length and w is the width of the garden. Solve for l in terms of P and w.

10. A drama club washes cars as a fund-raising activity. The club charges $6 to wash each car.

a. Write an equation to relate the club's income y to the number x of cars they wash.

b. Graph the equation.

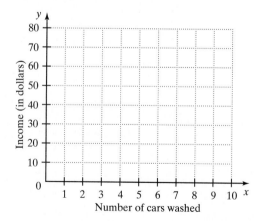

c. What are the x- and y-intercepts of the graph?

● *Check your answers on page A-18.*

Chapter 4
Solving Systems of Linear Equations

Economics and Linear Curves

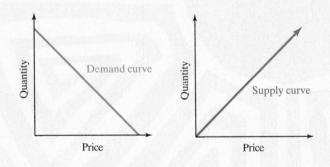

In a market, sellers can set the price at which their goods are offered for sale. How does this price affect the number of goods that buyers are willing to purchase? How does it affect the number of goods that producers are willing to supply the sellers?

Generally, as the *price* of an item increases, the *quantity* of items sold declines. This trend is captured in a **demand curve**—commonly approximated by a straight line with a negative slope. The coordinates of each point on this line correspond to the price at which retailers sell items and the quantity of items they sell.

By contrast, the **supply curve** has a positive slope, meaning that as selling prices increase, wholesalers are inclined to make more goods available to retailers. The coordinates of a point on this line represent the price at which retailers sell items and the quantity of items that wholesalers supply to the retailers.

Graphing both the supply curve and the demand curve on the same coordinate plane shows the price at which the market is **at equilibrium**. At this point of intersection, all items produced are sold, and all customers are satisfied.

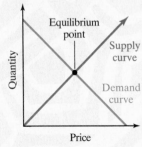

Chapter 4 Pretest

To see if you have already mastered the topics in this chapter, take this test.

1. Determine which of the following ordered pairs is a solution of the system

$$x + 2y = 5$$
$$5x - y = -8$$

   a. $(5, 0)$

   b. $(-1, 3)$

   c. $(1, -3)$

2. For the system graphed, indicate the number of solutions.

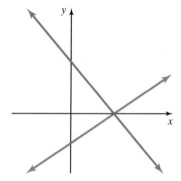

Solve each system by graphing.

3. $x + y = -2$
   $\quad y = x + 4$

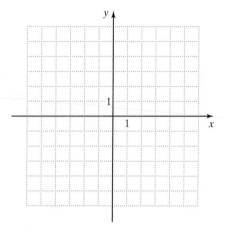

4. $x - 2y = 1$
   $\quad\quad y = 2$

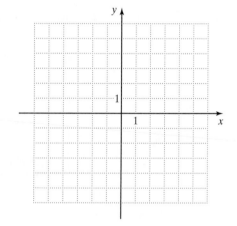

5. $9x + 3y = -6$
   $3x - 4y = 8$

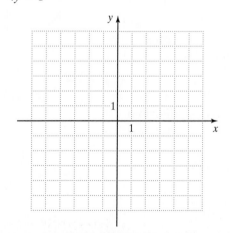

Solve each system by substitution.

6. $x - 2y = 7$
  $y = -11 - x$

7. $7x - 4y = 10$
  $x - 2y = 0$

8. $a + 3b = -2$
  $a = 2b - 7$

Solve each system by elimination.

9. $2x + 5y = -13$
  $-2x + 6y = -20$

10. $6x - 8y = 36$
  $1.5x - 2y = 9$

11. $3x - 7y = -19$
  $2x + 3y = -5$

Solve each system.

12. $4x + y = 0$
  $5y = 12 - 8x$

13. $-3n + 5m = 10$
  $-4m = -2(n + 1)$

14. $x + 9 = 2y$
  $8y - 13 = 4x$

15. $6x + 10y - 12 = 0$
  $3x + 2.5y - 6 = 0$

Solve.

16. At a college commencement, four times as many bachelor's degrees as associate's degrees were awarded to graduating students. If 3095 students graduated, how many bachelor's degrees and associate's degrees were awarded?

17. Ticket prices at a local movie theater are $6.50 for all shows before 5:00 P.M. and $10 for all shows after 5:00 P.M. The total revenue from ticket sales on Saturday was $17,650. If 1975 tickets were sold on Saturday, how many tickets were sold before 5:00 P.M.? After 5:00 P.M.?

18. For a student club fund-raiser, the number of $2 raffle tickets printed was three times the number of $5 tickets. If all of the tickets are sold, receipts from the $5 tickets will be $50 less than those from the $2 tickets. How many $5 tickets were printed?

19. A lottery winner invested $200,000 of her winnings in two funds earning 5% and 6% simple interest, respectively. If after one year she earned $11,200 in interest, how much did she invest in each fund?

20. On a boating trip, it took 2 hr to travel 13 mi with the current. It took the same amount of time to travel 11 mi against the current on the return trip. Find the speed of the boat and the speed of the current.

● *Check your answers on page A-18.*

4.1 Introduction to Systems of Linear Equations: Solving by Graphing

What Systems of Linear Equations Are and Why They Are Important

Recall from previous chapters that some situations are described by a linear equation in one variable, say $2x + 1 = 10$, whereas others are described by a single linear equation in *two* variables, for instance, $y = 3x - 5$.

Now let's consider situations in which the relationship between two variables is described by a *pair* of linear equations, for instance:

$$x + y = 7$$
$$x - y = 3$$

Groups of equations, called *systems*, serve as a model for a wide variety of applications in fields such as business and science.

In this chapter, we deal with three approaches to solving systems of linear equations, namely by *graphing*, *substitution*, and *elimination*.

Introduction to Systems of Linear Equations

We begin by focusing on the meaning of a system of equations.

> **Definition**
>
> A **system of equations** is a group of two or more equations solved simultaneously.

Systems of equations are sometimes written with large braces:

$$\begin{Bmatrix} x + y = 7 \\ x - y = 3 \end{Bmatrix} \quad \text{or} \quad \begin{cases} x + y = 7 \\ x - y = 3 \end{cases}$$

Braces are used to emphasize that any solution of a system must satisfy *all* the equations in the system. For instance, $x = \mathbf{5}$ and $y = \mathbf{2}$ is a solution of the system above, because when we substitute 5 for x and 2 for y into the equations, *both* equations are true:

$$x + y = 7 \longrightarrow 5 + 2 \stackrel{?}{=} 7 \quad \textbf{True.}$$
$$x - y = 3 \longrightarrow 5 - 2 \stackrel{?}{=} 3 \quad \textbf{True.}$$

A solution of a system of two equations is commonly represented as an ordered pair of numbers. For instance the solution of the system just mentioned can be written as $(5, 2)$. Can you explain why $(2, 5)$ is not a solution of this system?

Definition

A **solution** of a system of two equations in two variables is an ordered pair of numbers that makes both equations in the system true.

EXAMPLE 1

Consider the system:

$$x - 2y = 6$$
$$2x + 5y = 3$$

a. Is $(4, -1)$ a solution of the system?

b. Is $(2, -2)$ a solution of the system?

SOLUTION

a. To decide if the ordered pair $(4, -1)$ is a solution of this system, we substitute the x-coordinate 4 for x and the y-coordinate -1 for y in the equations and check if both equations are true.

$x - 2y = 6 \longrightarrow 4 - 2(-1) \stackrel{?}{=} 6 \xrightarrow{\text{simplifies to}} 6 = 6$ True.

$2x + 5y = 3 \longrightarrow 2(4) + 5(-1) \stackrel{?}{=} 3 \xrightarrow{\text{simplifies to}} 3 = 3$ True.

The ordered pair $(4, -1)$ satisfies both equations and so is a solution of the system.

b. To see if $(2, -2)$ is a solution, we substitute 2 for x and -2 for y in the equations and check if they are both true.

$x - 2y = 6 \longrightarrow 2 - 2(-2) \stackrel{?}{=} 6 \xrightarrow{\text{simplifies to}} 6 = 6$ True.

$2x + 5y = 3 \longrightarrow 2(2) + 5(-2) \stackrel{?}{=} 3 \xrightarrow{\text{simplifies to}} -6 = 3$ False.

The ordered pair $(2, -2)$ is not a solution of the system because it does not satisfy both equations.

PRACTICE 1

Consider the following system.

$$3x + 2y = 5$$
$$4x - 2y = -5$$

Determine whether the following ordered pairs are solutions of the system.

a. $(0, 2.5)$

b. $(1, -1)$

Number of Solutions of a System

In solving a system of linear equations, a question that immediately comes to mind is how many solutions the system has. Let's consider this question graphically. Since each equation is linear, both graphs are lines. Now suppose that we graph the two equations on the same coordinate plane. Any point at which the two graphs of the system intersect is a solution of the system, because that point must satisfy both equations.

For instance, let's again consider the system

$$x + y = 7$$
$$x - y = 3$$

and solve it by graphing both equations.

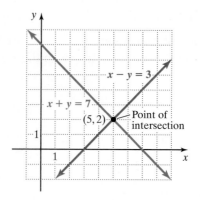

Note that the lines intersect at $(5, 2)$—precisely the ordered pair that we have previously determined to be a solution of this system. Since the two lines meet at a single point, the system has just one solution.

Not all systems have one solution. For instance, consider the following system in which there are *no* solutions:

$$3x - y = 2$$
$$3x - y = 4$$

Graphing this system, we get:

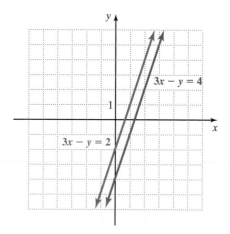

We observe that the lines are parallel and, therefore, do not intersect. So in this case, the system has no solutions.

Finally, let's examine a system that has more than one solution.

$$2x - 2y = 6$$
$$y = x - 3$$

The graph of this system is as follows:

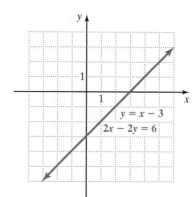

Note that only one line is shown. The reason is that both equations in the system have the same graph. Any point on this line, for instance $(3, 0)$, is a solution of both equations. A system such as this one has *infinitely many* solutions.

Every system of linear equations has one solution, no solution, or infinitely many solutions. The following table summarizes the main features of the three types of systems.

Number of Solutions	Description of the System's Graph	Possible Graph
One solution	The lines intersect at exactly one point.	
No solution	The lines are parallel.	
Infinitely many solutions	The lines coincide, that is, they are the the same line.	

EXAMPLE 2

For each system graphed, determine the number of solutions.

a.

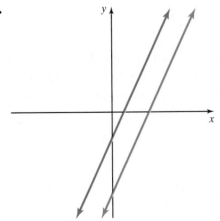

PRACTICE 2

Determine the number of solutions of each of the following systems:

a.

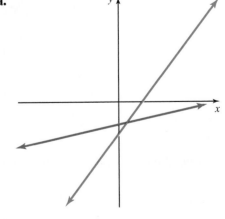

b.

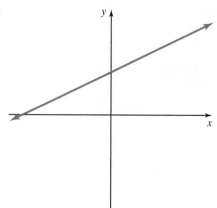

b.

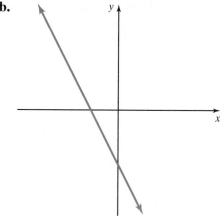

c.

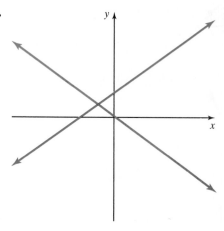

c.

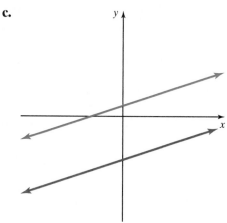

SOLUTION

a. The graph of the system consists of two lines that appear to be parallel. Since the lines do not intersect, the system has no solution.

b. This graph is a single line. Therefore, the system has infinitely many solutions.

c. The two lines in this graph intersect at a single point. So the system has one solution.

Solving Systems by Graphing

How exactly are systems of linear equations solved? In this chapter, we consider several methods of solving systems. Let's first discuss the **graphing method** in which we graph the equations that make up the system. Any point of intersection is a solution of the system.

EXAMPLE 3	PRACTICE 3
Solve the following system by graphing.	On the given coordinate plane, solve the following system by graphing.

Solve the following system by graphing.

$$x + y = 6$$
$$x - y = -4$$

SOLUTION Let's graph each linear equation by using the x- and y-intercept method and then sketching the line that passes through these points.

On the given coordinate plane, solve the following system by graphing.

$$x + y = 2$$
$$x - y = 4$$

$x + y = 6$ $x - y = -4$

x	y
0	6
6	0
3	3

x	y
0	4
-4	0
2	6

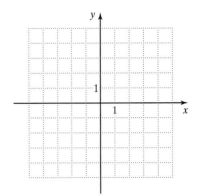

On the same coordinate plane, we plot the points and then graph both equations.

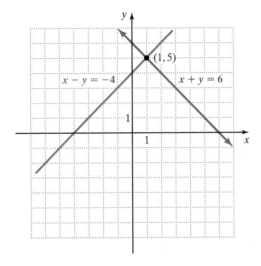

The corresponding lines appear to intersect at the point $(1, 5)$, giving $x = 1$ and $y = 5$.

CHECK Since solving a system of equations by graphing may result in approximate solutions, we confirm that $(1, 5)$ is the solution by substituting these values into the original equations:

$x + y = 6$ $\xrightarrow{\text{Substitute 1 for } x \text{ and 5 for } y.}$ $1 + 5 \overset{?}{=} 6$

$\qquad\qquad\qquad\qquad\qquad\qquad\qquad 6 = 6$ True.

$x - y = -4$ $\xrightarrow{\text{Substitute 1 for } x \text{ and 5 for } y.}$ $1 - 5 \overset{?}{=} -4$

$\qquad\qquad\qquad\qquad\qquad\qquad\qquad -4 = -4$ True.

So $(1, 5)$ is the solution of the system.

To Solve a System of Linear Equations by Graphing

- Graph both equations on the same coordinate plane.
- There are three possibilities:
  a. If the lines intersect, then the solution is the ordered pair of coordinates for the point of intersection. Check that these coordinates satisfy both equations.
  b. If the lines are parallel, then there is no solution of the system.
  c. If the lines coincide, then there are infinitely many solutions, namely, all the ordered pairs of coordinates that represent points on the line.

EXAMPLE 4

Solve by graphing.

$$y = 2x + 5$$
$$2x - y = 2$$

SOLUTION Graphing the two equations, we get:

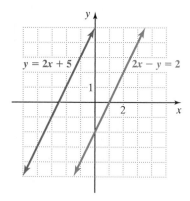

The lines appear to be parallel, which suggests that the system has no solution. To confirm that the lines are parallel, we can check that their slopes are equal. The graph of the first equation, $y = 2x + 5$, has slope 2. To find the slope of the second equation, we write $2x - y = 2$ in slope-intercept form, getting $y = 2x - 2$. The graph of this equation also has slope 2. Therefore, the lines are parallel and the system has no solution.

PRACTICE 4

Solve for x and y by graphing.

$$y = x - 6$$
$$x - y = 4$$

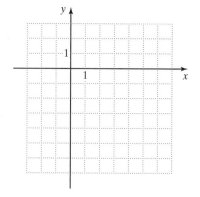

EXAMPLE 5

Solve by graphing.

$$2y = -8x + 2$$
$$-4x - y = -1$$

SOLUTION When we graph the two equations in this system, we get the same graph.

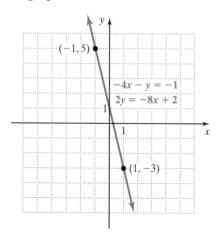

Note that when the two equations in the system are changed to slope-intercept form, the equations are identical.

PRACTICE 5

Solve by graphing.

$$6x = 15 - 3y$$
$$y = 5 - 2x$$

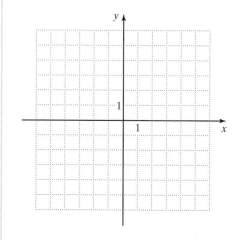

$$2y = -8x + 2 \quad \xrightarrow{\text{Isolate } y,} \quad y = -4x + 1$$
$$-4x - y = -1 \quad \xrightarrow{\text{Isolate } y,} \quad y = -4x + 1$$

We conclude that the system has infinitely many solutions. All points on the graph, some of which are indicated, are solutions. Can you identify another point on the graph and confirm that it is a solution to the system?

EXAMPLE 6

The U.S. House of Representatives has 435 members. On a certain bill, all the representatives voted, and 15 more representatives voted for the bill than against the bill. (There were no abstentions.)

a. If s represents the number of representatives who *supported* the bill, and n the number of representatives who did *not* support the bill, express the given information as a system of equations.

b. On a coordinate plane, graph the system found in part (a).

c. Find the coordinates of the point of intersection.

d. In this problem, what is the significance of the coordinates of the point of intersection?

SOLUTION

a. The given information can be expressed algebraically as

$$s + n = 435$$
$$s = n + 15$$

b. Let's graph s along the vertical axis and n along the horizontal axis. Since the number of representatives voting for or against a bill is between 0 and 435, we choose an appropriate scale and label the two axes accordingly. Next we graph the two equations.

c. The lines appear to intersect approximately at the point $(210, 225)$, that is, $n = 210$ and $s = 225$.

d. We conclude that about 210 representatives voted against the bill and 225 voted for the bill.

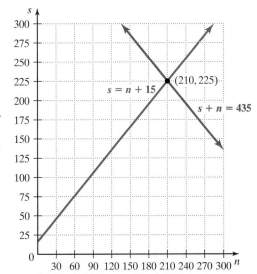

PRACTICE 6

A liberal arts student transfering to a four-year institution took a test of verbal skills and a test of mathematical skills. Her total score was 1150, and the verbal score v was 100 less than the math score m.

a. Express the given information as a system of equations.

b. On a coordinate plane, graph the system found in part (a).

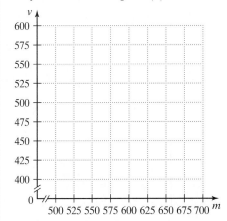

c. Name the coordinates of the point of intersection.

d. In this situation, what is the significance of the coordinates of the point of intersection?

When running a business, it is important to determine both the income that the business makes and the expenses that it takes to run the business. The business's income and its expenses depend on the number of items produced and sold. These quantities can be graphed on a coordinate plane, as shown in the next example. The point at which the income for a business equals its expenses is called the *break-even point*.

EXAMPLE 7

For a start-up business, an entrepreneur determined that to produce computer-generated, silk-screen T-shirts it will cost $3.25 a shirt plus $450 in fixed overhead. Each shirt produced is sold at $5.50.

a. If x represents the number of T-shirts sold and y is the amount it costs to produce the T-shirts, write an equation that relates x and y.

b. If x represents the number of T-shirts produced and y is the amount of income from selling the T-shirts, write an equation that relates x and y.

c. On a coordinate plane, graph the lines found in parts (a) and (b).

d. Find the break-even point for producing the T-shirts. Explain its significance in terms of the x- and y-coordinates.

SOLUTION

a. The given information can be expressed as

$$y = 3.25x + 450.$$

b. We can write the given information as

$$y = 5.50x.$$

c.

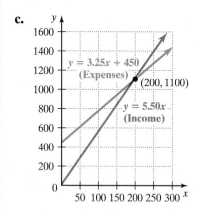

d. Since the break-even point is the point where the income equals the expenses, we must find the point of intersection of the lines $y = 3.25x + 450$ and $y = 5.50x$. The intersection of the lines is the point $(200, 1100)$, which is the break-even point. So when 200 shirts are produced, the income and the expenses will be the same, $1100. After 200 shirts are produced, the business will start making a profit.

PRACTICE 7

To print a newsletter costs $450 fixed overhead plus $1.50 a copy. Every printed copy of the newsletter is sold at $3 apiece.

a. If x represents the number of copies printed and y is the amount of money it costs to print the newsletter, write an equation that relates x and y.

b. If x represents the number of copies printed and y is the amount of income from newsletter sales, write an equation that relates x and y.

c. On the coordinate plane below, graph the lines found in parts (a) and (b).

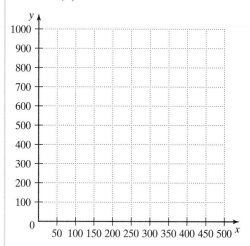

d. Find the break-even point for printing the newsletter.

In this section, we have examined the graphing method of solving systems of linear equations. A major advantage of this method over alternative methods is that it helps us to visualize the problem and its solution. However, a disadvantage of this approach is that our reading of a graph may be inaccurate, particularly when a coordinate of the point of intersection is not an integer or is very large. So a solution found by the graphing method may not be exact.

 ## Solving Systems of Linear Equations on a Grapher

Both graphing calculators and computers with graphing software can help facilitate the process of solving systems of linear equations. As with the paper-and-pencil approach, a grapher displays the graphs of the equations that make up a system on the same coordinate plane. We can then use one of the special features of the grapher to read the coordinates of the point at which the graphed lines intersect, that is, the solution of the system.

The most common features of a grapher that help us to read the coordinates of the point of intersection are **TRACE**, **ZOOM**, and **INTERSECT**.

- With the **TRACE** feature, the cursor runs along either of the graphed lines until it is positioned on or near the point of intersection; the coordinates of that point are then displayed.

- The **ZOOM** feature lets us position the cursor as close as we want to the point of intersection.

- The **INTERSECT** feature automatically calculates the point of intersection.

Note that each of the features may give only an approximation for the point of intersection. However, the most accurate approximation of the point of intersection is given by the **INTERSECT** feature.

EXAMPLE 8

Use either a graphing calculator or graphing software to solve.

$$4x - y = 11$$
$$x = y + 6$$

SOLUTION Begin by solving each equation for y.

$$4x - y = 11 \quad \xrightarrow{\text{Isolate } y.} \quad y = 4x - 11$$
$$x = y + 6 \quad \xrightarrow{\text{Isolate } y.} \quad y = x - 6$$

Then press the $\boxed{Y=}$ key, and enter $4x - 11$ to the right of **Y1 =** and $x - 6$ to the right of **Y2 =**. Set the viewing window. Then press the $\boxed{\text{GRAPH}}$ key to display the coordinate plane on which the two equations are graphed. The **TRACE** feature can be used to move a cursor along one of the lines toward the intersection of the graphs by holding down an arrow key. Note that as the cursor is moved, the changing coordinates of its position will be displayed on the screen. Once the cursor reaches the point of intersection, we can read the coordinates on the screen.

PRACTICE 8

Use a grapher to solve the following system of equations.

$$8x - y = 1$$
$$y = x + 5$$

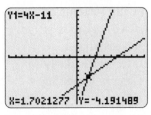

Using the TRACE feature

To get a better approximation of the solution, we can either activate the **ZOOM** feature to zoom in on the intersection point or activate the **INTERSECT** feature.

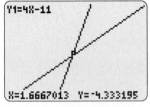

Using the ZOOM feature

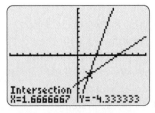

Using the INTERSECT feature

So the approximate solution here is $(1.667, -4.333)$.

Exercises 4.1

FOR EXTRA HELP

📖 *Student's Solutions Manual*

🎧 *Addison-Wesley Math Tutor Center*

🚪 *MyMathLab*

📼 *Videotape 4/DVT 4*

Indicate whether each ordered pair is or is not a solution to the given system.

1. $x + y = 3$
$2x - y = 6$

   a. $(0, 3)$ _____

   b. $(3, 3)$ _____

   c. $(3, 0)$ _____

2. $x - 6y = 3$
$x - y = -7$

   a. $(-2, -9)$ _____

   b. $(-9, -2)$ _____

   c. $(9, -2)$ _____

3. $4x + 5y = 0$
$7x - y = 0$

   a. $(1, 7)$ _____

   b. $(-5, 4)$ _____

   c. $(0, 0)$ _____

4. $2x - 2y = 30$
$8x + 2y = -10$

   a. $(1, -9)$ _____

   b. $(16, 1)$ _____

   c. $(2, -11)$ _____

Match each system with the appropriate graph.

5. a. A system with solution $(1, 3)$

   b. A system with solution $(-1, 3)$

   c. A system with infinitely many solutions

   d. A system with no solution

I
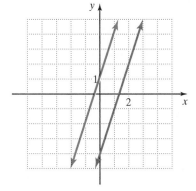

II
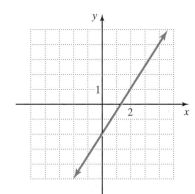

continued

III

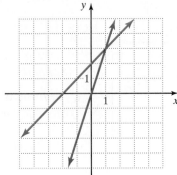

IV

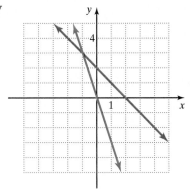

6. a. A system with solution $\left(-\frac{1}{4}, -1\frac{1}{4}\right)$

   b. A system with solution $(-1, 3)$

   c. A system with infinitely many solutions

   d. A system with no solution

I

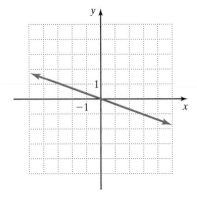

II

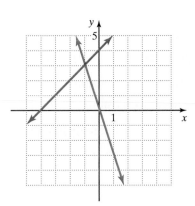

III

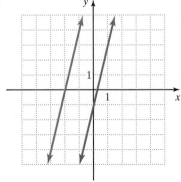

IV

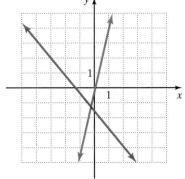

Solve by graphing.

7. $x - y = 2$
$x + y = 4$

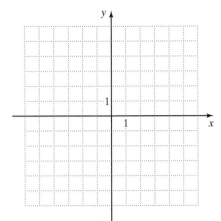

8. $x + 2y = 3$
$x + y = 2$

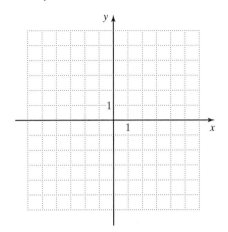

9. $y = x + 4$
$x + y = 4$

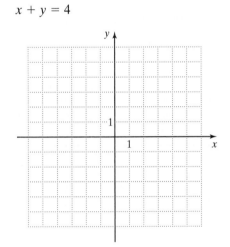

10. $-5 = 2x + y$
$y = -x$

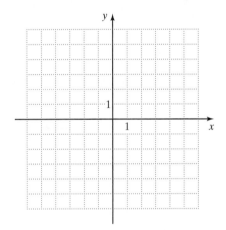

11. $y = -x + 6$
$y = -3x + 8$

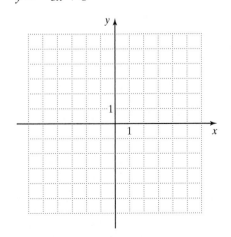

12. $y = x + 1$
$y = -x - 3$

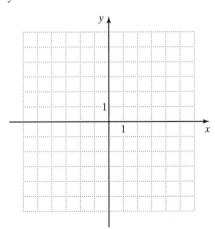

13. $y = -\frac{1}{2}x + 1$
$y = 2x + 1$

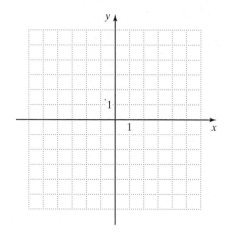

14. $y = 2x - 6$
$y = 3 - \frac{1}{4}x$

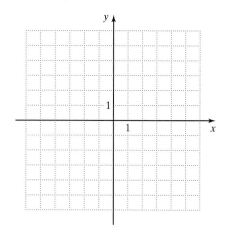

15. $y = 5 + 3x$
$x + y = -3$

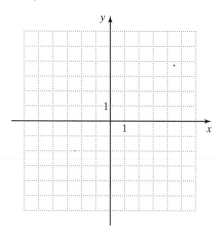

16. $2x + y = -3$
$y = -(x + 4)$

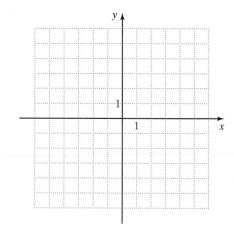

17. $2y = 6x + 2$
$3y - 9x = 3$

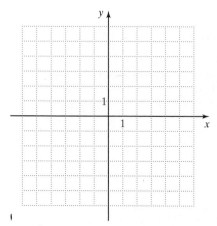

18. $4x = 8y + 4$
$5x - 10y = 5$

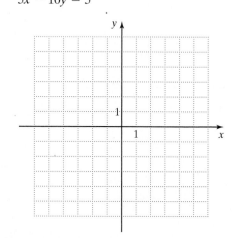

19. $2x + y = -4$
    $y = -2x + 3$

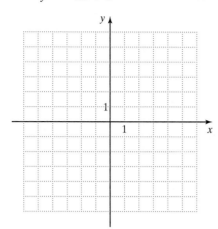

20. $3x - y = 1$
    $6x + 4 = 2y$

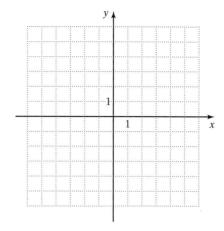

21. $x = 5 + y$
    $-2x + 2y = -10$

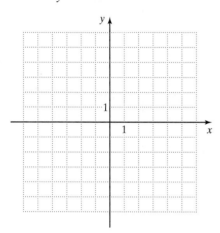

22. $x + y = 6$
    $3y - 18 = -3x$

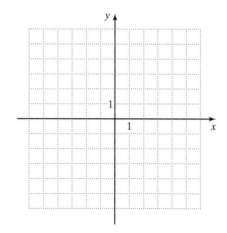

23. $x - y = -1$
    $x - y = 4$

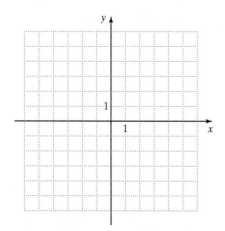

24. $x + 5y = 6$
    $x + 5y = 0$

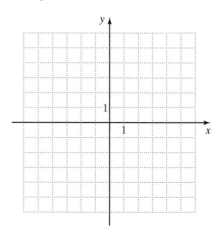

25. $3x + 2y = -10$
$5x - y = -8$

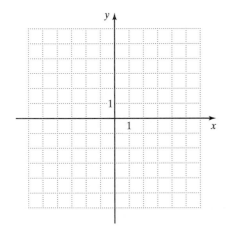

26. $-x - 2y = 8$
$-6x + 4y = 0$

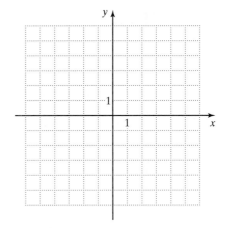

27. $-3x + y - 14 = 0$
$3x - y - 11 = 0$

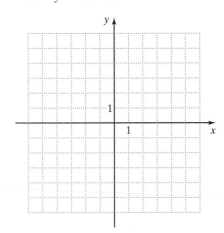

28. $7x - y - 2 = 0$
$14x - 2y - 12 = 0$

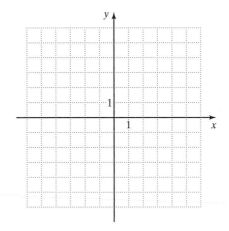

29. $10x + 2y = -6$
$y = 2$

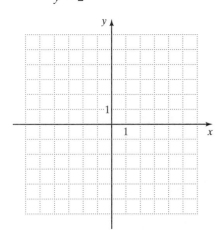

30. $x + 5y = -15$
$x = 5$

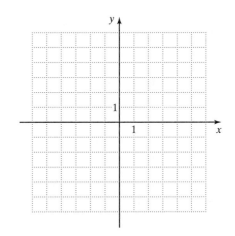

31. $x = 0$
$x - 2y = 4$

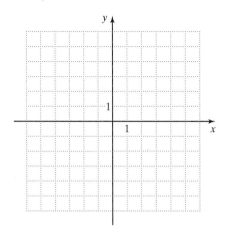

32. $y = -3$
$y = 2x + 3$

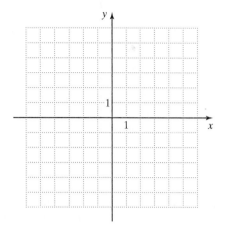

33. $4x - 4y = -8$
$y = \dfrac{2}{3}x$

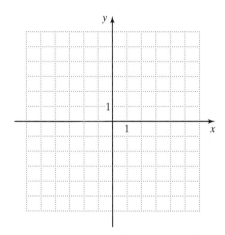

34. $3x + 2y = 6$
$y = -\dfrac{3}{4}x$

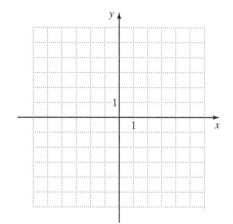

Applications

Solve.

35. A young married couple had a combined annual income of $57,000.

    a. If the wife made $3000 more than the husband, write these relationships as a system of equations.

b. Graph the equations.

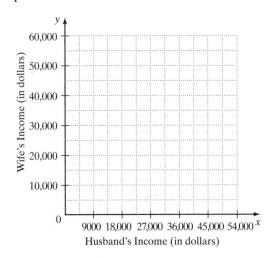

c. Find the two incomes.

36. A plane flying with a tailwind flew at a speed of 450 mph, relative to the ground. When flying against the tailwind, it flew at a speed of 350 mph.

a. Express these relationships as equations.

b. Graph these equations.

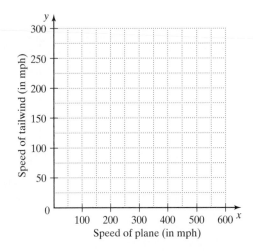

c. Find the speed of the plane in calm air and the speed of the wind.

37. Mike the plumber charges $75 for a house call and then $40 per hour for labor. Sally the plumber charges $100 for a house call, and then $30 per hour for labor.

a. Write a cost equation for each plumber, where y is the total cost of plumbing repairs and x is the number of hours of labor.

b. Graph the two equations.

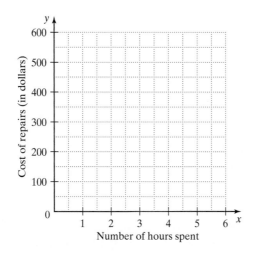

c. Determine the number of hours of plumbing repairs that would be required for the two plumbers to charge the same amount.

d. Determine from the graph which plumber charges less if the estimated amount of time to carry out the plumbing repairs is 5 hr.

38. To connect to the Web, you must choose between two Internet service providers (ISPs). Flat ISP charges a monthly flat fee of $20 regardless of how many hours you connect to the Web. A competing company, Variable ISP, charges $2.50 per month plus $0.50 for each hour of connection time.

a. Express each company's price structure, p, in terms of hours-connected, h.

b. Draw a graph that shows how each company's price structure relates to connection time.

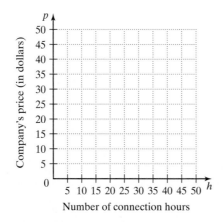

c. For which connection time do the two companies charge the same?

39. A small company duplicates DVDs. The cost of duplicating is $30 fixed overhead plus $0.25 per DVD duplicated. The company generates revenues of $1.50 per DVD. Use a graph to determine the break-even point for duplicating DVDs.

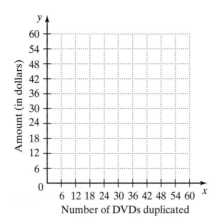

40. A clothing company sells jackets for $140 per jacket. The company's fixed costs are $9000 and the variable costs are $50 per jacket. Use a graph to determine the break-even point for production.

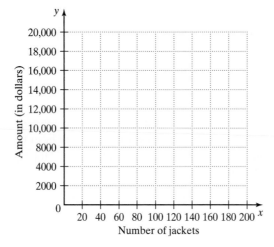

41. A movie fan rented 6 films at a local video store for one day. The daily rental charge was $2 on some films and $4 on others. If the total rental charge was $22, how many $4 films were rented?

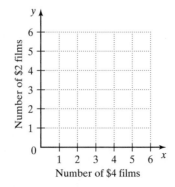

42. An appliance store sells washer-dryer combinations. If the washer costs $200 more than the dryer, find the cost of each appliance.

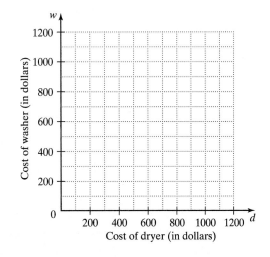

43. Silver's Gym charges a $300 initiation fee plus $30 per month. DeLuxe Fitness Center has an initial charge of $400 but only charges $25 per month. Use a graph to determine for what number of months both health clubs will charge the same amount.

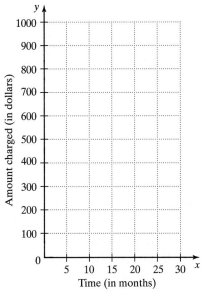

44. A plant nursery is selling a 7-ft specimen of a tree that grows about 1.5 ft per year and a 6-ft specimen of a tree that grows 2 ft per year. Use a graph to determine in how many years the two trees will be the same height.

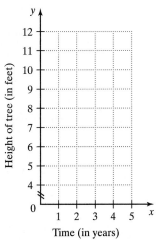

• *Check your answers on page A-19.*

Mindstretchers

CRITICAL THINKING

1. Write a system of linear equations that has (2, 5) as its only solution.

WRITING

2. Is it possible for a system of two linear equations to have exactly two solutions? If not, explain why.

_____

_____

_____

MATHEMATICAL REASONING

3. Not every system of equations is linear. For example the system

$$y = 2x$$
$$y = x^2$$

has the following graph.

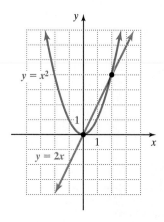

How many solutions does this system have? Explain how you know.

_____

_____

_____

4.2 Solving Systems of Linear Equations by Substitution

This section deals with solving a system of equations by the **substitution method**. As in the previous section, we restrict the discussion to systems of two linear equations in two variables. In applying the substitution method, we solve such a system by first solving one linear equation in one variable—a much simpler problem. As compared with the graphing method, the substitution method has the advantage of being faster and also of giving us an exact solution. The substitution method particularly lends itself to solving systems in which a variable is isolated in one of the equations.

To see how solving by substitution works, let's look at some examples.

OBJECTIVES

- *To solve a system of linear equations by substitution*
- *To solve applied problems involving systems of linear equations*

EXAMPLE 1

Solve by substitution:

$$\textbf{(1)} \quad x + y = 10$$
$$\textbf{(2)} \quad y = 2x + 4$$

SOLUTION Notice that Equation (2) is solved for y in terms of x. So we can substitute the expression $2x + 4$ from Equation (2) for y in Equation (1).

$$\textbf{(1)} \quad x + y = 10$$
$$x + (2x + 4) = 10 \quad \text{Substitute } 2x + 4 \text{ for } y.$$

We now have an equation that contains only one variable, namely x, and so is easy to solve.

$$x + (2x + 4) = 10$$
$$3x + 4 = 10$$
$$3x = 6$$
$$x = 2$$

Now that we have found the value of x, let's substitute it in either of the original equations in order to determine the corresponding value of y. Substituting 2 for x in Equation (2), we get:

$$\textbf{(2)} \quad y = 2x + 4$$
$$= 2(2) + 4$$
$$= 8$$

So the solution to the system is $(2, 8)$, that is, $x = 2$ and $y = 8$.

CHECK We can check the solution by substituting 2 for x and 8 for y in the original equations.

$$\textbf{(1)} \quad x + y = 10 \qquad \textbf{(2)} \quad y = 2x + 4$$
$$2 + 8 \stackrel{?}{=} 10 \qquad\qquad 8 \stackrel{?}{=} 2 \cdot 2 + 4$$
$$10 = 10 \quad \text{True.} \qquad\quad 8 = 8 \qquad\qquad \text{True.}$$

The check confirms the solution $(2, 8)$.

PRACTICE 1

Use the substitution method to solve.

$$\textbf{(1)} \quad x - y = 7$$
$$\textbf{(2)} \quad x = -y + 1$$

In Example 1, would we have gotten the same solution if we had solved for y in the *first* equation and then replaced y in the second equation?

The preceding example suggests the following procedure for solving systems of linear equations in two variables.

To Solve a System of Linear Equations by Substitution

- In one of the equations, solve for either variable in terms of the other variable.
- In the other equation, substitute the expression equal to the variable found in the previous step. Then solve the resulting equation for the remaining variable.
- Substitute the value found in the previous step in either of the original equations and solve for the other variable.
- Check by substituting the values in both equations of the original system.

EXAMPLE 2

Use the substitution method to solve the following system.

$$\begin{array}{ll} \textbf{(1)} & d = 3q - 8 \\ \textbf{(2)} & 3d - 4q = 10 \end{array}$$

SOLUTION Since d is isolated in Equation (1), we can substitute the expression $3q - 8$ for d in Equation (2).

$$\begin{array}{rl} \textbf{(2)} & 3d - 4q = 10 \\ & 3(3q - 8) - 4q = 10 \qquad \text{Substitute } 3q - 8 \text{ for } d. \\ & 9q - 24 - 4q = 10 \\ & 5q - 24 = 10 \\ & 5q = 34 \\ & q = \dfrac{34}{5}, \quad \text{or } 6.8 \end{array}$$

Now let's solve for d by substituting 6.8 for q in Equation (1).

$$\begin{array}{rl} \textbf{(1)} \quad d & = 3q - 8 \\ & = 3(6.8) - 8 \\ & = 20.4 - 8 \\ & = 12.4 \end{array}$$

The solution is $q = 6.8$ and $d = 12.4$. Note that neither value is an integer. So if we solve this system by the graphing method, we have to estimate the coordinates of a point.

PRACTICE 2

Solve for m and n by substitution.

$$\begin{array}{ll} \textbf{(1)} & m = -5n + 1 \\ \textbf{(2)} & 2m + 3n = 7 \end{array}$$

CHECK We can confirm the solution by substituting these values in both of the original equations.

(1) $d = 3q - 8$

$12.4 \stackrel{?}{=} 3(6.8) - 8$

$12.4 \stackrel{?}{=} 20.4 - 8$

$12.4 = 12.4$ True.

(2) $3d - 4q = 10$

$3(12.4) - 4(6.8) \stackrel{?}{=} 10$

$37.2 - 27.2 \stackrel{?}{=} 10$

$10 = 10$ True.

So the solution is confirmed.

In Example 2, would we have gotten the same solution to the system if the variables had been called x and y instead of q and d? Explain.

EXAMPLE 3

Solve the system by substitution.

(1) $5x - 3y = 5$
(2) $2x - y = 1$

SOLUTION We first need to solve for x or y in either of the equations. Let's solve for y in Equation (2) where the coefficient of y is -1.

(2) $2x - y = 1$

$-y = -2x + 1$

$y = 2x - 1$ Divide each side by -1.

Next we substitute the expression $2x - 1$ for y in Equation (1) and solve for x.

(1) $5x - 3y = 5$

$5x - 3(2x - 1) = 5$ Substitute $2x - 1$ for y.

$5x - 6x + 3 = 5$

$-x + 3 = 5$

$-x = 2$

$x = -2$

Now we can solve for y by substituting -2 for x in Equation (2).

(2) $2x - y = 1$

$2(-2) - y = 1$

$-4 - y = 1$

$-y = 5$

$y = -5$

So the solution is $(-2, -5)$. Check this in the original system.

PRACTICE 3

Solve by substitution.

(1) $2x - 7y = 7$
(2) $6x - y = 1$

EXAMPLE 4

Solve by substitution.

$$\begin{aligned}\textbf{(1)} \quad x - 4y &= 15 \\ \textbf{(2)} \quad -2x + 8y &= 5\end{aligned}$$

SOLUTION We first need to solve for either x or y in one of the equations. Let's solve for x in Equation (1) since the coefficient of x in this equation is 1.

$$\begin{aligned}\textbf{(1)} \quad x - 4y &= 15 \\ x &= 4y + 15\end{aligned}$$

Next, we substitute the expression $4y + 15$ for x in equation (2).

$$\begin{aligned}\textbf{(2)} \qquad -2x + 8y &= 5 \\ -2(4y + 15) + 8y &= 5 \qquad \text{Substitute } 4y + 15 \text{ for } x. \\ -8y - 30 + 8y &= 5 \\ -30 &= 5 \qquad \text{False.}\end{aligned}$$

Getting a false statement means that there is no value of y that makes this last equation true. So the original system has no solution.

PRACTICE 4

Use the substitution method to solve the following system.

$$\begin{aligned}\textbf{(1)} \quad 3x + y &= 10 \\ \textbf{(2)} \quad -6x - 2y &= 1\end{aligned}$$

What do you think the graph of the system in Example 4 looks like?

EXAMPLE 5

Solve by substitution.

$$\begin{aligned}\textbf{(1)} \quad 6x + 2y &= 4 \\ \textbf{(2)} \quad -y &= 3x - 2\end{aligned}$$

SOLUTION Since the coefficient of y in Equation (2) is -1, let's solve this equation for y.

$$\begin{aligned}\textbf{(2)} \quad -y &= 3x - 2 \\ y &= -3x + 2 \qquad \text{Divide each side by } -1.\end{aligned}$$

Next, we substitute $-3x + 2$ for y in Equation (1).

$$\begin{aligned}\textbf{(1)} \qquad 6x + 2y &= 4 \\ 6x + 2(-3x + 2) &= 4 \qquad \text{Substitute } -3x + 2 \text{ for } y. \\ 6x - 6x + 4 &= 4 \\ 4 &= 4 \qquad \text{True.}\end{aligned}$$

Getting a true statement means that every value of x makes the last equation true. Therefore, the original system has infinitely many solutions.

PRACTICE 5

Solve for x and y.

$$\begin{aligned}\textbf{(1)} \quad y &= -2x + 4 \\ \textbf{(2)} \quad 10x + 5y &= 20\end{aligned}$$

In Example 5, what do you think the graph of the system looks like? Can you identify a particular solution to the system?

TIP When solving a system of linear equations in two variables by substitution

- if we get a false statement, then the system has no solution;
- if we get a true statement, then the system has infinitely many solutions.

Now let's use the substitution method to solve some applications.

EXAMPLE 6

A car rental agency has two plans:

- In the Ambassador Plan, renting a car for one day costs $35 plus $0.25 per mile driven.
- In the Diplomat Plan, a one-day car rental costs $50 plus $0.10 per mile driven.

a. For each plan, write a linear equation that relates a day's price p for renting a car to the number of miles driven n. Express the given information as a system of equations.

b. Use the substitution method to solve the system of linear equations.

c. In the context of this problem, what is the significance of the solution?

SOLUTION

a. The Ambassador Plan can be expressed as $p = 0.25n + 35$; the Diplomat Plan becomes $p = 0.10n + 50$. The system representing both plans is therefore

$$(1) \quad p = 0.25n + 35$$
$$(2) \quad p = 0.10n + 50$$

b. To solve the system, we can set the two expressions for p equal to each other.

$$0.25n + 35 = 0.10n + 50$$

Solving for n gives us:

$$0.25n + 35 = 0.10n + 50$$
$$0.15n = 15$$
$$n = \frac{15}{0.15}$$
$$n = 100$$

To solve for p, we can substitute 100 for n in Equation (1).

$$(1) \quad p = 0.25n + 35$$
$$= 0.25(\mathbf{100}) + 35$$
$$= 25 + 35$$
$$= 60$$

So the solution to the system is $n = 100$ and $p = 60$.

PRACTICE 6

To watch movies on premium channels, a couple decides to choose between two television cable deals:

- the TV Deal that costs $20 installation and $35 per month, and
- the Movie Deal that costs $30 installation and $25 per month

a. Write an equation for each deal, expressing the cost of a deal c in terms of the number of months n for which the couple signs up.

b. Solve the system of linear equations by substitution.

c. In the context of this problem, what is the significance of the solution?

c. With the appropriate units, the solution is $n = 100$ mi and
$p = \$60$. This means that the cost of a one-day rental on
the two plans is the same amount of money, namely $60,
only when the car is driven 100 mi. For other distances
driven, the plans charge different amounts.

Recall that we discussed mixture problems involving a single equation in Section 2.5. The following example shows how we can apply our knowledge of solving systems of linear equations to these problems.

EXAMPLE 7	PRACTICE 7

How much 30% alcohol solution and 50% alcohol solution
must be mixed to get 10 gal of 42% solution?

SOLUTION We solve this problem as we did earlier mixture
problems, namely by organizing the given information in a
table. Let's represent the amount of 30% solution by x and the
amount of 50% solution by y.

Action	Percent of Alcohol	Amount of Solution (gal)	Amount of Alcohol (gal)
Start with	30%	x	$0.3x$
Add	50%	y	$0.5y$
Finish with	42%	10	0.42 (10), or 4.2

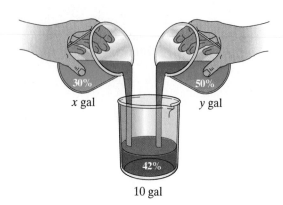

10 gal

The amount of alcohol in the 30% solution is 30% of x, or
$0.3x$. The amount of alcohol in the 50% solution is 50% of y,
or $0.5y$. The amount of alcohol in the 42% solution is 42% of
10, or 4.2. Since the total amount of the combined solutions is
10 gal and the total amount of alcohol is 4.2 gal, we get the following system.

$$\textbf{(1)} \qquad x + y = 10$$
$$\textbf{(2)} \quad 0.3x + 0.5y = 4.2$$

In applying the substitution method, we begin by solving for y
in Equation (1).

$$\textbf{(1)} \quad x + y = 10$$
$$y = -x + 10$$

(Practice 7 column:)

A chemist wishes to combine an alloy
that is 20% copper with one that is
50% copper to obtain 15 oz of an
alloy that is 25% copper. Find the
quantities of the alloys required.

We then substitute $-x + 10$ for y in Equation (2).

$$
\begin{align*}
\textbf{(2)} \qquad\qquad 0.3x + 0.5y &= 4.2 \\
0.3x + 0.5(-x + 10) &= 4.2 \\
0.3x - 0.5x + 5 &= 4.2 \\
-0.2x &= -0.8 \\
x &= \frac{-0.8}{-0.2} \\
x &= 4
\end{align*}
$$

After replacing x by 4 in Equation (1), we solve for y.

$$
\begin{align*}
\textbf{(1)} \quad x + y &= 10 \\
4 + y &= 10 \\
y &= 6
\end{align*}
$$

So the solution to the system is $(4, 6)$. In other words, 4 gal of 30% solution and 6 gal of 50% solution are needed to produce 10 gal of the 42% solution.

A system of linear equations can also serve as a model for investment problems, as the following example illustrates.

EXAMPLE 8

A stockbroker had $10,000 to invest for her client. The broker invested part of this amount at a low-risk, low-yield 5% rate of return per year and the rest at a high-risk, high-yield 7% rate. If the client earned a return of $550 in one year, how much money did the broker invest at each rate?

SOLUTION The following table reflects the given information. Here, x stands for the amount of the investment at a 5% return, and y the investment at a 7% return.

Rate of Return	Amount of Investment ($)	Amount of Return ($)
5%	x	$0.05x$
7%	y	$0.07y$
TOTAL	10,000	550

The amount of return on each investment is the product of the rate of return and the amount of the investment. We add the amount of the individual investments to find the total investment, and the amount of returns on each investment to find the total amount of return. Since the total investment is $10,000 and the total return is $550, we get the following system:

$$
\begin{align*}
\textbf{(1)} \qquad\qquad x + y &= 10{,}000 \\
\textbf{(2)} \quad 0.05x + 0.07y &= 550
\end{align*}
$$

PRACTICE 8

The manager of a city pension fund splits $198,000 between two investments. The first investment pays 4% in simple interest per year, and the second pays 5% in simple interest per year. At the end of the first year, the two investments return the same amount of interest. How much money did the manager put into each investment?

Now let's solve for y in Equation (1).

(1) $x + y = 10{,}000$

$$y = 10{,}000 - x$$

We then substitute $10{,}000 - x$ for y in Equation (2).

(2)
$$0.05x + 0.07y = 550$$
$$0.05x + 0.07(\mathbf{10{,}000} - x) = 550$$
$$0.05x + 700 - 0.07x = 550$$
$$-0.02x + 700 = 550$$
$$-0.02x = -150$$
$$x = \frac{-150}{-0.02}$$
$$x = 7500$$

After substituting 7500 for x in Equation (1), we solve for y.

(1)
$$x + y = 10{,}000$$
$$\mathbf{7500} + y = 10{,}000$$
$$y = 2500$$

Therefore, the solution to the system is (7500, 2500). In other words, $7500 was invested at 5% and $2500 at 7%.

Exercises 4.2

FOR EXTRA HELP

📖 Student's Solutions Manual

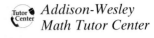 Addison-Wesley Math Tutor Center

🚪 MyMathLab

📼 Videotape 4/DVT 4

Solve by substitution and check.

1. $x + y = 10$
  $y = 2x + 1$

2. $x - y = 7$
  $x = 5y + 3$

3. $y = -3x - 15$
  $y = -x - 7$

4. $y = -2x - 21$
  $y = 5x$

5. $-x - y = 8$
  $x = -3y$

6. $x - y = 15$
  $y = -4x$

7. $4x + 2y = 10$
  $x = 2$

8. $2y + x = 10$
  $y = -5$

9. $-x + 20y = 0$
  $x - y = 0$

10. $5x + 3y = 0$
  $x + y = 0$

11. $6x + 4y = 2$
  $2x + y = 0$

12. $x - 3y = 0$
  $2x - 3y = 6$

13. $3x + 5y = -12$
  $x + 2y = -6$

14. $3x + 5y = -1$
  $3x + y = -5$

15. $7x - 3y = 26$
  $3x - y = 11$

16. $x + 3y = 1$
  $-3x - 5y = -2$

17. $8x + 2y = -1$
  $y = -4x + 1$

18. $4x + 2y = 4$
  $y = 5 - 2x$

19. $6x - 2y = 2$
  $y = 3x - 1$

20. $2x - 6y = -12$
  $x = 3y - 6$

21. $p + 2q = 13$
  $q + 7 = 4p$

22. $a - b = -1$
  $6b = 5a$

23. $s - 3t + 5 = 0$
  $-4s + t - 9 = 0$

24. $2l - 3w + 6 = 0$
  $l - w - 10 = 0$

Applications

Solve.

25. Two taxi companies compete in the same neighborhood. One of these companies charges $3 for the taxi drop plus $1.25 for each mile driven, while the other charges $2 for the taxi drop, plus $1.50 for each mile driven.

  a. Express these relationships as an algebraic system.

  b. Solve the system and interpret the results.

26. Two electricians make house calls. One charges $75 for a visit plus $50 per hour of work. The other charges $95 per visit plus $40 per hour of work.

    a. Write a linear equation for each electrician that relates the charge for a house call in terms of the length of a visit.

    b. For how many hours of work do the two electricians charge the same?

27. On a particular airline route, a full-price coach ticket costs $310 and a discounted coach ticket costs $210. On one of these flights, there were 172 passengers in coach, which resulted in a total ticket income of $44,120. How many full-price tickets were sold?

28. During a sale, a store sells red-dot items at a 30% discount and yellow-dot items at a 20% discount. A shopper bought red- and yellow-dot items with a combined regular price of $40. If the total discount was $9.80, how much did the shopper spend on each kind of item?

29. A laboratory technician needs to make a 10-liter batch of antiseptic that is 60% alcohol. How can she combine a batch of antiseptic that is 30% alcohol with another that is 70% to get the desired concentration?

30. A bottle of fruit juice contains 20% water. How much water must be added to this bottle to produce 8 L of fruit juice that is 50% water?

31. A corporation merged two departments into one. In one department, 5% of the employees were women, whereas in the other department, 80% were women. When the departments were merged, 50% of the 150 employees were women. How many women were in each department before the merger?

32. A hospital needs 30 L of a 10% solution of disinfectant. How many liters of a 20% solution and a 4% solution should be mixed to obtain this 10% solution?

33. A student took out two loans totaling $5000. She borrowed the maximum amount she could at 6% and the remainder at 7% interest per year. At the end of the first year, she owed $310 in interest. How much was loaned at each rate?

34. A man invested three times as much money in a bond fund that earned 8% in a year as he did in a mutual fund that returned 4% in the year. How much money did he invest in each fund if the total earnings for the year were $112?

35. A $40,000 investment was split so that part was invested at a 7% annual rate of interest and the rest at 9%. If the total annual earnings were $3140, how much money was invested at each rate?

36. A financial adviser counseled a client to invest $15,000, split between two stocks. At the end of one year, the investment in one stock increased in value by 4%, and the investment in the second stock increased in value by 8%. If the total increase in value of the investment was $1120, how much money was invested in each stock?

● *Check your answers on page A-21.*

Mindstretchers

GROUPWORK

1. Cramer's Rule is a formula that can be used to solve a system of linear equations for x and y. Consider the following system.

$$ax + by = c$$
$$dx + ey = f$$

The formula states that $x = \dfrac{ce - bf}{ae - bd}$ and $y = \dfrac{af - cd}{ae - bd}$. Note that this mechanical approach allows machines to solve systems of equations.

a. Working with a partner, make up your own values for a, b, c, d, e, and f, and substitute these values in the system.

$$\underline{\hspace{1cm}} x + \underline{\hspace{1cm}} y = \underline{\hspace{1cm}}$$
$$\underline{\hspace{1cm}} x + \underline{\hspace{1cm}} y = \underline{\hspace{1cm}}$$

b. Use Cramer's Rule to calculate x and y.

$$x = \frac{ce - bf}{ae - bd} = \underline{\hspace{2cm}}$$

$$y = \frac{af - cd}{ae - bd} = \underline{\hspace{2cm}}$$

c. By substitution, check whether (x, y) is in fact a solution to the system.

MATHEMATICAL REASONING

2. On the coordinate plane, consider the quadrilateral $ABCD$ shown. At what point do the diagonals $\overline{AC}$ and $\overline{BD}$ intersect? Explain how to find the answer exactly.

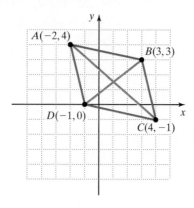

_____

_____

_____

_____

CRITICAL THINKING

3. For what value of k will the system shown have infinitely many solutions?

$$kx - 2y = 10$$
$$4x - y = 5$$

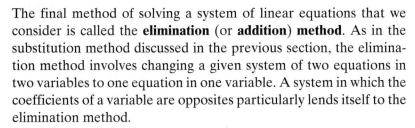

4.3 Solving Systems of Linear Equations by Elimination

OBJECTIVES

- *To solve a system of linear equations by elimination*

- *To solve applied problems involving systems of linear equations*

The final method of solving a system of linear equations that we consider is called the **elimination** (or **addition**) **method**. As in the substitution method discussed in the previous section, the elimination method involves changing a given system of two equations in two variables to one equation in one variable. A system in which the coefficients of a variable are opposites particularly lends itself to the elimination method.

Recall that in solving linear equations in one variable, we frequently used the addition property of equality: If $a = b$, then $a + c = b + c$. That is, if we add the same number to both sides of an equation, we get an equivalent equation.

The elimination method for solving *systems* is based on a closely related property of equality: If $a = b$ and $c = d$, then $a + c = b + d$. This property allows us to "add equations".

Let's look at some examples of applying this property in the elimination method.

EXAMPLE 1	PRACTICE 1

Solve the following system by the elimination method.

$$\textbf{(1)} \quad x + y = 4$$
$$\textbf{(2)} \quad x - y = 2$$

SOLUTION First we decide which variable to eliminate. Since the coefficients of the y-terms in the two equations are opposites (namely $+1$ and -1), we eliminate y if we add the equations.

$$\textbf{(1)} \quad x + y = 4$$
$$\textbf{(2)} \quad \underline{x - y = 2}$$
$$2x + 0y = 6$$
$$2x = 6$$
$$x = 3$$

To find y, we substitute 3 for x in either of the original equations. Substituting in Equation (1) we get:

$$\textbf{(1)} \quad x + y = 4$$
$$3 + y = 4$$
$$y = 4 - 3$$
$$y = 1$$

So $x = 3$ and $y = 1$. That is, the solution is (3, 1).

CHECK We check the solution by substituting these values for x and y in both of the original equations.

$$\textbf{(1)} \quad x + y = 4 \qquad\qquad \textbf{(2)} \quad x - y = 2$$
$$3 + 1 \overset{?}{=} 4 \qquad\qquad\qquad 3 - 1 \overset{?}{=} 2$$
$$4 = 4 \quad \text{True.} \qquad\qquad 2 = 2 \quad \text{True.}$$

So our solution (3, 1) is confirmed.

Solve for x and y.

$$\textbf{(1)} \quad x + y = 6$$
$$\textbf{(2)} \quad x - y = -10$$

EXAMPLE 2

Use the elimination method to solve for x and y.

$$\textbf{(1)} \quad 3x + 2y = 14$$
$$\textbf{(2)} \quad 5x + 2y = -8$$

SOLUTION In this system, adding the two given equations does not eliminate either variable. However, we note that the two y-terms have the same coefficient, namely 2. So if we multiply Equation (1) by -1 and then add the equations, the y-terms will cancel out.

$$
\begin{array}{ll}
\textbf{(1)} \quad 3x + 2y = 14 & \xrightarrow{\text{Multiply by }-1.} \quad -3x - 2y = -14 \\
\textbf{(2)} \quad 5x + 2y = -8 & \hspace{3.5cm} \underline{5x + 2y = -8} \quad \text{Add the equations.} \\
& \hspace{3.8cm} 2x \hspace{1.1cm} = -22 \\
& \hspace{4.6cm} x = -11
\end{array}
$$

Next we substitute -11 for x in either of the original equations. Let's choose Equation (1), and then solve for y.

$$
\begin{aligned}
\textbf{(1)} \quad 3x + 2y &= 14 \\
3(-11) + 2y &= 14 \\
-33 + 2y &= 14 \\
2y &= 14 + 33 \\
2y &= 47 \\
y &= \frac{47}{2} = 23.5
\end{aligned}
$$

So the solution is $(-11, 23.5)$.

PRACTICE 2

Solve the following system using the elimination method.

$$\textbf{(1)} \quad 4x + 3y = -7$$
$$\textbf{(2)} \quad 5x + 3y = -5$$

EXAMPLE 3

Solve.

$$\textbf{(1)} \quad 3x - y = -2$$
$$\textbf{(2)} \quad x + 5y = 10$$

SOLUTION Note that the coefficient of x in Equation (2) is $+1$. By multiplying this equation by -3 and then adding the two equations, we eliminate the x-terms.

$$
\begin{array}{ll}
\textbf{(1)} \quad 3x - y = -2 & \hspace{2.2cm} 3x - y = -2 \\
\textbf{(2)} \quad x + 5y = 10 & \xrightarrow{\text{Multiply by }-3.} \quad \underline{-3x - 15y = -30} \\
& \hspace{3.2cm} -16y = -32 \quad \text{Add the equations.} \\
& \hspace{3.6cm} y = 2
\end{array}
$$

Next, we substitute 2 for y in Equation (2), and then solve for x.

$$
\begin{aligned}
\textbf{(2)} \quad x + 5y &= 10 \\
x + 5(2) &= 10 \\
x + 10 &= 10 \\
x &= 0
\end{aligned}
$$

So the solution is $(0, 2)$.

PRACTICE 3

Solve for x and y.

$$\textbf{(1)} \quad x - 3y = -18$$
$$\textbf{(2)} \quad 5x + 2y = 12$$

How could we have solved the system in Example 3 another way?

EXAMPLE 4

Use the elimination method to solve the following system of linear equations.

$$(1) \quad 4x + 3y = -19$$
$$(2) \quad 3x - 2y = -10$$

SOLUTION This system is more complicated to solve than the previous examples because there is no single integer that we can multiply either equation by that will eliminate a variable when we add the equations. Instead, we must multiply *both* equations by integers that lead to the elimination of a variable. There are a number of possible strategies to accomplish this. We can, for instance, multiply Equation (1) by 2 and Equation (2) by 3 to eliminate the y-terms when the equations are added.

$$(1) \quad 4x + 3y = -19 \quad \xrightarrow{\text{Multiply by 2.}} \quad 8x + 6y = -38$$
$$(2) \quad 3x - 2y = -10 \quad \xrightarrow{\text{Multiply by 3.}} \quad \underline{9x - 6y = -30}$$
$$17x \qquad = -68 \quad \text{Add the equations.}$$
$$x = -4$$

Now let's substitute -4 for x in Equation (1), and then solve for y.

$$(1) \qquad 4x + 3y = -19$$
$$4(-4) + 3y = -19$$
$$-16 + 3y = -19$$
$$3y = 16 + (-19)$$
$$3y = -3$$
$$y = -1$$

So the solution is $(-4, -1)$.

PRACTICE 4

Solve by elimination.

$$(1) \quad 5x - 7y = 24$$
$$(2) \quad 3x - 5y = 16$$

How could we have solved the system in Example 4 by eliminating x instead of y?

To Solve a System of Linear Equations by Elimination

- Write both equations in the general form $Ax + By = C$.
- Choose the variable that you want to eliminate.
- If necessary, multiply one or both equations by appropriate numbers so that the coefficients of the variable to be eliminated are opposites.
- Add the equations. Then solve the resulting equation for the remaining variable.
- Substitute the value found in the previous step in either of the original equations and solve for the other variable.
- Check by substituting the values in both equations of the original system.

EXAMPLE 5

Solve by elimination.

$$\textbf{(1)} \qquad 5x = 3y$$
$$\textbf{(2)} \quad -3x + 2y = 9$$

SOLUTION Equation (1) is not in the form $Ax + By = C$, so let's begin by rewriting it in general form.

$$\textbf{(1)} \qquad 5x = 3y \quad \xrightarrow{\text{Write in general form.}} \quad 5x - 3y = 0$$
$$\textbf{(2)} \quad -3x + 2y = 9 \qquad\qquad\qquad -3x + 2y = 9$$

Now suppose we choose to eliminate the x-terms. To do this, we can multiply Equation (1) by 3, Equation (2) by 5, and then add the equations.

$$\textbf{(1)} \quad 5x - 3y = 0 \quad \xrightarrow{\text{Multiply by 3.}} \quad 15x - 9y = 0$$
$$\textbf{(2)} \quad -3x + 2y = 9 \quad \xrightarrow{\text{Multiply by 5.}} \quad \underline{-15x + 10y = 45} \quad \text{Add the equations.}$$
$$y = 45$$

To solve for x, let's substitute 45 for y in Equation (1).

$$\textbf{(1)} \quad 5x = 3y$$
$$5x = 3(45)$$
$$5x = 135$$
$$x = 27$$

So the solution is $(27, 45)$.

PRACTICE 5

Use the elimination method to solve the following system.

$$\textbf{(1)} \quad -2x + 5y = 20$$
$$\textbf{(2)} \qquad 3x = 7y - 26$$

EXAMPLE 6

Solve by elimination.

$$\textbf{(1)} \quad 4x - 6y + 12 = 0$$
$$\textbf{(2)} \quad 2x - 3y \quad\;\; = -4$$

SOLUTION We begin by writing Equation (1) in general form.

$$\textbf{(1)} \quad 4x - 6y + 12 = 0 \quad \xrightarrow{\text{Write in general form.}} \quad 4x - 6y = -12$$
$$\textbf{(2)} \qquad 2x - 3y = -4 \qquad\qquad\qquad 2x - 3y = -4$$

Now let's eliminate the y-terms. To do this, we can multiply Equation (2) by -2, and then add the equations.

$$\textbf{(1)} \quad 4x - 6y = -12 \qquad\qquad\qquad 4x - 6y = -12$$
$$\textbf{(2)} \quad 2x - 3y = \;\; -4 \quad \xrightarrow{\text{Multiply by }-2.} \quad \underline{-4x + 6y = 8}$$
$$0 = -4 \quad \text{False.}$$

Since adding the equations yields a false statement, the original system has no solution.

PRACTICE 6

Solve:

$$3x = 4 + y$$
$$9x - 3y = 12$$

Let's use our knowledge of the elimination method to solve some applied problems, beginning with a motion problem.

EXAMPLE 7	PRACTICE 7

It takes a plane 3 hr to fly between two airports, traveling with a tailwind at a ground speed of 500 mph. The plane then takes 4 hr to make the return trip against the same wind. What is the speed of the plane in still air? What is the speed of the wind?

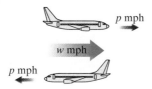

SOLUTION Let p represent the speed of the plane in still air and w represent the speed of the wind. On the initial flight, the wind is with the plane so its speed relative to the ground is $p + w$. When returning, the wind is against the plane so its ground speed is $p - w$. We can organize the given information in the following table:

	Ground speed ·	Time =	Distance
Going	$p + w$	3	$3(p + w)$
Returning	$p - w$	4	$4(p - w)$

Note that since the distance the plane travels is the product of its ground speed and the time it travels, we can compute each entry in the distance column of the table by multiplying the corresponding entries in the groundspeed and the time columns.

Since we are told that the speed going is 500 mph, we have

$$p + w = 500$$

But the distance going and the distance returning are equal, so

$$3(p + w) = 4(p - w)$$

Now we have a system of two equations, which we must solve.

$$\textbf{(1)} \qquad p + w = 500$$
$$\textbf{(2)} \quad 3(p + w) = 4(p - w)$$

We can write Equation (2) in general form, by simplifying.

$$3(p + w) = 4(p - w)$$
$$3p + 3w = 4p - 4w$$
$$3p - 4p + 3w + 4w = 0$$
$$-p + 7w = 0$$

A whale swimming with the current traveled 80 mi in 2 hr. Swimming against the current, the whale traveled only 40 mi in the same amount of time. Find the whale's speed in calm water and the speed of the current.

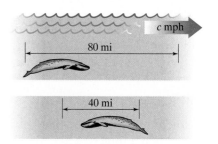

The system then becomes

> **(1)** $p + w = 500$
> **(2)** $-p + 7w = 0$

Adding the equations eliminates the p-terms.

$$8w = 500$$
$$w = 62.5$$

Finally, let's substitute 62.5 for w in Equation (1) and solve for p.

> **(1)** $p + 62.5 = 500$
> $p = 437.5$

So the wind speed is 62.5 mph, and the speed of the plane in still air is 437.5 mph.

EXAMPLE 8	PRACTICE 8

EXAMPLE 8

A student had two part-time jobs in a restaurant. One week she earned a total of $306, working 12 hr as a cashier and 10 hr as a cook. The next week, she worked 14 hr as a cashier and 22 hr cooking, earning $512. What is her hourly wage as a cashier? As a cook?

SOLUTION Let x represent the student's hourly wage as a cashier and y represent the student's hourly wage as a cook. The first week, the student earned $306, and the second week, $512. So we must solve the following system.

> **(1)** $12x + 10y = 306$
> **(2)** $14x + 22y = 512$

We can divide each equation by 2 to simplify.

> **(1)** $6x + 5y = 153$
> **(2)** $7x + 11y = 256$

PRACTICE 8

Admission prices at a football game were $10 for adults and $6 for children. The total value of the 175 tickets sold was $1450. How many adults and how many children attended the game?

Let's eliminate the x-terms by multiplying Equation (1) by 7 and Equation (2) by -6. Then we add the equations.

$$
\begin{array}{lll}
\textbf{(1)} & 6x + 5y = 153 & \xrightarrow[\text{Multiply by }-6.]{\text{Multiply by 7.}} & 42x + 35y = 1071 \\
\textbf{(2)} & 7x + 11y = 256 & & -42x - 66y = -1536
\end{array}
$$

Adding the equations eliminates the x-terms.

$$-31y = -465$$
$$y = \frac{-465}{-31}$$
$$y = 15$$

Finally, we substitute 15 for y in the original Equation (1) and solve for x.

$$
\begin{aligned}
\textbf{(1)} \quad 12x + 10y &= 306 \\
12x + 10(15) &= 306 \\
12x + 150 &= 306 \\
12x &= 156 \\
x &= \frac{156}{12} \\
x &= 13
\end{aligned}
$$

So the student earned $13 per hour as a cashier and $15 per hour as a cook.

In this chapter, we have discussed three methods of solving a system of linear equations—the graphing method, the substitution method, and the elimination (or addition) method. The following table lists some advantages and disadvantages of each method, to help in deciding which method to apply in a given problem.

Method	Advantages	Disadvantages
Graphing Method	● Provides a picture that makes relationships understandable.	● Approximates solutions, particularly when they are not integers or are large. ● Can be time consuming if not using a grapher.
Substitution Method	● Gives exact solutions. ● Is easy to use when a variable in one of the original equations is isolated.	● No picture. ● Can result in complicated equations with parentheses and with fractions.
Elimination Method	● Gives exact solutions. ● Is easy to use when the two coefficients of a variable are opposites.	● No picture.

Exercises 4.3

FOR EXTRA HELP

 Student's Solutions Manual

 Addison-Wesley Math Tutor Center

MyMathLab

Videotape 4/DVT 4

Solve.

1. $x + y = 3$
$x - y = 7$

2. $x - y = 10$
$x + y = -8$

3. $x + y = -4$
$-x + 3y = -6$

4. $5x - y = 8$
$2x + y = -1$

5. $10p - q = -14$
$-4p + q = -4$

6. $a + b = -4$
$-a + 2b = -8$

7. $3x + y = -3$
$4x + y = -4$

8. $x + 4y = -3$
$x - 7y = 19$

9. $3x + 5y = 10$
$3x + 5y = -5$

10. $8x + 2y = 3$
$4x + y = -9$

11. $9x + 6y = -15$
$-3x - 2y = 5$

12. $4x + y = -3$
$8x + 2y = -6$

13. $5x + 2y = -9$
$-5x + 2y = 11$

14. $7x + 4y = -6$
$-x + 4y = 10$

15. $2s + d = -2$
$5s + 3d = -6$

16. $-5x + 8y = -7$
$-6x + 9y = -9$

17. $3x - 5y = 1$
$7x - 8y = 17$

18. $3x + 2y = 9$
$-2x + 3y = -19$

19. $5x + 2y = -1$
$4x - 5y = -14$

20. $10x - 3y = 9$
$3x - 2y = -5$

21. $7p + 3q = 15$
$-5p - 7q = 16$

22. $8a + 2b = 18$
$4a - 3b = -15$

23. $6x + 5y = -8.5$
$8x + 10y = -3$

24. $6x - 6y = -3.6$
$-4x + 8y = -16$

25. $3.5x + 5y = -3$
$2x = -2y$

26. $3x - 3y = 0$
$1.5y = -6x + 30$

27. $2x - 4 = -y$
$x + 2y = 0$

28. $y = -3x + 7$
$4x + 2y = 11$

29. $8x + 10y = 1$
$-4x - 5y + 6 = 0$

30. $x - y = 6$
$3x = 3y + 10$

Applications

Solve.

31. A quarterback throws a pass that travels 40 yd with the wind in 2.5 sec. If he had thrown the same pass against the wind, the football would have traveled 20 yd in 2 sec. Find the speed of a pass that the quarterback would throw if there were no wind.

32. A crew team rows in a river with a current. When the team rows with the current, the boat travels 14 mi in 2 hr. Against the current, the team rows 6 mi in the same amount of time. At what speed does the team row in still water?

33. To enter a zoo, adult visitors must pay $5, whereas children and seniors pay only half price. On one day, the zoo collected a total of $765. If the zoo had 223 visitors that day, how many half-price admissions and how many full-price admissions did the zoo collect?

34. Compact discs are stored in single jewel cases, which are 0.375 in. thick, and in multiple-CD jewel cases, which have a thickness of 0.875 in. If 86 of these jewel cases exactly fit on the storage shelf shown, how many of the jewel cases are single?

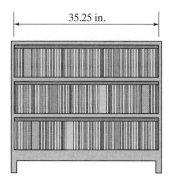

35.25 in.

35. The annual salaries of a congressman and a senator total $227,000. If the senator makes $23,200 more than the congressman, find each of their salaries.

36. The height of the picture shown to the right is double its width. It took molding 180 in. long to frame the picture. Find the dimensions of the frame.

37. A particular computer takes 43 nanoseconds to carry out 5 sums and 7 products, and 42 nanoseconds to perform 2 sums and 9 products. How long does the computer take to carry out one sum? To carry out one product?

38. A wholesale novelty shop sells some embroidered scarves for $12 each and others for $15 each. A customer pays $234 for 17 scarves. How many scarves at each price did she buy?

39. One issue of a journal has 3 full-page ads and 5 half-page ads, generating $6075 in revenue. The next issue has 4 full-page ads and 4 half-page ads, resulting in advertising revenue of $6380. Determine the advertising rates in this journal for full-page and half-page ads.

40. According to a law of physics, the lever shown will balance when the products of each weight and the length of its force arm are equal.

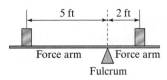

The weights shown above balance. If 10 lb are added to the left weight, which is then moved 1 ft closer to the fulcrum, the lever will again balance. Find the two original weights.

• *Check your answers on page A-21.*

Mindstretchers

GROUPWORK

1. Your friend performs the following magic trick: She asks you to think of two numbers but not to tell you what they are. Instead, you tell her the sum and the difference of the two numbers. She promptly tells you what the two original numbers were. Explain how your friend does the trick. Working with partners, try to perform this trick.

_____

_____

_____

_____

_____

WRITING

2. Consider the system of equations

$$\textbf{(1)} \quad 5x - 8y = 4$$
$$\textbf{(2)} \quad 12x + 24y = 11$$

Explain how the concept of LCM relates to solving this system by elimination.

_____

_____

_____

_____

_____

_____

_____

MATHEMATICAL REASONING

3. The elimination method can be extended to three linear equations in three variables. Solve the following system:

$$4x - y - 3z = 30$$
$$3x - 2y - 6z = -5$$
$$x - z = 5$$

Cultural Note

Sources: Roger Cooke, *The History of Mathematics*, John Wiley, New York, 1997; D. E. Smith, *History of Mathematics*, Dover Publications, New York, 1923

Carl Friedrich Gauss (1777–1855) is generally considered to be one of the greatest mathematicians in history. Among his many mathematical contributions was the *Gaussian elimination method* of solving systems of linear equations, discussed in this chapter. Gauss (rhymes with "house") is credited with being the first to prove the major mathematical result known as the Fundamental Theorem of Algebra. He was also an important scientist. In astronomy, he laid the theoretical foundation for predicting a planet's orbit. To honor this German's groundbreaking work in physics, his name is given to the unit (*gauss*) used today to express the strength of a magnetic field.

Key Concepts and Skills

	= CONCEPT		= SKILL

CONCEPT/SKILL	DESCRIPTION	EXAMPLE
[4.1] System of equations	Two or more equations considered simultaneously, that is, together.	$x + y = 7$ $x - y = 1$
[4.1] Solution of a system of equations in two variables	An ordered pair of numbers that satisfies both equations in the system.	Is (4, 3) a solution of the following system? $x + y = 7 \rightarrow 4 + 3 \overset{?}{=} 7$ True. $x - y = 1 \rightarrow 4 - 3 \overset{?}{=} 1$ True. Yes, (4, 3) is a solution of the system.
[4.1] To solve a system of linear equations by graphing	• Graph both equations on the same coordinate plane. • There are three possibilities: **a.** If the lines intersect, then the solution is the ordered pair of coordinates for the point of intersection. Check that these coordinates satisfy both equations. **b.** If the lines are parallel, then there is no solution of the system. **c.** If the lines coincide, then there are infinitely many solutions, namely all the ordered pairs of coordinates that represent points on the line.	$x + y = 7$ $x - y = 3$ 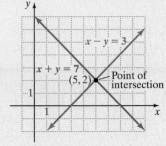 $3x - y = 2$ $3x - y = 4$ 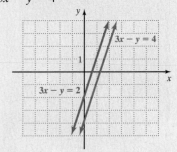 $x - y = 3$ $2x - 2y = 6$ 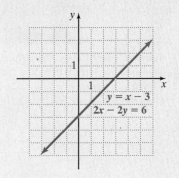

continued

III

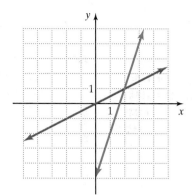

IV

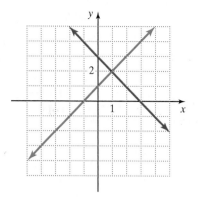

Solve each system by graphing.

4. $x + y = 6$
$\quad x - y = -4$

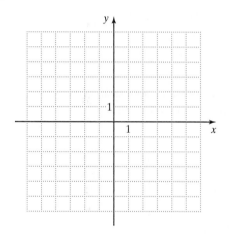

5. $\quad\quad y = 2x$
$\quad 6x - 3y = 3$

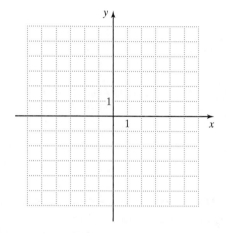

6. $\quad\quad 2y = -8x + 2$
$\quad -4x - y = -1$

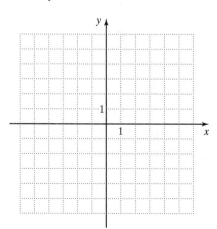

7. $x - 3y = -15$
$\quad y - \; x = 5$

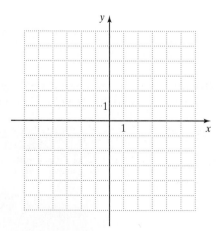

[4.2]

Solve each system by substitution.

8. $x + y = 3$
   $y = 2x + 6$

9. $a = 3b - 4$
   $a + 4b = 10$

10. $x - 3y = 1$
   $-2x + 6y = 7$

11. $10x + 2y = 14$
   $-y = 5x - 7$

[4.3]

Solve each system by elimination.

12. $x + y = 1$
   $x - y = 7$

13. $2x + 3y = 8$
   $4x + 6y = 16$

14. $4x = 9 - 5y$
   $2x + 3y = 3$

15. $3x + 2y = -4$
   $4x - 3y = 23$

Mixed Applications

Solve.

16. A student starts a typing service. He buys a computer and a printer for $1750, and then charges $5.50 per page for typing. Expenses for ink, paper, and electricity amount to $0.50 per page.

   a. Write the given information as a system of equations.

   b. How many pages must the student type to break even?

17. A job applicant must choose between two sales positions. One position pays $10 per hour, and the other $8 per hour plus a base pay of $50 per week.

   a. Express the weekly salaries of the two positions as a system of equations.

   b. How many hours would the applicant have to work per week in order to earn the same amount of money at each position?

18. The movie screen shown has a perimeter of 332 ft. If the length is 26 ft more than the width, find the area of the screen.

19. A doubles tennis court is 51 ft longer than it is wide. If the court's perimeter is 228 ft, find its dimensions.

20. The coin box of a vending machine contains only nickels and dimes. There are 350 coins worth $25. How many nickels and how many dimes did the box contain?

21. Two trains start 500 mi apart and speed toward each other. The difference between the average speeds of the trains is 5 mph. If they pass one another after 4 hr, find the rate of each train.

22. During a season, a college basketball team scored 2437 points on a combination of three-point and two-point baskets. If the team made 1085 baskets, how many two-point baskets and how many three-point baskets did the team make?

23. A pharmacist has 10% and 30% alcohol solutions in stock. To prepare 200 ml of a 25% solution, how much of each should the pharmacist mix?

24. A farmer is preparing an insecticide by mixing a 50% solution with water. How much of this solution and how much water are needed to fill a 2000-liter tank with a 35% solution?

25. Last year, a financial adviser recommended that her client invest part of his $50,000 in secure municipal bonds that paid 6% and the rest in corporate stocks that paid 8%. How much money did the client put into each type of investment if the total annual return was $3200?

26. An investor split $10,000 between a high-risk mutual fund and a low-risk mutual fund. Last year, the high-risk fund paid 12% and the low-risk fund paid 2%, for a total of $900. How much money was invested in each fund?

27. Two airplanes leave an airport at the same time, one flying 100 mph faster than the other. The planes travel in opposite directions and after 2 hr they are 1800 mi apart. Determine the speed of the slower plane.

28. Flying with the wind, a bird flew 13 mi in half an hour. On the return trip against the wind, it was able to travel only 8 mi in the same amount of time. Find the speed of the bird in calm air and the speed of the wind.

29. The U.S. Senate has 100 members. After debating the merits of a treaty, all the senators voted, and 14 more voted for the treaty than against. None of the senators abstained.

   a. How many senators voted *for* the treaty?

   b. How many senators voted *against* the treaty?

30. In a chemistry lab, a piece of copper starting at 2°C is heated at the rate of 3° per minute. At the same time, a piece of iron starting at 86°C is being cooled at the rate of 4° per minute.

   a. After how much time will the two metals be at the same temperature?

   b. After how much time will the iron be 14° colder than the copper?

● Check your answers on page A-21.

Chapter 4 Posttest

To see if you have mastered the topics in this chapter, take this test.

1. Indicate which of the following ordered pairs is a solution of the system

$$x + y = -1$$
$$3x - y = 1$$

   a. $(0, -1)$

   b. $(-1, 0)$

   c. $(2, -3)$

2. How many solutions does the graphed system appear to have?

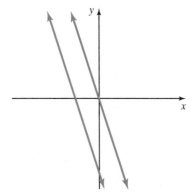

Solve each system by graphing.

3. $x - y = 3$
   $x + y = 3$

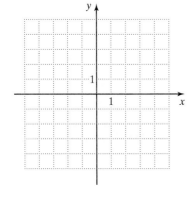

4. $5 = 2x - y$
   $y = 2x$

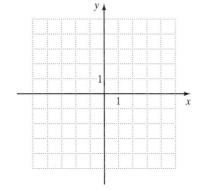

5. $2x + 3y = 4$
   $3x - y = -5$

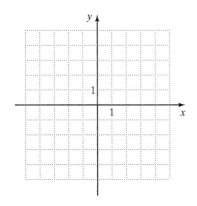

Solve each system by substitution.

6. $x = 3y - 7$
  $y = x + 5$

7. $3x - 5y = -12$
  $x + 2y = 7$

8. $u - 3v = -12$
  $5u + v = 8$
  $u = \frac{3}{4}, v = \frac{17}{4}$

Solve each system by elimination.

9. $4x + y = 3$
  $7x - y = 19$

10. $x - y = 5$
  $2x - 2y = 5$

11. $-5p + 2q = 1$
  $4p + 3q = 1.5$

Solve each system.

12. $5x = 3y$
  $-3x + 2y = 9$

13. $4l = -(m + 3)$
  $8l + 2m = -6$

14. $5x + 2y = -1$
  $x - 1 = y$

15. $5x + 3y - 9 = 0$
  $2x - 7y - 20 = 0$

Solve.

16. In a local election, the ratio of votes for the winning candidate to the losing candidate was 2 to 1. If 6306 votes were cast in the election, how many votes did the winning candidate get?

17. The following table gives nutritional information for servings of turkey and of salmon:

	Turkey, light meat (3 oz)	Salmon (3 oz)
Fat (grams)	3	3
Calories	135	99

How many servings of turkey and of salmon would it take to get 9 g of fat and 333 cal?

18. A businesswoman has twice as much money invested at 7.5% as she has at 6%. The year-long income from both investments is $840. How much has she invested at each rate?

19. A 20% iodine solution is mixed with a 60% iodine solution to produce 4 gal of a 50% iodine solution. How many gallons of each solution are needed?

20. A small airplane traveled 170 mph with a tailwind and 130 mph with a headwind. Find the speed of the wind and the speed of the airplane in still air.

• *Check your answers on page A-22.*

Cumulative Review Exercises

To help you review, solve the following.

1. Calculate: $-4 \div 2 + 3\,(-1)(8)$

2. True or false: $-6 < -5$

3. Is 5 a solution of the equation $3p + 1 = 9 - p$?

4. Solve: $5(x + 1) - (x - 2) = x - 2$

5. Solve and graph: $3x - 7 < 4(x - 2)$

6. Find the slope of the line shown:

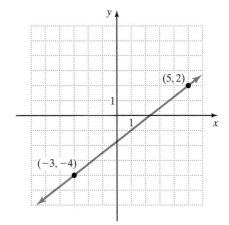

7. Find the slope and *y*-intercept of the graph whose equation is $3x + 6y = 12$.

8. Graph: $y = -4x + 2$

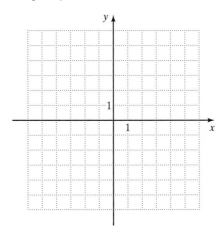

9. The maximum speed of a supersonic airplane S in miles per hour is commonly represented by its Mach number, M, where

$$M = \frac{S}{740}.$$

What is the maximum speed of an airplane flying at Mach 2.1?

10. In renting a car for a day, you must choose between two local car agencies. One agency charges $35 per day plus $0.20 per mile and the other charges $50 per day plus $0.15 per mile. Under what circumstances do the two agencies charge the same amount for a one-day rental?

Chapter 5

Exponents and Polynomials

Layoffs and Polynomials

Layoffs are common whenever the economy contracts. For instance, in 1933, the worst year of the Great Depression, so many American workers were laid off that one-fourth of the U.S. labor force was unemployed.

Suppose that 100 employees work in a factory. If the fraction f of these employees are laid off, the factory will still employ $100(1 - f)$, or $100 - 100f$, workers. If the factory again lays off the same fraction of employees, the remaining number of workers can be represented by $100(1 - f)(1 - f)$, an expression that can also be written as the *polynomial* $100 - 200f + 100f^2$.

(*Source:* Michael Parkin, *Economics*, Addison-Wesley, 1999)

To see if you have already mastered the topics in this chapter, take this test.

Simplify.

1. $x^5 \cdot x^4$

2. $y^7 \div y^3$

3. $-3a^0$

4. $(4x^4y^3)^2$

5. $\left(\dfrac{a}{b^5}\right)^3$

6. $(5x^{-1}y^4)^{-2}$

7. For the polynomial $6x^4 + 5x^3 + x^2 - 7x + 8$, name:

   a. the terms _____

   b. the coefficients _____

   c. the degree _____

   d. the constant term _____

8. Find the sum: $(2n^2 + 7n - 10) + (n^2 - 6n + 12)$

9. Subtract: $(8x^2 - 9) - (7x^2 - x - 5)$

10. Combine: $(6a^2b + ab - a^2) + (2a^2 + 3a^2b - 5b^2) - (7a^2 - 2ab - b^2)$

Multiply.

11. $3x^2(x^2 - 4x + 9)$

12. $(n + 3)(2n^2 + n - 6)$

13. $(4x + 9)(x - 3)$

14. $(3y - 7)(3y + 7)$

15. $(5 - 2n)^2$

Divide.

16. $\dfrac{9t^4 - 18t^3 - 45t^2}{9t^2}$

17. $(4x^2 - 3x - 10) \div (x - 2)$

Solve.

18. In chemistry, a mole (mol) of any material contains 6×10^{23} molecules. Express in scientific notation the number of molecules that 200 mol of hydrogen will contain. (*Source:* Karen Timberlake, *Chemistry: An Introduction to General Organic and Biological Chemistry*, Addison-Wesley, 1999)

19. The average monthly cellular telephone bill is approximated by the polynomial

$$-0.535t^2 + 2.64t + 45.3,$$

where t represents the number of years since 2000. What was the average monthly cellular telephone bill in 2002? (*Source:* Cellular Telecommunications and Internet Association)

20. The owner of a daycare center plans to have a rectangular sandbox built in the outdoor play area. The width (in feet) of the sandbox is given by the polynomial $2x - 5$, as shown. If the length of the sandbox is designed to be 10 ft longer than the width, write a polynomial that represents the area of the sandbox.

$2x - 5$

● *Check your answers on page A-22.*

5.1 Laws of Exponents

OBJECTIVES

- *To simplify expressions by using the product and quotient rules of exponents*
- *To simplify expressions with exponent zero*
- *To simplify expressions with negative exponents*
- *To solve applied problems involving exponents*

What Exponents Are and Why They Are Important

In Section 1.7, we evaluated expressions involving exponents. In this chapter, we discuss a particular kind of expression called a *polynomial* and operations involving polynomials. Central to our discussion of these operations is a thorough understanding of the laws of exponents.

Exponents play an important role in arithmetic and algebra. Powers of 10 are key to the decimal place-value system that underlies the reading, writing, and computation of real numbers. In scientific notation, exponents are used to represent very large and very small numbers. There are many other applications of exponents in the sciences and in business.

Exponents

Recall the definition of an exponent from Chapter 1: An exponent (or power) is a number that indicates how many times another number (called the *base*) is used as a factor. For instance,

$$\underset{\text{Base}}{\underbrace{5}}{}^{\overset{\text{Exponent}}{3}} = \underbrace{5 \cdot 5 \cdot 5}_{\text{3 factors of 5}}$$

In general, if a is a positive integer, the expression x^a means

$$x^a = \underbrace{x \cdot x \cdot x \cdot \cdots \cdot x}_{a \text{ factors}},$$

where the exponent a indicates that there are a factors of x.

Exponent of One

For any real number x, $x^1 = x$.

Any number raised to the power 1 is the number itself. For example, $7^1 = 7$, $(-5)^1 = -5$, and $x^1 = x$.

EXAMPLE 1	PRACTICE 1
Multiply.	Multiply.
a. 2^5	**a.** 10^4
b. $\left(-\dfrac{1}{3}\right)^4$	**b.** $\left(-\dfrac{1}{2}\right)^5$
c. $(-x)^1$	**c.** $(-y)^6$
d. $(-x)^2$	**d.** $(-y)^1$

SOLUTION

a. $2^5 = 2 \cdot 2 \cdot 2 \cdot 2 \cdot 2 = 32$

b. $\left(-\dfrac{1}{3}\right)^4 = \left(-\dfrac{1}{3}\right)\left(-\dfrac{1}{3}\right)\left(-\dfrac{1}{3}\right)\left(-\dfrac{1}{3}\right) = \dfrac{1}{81}$

c. $(-x^1) = -x$

d. $(-x)^2 = (-x)(-x) = x^2$

The expression 10^0 involves raising a number to the zero power. To understand the value of this expression, consider the following pattern:

$$10^5 = 10 \cdot 10 \cdot 10 \cdot 10 \cdot 10 = 100{,}000$$
$$10^4 = 10 \cdot 10 \cdot 10 \cdot 10 = 10{,}000$$
$$10^3 = 10 \cdot 10 \cdot 10 = 1000$$
$$10^2 = 10 \cdot 10 = 100$$
$$10^1 = 10$$
$$10^0 = ?$$

Note that to go from 10^5 to 10^4 we can divide 10^5 by 10. The pattern continues, and going from 10^2 to 10^1, we can divide 10^2 by 10. So to go from 10^1 to 10^0, it seems reasonable for us to divide 10^1 by 10, which is 1. Thus, we take 10^0 to be equal to 1. Would we have gotten the same result had we considered powers of 2 instead of powers of 10 in order to determine the value of 2^0?

Exponent of Zero

For any nonzero real number x, $x^0 = 1$.

Note that the expression 0^0 is undefined. Throughout the remainder of this text, we will assume that any variable raised to the 0 power represents a nonzero number.

EXAMPLE 2	PRACTICE 2
Simplify.	Simplify.
a. 25^0	**a.** 8^0
b. $(-3.5)^0$	**b.** $\left(-\dfrac{2}{3}\right)^0$
c. a^0	**c.** y^0
d. $-a^0$	**d.** $-y^0$
SOLUTION	
a. $25^0 = 1$	
b. $(-3.5)^0 = 1$	
c. $a^0 = 1$	
d. $-a^0 = -1 \cdot a^0 = -1 \cdot 1 = -1$	

Laws of Exponents

The laws of exponents are rules that apply to exponents. These rules are not arbitrary but follow logically from the definition of exponent.

Let's first discuss the *product rule*. This rule applies when we multiply two powers with the same base. Consider the expression $x^4 \cdot x^6$. Using the definition of an exponent we get:

$$x^4 \cdot x^6 = \underbrace{\overbrace{(x \cdot x \cdot x \cdot x)}^{\text{4 factors}} \overbrace{(x \cdot x \cdot x \cdot x \cdot x \cdot x)}^{\text{6 factors}}}_{\text{10 factors}} = x^{10}$$

Since 4 factors of x and 6 additional factors of x make 10 factors of x, it follows that

$$x^4 \cdot x^6 = x^{4+6} = x^{10}.$$

This result can be generalized as follows.

> **Product Rule of Exponents**
>
> For any nonzero real number x and for any positive integers a and b,
>
> $$x^a \cdot x^b = x^{a+b}.$$

The product rule states that when we multiply powers of the same base, we add the exponents and leave the base the same.

EXAMPLE 3	PRACTICE 3

EXAMPLE 3

Simplify using the product rule, if possible.

a. $2^3 \cdot 2^5$

b. $(-5)^2 \cdot (-5)^8$

c. $x^8 \cdot x^{10}$

d. $m^4 \cdot m$

e. $x^2 \cdot y^3$

SOLUTION When we multiply powers of the same base, the product rule tells us to add the exponents but *not to change the base*.

a. $2^3 \cdot 2^5 = 2^{3+5} = 2^8$

b. $(-5)^2 \cdot (-5)^8 = (-5)^{2+8} = (-5)^{10}$

c. $x^8 \cdot x^{10} = x^{8+10} = x^{18}$

d. $m^4 \cdot m = m^4 \cdot m^1 = m^{4+1} = m^5$

e. In the expression $x^2 \cdot y^3$, we cannot apply the product rule because the bases are not the same.

PRACTICE 3

Simplify using the product rule, if possible.

a. $10^8 \cdot 10^4$

b. $(-4)^3 \cdot (-4)^3$

c. $n^3 \cdot n^7$

d. $y^5 \cdot y^0$

e. $a \cdot b^4$

Now we discuss another law of exponents—the *quotient rule*. This rule applies when we divide two powers of the same base. Consider the expression $\dfrac{x^6}{x^2}$. Using the definition of exponent, we get:

$$\frac{x^6}{x^2} = \frac{\overbrace{x \cdot x \cdot x \cdot x \cdot \overset{1}{\cancel{x}} \cdot \overset{1}{\cancel{x}}}^{6 \text{ factors}}}{\underset{\underset{2 \text{ factors}}{\underset{1}{\cancel{x}} \cdot \underset{1}{\cancel{x}}}}{}} = \underbrace{x \cdot x \cdot x \cdot x}_{4 \text{ factors}} = x^4$$

So

$$\frac{x^6}{x^2} = x^{6-2} = x^4,$$

which suggests the following rule.

Quotient Rule of Exponents

For any nonzero real number x and for any positive integers a and b,

$$\frac{x^a}{x^b} = x^{a-b}.$$

The quotient rule states that when we divide powers of the same base, we subtract the exponent in the denominator from the exponent in the numerator and leave the base the same.

EXAMPLE 4

Simplify using the quotient rule, if possible.

a. $\dfrac{10^5}{10^2}$

b. $(-2)^5 \div (-2)^5$

c. $\dfrac{p^{12}}{p^7}$

d. $\dfrac{y^{13}}{y}$

e. $\dfrac{x^4}{y^2}$

SOLUTION When we divide powers of the same base, the quotient rule tells us to subtract the exponents but *not to change the base.*

a. $\dfrac{10^5}{10^2} = 10^{5-2} = 10^3$

b. $(-2)^5 \div (-2)^5 = \dfrac{(-2)^5}{(-2)^5} = (-2)^{5-5} = (-2)^0 = 1$

PRACTICE 4

Simplify using the quotient rule, if possible.

a. $\dfrac{7^7}{7^2}$

b. $(-9)^6 \div (-9)^5$

c. $\dfrac{s^{10}}{s^{10}}$

d. $\dfrac{r^8}{r}$

e. $\dfrac{a^5}{b^3}$

c. $\dfrac{p^{12}}{p^{7}} = p^{12-7} = p^{5}$

d. $\dfrac{y^{13}}{y} = \dfrac{y^{13}}{y^{1}} = y^{13-1} = y^{12}$

e. In the expression $\dfrac{x^{4}}{y^{2}}$, we cannot apply the quotient rule because the bases are not the same.

Note in Example 4(b) that the quotient rule confirms the fact that any nonzero real number raised to the zero power is 1. That is,

$$\frac{(-2)^{5}}{(-2)^{5}} = \frac{-32}{-32} = 1 \qquad \text{and} \qquad \frac{(-2)^{5}}{(-2)^{5}} = (-2)^{5-5} = (-2)^{0} = 1.$$

EXAMPLE 5

Simplify.

a. $x^{3} \cdot x \cdot x^{5}$

b. $(a^{2}b)(ab^{4})$

c. $\dfrac{t^{3} \cdot t^{5}}{t^{2}}$

PRACTICE 5

Simplify.

a. $y^{2} \cdot y^{3} \cdot y^{4}$

b. $(x^{3}y^{3})(x^{2}y^{3})$

c. $\dfrac{a^{7}}{a \cdot a^{4}}$

SOLUTION

a. $x^{3} \cdot x \cdot x^{5} = x^{9}$ Use the product rule.

b. $(a^{2}b)(ab^{4}) = a^{2} \cdot a^{1} \cdot b^{1} \cdot b^{4}$ Rearrange the factors.

                 $= a^{3}b^{5}$ Use the product rule.

c. $\dfrac{t^{3} \cdot t^{5}}{t^{2}} = \dfrac{t^{8}}{t^{2}} = t^{6}$ Use the product rule in the numerator.

                         Use the quotient rule.

Negative Exponents

Until now, we have only considered exponents that were either positive integers or 0. What meaning should we give to *negative exponents*?

The quotient rule is the key to answering this question. Consider, for instance, the quotient $\dfrac{6^{4}}{6^{7}}$. On the one hand, we can simplify this fraction by using the definition of exponent and canceling the common factors, getting:

$$\frac{6^{4}}{6^{7}} = \frac{\overset{1}{\cancel{6}} \cdot \overset{1}{\cancel{6}} \cdot \overset{1}{\cancel{6}} \cdot \overset{1}{\cancel{6}}}{\underset{1}{\cancel{6}} \cdot \underset{1}{\cancel{6}} \cdot \underset{1}{\cancel{6}} \cdot \underset{1}{\cancel{6}} \cdot 6 \cdot 6 \cdot 6} = \frac{1}{6^{3}}$$

On the other hand, we can simplify by using the quotient rule, getting:

$$\frac{6^{4}}{6^{7}} = 6^{4-7} = 6^{-3}$$

Since

$$\frac{6^4}{6^7} = 6^{-3} \quad and \quad \frac{6^4}{6^7} = \frac{1}{6^3},$$

we conclude that $6^{-3} = \dfrac{1}{6^3}$, which leads us to the following:

Negative Exponent

For any nonzero real number x and for any integer a,

$$x^{-a} = \frac{1}{x^a}.$$

In general, an expression with exponents is considered *simplified* when it is written with only positive exponents.

EXAMPLE 6	PRACTICE 6
Simplify.	Simplify.
a. 5^{-2}	**a.** 9^{-2}
b. p^{-8}	
c. $-(8x)^{-1}$	**b.** n^{-5}
d. $(-4)^{-2}$	
SOLUTION	**c.** $-(3y)^{-1}$
a. $5^{-2} = \dfrac{1}{5^2} = \dfrac{1}{25}$	**d.** $(5)^{-3}$
b. $p^{-8} = \dfrac{1}{p^8}$	
c. $-(8x)^{-1} = -1(8x)^{-1} = \dfrac{-1}{(8x)^1} = -\dfrac{1}{8x}$	
d. $(-4)^{-2} = \dfrac{1}{(-4)^2} = \dfrac{1}{16}$	

TIP A negative exponent indicates a reciprocal. For example, $5^{-2} = \dfrac{1}{25}$.

The product rule of exponents and the quotient rule of exponents, which were defined for positive-integer exponents, also hold for negative-integer exponents.

EXAMPLE 7

Simplify by writing each expression using only positive exponents.

a. $2^{-1}q$ **b.** $5x^{-2}$ **c.** $\dfrac{y^6}{y^{10}}$

d. $4^{-1} \cdot x^{-5} \cdot x^2$ **e.** $\dfrac{1}{x^{-2}}$

SOLUTION

a. $2^{-1}q = \dfrac{1}{2} \cdot q = \dfrac{q}{2}$

b. $5x^{-2} = 5 \cdot \dfrac{1}{x^2} = \dfrac{5}{x^2}$

c. $\dfrac{y^6}{y^{10}} = y^{6-10} = y^{-4} = \dfrac{1}{y^4}$

d. $4^{-1} \cdot x^{-5} \cdot x^2 = 4^{-1} \cdot x^{-5+2} = \dfrac{1}{4}x^{-3} = \dfrac{1}{4} \cdot \dfrac{1}{x^3} = \dfrac{1}{4x^3}$

e. $\dfrac{1}{x^{-2}} = 1 \div x^{-2} = 1 \div \dfrac{1}{x^2} = 1 \cdot x^2 = x^2$

PRACTICE 7

Rewrite as expressions using only positive exponents.

a. $8^{-1}s$

b. $3x^{-1}$

c. $\dfrac{r^3}{r^9}$

d. $3^2 \cdot g^{-1} \cdot g^{-4}$

e. $\dfrac{1}{x^{-3}}$

The definition of a negative exponent and Example 7(e), in which we saw that $\dfrac{1}{x^{-2}} = x^2$, suggest the following.

Reciprocal of x^{-a}

For any nonzero real number x and any positive integer a,

$$\frac{1}{x^{-a}} = x^a.$$

EXAMPLE 8

Rewrite as an expression using positive exponents.

a. $\dfrac{5}{x^{-4}}$

b. $\dfrac{1}{3y^{-1}}$

c. $\dfrac{a^2}{b^{-3}}$

PRACTICE 8

Rewrite as an expression using positive exponents.

a. $\dfrac{1}{a^{-3}}$

b. $\dfrac{2}{5x^{-2}}$

c. $\dfrac{r^3}{2s^{-1}}$

SOLUTION

a. $\dfrac{5}{x^{-4}} = 5 \cdot \dfrac{1}{x^{-4}} = 5 \cdot x^4 = 5x^4$

b. $\dfrac{1}{3y^{-1}} = \dfrac{1}{3} \cdot \dfrac{1}{y^{-1}} = \dfrac{1}{3} \cdot y^1 = \dfrac{y}{3}$

c. $\dfrac{a^2}{b^{-3}} = a^2 \cdot \dfrac{1}{b^{-3}} = a^2 \cdot b^3 = a^2b^3$

EXAMPLE 9

Physicists study different kinds of electromagnetic waves, including radio waves, light waves, X-rays, and gamma rays. The diagram below, called the *electromagnetic spectrum*, shows the relationship among the wavelengths of these waves.

Consider a particular X-ray whose wavelength is 10^{-10} m and a gamma ray whose wavelength is 10^{-15} m. (*Source:* Arthur Beiser, *The Mainstream of Physics*, Addison-Wesley, 1962)

a. Which of these rays has a greater length?

b. What is the ratio of the longer to the shorter wavelength?

SOLUTION

a. The wavelengths are 10^{-10} m for the X-ray and 10^{-15} m for the gamma ray. Converting these expressions with negative exponents to equivalent expressions with positive exponents, the wavelengths can be written as $\dfrac{1}{10^{10}}$ m and $\dfrac{1}{10^{15}}$ m, respectively. Since $\dfrac{1}{10^{10}}$ has the smaller denominator, it is the larger number. Therefore the X-ray has the greater wavelength.

b. We use the quotient rule to compute the ratio of the greater wavelength, 10^{-10} m, to the shorter wavelength, 10^{-15} m:

$$\frac{10^{-10}}{10^{-15}} = 10^{(-10)-(-15)} = 10^{-10+15} = 10^5$$

So the ratio is 10^5.

PRACTICE 9

A computer's memory is often measured in *bits*, *bytes*, and *megabytes*. A bit (short for binary digit) is the smallest unit of data in the memory of the computer. A byte is equal to 2^3 bits, whereas a megabyte (MB) is equal to 2^{20} bytes.

a. How many bits are in a megabyte? Write the answer as a power of 2.

b. In most computers, the hard drive's capacity is expressed in *gigabytes*. A gigabyte (GB) is 2^{10} megabytes. How many bytes are there in a gigabyte? Express the result as a power of 2.

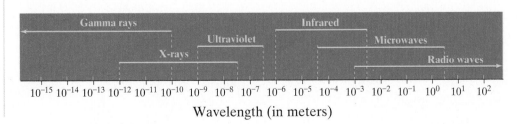

Wavelength (in meters)

Exercises 5.1

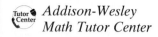

Multiply.

1. 5^3

2. 1^8

3. $-(0.5)^2$

4. $(-0.3)^2$

5. $(-2)^3$

6. -2^3

7. $\left(-\dfrac{1}{2}\right)^3$

8. $\left(-\dfrac{4}{5}\right)^2$

9. $(-x)^4$

10. $(-y)^3$

Simplify.

11. $(pq)^1$

12. $(-4xy)^1$

13. $(-3)^0$

14. -3^0

15. $-a^0$

16. b^0

Simplify using the product rule, if possible.

17. $10^9 \cdot 10^2$

18. $5^2 \cdot 5^3$

19. $a^4 \cdot a^2$

20. $x \cdot x^8$

21. $x^3 \cdot y^5$

22. $a^4 \cdot b^5$

23. $n^6 \cdot n$

24. $y \cdot y^0$

25. $x^2 y$

26. $a^4 b^3$

Simplify using the quotient rule, if possible.

27. $\dfrac{8^5}{8^3}$

28. $\dfrac{3^8}{3^2}$

29. $\dfrac{y^6}{y^5}$

30. $\dfrac{x^{12}}{x^{12}}$

31. $\dfrac{a^{10}}{a^4}$

32. $\dfrac{x^7}{x^5}$

33. $\dfrac{y^8}{x^4}$

34. $\dfrac{a^5}{b}$

35. $\dfrac{x^6}{x^6}$

36. $r^4 \div r^0$

Simplify.

37. $y^2 \cdot y^3 \cdot y$

38. $t \cdot t \cdot t^2$

39. $(p^2 q^3)(p^5 q^2)$

40. $(xy^2)(x^2 y^6)$

41. $(yx^2)(xz^2)(yz)$

42. $a(a^4b^2)(bc^3)$

43. $\dfrac{a^2 \cdot a^3}{a^4}$

44. $\dfrac{t^4}{t^3 \cdot t}$

45. $\dfrac{x^2 \cdot x^4}{x^3 \cdot x}$

46. $\dfrac{y^5 \cdot y^5}{y^2 \cdot y^3}$

Rewrite as an expression using only positive exponents.

47. 5^{-1}

48. 7^{-1}

49. x^{-1}

50. a^{-1}

51. $(-3a)^{-1}$

52. $-(5y)^{-1}$

53. 2^{-4}

54. 7^{-3}

55. -3^{-4}

56. -5^{-2}

57. $(-4)^{-2}$

58. $(-2)^{-4}$

59. $8n^{-3}$

60. $-2y^{-3}$

61. $(-x)^{-2}$

62. $(-a)^{-4}$

63. $-x^{-2}$

64. $-a^{-4}$

65. $-3^{-2}x$

66. $-4^{-1}y$

67. $x^{-2}y^3$

68. xy^{-3}

69. qr^{-1}

70. rs^{-1}

71. $4x^{-1}y^2$

72. $-5a^2b^{-4}$

73. $p^{-2} \cdot p^{-3}$

74. $t^{-3} \cdot t^{-3}$

75. $p^{-1} \cdot p^4$

76. $s^4 \cdot s^{-2}$

77. $\dfrac{a^3}{a^4}$

78. $\dfrac{n}{n^5}$

79. $\dfrac{2}{n^{-4}}$

80. $\dfrac{3}{n^{-1}}$

81. $\dfrac{1}{2p^{-5}}$

82. $\dfrac{2}{3x^{-4}}$

83. $\dfrac{p^4}{q^{-1}}$

84. $\dfrac{a}{b^{-6}}$

85. $\dfrac{t^{-2}}{t^3}$

86. $\dfrac{x^{-2}}{x^5}$

87. $\dfrac{x^5}{x^{-2}}$

88. $\dfrac{n^7}{n^{-1}}$

89. $\dfrac{a^{-4}}{a^{-5}}$

90. $\dfrac{y^{-1}}{y^{-6}}$

91. $\dfrac{a^{-3}}{b^{-3}}$

92. $\dfrac{x^{-4}}{y^{-2}}$

Applications

Solve.

93. The first day of an epidemic, 35 people got sick. Each day thereafter, the number of people who got ill doubled.

  a. How many people were ill on the sixth day of the epidemic? On the tenth day?

  b. How many times as great was the number of people ill on the tenth day as compared to the number ill on the sixth day?

94. The value of a new car t years after it is purchased is given by the expression $28{,}000(1.25)^{-t}$.

  a. What is the value of the car one year after it was purchased?

  b. Evaluate the expression for $t = 0$. Explain the significance of this value.

95. The concentration of a pollutant in a pond is 60 parts per million (ppm). The pollution level drops by 5% each month, so that the amount of pollutant each month is 95% of the amount in the previous month, as shown in the following table.

Month	Pollution Level
1	60 ppm
2	60×0.95 ppm
3	$60 \times (0.95)^2$ ppm
4	$60 \times (0.95)^3$ ppm
5	$60 \times (0.95)^4$ ppm
6	$60 \times (0.95)^5$ ppm
7	$60 \times (0.95)^6$ ppm

What will the pollution level be in the twelfth month?

96. The population of the United States in 1820 was approximately 10^7. One hundred years later, it was approximately 10^8. By what factor did the U.S. population grow during this century? (*Source:* U.S. Bureau of the Census)

97. A small, cube-shaped box is packed within a larger, cube-shaped box and is surrounded by Styrofoam peanuts. The side length of the larger box is $\frac{5}{2}$ that of the smaller box.

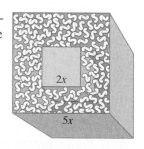

  a. Write an expression for the volume of each box.

  b. How many times the volume of the small box is the volume of the large box?

98. The cylindrical storage vat pictured has a base with area πr^2 and a height of r. The volume of the vat is the product of its height and the area of the base. Find the volume.

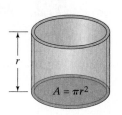

● *Check your answers on page A-22.*

Mindstretchers

WRITING

1. Identify the errors that were made resulting in the following false statements.

a. $4^{-3} = -\dfrac{1}{64}$

_____

_____

b. $x^{-2} \cdot x^{-3} = x^6$

_____

_____

c. $4^3 \cdot 4^{-5} = 16^{-2}$

_____

_____

d. $5^4 \div 5 = 1^4$

_____

_____

GROUPWORK

2. Which is larger: x^2 or x^{-2}? Explain your answer, and give some examples.

MATHEMATICAL REASONING

3. The expression 0^0 is undefined. Can you explain why?

5.2 More Laws of Exponents and Scientific Notation

OBJECTIVES

- *To simplify expressions by using the power rule*
- *To simplify expressions by raising a product to a power*
- *To simplify expressions by raising a quotient to a power*
- *To write a number in scientific notation*
- *To solve applied problems involving laws of exponents and scientific notation*

In this section, we consider several additional laws of exponents, as well as an important application of exponents known as scientific notation.

Additional Laws of Exponents

In the previous section, we discussed the product rule for the product of powers and the quotient rule for the quotient of powers. We now consider a third rule known as the *power rule*. The power rule deals with expressions in which a power is raised to a power.

Let's consider, for instance, the expression $(x^2)^3$. Using the definition of an exponent gives us:

$$(x^2)^3 = \underbrace{x^2 \cdot x^2 \cdot x^2}_{3 \text{ factors of } x^2} = x^{2+2+2} = x^6$$

So $(x^2)^3 = x^6$. We can generalize this result as follows.

Power Rule of Exponents

For any nonzero real number x and any integers a and b,

$$(x^a)^b = x^{ab}.$$

In words, the power rule says that when raising a power to a power, we *multiply* the exponents and *leave the base the same*.

EXAMPLE 1

Simplify using the power rule of exponents.

a. $(5^2)^2$ b. $(2^{-3})^2$

c. $-(p^4)^5$ d. $(q^2)^{-1}$

SOLUTION We apply the power rule and then simplify.

a. $(5^2)^2 = 5^{2 \cdot 2} = 5^4 = 625$

b. $(2^{-3})^2 = 2^{-3 \cdot 2}$

$= 2^{-6}$

$= \dfrac{1}{2^6}$ Use the definition of a negative exponent.

$= \dfrac{1}{64}$

c. $-(p^4)^5 = -(p^{4 \cdot 5}) = -p^{20}$

d. $(q^2)^{-1} = q^{2 \cdot (-1)} = q^{-2} = \dfrac{1}{q^2}$

PRACTICE 1

Simplify using the power rule of exponents.

a. $(2^3)^2$

b. $(7^3)^{-1}$

c. $(q^2)^4$

d. $-(p^3)^{-5}$

TIP Be sure to distinguish between the *product* rule and the *power* rule.

Product rule: $x^a \cdot x^b = x^{a+b}$ **Power rule:** $(x^a)^b = x^{ab}$

Add the exponents. ⌐   Multiply the exponents. ⌐

Another law of exponents has to do with *raising a product to a power*.

For instance, consider the expression $(5x)^3$.

Rearrange the factors.

$$(5x)^3 = (5x)(5x)(5x) = (5 \cdot 5 \cdot 5)(x \cdot x \cdot x) = 5^3 \cdot x^3 = 125x^3$$

So we see that $(5x)^3$ is the same as 5^3 times x^3. We can generalize this result as follows.

Raising a Product to a Power

For any nonzero real numbers x and y and any integer a,

$$(xy)^a = x^a \cdot y^a.$$

This rule states that to raise a product to a power we raise each factor to that power.

EXAMPLE 2

Simplify using the rule for raising a product to a power.

a. $(2y)^4$

b. $(-3a)^2$

c. $-(3a)^2$

SOLUTION We apply the rule for raising a product to a power and then simplify.

a. $(2y)^4 = 2^4 \cdot y^4 = 16y^4$

b. $(-3a)^2 = (-3)^2(a)^2 = 9a^2$

c. $-(3a)^2 = -3^2a^2 = -9a^2$

PRACTICE 2

Simplify.

a. $(7a)^2$

b. $(-4x)^3$

c. $-(4x)^3$

EXAMPLE 3

Simplify.

a. $(2x^4)^5$

b. $(p^3q^5)^3$

c. $-7(m^5n^{10})^2$

d. $(5a^{-2}c^4)^{-2}$

PRACTICE 3

Simplify.

a. $(-6a^9)^2$

b. $(q^8r^{10})^2$

c. $-2(ab^7)^3$

d. $(7a^{-1}c^{-5})^2$

SOLUTION

a. $(2x^4)^5 = 2^5(x^4)^5$ Use the rule for raising a product to a power.

$\qquad = 32x^{20}$ Use the power rule.

b. $(p^3q^5)^3 = (p^3)^3(q^5)^3 = p^9q^{15}$

c. $-7(m^5n^{10})^2 = -7(m^5)^2(n^{10})^2 = -7m^{10}n^{20}$

d. $(5a^{-2}c^4)^{-2} = 5^{-2}(a^{-2})^{-2}(c^4)^{-2}$ Use the rule for raising a product to a power.

$\qquad = 5^{-2}(a^4)(c^{-8})$ Use the power rule.

$\qquad = \dfrac{1}{25} \cdot a^4 \cdot \dfrac{1}{c^8}$ Use the definition of a negative exponent.

$\qquad = \dfrac{a^4}{25c^8}$

The final law of exponents that we discuss is *raising a quotient to a power*. For instance, consider the expression $\left(\dfrac{a}{b}\right)^4$, where a divided by b is raised to the fourth power. By the definition of exponent, we get

$$\left(\frac{a}{b}\right)^4 = \frac{a}{b} \cdot \frac{a}{b} \cdot \frac{a}{b} \cdot \frac{a}{b} = \frac{a \cdot a \cdot a \cdot a}{b \cdot b \cdot b \cdot b} = \frac{a^4}{b^4}.$$

So $\left(\dfrac{a}{b}\right)^4 = \dfrac{a^4}{b^4}$. We generalize this result as follows.

Raising a Quotient to a Power

For any nonzero real numbers x and y and any integer a,

$$\left(\frac{x}{y}\right)^a = \frac{x^a}{y^a}.$$

This rule states that to raise a quotient to a power, we raise both the numerator and the denominator to that power.

EXAMPLE 4	**PRACTICE 4**
Simplify by using the rule for raising a quotient to a power.	Simplify.
a. $\left(\dfrac{x}{5}\right)^3$	**a.** $\left(\dfrac{y}{3}\right)^2$
b. $\left(\dfrac{-a}{b}\right)^4$	**b.** $\left(\dfrac{-u}{v}\right)^{10}$
c. $\left(\dfrac{5}{x}\right)^{-3}$	**c.** $\left(\dfrac{3}{y}\right)^{-2}$
d. $\left(\dfrac{-3r^2}{st^4}\right)^3$	**d.** $\left(\dfrac{-10a^5}{3b^2c}\right)^2$
e. $\left(\dfrac{9u}{v^{-1}}\right)^2$	**e.** $\left(\dfrac{5x}{y^{-2}}\right)^3$

SOLUTION Here we use the rule for raising a quotient to a power and then simplify.

a. $\left(\dfrac{x}{5}\right)^3 = \dfrac{x^3}{5^3} = \dfrac{x^3}{125}$

b. $\left(\dfrac{-a}{b}\right)^4 = \dfrac{(-a)^4}{b^4} = \dfrac{a^4}{b^4}$

c. $\left(\dfrac{5}{x}\right)^{-3} = \dfrac{5^{-3}}{x^{-3}}$

$\qquad = 5^{-3} \cdot \dfrac{1}{x^{-3}}$

$\qquad = \dfrac{1}{5^3} \cdot x^3$

$\qquad = \dfrac{x^3}{125}$

d. $\left(\dfrac{-3r^2}{st^4}\right)^3 = \dfrac{(-3r^2)^3}{(st^4)^3} = \dfrac{(-3)^3(r^2)^3}{s^3(t^4)^3} = \dfrac{-27r^6}{s^3t^{12}}$

e. $\left(\dfrac{9u}{v^{-1}}\right)^2 = \dfrac{(9u)^2}{(v^{-1})^2}$

$\qquad = \dfrac{9^2u^2}{v^{-2}}$

$\qquad = 81u^2 \cdot \dfrac{1}{v^{-2}}$

$\qquad = 81u^2v^2$

Note that the simplified form of the expression in Example 4(a) is the same as the simplified form of the expression in Example 4(c). Since $\left(\dfrac{5}{x}\right)^{-3} = \dfrac{x^3}{125}$ and $\left(\dfrac{x}{5}\right)^3 = \dfrac{x^3}{125}$, we conclude that $\left(\dfrac{5}{x}\right)^{-3} = \left(\dfrac{x}{5}\right)^3$. This conclusion leads us to another law of exponents—*raising a quotient to a negative power.*

Raising a Quotient to a Negative Power

For any nonzero real numbers x and y and any integer a,

$$\left(\dfrac{x}{y}\right)^{-a} = \left(\dfrac{y}{x}\right)^{a}.$$

EXAMPLE 5

Simplify.

a. $\left(\dfrac{2}{x}\right)^{-3}$

b. $\left(\dfrac{3r}{10s}\right)^{-1}$

c. $\left(\dfrac{x^4}{y^2}\right)^{-2}$

PRACTICE 5

Simplify.

a. $\left(\dfrac{5}{a}\right)^{-2}$

b. $\left(\dfrac{4u}{v}\right)^{-1}$

c. $\left(\dfrac{a^5}{b^3}\right)^{-2}$

SOLUTION Use the rule for raising a quotient to a negative power.

a. $\left(\dfrac{2}{x}\right)^{-3} = \left(\dfrac{x}{2}\right)^{3} = \dfrac{x^3}{2^3} = \dfrac{x^3}{8}$

b. $\left(\dfrac{3r}{10s}\right)^{-1} = \left(\dfrac{10s}{3r}\right)^{1} = \dfrac{10s}{3r}$

c. $\left(\dfrac{x^4}{y^2}\right)^{-2} = \left(\dfrac{y^2}{x^4}\right)^{2} = \dfrac{(y^2)^2}{(x^4)^2} = \dfrac{y^4}{x^8}$

Scientific Notation

Scientific notation is an important application of exponents—whether they are positive, negative, or zero. Scientists use this notation to abbreviate very large or very small numbers.

Example	Standard Notation	Scientific Notation
The speed of light	983,000,000 ft/sec	9.83×10^8 ft/sec
The length of a virus	0.000000000001 m	1×10^{-12} m

Note that scientific notation is based on powers of 10.

> **Definition**
>
> A number is in **scientific notation** if it is written in the form
> $$a \times 10^n,$$
> where n is an integer and a is greater than or equal to 1 but less than 10 ($1 \le a < 10$).

Note that any value of a that satisfies the inequality $1 \le a < 10$ must have *one nonzero digit* to the left of the decimal point. For instance, 7.3×10^5 is written in scientific notation. Do you see why the numbers 0.83×10^2, 5×3^7, and 13.8×10^{-4} are *not* written in scientific notation?

TIP When written in scientific notation, large numbers have positive powers of 10, whereas small numbers have negative powers of 10. For instance, 3×10^{23} is large, while 3×10^{-23} is small.

Let's now consider how to change a number from scientific notation to standard notation.

EXAMPLE 6

Change the number 2.41×10^5 from scientific notation to standard notation.

SOLUTION To express this number in standard notation, we need to multiply 2.41 by 10^5. Since $10^5 = 100,000$, multiplying 2.41 by 100,000 gives:

$$2.41 \times 10^5 = 2.41 \times 100,000 = 241,000.00 = 241,000$$

The number 241,000 is written in standard notation.

Note that the power of 10 here is *positive* and that the decimal point is moved five places *to the right*. So a shortcut for expressing 2.41×10^5 in standard notation is to move the decimal point in 2.41 five places to the right.

$$2.41 \times 10^5 = 2.41\,0\,0\,0 = 241,000.$$

PRACTICE 6

Express 2.539×10^2 in standard notation.

EXAMPLE 7

Convert 3×10^{-5} to standard notation.

SOLUTION Using the definition of a negative exponent, we get:

$$3 \times 10^{-5} = 3 \times \frac{1}{10^5}, \text{ or } \frac{3}{10^5}$$

Since $10^5 = 100,000$, dividing 3 by 100,000 gives us

$$\frac{3}{10^5} = \frac{3}{100,000} = 0.00003$$

Here we note that the power of 10 is *negative* and that the decimal point, which is understood to be at the right end of a whole number, is moved five places *to the left*. So a shortcut for expressing 3×10^{-5} in standard notation is to move the decimal point in 3. five places to the left.

$$3 \times 10^{-5} = 3. \times 10^{-5} = 0\,0\,0\,0\,3. = .00003, \text{ or } 0.00003$$

PRACTICE 7

Change 4.3×10^{-9} to standard notation.

TIP When converting a number from scientific notation to standard notation, move the decimal point to the *right* if the power of 10 is *positive* and to the *left* if the power of 10 is *negative*.

Now let's consider the reverse situation, namely, changing a number in standard notation to scientific notation.

EXAMPLE 8

Express 37,000,000,000 in scientific notation.

SOLUTION For a number to be written in scientific notation, it must be of the form

$$a \times 10^n,$$

where n is an integer and $1 \le a < 10$. We know that 37,000,000,000 and 37,000,000,000. are the same. We move the decimal point *to the left* so that there is one nonzero digit to the left of the decimal point. The power of 10 we need to multiply by is the same as the number of places moved.

Move 10 places to the *left*.

$$37,000,000,000 = 3\overset{\frown}{7000000000.} \times 10^{10}$$
$$= 3.7 \times 10^{10}$$

Since 3.7 and 3.7000000000 are equivalent, we can drop the trailing zeros. So 37,000,000,000 expressed in scientific notation is 3.7×10^{10}.

PRACTICE 8

Write 8,000,000,000,000 in scientific notation.

EXAMPLE 9

Convert 0.00000000000000002 to scientific notation.

SOLUTION We must write the number 0.00000000000000002 in the form

$$a \times 10^n,$$

where n is an integer and $1 \le a < 10$. We move the decimal point *to the right* so that there is one nonzero digit to the left of the decimal point. The number of places moved, preceded by a *negative* sign, is the power of 10 that we need.

Move 17 places to the *right*.

$$0.00000000000000002 = 0.\overset{\frown}{00000000000000002} \times 10^{-17}$$
$$= 2 \times 10^{-17}$$

PRACTICE 9

Express 0.000000000071 in scientific notation.

Next, let's consider calculations involving numbers written in scientific notation.

EXAMPLE 10

Calculate, writing the result in scientific notation.

a. $(4 \times 10^{-1})(2.1 \times 10^6)$
b. $(1.2 \times 10^5) \div (2 \times 10^{-4})$

PRACTICE 10

Calculate, writing the result in scientific notation.

a. $(7 \times 10^{-2})(3.52 \times 10^3)$

b. $(2.4 \times 10^3) \div (6 \times 10^{-9})$

SOLUTION

a. $(4 \times 10^{-1})(2.1 \times 10^6)$

$\qquad = (4 \times 2.1)(10^{-1} \times 10^6)$ Regroup the factors.

$\qquad = 8.4 \times 10^{-1+6}$ Use the product rule.

$\qquad = 8.4 \times 10^5$

b. $(1.2 \times 10^5) \div (2 \times 10^{-4}) = \dfrac{1.2 \times 10^5}{2 \times 10^{-4}}$

$\qquad = \dfrac{1.2}{2} \times \dfrac{10^5}{10^{-4}}$ Rewrite the quotient as a product of quotients.

$\qquad = 0.6 \times 10^{5-(-4)}$ Use the quotient rule.

$\qquad = 0.6 \times 10^9$

Note that 0.6×10^9 is not in scientific notation because 0.6 is not between 1 and 10, that is, it does not have one nonzero digit to the left of the decimal point. To write 0.6×10^9 in scientific notation, we convert 0.6 to scientific notation and then simplify the product.

$0.6 \times 10^9 = (6 \times 10^{-1}) \times 10^9$ Convert 0.6 to scientific notation.

$\qquad = 6 \times (10^{-1} \times 10^9)$

$\qquad = 6 \times 10^8$ Use the product rule.

The answer is 6×10^8.

EXAMPLE 11

There are about 5×10^6 red blood cells per cubic millimeter of blood. Each of these red blood cells contains about 2×10^8 hemoglobin molecules. Calculate the approximate number of hemoglobin molecules per cubic millimeter of blood, writing the result in scientific notation. (*Source:* S. Mader, *Inquiry into Life*, William C. Brown, 1991)

SOLUTION We need to find the product of the number of red blood cells per cubic millimeter of blood and the number of hemoglobin molecules per red blood cell:

$$(5 \times 10^6)(2 \times 10^8) = \underbrace{(5 \times 2)}\underbrace{(10^6 \times 10^8)}$$

$$= \quad 10 \quad \times \quad 10^{6+8}$$

$$= \quad 10 \quad \times \quad 10^{14}$$

To write this number in scientific notation, we convert 10 to scientific notation and then simplify the product.

$$10 \times 10^{14} = (1.0 \times 10^1) \times 10^{14}$$

$$= 1.0 \times (10^1 \times 10^{14})$$

$$= 1.0 \times 10^{15}$$

So there are approximately 1×10^{15} hemoglobin molecules per cubic millimeter of blood.

PRACTICE 11

The number of hairs on the average human head is estimated to be about 1.5×10^5. If there are approximately 6×10^9 people in the world, estimate the number of human hairs in the world. (*Source:* Time Almanac 2000)

EXAMPLE 12

A CD-ROM contains 600 million bytes of information. Use scientific notation to determine the number of files, each containing 30,000 bytes, that a CD-ROM will hold.

SOLUTION The CD-ROM houses 600 million, or 6×10^8, bytes. We are considering files containing 30,000, or 3×10^4, bytes. To determine the number of files that will fit on the CD-ROM, we divide.

$$(6 \times 10^8) \div (3 \times 10^4) = \frac{6 \times 10^8}{3 \times 10^4}$$
$$= \frac{6}{3} \times \frac{10^8}{10^4}$$
$$= 2 \times 10^{8-4}$$
$$= 2 \times 10^4$$

So 2×10^4, or 20,000, files will fit on the CD-ROM.

PRACTICE 12

At the very best, a light microscope can distinguish points 2×10^{-7} m apart, whereas an electronic microscope can distinguish points that are 2×10^{-10} m apart. The second number is how many times as great as the first number? (*Source:* S. Mader, *Inquiry into Life*, William C. Brown, 1991)

 Calculators and Scientific Notation

Calculators vary as to how numbers are displayed or entered in scientific notation.

Display

In order to avoid an overflow error, many calculator models change to scientific notation an answer that is either too small or too large to fit into the calculator's display. Calculators generally use the base 10 without displaying it. Some calculators display scientific notation with either an *E* or *e*, and others show a space. For example, 3.1E–4 or 3.1 ▪–4 can represent 3.1×10^{-4}. What other differences do you see between written scientific notation and displayed scientific notation?

EXAMPLE 13

Multiply 1,000,000,000 by 2,000,000,000.

SOLUTION

Input	1000000000		×		2000000000		=	
Display	1000000000.	1000000000.		1000000000.	2000000000.			2E18

Does your calculator display the product in scientific notation, that is, as 2E18, 2e18, or 2.▪18?

PRACTICE 13

Square 0.000000005. How is the answer displayed?

Enter

Some calculators give the wrong answer to a computation if very large or very small numbers are *entered* in standard form rather than in scientific notation. To enter a number in scientific notation, many calculators have a key labeled EE , EXP , or EEX . For a negative exponent, a key labeled +/− or (−) must be pressed either before or after the exponent key, depending on the calculator.

EXAMPLE 14

Enter the number 5,000,000,000 in scientific notation.

SOLUTION

Input	5	EE	9
Display	5.	5.00	5.E9

PRACTICE 14

In your calculator, enter in scientific notation the number 0.00000000073.

EXAMPLE 15

Multiply 3.5×10^4 by 2.1×10^7 on a calculator.

SOLUTION

Input	3.5	EE	4	×	2.1	EE	7	=
Display	3.5	3.5 00	3.5 04	35000	2.1	2.1 00	2.1 07	7.35 11

So the answer is 7.35×10^{11}. If your calculator has enough places in the display, it may give the answer to this problem in standard form: 735,000,000,000.

PRACTICE 15

Use a calculator to divide 9.2×10^{12} by 2×10^4.

Exercises 5.2

FOR EXTRA HELP

📖 *Student's Solutions Manual*

Tutor Center 🔊 *Addison-Wesley Math Tutor Center*

🚪 *MyMathLab*

📼 *Videotape 5/DVT 5*

Simplify.

1. $(2^2)^4$

2. $(3^3)^2$

3. $(10^5)^2$

4. $(0^5)^3$

5. $(4^{-2})^2$

6. $(2^3)^{-4}$

7. $(x^4)^6$

8. $(p^2)^{10}$

9. $(y^4)^2$

10. $(n^3)^3$

11. $(x^{-2})^3$

12. $(y^5)^{-6}$

13. $(n^{-2})^{-2}$

14. $(a^{-5})^{-4}$

15. $(4x)^3$

16. $(2y)^5$

17. $(-8y)^2$

18. $(-7a)^2$

19. $-(4n^5)^3$

20. $-(5x^3)^3$

21. $4(-2y^2)^4$

22. $2(-3t)^3$

23. $(3a)^{-2}$

24. $-(5t)^{-3}$

25. $(pq)^{-7}$

26. $(mn)^{-6}$

27. $(r^2t)^6$

28. $(a^3b^5)^4$

29. $(-2p^5q)^2$

30. $(-3a^2b^3)^4$

31. $-2(m^4n^8)^3$

32. $4(x^2y^3)^2$

33. $(-4m^5n^{-10})^3$

34. $(3a^{-3}c^8)^2$

35. $(a^3b^2)^{-4}$

36. $(p^{-3}q^{-4})^2$

37. $(4x^{-2}y^3)^2$

38. $(-2x^{-2}y^3)^{-3}$

39. $\left(\dfrac{5}{b}\right)^3$

40. $\left(\dfrac{x}{4}\right)^2$

41. $\left(\dfrac{c}{b}\right)^2$

42. $\left(\dfrac{t}{s}\right)^5$

43. $-\left(\dfrac{a}{b}\right)^7$

44. $-\left(\dfrac{x}{y}\right)^3$

45. $\left(\dfrac{a^2}{3}\right)^3$

46. $\left(\dfrac{4}{y^6}\right)^3$

47. $\left(-\dfrac{p^3}{q^2}\right)^5$

48. $\left(\dfrac{x^2}{y^3}\right)^4$

49. $\left(\dfrac{a}{4}\right)^{-1}$

50. $\left(-\dfrac{b}{3}\right)^{-1}$

51. $\left(\dfrac{2x^5}{y^2}\right)^3$

52. $\left(\dfrac{n^2}{3w^5}\right)^2$

53. $\left(\dfrac{pq}{p^2q^2}\right)^5$

54. $\left(\dfrac{-s^2t^3}{st^2}\right)^2$ **55.** $\left(\dfrac{3x}{y^{-3}}\right)^4$ **56.** $\left(\dfrac{p^{-1}}{5q^5}\right)^2$ **57.** $\left(\dfrac{-u^2v^3}{4vu^4}\right)^2$

58. $\left(\dfrac{2xy^3}{xy^2}\right)^4$ **59.** $\left(-\dfrac{x^{-2}y}{2z^{-4}}\right)^4$ **60.** $-\left(\dfrac{4a^{-4}}{bc^{-2}}\right)^2$ **61.** $\left(\dfrac{r^5}{t^6}\right)^{-2}$

62. $-\left(\dfrac{y^3}{x^3}\right)^{-2}$ **63.** $\left(\dfrac{-2a^4}{b^2}\right)^{-3}$ **64.** $\left(\dfrac{q^5}{5p^4}\right)^{-2}$

Express in standard notation.

65. 3.17×10^8 **66.** 9.1×10^5 **67.** 1×10^{-6} **68.** 8.33×10^{-4}

69. 6.2×10^6 **70.** 7.55×10^{10} **71.** 4.025×10^{-5} **72.** 2.1×10^{-3}

Express in scientific notation.

73. 420,000,000 **74.** 100,000,000 **75.** 0.0000035 **76.** 0.00017

77. 217,000,000,000 **78.** 154,800,000,000 **79.** 0.00000000731 **80.** 0.00000005672

Complete the following tables.

81.

Standard Notation	Scientific Notation (written)	Scientific Notation (displayed on a calculator)
975,000,000		
	4.87×10^8	
		1.652E−10
0.000000067		
	1×10^{-13}	
		3.281E9

82.

Standard Notation	Scientific Notation (written)	Scientific Notation (displayed on a calculator)
975,000,000,000		
	5×10^8	
		4.988E−7
0.0000048		
	9.34×10^{-9}	
		9.772E6

Calculate, writing the result in scientific notation.

83. $(3 \times 10^2)(3 \times 10^5)$

84. $(5 \times 10^4)(7.1 \times 10^3)$

85. $(2.5 \times 10^{-2})(8.3 \times 10^{-3})$

86. $(2.1 \times 10^4)(8 \times 10^{-4})$

87. $(8.6 \times 10^9)(4.4 \times 10^{-12})$

88. $(9.1 \times 10^{-13})(6.3 \times 10^{-10})$

89. $(2.5 \times 10^8) \div (2 \times 10^{-2})$

90. $(3.0 \times 10^4) \div (1 \times 10^3)$

91. $(6 \times 10^5) \div (2 \times 10^3)$

92. $(4.8 \times 10^{-3}) \div (8 \times 10^2)$

93. $(9.6 \times 10^{20}) \div (3.2 \times 10^{12})$

94. $(8.4 \times 10^6) \div (4.2 \times 10^7)$

Applications

Solve.

95. A DVD holds between 4×10^9 and 1.7×10^{10} bytes of data. Express these quantities in standard notation.

96. The infectious part of a virus is typically between 2.5×10^{-8} m and 2×10^{-7} m in size. Express these quantities in standard notation. (*Source:* S. Mader, *Inquiry into Life*, William C. Brown, 1991)

97. The wavelength of red light is 0.0000007 m. Write this length in scientific notation.

98. In a recent year, retail sales in U.S. shopping centers totaled $1,030,000,000,000. Express this amount in scientific notation. (*Source: The 1999 Statistical Abstract of the United States*)

99. The cell is considered the basic unit of life. Each day, the body destroys and replaces more than 200 billion cells. Write this quantity in scientific notation.

100. The area of the United States is approximately 3.7×10^6 sq mi. Express this area in standard notation. (*Source: The New York Times Almanac,* 2000)

101. The mass of a proton is about 1.7×10^{-24} g. Rewrite this quantity in standard notation. (*Source:* Karen Timberlake, *Chemistry,* Addison-Wesley, 1999)

102. To measure vast distances, astronomers use a unit called a *parsec*, which is equal to about 3.086×10^{18} cm. Express this quantity in standard form. (*Source:* D. McNally, *Positional Astronomy,* 1974)

103. The population of Africa in a recent year was about 7.8×10^8. What was this population expressed in standard notation? (*Source: New York Times 2000 Almanac*)

104. A supercomputer carries out 3,600,000,000 operations per second. Rewrite this capability in scientific notation. (*Source:* Apple Computer)

105. For each pound of body weight, a human body contains about 3.2×10^4 microliters (μL) of blood. In turn, a microliter of blood contains about 5×10^6 red blood cells. A person weighing 100 lb has approximately how many red blood cells?

106. On the television series *Star Trek: The Next Generation*, the android Data could carry out 60 trillion operations per second. Express this rate in scientific notation.

107. Light travels through a vacuum at a speed of 186,000 mi per sec.

a. Express this speed in scientific notation.

b. Estimate mentally how long it will take for light to travel from the star Vega, which is 1.58×10^{14} mi from Earth. (*Source: The New York Times 2000 Almanac*)

 108. There are 26,890,000,000,000,000,000 molecules of a gas in a cubic meter.

a. Rewrite this quantity in scientific notation.

b. What volume is required for 3.4×10^{20} molecules of the gas?

• *Check your answers on page A-23.*

Mindstretchers

INVESTIGATION

1. On a scientific calculator, enter the number 2. Double that number. Then keep doubling the result. After how many doublings does your calculator display the number in scientific notation? Explain how you could have predicted that result.

_____

CRITICAL THINKING

2. What is the mathematical relationship between $(a^m)^n$ and $(a^m)^{-n}$? Justify your answer.

_____

_____

RESEARCH

3. In your college library or on the Web, determine the annual national debt for the United States for five consecutive years. Would you use scientific notation or standard notation to express these amounts? Explain why.

_____

5.3 Basic Concepts of Polynomials

What Polynomials Are and Why They Are Important

In Chapter 1, we discussed algebraic expressions in general. We now consider a particular kind of algebraic expression called a *polynomial*.

Just as whole numbers are fundamental to arithmetic, polynomials play a similarly key role in algebra.

OBJECTIVES

- *To classify polynomials*
- *To simplify polynomials*
- *To evaluate polynomials*
- *To solve applied problems involving polynomials*

Whole number: $3 \cdot 10^2 + 7 \cdot 10^1 + 8 \cdot 10^0 = 378$

Polynomial: $3 \cdot x^2 + 7 \cdot x^1 + 8 \cdot x^0 = 3x^2 + 7x + 8$

In fact, a good deal of algebra is devoted to studying properties of polynomials and operations on polynomials.

Many phenomena in the sciences and business can be described by polynomial expressions. Even when the description is only approximate, the polynomial approximation is often a good one.

Monomials

We begin by considering algebraic expressions called *monomials*.

> **Definition**
>
> A **monomial** is an expression that is the product of a real number and variables raised to nonnegative integer powers.

Some examples of monomials are:

$$5x \qquad -7t^4 \qquad \frac{4}{5}x^2 \qquad -2p^2q^5$$

Recall that in the expression $5x$, 5 is called the **coefficient**.

Note that a constant such as -12 can be thought of as $-12x^0$. So any constant is also considered a monomial.

The expression $5x + 3$ is not a monomial, since it has two terms, $5x$ and 3. Can you explain whether $\frac{2}{x}$ is a monomial?

Monomials serve as building blocks (or terms) for the larger set of polynomials. Polynomials are formed by adding and subtracting monomial terms.

> **Definition**
>
> A **polynomial** is an algebraic expression with one or more monomials added or subtracted.

Here are some examples of polynomials:

$3x^2 - 5x + 7$

$4t^2 - 3$

$-8x^2$

$17x^4 + 5x^3 - 8x^2 + x - 1$

$20pq - p^2 - 7q^2 + 6$

Here are some examples of algebraic expressions that are *not* polynomials:

$2x^{-1}$

$\dfrac{t^2}{3} + \dfrac{4}{t}$

$\dfrac{5x^2}{2x + 9}$

$2\sqrt{x} + 1$

EXAMPLE 1	PRACTICE 1
Consider the polynomial $3x^5 + 2x^3 - 8$.	For the polynomial $-10x^2 + 4x + 20$, find (a) the terms and (b) their coefficients.

a. Identify the terms of the polynomial.

b. For each term, identify its coefficient.

SOLUTION

a. The terms are $3x^5$, $2x^3$, and -8.

b. The coefficients of the terms are $3, 2$, and -8, respectively.

Classification of Polynomials

There are several ways to classify polynomials. One way is according to the number of variables in the polynomial and another is according to the number of terms in the polynomial. Finally, a third kind of classification is according to the degree of the polynomial. We consider each of these classifications in turn.

Number of Variables

A polynomial such as $3x^2 - 6x + 9$ is said to be *in one variable,* namely in x. The polynomial $t^5 + 11t^4 - 7t^3 - t^2 + 10t - 50$ is also in one variable, namely in t. On the other hand, the polynomial $3x^4y - 5x^2y^3 + 9$ is in *two* variables, x and y. Throughout this text, we focus on polynomials in one variable.

Number of Terms

As we have seen, a polynomial with just one term is called a *monomial.* A polynomial with *two* terms is called a **binomial**. A **trinomial** is a polynomial with *three* terms. Polynomials with four or more terms are simply called *polynomials.*

$$
\begin{array}{ll}
10x & \longleftarrow \quad \text{Monomial} \\
3x - 2 & \longleftarrow \quad \text{Binomial} \\
x^2 + 9x + 6 & \longleftarrow \quad \text{Trinomial} \\
-x^3 + 8x^2 + x - 19 & \longleftarrow \quad \text{Polynomial}
\end{array}
$$

EXAMPLE 2

Classify each polynomial according to the number of terms.

Polynomial	Monomial	Binomial	Trinomial	Other Polynomial
$3x - 5$				
$7x^2 - 3x + 10$				
$10a^2$				
$x^4 - 6x^2 + 8x + 13$				

SOLUTION

Poynomial	Monomial	Binomial	Trinomial	Other Polynomial
$3x - 5$		✓		
$7x^2 - 3x + 10$			✓	
$10a^2$	✓			
$x^4 - 6x^2 + 8x + 13$				✓

PRACTICE 2

Classify each polynomial according to the number of terms.

Polynomial	Monomial	Binomial	Trinomial	Other Polynomial
$2x + 9$				
$-4x^2$				
$12p - 1$				
$3x^4 - 6x^2 + 9x + 1$				

Degree and Order of Terms

Let's consider a *monomial* in one variable. The **degree** of the monomial is the power of the variable in the monomial.

$$3x^4 \longleftarrow \text{Of the fourth degree or of degree 4}$$
$$-7y^2 \longleftarrow \text{Of the second degree or of degree 2}$$

Recall that a constant, such as 3, can be thought of as $3x^0$ and so is considered to be of degree 0.

8 is a monomial of degree 0

-12 is a monomial of degree 0

Polynomials are also classified by their degree. The degree of a polynomial is the highest degree of any of its terms. For instance, the degree of $8x^3 + 9x^2 - 7x - 1$ is 3 since 3 is the highest degree of any term.

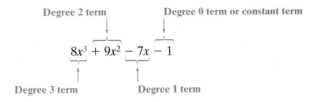

Degree 2 term   Degree 0 term or constant term

$$8x^3 + 9x^2 - 7x - 1$$

Degree 3 term   Degree 1 term

EXAMPLE 3

Identify the degree of each polynomial.

a. $-20x^3$

b. $5 + x$

c. $-7x^2 + 3x + 10$

d. -36

SOLUTION

a. $-20x^3$ is of degree 3.

b. $5 + x = 5 + x^1$, which is of degree 1.

c. $-7x^2 + 3x + 10$ is of degree 2.

d. $-36 = -36x^0$, which is of degree 0.

PRACTICE 3

Indicate the degree of each polynomial.

a. $7n$

b. $x - x^2$

c. $2 + 4x^2 - 10x^3$

d. -8

The **leading term** of a polynomial is the term in the polynomial with the highest degree, and the coefficient of that term is called the **leading coefficient**. The term of degree 0 is called the **constant term**. So in the polynomial $3t^2 - 8t + 1$, the leading term is $3t^2$, the leading coefficient is 3, and the constant term is 1.

EXAMPLE 4

Complete the following table.

Polynomial	Constant Term	Leading Term	Leading Coefficient
$2x^{10}$			
$4x + 25$			
$3 - 10x + 8x^2$			
$7x^3 - x - 8$			

PRACTICE 4

Complete the following table.

Polynomial	Constant Term	Leading Term	Leading Coefficient
$-3x^7 + 9$			
x^5			
$x^4 - 7x - 1$			
$3x + 5x^3 + 20$			

SOLUTION

Polynomial	Constant Term	Leading Term	Leading Coefficient
$2x^{10}$	0	$2x^{10}$	2
$4x + 25$	25	$4x$	4
$3 - 10x + 8x^2$	3	$8x^2$	8
$7x^3 - x - 8$	-8	$7x^3$	7

The terms of a polynomial are usually arranged in *descending order of degree*. That is, we write the leading term on the left, then the term of the next highest degree, and so forth.

$$2x^3 + 5x^2 - 3x - 10 \qquad \text{Descending order of degree—the exponents get smaller from left to right}$$

Occasionally, however, the terms of a polynomial are written in *ascending order of degree*.

$$-10 - 3x + 5x^2 + x^3 \qquad \text{Ascending order of degree—the exponents get larger from left to right}$$

EXAMPLE 5

Rearrange each polynomial in descending order.

a. $3x^4 + 9x^2 - 7x^3 + x + 10$

b. $-7x + 6x^3 + 10$

SOLUTION

a. We rewrite the polynomial so that the term with the highest exponent of x is on the left, the next highest exponent comes second, and so on.

$$3x^4 + 9x^2 - 7x^3 + x + 10 = 3x^4 - 7x^3 + 9x^2 + x^1 + 10x^0$$
$$= 3x^4 - 7x^3 + 9x^2 + x + 10$$

b. We rewrite the polynomial so that the exponents get smaller from left to right.

$$\underset{\substack{\uparrow \\ \text{Degree 2} \qquad \text{Degree 0}}}{\overset{\substack{\text{Degree 3} \qquad \text{Degree 1} \\ \downarrow \qquad\qquad \downarrow}}{-7x + 6x^3 + 10 = 6x^3 + \boxed{} - 7x + 10}}$$

PRACTICE 5

Write each polynomial in descending order.

a. $-8x + 9x^5 - 7x^4 + 9x^2 - 6$

b. $x^3 + 7x^5 - 3x^2 + 8$

Note that a term with coefficient 0 is usually not written. The unwritten term is said to be a *missing term*. For instance, in the polynomial

$$6x^3 - 7x + 10,$$

$0x^2$ is the missing term. So we can write this polynomial as $6x^3 + 0x^2 - 7x + 10$.

The concept of missing terms is important in the division of polynomials, as we will see later in this chapter.

Simplifying and Evaluating Polynomials

Recall that in Section 1.8, we discussed how to simplify algebraic expressions by combining like terms.

EXAMPLE 6	PRACTICE 6
Simplify and then put in descending order.	Combine like terms and then write in descending order.
$$8 + 3x^3 + 9x + 1 - 8x + 7x^2 - 3x^2$$	$$2x^2 + 3x - x^2 + 5x^3 + 3x - 5x^3 + 20$$
SOLUTION	

$8 + 3x^3 + 9x + 1 - 8x + 7x^2 - 3x^2$

$\quad = 8 + 3x^3 + 9x + 1 - 8x + 7x^2 - 3x^2$

$\quad = 9 + 3x^3 + x + 4x^2$ **Combine like terms.**

$\quad = 3x^3 + 4x^2 + x + 9$

Recall our discussion of evaluating algebraic expressions in Section 1.8. Polynomials, like other algebraic expressions, are evaluated by replacing each variable with the given number and then carrying out the computation.

EXAMPLE 7	PRACTICE 7
Find the value of $2x^2 - 8x - 5$ when	Find the value of $x^2 - 5x + 5$ when
a. $x = 3$.	**a.** $x = 2$.
b. $x = -3$.	**b.** $x = -2$.
SOLUTION	

a. $2x^2 - 8x - 5 = 2(3)^2 - 8(3) - 5$ **Substitute 3 for x.**

$\qquad\qquad\qquad\quad = 2(9) - 8(3) - 5$

$\qquad\qquad\qquad\quad = 18 - 24 - 5 = -11$

b. $2x^2 - 8x - 5 = 2(-3)^2 - 8(-3) - 5$ Substitute -3 for x.
$$= 2(9) - 8(-3) - 5$$
$$= 18 + 24 - 5$$
$$= 37$$

EXAMPLE 8

If \$1000 is deposited in a savings account that pays compound interest at a rate r compounded annually, then after two years the balance in the account will be represented by the polynomial $(1000r^2 + 2000r + 1000)$ dollars. Find the balance if $r = 0.05$.

SOLUTION We need to replace r by 0.05 in the polynomial.

$$1000r^2 + 2000r + 1000 = 1000(0.05)^2 + 2000(0.05) + 1000$$
$$= 1000(0.0025) + 2000(0.05) + 1000$$
$$= 2.5 + 100 + 1000$$
$$= 1102.5$$

So the account balance is \$1102.50.

PRACTICE 8

If an object is dropped from a height of 500 ft above the ground, its height in feet above the ground after t sec is given by the expression $500 - 16t^2$. How high above the ground is the object after 3 sec?

Exercises 5.3

FOR EXTRA HELP

📖 *Student's Solutions Manual*

Tutor Center *Addison-Wesley Math Tutor Center*

🚪 *MyMathLab*

📼 *Videotape 5/DVT 5*

Indicate whether each of the following is a polynomial.

1. $7x^2$

2. $\dfrac{x^3}{3} - 2x^2 + 9x - 4$

3. $x - 7\sqrt{x} + 1$

4. $10p + q$

5. $4a - 3a^2 + 8$

6. $2xy - x^2$

7. $\dfrac{2}{x + 3}$

8. $3y^{-1} + y$

Classify each polynomial according to the number of terms.

9.

Polynomial	Monomial	Binomial	Trinomial	Other Polynomial
$5x - 1$		✓		
$-5a^2$	✓			
$-6a + 3$		✓		
$x^3 + 4x^2 + 2$			✓	

10.

Polynomial	Monomial	Binomial	Trinomial	Other Polynomial
$5x + x^2$		✓		
$3x$	✓			
$12p - 1$		✓		
$2x^5 - x^3 + x + 5$				✓

Rearrange each polynomial in descending order, and then identify its degree.

11. $3x^2 - 2x + 8 - 4x^3$

12. $5x^3 + 7x + 1 - 7x^2$

13. $2 - 3y$

14. $4p^2 - p^4 + 3p^3 + 10 - p$

15. $7x - 5x^2$

16. $-8x^2 + 6x - 2$

17. $-y^3 - 2y + 2 - 4y^5$

18. $5x^3 + 3x^5 + 8x + 3$

19. $5a^2 - a$

20. $25 - y + 2y^2 + y^3 - 3y^4$

21. $9p + 3p^3$

22. $5x^2$

Complete the following table.

23.

Polynomial	Constant Term	Leading Term	Leading Coefficient
$-x^7 + 2$	2	$-x^7$	-1
$2x - 30$	-30	$2x$	2
$-5x + 1 + x^2$	1	$-5x$	-5
$7x^3 - 2x - 3$	3	$7x^3$	7

24.

Polynomial	Constant Term	Leading Term	Leading Coefficient
$5x^3 + 8$	8	$5x^3$	5
$-x + 10$	10	$-x$	-1
$2x^2 - 3x + 4$	4	$2x^2$	2
$-5x + x^4 - 9$	-9	x^4	1

Simplify.

25. $9x^3 - 7x^2 + 1 + x^3 + 10x + 5$

26. $2y^3 - 7y^2 + 1 + 2y^2 + 3y + 8$

27. $r^3 + 2r^2 + 15 + r^2 - 8r - 1$

28. $n^4 - n^3 - 7n^2 + n^2 + 10n + 3$

Identify the missing terms of each polynomial.

29. $x^3 - 7x - 2$

30. $n^2 + 7n$

31. $6x^3 + 8x^2 + 1$

32. $x^4 - 3x$

Find the value of each polynomial for the given values of the variable.

33. $7x - 3$, for $x = 2$ and $x = -2$

34. $5a + 11$, for $a = 0$ and $a = 2$

35. $n^2 - 3n + 9$, for $n = 7$ and $n = -7$

36. $3y^2 + 2y + 1$, for $y = 2$ and $y = -1$

37. $2.1x^2 + 3.9x - 7.3$, for $x = 2.37$ and $x = -2.37$

38. $0.1x^3 + 4.1x - 9.1$, for $x = 3.14$ and $x = -3.14$

Combine like terms. Then write the polynomial in descending order of powers.

39. $4x^2 - 2x - x^2 - 10 - 3x + 4$

40. $x^3 + 5x - 7x^2 - 1 - x^3 + x$

41. $6n^3 + 20n - n^2 + 2 - 4n^3 + 15n^2 + 8$

42. $8y^2 + y^3 - 8y + 20 + 3y + 9y^2$

Applications

Solve.

43. The polynomial $1 + x^2 + x^{15} + x^{16}$ is used by computer scientists to detect errors in computer data. Classify this polynomial in terms of its variables and its degree.

44. The owner of a factory estimates that her profit (in dollars) is

$$0.003x^3 - 1.4x^2 + 300x - 1000,$$

where x is the number of items that the factory produces. Describe this polynomial in terms of its variables and its degree.

45. The polynomial $x + \dfrac{x^2}{20}$ is the *stopping distance* of a car in feet after the brakes are applied, where the variable x is the speed of the car in miles per hour before braking. Find the stopping distance for a car that had been traveling at 40 mph.

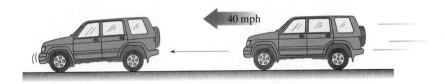

40 mph

46. There are n teams that compete in a sports league, where each team plays every other team once. The following polynomial gives the total number of games that must be played:

$$0.5n^2 - 0.5n$$

If the league has 20 teams, how many games are played?

47. The polynomial $72x + 2342$ approximates the world population (in millions), where x represents the number of years since 1950. According to this model, what was the world population in 2000? (*Source:* U.S. Bureau of the Census)

48. The percent of U.S. households with Web access is approximated by $0.45x^2 + 6.75x + 26.2$, where x represents the number of years since 1998. Estimate the percent of U.S. households with Web access in 2003.
(*Source:* U.S. Department of Commerce)

49. The number of U.S. radio stations with a rock music format is approximated by the polynomial $1.68x^3 + 9.95x^2 - 11.6x + 730$, where x represents the number of years since 1999. To the nearest whole number, estimate the number of U.S. radio stations with a rock music format in 2003. (*Source:* M Street Corporation)

50. The number (in thousands) of U.S. households with cable television can be approximated by the expression $24.5t^3 - 253t^2 + 2043t + 60,920$, where t represents the number of years since 1995. According to this model, how many U.S. households were there with cable television in 2004? (*Source: Statistical Abstract of the United States*)

• *Check your answers on page A-23.*

Mindstretchers

1. The following prefixes are used with polynomials. Use a dictionary to fill in the following table.

Prefix	Meaning of This Prefix	Three Words Beginning with This Prefix
Mono-		
Bi-		
Tri-		
Poly-		

2. There are some polynomials whose value is a prime number for many values of the variable. For instance, consider the second-degree polynomial $n^2 + n + 41$.

a. Check that for n equal to a whole number between 0 and 39, the value of this polynomial is a prime number.

_____

_____

_____

_____

_____

_____

b. Is the value of this polynomial a prime number for $n = 40$? Explain your answer.

_____

PATTERNS

3. The degree of a monomial in more than one variable is the sum of the powers of the variables in that term. Recall that the degree of a polynomial is the highest degree of any of its terms. The following tables show polynomials that represent the area or the volume of various common geometric figures.

AREA

Geometric Figure	Polynomial	Degree of the Polynomial
Square	s^2	
Triangle	$0.5bh$	
Trapezoid	$0.5hb + 0.5hB$	
Circle	$3.14r^2$	
Rectangle	lw	

VOLUME

Geometric Figure	Polynomial	Degree of the Polynomial
Cube	e^3	
Rectangle solid	lwh	
Sphere	$\dfrac{4}{3}\pi r^3$	
Cylinder	$\pi r^2 h$	

a. Complete the tables by finding the degree of each polynomial.

b. Describe the pattern you observe in the table for area. Explain your observation.

_____

_____

_____

c. Describe the pattern you observe in the table for volume. Explain your observation.

_____

_____

_____

Cultural Note

Muhammad ibn Musa al-Khwarizmi, a ninth-century mathematician, wrote *al-Kitab al-mukhtasar fi hisab al-jabr wa'l-muqabala* (*The Compendious Book on Calculation by Completion and Balancing*)—one of the earliest treatises on algebra and the source of the word *algebra*. This work dealt with solving equations as well as with practical applications of algebra to measurement and legacies. al-Khwarizmi, from whose name the word *algorithm* derives, also wrote influential works on astronomy and on the Hindu numeration system.

Sources:

Jan Gullberg, *Mathematics From the Birth of Numbers* (W. W. Norton, 1997).

Morris Kline, *Mathematics, A Cultural Approach* (Addison-Wesley, 1962).

5.4 Addition and Subtraction of Polynomials

OBJECTIVES

- *To add polynomials*
- *To subtract polynomials*
- *To solve applied problems involving the addition or subtraction of polynomials*

In this section, we consider the addition and subtraction of polynomials and their applications to real-world situations. As our discussion proceeds, note the similarity between adding and subtracting whole numbers in arithmetic and these operations on polynomials in algebra.

Adding Polynomials

Recall from Section 1.8 that we can simplify algebraic expressions by combining like terms. We use the same approach when combining polynomials.

To Add Polynomials

- Add the like terms.

As with whole numbers, we can add polynomials using either a horizontal or vertical format. To add polynomials horizontally, we simply remove the parentheses and combine like terms.

EXAMPLE 1

Find the sum: $(8x^2 + 3x + 4) + (-12x^2 + 7)$

SOLUTION Recall that when a plus sign precedes terms in parentheses, we remove the parentheses and keep the sign of each term.

$$\underbrace{(8x^2 + 3x + 4)}_{\substack{\text{First} \\ \text{polynomial}}} + \underbrace{(-12x^2 + 7)}_{\substack{\text{Second} \\ \text{polynomial}}}$$

$$= 8x^2 + 3x + 4 - 12x^2 + 7 \qquad \text{Remove parentheses.}$$

$$= -4x^2 + 3x + 11 \qquad \text{Combine like terms.}$$

PRACTICE 1

Add: $6x - 3$ and $9x^2 - 3x - 40$

EXAMPLE 2

Combine: $(3st^2 - 4st + t^2) + (8s^2t - 3t^2) + (10t^2 - 5st + 7s^2)$

SOLUTION

$(3st^2 - 4st + t^2) + (8s^2t - 3t^2) + (10t^2 - 5st + 7s^2)$

$$= 3st^2 - 4st + t^2 + 8s^2t - 3t^2 + 10t^2 - 5st + 7s^2$$

$$= 3st^2 + 8s^2t - 9st + 7s^2 + 8t^2$$

PRACTICE 2

Combine: $(9p^2 + 4pq + 2q^2) + (-p^2 - 5q^2) + (2p^2 - 3pq - 7q^2)$

417

Now let's look at how to add polynomials in a vertical format. Recall that in adding whole numbers, for instance 329 and 50, we position the addends so that digits with the same place value are in the same column.

$$\begin{array}{r} \text{hundreds} \underset{\downarrow\;\downarrow\;\downarrow}{\overset{\text{tens}}{\underset{}{\rule{0pt}{0pt}}}} \text{ones} \\ 329 \\ +\;50 \end{array}$$

Similarly, when we add polynomials vertically, we position the polynomials so that like terms are in the same column. Suppose, for example, we want to add $7x^5 + x^3 - 3x^2 + 8$ and $2x^5 - 7x^4 + 9x - 9$. In general, a polynomial is considered to be in simplest form when each term is simplified and like terms are combined. Usually the terms are then rearranged in descending order. So, first we make sure that both polynomials are in descending order. Then we write the polynomials as follows:

$$\begin{array}{l} 7x^5 + 0x^4 +\;\;\; x^3 - 3x^2 + 0x + 8 \\ \underline{2x^5 - 7x^4 + 0x^3 + 0x^2 + 9x - 9} \end{array}$$

Note that we could have just left a space for each missing term of the polynomials. Do you see that each column contains like terms? We then add the terms in each column, as shown.

$$\begin{array}{l} 7x^5 \qquad\quad + x^3 - 3x^2 \qquad + 8 \\ \underline{2x^5 - 7x^4 \qquad\qquad\qquad + 9x - 9} \\ 9x^5 - 7x^4 + x^3 - 3x^2 + 9x - 1 \end{array}$$

So the sum is $9x^5 - 7x^4 + x^3 - 3x^2 + 9x - 1$.

Let's consider some more examples.

EXAMPLE 3

Add vertically: $3x^2 - 5x - 6$ and $10x + 20$

SOLUTION First we check that both polynomials are in descending powers of x. Next we rewrite the polynomials vertically, with like terms positioned in the same column:

$$\begin{array}{r} \text{Second-degree term} \underset{}{\overset{\text{First-degree}}{\underset{\text{terms}}{\rule{0pt}{0pt}}}} \text{Zero-degree (constant) terms} \\ 3x^2 - 5x -\;\; 6 \\ \underline{10x + 20} \end{array}$$

We add within columns.

$$\begin{array}{r} 3x^2 - 5x \;-\; 6 \\ \underline{10x \;+\; 20} \\ 3x^2 + 5x \;+\; 14 \end{array}$$

The sum is $3x^2 + 5x + 14$, which is in simplest form.

PRACTICE 3

Find the sum of $8n^2 + 2n - 1$ and $3n^2 - 2$ using a vertical format.

EXAMPLE 4

Find the sum of $7x^3 - 10x^2y + 8xy^2 + 13y^3$, $14xy^2 - 1$ and $3x^2y - 5xy^2 - y^3 + 2$ using a vertical format.

SOLUTION

$$
\begin{array}{l}
7x^3 - 10x^2y + 8xy^2 + 13y^3 \\
\phantom{7x^3 - 10x^2y + {}}14xy^2 \quad -1 \\
\underline{3x^2y - 5xy^2 - y^3 \quad +2} \\
7x^3 - 7x^2y + 17xy^2 + 12y^3 \quad +1
\end{array}
$$

Is the sum in Example 4 in simplified form? Explain.

PRACTICE 4

Add vertically:

$7p^3 - 8p^2q - 3pq^2 + 20,$

$10p^2q + pq^2 - q^3 + 5$, and $p^3 - q^3$

Subtracting Polynomials

Recall from Section 1.8 that when a minus sign precedes terms in parentheses, we remove the parentheses and change the signs of each term.

EXAMPLE 5

Remove parentheses and simplify.

a. $2x - (3x + 4y)$

b. $(5n + 2m) - (n + m) + (3n - 4m)$

SOLUTION

a. In the expression $2x - (3x + 4y)$, since $(3x + 4y)$ is preceded by a minus sign, we remove the parentheses and change the sign of each term in parentheses. Then we combine like terms.

$$
\begin{aligned}
2x - (3x + 4y) &= 2x - 3x - 4y \\
&= -x - 4y
\end{aligned}
$$

b. $(5n + 2m) \underbrace{- (n + m)}_{\substack{\text{For a polyno-}\\\text{mial preceded}\\\text{by a minus,}\\\textit{change}\text{ signs}\\\text{of terms.}}} \underbrace{+ (3n - 4m)}_{\substack{\text{For a polyno-}\\\text{mial preceded}\\\text{by a plus sign,}\\\textit{keep}\text{ signs of}\\\text{terms.}}} = 5n + 2m - n - m$

$$+ 3n - 4m = 7n - 3m$$

PRACTICE 5

Remove parentheses and simplify.

a. $-(4r - 3s) + 7r$

b. $(2p + 5q) + (p - 6q) - (3p + 2q)$

To subtract real numbers, we change the number being subtracted to its opposite, and then add. Subtraction of polynomials works very much in the same way.

To Subtract Polynomials
- Change the sign of each term of the polynomial being subtracted.
- Then add.

For instance, suppose that we want to subtract the polynomial $2x^4 - 5x^3 + 4x^2 + x + 1$ from $3x^4 + x^3 - 4x^2 + 8x - 9$.

The polynomial from which we are subtracting

The polynomial being subtracted

$$(3x^4 + x^3 - 4x^2 + 8x - 9) - (2x^4 - 5x^3 + 4x^2 + x + 1)$$

$$= (3x^4 + x^3 - 4x^2 + 8x - 9) + (-2x^4 + 5x^3 - 4x^2 - x - 1)$$

Change the sign of each term of the polynomial being subtracted, and then add.

$$= 3x^4 + x^3 - 4x^2 + 8x - 9 - 2x^4 + 5x^3 - 4x^2 - x - 1$$

Remove parentheses.

$$= x^4 + 6x^3 - 8x^2 + 7x - 10$$

Combine like terms.

EXAMPLE 6

Subtract: $(5x^2 - 3x + 7) - (-2x^2 + 8x + 9)$

SOLUTION

$$(5x^2 - 3x + 7) - (-2x^2 + 8x + 9) = (5x^2 - 3x + 7) + (2x^2 - 8x - 9)$$
$$= 5x^2 - 3x + 7 + 2x^2 - 8x - 9$$
$$= 7x^2 - 11x - 2$$

PRACTICE 6

Find the difference:
$(2x - 1) - (3x^2 + 15x - 1)$

Thus far, we have subtracted polynomials using a horizontal format. However, we can also subtract polynomials vertically, a skill that comes up when dividing polynomials. As in the case of the vertical addition of polynomials, the key in vertical subtraction is to position the polynomials so that like terms are in the same column. Then we change the sign of each term of the polynomial being subtracted, and add.

EXAMPLE 7

Subtract using a vertical format: $(7x^2 - 3x + 7) - (x^2 + 8x - 9)$

SOLUTION

$$\begin{array}{r} 7x^2 - 3x + 7 \\ -(x^2 + 8x - 9) \end{array}$$

Position like terms in the same columns.

$$\begin{array}{r} 7x^2 - 3x + 7 \\ - x^2 - 8x + 9 \end{array}$$

Change the sign of each term of the polynomial being subtracted.

$$\begin{array}{r} 7x^2 - 3x + 7 \\ - x^2 - 8x + 9 \\ \hline 6x^2 - 11x + 16 \end{array}$$

Add.

PRACTICE 7

Subtract vertically:
$(20x - 13) - (5x^2 - 12x + 13)$

EXAMPLE 8

Subtract $10x^2 + 8xy + y^2$ from $4y^2 - 9x^2$, using a vertical format.

SOLUTION

$$
\begin{array}{l}
\quad\; -9x^2 \qquad\quad + 4y^2 \\
-(10x^2 + 8xy + \; y^2)
\end{array}
$$
Position like terms in the same column.

$$
\begin{array}{l}
\quad\; -9x^2 \qquad\quad + 4y^2 \\
-10x^2 - 8xy - \; y^2
\end{array}
$$
Change the signs of the terms in the polynomial being subtracted.

$$
\begin{array}{l}
\quad\; -9x^2 \qquad\quad + 4y^2 \\
-10x^2 - 8xy \;\; - \; y^2 \\
\hline
-19x^2 - 8xy \;\; + 3y^2
\end{array}
$$
Add.

PRACTICE 8

Find the difference using a vertical format:
$$(2p^2 - 7pq + 5q^2)$$
$$- (3p^2 + 4pq - 12q^2)$$

EXAMPLE 9

The polynomial $0.1x + 25.6$ approximates the number of Americans (in millions) who voted for the Democratic candidate in the presidential election that took place x years after 1936. The corresponding polynomial for the Republican candidate is $x + 16$. Find the polynomial that approximates the number of Americans who voted for either the Democratic or the Republican candidate. (*Source: Congressional Quarterly*)

SOLUTION To determine the number of Americans who voted for either the Democratic or the Republican candidate, we add the number who voted for the Democratic candidate and the number who voted for the Republican candidate. These numbers are approximated by the given polynomials.

$$
\begin{array}{r}
0.1x + 25.6 \\
x + 16 \\
\hline
1.1x + 41.6
\end{array}
$$

So $1.1x + 41.6$ represents the number of Americans who voted for either the Democratic or Republican candidate.

PRACTICE 9

The polynomial $0.3x + 67.2$ approximates the life expectancy (in years) at birth for males born x years after 1970. The corresponding polynomial for females is $0.3x + 74.8$. Find the polynomial that approximates how much greater the life expectancy is for females than for males.

(*Source:* U.S. National Center for Health Statistics, *Vital Statistics of the United States*)

Exercises 5.4

FOR EXTRA HELP

📖 *Student's Solutions Manual*

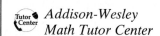 *Addison-Wesley Math Tutor Center*

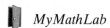 *MyMathLab*

📼 *Videotape 5/DVT 5*

Add horizontally.

1. $3x^2 + 6x - 5$ and $-x^2 + 2x + 7$

2. $10x^2 + 3x + 9$ and $-x^2 - 5x + 1$

3. $2n^3 + n$ and $3n^3 + 8n$

4. $9y + 2y^2$ and $-y - 3y^2$

5. $10p + 3 + p^2$ and $p^2 - 7p - 4$

6. $x^2 + 3x - 8$ and $10 - 3x + 4x^2$

7. $8x^2 + 7xy - y^2$ and $3x^2 - 10xy + 3y^2$

8. $20p^2 + 15q^4 + 30pq$ and $-4pq + 10q^4 - p^2$

9. $2p^3 - p^2q - 5pq^2 + 1$, $3p^2q + 2pq^2 - 4q^3 + 4$, and $p^3 + q^3$

10. $2x^3 - 4x^2y + xy^2 + y^3$, $3xy^2 - 6$, and $2x^2y - xy^2 - 2y^3 + 3$

Add vertically.

11. $10x^2 - 3x - 8$ and $20x + 3$

12. $t^2 + 4t + 5$ and $-t + 10$

13. $5x^3 + 7x - 1$ and $x^2 + 2x + 3$

14. $2r^3 + r + 2$ and $-r^3 - 8r^2 + 5r - 6$

15. $5ab^2 - 3a^2 + a^3$ and $2ab^2 + 9a^2 - 4a^3$

16. $p^2q^3 - p^2 - q^3$ and $5p^2q^3 + p^2 + q^3$

Subtract horizontally.

17. $2x^2 + 3x - 7$ from $x^2 + x + 4$

18. $2x^3 + 7x^2 + 3x$ from $8x^3 - 10x^2 + x$

19. $3x^3 + x^2 + 5x - 8$ from $x^3 + 10x^2 - 8x + 3$

20. $5t^2 - 7t - 1$ from $8t^2 - 3t + 2$

21. $5x + 9$ from $x^2 + 3x$

22. $3x - 7$ from $x^2 - x + 4$

23. $4y^2 - 6xy - 3$ from $1 - 6xy + 5x^2 - y^2$

24. $p^4 - 7p^2q^2 + q^4$ from $8p^4 - 3q^4$

Subtract vertically.

25. $7p^2 - 10p - 1$ from $2p^2 - 3p + 5$

26. $x^2 - 5x + 2$ from $3x^2 + 10x - 2$

27. $8t^3 - 5$ from $9t^3 - 12t^2 + 3$

28. $10x + 7$ from $x^2 + 2x - 6$

29. $r^3 - 3r^2s - 5$ from $4r^3 - 20r^2s - 7$

30. $-5x^3 - 2y^2$ from $13xy^3 + 7x^3 - 10y^2$

Remove the parentheses and simplify, if possible.

31. $7x - (8x + r)$

32. $-(3x + 2y) + (4x - 5)$

33. $2p - (3q + r)$

34. $t - (4r - s)$

35. $(4y - 1) + (3y^2 - y + 5)$

36. $(2x + 6) + (x^2 - 4x + 3)$

37. $(m^3 - 6m + 7) - (-9 + 6m)$

38. $(p^2 + 3p - 5) + (p^3 + 6 - p^2)$

39. $(2x^3 - 7x + 8) - (5x^2 + 3x - 1)$

40. $(n^3 - 4n + 2) - (n^2 - 8n + 1)$

41. $(8x^2 + 3x) + (x - 2) + (x^2 + 9)$

42. $(5y^2 + y) + (9y - 1) + (y^2 + 2)$

43. $(3x - 7) + (2x + 9) - (7x - 10)$

44. $(5n + 1) - (3n + 1) + (2n + 5)$

45. $(7x^2y^2 - 10xy + 4) - (2xy + 8) + (x^2y^2 - 10)$

46. $(2m^2n^2 - mn + 7) - (mn - 3) + (m^2n^2 + 7)$

Applications

Solve.

47. The surface area of the cylindrical can shown is approximated by the polynomial expression $3.14r^2 + 3.14r^2 + 6.28rh$.

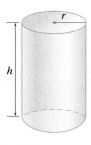

   a. Simplify this polynomial expression.

   b. Find a polynomial expression for the surface area of a can where the radius and height are equal.

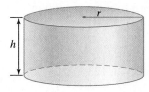

48. The room shown is in the shape of a cube.

   a. Write a simplified expression for the surface area of the four walls.

   b. Find the surface area of the four walls when *e* is 9 ft, *x* is 3 ft, and *y* is 7 ft.

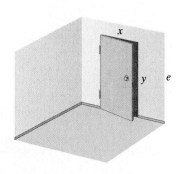

49. The total U.S. imports of petroleum (in millions of barrels per day) in a given year is approximated by the polynomial $31x^3 - 522x^2 + 2083x + 6051$, where x represents the number of years since 1975. The corresponding total of exports of petroleum is $-x^3 + 16x^2 + 22x + 189$. Write a polynomial that represents how many more barrels per day were imported than exported in a given year. (*Source:* U.S. Department of Energy's *Monthly Energy Review*)

50. The number (in thousands) of male commissioned officers in the U.S. Department of Defense in a given year is approximated by $-0.1x^2 + 5.4x + 18.3$, where x represents the number of years since 1940. The corresponding polynomial for female commissioned officers is $0.2x + 1.3$. Find the polynomial that represents, for a given year, how many more male commissioned officers than female commissioned officers there were. (*Source:* U.S. Department of Defense)

51. The number (in millions) of compact discs sold in a given year is approximated by $2x^3 - 27x^2 + 172x + 391$, where x represents the number of years since 1992. The corresponding polynomial for cassettes is $2x^3 - 22x^2 + 18x + 360$. Find the polynomial that represents how many more CDs than cassettes were sold in a given year. (*Source:* Recording Industry Association of America)

52. The total expenses (in billions of dollars) in federal U.S. hospitals can be modeled by the polynomial $0.8t + 4$, where t is the number of years since 1975. For nonfederal U.S. hospitals, the corresponding polynomial is $13t + 27$. Write a polynomial that represents the total expenses for all U.S. hospitals. (*Source:* U.S. National Center for Health Statistics)

• *Check your answers on page A-24.*

Mindstretchers

PATTERNS

1. A Fibonacci sequence is a list of numbers with the following property: After the first two numbers, every other number on the list is the sum of the two previous numbers. The following, for example, is a Fibonacci sequence:

$$7 + 11$$
$$\downarrow$$
$$7, 11, 18, 29, 47, 76, 123, \ldots$$
$$\uparrow$$
$$11 + 18$$

a. What is the next number in this sequence?

_____

b. If the first two numbers in a Fibonacci sequence are *a* and *b*, find the third and fourth numbers. Check that the tenth number in the sequence is given by the polynomial $21a + 34b$.

_____

_____

_____

_____

_____

MATHEMATICAL REASONING

2. Is it possible to add two polynomials, each of degree 4, and have the sum be a polynomial of degree 2? If so, give an example. If not, explain why not.

_____

_____

CRITICAL THINKING

3. Is the subtraction of polynomials a commutative operation? Give an example to support your answer.

_____

_____

_____

_____

_____

5.5 Multiplication of Polynomials

In this section, we discuss how to multiply polynomials. We start with finding the product of two monomials.

OBJECTIVES

- *To multiply monomials*
- *To multiply a monomial by a polynomial*
- *To multiply binomials*
- *To multiply polynomials in general*
- *To solve applied problems involving the multiplication of polynomials*

Multiplying Monomials

When multiplying monomials such as $3x^2$ and $2x^5$, the product rule of exponents helps us to find the product.

$$(3x^2)(2x^5) = (3 \cdot 2) \cdot (x^2 \cdot x^5)$$ The commutative and associative properties of multiplication

$$= (3 \cdot 2) \cdot (x^{2+5})$$ The product rule of exponents
$$= 6x^7$$

To Multiply Monomials
- Multiply the coefficients.
- Then multiply the variables, using the product rule of exponents.

EXAMPLE 1

Multiply: $-2x \cdot 8x$

SOLUTION

$$-2x \cdot 8x = (-2 \cdot 8) \cdot (x \cdot x)$$
$$= (-2 \cdot 8)(x^{1+1})$$
$$= -16x^2$$

PRACTICE 1

Find the product of $(-10x^2)$ and $(-4x^3)$.

EXAMPLE 2

Multiply: $(-2x^3y)(-4x^2y^4)(10xy)$

SOLUTION

$$(-2x^3y)(-4x^2y^4)(10xy) = (-2 \cdot -4 \cdot 10) \cdot (x^3 \cdot x^2 \cdot x) \cdot (y \cdot y^4 \cdot y)$$
$$= 80(x^{3+2+1})(y^{1+4+1})$$
$$= 80x^6y^6$$

Note that the variables in a product are generally written in alphabetical order.

PRACTICE 2

Find the product:
$(7ab^2)(10a^2b^3)(-5a)$

EXAMPLE 3	PRACTICE 3
Simplify: $(-3p^2r)^3$	Find the square of $-5xy^2$.

SOLUTION

$(-3p^2r)^3 = (-3)^3(p^2)^3(r)^3$ Use the rule for raising a product to a power.

$\qquad\qquad = -27p^6r^3$

Multiplying a Monomial by a Polynomial

Now let's use our knowledge of multiplying monomials to find the product of a monomial and a polynomial.

Consider, for instance, the product $(7x)(9x^2 + 5)$. We use the distributive property to find this product.

$$(7x)(9x^2 + 5) = (7x)(9x^2) + (7x)(5) = 63x^3 + 35x$$

Let's look at some more examples.

EXAMPLE 4	PRACTICE 4
Multiply: $(-8x + 9)(-3x^2)$	Find the product: $(10s^2 - 3)(7s)$

SOLUTION

$$\begin{aligned}(-8x + 9)(-3x^2) &= (-3x^2)(-8x + 9)\\ &= (-3x^2)(-8x) + (-3x^2)(9)\\ &= 24x^3 - 27x^2\end{aligned}$$

EXAMPLE 5	PRACTICE 5
Multiply: $3p^2q(5p^3 - 2pq + q^3)$	Simplify: $-2m^3n^2(-6m^3n^5 + 2mn^2 + n)$

SOLUTION

$$\begin{aligned}3p^2q(5p^3 - 2pq + q^3) &= 3p^2q(5p^3) + 3p^2q(-2pq) + 3p^2q(q^3)\\ &= 15p^5q - 6p^3q^2 + 3p^2q^4\end{aligned}$$

EXAMPLE 6	PRACTICE 6
Simplify: $8x^2(3x + 1) + x^2(5x^2 - 6x + 5)$	Simplify: $7s^3(-2s^2 + 5s + 4) - s^2(s^2 + 6s - 1)$

SOLUTION

$$\begin{aligned}8x^2(3x &+ 1) + x^2(5x^2 - 6x + 5)\\ &= 8x^2(3x) + 8x^2(1) + x^2(5x^2) + x^2(-6x) + x^2(5)\\ &= 24x^3 + 8x^2 + 5x^4 - 6x^3 + 5x^2\\ &= 5x^4 + 18x^3 + 13x^2 \qquad \text{Combine like terms.}\end{aligned}$$

Multiplying Two Binomials

Now we extend the discussion to the multiplication of binomials. As in the case of multiplying monomials and binomials, we use the distributive property.

Consider, for example, the product $(x + 4)(7x + 2)$. To apply the distributive property, we can think of the first factor, $(x + 4)$, as a single number multiplied by the binomial $(7x + 2)$.

$$(a) \quad (b + c) = \quad (a) \quad (b) + \quad (a) \quad (c)$$

$(x + 4)(7x + 2) = (x + 4)(7x) + (x + 4)(2)$	Use the distributive property.
$= 7x(x + 4) + 2(x + 4)$	Use the commutative property.
$= 7x \cdot x + 7x \cdot 4 + 2 \cdot x + 2 \cdot 4$	Use the distributive property.
$= 7x^2 + 28x + 2x + 8$	
$= 7x^2 + 30x + 8$	Combine like terms.

Would we get the same answer if we multiplied $(7x + 2)$ by $(x + 4)$?

Let's consider some other examples.

EXAMPLE 7

Find the product: $(3x + 1)(5x - 2)$

SOLUTION

$$\begin{aligned}
(3x + 1)(5x - 2) &= (3x + 1)(5x) + (3x + 1)(-2) \\
&= 5x(3x + 1) + (-2)(3x + 1) \\
&= 5x \cdot 3x + 5x \cdot 1 + (-2) \cdot 3x + (-2) \cdot 1 \\
&= 15x^2 + 5x - 6x - 2 \\
&= 15x^2 - x - 2
\end{aligned}$$

PRACTICE 7

Multiply: $(a - 1)(2a + 3)$

Another way to multiply two binomials is called the **FOIL method,** which is derived from the distributive property. With this method, we can memorize a formula that makes multiplying binomials quick and easy.

FOIL stands for **F**irst, **O**uter, **I**nner, and **L**ast. Let's see how this method works, applying it to the product $(x + 4)(7x + 2)$ that we discussed above.

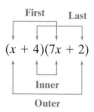

The two **first** terms in the binomials are x and $7x$, and their product is $7x^2$.

$$\text{First}$$
$$(x + 4)(7x + 2) \qquad x \cdot 7x = 7x^2$$

The two **outer** terms are x and 2, and their product is $2x$.

$$(x + 4)(7x + 2) \qquad x \cdot 2 = 2x$$

Outer

The two **inner** terms are 4 and $7x$, and their product is $28x$.

$$(x + 4)(7x + 2) \qquad 4 \cdot 7x = 28x$$

Inner

Next, the two **last** terms are 4 and 2, and their product is 8.

Last

$$(x + 4)(7x + 2) \qquad 4 \cdot 2 = 8$$

Finally, we add the four products, combining any like terms.

$$7x^2 + 2x + 28x + 8 = 7x^2 + 30x + 8$$

Note that, as expected, this answer is the same as the one found using the distributive property.

To Multiply Two Binomials Using the FOIL Method

Consider $(a + b)(c + d)$.

- Multiply the two first terms in the binomials.

$$(a + b)(c + d) \qquad \text{Product is } ac.$$

F

- Multiply the two outer terms.

$$(a + b)(c + d) \qquad \text{Product is } ad.$$

O

- Multiply the two inner terms.

$$(a + b)(c + d) \qquad \text{Product is } bc.$$

I

- Multiply the two last terms.

$$(a + b)(c + d) \qquad \text{Product is } bd.$$

L

- Find the sum of these four products.

$$(a + b)(c + d) = ac + ad + bc + bd$$

With some practice, the FOIL method can be done mentally.

EXAMPLE 8

Multiply: $(8x - 3)(2x - 1)$

SOLUTION Using the FOIL method, we get:

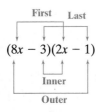

$$
\begin{array}{ll}
\text{F:} & (8x)(2x) = 16x^2 \\
\text{O:} & (8x)(-1) = -8x \\
\text{I:} & (-3)(2x) = -6x \\
\text{L:} & (-3)(-1) = 3
\end{array}
$$

So $(8x - 3)(2x - 1) = 16x^2 - 8x - 6x + 3 = 16x^2 - 14x + 3$. Note that the middle term, $-14x$, is the sum of the outer and inner products, which are like terms.

PRACTICE 8

Find the product of $8x + 3$ and $2x - 1$.

EXAMPLE 9

Multiply: $(3a + b)(2a - b)$

SOLUTION

$$
\begin{array}{l}
\qquad\quad\; \text{F} \qquad\;\; \text{O} \qquad\;\; \text{I} \qquad\;\; \text{L} \\
(3a + b)(2a - b) = (3a)(2a) + (3a)(-b) + (b)(2a) + (b)(-b) \\
\qquad\qquad\qquad\quad = 6a^2 - 3ab + 2ab - b^2 \\
\qquad\qquad\qquad\quad = 6a^2 - ab - b^2
\end{array}
$$

PRACTICE 9

Find the product: $(7m - n)(2m + n)$

Multiplying Polynomials

Finally, let's consider multiplying polynomials in general. Here we extend the previous discussion of multiplying binomials to multiplying polynomials that can have any number of terms. Let's consider, for instance, the product of $x^2 + 3x - 1$ and $x + 2$.

$$
\begin{array}{ll}
(x^2 + 3x - 1)(x + 2) = (x^2 + 3x - 1)(x) + (x^2 + 3x - 1)(2) & \text{Use the distributive property.} \\
\qquad\qquad\qquad\quad\; = (x^3 + 3x^2 - x) + (2x^2 + 6x - 2) & \text{Use the distributive property.} \\
\qquad\qquad\qquad\quad\; = x^3 + 5x^2 + 5x - 2 & \text{Combine like terms.}
\end{array}
$$

Instead of multiplying horizontally, we can multiply two polynomials in a vertical format similar to that used for multiplying whole numbers.

$$
\begin{array}{r}
x^2 + 3x - 1 \\
x + 2 \\
\hline
2x^2 + 6x - 2 \\
x^3 + 3x^2 - x \quad\; \\
\hline
x^3 + 5x^2 + 5x - 2
\end{array}
$$

Multiply $x^2 + 3x - 1$ by 2.

Multiply $x^2 + 3x - 1$ by x.

Add like terms.

Note that we positioned the terms of the two "partial products" in the shaded area so that each column contains like terms. Finally, to find the product of the original polynomials, we add down each column in the shaded area.

EXAMPLE 10

Find the product of $3y^2 + y + 5$ and $4y - 1$.

SOLUTION We begin by rewriting the problem in a vertical format.

$$
\begin{array}{r}
3y^2 + y + 5 \\
4y - 1 \\
\hline
-3y^2 - y - 5 \\
12y^3 + 4y^2 + 20y \phantom{{}-5} \\
\hline
12y^3 + y^2 + 19y - 5
\end{array}
$$

So we conclude that

$$(3y^2 + y + 5)(4y - 1) = 12y^3 + y^2 + 19y - 5.$$

PRACTICE 10

Multiply: $(8n^2 - n + 3)(n + 2)$

EXAMPLE 11

Multiply: $(4x^3 - 2x + 1)(x + 5)$

SOLUTION Let's multiply vertically.

Use $+ 0x^2$ for the missing x^2 term.

$$
\begin{array}{r}
4x^3 + 0x^2 - 2x + 1 \\
x + 5 \\
\hline
20x^3 + 0x^2 - 10x + 5 \\
4x^4 + 0x^3 - 2x^2 + x \phantom{{}+5} \\
\hline
4x^4 + 20x^3 - 2x^2 - 9x + 5
\end{array}
$$

Note that we wrote $0x^2$ for the missing second-degree term in the top polynomial. (Alternatively, we could have left a blank space there.) Similarly, we write a term with a 0 coefficient for each missing term in the partial products.

PRACTICE 11

Find the product of $8x^3 + 9x - 1$ and $3x + 7$.

EXAMPLE 12

Find the product of $a^2 + 2ab + b^2$ and $a + b$.

SOLUTION

$$
\begin{array}{r}
a^2 \phantom{{}+} + 2ab \phantom{{}+} + b^2 \\
a \phantom{{}+} + b \\
\hline
a^2b + 2ab^2 + b^3 \\
a^3 + 2a^2b + ab^2 \phantom{{}+b^3} \\
\hline
a^3 + 3a^2b + 3ab^2 + b^3
\end{array}
$$

PRACTICE 12

Multiply $p^2 - 2pq + q^2$ by $p - q$.

EXAMPLE 13

The polynomial $0.5n(n + 1)$ represents the sum of the first n whole numbers. Rewrite this polynomial without parentheses.

SOLUTION To remove the parentheses, we multiply the monomial $0.5n$ by each term in the binomial, and then write the sum.

$$0.5n(n + 1) = 0.5n^2 + 0.5n$$

PRACTICE 13

At the end of two years, the amount of money in a savings account is given by

$$(P + Pr) + (P + Pr)r,$$

where P is the initial balance and r is the annual rate of interest compounded annually. Rewrite this expression by removing parentheses and simplifying.

Exercises 5.5

FOR EXTRA HELP

📖 *Student's Solutions Manual*

☎ *Addison-Wesley Math Tutor Center*

🚪 *MyMathLab*

📼 *Videotape 5/DVT 5*

Multiply.

1. $(6x)(-4x)$

2. $(-3x)(2x)$

3. $(9t^2)(-t^3)$

4. $(-6y^2)(7y^5)$

5. $(-5x^2)(-4x^4)$

6. $(-2h^2)(-3h^3)$

7. $(10x^3)(-7x^5)$

8. $(20a)(-5a^{99})$

9. $(-4pq^2)(-4p^2qr^2)$

10. $(8st^2)(6s^4t^7)$

11. $(-8x)^2$

12. $(-10p)^2$

13. $\left(\frac{1}{2}t^4\right)^3$

14. $\left(\frac{1}{3}n^3\right)^3$

15. $(7a)(10a^2)(-5a)$

16. $(-8n^3)(2n^3)(-n)$

17. $(2ab^2)(-3abc)(4a^2)$

18. $(4mn^3)(-m)(7mn^2)$

Find the product.

19. $(7x - 5)\,x$

20. $(y)(3y - 7)$

21. $(9t + t^2)\,(5t)$

22. $(5x - x^2)(4x)$

23. $6a^3(4a^2 - 7a)$

24. $2y(8y - y^3)$

25. $4x^2(3x - 2)$

26. $-5p^7(9p - 3)$

27. $x^3(x^2 - 2x + 4)$

28. $t^2(t^2 + 8t + 1)$

29. $5x(3x^2 + 5x + 6)$

30. $-4x(3x^2 - x + 2)$

31. $(5x^2 - 3x - 7)(-9x)$

32. $(10x^2 + x - 1)(2x)$

33. $6x^2(x^3 + 4x^2 - x - 1)$

34. $(x^3 + 6x^2 - 9x + 10)(-3x^4)$

35. $4p(7q - p^2)$

36. $-pq^2(3p^3 - 9q)$

37. $(v + 3w^2)(-7v)$

38. $(m^2 + n^2)\,3mn^5$

39. $2a^2b^3(3a^4b^2 + 10ab^5)$

40. $-4x^2y^2(7x^2y^3 - 4x^3y^4)$

Simplify.

41. $10x + 2x(-3x + 8)$

42. $-7x + 3x(5x - 9)$

43. $-x + 8x(x^2 - 2x + 1)$

44. $2x(8x^2 + 7x - 2) - 6x^2$

45. $9x(x^2 + 3x - 5) + 8x(-4x^2 + x)$

46. $x(x^2 + 11x) - 10x(2x^2 + 3)$

47. $-4xy(2x^2 + 4xy) + x^2y(7x^2 - 2y)$

48. $2s^3t(5s - t^2) - 7s^2t^2(9s^2 - 10t)$

49. $5a^2b^2(3ab^4 - a^3b^2) + 4a^2b^2(9ab^4 - 10a^3b^2)$

50. $(3p - 8pq)(5p^2) - (4p^3 + 1)(7q)$

Multiply.

51. $(y + 2)(y + 3)$

52. $(x + 1)(x + 4)$

53. $(x - 3)(x - 5)$

54. $(n - 4)(n - 2)$

55. $(a - 2)(a + 2)$

56. $(x + 3)(x - 3)$

57. $(w + 3)(2w - 7)$

58. $(8x + 5)(x + 4)$

59. $(3 - 2y)(5y - 1)$

60. $(4u - 1)(3 - 2u)$

61. $(10p - 4)(2p - 1)$

62. $(7x + 1)(7x - 3)$

63. $(u + v)(u - v)$

64. $(x + y)(x - y)$

65. $(2p - q)(q - p)$

66. $(x + 4y)(x - y)$

67. $(3a - b)(a - 2b)$

68. $(5x + 4y)(x - y)$

69. $(p - 8)(4q + 3)$

70. $(x + 7)(6y - 1)$

71. $(x - 3)(x^2 - 3x + 1)$

72. $(a + 2)(a^2 - 4a + 4)$

73. $(2x - 1)(x^2 + 3x - 5)$

74. $(8n + 3)(2n^2 - 9n - 1)$

75. $(a - b)(a^2 + ab + b^2)\cdot$

76. $(x^2 + xy + y^2)(y - x)$

77. $(3x)(x + 5)(x - 7)$

78. $(y^2)(8 - 3y)(8 + y)$

Applications

Solve.

79. Backgammon is one of the world's oldest board games. The length and width of the distinctive board (shown below) differ by 30 mm. Find the area of the board in terms of x without using parentheses.

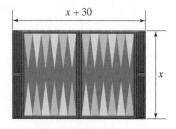

80. To lift an object of mass m from level y_1 to level y_2 requires energy in the amount $mg(y_2 - y_1)$. Write this expression without parentheses.

81. A factory has been selling 1000 color laser printers per year for $1500 each. The company's market research indicates that for each $100 that the price is raised, sales will fall by 30 units. The expression $(1500 + 100x)(1000 - 30x)$ gives the estimated revenue that the company will take in if it adjusts the price of a printer, where x represents the number of $100 increases in the price. Rewrite this expression, multiplying out the factors.

82. A company's total revenue R is given by the equation

$$R = px,$$

where p is the price of each item and x is the number of items sold. Write a polynomial for the revenue if $x = -\dfrac{1}{4}p + 100$.

83. Investment brokers use the formula $A = P(1 + r)^t$ for the amount of money A in a client's account that earns compound interest. In this formula, P is the principal (the original amount of money that the client invested), r is the rate of return per time period (in decimal form), and t is the number of time periods that the money has been invested.

   a. If the client invested $5000 for 3 periods, write this formula as a polynomial in r without parentheses.

   b. If a client invested $5000, how much greater is the amount of money in the account after 3 periods as compared with 2 periods? Write your answer without parentheses.

   c. If the client's rate of return on the investment is 10%, how much money is represented by the expression in part (b)?

84. The expression for the volume of a sphere is $\dfrac{4}{3}\pi r^3$, where r is the radius of the sphere. Assume that the shape of the Earth is approximately a sphere of radius r miles.

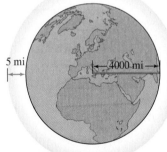

Not to scale

5 mi | 4000 mi

   a. Find and simplify the expression for the volume of the sphere formed by everywhere rising 5 mi above the surface of the Earth.

   b. Find and simplify the expression for the volume of the sphere formed by everywhere descending 5 mi below the surface of the Earth.

   c. According to some scientists, all the life discovered so far in the Universe is found in the layer around the Earth that extends 5 mi above the Earth's surface to 5 mi below. What is the volume of this layer?

   d. If the radius of the Earth is approximately 4000 mi, find the approximate volume of the layer described in part (c).

• *Check your answers on page A-24.*

Mindstretchers

MATHEMATICAL REASONING

1. We can draw rectangles to visualize the product of two binomials. Consider, for example, the product $(x + 9)(x + 2)$. Using the diagram shown, explain how the product can be expressed as the sum of four areas.

	x	9
x	x^2	$9x$
2	$2x$	18

_____

_____

_____

_____

_____

Compare your answer with the result of using the FOIL method to multiply the two binomials.

_____

_____

PATTERNS

2. Simplify the following polynomials:

$$(x + y)^0 =$$
$$(x + y)^1 =$$
$$(x + y)^2 =$$
$$(x + y)^3 =$$

In the following table, enter the coefficients from these polynomials. What pattern (known as Pascal's Triangle) do you observe in this table?

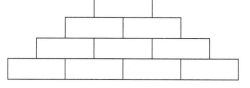

_____

_____

3. Lattice multiplication is a procedure that originated in India in the twelfth century. In this procedure, whole numbers are multiplied as if they were binomials. Each digit of each factor is multiplied separately. The products are recorded in little cells within a lattice, and then added along the diagonals. For instance, to find 29 · 47, the four products are placed in the small, diagonally split squares. The product of 2 and 4, shown in red, is 8.

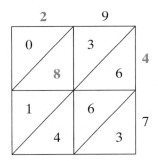

In the following diagram, the square in the upper left shows $^0/_8$, which represents 8. Since the product of 9 and 4 is 36, the square in the upper right contains $^3/_6$. The lower products are $^1/_4$ or 14 and $^6/_3$ or 63. These products are all added along the diagonal. For instance in the diagonal shaded green, the sum 6 + 6 + 4 is 16; the 6 is written below and the 1 is carried into the diagonal above and added into that diagonal: 1 + (3 + 8 + 1). The product 1363 appears down the left side of the lattice and across the bottom.

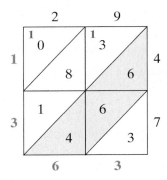

Use lattice multiplication to find the following products:

a. 53 · 89

b. 61 · 94

5.6 Special Products

Recall that in the previous section, we discussed two ways of multiplying binomials—first by directly applying the distributive property, and second by using the FOIL method. In this section, we focus on yet a third approach—using formulas. These formulas provide a shortcut for finding special products, that is, special cases of multiplying binomials.

The Square of a Binomial

To square a binomial means to multiply that binomial by itself. Consider, for instance, $(x + 5)^2$, in which we square the *sum* of two terms. We can rewrite this expression as a binomial multiplied by itself and then use the FOIL method to find the product.

$$(x + 5)^2 = (x + 5)(x + 5)$$
$$= x^2 + 5x + 5x + 25$$
$$= x^2 + 10x + 25$$

Note that the expression $x^2 + 10x + 25$ is equal to $(x)^2 + 2(x)(5) + (5)^2$. So the square of the sum of x and 5 equals the square of x plus twice the product of x and 5 plus the square of 5. This observation leads us to the formula for squaring the sum of two terms.

The Square of a Sum

$$(a + b)^2 = a^2 + 2ab + b^2$$

This formula states that the square of the *sum* of two terms is equal to the square of the first term plus twice the product of the two terms plus the square of the second term. Can you explain why this rule follows from the FOIL method of multiplying binomials?

Memorize the formula for the square of a sum now. With sufficient practice, you will be able to square a binomial sum mentally.

EXAMPLE 1

Simplify: $(x + 7)^2$

SOLUTION Since we are squaring the sum of x and 7, we can use the formula for the square of a sum.

First term → x
Second term → 7
The square of the first term → x^2
The square of the second term → $(7)^2$

$$(x + 7)^2 = x^2 + \underline{2(x)(7)} + (7)^2$$

Twice the product of the two terms

$$= x^2 + 14x + 49$$

PRACTICE 1

Simplify: $(p + 10)^2$

Note in Example 1 that $(x + 7)^2 = x^2 + 14x + 49$, whereas $x^2 + 7^2 = x^2 + 49$. So we see that $(x + 7)^2 \neq x^2 + (7)^2$.

TIP It is important to distinguish between the *square of the sum* of two terms and the *sum of the squares* of the terms: $(x + y)^2 \neq x^2 + y^2$

EXAMPLE 2

Simplify: $(p + q)^2$

SOLUTION In $(p + q)^2$, the first term is p and the second term is q.

First term	Second term	The square of the first term		The square of the second term
↓	↓	↓		↓

$$(p + q)^2 = p^2 + \underbrace{2(p)(q)}_{\substack{\text{Twice the product of} \\ \text{the two terms}}} + q^2$$

$$= p^2 + 2pq + q^2$$

PRACTICE 2

Simplify: $(s + t)^2$

EXAMPLE 3

Simplify: $(2x + 3y)^2$

SOLUTION

$$(2x + 3y)^2 = (2x)^2 + 2(2x)(3y) + (3y)^2$$
$$= 4x^2 + 12xy + 9y^2$$

PRACTICE 3

Simplify: $(4p + 5q)^2$

Now let's examine a second and related formula, which involves the square of the *difference* of two terms rather than their sum. For instance, consider $(x - 5)^2$. Again, we rewrite the square of the binomial and then apply the FOIL method:

$$(x - 5)^2 = (x - 5)(x - 5)$$
$$= x^2 - 5x - 5x + 25$$
$$= x^2 - 10x + 25$$

Note that the expression $x^2 - 10x + 25$ is equal to $x^2 - 2(x)(5) + 25$. So the square of the difference of x and 5 equals the square of x minus twice the product of x and 5 plus the square of 5. This example leads us to the formula for squaring the difference of two terms.

The Square of a Difference

$$(a - b)^2 = a^2 - 2ab + b^2$$

This formula states that the square of the difference of two terms is equal to the square of the first term minus twice the product of the two terms plus the square of the second term.

If we compare the formula for the square of a sum with the formula for the square of a difference, we see that the signs of the middle term of the resulting trinomial differ. That is, for $(a + b)^2$, the middle term is positive, whereas for $(a - b)^2$, the middle term is negative.

EXAMPLE 4

Simplify: $(8a - 1)^2$

SOLUTION Here we are squaring the difference of two terms, so we use the formula for the square of a difference.

First term	Second term		The square of the first term		The square of the second term

$$(8a - 1)^2 = (8a)^2 - \underbrace{2(8a)(1)}_{\substack{\text{Twice the product of} \\ \text{the two terms}}} + 1^2$$

$$= 64a^2 - 16a + 1$$

PRACTICE 4

Simplify: $(5x - 2)^2$

Another way to simplify the expression $(8a - 1)^2$ in Example 4 is to rewrite $(8a - 1)^2$ as $[8a + (-1)]^2$, and then apply the formula for squaring a sum. Can you explain how we would get the same answer with this approach?

EXAMPLE 5

Simplify: $(p - q)^2$

SOLUTION
$$(p - q)^2 = p^2 - 2(p)(q) + q^2$$
$$= p^2 - 2pq + q^2$$

PRACTICE 5

Simplify: $(u - v)^2$

EXAMPLE 6

Simplify: $(3a - 4b)^2$

SOLUTION
$$(3a - 4b)^2 = (3a)^2 - 2(3a)(4b) + (4b)^2$$
$$= 9a^2 - 24ab + 16b^2$$

PRACTICE 6

Simplify: $(2x - 9y)^2$

The Product of the Sum and Difference of Two Terms

The third special binomial formula relates to multiplying *the sum of two terms by the difference of the same two terms*. Explain why neither of the two previous formulas applies in this situation.

For example, consider the product $(x + 5)(x - 5)$. Using the FOIL method we get:

$$(x + 5)(x - 5) = x \cdot x + x \cdot (-5) + 5 \cdot x - 5 \cdot 5$$
$$= x^2 - 5x + 5x - 25$$
$$= x^2 - 25$$

The middle terms cancel each other out.

The Product of the Sum and Difference of Two Terms

$$(a + b)(a - b) = a^2 - b^2$$

This formula states that the product of the sum and difference of the *same* two terms is equal to the square of the first term minus the square of the second term.

EXAMPLE 7

Multiply: $(x + 11)(x - 11)$

SOLUTION

First term	Second term		The square of the first term	The square of the second term

$$(x + 11)(x - 11) = x^2 - (11)^2$$
$$= x^2 - 121$$

PRACTICE 7

Find the product of $(t + 10)$ and $(t - 10)$.

EXAMPLE 8

Multiply.

a. $(p - q)(p + q)$

b. $(3m + 2n)(3m - 2n)$

SOLUTION

a. Since $(p - q)(p + q) = (p + q)(p - q)$, the formula for finding the product of the sum and difference of two terms applies.

$$(p - q)(p + q) = p^2 - q^2$$

b. $(3m + 2n)(3m - 2n) = (3m)^2 - (2n)^2 = 9m^2 - 4n^2$

PRACTICE 8

Find the product.

a. $(r - s)(r + s)$

b. $(8s - 3t)(8s + 3t)$

EXAMPLE 9

Find the product: $(3a^2 - 5)(3a^2 + 5)$

SOLUTION

$$(3a^2 - 5)(3a^2 + 5) = (3a^2)^2 - (5)^2 = 9a^4 - 25$$

PRACTICE 9

Multiply: $(10 - 7k^2)(10 + 7k^2)$

Were you able to find the products in the last few examples mentally? If not, set this as a personal goal when doing similar exercises at the end of this section.

EXAMPLE 10

The nineteenth-century French physician Jean Louis Poiseuille investigated the flow of blood in the smaller blood vessels of the body. He discovered that the speed of blood varies from point to point within a blood vessel. In a blood vessel of radius r at a point b units from the center of the blood vessel, the blood flow speed is given by the expression $k(r + b)(r - b)$, where k is a constant. Rewrite this expression without parentheses.

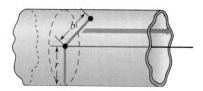

SOLUTION We need to multiply out $k(r + b)(r - b)$.

$$k(r + b)(r - b) = k(r^2 - b^2)$$
$$= kr^2 - kb^2$$

So the rewritten expression is $kr^2 - kb^2$.

PRACTICE 10

The area of the square wooden frame shown can be represented by the polynomial $(S + s)(S - s)$, where s is the side length of the smaller square and S is the side length of the larger square. Rewrite this expression without parentheses.

Exercises 5.6

FOR EXTRA HELP

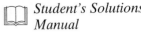 Student's Solutions Manual

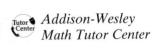 Addison-Wesley Math Tutor Center

MyMathLab

Videotape 5/DVT 5

Simplify.

1. $(y + 2)^2$

2. $(a + 3)^2$

3. $(x + 4)^2$

4. $(n + 8)^2$

5. $(x - 11)^2$

6. $(b - 10)^2$

7. $(6 - n)^2$

8. $(9 - y)^2$

9. $(x + y)^2$

10. $(s - t)^2$

11. $(3x + 1)^2$

12. $(5x + 3)^2$

13. $(4n - 5)^2$

14. $(2x - 1)^2$

15. $(9x + 2)^2$

16. $(11m + 3)^2$

17. $\left(a + \dfrac{1}{2}\right)^2$

18. $(b - 0.2)^2$

19. $(8b + c)^2$

20. $(3s + t)^2$

21. $(5x - 2y)^2$

22. $(3m - 4n)^2$

23. $(-x + 3y)^2$

24. $(-p + 2q)^2$

25. $(4x^3 + y^4)^2$

26. $(5a^2 - c^2)^2$

Multiply.

27. $(a + 1)(a - 1)$

28. $(8 + r)(8 - r)$

29. $(4x - 3)(4x + 3)$

30. $(7y - 2)(7y + 2)$

31. $(10 + 3y)(3y - 10)$

32. $(-1 + 9x)(9x + 1)$

33. $\left(m - \dfrac{1}{2}\right)\left(m + \dfrac{1}{2}\right)$

34. $(n + 0.3)(n - 0.3)$

35. $(4a + b)(4a - b)$

36. $(p - 3q)(p + 3q)$

37. $(3x - 2y)(3x + 2y)$

38. $(10t + 3s)(10t - 3s)$

39. $(1 - 5n)(5n + 1)$

40. $(2s + 3)(3 - 2s)$

41. $x(x + 5)(x - 5)$

42. $y(y - 7)(y + 7)$

43. $5n^2(n + 7)^2$

44. $-8y^3(2y - 1)^2$

45. $(n^2 - m^4)(n^2 + m^4)$

46. $(x^3 + y^5)(x^3 - y^5)$

47. $(a - b)(a + b)(a^2 + b^2)$

48. $(x + y)(x - y)(x^2 + y^2)$

Applications

Solve.

49. A city laid out on a grid plans for a square-shaped park, as shown.

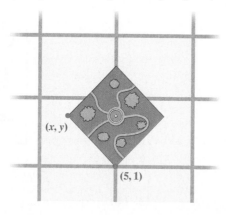

The area of the park can be modeled by the expression $(x - 5)^2 + (y - 1)^2$. Rewrite this expression by removing parentheses and simplifying.

50. A student deposits $100 in an account at interest rate r (in decimal form). If the interest earned is compounded annually, the amount in the account after two years is given by

$$A = 100(1 + r)^2.$$

Write A as a polynomial in r without parentheses.

51. An investment of A dollars increases in value by $P\%$ for each of two years. The value of the investment at the end of the two years can be represented by

$$A\left(1 + \frac{P}{100}\right)\left(1 + \frac{P}{100}\right).$$

Multiply out this expression.

52. In measuring the lengths of the sides of a square piece of wood, a carpenter can be off by length e. The carpenter measures the side of the wooden square to be x.

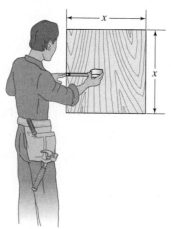

a. What are the longest possible true dimensions of the wooden square? The shortest possible true dimensions?

b. What is the difference in area between the longest possible wooden square and the shortest possible wooden square in terms of e and x?

53. To measure the spread of data, statisticians compute the sample variance of the data. For a sample of size 3, they use the following formula.

$$\text{Sample variance} = \frac{(a - m)^2 + (b - m)^2 + (c - m)^2}{2}$$

Rewrite this formula without parentheses, combining like terms.

54. As the temperature of a lightbulb's filament changes from T_1 to T_2, the energy that the filament radiates changes by the quantity

$$a(T_1 - T_2)(T_1 + T_2)(T_1^2 + T_2^2).$$

Multiply to find this change.

● *Check your answers on page A-24.*

Mindstretchers

PATTERNS

1. Mentally compute each product. (*Hint:* Think of these computations as "special products.")

a. $9999 \times 10{,}001$ _____

b. $30\frac{1}{10} \times 29\frac{9}{10}$ _____

MATHEMATICAL REASONING

2. Suppose that you square two consecutive whole numbers and subtract the smaller square from the larger. Is it possible that the difference is an even number? Explain your answer.

_____

_____

_____

_____

_____

3. By the year 2000 B.C., the astronomers of Mesopotamia knew the relationship $(a - b)(a + b) = a^2 - b^2$. They could demonstrate this relationship by a geometric model. Find the area of the remaining region if the yellow square is removed from the figure shown. Show that this model verifies the relationship $(a - b)(a + b) = a^2 - b^2$. (*Hint:* Find the area in two ways.)

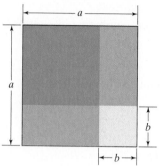

5.7 Division of Polynomials

In the final section of this chapter, we deal with dividing polynomials. We progress from dividing a monomial by another monomial to dividing a polynomial by a binomial.

OBJECTIVES

- *To divide monomials*
- *To divide a polynomial by a monomial*
- *To divide a polynomial by a binomial*
- *To solve applied problems involving the division of polynomials*

Dividing Monomials

The ability to divide monomials—the simplest of polynomial divisions—depends on our knowledge of both fractions and exponents, as the following example illustrates.

EXAMPLE 1

Simplify: $8x^6 \div 4x^2$

SOLUTION We begin by rewriting the problem in fractional form.

$$8x^6 \div 4x^2 = \frac{8x^6}{4x^2}$$

$$\frac{8x^6}{4x^2} = \frac{8}{4} \cdot \frac{x^6}{x^2}$$

$$= 2x^{6-2} \quad \text{Divide the coefficients and use the}$$
$$= 2x^4 \quad \text{quotient rule of exponents.}$$

PRACTICE 1

Find the quotient: $-12n^6 \div 3n$

EXAMPLE 2

Divide: $\dfrac{-15a^2b^3c}{10ab^2}$

SOLUTION

$$\frac{-15a^2b^3c}{10ab^2} = \frac{-15}{10} \cdot \frac{a^2b^3c}{ab^2}$$

$$= \frac{-3}{2} \cdot a^{2-1}b^{3-2}c$$

$$= \frac{-3}{2}abc$$

$$= -\frac{3abc}{2}$$

PRACTICE 2

Find the quotient:

$(20p^3q^2r^4) \div (-5p^2q^2r)$

Dividing a Polynomial by a Monomial

Now we extend our discussion of division to finding the quotient of a polynomial divided by a monomial. We consider an example, written in fractional form.

EXAMPLE 3

Simplify the quotient: $(10x^2 + 15x) \div (5x)$

SOLUTION Let's write the given expression in fractional form.

$$(10x^2 + 15x) \div (5x) = \overset{\text{Polynomial}}{\overbrace{\underset{\underset{\text{Monomial}}{\smile}}{\dfrac{10x^2 + 15x}{5x}}}}$$

Since we are dividing a polynomial by a monomial, we can rewrite this fraction as the sum of two fractions. Then we simplify each fraction.

$$\frac{10x^2 + 15x}{5x} = \frac{10x^2}{5x} + \frac{15x}{5x}$$
$$= 2x + 3$$

Example 3 suggests that when dividing a polynomial by a monomial, we can divide each term in the polynomial by the monomial and then add. Let's apply this shortcut in the following examples.

EXAMPLE 4

Divide: $\dfrac{9x^4 - 6x^3 + 12x^2}{-3x^2}$

SOLUTION Divide each term in the numerator by the denominator. Then add the quotients:

$$\frac{9x^4 - 6x^3 + 12x^2}{-3x^2} = \frac{9x^4}{-3x^2} - \frac{6x^3}{-3x^2} + \frac{12x^2}{-3x^2}$$
$$= -3x^2 + 2x - 4$$

EXAMPLE 5

Divide: $\dfrac{10p^4q^5 + 12p^2q^4 - pq^3}{2pq^2}$

SOLUTION

$$\frac{10p^4q^5 + 12p^2q^4 - pq^3}{2pq^2} = \frac{10p^4q^5}{2pq^2} + \frac{12p^2q^4}{2pq^2} - \frac{pq^3}{2pq^2}$$
$$= 5p^3q^3 + 6pq^2 - \frac{q}{2}$$

PRACTICE 3

Divide: $(21x^3 - 14x^2)$ by $7x$

PRACTICE 4

Simplify: $\dfrac{14x^8 + 10x^5 - 8x^3}{-2x^3}$

PRACTICE 5

Find the quotient:

$$\frac{-5a^7b^6 + a^2b^4 - 15ab^3}{5ab^3}$$

Dividing a Polynomial by a Binomial

Now let's take a look at the general case—how to divide one polynomial by another polynomial. We will restrict our attention to dividing a polynomial by a *binomial*, but these remarks apply to dividing by polynomials with three or more terms as well.

The procedure for dividing a polynomial by a binomial is similar to that of dividing whole numbers, which is commonly called *long division.*

$$
\begin{array}{r}
\text{Divisor} \longrightarrow 13\overline{)156} \\
\end{array}
$$

Divisor $\longrightarrow$ $13\overline{)\,156}$ $\longleftarrow$ Quotient is 12, Dividend 156

$$
\begin{array}{r}
12 \quad \longleftarrow \text{Quotient}\\
13\overline{)\,156} \quad \longleftarrow \text{Dividend}\\
-13\\
\hline
26\\
-26\\
\hline
0 \quad \longleftarrow \text{Remainder}
\end{array}
$$

So $156 \div 13 = 12$ with remainder 0.

Now let's consider the following problem in dividing polynomials.

$$(x^2 - 5x - 24) \div (x + 3)$$

We set up the problem just as if we were dividing whole numbers, being careful to correctly distinguish between the dividend and the divisor. In this case, $x^2 - 5x - 24$ is the dividend and $x + 3$ is the divisor.

$$
\begin{array}{r}
x\\
x + 3\overline{)x^2 - 5x - 24}\\
x^2 + 3x\\
\end{array}
$$

Divide the first term in the dividend by the first term in the divisor: Think $x \div x = x$. Place x in the quotient above the x term in the dividend. Then *multiply* x in the quotient by the divisor: $x(x + 3) = x^2 + 3x$.

$$
\begin{array}{r}
x\\
x + 3\overline{)x^2 - 5x - 24}\\
x^2 + 3x\\
\hline
-8x - 24\\
\end{array}
$$

Subtract $(x^2 + 3x)$ from $(x^2 - 5x)$ by changing the signs of each term in $(x^2 + 3x)$ and then adding to get $-8x$. Bring down the next term, -24.

$$
\begin{array}{r}
x - 8\\
x + 3\overline{)x^2 - 5x - 24}\\
x^2 + 3x\\
\hline
-8x - 24\\
-8x - 24\\
\hline
0\\
\end{array}
$$

The remainder is 0.

Divide x into $-8x$: Think $-8x \div x = -8$. Place -8 in the quotient above the constant term in the dividend. Then *multiply* -8 in the quotient by the divisor: $-8(x + 3) = -8x - 24$. Finally, *subtract* $(-8x - 24)$ from $(-8x - 24)$ by changing the signs of each term in $(-8x - 24)$ and then adding to get 0.

Note that the degree of the remainder (degree 0) is less than the degree of the divisor (degree 1).

So $(x^2 - 5x - 24) \div (x + 3) = x - 8$. Can you explain how you would check this quotient?

This example suggests the following general method for dividing a polynomial by a polynomial.

To Divide a Polynomial by a Polynomial

- Arrange each term of the dividend and divisor in descending order.
- Divide the first term of the dividend by the first term of the divisor. The result is the first term of the quotient.
- Multiply the first term of the quotient by the divisor and place the product under the dividend.
- Subtract the product, found in the previous step, from the dividend.
- Bring down the next term to form a new dividend.
- Repeat the process until the degree of the remainder is less than the degree of the divisor.

EXAMPLE 6

$$2x - 1 \overline{)6x^2 + 9x - 6}$$

SOLUTION The dividend and divisor are already in descending order.

$$
\begin{array}{r}
3x \\
2x - 1 \overline{)6x^2 + 9x - 6} \\
\underline{6x^2 - 3x} \\
12x - 6
\end{array}
$$

Divide $6x^2$ by $2x$, getting $3x$.

Multiply $3x$ by $(2x - 1)$, getting $(6x^2 - 3x)$.

Subtract $(6x^2 - 3x)$ from $(6x^2 + 9x)$ and bring down -6.

$$
\begin{array}{r}
3x + 6 \\
2x - 1 \overline{)6x^2 + 9x - 6} \\
\underline{6x^2 - 3x} \\
12x - 6 \\
\underline{12x - 6} \\
0
\end{array}
$$

Divide $12x$ by $2x$, getting 6.

Multiply 6 by $(2x - 1)$, getting $(12x - 6)$.

Subtract $(12x - 6)$ from $(12x - 6)$.

The degree of 0 is less than the degree of $(2x - 1)$, so the process stops.

So $(6x^2 + 9x - 6) \div (2x - 1) = 3x + 6$.

PRACTICE 6

Find the quotient:
$(10x^2 + 17x + 3) \div (5x + 1)$

TIP We place each term in the quotient above a term in the dividend of the same degree.

Now we focus on problems in dividing polynomials that have *remainders*.

Dividing whole numbers:

$$45\overline{)956}$$ quotient 21

$$\frac{90}{56}$$
$$\frac{45}{11} \leftarrow \text{Remainder}$$

CHECK

$$45 \cdot 21 + 11 \stackrel{?}{=} 956$$
$$956 = 956 \qquad \text{True.}$$

So $956 \div 45 = 21\frac{11}{45}$.

Dividing polynomials:

$$x + 5\overline{)x^2 + 8x + 16}$$ quotient $x+3$

$$\frac{x^2 + 5x}{3x + 16}$$
$$\frac{3x + 15}{1} \leftarrow \text{Remainder}$$

CHECK

$$(x + 5)(x + 3) + 1 \stackrel{?}{=} x^2 + 8x + 16$$
$$x^2 + 8x + 16 = x^2 + 8x + 16 \qquad \text{True.}$$

So $(x^2 + 8x + 16) \div (x + 5) = x + 3 + \dfrac{1}{x + 5}$.

Note that we can check a problem involving division of polynomials in the same way that we check division of whole numbers:

$$\text{Divisor} \cdot \text{quotient} + \text{remainder} = \text{Dividend}$$

EXAMPLE 7

Find the quotient: $(x^3 + 3x^2 - 8x + 2) \div (x + 5)$

SOLUTION

$$x + 5\overline{)x^3 + 3x^2 - 8x + 2}$$ quotient $x^2 - 2x + 2$

$$\frac{x^3 + 5x^2}{-2x^2 - 8x}$$
$$\frac{-2x^2 - 10x}{2x + 2}$$
$$\frac{2x + 10}{-8}$$

Since the degree of the remainder is less than the degree of the divisor, we stop.

CHECK

$$(x + 5)(x^2 - 2x + 2) + (-8) \stackrel{?}{=} x^3 + 3x^2 - 8x + 2$$
$$x^3 + 3x^2 - 8x + 2 = x^3 + 3x^2 - 8x + 2 \qquad \text{True.}$$

So we write the answer as

$$x^2 - 2x + 2 + \frac{-8}{x + 5}$$

PRACTICE 7

Divide $(3x^3 + 7x^2 + 11x + 5)$ by $(3x + 1)$.

Some problems in dividing polynomials involve terms that are not in *descending order*.

EXAMPLE 8

Divide $(6 + 8x^2 - 14x)$ by $(2x - 3)$.

SOLUTION Before dividing, we place the terms in both the divisor and the dividend in descending order. Here we need to rearrange the terms in the dividend:

$$
\begin{array}{r}
4x - 1 \\
2x - 3 \overline{)8x^2 - 14x + 6} \\
\underline{8x^2 - 12x} \\
-2x + 6 \\
\underline{-2x + 3} \\
3
\end{array}
$$

The remainder is 3.

So $(8x^2 - 14x + 6) \div (2x - 3) = 4x - 1 + \dfrac{3}{2x - 3}$.

We leave the check to you.

In dividing polynomials, we may have *missing terms* in the dividend, as shown in the following example.

EXAMPLE 9

$x + 3 \overline{)2x^3 + 7x^2 - 9}$

SOLUTION Since there is no x-term in the dividend, we can insert $0x$ as a placeholder for the missing term.

$$
\begin{array}{r}
2x^2 + x - 3 \\
x + 3 \overline{)2x^3 + 7x^2 + 0x - 9} \\
\underline{2x^3 + 6x^2} \\
x^2 + 0x \\
\underline{x^2 + 3x} \\
-3x - 9 \\
\underline{-3x - 9} \\
0
\end{array}
$$

So $\dfrac{2x^3 + 7x^2 - 9}{x + 3} = 2x^2 + x - 3$.

PRACTICE 8

Divide: $(-21s + 10 + 9s^2) \div (3s - 2)$

PRACTICE 9

Divide: $\dfrac{4n^3 - 19n^2 - 4}{4n - 3}$

EXAMPLE 10

To find the length l of a rectangular-shaped object, we can use the formula $A = lw$, where the area A and width w are given.

a. Solve $A = lw$ for l.

b. If the area of the rectangular top of a billiard table is given by the polynomial $(5x^2 + 13x + 6)$ ft, find the length when the width is $(x + 2)$ ft.

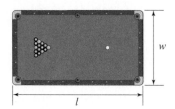

SOLUTION

a. Since $A = lw$, $l = \dfrac{A}{w}$.

b. Using $l = \dfrac{A}{w}$, we conclude that $l = \dfrac{5x^2 + 13x + 6}{x + 2}$. Dividing the numerator by the denominator, we find that $l = 5x + 3$. So the length is $(5x + 3)$ ft.

PRACTICE 10

If \$10 is invested at an interest rate of r per year and compounded annually, the future value S in dollars at the end of the nth year is given by

$$S = 10(1 + r)^n$$

a. What is the future value of the investment after 1 year? After 2 years?

b. Write the answers to part (a) without parentheses and in descending order.

c. Using your answer in part (b), determine how many times as great the future value of the investment is after 2 years as compared to the future value after 1 year.

Exercises 5.7

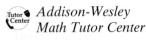

Simplify.

1. $\dfrac{10x^4}{5x^2}$

2. $\dfrac{6x^3}{2x^2}$

3. $\dfrac{16a^8}{-4a}$

4. $\dfrac{-35y^2}{7y}$

5. $\dfrac{8x^5}{-6x^4}$

6. $\dfrac{-9p^5}{-12p^2}$

7. $\dfrac{12p^2q^3}{3p^2q}$

8. $\dfrac{9a^4b}{3a^2b}$

9. $\dfrac{-24u^6v^4}{-8u^4v^2}$

10. $\dfrac{4x^5y^4}{2x^2y}$

11. $\dfrac{-15a^2b^5}{7ab^3}$

12. $\dfrac{21x^3y^5}{-10xy^2}$

13. $\dfrac{-6u^5v^3w^3}{4u^2vw^3}$

14. $\dfrac{-10x^3yz^2}{8x^2yz}$

Divide.

15. $\dfrac{6n^2 + 10n}{2n}$

16. $\dfrac{12m^4 - 15m^3}{3m}$

17. $\dfrac{20b^4 - 10b}{10b}$

18. $\dfrac{2x^2 - 8x}{2x}$

19. $\dfrac{18a^2 + 12a}{-3a}$

20. $\dfrac{16x^2 - 10x}{-2x}$

21. $\dfrac{9x^5 - 6x^7}{3x^5}$

22. $\dfrac{6a^3 - 4a^2}{2a^2}$

23. $\dfrac{12a^4 - 18a^3 + 30a^2}{6a^2}$

24. $\dfrac{8x^5 + 4x^4 - 16x^3}{4x^2}$

25. $\dfrac{n^5 - 10n^4 - 5n^3}{-5n^3}$

26. $\dfrac{9y^6 - 3y^5 - 2y^4}{-3y^4}$

27. $\dfrac{20a^2b + 4ab^3}{8ab}$

28. $\dfrac{14xy^2 - 21x^3y^4}{-7xy^2}$

29. $\dfrac{12x^2y^3 - 9xy - 3xy^2}{-3xy}$

30. $\dfrac{10ab^8 - 4ab^6 + 6ab^4}{2ab^4}$

31. $\dfrac{8p^2q^3 - 4p^3q^3 + 6p^4q}{4p^2q}$

32. $\dfrac{6x^2y^3 - 18x^3y^4 + 9x^4y^5}{6x^2y^3}$

Find the quotient.

33. $(x^2 - 4x - 21) \div (x + 3)$

34. $(x^2 - 6x - 40) \div (x - 10)$

35. $(56x^2 - 23x + 2) \div (8x - 1)$

36. $(30x^2 + 23x + 3) \div (6x + 1)$

37. $(6x^2 + 13x - 5) \div (2x + 5)$

38. $(10x^2 - x - 2) \div (5x + 2)$

39. $(-2x + 5x^2 - 3) \div (x - 1)$

40. $(19x + 2x^2 + 35) \div (x + 7)$

41. $(4 + 20x + 21x^2) \div (2 + 3x)$

42. $(-3 + x + 2x^2) \div (3 + 2x)$

Divide.

43. $\dfrac{x^2 + 2x - 5}{x + 2}$

44. $\dfrac{x^2 + 2x + 7}{x - 2}$

45. $\dfrac{-3 - 5x + 2x^2}{x - 3}$

46. $\dfrac{-2x + 5x^2 - 3}{x - 1}$

47. $\dfrac{8x^2 - 6x - 7}{4x + 3}$

48. $\dfrac{3x^2 - x - 8}{3x - 1}$

49. $\dfrac{-x + x^3 - 5x^2 + 5}{x + 1}$

50. $\dfrac{-5 + 11x - 7x^2 + x^3}{x - 5}$

51. $\dfrac{6x^3 - 11x^2 - 5x + 19}{3x - 4}$

52. $\dfrac{2x^3 + x^2 - 4x - 8}{2x + 1}$

53. $\dfrac{5x^2 - 2}{x - 4}$

54. $\dfrac{10x^2 - 2x}{x + 3}$

55. $\dfrac{4x^3 - x + 3}{2x - 3}$

56. $\dfrac{3x^3 + x^2 - 4}{x + 1}$

57. $\dfrac{x^3 + 27}{x + 3}$

58. $\dfrac{x^3 - 1}{x - 1}$

Applications

Solve.

59. The formula $d = rt$ can be used to find the time t when given the distance d and the rate r.

   a. Solve the equation $d = rt$ for t.

   b. Use the answer from part (a) to find an expression for the time it takes to travel a distance of $(t^3 - 6t^2 + 7t + 14)$ mi at a rate of $(t + 1)$ mph.

60. A *geometric series* is a sum of terms where each term is formed by multiplying the previous term by a constant. For example, the series $5 + 5r + 5r^2$ has three terms where the first term is 5 and each of the other terms is r times the previous term. Use long division to show that the sum of the first three terms can be calculated from the formula $\dfrac{-5r^3 + 5}{-r + 1}$.

61. A city or county cellular telephone system is divided into cells, each of which is equipped with a low-powered radio transmitter/receiver. When a cell phone moves from one cell toward another, a computer transfers the phone call to the new cell. If x is the number of years since 1984, then the number of cell systems in the United States can be modeled by the polynomial $200x - 300$ and the number of thousands of U.S. cell phone subscribers can be approximated by $600x^2 - 3700x + 4400$. Find a polynomial to model the average number of subscribers per cell system. (Ignore any remainder.) (*Source:* Cellular Telecommunications and Internet Association)

62. The United States is the world's leading producer of wheat. If x is the number of years since 1997, then the annual wheat production (in millions of bushels) of leading American states can be modeled by the polynomial $8x^3 - 150x^2 + 218x + 2520$ and the wheat acreage harvested annually (in millions of acres) by $-4x + 63$. Find a polynomial that represents the annual yield per acre of wheat harvested. (Ignore any remainder.) (*Source:* U.S. Department of Agriculture)

● *Check your answers on page A-25.*

Mindstretchers

MATHEMATICAL REASONING

1. When you divide a polynomial by a trinomial, explain how you know if the trinomial is a factor of the polynomial.

_____

_____

PATTERNS

2. Consider the following table.

Divisor	Dividend	Quotient
$x + 1$	$x^2 - x + 1$	
$x + 1$	$x^3 - x^2 + x - 1$	
$x + 1$	$x^4 - x^3 + x^2 - x + 1$	

   a. Complete the table by dividing each dividend by the divisor.

   b. Predict the result of dividing $x^5 - x^4 + x^3 - x^2 + x - 1$ by $x + 1$. Verify your prediction.

_____

CRITICAL THINKING

3. Divide $(2y^2 + 5y + 3)$ by $(y + 1)$. For which values of y is the quotient larger in value than the divisor?

_____

Key Concepts and Skills

| | = CONCEPT | | = SKILL |

CONCEPT/SKILL	DESCRIPTION	EXAMPLE
[5.1] Exponent (or Power)	A number that indicates how many times another number (called the *base*) is used as a factor.	Exponent $4^3 = 4 \cdot 4 \cdot 4$ Base — 3 factors
[5.1] Exponent of One	For any real number x, $x^1 = x$.	$2^1 = 2$ $(ab)^1 = ab$
[5.1] Exponent of Zero	For any nonzero real number x, $x^0 = 1$.	$5^0 = 1$ $(ab)^0 = 1$
[5.1] Product Rule of Exponents	For any nonzero real number x and for any integers a and b, $$x^a \cdot x^b = x^{a+b}$$	$3^2 \cdot 3^3 = 3^{2+3} = 3^5 = 243$ $x \cdot x = x^{1+1} = x^2$
[5.1] Quotient Rule of Exponents	For any nonzero real number x and for any integers a and b, $$\frac{x^a}{x^b} = x^{a-b}$$	$2^5 \div 2^3 = \frac{2^5}{2^3} = 2^{5-3} = 2^2 = 4$ $\frac{x^6}{x} = x^{6-1} = x^5$
[5.1] Negative Exponents	For any nonzero real number x and for any integer a, $$x^{-a} = \frac{1}{x^a}$$	$6^{-2} = \frac{1}{6^2} = \frac{1}{36}$ $(2x)^{-2} = \frac{1}{(2x)^2} = \frac{1}{4x^2}$
[5.1] Reciprocal of x^{-a}	For any nonzero real number x and for any integer a, $$\frac{1}{x^{-a}} = x^a$$	$\frac{1}{5^{-3}} = 5^3 = 125$ $\frac{x^3}{y^{-2}} = x^3 y^2$
[5.2] Power Rule of Exponents	For any nonzero real number x and for any integers a and b, $$(x^a)^b = x^{ab}$$	$(2^3)^2 = 2^{3 \cdot 2} = 2^6 = 64$ $(p^7)^3 = p^{7 \cdot 3} = p^{21}$
[5.2] Raising a Product to a Power	For any nonzero real numbers x and y and any integer a, $$(xy)^a = x^a \cdot y^a$$	$(4y)^3 = 4^3 y^3 = 64y^3$ $(c^4 d^3)^5 = c^{4 \cdot 5} d^{3 \cdot 5}$ $= c^{20} d^{15}$
[5.2] Raising a Quotient to a Power	For any nonzero real numbers x and y and any integer a, $$\left(\frac{x}{y}\right)^a = \frac{x^a}{y^a}$$	$\left(\frac{2}{3}\right)^3 = \frac{2^3}{3^3} = \frac{8}{27}$ $\left(\frac{-5}{b}\right)^4 = \frac{(-5)^4}{b^4} = \frac{625}{b^4}$

continued

CONCEPT/SKILL	DESCRIPTION	EXAMPLE
[5.2] Raising a Quotient to a Negative Power	For any nonzero real numbers x and y and any integer a, $$\left(\frac{x}{y}\right)^{-a} = \left(\frac{y}{x}\right)^{a}$$	$$\left(\frac{2}{3}\right)^{-1} = \left(\frac{3}{2}\right)^{1} = \frac{3}{2}$$ $$\left(\frac{p}{q}\right)^{-3} = \left(\frac{q}{p}\right)^{3} = \frac{q^3}{p^3}$$
[5.2] Scientific Notation	A number is in scientific notation if it is written in the form $$a \times 10^n,$$ where n is an integer and a is greater than or equal to 1 but less than 10 $(1 \le a < 10)$.	5.3×10^9 and 2.41×10^{-5} are in scientific notation.
[5.3] Monomial	An expression that is the product of a real number and variables raised to nonnegative integer powers.	$3x^3$ $-4a^2b$
[5.3] Polynomial	An algebraic expression with one or more monomials added or subtracted.	$-5x$ ← monomial $2x + 1$ ← binomial $x^2 - 9x + 2$ ← trinomial $-x^3 + 7x^2 - x + 19$ ← polynomial
[5.4] To Add Polynomials	• Add the like terms.	Find the sum horizontally: $$(5x^2 + 6x - 9) + (-10x^2 + 7)$$ $$= 5x^2 + 6x - 9 - 10x^2 + 7$$ $$= -5x^2 + 6x - 2$$ Add vertically: $$(5x^2 + 6x - 9) + (-10x^2 + 7)$$ $$\begin{array}{r} 5x^2 + 6x - 9 \\ -10x^2 \quad\;\; + 7 \\ \hline -\,5x^2 + 6x - 2 \end{array}$$
[5.4] To Subtract Polynomials	• Change the signs of each term of the polynomial being subtracted. • Then add.	Subtract horizontally: $$(2x^2 - 6x + 1) - (-x^2 + 4x + 5)$$ $$= 2x^2 - 6x + 1 + x^2 - 4x - 5$$ $$= 3x^2 - 10x - 4$$ Subtract vertically: $$(2x^2 - 6x + 1) - (-x^2 + 4x + 5)$$ $$\begin{array}{rr} 2x^2 - 6x + 1 & 2x^2 - \;6x + 1 \\ -(-x^2 + 4x + 5) & \underline{x^2 - \;4x - 5} \\ & 3x^2 - 10x - 4 \end{array}$$
[5.5] To Multiply Monomials	• Multiply the coefficients. • Then multiply the variables, using the product rule of exponents.	Multiply: $(-3x^2y)(5x^3y^2)$ $= (-3 \cdot 5)(x^2 \cdot x^3)(y \cdot y^2) = -15x^5y^3$

☐ = CONCEPT   ☐ = SKILL

CONCEPT/SKILL	DESCRIPTION	EXAMPLE
[5.5] To Multiply Two Binomials Using the FOIL Method	Consider $(a + b)(c + d)$. ● Multiply the two first terms in the binomials. $(a + b)(c + d)$ Product is ac. F ● Multiply the two outer terms. $(a + b)(c + d)$ Product is ad. O ● Multiply the two inner terms. $(a + b)(c + d)$ Product is bc. I ● Multiply the two last terms. $(a + b)(c + d)$ Product is bd. L The product of the two binomials is the sum of these four products. $(a + b)(c + d) = ac + ad + bc + bd$	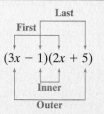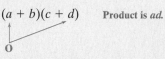 F $(3x)(2x) = 6x^2$ O $(3x)(5) = 15x$ I $(-1)(2x) = -2x$ L $(-1)(5) = -5$ The product $(3x - 1)(2x + 5)$ is the sum of these four products: $6x^2 + 15x - 2x - 5$ $= 6x^2 + 13x - 5$
[5.6] The Square of a Sum	$(a + b)^2 = a^2 + 2ab + b^2$	$(x + 3)^2 = x^2 + 2(x)(3) + (3)^2$ $= x^2 + 6x + 9$ $(7y + 5)^2 = (7y)^2 + 2(7y)(5) + (5)^2$ $= 49y^2 + 70y + 25$
[5.6] The Square of a Difference	$(a - b)^2 = a^2 - 2ab + b^2$	$(y - 6)^2 = y^2 - 2(y)(6) + (6)^2$ $= y^2 - 12y + 36$ $(4x - 1)^2 = (4x)^2 - 2(4x)(1) + (1)^2$ $= 16x^2 - 8x + 1$
[5.6] The Product of the Sum and Difference of Two Terms	$(a + b)(a - b) = a^2 - b^2$	$(2t + s)(2t - s) = (2t)^2 - (s)^2$ $= 4t^2 - s^2$
[5.7] To Divide a Polynomial by a Polynomial	● Arrange each term of the dividend and divisor in descending order. ● Divide the first term of the dividend by the first term of the divisor. The result is the first term of the quotient. ● Multiply the first term of the quotient by the divisor and place the product under the dividend. ● Subtract the product, found in the previous step, from the dividend. ● Bring down the next term to form a new dividend. ● Repeat the process until the degree of the remainder is less than the degree of the divisor.	$(3y^2 - 4y - 7) \div (y - 2)$ Quotient $3y + 2$ Divisor $\quad y - 2\overline{)3y^2 - 4y - 7}$ ← Dividend $\underline{3y^2 - 6y}$ $2y - 7$ $\underline{2y - 4}$ Remainder → -3

Chapter 5 Review Exercises

To help you review this chapter, solve these problems.

[5.1]

Simplify.

1. $(-x)^3$

2. -31^0

3. $n^4 \cdot n^7$

4. $x^6 \cdot x$

5. $\dfrac{n^8}{n^5}$

6. $p^{10} \div p^7$

7. $y^4 \cdot y^2 \cdot y$

8. $(a^2b)(ab^2)$

9. x^0y

10. $\dfrac{n^4 \cdot n^7}{n^9}$

Write as an expression using only positive exponents.

11. $(5x)^{-1}$

12. $-3n^{-2}$

13. $8^{-2}v^4$

14. $\dfrac{1}{y^{-4}}$

15. $x^{-8} \cdot x^7$

16. $5^{-1} \cdot y^6 \cdot y^{-3}$

17. $\dfrac{a^5}{a^{-5}}$

18. $\dfrac{t^{-2}}{t^4}$

19. $\dfrac{x^{-2}}{y}$

20. $\dfrac{x^2}{y^{-1}}$

[5.2]

Simplify.

21. $(10^2)^4$

22. $-(x^3)^3$

23. $(2x^3)^2$

24. $(-4m^5n)^3$

25. $3(x^{-2})^6$

26. $(a^3b^{-4})^{-2}$

27. $\left(\dfrac{x}{3}\right)^4$

28. $\left(\dfrac{-a}{b^3}\right)^2$

29. $\left(\dfrac{x}{y}\right)^{-6}$

30. $\left(\dfrac{x^2}{y^{-1}}\right)^5$

31. $\left(\dfrac{4a^3}{b^4c}\right)^2$

32. $\left(\dfrac{-u^{-5}v^2}{7w}\right)^2$

Express in standard notation.

33. 3.7×10^{10}

34. 1.63×10^9

35. 5.022×10^{-5}

36. 6×10^{-11}

Express in scientific notation.

37. $1,200,000,000,000$

38. $427,000,000$

39. 0.00000000000004

40. 0.00000056

Perform the indicated operation. Then write the result in scientific notation.

41. $(1.4 \times 10^6)(4.2 \times 10^3)$

42. $(3 \times 10^{-2})(2.1 \times 10^5)$

43. $(1.8 \times 10^4) \div (3 \times 10^{-3})$

44. $(9.6 \times 10^{-4}) \div (1.6 \times 10^6)$

[5.3]

Indicate whether the expression is a polynomial.

45. $3x^4 - 5x^3 + \dfrac{x^2}{4} - 8$

46. $-2x^2 - \dfrac{7}{x} + 1$

Classify each polynomial according to the number of terms.

47. $2x^5 + 7x^2 - 5$

48. $16 - 4t^2$

Write the polynomial in descending order. Then identify the degree, leading term, and leading coefficient of the polynomial.

49. $8y - 3y^3 + y^2 - 1$

50. $n^4 - 6n^2 - 7n^3 + n$

Simplify. Then write the polynomial in descending order of powers.

51. $10x - 8x^2 - 8x + 9x^2 - x^3 + 13$

52. $4n^3 - 7n + 9 - 3n^2 - n^3 + 7n^2 - 5 + n$

Evaluate the polynomial for the given values of the variable.

53. $2n^2 - 7n + 3$ for $n = -1$ and $n = 3$

54. $x^3 - 8$ for $x = 2$ and $x = -2$

[5.4]

Perform the indicated operations.

55. $(4x^2 - x + 4) + (-3x^2 + 9)$

56. $(5y^4 - 2y^3 + 7y - 11) + (6 - 8y - y^2 - 5y^4)$

57. $(a^2 + 5ab + 6b^2) + (3a^2 - 9b^2) + (-7ab - 3a^2)$

58. $(5s^3t - 2st + t^2) + (s^2t - 5t^2) + (t^2 - 4st + 9s^2)$

59. $(x^2 - 5x + 2) - (-x^2 + 3x + 10)$

60. $(10n^3 + n^2 - 4n + 1) - (11n^3 - 2n^2 - 5n + 1)$

61.
$$\begin{array}{r} 5y^4 - 4y^3 + y - 6 \\ -(y^3 - 2y^2 + 7y - 3) \\ \hline \end{array}$$

62.
$$\begin{array}{r} -9x^3 + 8x^2 - 11x - 12 \\ +11x^3 - x + 15 \\ \hline \end{array}$$

Simplify.

63. $14t^2 - (10t^2 - 4t)$

64. $-(5x - 6y) + (3x - 7y)$

65. $(3y^2 - 1) - (y^2 + 3y + 2) + (-2y + 5)$

66. $(1 - 4x - 6x^2) - (7x - 8) - (-11x - x^2)$

[5.5]

Multiply.

67. $-3x^4 \cdot 2x$

68. $(3ab)(8a^2b^3)(-6b)$

69. $2xy^2(4x - 5y)$

70. $(x^2 - 3x + 1)(-5x^2)$

71. $(n + 3)(n + 7)$

72. $(3x - 9)(x + 6)$

73. $(2x - 1)(4x - 1)$

74. $(3a - b)(3a + 2b)$

75. $(2x^3 - 5x + 2)(x + 3)$

76. $(y - 2)(y^2 - 7y + 1)$

Simplify.

77. $-y + 2y(-3y + 7)$

78. $4x^2(2x - 6) - 3x(3x^2 - 10x + 2)$

[5.6]

Simplify.

79. $(a - 1)^2$

80. $(s + 4)^2$

81. $(2x + 5)^2$

82. $(3 - 4t)^2$

83. $(5a - 2b)^2$

84. $(u^2 + v^2)^2$

Multiply.

85. $(m + 4)(m - 4)$

86. $(6 - n)(6 + n)$

87. $(7n - 1)(7n + 1)$

88. $(2x + y)(2x - y)$

89. $(4a - 3b)(4a + 3b)$

90. $x(x + 10)(x - 10)$

91. $-3t^2(4t - 5)^2$

92. $(p^2 - q^2)(p + q)(p - q)$

[5.7]

Divide.

93. $12x^4 \div 4x^2$

94. $\dfrac{-20a^3b^5c}{10ab^2}$

95. $(18x^3 - 6x) \div (3x)$

96. $\dfrac{10x^5 + 6x^4 - 4x^3 - 2x^2}{2x^2}$

97. $(3x^2 + 8x - 35) \div (x + 5)$

98. $\dfrac{13 - 5x^2 + 2x^3}{2x - 1}$

Mixed Applications

Solve.

99. The half-life of the element thorium-232 is 13,900,000,000 yr. Express this length of time in scientific notation. (*Source:* Peter J. Nolan, *Fundamentals of College Physics*)

100. Physicists use both the joule (J) and the electron volt (eV) as units of work, where 1 J is equal to 6.24×10^{18} eV. Rewrite this quantity in standard notation. (*Source:* Peter J. Nolan, *Fundamentals of College Physics*)

101. A grain of bee pollen is about 0.00003 m in diameter. Express this length in scientific notation.

102. The diameter of an atom is about 1.1×10^{-10} m. What is this quantity in standard notation? (*Source:* Peter J. Nolan, *Fundamentals of College Physics*)

103. At a party there are n people present. If everyone shakes hands with everyone else, then the polynomial

$$\frac{n^2}{2} - \frac{n}{2}$$

gives the total number of handshakes. If 9 people are at the party, how many handshakes will there be?

104. An object falling from an altitude of 500 m will be $-4.9t^2 + 500$ m above the ground after t sec. What is the altitude of the object 2 sec into the fall?

105. The number of divorces in the United States (in thousands) in various years is approximated by the polynomial $-0.3x^2 + 36.7x + 213$, where x represents the number of years since 1950. According to this model, how many divorces to the nearest thousand were there in 1951? (*Source:* U.S. National Center for Health Statistics, *Vital Statistics of the United States*)

106. The polynomial $-0.8x^2 + 41.5x + 898.6$ approximates the number of two-year colleges in the United States in a given year, where x represents the number of years since 1970. Use this polynomial to estimate to the nearest whole number how many two-year colleges there were in the United States in the year 1970. (*Source:* U.S. National Center for Education Statistics)

107. A rectangular swimming pool is surrounded by a 6-ft-wide concrete walk as shown in the figure.

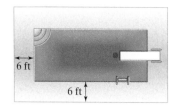

a. If the length of the pool is 10 feet less than three times the width w, find a polynomial that represents the area of the swimming pool.

b. Write a polynomial that represents the area of the concrete walk.

c. Use your expression from part (b) to find the area of the concrete walk if the width of the swimming pool is 12 ft.

108. The volume of a rectangular box can be found by multiplying the height of the box by the area of its base. If the volume of the box shown is given by the polynomial $2x^3 + 5x^2 - 4x - 12$, find the area of the square base.

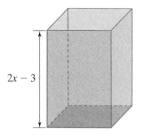

● *Check your answers on page A-25.*

Chapter 5 Posttest

To see if you have mastered the topics in this chapter, take this test.

Simplify.

1. $x^6 \cdot x$

2. $n^{10} \div n^4$

3. $7a^{-1}b^0$

4. $(-3x^2y)^3$

5. $\left(\dfrac{x^2}{y^3}\right)^4$

6. $\left(\dfrac{3x^2}{y}\right)^{-3}$

7. For the polynomial $-x^3 + 2x^2 + 9x - 1$, name:

    a. the terms _____

    b. the coefficients _____

    c. the degree _____

    d. the constant term _____

8. Find the sum: $(y^2 - 1) + (y^2 - y + 6)$

9. Subtract: $(x^2 - 7x - 4) - (2x^2 - 8x + 5)$

10. Combine: $(4x^2y^2 - 6xy - y^2) - (3x^2 + x^2y^2 - 2y^2)$
      $- (x^2 - 6xy + y^2)$

Multiply.

11. $(2mn^2)(5m^2n - 10mn + mn^2)$

12. $(y^3 - 2y^2 + 4)(y - 1)$

13. $(3x - 1)(2x + 7)$

14. $(7 - 2n)(7 + 2n)$

15. $(2m - 3)^2$

Divide.

16. $\dfrac{12s^3 + 15s^2 - 27s}{-3s}$

17. $(3t^3 - 5t^2 - t + 6) \div (3t - 2)$

Solve.

18. Medical X-rays, with a wavelength of about 10^{-10} m, can penetrate the flesh (but not the bones) of your body. Ultraviolet rays, which cause sunburn by penetrating only the top layer of skin, have a wavelength about 1000 times as long as X-rays. Find the length of ultraviolet rays. Write the answer in scientific notation. (*Source:* Peter J. Nolan, *Fundamentals of College Physics*, 1993)

19. A real estate broker sells two houses. The first house sells for $140,000 and is expected to increase in value by $1500 per year. The second house is purchased for $90,000 and will likely appreciate by $800 per year.

   a. Write an expression for the value of each house after x years.

   b. Write an expression that represents the combined value of both houses after x years.

20. A young couple is saving up to purchase a car. They deposit $1000 in an account that has an annual interest rate of r (in decimal form). At the end of two years, the value of the account will be $1000(1 + r)^2$ dollars. Find the account balance at that time if the interest rate is 3%.

● *Check your answers on page A-25.*

Cumulative Review Exercises

To help you review, solve the following.

1. Solve $y = mx + b$ for m.

2. Evaluate $3a^2 - 5ab + b^2$ for $a = -3$ and $b = 2$.

3. Solve for x: $2x + 12 - 9x = 5(4 - 3x) + 6x$

4. Find the slope and y-intercept of the line $2x - 3y = 6$.

5. Graph the inequality: $y < 2x + 1$.

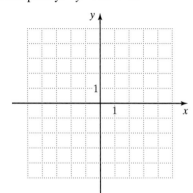

6. Solve by elimination:
$$3x - 2y = 10$$
$$2x + 3y = -2$$

7. Find the difference:
$(3m^2 - 8m + 7) - (2m^2 + 8m - 9)$

8. According to Albert Einstein's famous equation $E = mc^2$, all objects, even resting ones, contain energy E. If the mass m of a raisin is 10^{-3} kg, and the speed c of light is about 3×10^8 m/sec, find the amount of energy the raisin contains. Write the answer in scientific notation.

9. The Winter Olympics occur every 4 years.

   a. If x represents the first year that they took place, write expressions for the next three Winter Olympic years.

   b. If Winter Olympics were held in 1972, were they also held in 1980? Explain.

10. An executive goes out to dinner and leaves a 20% tip for the service.

   a. The bill for the meal without tip is represented by b. Write an expression for the amount of the tip in terms of b.

   b. The total cost c of the meal is the original bill plus the tip. Write an equation describing this situation.

• *Check your answers on page A-25.*

Chapter 6

Factoring Polynomials

Factoring and Cryptography

Cryptography, the science of coding and decoding messages, has been important throughout history. Sending secret messages in concealed form is particularly useful during wartime. For instance, the United States entered World War I in part because British intelligence intercepted and deciphered a message sent to the German minister in Mexico; the message called for a German–Mexican alliance against the United States. During World War II, the ability of the Allies to decode Nazi secrets allowed their commanders to eavesdrop on German plans and may have shortened the war by several years.

In peacetime, cryptographic techniques, used in electronic banking and in Web-based credit card purchases, play an increasingly important role in our lives. Of the numerous cryptographic techniques for coding messages today, one important technique is *prime number encryption*. To crack a message coded in this way depends on finding the prime factors of a given, very large, whole number. Whereas multiplying two prime numbers is easy, reversing the process is difficult and drawn out. For instance, it has been estimated that finding the prime factorization of a five-digit whole number takes some 14 billion mathematical steps.

(**Sources:** Rudolf Kippenhahn, *Code Breaking: A History and Exploration*, The Overlook Press, 1999; F. H. Hinsley and Alan Stripp (Editors), *Codebreakers: The Inside Story of Bletchley Park*, Oxford University Press, 1994)

Chapter 6 Pretest

To see if you have already mastered the topics in this chapter, take this test.

1. Find the greatest common factor of $18ab$ and $36a^4$.

Factor.

2. $4pq + 16p$

3. $10x^2y - 5x^3y^3 + 5xy^2$

4. $3x^2 + 6x + 2x + 4$

5. $n^2 - 11n + 24$

6. $4a + a^2 - 21$

7. $9y - 12y^2 + 3y^3$

8. $5a^2 + 6ab - 8b^2$

9. $-12n^2 + 38n + 14$

10. $4x^2 - 28x + 49$

11. $25n^2 - 9$

12. $x^2y - 4y^3$

13. $y^6 - 9y^3 + 20$

Solve.

14. $n(n - 6) = 0$

15. $3x^2 + x = 2$

16. $(y + 4)(y - 2) = 7$

17. The lateral surface area of a rectangular solid is given by the formula $A = 2lw + 2lh + 2wh$. Solve this formula for h in terms of A, w, and l.

18. A baseball player hits a pop-up fly ball with an initial velocity of 63 ft/sec from a height of 4 ft above the ground. The height of the ball (in feet) t sec after it is hit is given by the expression $-16t^2 + 63t + 4$. Write this expression in factored form.

19. A homeowner wants to fence off part of her yard to build a 15-ft by 15-ft square play area for her children. Write an expression, in factored form, for the area of the yard not covered by the play area.

20. Find the dimensions of the 40-in. plasma television screen shown if the length is 8 in. longer than the height.

S

15 ft

15 ft

S

S

• Check your answers on page A-25.

470

6.1 Common Factoring and Factoring by Grouping

OBJECTIVES

- *To find the greatest common factor (GCF) of two or more integers or terms*
- *To factor out the greatest common factor from a polynomial*
- *To factor by grouping*
- *To solve applied problems involving factoring*

What Factoring Is and Why It Is Important

In the previous chapter, we discussed how to *multiply* two factors in order to find their polynomial product.

Multiplying

$$\underbrace{(3x + 4)}_{\text{Factor}} \underbrace{(2x + 1)}_{\text{Factor}} = \underbrace{6x^2 + 11x + 4}_{\text{Product}}$$

In this chapter, we reverse the process beginning with a polynomial and expressing it as a product of factors. Rewriting a polynomial as a product is called *factoring* the polynomial.

Factoring

$$\underbrace{6x^2 + 11x + 4}_{\text{Polynomial}} = \underbrace{(3x + 4)}_{\text{Factor}} \underbrace{(2x + 1)}_{\text{Factor}}$$

Just as factoring integers plays a key role in arithmetic, so factoring polynomials is an important skill in algebra. Factoring polynomials helps us to simplify certain algebraic expressions and also to solve various types of equations.

Finding the Greatest Common Factor of Two or More Integers or Terms

We have already shown that every composite number can be written as the product of prime factors, called its *prime factorization*. For instance, the prime factorization of 15 is $3 \cdot 5$, and the prime factorization of 35 is $5 \cdot 7$. Since 5 appears in both factorizations, 5 is said to be a *common factor* of 15 and 35.

> **Definition**
>
> A **common factor** of two or more integers is an integer that is a factor of each integer.

We can use the concept of common factor to find a *greatest common factor*.

> **Definition**
>
> The **greatest common factor (GCF)** of two or more integers is the greatest integer that is a factor of each integer.

Let's consider an example of finding the greatest common factor of three numbers.

EXAMPLE 1

Find the GCF of 45, 63, and 81.

SOLUTION First we find the prime factorization of each number.

$$45 = 3 \cdot 3 \cdot 5 = 3^2 \cdot 5$$
$$63 = 3 \cdot 3 \cdot 7 = 3^2 \cdot 7$$
$$81 = 3 \cdot 3 \cdot 3 \cdot 3 = 3^4$$

Then we look for the greatest common factor. We see that $3 \cdot 3 = 3^2$ is a factor of each number. Since no power of 3 higher than 3^2 and no prime number other than 3 is a factor of *all* three numbers, the GCF of 45, 63, and 81 is 3^2, or 9.

PRACTICE 1

What is the GCF of 24, 72, and 96?

We can extend the concept of greatest common factor to monomials. For instance, to find the greatest common factor of $-21x^2$ and $35xy^2$, we begin by writing the monomials in factored form.

$$-21x^2 = -1 \cdot 3 \cdot 7 \cdot x \cdot x$$
$$35xy^2 = 5 \cdot 7 \cdot x \cdot y \cdot y$$

From the factorizations we see that each monomial has a factor of 7 and a factor of x in common. Since 7 is the greatest factor of the coefficients and x^1 is the highest power of x that is a factor of each monomial, the product of 7 and x, or $7x$, is the greatest common factor of $-21x^2$ and $35xy^2$.

EXAMPLE 2

Find the GCF of x^4, x^3, and x^2.

SOLUTION We write each monomial in factored form.

$$x^4 = x \cdot x \cdot x \cdot x$$
$$x^3 = x \cdot x \cdot x$$
$$x^2 = x \cdot x$$

From the factored forms, we see that the monomials have at most two factors of x in common. So the GCF of x^4, x^3, and x^2 is $x \cdot x$, or x^2.

PRACTICE 2

What is the GCF of a^3, a^2, and a?

Note that we could have written the factored forms of the monomials in Example 2 as

$$x^4 = x^2 \cdot x^2$$
$$x^3 = x^2 \cdot x^1$$
$$x^2 = x^2$$

From these factored forms we see that x^2 is the highest power of the variable factor common to all three monomials.

> **Definition**
>
> The **greatest common factor (GCF) of two or more monomials** is the product of the greatest common factor of the coefficients and the highest powers of the variable factors common to all of the monomials.

Next let's consider the greatest common factor of expressions involving more than one variable.

EXAMPLE 3	**PRACTICE 3**
Identify the GCF of $3a^3b$ and $-15a^2b^4$.	Find the GCF of $-18x^3y^4$ and $12xy^2$.

SOLUTION First, we write each monomial in factored form.

$$3a^3b = 3 \cdot a^2 \cdot a \cdot b$$
$$-15a^2b^4 = -1 \cdot 3 \cdot 5 \cdot a^2 \cdot b \cdot b^3$$

The greatest common factor of the coefficients is 3 and the highest powers of the common variable factors are a^2 and b. So the GCF of $3a^3b$ and $-15a^2b^4$ is $3a^2b$.

Factoring Out the Greatest Common Factor from a Polynomial

Recall from the previous chapter that we used the distributive property to multiply a monomial by a polynomial. For example, consider the product of $2x$ and $(x + 7)$.

$$2x(x + 7) = 2x \cdot x + 2x \cdot 7 = 2x^2 + 14x$$

When the terms of a polynomial have common factors, we can factor the polynomial by reversing this process. So we can write $2x^2 + 14x$ in factored form by dividing out $2x$, the GCF of the terms $2x^2$ and $14x$.

$$2x^2 + 14x = 2x \cdot x + 2x \cdot 7 = 2x(x + 7)$$
$$\uparrow$$
$$\text{GCF}$$

So the factored form of $2x^2 + 14x$ is $2x(x + 7)$.

EXAMPLE 4	**PRACTICE 4**
Factor: $25x^3 + 10x^2$	Factor: $10y^2 + 8y^5$

SOLUTION The GCF of $25x^3$ and $10x^2$ is $5x^2$.

$25x^3 + 10x^2 = 5x^2(5x) + 5x^2(2)$ Factor out the GCF $5x^2$ from each term.

$\qquad\qquad = 5x^2(5x + 2)$ Use the distributive property.

So the factorization of $25x^3 + 10x^2$ is $5x^2(5x + 2)$.

Now let's consider some examples of factoring polynomials in more than one variable.

EXAMPLE 5

Factor: $12c^2 - 2cd$

SOLUTION The GCF of $12c^2$ and $-2cd$ is $2c$.

$$12c^2 - 2cd = 2c(6c) - 2c(d) \quad \text{Factor out the GCF } 2c \text{ from each term.}$$
$$= 2c(6c - d) \quad \text{Use the distributive property.}$$

PRACTICE 5

Factor: $21a^2b - 14a$

EXAMPLE 6

Factor: $3x^2y^4 + 9xy^2$

SOLUTION

$$3x^2y^4 + 9xy^2 = 3xy^2(xy^2) + 3xy^2(3)$$
$$= 3xy^2(xy^2 + 3)$$

PRACTICE 6

Factor: $8a^2b^2 - 6ab^3$

EXAMPLE 7

Express in factored form: $20y^2 - 5y + 15$

SOLUTION

$$20y^2 - 5y + 15 = 5(4y^2) - 5(y) + 5(3)$$
$$= 5(4y^2 - y + 3)$$

PRACTICE 7

Factor: $24a^2 - 48a + 12$

When solving some literal equations, it may be necessary to factor out common monomial factors.

EXAMPLE 8

Solve $m_1x + b_1 = m_2x + b_2$ for x in terms of m_1, m_2, b_1, and b_2.

SOLUTION To solve for x, we bring all the terms involving x to the left side of the equation and the other terms to the right side of the equation.

$$m_1x + b_1 = m_2x + b_2$$

$$m_1x + b_1 - b_1 = m_2x + b_2 - b_1 \quad \begin{array}{l}\text{Subtract } b_1 \text{ from each side of}\\ \text{the equation.}\end{array}$$

$$m_1x = m_2x + b_2 - b_1$$

$$m_1x - m_2x = m_2x - m_2x + b_2 - b_1 \quad \begin{array}{l}\text{Subtract } m_2x \text{ from each side of}\\ \text{the equation.}\end{array}$$

$$m_1x - m_2x = b_2 - b_1$$

$$x(m_1 - m_2) = b_2 - b_1 \quad \begin{array}{l}\text{Factor out } x \text{ on the left side}\\ \text{of the equation.}\end{array}$$

$$\frac{x(m_1 - m_2)}{m_1 - m_2} = \frac{b_2 - b_1}{m_1 - m_2} \quad \begin{array}{l}\text{Divide each side of the}\\ \text{equation by } (m_1 - m_2), \text{ the}\\ \text{coefficient of } x.\end{array}$$

$$x = \frac{b_2 - b_1}{m_1 - m_2}$$

PRACTICE 8

Solve $ab = s^2 - ac$ for a in terms of b, c, and s.

Factoring by Grouping

Recall that the factorization of $2x^2 + 14x$ is $2x(x + 7)$. The factor $(x + 7)$ is called a *binomial* factor. The distributive property can be used to divide out not only a common monomial factor but also a common binomial factor, if there is one. For instance, let's consider the expression $x(x + 5) + 2(x + 5)$.

$$\underbrace{x(x + 5)}_{\text{First term}} + \underbrace{2(x + 5)}_{\text{Second term}}$$

In this polynomial, the binomial $(x + 5)$ is common to both terms. Using the distributive property, we can factor out $(x + 5)$. That is,

$$x(x + 5) + 2(x + 5) = (x + 5)(x + 2).$$

So the factored form of $x(x + 5) + 2(x + 5)$ is $(x + 5)(x + 2)$.

EXAMPLE 9

Factor: $x(x + 4) - 5(x + 4)$

SOLUTION Using the distributive property, we get:

$$x(x + 4) - 5(x + 4) = (x + 4)(x - 5)$$

PRACTICE 9

Factor: $4(y - 3) + y(y - 3)$

In some algebraic expressions, such as $x(a - 7) + 3(7 - a)$, the binomial factors are opposites. Before we can factor out a common binomial factor, we must rewrite one of the binomials by factoring out -1, as shown in the next example.

EXAMPLE 10

Factor: $x(a - 7) + 3(7 - a)$

SOLUTION The binomial factors $(a - 7)$ and $(7 - a)$ are opposites, so we factor out -1 from the binomial $(7 - a)$ and rewrite the original expression.

$$\begin{aligned} x(a - 7) + 3(7 - a) &= x(a - 7) + 3\,[-1(a - 7)] && \text{Factor out } -1 \text{ from} \\ &&& (7 - a). \\ &= x(a - 7) - 3(a - 7) && \text{Simplify.} \\ &= (a - 7)(x - 3) && \text{Use the distributive} \\ &&& \text{property.} \end{aligned}$$

PRACTICE 10

Factor: $3y(x - 1) + 2(1 - x)$

EXAMPLE 11

Factor: $5n(4n - 1) - (4n - 1)$

SOLUTION

$$\begin{aligned} 5n(4n - 1) - (4n - 1) &= 5n(4n - 1) - 1(4n - 1) \\ &= (4n - 1)(5n - 1) \end{aligned}$$

PRACTICE 11

Factor: $(4 - 3x) + 2x(4 - 3x)$

When trying to factor a polynomial that has four terms, it may be possible to group pairs of terms in such a way that a common binomial factor can be found. This method is called **factoring by grouping**.

EXAMPLE 12

Factor: $y^2 + 6y - xy - 6x$

SOLUTION

$$y^2 + 6y - xy - 6x = (y^2 + 6y) + (-xy - 6x) \qquad \text{Group the first two terms and the last two terms.}$$

$$= (y^2 + 6y) - (xy + 6x) \qquad \text{Factor out } -1 \text{ in the second group:} \\ -xy - 6y = -(xy + 6y)$$

$$= y(y + 6) - x(y + 6) \qquad \text{Factor out the the GCF from each group.}$$

$$= (y + 6)(y - x) \qquad \text{Write in factored form.}$$

PRACTICE 12

Factor: $a^2 + 2a - 2ab - 4b$

EXAMPLE 13

Express in factored form: $6h - 6k - h^4 + h^3k$

SOLUTION

$$6h - 6k - h^4 + h^3k = (6h - 6k) + (-h^4 + h^3k) \qquad \text{Group the first two terms and the last two terms.}$$

$$= (6h - 6k) - (h^4 - h^3k) \qquad -h^4 + h^3k = -(h^4 - h^3k)$$

$$= 6(h - k) - h^3(h - k) \qquad \text{Factor out the GCF from each group.}$$

$$= (h - k)(6 - h^3) \qquad \text{Write in factored form.}$$

PRACTICE 13

Factor: $5y - 5z - y^5 + y^4z$

EXAMPLE 14

Each week, a sales associate receives a salary of d dollars as well as 5% commission on the value of the sales that she makes. Last week, sales amounted to x dollars, and this week, sales rose to y dollars. How much greater was the sales associate's total income this week than last week? Express this amount in factored form.

SOLUTION Last week, the sales associate made d dollars in salary and $0.05x$ in commission. This week, the associate made d dollars in salary and $0.05y$ in commission. So the difference in total income is:

$$(d + 0.05y) - (d + 0.05x) = d + 0.05y - d - 0.05x$$

$$= 0.05y - 0.05x$$

$$= 0.05(y - x)$$

So the sales associate made $0.05(y - x)$ dollars more this week than last week.

PRACTICE 14

The distance an object under constant acceleration travels in time t is given by the expression $v_0 t + \frac{1}{2}at^2$, where v_0 is the object's initial velocity and a is its acceleration. Factor this expression.

Exercises 6.1

FOR EXTRA HELP

📖 Student's Solutions Manual

📞 Addison-Wesley Math Tutor Center

🚪 MyMathLab

📼 Videotape 6/DVT 6

Find the greatest common factor of each group of terms.

1. 27, 54, and 81

2. 28, 35, 63

3. x^4, x^6, x^3

4. y^2, y, y^5

5. $16b, 8b^3, 12b^2$

6. $3a, 7a^2, 5a^4$

7. $-12x^5y^7, 4y^3$

8. $9m^3, 6m^2n$

9. $18a^5b^4, -6a^4b^3, 9a^2b^2$

10. $24mn, 32mn^2, 16m^2n$

11. $x(3x - 1)$ and $8(3x - 1)$

12. $6(5n + 2)$ and $n(5n + 2)$

13. $4x(x + 7)$ and $9x(x + 7)$

14. $y(y - 4)$ and $6y(y - 4)$

Factor out the greatest common factor.

15. $3x + 6$

16. $10y + 15$

17. $24x^2 + 8$

18. $30y^2 - 6$

19. $27m + 9n$

20. $16r - 8t$

21. $2x - 7x^2$

22. $5b^2 - 6b^3$

23. $4z^5 + 12z^2$

24. $3b^2 - 18b$

25. $10x^3 - 15x$

26. $12a^2 + 18a$

27. $a^2b^2 - ab$

28. $xy + x^2y^2$

29. $6xy^2 + 7x^2y$

30. $3p^3q^2 - 5p^2q^3$

31. $27pq^2 + 18p^2q$

32. $45c^2d - 15cd^2$

33. $2x^3y - 12x^3y^4$

34. $7a^2b^3 + 9a^4b^3$

35. $3c^3 + 6c^2 + 12$

36. $5y^2 - 20y + 10$

37. $9b^4 - 3b^3 + b^2$

38. $8y^5 - y^4 - 4y^2$

39. $2m^4 + 10m^3 - 6m^2$

40. $3x^3 - 9x^2 - 27x$

41. $5b^5 - 3b^3 + 2b^2$

42. $9c^4 + c^3 + 6c^2$

43. $15x^4 - 10x^3 - 25x$

44. $12m^6 + 9m^5 + 15m^3$

45. $4a^2b + 8a^2b^2 - 12ab$

46. $5m^2n - 15mn^2 + 10mn$

47. $9c^2d^2 + 12c^3d + 3cd^3$

48. $18x^2y^4 - 24xy^3 + 30x^3y$

Factor by grouping.

49. $x(x - 1) + 3(x - 1)$

50. $2(n + 4) + n(n + 4)$

51. $5a(a - 1) - 3(a - 1)$

52. $4x(x + 3) - 7(x + 3)$

53. $r(s + 7) - 2(7 + s)$

54. $a(6 + b) - 7(b + 6)$

55. $a(x - y) - b(x - y)$

56. $y(a - z) - x(a - z)$

57. $3x(y + 2) - (y + 2)$

58. $(n - 1) - 2m(n - 1)$

59. $b(b - 1) + 5(1 - b)$

60. $x(x - 3) + 2(3 - x)$

61. $y(y - 1) - 5(1 - y)$

62. $n(n - 9) - 4(9 - n)$

63. $(t - 3) - t(3 - t)$

64. $w(w - 4) + (4 - w)$

65. $9a(b - 7) + 2(7 - b)$

66. $2y(x - 2) + 3(2 - x)$

67. $rs + 3s + rt + 3t$

68. $mn + 2m + np + 2p$

69. $xy + 6y - 4x - 24$

70. $ab - 5b - 2a + 10$

71. $15xy - 9yz + 20xz - 12z^2$

72. $6ab + 12ac - 5bc - 10c^2$

73. $2xz + 8x + 5yz + 20y$

74. $3ab + 9a + 4bc + 12c$

Solve for the indicated variable.

75. $TM = PC + PL$ for P

76. $S = a + Nd - d$ for d

77. $S = 2lw + 2lh + 2wh$ for l

78. $S = a + ar^n$ for a

Applications

Solve.

79. When an object with mass m increases in velocity from v_1 to v_2, its momentum increases by $mv_2 - mv_1$. Factor this expression.

80. One item sells for p dollars and another for q dollars. In addition, an 8% sales tax is charged on all items sold. An expression for the total selling price is $1.08p + 1.08q$. Write this expression in factored form.

81. In a meeting of diplomats, all diplomats must shake hands with one another. If there are n diplomats, the expression $0.5n^2 - 0.5n$ represents the total number of handshakes at the meeting. Factor this expression.

82. For an investment earning simple interest, the future value of the investment is represented by the expression $P + Prt$, where P is the present value of the investment, r is the annual interest rate, and t is the time in years. Factor this expression.

83. In a polygon with n sides, the number of diagonals is given by the expression $\frac{1}{2}n^2 - \frac{3}{2}n$. Write this expression in factored form.

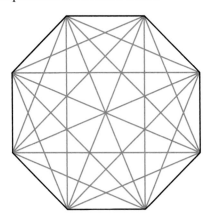

84. In a polygon with n sides, the interior angles (measured in degrees) add up to $180n - 360$. Find an equivalent expression by factoring out the GCF.

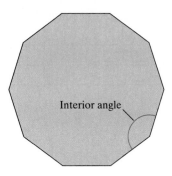

Interior angle

85. Consider the formula $P = nC + nT + D$, where P is the total price of a purchase, n is the number of items purchased, C is the cost per item, T is the tax on each item, and D is the total delivery charge. Solve for n in terms of P, C, T, and D.

86. The *harmonic mean H* of two numbers x and y is a kind of average. Solve for H in the formula $Hx + Hy = 2xy$.

● *Check your answers on page A-26.*

Mindstretchers

MATHEMATICAL REASONING

1. A four-digit whole number can be represented by the expression

$$1000d + 100c + 10b + a,$$

where a is the digit in the unit's place, b is the digit in the ten's place, c is the digit in the hundred's place, and d is the digit in the thousand's place.

a. Consider such a four-digit whole number (for instance, 8351). Then reverse the order of the digits, forming a second number $1000a + 100b + 10c + d$ (here, 1538). Subtract the smaller number from the larger ($8351 - 1538 = 6813$). Then check whether this difference is divisible by 9.

_____

b. Show that when you reverse the order of the digits of *any* four-digit whole number and subtract the two four-digit numbers, their difference must be divisible by 9.

_____

_____

_____

_____

_____

CRITICAL THINKING

2. Factor the expression $a^{n+2}b^n - a^n b^{n+1}$.

_____

GROUPWORK

3. Working with a partner, for each polynomial list three numbers or monomials that when placed in the [ ] will make the polynomial factorable.

a. $2xy - 7x + \boxed{} - 14$ _____

b. $xy^2 + \boxed{} + 3y^2 - 48$ _____

6.2 Factoring Trinomials Whose Leading Coefficient Is 1

In this section, we move on to another kind of factoring—factoring trinomials of the form $ax^2 + bx + c$, where $a = 1$. Recall that the coefficient a of the leading term, ax^2, is called the *leading* coefficient. In other words, we are examining trinomials of the form $x^2 + bx + c$, where the leading coefficient is 1. First, we factor trinomials in which the constant term is positive. For example, we factor trinomials such as

$$x^2 + 5x + 6 \quad \text{and} \quad x^2 - 8x + 16$$

Constant term

Next we factor trinomials in which the constant term is negative. For example, we factor trinomials such as

$$x^2 + 3x - 10 \quad \text{and} \quad x^2 - 5x - 24$$

Constant term

In Section 6.5, we will see how factoring trinomials helps us to solve related equations and applied problems.

Factoring $x^2 + bx + c$, c Positive

Recall from Section 5.5 the FOIL method of multiplying two binomials.

$$
\begin{array}{cccc}
\text{F} & \text{O} & \text{I} & \text{L}
\end{array}
$$
$$(x + 2)(x + 3) = x^2 + 3x + 2x + 6$$
$$= x^2 + 5x + 6$$

Note that when multiplying these two binomials, we get a trinomial. Also note that the leading coefficient of both binomial factors here is 1.

This suggests that factoring a trinomial of the form $x^2 + bx + c$ gives the product of two binomials of the form $(x + ?)(x + ?)$, where each question mark represents an integer. To find the binomials, we apply the FOIL method in reverse.

For instance, let's factor $x^2 + 5x + 6$. Since the leading term of the trinomial is x^2, we apply the FOIL method to two binomial factors, placing x as the first term in each of the factors.

$$
\begin{array}{cccc}
\text{F} & \text{O} & \text{I} & \text{L}
\end{array}
$$
$$x^2 + 5x + 6 = (x + ?)(x + ?) = x^2 + 5x + 6$$

We see that the product of the constant terms of the binomial factors must be 6, the constant term of the trinomial. The sum of the outer and inner products must be $5x$. So we need to find two integers whose product is 6 and whose sum is 5.

To find these integers, consider all possible factors of 6, that is, of $+6$.

Factors of 6	Possible Binomial Factors	Sum of Outer and Inner Products	
1, 6	$(x + 1)(x + 6)$	$6x + x = 7x$	
-1, -6	$(x - 1)(x - 6)$	$-6x - x = -7x$	
2, 3	$(x + 2)(x + 3)$	$3x + 2x = 5x$	←——The correct middle term
-2, -3	$(x - 2)(x - 3)$	$-3x - 2x = -5x$	

So $x^2 + 5x + 6 = (x + 2)(x + 3)$.

We check that the factors are correct by multiplying.

$$(x + 2)(x + 3) = x^2 + \underbrace{3x + 2x}_{} + 6 = x^2 + \underbrace{5x}_{} + 6$$

Sum of the outer and inner products   **Middle term**

This way of factoring a trinomial, listing all the possibilities, is sometimes called the *trial-and-error method*. Factoring a trinomial by the trial-and-error method involves recognizing patterns, looking for clues, and, once the factorization is found, multiplying to check. Note that by the commutative property of multiplication, we can also write the product $(x + 2)(x + 3)$ as $(x + 3)(x + 2)$.

EXAMPLE 1

Factor: $y^2 + 7y + 10$

SOLUTION Applying the FOIL method in reverse, we know that the first term of each factor is y. So the factors are of the form $(y + ?)(y + ?)$. Using the trial-and-error method, we need to find two integers whose product is 10 and whose sum is 7. The following table shows how to test pairs of factors of 10, the constant term of the trinomial.

Factors of 10	Sum of Factors	
1, 10	11	
-1, -10	-11	
2, 5	7	←——— Factors 2 and 5 have a sum of 7.
-2, -5	-7	

So $y^2 + 7y + 10 = (y + 2)(y + 5)$, or $(y + 5)(y + 2)$.

—————— Same sign ——————

PRACTICE 1

Factor: $x^2 + 5x + 4$

Can you explain why in the preceding list of possible factors we need only have tested the positive factors of the constant term?

EXAMPLE 2

Factor: $x^2 - 10x + 16$

SOLUTION The constant term of the trinomial is positive and the coefficient of the x-term is negative. So the constant terms of the binomial factors must both be negative.

$$x^2 - 10x + 16 = (x - ?)(x - ?)$$

We need to find two negative integers whose product is 16 and whose sum is -10. In this case we need to consider only negative factors of 16.

Factors of 16	Sum of Factors	
$-1, -16$	-17	
$-2, -8$	-10	← Factors -2 and -8 have a sum of -10.
$-4, -4$	-8	

So $x^2 - 10x + 16 = (x - 2)(x - 8)$, or $(x - 8)(x - 2)$.

PRACTICE 2

Factor: $y^2 - 9y + 20$

TIP When the constant term c of the trinomial $x^2 + bx + c$ is positive,

- the constant terms of the binomial factors are both positive when b, the coefficient of the x-term in the trinomial, is positive, and
- the constant terms are both negative when b is negative.

Not every trinomial can be expressed as the product of binomial factors with coefficients that are integers. Polynomials that are not factorable are called **prime polynomials**. For instance, the trinomial $x^2 + 5x + 1$ is a prime polynomial. Can you explain why this trinomial is prime?

EXAMPLE 3

Factor: $x^2 + 4x + 6$

SOLUTION Both the constant term 6 and the coefficient of the x-term 4 are positive. So if the trinomial is factorable, the constant terms of its binomial factors must both be positive as well.

$$x^2 + 4x + 6 = (x + ?)(x + ?)$$

We need to find two positive integers whose product is 6 and whose sum is 4.

Factors of 6	Sum of Factors
1, 6	7
2, 3	5

Since neither sum of the factors yields the correct coefficient of the x-term, we can conclude that the polynomial is not factorable. Therefore, this is a *prime polynomial*.

PRACTICE 3

Factor: $x^2 + 3x + 5$

When the terms of a trinomial are not in descending order, we usually rewrite the trinomial before factoring, as shown in the next example.

EXAMPLE 4

Factor: $12 - 8x + x^2$

SOLUTION We begin by writing the terms in descending order.

$$12 - 8x + x^2 = x^2 - 8x + 12$$
$$= (x - ?)(x - ?)$$

Since the middle term of the trinomial is negative and the constant term is positive, we are looking for two negative integers. So we need to consider only negative factors of 12.

Factors of 12	Sum of Factors
−1, −12	−13
−2, −6	−8 ← Factors −2 and −6 have a sum of −8.
−3, −4	−7

So $x^2 - 8x + 12 = (x - 2)(x - 6)$.

PRACTICE 4

Factor: $32 - 12y + y^2$

Note that in Example 4, we could also have factored $12 - 8x + x^2$ as $(2 - x)(6 - x)$, without rearranging the terms of the trinomial. Can you explain why our two solutions $(x - 2)(x - 6)$ and $(2 - x)(6 - x)$ are equal?

Now let's consider a trinomial of the form $x^2 + bxy + cy^2$. We note that this trinomial contains more than one variable. When factoring these trinomials, we use the trial-and-error method where the binomial factors are of the form $(x + ?y)(x + ?y)$ and the question marks represent factors of c, the coefficient of the y^2 term, whose sum is b, the coefficient of the xy-term.

EXAMPLE 5

Factor: $x^2 + 3xy + 2y^2$

SOLUTION $x^2 + 3xy + 2y^2 = (x + ?y)(x + ?y)$

Since the middle term and the last term are both positive, we look for only positive factors of 2, the coefficient of y^2, whose sum is 3, the coefficient of the xy-term.

Factors of 2	Sum of Factors
1, 2	3

So $x^2 + 3xy + 2y^2 = (x + 1y)(x + 2y) = (x + y)(x + 2y)$, or $(x + 2y)(x + y)$.

PRACTICE 5

Factor: $p^2 - 4pq + 3q^2$

Factoring $x^2 + bc + c$, c Negative

Now let's consider how to factor trinomials in which the coefficient of the first term is 1 and the sign of the constant term is negative.

EXAMPLE 6	PRACTICE 6
Factor: $x^2 + 2x - 3$	Factor: $x^2 + x - 6$

SOLUTION We must find factors of -3 whose sum is 2.

Factors of -3	Sum of Factors
$-1, 3$	2 ← Factors -1 and 3 have a sum of 2.
$1, -3$	-2

So $x^2 + 2x - 3 = (x - 1)(x + 3)$.

CHECK We check by multiplying.

$$(x - 1)(x + 3) = x^2 + \underbrace{3x - x}_{\substack{\text{Sum of the} \\ \text{outer and} \\ \text{inner products}}} - 3 = x^2 + \underbrace{2x}_{\substack{\text{Middle} \\ \text{term}}} - 3$$

TIP When the constant term c of the trinomial $x^2 + bx + c$ is negative, the constant terms of the binomial factors have opposite signs.

EXAMPLE 7	PRACTICE 7
Factor: $y^2 - 3y - 10$	Factor: $x^2 - 21x - 46$

SOLUTION We must find two integers whose product is -10 and whose sum is -3. Since -10 is negative, one of its factors must be positive and the other negative.

Factors of -10	Sum of Factors
$1, -10$	-9
$-1, 10$	9
$2, -5$	-3 ← Factors 2 and -5 have a sum of -3.
$-2, 5$	3

So $y^2 - 3y - 10 = (y + 2)(y - 5)$.

Note that since the sum of the two factors of -10 is -3, the negative factor must have a larger absolute value than the positive factor.

EXAMPLE 8

Factor: $x^2 - 12 + x$

SOLUTION

$x^2 - 12 + x = x^2 + x - 12$ Write the terms in descending order.

$\qquad\qquad = (x + ?)(x - ?)$ Since the constant term is negative, one of its factors is positive and the other factor is negative.

Now we must find two factors of -12 whose sum is 1. So the positive factor must have a larger absolute value than the negative factor. Thus, we consider only factors of -12 for which the positive factor has the larger absolute value.

Factors of -12	Sum of Factors
$-1, 12$	11
$-2, 6$	4
$-3, 4$	1 ←——— Factors -3 and 4 have a sum of 1.

So $x^2 + x - 12 = (x - 3)(x + 4)$.

PRACTICE 8

Factor: $y^2 - 24 + 2y$

Next we consider factoring a trinomial in two variables.

EXAMPLE 9

Factor: $x^2 - 5xy - 14y^2$

SOLUTION $x^2 - 5xy - 14y^2 = (x + ?\,y)(x - ?\,y)$

We must find two factors of -14 whose sum is -5. Since the product of these factors is a negative number, one of the factors must be positive and the other negative. Since the sum of the factors is negative, the negative factor must have a larger absolute value than the positive factor. Thus, we consider only factors of -14 for which the negative factor has the larger absolute value.

Factors of -14	Sum of Factors
$1, -14$	-13
$2, -7$	-5 ←——— Factors 2 and -7 have a sum of -5.

So $x^2 - 5xy - 14y^2 = (x + 2y)(x - 7y)$.

PRACTICE 9

Factor: $a^2 - 5ab - 24b^2$

Some trinomials have a common factor. When factoring such a trinomial, we factor out the GCF before we try factoring the trinomial into the product of two binomials.

EXAMPLE 10

Factor: $3x^2 + 6x - 24$

SOLUTION Each term of the trinomial has a common factor of 3, so we begin by factoring out this factor.

$$3x^2 + 6x - 24 = 3(x^2 + 2x - 8) = 3(x + ?)(x - ?)$$

Since the product of the two missing integers is negative, we need to consider only factors of -8, one positive and the other negative, where the positive factor has a larger absolute value than the negative factor.

Factors of -8	Sum of Factors
$-1, 8$	7
$-2, 4$	2 ←——— Factors -2 and 4 have a sum of 2.

So $3x^2 + 6x - 24 = 3(x^2 + 2x - 8) = 3(x + 4)(x - 2)$.

Note that after factoring out the GCF, 3, neither of the remaining factors of the polynomial has a common factor.

PRACTICE 10

Factor: $y^3 - 9y^2 - 10y$

EXAMPLE 11

Express in factored form: $3a^4 + 27a^3 + 24a^2$

SOLUTION

$$3a^4 + 27a^3 + 24a^2 = 3a^2(a^2 + 9a + 8) \qquad \text{Factor out the GCF } 3a^2 \text{ from each term.}$$

$$= 3a^2(a + 1)(a + 8) \qquad \text{Factor } a^2 + 9a + 8.$$

So $3a^4 + 27a^3 + 24a^2 = 3a^2(a + 1)(a + 8)$.

PRACTICE 11

Factor: $8x^3 - 24x^2 + 16x$

As in the previous examples, after factoring out the GCF the remaining trinomial can sometimes still be factored. A polynomial is **factored completely** when it is expressed as the product of a monomial and one or more prime polynomials. Throughout the remainder of this text, factor means to factor completely.

EXAMPLE 12

Factor: $-x^2 + 9x - 14$

SOLUTION

$-x^2 + 9x - 14 = -1(x^2 - 9x + 14)$ Factor out -1 so that the leading coefficient is 1.

$= -1(x - 7)(x - 2)$

We can also express the solution two other ways by multiplying either binomial by -1.

$-x^2 + 9x - 14 = -1(x - 7)(x - 2)$

$= (-x + 7)(x - 2)$ Multiply $(x - 7)$ by -1.

$= (x - 7)(-x + 2)$ Multiply $(x - 2)$ by -1.

PRACTICE 12

Write in factored form:
$-x^2 - 10x + 11$

EXAMPLE 13

Show that for any whole number n, the number represented by $n^2 + 7n + 12$ can be expressed as the product of two consecutive whole numbers.

SOLUTION Since we want to represent the expression $n^2 + 7n + 12$ as a product, we factor it.

$$n^2 + 7n + 12 = (n + 3)(n + 4)$$

Note that the two factors, $n + 3$ and $n + 4$, are whole numbers that differ by 1.

$$(n + 4) - (n + 3) = n + 4 - n - 3 = 1$$

So $n^2 + 7n + 12$ can be expressed as the product of two consecutive whole numbers.

PRACTICE 13

A ball is tossed upward with a velocity of 32 ft/sec from a roof 48 ft above the ground. The expression $-16t^2 + 32t + 48$ approximates the height of the ball above the ground in feet after t sec. Factor this expression.

Exercises 6.2

Match each trinomial with its binomial factors.

1. $x^2 - 16x + 28$ **a.** $(x - 1)(x + 28)$

2. $x^2 + 12x - 28$ **b.** $(x - 7)(x + 4)$

3. $x^2 + 29x + 28$ **c.** $(x - 4)(x - 7)$

4. $x^2 + 27x - 28$ **d.** $(x - 2)(x + 14)$

5. $x^2 - 3x - 28$ **e.** $(x + 28)(x + 1)$

6. $x^2 - 11x + 28$ **f.** $(x - 14)(x - 2)$

Find the missing factor.

7. $x^2 - 3x - 10 = (x + 2)$
$(\quad)$

8. $x^2 - 11x + 18 = (x - 9)$
$(\quad)$

9. $x^2 + 5x + 4 = (x + 1)$
$(\quad)$

10. $x^2 - x - 12 = (x - 4)$
$(\quad)$

11. $x^2 + 5x - 6 = (x + 6)$
$(\quad)$

12. $x^2 + 4x - 21 = (x - 3)$
$(\quad)$

Factor, if possible.

13. $x^2 + 6x + 8$ **14.** $x^2 + 9x + 8$ **15.** $x^2 + 5x - 6$

16. $x^2 + 2x - 3$ **17.** $x^2 + x + 2$ **18.** $x^2 + 2x - 8$

19. $x^2 + 5x + 4$ **20.** $x^2 + 13x + 7$ **21.** $x^2 - 4x + 3$

22. $x^2 - 6x + 5$ **23.** $y^2 - 12y + 32$ **24.** $m^2 - 5m + 4$

25. $t^2 - 4t - 5$ **26.** $s^2 - 4s - 12$ **27.** $n^2 - 9n - 36$

28. $y^2 - 13y - 48$ **29.** $x^2 + 4x - 45$ **30.** $x^2 + 3x - 18$

31. $y^2 - 9y + 20$ **32.** $a^2 - 7a + 10$ **33.** $b^2 + 11b + 28$

34. $p^2 + 13p + 22$ **35.** $m^2 - 15m + 44$ **36.** $x^2 - 12x + 36$

37. $-y^2 + 5y + 50$ **38.** $-x^2 + 5x + 84$ **39.** $x^2 + 64 - 16x$

40. $a^2 + 20 - 12a$ **41.** $16 - 10x + x^2$ **42.** $20 + b^2 - 21b$

43. $81 - 30w + w^2$ **44.** $y^2 + 72 - 17y$ **45.** $p^2 - 8pq + 7q^2$

46. $s^2 - 10st + 25t^2$ **47.** $p^2 - 4pq - 5q^2$ **48.** $x^2 - 4xy - 12y^2$

49. $m^2 - 12mn + 35n^2$ **50.** $r^2 - rs - 30s^2$ **51.** $x^2 + 9xy + 8y^2$

52. $a^2 + 12ab + 27b^2$

53. $5x^2 - 5x - 30$

54. $4y^2 + 12y - 40$

55. $2x^2 + 10x - 28$

56. $8r^2 - 56r - 64$

57. $12 - 18t + 6t^2$

58. $8 - 10x + 2x^2$

59. $3x^2 + 24 + 18x$

60. $5z^2 - 15 - 10z$

61. $y^3 + 3y^2 - 10y$

62. $x^3 - 6x^2 - 7x$

63. $a^3 + 8a^2 + 15a$

64. $q^3 - q^2 - 42q$

65. $t^4 - 14t^3 + 24t^2$

66. $x^4 + 6x^3 - 27x^2$

67. $4a^3 - 12a^2 + 8a$

68. $3y^3 - 18y^2 + 24y$

69. $2x^3 + 30x + 16x^2$

70. $5b^3 + 10b + 15b^2$

71. $4x^3 + 48x - 28x^2$

72. $3r^3 - 42r + 15r^2$

73. $-56s + 6s^2 + 2s^3$

74. $-20y - 16y^2 + 4y^3$

75. $2c^4 + 4c^3 - 70c^2$

76. $4t^4 + 24t^3 - 64t^2$

77. $ax^3 - 18ax^2 + 32ax$

78. $b^2y^3 - 5b^2y^2 - 36b^2y$

Applications

Solve.

79. Show that for any whole number n, the number represented by $n^2 + 11n + 30$ can be expressed as the product of two consecutive whole numbers.

80. A child throws a stone downward with an initial velocity of 48 ft/sec from a height of 160 ft. One step in figuring out how long it takes for the stone to reach the ground is to factor the expression $16t^2 + 48t - 160$. What is its factorization?

81. A statistician found that the cost in dollars for a company to produce x units of a certain product can be approximated by $C = x^2 - 14x + 45$. Factor the expression on the right side of this equation.

82. Show that for any whole number n, the number represented by $4n^2 + 20n + 24$ can be expressed as the product of two consecutive even numbers.

• *Check your answers on page A-26.*

Mindstretchers

GROUPWORK

1. Work with a partner. Next to each trinomial, list at least two integers that when inserted in the box will make the trinomial factorable.

_____

a. $x^2 + \boxed{} x + 60$ _____

b. $x^2 - x + \boxed{}$ _____

INVESTIGATION

2. Copy or trace the following algebra tiles onto a piece of paper. Then cut out each tile separately. Finally position all the tiles like a jigsaw puzzle so as to form a rectangle. (*Hint:* Factor the polynomial $x^2 + 5x + 6$.)

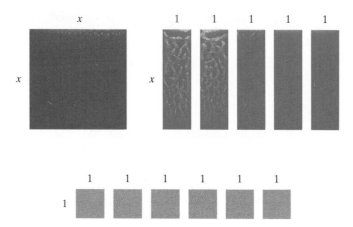

MATHEMATICAL REASONING

3. In arithmetic, we simplify a fraction such as $\dfrac{20}{24}$ by writing the numerator and denominator in factored form and then dividing out common factors. For example, $\dfrac{20}{24} = \dfrac{\cancel{2} \cdot \cancel{2} \cdot 5}{\cancel{2} \cdot \cancel{2} \cdot 2 \cdot 3} = \dfrac{5}{6}$. Assuming $x \neq 1$ and $x \neq 3$, simplify $\dfrac{x^2 - 3x + 2}{x^2 - 4x + 3}$.

6.3 Factoring Trinomials Whose Leading Coefficient Is Not 1

OBJECTIVES

- *To factor trinomials of the form $ax^2 + bx + c$, where $a \neq 1$*

- *To solve applied problems involving factoring*

In the previous section we discussed factoring trinomials of the form $ax^2 + bx + c$, where $a = 1$. Here, we consider polynomials whose leading coefficient is not 1. That is, we factor trinomials such as

$$2x^2 + 5x + 3 \qquad \text{and} \qquad 5x^2 - 13x - 6$$
↑ ↑

The coefficient of the leading term is not 1.

The method of factoring that we use is, again, trial and error. However, we also discuss an alternative procedure that is based on factoring by grouping, a method that we discussed in Section 6.1.

Factoring $ax^2 + bx + c$, $a \neq 1$

Let's consider the product of two binomials.

$$
\begin{array}{cccc}
\text{F} & \text{O} & \text{I} & \text{L}
\end{array}
$$
$$(2x + 3)(x + 1) = (2x)(x) + (2x)(1) + (3)(x) + (3)(1)$$
$$= 2x^2 \quad + \quad 2x \quad + \quad 3x \quad + \quad 3$$
$$= 2x^2 + 5x + 3$$

Now let's reverse the process: We start with the product $2x^2 + 5x + 3$, which we must factor. First, we check for common factors. Since there are no common factors other than 1 and -1, we use the process discussed in the last section for factoring trinomials, applying the FOIL method in reverse. Here, however, the leading coefficient is not 1, so we need to consider the factors of both 2 and 3. We then list and test all combinations of these factors to see if any will give us the desired middle term, $5x$. In other words, we are looking for four integers so that:

$$2x^2 + 5x + 3 = (?x + ?)(?x + ?)$$

Factors of 2	Factors of 3	Possible Binomial Factors	Sum of Outer and Inner Products	
2, 1	3, 1	$(2x + 3)(x + 1)$	$2x + 3x = 5x$	← Correct middle term
		$(2x + 1)(x + 3)$	$6x + x = 7x$	
2, 1	$-3, -1$	$(2x - 3)(x - 1)$	$-2x - 3x = -5x$	
		$(2x - 1)(x - 3)$	$-6x - x = -7x$	

Using this trial-and-error method, we find that $(2x + 3)(x + 1)$ is the correct factorization.

Note that this trial-and-error method for factoring a trinomial such as $2x^2 + 5x + 3$ is similar to the method for factoring trinomials with leading coefficient 1: We list and test all the possible factors of both the leading term and the constant term of the trinomial. We are looking for a combination of factors where the sum of the outer and inner products is the middle term of the trinomial. Practice and experience will shorten the process.

EXAMPLE 1

Factor: $3x^2 + 11x + 10$

SOLUTION The terms of $3x^2 + 11x + 10$ have no common factors. So we proceed to use the trial-and-error method to factor this trinomial. Note that both the middle term, $11x$, and the constant term, 10, are positive. So we need to consider only combinations of the positive factors of 3 and of 10 that will give us a middle term with coefficient 15.

$$3x^2 + 11x + 10 = (?x + ?)(?x + ?)$$

Factors of 3	Factors of 10	Possible Binomial Factors	Middle Term
3, 1	2, 5	$(3x + 2)(x + 5)$	$15x + 2x = 17x$
		$(3x + 5)(x + 2)$	$6x + 5x = 11x$ ← Correct middle term
	10, 1	$(3x + 10)(x + 1)$	$3x + 10x = 13x$
		$(3x + 1)(x + 10)$	$30x + x = 31x$

So $3x^2 + 11x + 10 = (3x + 5)(x + 2)$.

PRACTICE 1

Factor: $5x^2 + 14x + 8$

EXAMPLE 2

Express in factored form: $15 - 17x + 4x^2$

SOLUTION First, we rewrite the terms of the trinomial in descending order: $4x^2 - 17x + 15$. These terms have no common factor. To find the factorization of $4x^2 - 17x + 15$, we consider combinations of factors of 4 and of 15 that will result in a middle term with the coefficient -17.

Factors of 4	Factors of 15	Possible Binomial Factors	Middle Term
2, 2	$-3, -5$	$(2x - 3)(2x - 5)$	$-10x - 6x = -16x$
	$-15, -1$	$(2x - 15)(2x - 1)$	$-2x - 30x = -32x$
4, 1	$-3, -5$	$(4x - 3)(x - 5)$	$-20x - 3x = -23x$
		$(4x - 5)(x - 3)$	$-12x - 5x = -17x$ ← Correct middle term
	$-15, -1$	$(4x - 15)(x - 1)$	$-4x - 15x = -19x$
		$(4x - 1)(x - 15)$	$-60x - x = -61x$

So $4x^2 - 17x + 15 = (4x - 5)(x - 3)$.

PRACTICE 2

Factor: $21 - 25x + 6x^2$

Note that in Examples 1 and 2 we could have stopped the process of testing possible factorizations after finding the correct middle term.

EXAMPLE 3

Factor: $2y^2 + 19y - 10$

SOLUTION The terms of $2y^2 + 19y - 10$ have no common factors. So we factor the trinomial by considering combinations of the factors of 2 and of -10 that will give us the middle term with coefficient 19.

Factors of 2	Factors of -10	Possible Binomial Factors	Middle Term
2, 1	2, -5	$(2y + 2)(y - 5)$	$-10y + 2y = -8y$
		$(2y - 5)(y + 2)$	$4y - 5y = -y$
	$-2, 5$	$(2y - 2)(y + 5)$	$10y - 2y = 8y$
		$(2y + 5)(y - 2)$	$-4y + 5y = y$
	10, -1	$(2y + 10)(y - 1)$	$-2y + 10y = 8y$
		$(2y - 1)(y + 10)$	$20y - y = 19y$ ← Correct middle term
	$-10, 1$	$(2y + 1)(y - 10)$	$-20y + y = -19y$
		$(2y - 10)(y + 1)$	$2y - 10y = -8y$

So $2y^2 + 19y - 10 = (2y - 1)(y + 10)$.

PRACTICE 3

Factor: $7y^2 + 47y - 14$

Can you explain why $(2y + 2)$, $(2y - 2)$, $(2y + 10)$, and $(2y - 10)$ can be immediately eliminated as possible factors of $2y^2 + 19y - 10$ in Example 3?

Consider the following possible binomial factors in Example 3.

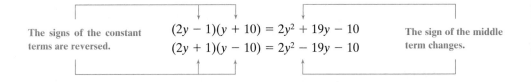

The signs of the constant terms are reversed.

$(2y - 1)(y + 10) = 2y^2 + 19y - 10$
$(2y + 1)(y - 10) = 2y^2 - 19y - 10$

The sign of the middle term changes.

Comparing these possible factors suggest the following shortcut.

TIP Reversing the signs of the constant terms in binomial factors has the effect of switching the sign of the middle term in their product.

EXAMPLE 4

Factor: $5x^2 - 13x - 6$

SOLUTION Since the terms of $5x^2 - 13x - 6$ have no common factors, let's look at the combinations of factors of 5 and of -6 that will give us the middle term with coefficient -13.

Factors of 5	Factors of -6	Possible Binomial Factors	Middle Term	
5, 1	2, -3	$(5x + 2)(x - 3)$	$-15x + 2x = -13x$	← Correct middle term
		$(5x - 3)(x + 2)$	$10x - 3x = 7x$	
	$-2, 3$	$(5x - 2)(x + 3)$	$15x - 2x = 13x$	
		$(5x + 3)(x - 2)$	$-10x + 3x = -7x$	
	$-6, 1$	$(5x - 6)(x + 1)$	$5x - 6x = -x$	
		$(5x + 1)(x - 6)$	$-30x + x = -29x$	
	6, -1	$(5x + 6)(x - 1)$	$-5x + 6x = x$	
		$(5x - 1)(x + 6)$	$30x - x = 29x$	

So $5x^2 - 13x - 6 = (5x + 2)(x - 3)$. Note that it was unnecessary to examine any factors after the first trial, since we found the correct combination for the middle term, $-13x$.

PRACTICE 4

Factor: $2x^2 - x - 10$

EXAMPLE 5

Factor: $12y^3 + 2y^2 - 2y$

SOLUTION Since $2y$ is the GCF of the trinomial, first we factor it out getting:

$$12y^3 + 2y^2 - 2y = 2y(6y^2 + y - 1)$$

Next, we factor $6y^2 + y - 1$, looking for a combination of factors of 6 and -1 that will give us the middle term with coefficient 1.

Factors of 6	Factors of -1	Possible Binomial Factors	Middle Term	
6, 1	1, -1	$(6y + 1)(y - 1)$	$-6y + y = -5y$	
		$(6y - 1)(y + 1)$	$6y - y = 5y$	
3, 2	1, -1	$(3y + 1)(2y - 1)$	$-3y + 2y = -y$	
		$(3y - 1)(2y + 1)$	$3y - 2y = y$	← Correct middle term

So $12y^3 + 2y^2 - 2y = 2y(6y^2 + y - 1) = 2y(3y - 1)(2y + 1)$.

PRACTICE 5

Factor: $18x^3 - 21x^2 - 9x$

Now we consider factoring a trinomial of the form $ax^2 + bxy + cy^2$. This type of trinomial contains more than one variable, so we need to look for a factorization of the form $(?x + ?y)(?x + ?y)$.

EXAMPLE 6

Factor: $12x^2 + 28xy + 8y^2$

SOLUTION Since 4 is the GCF of the trinomial, let's first factor it out.

$$12x^2 + 28xy + 8y^2 = 4(3x^2 + 7xy + 2y^2)$$

Next we factor $3x^2 + 7xy + 2y^2$. We look for the combination of factors of 3 and 2 that will give us the middle term $7xy$.

$$4(3x^2 + 7xy + 2y^2) = 4(?x + ?y)(?x + ?y)$$

Factors of 3	Factors of 2	Possible Binomial Factors	Middle Term
3, 1	2, 1	$(3x + 2y)(x + y)$	$3xy + 2xy = 5xy$
		$(3x + y)(x + 2y)$	$6xy + xy = 7xy$ ←——Correct middle term

So $12x^2 + 28xy + 8y^2 = 4(3x^2 + 7xy + 2y^2) =$
$4(3x + y)(x + 2y)$.

Now let's consider an alternative procedure for factoring a trinomial $ax^2 + bx + c$ based on *grouping*. This method, which the next example illustrates, is sometimes called the *ac method*.

EXAMPLE 7

Factor: $2x^2 + 5x - 3$

SOLUTION First, we check that the terms of $2x^2 + 5x - 3$ have no common factors. Next, instead of listing the factors of 2 and -3 as in the trial-and-error method, we begin by finding their product:

$$ac = (2)(-3) = -6$$

We then look for two factors of the number ac that add up to b, that is, to 5. The numbers 6 and -1 satisfy these conditions, since $(6)(-1) = -6$ and $(6) + (-1) = 5$. Using these factors to split up the middle term in the original trinomial, we rewrite the trinomial.

$2x^2 + 5x - 3 = 2x^2 + 6x + (-1)x - 3$	Split up the middle term.
$= [2x^2 + 6x] + [(-1)x - 3]$	Group the first two terms and the last two terms.
$= 2x(x + 3) + (-1)(x + 3)$	Factor out the GCF from each group.
$= (x + 3)(2x - 1)$	Write in factored form.

So $2x^2 + 5x - 3 = (x + 3)(2x - 1)$. As usual, we can check that this factorization is correct by multiplication.

PRACTICE 6

Factor: $36c^2 - 12cd - 15d^2$

PRACTICE 7

Factor: $2x^2 - 7x - 4$

Now let's solve some applied problems involving the factoring of trinomials.

EXAMPLE 8

Suppose a ball is thrown upward at 40 ft/sec from the top of a building 24 ft above the ground. Then the height of the ball above the ground in feet t sec after the ball is thrown is given by the expression $-16t^2 + 40t + 24$. Write this expression in factored form.

SOLUTION We factor the expression $-16t^2 + 40t + 24$:

$$-16t^2 + 40t + 24 = -8(2t^2 - 5t - 3)$$
$$= -8(2t + 1)(t - 3)$$

So the factorization of $-16t^2 + 40t + 24$ is $-8(2t + 1)(t - 3)$, which can also be written $8(-2t - 1)(t - 3)$, or $8(2t + 1)(-t + 3)$.

PRACTICE 8

A bin is made from a 7-ft by 5-ft sheet of metal by cutting out squares of equal size from each corner and then turning up the sides. The volume of the resulting bin can be represented by the expression $4x^3 - 24x^2 + 35x$. Rewrite this expression in factored form.

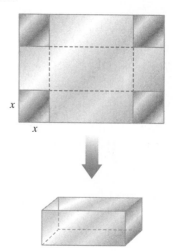

Exercises 6.3

Match each trinomial with its binomial factors.

1. $2x^2 + 3x - 9$

2. $2x^2 - 19x + 9$

3. $2x^2 - 11x + 9$

4. $2x^2 - 3x - 9$

5. $2x^2 - 17x - 9$

6. $2x^2 - 7x - 9$

a. $(2x - 9)(x + 1)$

b. $(2x - 9)(x - 1)$

c. $(x - 9)(2x + 1)$

d. $(x - 9)(2x - 1)$

e. $(2x - 3)(x + 3)$

f. $(x - 3)(2x + 3)$

Find the missing factor.

7. $3x^2 + 16x + 5 = (x + 5)$
   ( )

8. $2x^2 - 5x - 12 = (2x + 3)$
   ( )

9. $5x^2 - 13x - 6 = (5x + 2)$
   ( )

10. $2x^2 + x - 6 = (x + 2)$
   ( )

11. $3x^2 - 11x + 6 = (3x - 2)$
   ( )

12. $6x^2 - 7x + 2 = (2x - 1)$
   ( )

Factor, if possible.

13. $3x^2 + 8x + 5$

14. $2x^2 + 15x + 7$

15. $2y^2 - 11y + 5$

16. $3y^2 - 10y + 7$

17. $3x^2 + 14x + 8$

18. $2x^2 + 11x + 9$

19. $5x^2 + 9x - 6$

20. $5x^2 + 17x - 12$

21. $6y^2 - y - 5$

22. $4y^2 - 16y - 7$

23. $2y^2 - 11y + 14$

24. $7y^2 - 19y + 10$

25. $9a^2 - 18a - 16$

26. $10m^2 - m - 21$

27. $4x^2 - 13x + 3$

28. $4n^2 - 9n + 2$

29. $6 + 17y + 12y^2$

30. $4 + 16n + 15n^2$

31. $-17m + 21 + 2m^2$

32. $-16x + 5 + 3x^2$

33. $-6a^2 - 7a + 3$

34. $-5b^2 - 14b + 3$

35. $8y^2 + 5y - 22$

36. $6x^2 + 5x - 25$

37. $7y^2 + 36y - 5$

38. $2y^2 + 27y + 14$

39. $8a^2 + 65a + 8$

40. $8n^2 + 33n + 4$

41. $6x^2 + 25x - 9$

42. $10x^2 + 21x - 10$

43. $8y^2 - 26y + 15$

44. $4m^2 - 16m - 9$

45. $14y^2 - 38y + 20$

46. $9y^2 - 24y + 15$

47. $28a^2 + 24a - 4$

48. $6x^2 + 40x - 14$

49. $-6b^2 + 40b + 14$

50. $-25m^2 + 65m + 30$

51. $12y^3 + 50y^2 + 28y$

52. $6x^3 + 45x^2 + 21x$

53. $14a^4 - 38a^3 + 20a^2$

54. $10n^4 - 35n^3 + 15n^2$

55. $2x^3y + 13x^2y + 15xy$

56. $3xy^3 + 10xy^2 + 3xy$

57. $6ab^3 - 44ab^2 + 14ab$

58. $12a^3b - 34a^2b + 24ab$

59. $20c^2 - 9cd + d^2$

60. $12a^2 - 25ab + 12b^2$

61. $2x^2 - 5xy - 3y^2$

62. $6s^2 - st - 12t^2$

63. $8a^2 - 6ab + b^2$

64. $3m^2 - 8mn + 5n^2$

65. $18x^2 + 3xy - 6y^2$

66. $4s^2 + 10st - 24t^2$

67. $16c^2 - 44cd + 30d^2$

68. $16a^2 - 48ab + 36b^2$

69. $27u^2 + 18uv + 3v^2$

70. $4a^2 + 26ab - 48b^2$

71. $42x^3 + 45x^2y - 27xy^2$

72. $60p^3 + 28p^2q - 16pq^2$

73. $-30x^4y + 35x^3y^2 + 15x^2y^3$

74. $-24x^3y^2 - 6x^2y^3 + 18xy^4$

75. $5ax^2 - 28axy - 12ay^2$

76. $3cx^2 + 7cxy - 20cy^2$

Applications

Solve.

77. An object is thrown upward so that its height in meters above the ground at time t seconds is represented by the expression $-5t^2 - 21t + 20$. Factor this expression.

78. A box with width w has a volume that can be expressed as $3w^3 - 2w^2 - w$. Rewrite this expression in factored form.

79. Show that the expression $4n^2 - 12n + 5$ can be written as the product of two integers that differ by 4, no matter what integer n represents.

80. The squares of the first n whole numbers add up to $\dfrac{2n^3 + 3n^2 + n}{6}$. Write this expression so that the numerator is in factored form.

• *Check your answers on page A-26.*

Mindstretchers

GROUPWORK

1. Work with a partner. Next to each polynomial, list at least two integers that, when inserted in the box, will make the polynomial factorable.

_____

a. $2x^2 +$ ☐ $x + 5$ _____

b. ☐ $x^2 - 4x + 1$ _____

c. $3x^2 - x +$ ☐   _____

INVESTIGATION

2. Copy or trace the following algebra tiles onto a piece of paper. Then cut out each tile separately. Finally position all the tiles like a jigsaw puzzle so as to form a rectangle. (*Hint:* Factor the polynomial $2x^2 + 7x + 3$.)

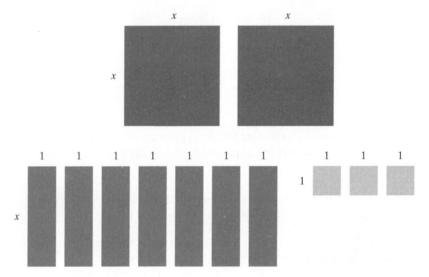

WRITING

3. Do you prefer to factor trinomials using the trial-and-error method or the *ac* method? Explain why.

_____

_____

_____

EXAMPLE 2

Factor: $x^2 + 12x + 36$

SOLUTION For the trinomial $x^2 + 12x + 36$, the first term x^2 and the last term 36, or 6^2, are perfect squares. The middle term, $12x$, or $2 \cdot x \cdot 6$, is twice the product of x and 6. It follows that $x^2 + 12x + 36$ is a perfect square trinomial. Since its middle term is positive, we apply the formula for the square of a sum.

$$x^2 + 12x + 36 = x^2 + \underbrace{2 \cdot x \cdot 6} + (6)^2 = (x + 6)^2$$

$$a^2 \; + \; 2ab \; + \; b^2 \; = \; (a + b)^2$$

CHECK We can confirm our answer by multiplying out $(x + 6)^2$.

$$(x + 6)^2 = (x + 6)(x + 6) = x^2 + 2 \cdot 6x + 36 = x^2 + 12x + 36$$

PRACTICE 2

Factor: $n^2 + 20n + 100$

EXAMPLE 3

Write as the square of a binomial: $x^2 + 9 - 6x$

SOLUTION Let's begin by rewriting the trinomial in descending order: $x^2 - 6x + 9$.

$$x^2 - 6x + 9 = x^2 - \underbrace{2 \cdot x \cdot 3} + (3)^2 = (x - 3)^2$$

$$a^2 \; - \; 2ab \; + \; b^2 \; = \; (a - b)^2$$

PRACTICE 3

Factor: $t^2 + 4 - 4t$

EXAMPLE 4

Express $9x^2 - 6xy + y^2$ as the square of a binomial.

SOLUTION Here the trinomial contains more than one variable.

$$9x^2 - 6xy + y^2 = (3x)^2 - \underbrace{2 \cdot 3x \cdot y} + y^2 = (3x - y)^2$$

$$a^2 \; - \; 2ab \; + \; b^2 \; = \; (a - b)^2$$

PRACTICE 4

Write $25c^2 - 40cd + 16d^2$ as the square of a binomial.

EXAMPLE 5

Factor: $y^{10} + 16y^5 + 64$

SOLUTION Since $y^{10} = (y^5)^2$ and $64 = (8)^2$, we know that y^{10} and 64 are perfect squares. Also, since $16y^5 = 2 \cdot 8 \cdot y^5$, that is, $16y^5$ is twice the product of y^5 and 8, we conclude that $y^{10} + 16y^5 + 64$ is a perfect square trinomial.

$$y^{10} + 16y^5 + 64 = (y^5)^2 + 2 \cdot 8 \cdot y^5 + (8)^2 = (y^5 + 8)^2$$

$$\underset{a^2 \quad + \quad 2ab \quad + \quad b^2 \quad = \quad (a+b)^2}{\uparrow \qquad \uparrow \qquad \uparrow \qquad \uparrow \quad \uparrow}$$

PRACTICE 5

Express $x^4 + 8x^2 + 16$ as the square of a binomial.

In factoring a perfect square trinomial, how do we know whether the binomial squared is the sum or the difference of two terms?

Factoring the Difference of Squares

Recall from Section 5.6 that when finding the product of the sum and the difference of the same terms, we get:

$$(a + b)(a - b) = a^2 - b^2$$

The product is a binomial that is called a **difference of squares**. We can factor such binomials by reversing the multiplication process.

> **Factoring the Difference of Squares**
> $$a^2 - b^2 = (a + b)(a - b)$$

This formula is a shortcut for factoring a binomial equal to the square of one term *minus* the square of another term. The terms are a and b, and so their squares are a^2 and b^2. The formula says that the factorization of a binomial that is the difference of the squares of two terms is the sum of the two terms times the difference of the same two terms, that is, $(a + b)(a - b)$.

EXAMPLE 6

Indicate whether each binomial is a difference of squares.

a. $x^2 - 81$

b. $x^2 + y^2$

c. $x^2 - y^3$

d. $4p^6 - q^2$

PRACTICE 6

Determine whether each binomial is a difference of squares.

a. $x^2 - 64$

b. $x^2 + 49$

SOLUTION

a. In the binomial $x^2 - 81$, both x^2 and 81 are perfect squares and correspond to a^2 and b^2, respectively, in our formula.

$$x^2 - 81 = x^2 - 9^2$$
$$\uparrow \quad \uparrow$$
$$a^2 - b^2$$

Here, a corresponds to x, and b corresponds to 9.
So $x^2 - 81$ is a difference of squares.

b. In the expression $x^2 + y^2$, both x^2 and y^2 are perfect squares, where x corresponds to a and y to b. However, the binomial is the sum and not the difference of squares.

c. For $x^2 - y^3$, x^2 is a perfect square, but y^3 is not. So $x^2 - y^3$ is not a difference of squares.

d. The binomial $4p^6 - q^2$ can be rewritten as $(2p^3)^2 - q^2$, and so is a difference of squares.

c. $x^3 - 16$

d. $r^4 - 9s^6$

Note, as the preceding example suggests, that even powers of a variable are perfect squares whereas odd powers of a variable are not. Can you explain why?

EXAMPLE 7

Factor: $x^2 - 100$

SOLUTION Since x^2 and 100 are perfect squares, $x^2 - 100$ is a difference of squares:

$$x^2 - 100 = x^2 - 10^2 = (x + 10)(x - 10)$$
$$\uparrow \quad \uparrow \qquad \uparrow \qquad \uparrow$$
$$a^2 - b^2 = (a + b) \ (a - b)$$

CHECK We can verify that $(x + 10)(x - 10)$ is the factorization of $x^2 - 100$ by multiplying.

$$(x + 10)(x - 10) = x^2 - 10x + 10x - 100 = x^2 - 100$$

PRACTICE 7

Factor: $y^2 - 121$

EXAMPLE 8

Write $16x^2 - 49y^2$ in factored form.

SOLUTION Since $16x^2 = (4x)^2$ and $49y^2 = (7y)^2$, we know that $16x^2$ and $49y^2$ are perfect squares. So $16x^2 - 49y^2$ is a difference of squares.

$$16x^2 - 49y^2 = (4x)^2 - (7y)^2 = (4x + 7y)(4x - 7y)$$
$$\uparrow \qquad \uparrow \qquad \uparrow \qquad \uparrow$$
$$a^2 - b^2 = (a + b) \quad (a - b)$$

PRACTICE 8

Express $9x^2 - 25y^2$ in factored form.

EXAMPLE 9

Factor: $4x^4 - 9y^6$

SOLUTION Because $4x^4 = (2x^2)^2$ and $9y^6 = (3y^3)^2$, we see that $4x^4$ and $9y^6$ are both perfect squares. So $4x^4 - 9y^6$ is a difference of squares.

$$4x^4 - 9y^6 = (2x^2)^2 - (3y^3)^2 = \underbrace{(2x^2 + 3y^3)}\underbrace{(2x^2 - 3y^3)}$$

$$\begin{array}{ccccc} \uparrow & & \uparrow & \uparrow & \uparrow \\ a^2 & - & b^2 & = & (a+b) & (a-b) \end{array}$$

PRACTICE 9

Factor: $64x^8 - 81y^2$

EXAMPLE 10

Find an expression for the area of the cross section of the pipe pictured. Write this expression in factored form.

SOLUTION The cross section is a ring-shaped region between two circles with the same center. The radius of the inner circle is r and the radius of the outer circle is R. Using the formula for the area of a circle helps us to find an expression for the area of the cross section:

Area of the cross section

= Area of the large circle − Area of the small circle

$= \quad \pi R^2 \quad - \quad \pi r^2$

$= \pi(R^2 - r^2)$

$= \pi(R + r)(R - r)$

So in factored form, the expression for the area of the cross section of the pipe is $\pi(R + r)(R - r)$.

PRACTICE 10

A stone is dropped from a bridge 256 ft above a river. The height of the stone above the river t sec after it is dropped is given by the expression $256 - 16t^2$. Factor this expression.

In this section, we have discussed how to factor some special types of polynomials, namely, perfect square trinomials and the difference of squares. There are, however, other special types of polynomials. Two of these special types, the difference of cubes and the sum of cubes, are discussed in Appendix A.3.

Exercises 6.4

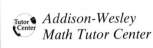
Determine whether each polynomial is a perfect square trinomial,
a difference of squares, or neither.

1. $x^2 + 2x + 1$

2. $y^2 + 8y + 16$

3. $-t^2 - 4t + 1$

4. $x^2 - 6x + 9$

5. $n^2 - 2n + 1$

6. $y^2 - 3y - 4$

7. $x^2 - 25$

8. $y^2 - 49$

9. $81x^2 - 36y^2$

10. $x^2 + y^2$

11. $25x^2 - 20x + 4$

12. $-y^2 + 2y + 9$

13. $y^2 + 1$

14. $4x^2 - 100y^2$

15. $25x^2 + 5xy + y^2$

16. $49x^2 + 14xy + y^2$

17. $x^3 - 1$

18. $x^4 + 9$

Factor, if possible.

19. $x^2 - 12x + 36$

20. $y^2 - 14y + 49$

21. $y^2 + 20y + 100$

22. $x^2 + 2x + 1$

23. $a^2 - 4a + 4$

24. $b^2 - 22b + 121$

25. $x^2 - 6x - 9$

26. $y^2 - 10y - 25$

27. $m^2 - 64$

28. $n^2 - 1$

29. $y^2 - 81$

30. $x^2 - 16$

31. $144 - x^2$

32. $225 - t^2$

33. $4a^2 - 36a + 81$

34. $25b^2 - 20b + 4$

35. $49x^2 + 28x + 4$

36. $9y^2 + 24y + 16$

37. $36 - 60x + 25x^2$

38. $49 - 42y + 9y^2$

39. $100m^2 - 81$

40. $16n^2 - 25$

41. $36x^2 + 121$

42. $64n^2 + 169$

43. $1 - 9x^2$

44. $81 - 4y^2$

45. $m^2 + 26mn + 169n^2$

46. $225a^2 - 30ab + b^2$

47. $4a^2 + 36ab + 81b^2$

48. $25s^2 - 40st + 16t^2$

49. $x^2 - 4y^2$

50. $49c^2 - d^2$

51. $100x^2 - 9y^2$

52. $36a^2 - 121b^2$

53. $y^6 + 2y^3 + 1$

54. $x^4 + 4x^2 + 4$

55. $64x^8 + 16x^4 + 1$

56. $16x^{10} + 8x^5 + 1$

57. $100x^{10} - 20x^5y^5 + y^{10}$

58. $9a^6 + 12a^3b^3 + 4b^6$

59. $25m^6 - 36$

60. $49n^8 - 16$

61. $x^4 - 144y^2$

62. $121y^6 - x^4$

63. $6x^2 + 12x + 6$

64. $12y^2 + 24y + 12$

65. $27m^3 - 36m^2 + 12m$

66. $48y^3 - 24y^2 + 3y$

67. $4s^2t^3 + 80s^2t^2 + 400s^2t$

68. $2x^3y^2 - 52x^2y^2 + 338xy^2$

69. $12x^6y^4 - 36x^3y^2 + 27$

70. $64c^6d^8 - 32c^3d^4 + 4$

71. $3k^3 - 147k$

72. $5m^3 - 125m$

73. $4y^4 - 36y^2$

74. $3t^5 - 300t^3$

75. $27x^2y - 3x^2y^3$

76. $50xy - 18x^3y$

77. $2a^2b^2 - 98$

78. $9x^4y^2 - 81$

79. $16b^4 - 121$

80. $9y^8 - 256$

81. $256 - r^4$

82. $625 - t^4$

83. $5x^4 - 80y^8$

84. $64s^4 - 4t^4$

85. $x^2(c - d) - 4(c - d)$

86. $y^2(a - b) - (a - b)$

87. $16(x - y) - a^2(x - y)$

88. $9(y - c) - x^2(y - c)$

Applications

Solve.

89. If the radius of a balloon decreases from radius r_1 to radius r_2, then the drop in the balloon's surface area is given by the expression $4\pi r_1^2 - 4\pi r_2^2$. Write this expression in factored form.

90. The height (in feet) of a stone dropped from a cliff 100 ft above a river, as shown in the illustration, is given by the expression $100 - 16t^2$, where t is time in seconds. Factor this expression.

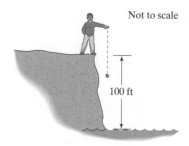

Not to scale

100 ft

91. A \$16,000 investment grew by an average annual rate of return of r. After two years, the value of the investment in dollars was $16{,}000 + 32{,}000r + 16{,}000r^2$. What is the factorization of this expression?

92. Find an expression, in factored form, for the area of the wooden border of the square picture frame shown.

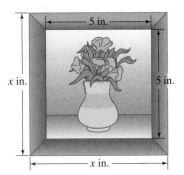

93. When the velocity of a rocket increases from v_1 to v_2, the force caused by air resistance increases by $kv_2^2 - kv_1^2$ for a constant k. Write this polynomial in factored form.

94. An open box is made from a 2-ft by 2-ft piece of cardboard by cutting out equal squares from each of the four corners and turning up the sides. The volume of the resulting box can be modeled by the polynomial $4x - 8x^2 + 4x^3$. Factor the expression.

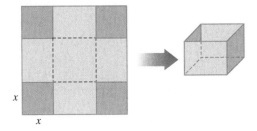

• *Check your answers on page A-26.*

Mindstretchers

PATTERNS

1. Find two factors of 3599 both of which are greater than 1. (*Hint:* 3599 = 3600 − 1.)

GROUPWORK

2. Try this trick with a partner:

a. Take your partner's age in years.

b. Square it.

c. Subtract 9.

d. Divide the result by 3 less than your partner's age.

e. Subtract 53.

f. Add your partner's age.

g. Divide by 2.

h. Add 5^2.

i. Check that you wind up where you started—with your partner's age.

continued

In the table, record the results for three different ages. Then in the fourth row, repeat the steps with a variable x representing your partner's age. Explain why this trick works.

(a)	(b)	(c)	(d)	(e)	(f)	(g)	(h)	(i)
x								

WRITING

3. In a few sentences, explain how the following diagram shows that $(a + b)^2 = a^2 + 2ab + b^2$.

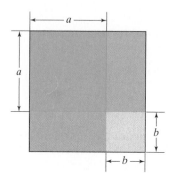

_____

_____

_____

_____

_____

6.5 Solving Quadratic Equations by Factoring

OBJECTIVES

• *To solve quadratic equations by factoring*

• *To solve applied problems using quadratic equations*

This section deals with a kind of equation that we have not previously considered, namely, a *quadratic equation*. Such equations come up in physics, in finance, and other fields as well.

Consider, for instance, a situation involving the movement of a rocket. If the rocket is shot straight upward from ground level with an initial velocity of 80 ft/sec, physicists approximate the rocket's height above the ground h by the expression $80t - 16t^2$, where t is the elapsed time in seconds and h is measured in feet. To find the time at which the rocket falls back and hits the ground (that is, when $h = 0$), we need to be able to solve the quadratic equation $80t - 16t^2 = 0$.

> **Definition**
>
> A **second-degree** or **quadratic equation** is an equation that can be written in the form $ax^2 + bx + c = 0$, where a, b, and c are real numbers and $a \neq 0$.

Some examples of quadratic equations are:

$$x^2 - x + 6 = 0 \qquad 3x^2 - 12 = 0 \qquad (x - 1)^2 = 0$$

Can you explain why these polynomials are of the second degree?

As in the case of a linear equation, a value is said to be a *solution* of a quadratic equation if substituting the value for the variable makes the equation a true statement.

Using Factoring to Solve Quadratic Equations

In this section, we consider those quadratic equations that can be solved by factoring. In Chapter 9, we will consider additional approaches to solving quadratic equations.

The key to solving quadratic equations by factoring is to apply the **zero-product property**.

> **The Zero-Product Property**
>
> If $ab = 0$, then $a = 0$ or $b = 0$, or both a and $b = 0$.

This property states that if the product of two factors is zero, then either one or both of the factors must be zero.

Consider these examples of the zero-product property.

- If $2x = 0$, then x must be 0 (since $2 \neq 0$).
- If $x(3x - 1) = 0$, then either $x = 0$ or $3x - 1 = 0$.
- If $(x - 3)(x + 2) = 0$, then either $x - 3 = 0$ or $x + 2 = 0$.

Let's see how to use the zero-product property to solve a quadratic equation that is already in factored form.

EXAMPLE 1

Solve: $(2x - 1)(x + 6) = 0$

SOLUTION Since $(2x - 1)(x + 6) = 0$, the zero-product property tells us that at least one of the factors must equal zero, that is either $2x - 1 = 0$ or $x + 6 = 0$.

$$(2x - 1)(x + 6) = 0$$

$2x - 1 = 0$	or $x + 6 = 0$	Set each factor equal to 0.
$2x = 1$	$x = -6$	Solve each equation for x.
$x = \dfrac{1}{2}$		

CHECK We replace x by the values $\frac{1}{2}$ and -6 in the original equation.

Substitute $\frac{1}{2}$ for x.

$$(2x - 1)(x + 6) = 0$$
$$\left[2 \cdot \left(\frac{1}{2}\right) - 1\right]\left(\frac{1}{2} + 6\right) \stackrel{?}{=} 0$$
$$(1 - 1)(6\tfrac{1}{2}) \stackrel{?}{=} 0$$
$$0 \cdot 6\tfrac{1}{2} \stackrel{?}{=} 0$$
$$0 = 0 \quad \text{True.}$$

Substitute -6 for x.

$$(2x - 1)(x + 6) = 0$$
$$[(2)(-6) - 1](-6 + 6) \stackrel{?}{=} 0$$
$$(-13)(0) \stackrel{?}{=} 0$$
$$0 = 0 \quad \text{True.}$$

So the solutions of the equation $(2x - 1)(x + 6) = 0$ are $\frac{1}{2}$ and -6.

PRACTICE 1

Solve: $(3x - 1)(x + 5) = 0$

In Example 1, note that we found the solutions of a quadratic equation by solving two linear equations: $2x - 1 = 0$ and $x + 6 = 0$. Explain how we know that these equations are linear.

When the quadratic expression in a second-degree equation is not given in factored form, we need to factor it before solving.

EXAMPLE 2

Solve: $y^2 - 5y = 0$

SOLUTION

$$y^2 - 5y = 0$$
$$y(y - 5) = 0 \qquad \text{Factor the left side of the equation.}$$

Next we set each factor equal to 0. Then we solve for x.

$$y = 0 \quad \text{or} \quad y - 5 = 0$$
$$y = 5$$

CHECK We verify our solutions in the original equation.

Substitute 0 for y. | Substitute 5 for y.

$$y^2 - 5y = 0 \qquad\qquad y^2 - 5y = 0$$
$$(0)^2 - 5(0) \stackrel{?}{=} 0 \qquad 5^2 - 5(5) \stackrel{?}{=} 0$$
$$0 - 0 \stackrel{?}{=} 0 \qquad\qquad 25 - 25 \stackrel{?}{=} 0$$
$$0 = 0 \quad \text{True.} \qquad\quad 0 = 0 \quad \text{True.}$$

The solutions are 0 and 5.

PRACTICE 2

Solve: $y^2 + 6y = 0$

In order to apply the zero-product property, the product of the factors of a quadratic must equal zero. This implies that a quadratic equation must be written in *standard form*, $ax^2 + bx + c = 0$, before it can be solved.

EXAMPLE 3

Solve: $2x^2 + x = 1$

SOLUTION

$$2x^2 + x = 1$$
$$2x^2 + x - 1 = 0 \qquad \text{Write in standard form by adding } -1 \text{ to each side.}$$
$$(2x - 1)(x + 1) = 0 \qquad \text{Factor the left side of the equation.}$$
$$2x - 1 = 0 \quad \text{or} \quad x + 1 = 0 \qquad \text{Set each factor to equal to 0.}$$
$$2x = 1 \qquad\qquad x = -1 \qquad \text{Solve for } x.$$
$$x = \frac{1}{2}$$

CHECK We verify our solutions in the original equation.

Substitute $\frac{1}{2}$ for x. | Substitute -1 for x.

$$2x^2 + x = 1 \qquad\qquad 2x^2 + x = 1$$
$$2\left(\frac{1}{2}\right)^2 + \frac{1}{2} \stackrel{?}{=} 1 \qquad 2(-1)^2 + (-1) \stackrel{?}{=} 1$$
$$2\left(\frac{1}{4}\right) + \frac{1}{2} \stackrel{?}{=} 1 \qquad 2(1) + (-1) \stackrel{?}{=} 1$$
$$1 = 1 \quad \text{True.} \qquad\qquad 1 = 1 \quad \text{True.}$$

So the solutions are $\frac{1}{2}$ and -1.

PRACTICE 3

Solve: $4y^2 - 11y = 3$

EXAMPLE 4

Solve: $2x(x - 3) = 8$

SOLUTION We begin by writing the equation in standard form.

$$2x(x - 3) = 8$$
$$2x^2 - 6x = 8 \qquad \text{Multiply.}$$
$$2x^2 - 6x - 8 = 0 \qquad \text{Write in standard form by adding } -8 \text{ to each side.}$$
$$2(x^2 - 3x - 4) = 0 \qquad \text{Factor out the GCF.}$$
$$2(x + 1)(x - 4) = 0 \qquad \text{Write in factored form.}$$

Next we set factors containing variables equal to 0. Then we solve for x.

$$x + 1 = 0 \quad \text{or} \quad x - 4 = 0$$
$$x = -1 \qquad\qquad x = 4$$

CHECK

Substitute -1 for x.

$$2x(x - 3) = 8$$
$$2(-1)(-1 - 3) \overset{?}{=} 8$$
$$(-2)(-4) \overset{?}{=} 8$$
$$8 = 8 \qquad \text{True.}$$

Substitute 4 for x.

$$2x(x - 3) = 8$$
$$2(4)(4 - 3) \overset{?}{=} 8$$
$$8(1) \overset{?}{=} 8$$
$$8 = 8 \qquad \text{True.}$$

So the solutions are -1 and 4.

PRACTICE 4

Solve: $3t(t + 4) = 15$

These examples lead us to the following strategy (or rule) for solving a quadratic equation by factoring.

To Solve a Quadratic Equation by Factoring
- If necessary, rewrite the equation in standard form with 0 on one side.
- Factor the other side.
- Use the zero-product property to get two simple linear equations.
- Solve the linear equations.
- Check by substituting the solutions in the original quadratic equation.

EXAMPLE 5

Suppose you have a square garden that you want to make longer. If you extend one side by 5 ft and the adjacent side by 2 ft, the resulting garden would be rectangular with an area of 130 sq ft. How much fencing will you need to enclose the enlarged garden?

PRACTICE 5

A framemaker is planning to frame a rectangular painting that has an area of 80 in^2.

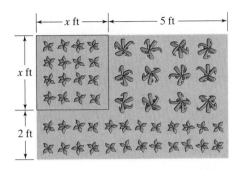

SOLUTION Let's represent the length of each side of the square by x. The resulting rectangular garden will have dimensions $(x + 5)$ and $(x + 2)$. The area of a rectangle can be computed by multiplying its length and its width, and we are told that this area is 130.

$$(x + 5)(x + 2) = 130$$
$$x^2 + 7x + 10 = 130$$
$$x^2 + 7x - 120 = 0$$
$$(x + 15)(x - 8) = 0$$
$$x + 15 = 0 \quad \text{or} \quad x - 8 = 0$$
$$x = -15 \qquad\qquad x = 8$$

If she has 3 ft of framing to put around the picture, what should the dimensions of the frame be? (Ignore the frame's thickness.)

CHECK

Substitute -15 for x.

$$(x + 5)(x + 2) = 130$$
$$(-15 + 5)(-15 + 2) \stackrel{?}{=} 130$$
$$(-10)(-13) \stackrel{?}{=} 130$$
$$130 = 130 \quad \text{True.}$$

Substitute 8 for x.

$$(x + 5)(x + 2) = 130$$
$$(8 + 5)(8 + 2) \stackrel{?}{=} 130$$
$$(13)(10) \stackrel{?}{=} 130$$
$$130 = 130 \quad \text{True.}$$

So the two solutions of the equation are -15 and 8. Since x represents a length, we can reject the negative solution -15. We conclude that the length of each side of the square is 8 ft. To compute the perimeter of the rectangle, we can substitute into the following formula:

$$P = 2l + 2w$$
$$= 2(8 + 5) + 2(8 + 2)$$
$$= 2(13) + 2(10)$$
$$= 26 + 20$$
$$= 46$$

Therefore, 46 ft of fencing is needed to enclose the enlarged garden.

We can also apply what we know about solving quadratic equations to problems involving the Pythagorean theorem. This theorem relates to the lengths of the three sides of a right triangle, which is illustrated on the next page.

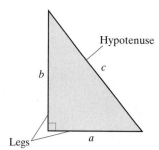

Hypotenuse

b c

Legs a

A right triangle has one 90° angle. The side opposite the 90° angle, the longest side, is called the *hypotenuse*. The other sides are called *legs*.

The Pythagorean theorem states that for every right triangle, the sum of the squares of the legs equals the square of the hypotenuse: $a^2 + b^2 = c^2$.

EXAMPLE 6

How far from the base of a building should a painter place a 17-ft ladder so that it reaches 15 ft up the building?

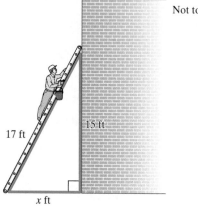

Not to scale

17 ft   15 ft

x ft

SOLUTION Let x represent the distance from the base of the building to the bottom of the ladder. Note that the ladder, the ground, and the building form a right triangle. Using the Pythagorean theorem, we get:

$$a^2 + b^2 = c^2$$
$$x^2 + 15^2 = 17^2$$
$$x^2 + 225 = 289$$
$$x^2 - 64 = 0$$
$$(x - 8)(x + 8) = 0$$
$$x - 8 = 0 \quad \text{or} \quad x + 8 = 0$$
$$x = 8 \qquad\qquad x = -8$$

Since x represents a distance, we consider only the positive value of x, namely, 8.

CHECK Substitute 8 for x.

$$x^2 + 15^2 = 17^2$$
$$8^2 + 15^2 \stackrel{?}{=} 17^2$$
$$64 + 225 \stackrel{?}{=} 289$$
$$289 = 289 \qquad \text{True.}$$

So the painter should place the ladder 8 ft from the base of the building.

PRACTICE 6

Two scooters, traveling at constant rates, leave an intersection at the same time. One scooter travels north while the other travels east. When the scooter traveling east has gone 5 mi, the distance between the two scooters is 13 mi. How far has the scooter going north traveled?

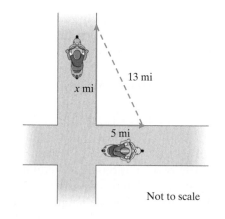

13 mi

x mi

5 mi

Not to scale

Exercises 6.5

FOR EXTRA HELP

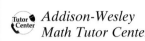

📖 *Student's Solutions Manual*

📞 *Addison-Wesley Math Tutor Center*

🚪 *MyMathLab*

📼 *Videotape 6/DVT 6*

Indicate whether each equation is linear or quadratic.

1. $x^2 - 3x + 2 = 0$

2. $x^2 = 6x$

3. $(x + 3)(x - 4) = x^2$

4. $\dfrac{x + 1}{4} = 2$

5. $2x^2 + 12x = -10$

6. $(x + 4)(x - 1) = 14$

Solve.

7. $(x + 3)(x - 4) = 0$

8. $(x - 2)(x - 1) = 0$

9. $y(3y + 5) = 0$

10. $2y(5y - 4) = 0$

11. $(2t + 1)(t - 5) = 0$

12. $(t - 3)(3t - 1) = 0$

13. $(2x + 3)(2x - 3) = 0$

14. $(5 - 4x)(5 + 4x) = 0$

15. $t(2 - 3t) = 0$

16. $t(1 + 2t) = 0$

17. $y^2 - 2y = 0$

18. $y^2 + 3y = 0$

19. $5x - 25x^2 = 0$

20. $3t + 6t^2 = 0$

21. $x^2 + 5x + 6 = 0$

22. $x^2 + x - 2 = 0$

23. $x^2 + x - 56 = 0$

24. $y^2 - y - 90 = 0$

25. $2x^2 - 5x - 3 = 0$

26. $2y^2 + 5y - 12 = 0$

27. $6x^2 - x - 2 = 0$

28. $4t^2 - 8t + 3 = 0$

29. $0 = 36x^2 - 12x + 1$

30. $0 = 25y^2 + 10y + 1$

31. $r^2 - 121 = 0$

32. $t^2 - 49 = 0$

33. $0 = (2x - 3)^2$

34. $0 = (4x + 1)^2$

35. $16x^2 - 16x + 4 = 0$

36. $9t^2 + 18t + 9 = 0$

37. $9m^2 + 15m - 6 = 0$

38. $6n^2 - 32n + 10 = 0$

39. $r^2 - r = 6$

40. $r^2 + 3r = 10$

41. $y^2 - 7y = -12$

42. $y^2 - y = 12$

43. $n^2 + 2n = 8$

44. $t^2 - 3t = 18$

45. $3y^2 + 4y = -1$

46. $3k^2 + 17k = -10$

47. $4x^2 + 6x = -2$

48. $12x^2 + 33x = 9$

49. $2n^2 = -10n$

50. $3m^2 = 6m$

51. $4x^2 = 1$

52. $9y^2 = 16$

53. $8y^2 = 2$

54. $12x^2 = 48$

55. $3r^2 + 6r = 2r^2 - 9$

56. $5n^2 + 36 = 12n + 4n^2$

57. $x(x - 1) = 12$

58. $r(r + 3) = 10$

59. $4t(t - 1) = 24$

60. $2n(n + 7) = -24$

61. $(y + 3)(y - 2) = 14$

62. $(m - 6)(m + 1) = -10$

63. $(3n - 2)(n + 5) = -14$

64. $(t - 5)(t + 2) = 18$

65. $(n + 2)(n + 4) = 12n$

66. $(3x + 5)(x - 1) = 16x$

67. $3x(2x - 5) = x^2 - 10$

68. $n^2 + 8 = 3n(n - 2)$

Applications

Solve.

69. In a certain league, the teams play each other twice in a season. It can be shown that if there are n teams in the league, the teams must play $n^2 - n$ games. If the league plays 210 games in a season, how many teams were in the league?

70. The number of ways to pair n students in a physics lab can be represented by the expression $\frac{1}{2}n(n - 1)$. If there are 325 different ways to pair students, how many students are in the lab?

71. Two cars leave an intersection, one traveling west and the other south. After some time, the faster car is 2 mi farther away from the intersection than the slower car. At that time, the two cars are 10 mi apart. How far did each car travel?

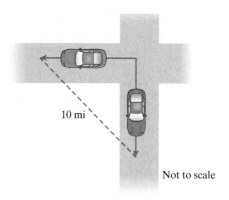

10 mi

Not to scale

72. The sail on a sailboat is a right triangle in which the hypotenuse is called the leech. A 12-ft tall mainsail has a leech length of 13 ft. If sailcloth costs $10 per square foot, what is the cost of a new mainsail?

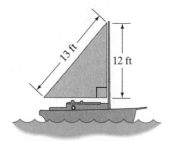

13 ft

12 ft

73. A bedroom is rectangular in shape, with length 4 ft more than its width. The area of the bedroom is 192 sq ft. Find the width and length of the room.

74. Suppose that you invested $8000 in a high-risk growth fund that after two years was worth $12,500. Your broker used the equation $8000(1 + r)^2 = 12,500$ to find the average annual rate of return. What is this rate?

75. A diver jumps from a diving board 24 ft above a pool. After t sec, the diver's height h above the water (in feet) is given by the expression $-16t^2 + 8t + 24$. In how many seconds will the diver hit the water ($h = 0$)?

76. The formula $h = v_0t - 16t^2$ gives the height h in feet of an object after t sec. Here, v_0 is the initial velocity of the object expressed in feet per second. Suppose a toy rocket was launched from the ground straight up with an initial velocity of 64 ft/sec. How many seconds after launch was the rocket 48 ft above the ground?

● *Check your answers on page A-27.*

Mindstretchers

MATHEMATICAL REASONING

1. Give an example of an equation:

a. whose solutions are 2 and 3. _____

b. whose only solution is 5. _____

c. whose solutions have opposite signs. _____

d. whose solutions are 2, 3, and 4. _____

TECHNOLOGY

2. Consider the quadratic equation $x^2 - 3x - 10 = 0$.

a. Solve this equation. _____

b. On a calculator or a computer, graph $y = x^2 - 3x - 10$. Use the graph to find the x-intercepts. _____

c. Explain how you can use these intercepts to solve the original equation $x^2 - 3x - 10 = 0$.

_____

_____

WRITING

3. Explain whether the zero-product property is true for more than two factors.

_____

_____

_____

Key Concepts and Skills

CONCEPT/SKILL	DESCRIPTION	EXAMPLE
[6.1] Common Factor of Two or More Integers	An integer that is a factor of each integer.	5 is a common factor of 15 and 50.
[6.1] Greatest Common Factor (GCF) of Two or More Integers	The greatest integer that is a factor of each integer.	The GCF of 45, 63, and 81 is 9.
[6.1] Greatest Common Factor (GCF) of Two or More Monomials	The product of the greatest common factor of the coefficients and the highest powers of the variable factors common to each monomial.	The GCF of $6x^4$, $8x^3$, and $12x^2$ is $2x^2$.
[6.1] Factoring By Grouping	Group pairs of terms and factor out a GCF in each group, if necessary. Then factor out the common binomial factor.	$xy + x - 4y - 4$ $= (xy + x) + (-4y - 4)$ $= x(y + 1) - 4(y + 1)$ $= (y + 1)(x - 4)$
[6.2] Factoring a Trinomial of the Form $ax^2 + bx + c$, Where $a = 1$	List and test the factors of c to find two integers for $(x + ?)(x + ?)$ whose product is c and whose sum is b.	$x^2 - 8x + 12 =$ $(x - 2)(x - 6)$ because

Factors of 12

$\overbrace{}$ $(-2) \cdot (-6) = 12$ and $(-2) + (-6) = -8$ $\underbrace{}$

Sum of factors |
| **[6.3] Factoring a Trinomial $ax^2 + bx + c$, Where $a \neq 1$ (Trial-and-Error Method)** | • List and test the factors of a and of c to find four integers for $(?x + ?)(?x + ?)$ so that the product of the leading coefficients of the binomial factors is a, the product of the constant terms of the binomial factors is c, and the coefficients of the inner and outer products add up to b. | $2x^2 + 15x + 7$ $= (2x + 1)(x + 7)$ because $2 \cdot 1 = 2,$ $1 \cdot 7 = 7,$ and $2 \cdot 7 + 1 \cdot 7 = 15.$ |
| **[6.3] Factoring a Trinomial $ax^2 + bx + c$, Where $a \neq 1$ (*ac* Method)** | • Form the product ac.
• Find two factors of ac that add up to b.
• Use these factors to split up the middle term in the original trinomial.
• Group the first two terms and the last two terms.
• From each group, factor out the common factor.
• Factor out the common binomial factor. | For $2x^2 + 15x + 7$, $ac = 2 \cdot 7 = 14$ $1 \cdot 14 = 14$ and $1 + 14 = 15$ $2x^2 + 15x + 7$ $= 2x^2 + x + 14x + 7$ $= (2x^2 + x) + (14x + 7)$ $= x(2x + 1) + 7(2x + 1)$ $= (2x + 1)(x + 7)$ |

continued

= CONCEPT = SKILL

CONCEPT/SKILL	DESCRIPTION	EXAMPLE
[6.4] **Factoring a Perfect Square Trinomial**	$a^2 + 2ab + b^2 = (a + b)^2$ $a^2 - 2ab + b^2 = (a - b)^2$	$x^2 + 12x + 36 = (x + 6)^2$ $x^2 - 6x + 9 = (x - 3)^2$
[6.4] **Factoring the Difference of Squares**	$a^2 - b^2 = (a + b)(a - b)$	$x^2 - 100 = (x + 10)(x - 10)$
[6.5] **Second-degree or Quadratic Equation**	An equation that can be written in the form $ax^2 + bx + c = 0$, where a, b, and c are real numbers and $a \neq 0$.	$x^2 - x + 6 = 0$
[6.5] **The Zero-Product Property**	If $ab = 0$, then $a = 0$ or $b = 0$, or both a and $b = 0$.	If $x(3x - 1) = 0$, then either $x = 0$ or $3x - 1 = 0$.
[6.5] **To Solve a Quadratic Equation by Factoring**	• If necessary, rewrite the equation in standard form with 0 on one side. • Factor the other side. • Use the zero-product property to get two simple linear equations. • Solve the linear equations. • Check by substituting the solutions in the original quadratic equation.	$x(x - 3) = 4$ $x^2 - 3x - 4 = 0$ $(x - 4)(x + 1) = 0$ $x - 4 = 0$ or $x + 1 = 0$ $x = 4$ $\quad$ $x = -1$ CHECK Substitute 4 for x. $4(4 - 3) \stackrel{?}{=} 4$ $4(1) \stackrel{?}{=} 4$ $4 = 4$ True. Substitute -1 for x. $(-1)(-1 - 3) \stackrel{?}{=} 4$ $(-1)(-4) \stackrel{?}{=} 4$ $4 = 4$ True.

Chapter 6 Review Exercises

To help you review this chapter, solve these problems.

[6.1]

1. Find the greatest common factor of 48, 36, and 60.

2. Find the greatest common factor of $9m^3n$, $24m^4$, and $15m^2n^2$.

Factor.

3. $3x - 6y$ **4.** $16p^3q^2 + 18p^2q - 4pq^2$ **5.** $(n - 1) + n(n - 1)$ **6.** $xb - 5b - 2x + 10$

Solve for the indicated variable.

7. $d = rt_1 + rt_2$ for r **8.** $ax + y = bx + c$ for x

[6.2]

Factor, if possible.

9. $x^2 + x + 1$ **10.** $m^2 - m + 3$ **11.** $y^2 + 42 + 13y$

12. $m^2 - 7mn + 10n^2$ **13.** $24 - 8x - 2x^2$ **14.** $-15xy^2 + 3x^3 - 12x^2y$

[6.3]

Factor, if possible.

15. $3x^2 + 5x - 2$ **16.** $5n^2 + 13n + 6$ **17.** $3n^2 - n - 1$

18. $6x^2 - x - 12$ **19.** $2a^2 + 3ab - 35b^2$ **20.** $16a - 4a^2 - 15$

21. $9y^3 - 21y + 60y^2$ **22.** $2p^2q - 3pq^2 - 2q^3$

[6.4]

Factor, if possible.

23. $b^2 - 6b + 9$ **24.** $64 - x^2$ **25.** $25y^2 - 20y + 4$

26. $9a^2 + 24ab + 16b^2$ **27.** $81p^2 - 100q^2$ **28.** $4x^8 - 28x^4 + 49$

29. $48x^4 - 3y^4$ **30.** $x^2(x - 1) - 9(x - 1)$

[6.5]

Solve.

31. $(x + 2)(x - 1) = 0$ **32.** $t(t - 4) = 0$ **33.** $3x^2 + 18x = 0$ **34.** $4x^2 + 4x + 1 = 0$

35. $y^2 - 10y = -16$ **36.** $3k^2 - k = 2$ **37.** $4n(2n + 3) = 20$ **38.** $(y - 1)(y + 2) = 10$

Mixed Applications

Solve.

39. The length of an object varies with its temperature. The expression $aLt_2 - aLt_1$ represents the change in the length of an object heated to temperature t_2, where L is its length at temperature t_1 and a is the *coefficient of linear expansion*, a constant that depends on the material that the object is made of. Write this expression in factored form.

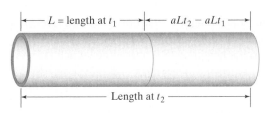

40. If a ball is thrown straight upward at a ft/sec, its height above the point of release is given by the expression $at - 16t^2$, where t is the number of seconds after release. Write an expression in factored form for the distance between the object's location at t_1 and at t_2.

41. Find the distance between the two intersections shown on the city grid pictured if each block is 500 ft long.

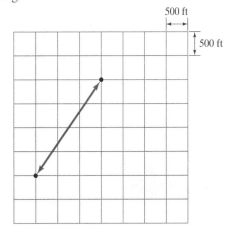

42. A kite maker designs the diamond-shaped kite shown. The diagonals of the kite cross at right angles. The vertical diagonal is 52 in. long. What is the length of the horizontal diagonal of the kite shown?

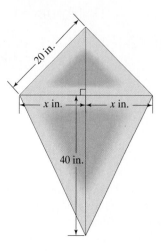

43. After t sec, the height of a rocket launched straight upward from ground level with an initial velocity of 76 ft/sec can be modeled by the polynomial $76t - 16t^2$. After how many seconds will the rocket reach a height of 18 ft above the launch (that is, equal to $+18$)?

44. The formula for the area of the trapezoid shown is $A = \frac{1}{2}hb + \frac{1}{2}hB$. Solve this formula for h in terms of A, b, and B.

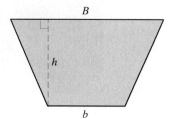

• *Check your answers on page A-27.*

Chapter 6 Posttest

To see whether you have mastered the topics in this chapter, take this test.

1. Find the greatest common factor of $12x^3$ and $15x^2$.

Factor.

2. $2xy - 14y$

3. $6pq^2 + 8p^3 - 16p^2q$

4. $ax - bx + by - ay$

5. $n^2 - 13n - 48$

6. $-8 + x^2 - 2x$

7. $15x^2 - 5x^3 + 20x$

8. $4x^2 + 13xy - 12y^2$

9. $-12x^2 + 36x - 27$

10. $9x^2 + 30xy + 25y^2$

11. $121 - 4x^2$

12. $p^2q^2 - 1$

13. $y^4 - 8y^2 + 16$

Solve.

14. $(n + 8)(n - 1) = 0$

15. $6x^2 + 10x = 4$

16. $(2n + 1)(n - 1) = 5$

17. In the right triangle shown, find the length of the missing side.

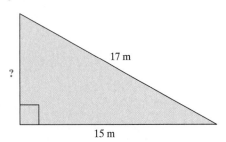

18. The energy it takes to lift an object of mass m from level y_1 to level y_2 is $mgy_2 - mgy_1$, where g is a constant. Factor this expression.

19. In a physics experiment, a weight is dropped from a platform 9 ft above the ground. The time t in seconds it takes the weight to reach the ground may be found by solving the equation $9 - 16t^2 = 0$. Solve for t.

20. A rectangular garden measures 25 ft by 30 ft. The gardener wishes to surround the garden with a border of mulch x feet wide, as shown.

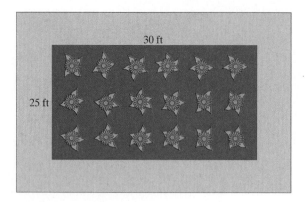

Write an expression in factored form for the area of the mulch border in terms of x.

● *Check your answers on page A-27.*

To help you review, solve the following:

1. Evaluate $2x + y - z$ if $x = -4$, $y = 0$, and $z = -5$.

2. Simplify: $5a + 2 - 2b + 3a + 9b$

3. Solve: $z + 4 = 5z - 2(z + 6)$

4. Graph the line $4x - 3y = 12$ on a coordinate plane.

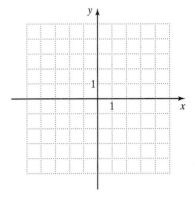

5. Solve the system:

$$\begin{aligned} \textbf{(1)} \quad & x + y = 6 \\ \textbf{(2)} \quad & y = 2x + 9 \end{aligned}$$

6. Simplify: $\dfrac{n^2 \cdot n^3 \cdot n}{n^5}$

7. Find the product: $(3x + 1)(7x - 2)$

8. A part-time college student pays a student fee of f dollars plus c dollars per credit. What is the charge for a student with an 8-credit schedule?

9. The owner of a shirt factory has fixed expenses of $500 per day. It costs the factory $15 to produce each shirt. If the shirts are sold wholesale at $25 apiece, how many shirts must be sold per day to break even?

10. An expression for the total surface area of a tin can is $2\pi r^2 + 2\pi rh$, where r is the radius and h is the height of the can. Rewrite this expression in factored form.

• *Check your answers on page A-27.*

Chapter 7

Rational Expressions and Equations

Rational Expressions and Grapes

Science plays a role in viticulture—the art of growing grapes. For instance, scientists have used DNA fingerprinting—the same technique used in paternity suits and criminal trials—to trace the parentage of numerous grape varieties.

Viticulture also makes use of algebra. Since much of the flavor and color of grapes is in their skin, wine growers want to raise grapes with an increased surface-to-volume ratio. This ratio is larger for smaller grapes, which have proportionately more skin than larger grapes.

We can see why this is true by assuming that a grape is approximately a sphere of radius r. The ratio of a sphere's surface area to its volume is represented by the rational expression $\dfrac{4\pi r^2}{\frac{4}{3}\pi r^3}$, which simplifies to $\dfrac{3}{r}$. Substituting smaller values for the radius r in this expression gives larger values of the expression. Thus, the smaller the grape is, the larger the surface-to-volume ratio.

(**Source:** David L. Wheeler, "Scholars Marry the Science and the Art of Winemaking," *Chronicle of Higher Education*, May 30, 1997)

529

To see if you have already mastered the topics in this chapter, take this test.

1. Identify the values for which the rational expression $\dfrac{5}{x+6}$ is undefined.

2. Show that the rational expressions $\dfrac{n^2-2n}{3n}$ and $\dfrac{n-2}{3}$ are equivalent.

Simplify.

3. $\dfrac{24x^2y^3}{6xy^5}$

4. $\dfrac{4a^2-8a}{a-2}$

5. $\dfrac{w^2-6w}{36-w^2}$

6. $\dfrac{\frac{5n}{8}}{\frac{n^3}{16}}$

7. Write $\dfrac{2}{3a}$ and $\dfrac{1}{9a-18}$ in terms of their LCD.

Perform the indicated operation.

8. $\dfrac{12y}{y+1}-\dfrac{7y+2}{y+1}$

9. $\dfrac{1}{6x^2}+\dfrac{5}{4x}$

10. $\dfrac{3}{c-3}-\dfrac{1}{c+3}$

11. $\dfrac{1}{x^2-2x+1}-\dfrac{2}{1-x^2}$

12. $\dfrac{15a^3b}{20n^4}\cdot\dfrac{16n^2}{9ab}$

13. $\dfrac{y-4}{5y^2+10y}\cdot\dfrac{y^2-2y-8}{y^2-16}$

14. $\dfrac{x^2-x-2}{x^2+5x+4}\div\dfrac{x^2-7x+10}{x-5}$

Solve and check.

15. $\dfrac{3x-8}{x^2-4}+\dfrac{2}{x-2}=\dfrac{7}{x+2}$

16. $\dfrac{x}{x+4}-1=\dfrac{2}{x-1}$

17. $\dfrac{9}{2x}=\dfrac{x}{x-1}$

Solve.

18. An ice cream company has fixed costs of $1500 and variable costs of $2 for each gallon of ice cream it produces. The cost per gallon of producing x gallons of ice cream is given by the expression $2 + \dfrac{1500}{x}$. Write this cost as a single rational expression.

19. On the first part of a 360-mi trip, a family drives 195 mi at an average speed of r mph. They drive the remainder of the trip at an average speed that is 10 mph less than their speed during the first part of the trip. If the entire trip took 6 hr, what was the average speed during each part of the trip?

20. It takes a photocopier t min to make 30 copies. If at the same rate it takes 5 min longer to make 90 copies, how long does it take the photocopier to make 30 copies?

• *Check your answers on page A-27.*

7.1 Rational Expressions

What Rational Expressions Are and Why They Are Important

In this chapter, we move beyond our previous discussion of polynomials to consider a broader type of algebraic expression, the *rational* expression. Rational expressions, sometimes called *algebraic fractions*, are useful in many disciplines, including the sciences, the social sciences, medicine, and business.

For instance, the work of some anthropologists who study the history of the human species involves rational expressions. In studying a fossil record, anthropologists examine ancient skulls and compute $\dfrac{100W}{L}$, the ratio of each skull's width W to its length L. This expression is an example of a rational expression.

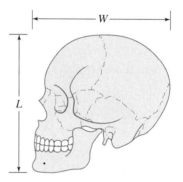

In this chapter, we discuss how to simplify rational expressions, as well as how to carry out operations on rational expressions. We also focus on how to solve equations involving rational expressions.

Introduction to Rational Expressions

Rational expressions in algebra are similar to fractions in arithmetic. In arithmetic, a fraction such as $\dfrac{3}{4}$ is the quotient of two integers, whereas in algebra, a rational expression such as $\dfrac{100W}{L}$ is the quotient of two polynomials.

> **Definition**
>
> A **rational expression**, $\dfrac{P}{Q}$, is an algebraic expression that can be written as the quotient of two polynomials, P and Q, where $Q \neq 0$.

Other examples of rational expressions are:

$$\frac{5}{x-2} \qquad \frac{n^2+2n-1}{n+1} \qquad \frac{-a^2}{7bc}$$

A rational expression can be written in terms of division. For example,

$$\frac{5}{x-2} \text{ can be written as } 5 \div (x-2), \text{ and}$$

$$\frac{n^2 + 2n - 1}{n + 1} \text{ can be written as } (n^2 + 2n - 1) \div (n + 1).$$

Since we can write a rational expression as division, we must be sure that its denominator does not equal 0. When a variable is replaced with a value that makes the denominator 0, the rational expression is undefined.

For instance, consider the rational expression $\frac{5}{x-2}$. For what values of x is this expression undefined? Setting the denominator $x - 2$ equal to 0, we get:

$$x - 2 = 0$$
$$x = 2$$

When x is replaced with 2 in the rational expression, we get:

$$\frac{5}{x-2} = \frac{5}{2-2} = \frac{5}{0} \quad \leftarrow \text{Undefined}$$

So $\frac{5}{x-2}$ is undefined when x is equal to 2.

EXAMPLE 1

Identify all numbers for which the following rational expressions are undefined.

a. $\dfrac{3}{x+5}$ **b.** $\dfrac{8x}{x^2 - 3x + 2}$

SOLUTION We find the values for which the rational expressions are undefined by setting each denominator equal to 0. Then we solve for x.

a. $\dfrac{3}{x+5}$

$$x + 5 = 0$$
$$x = -5$$

So $\dfrac{3}{x+5}$ is undefined when x is equal to -5.

b. $\dfrac{8x}{x^2 - 3x + 2}$

$$x^2 - 3x + 2 = 0$$
$$(x - 2)(x - 1) = 0 \qquad \text{Factor.}$$
$$x - 2 = 0 \quad \text{or} \quad x - 1 = 0 \qquad \text{Set each factor equal to 0.}$$
$$x = 2 \qquad\qquad x = 1 \qquad \text{Solve for } x.$$

So $\dfrac{8x}{x^2 - 3x + 2}$ is undefined when x is equal to 1 or 2.

PRACTICE 1

Indicate the values of the variable for which each rational expression is undefined.

a. $\dfrac{n+1}{n-3}$

b. $\dfrac{6}{n^2 - 9}$

Note that throughout the following discussion, we assume that all rational expressions are defined.

Equivalent Expressions

Recall from Chapter R that equivalent fractions, such as $\frac{1}{2}$ and $\frac{3}{6}$, are fractions that have the same value even though they are written differently. Similarly, equivalent rational expressions are rational expressions that have the same value, no matter what value replaces the variable.

To Find an Equivalent Rational Expression

Multiply the numerator and denominator of $\dfrac{P}{Q}$ by the same polynomial R.

$$\frac{P}{Q} = \frac{PR}{QR},$$

where $Q \neq 0$ and $R \neq 0$.

The rule for finding an equivalent rational expression allows us to multiply the numerator and denominator of a rational expression by the same nonzero polynomial.

EXAMPLE 2

Indicate whether each pair of rational expressions is equivalent.

a. $\dfrac{2}{3}$ and $\dfrac{2x}{3x}$

b. $\dfrac{d-5}{3}$ and $\dfrac{4d^2-20d}{12d}$

SOLUTION

a. If we *multiply* both the numerator and denominator of $\dfrac{2}{3}$ by x, we see that $\dfrac{2}{3} = \dfrac{2x}{3x}$. So the expressions $\dfrac{2}{3}$ and $\dfrac{2x}{3x}$ are equivalent.

b. If we *multiply* both the numerator and denominator of $\dfrac{d-5}{3}$ by $4d$, we get:

$$\frac{(d-5)\cdot 4d}{3\cdot 4d} = \frac{4d^2-20d}{12d}$$

So $\dfrac{d-5}{3}$ and $\dfrac{4d^2-20d}{12d}$ are equivalent.

PRACTICE 2

Determine whether each pair of rational expressions is equivalent.

a. $\dfrac{b}{3}$ and $\dfrac{3b^2}{9b}$

b. $\dfrac{5}{a+7}$ and $\dfrac{5a}{a^2+7a}$

Note that we can also use the rule to find an equivalent rational expression by dividing the numerator and denominator of the rational expression by the same nonzero polynomial.

$$\frac{x^2 - 4}{x^2 + 5x + 6} = \frac{(x - 2)(x + 2)}{(x + 3)(x + 2)} \qquad \text{Factor the numerator and denominator.}$$

$$= \frac{(x - 2)\overset{1}{\cancel{(x + 2)}}}{(x + 3)\underset{1}{\cancel{(x + 2)}}} \qquad \text{Divide out the common factor } (x + 2).$$

$$= \frac{x - 2}{x + 3}$$

So $\dfrac{x^2 - 4}{x^2 + 5x + 6}$ is equivalent to $\dfrac{x - 2}{x + 3}$.

A rational expression is said to be *in simplest form* (or *reduced to lowest terms*) when its numerator and denominator have no common factor other than 1 or -1. Throughout the remainder of this book, we generally simplify any answer that is a rational expression. Can you explain the similarities and differences in simplifying a fraction in arithmetic and simplifying a rational expression in algebra?

To Simplify a Rational Expression
- Factor the numerator and denominator.
- Divide out any common factors.

EXAMPLE 3

Write in simplest form.

a. $\dfrac{10x^2}{-5xy}$

b. $\dfrac{-4a^3b^2}{-2ab}$

SOLUTION

a. $\dfrac{10x^2}{-5xy} = \dfrac{5x(2x)}{5x(-y)} \qquad \text{Factor the numerator and denominator.}$

$\qquad = \dfrac{\overset{1}{\cancel{5x}}(2x)}{\underset{1}{\cancel{5x}}(-y)} \qquad \text{Divide out the common factor } 5x.$

$\qquad = -\dfrac{2x}{y} \qquad \text{Simplify.}$

b. $\dfrac{-4a^3b^2}{-2ab} = \dfrac{-2ab(2a^2b)}{-2ab}$

$\qquad = \dfrac{\overset{1}{\cancel{-2ab}}(2a^2b)}{\underset{1}{\cancel{-2ab}}}$

$\qquad = 2a^2b$

PRACTICE 3

Express in lowest terms.

a. $\dfrac{-12n^3}{-6mn}$

b. $\dfrac{-3x^4y}{2x^2y}$

EXAMPLE 4

Write in simplest form, if possible.

a. $\dfrac{3x - 6}{9x + 12}$

b. $\dfrac{n + 3}{2n + 6}$

c. $\dfrac{t + 3}{t - 1}$

SOLUTION

a. $\dfrac{3x - 6}{9x + 12} = \dfrac{3(x - 2)}{3(3x + 4)}$ Factor the numerator and the denominator.

$= \dfrac{\overset{1}{\cancel{3}}(x - 2)}{\underset{1}{\cancel{3}}(3x + 4)}$ Divide out the common factor 3.

$= \dfrac{x - 2}{3x + 4}$

b. $\dfrac{n + 3}{2n + 6} = \dfrac{n + 3}{2(n + 3)}$ Factor the denominator.

$= \dfrac{\overset{1}{\cancel{n + 3}}}{2(\underset{1}{\cancel{n + 3}})}$ Divide out the common factor $n + 3$.

$= \dfrac{1}{2}$

c. $\dfrac{t + 3}{t - 1}$ The numerator $t + 3$ and the denominator $t - 1$ have no common factor (other than 1). This expression cannot be simplified.

PRACTICE 4

Rewrite in lowest terms.

a. $\dfrac{2y - 8}{4y + 6}$

b. $\dfrac{v - 4}{v + 3}$

c. $\dfrac{x + 2}{3x + 6}$

TIP When simplifying a rational expression, do not divide out common terms in a sum or difference in the numerator and denominator of the expression. For instance, do not divide out the x's in $\dfrac{x + 2}{x - 3}$.

EXAMPLE 5

Simplify.

a. $\dfrac{ab - ac}{ax + 2ay}$ **b.** $\dfrac{2t^2 - 2}{t^2 + t - 2}$ **c.** $\dfrac{3x^2 + 2x - 1}{3x^2 - 4x + 1}$

SOLUTION

a. $\dfrac{ab - ac}{ax + 2ay} = \dfrac{a(b - c)}{a(x + 2y)}$

$= \dfrac{\overset{1}{\cancel{a}}(b - c)}{\underset{1}{\cancel{a}}(x + 2y)}$

$= \dfrac{b - c}{x + 2y}$

PRACTICE 5

Simplify.

a. $\dfrac{wt - wx}{wz - 3wg}$

b. $\dfrac{4n^2 - 4}{n^2 + 3n + 2}$

c. $\dfrac{2y^2 - y - 1}{2y^2 + 7y + 3}$

b. $\dfrac{2t^2 - 2}{t^2 + t - 2} = \dfrac{2(t^2 - 1)}{(t - 1)(t + 2)}$

$= \dfrac{2(t - 1)(t + 1)}{(t - 1)(t + 2)}$

$= \dfrac{2(\overset{1}{\cancel{t - 1}})(t + 1)}{(\underset{1}{\cancel{t - 1}})(t + 2)}$

$= \dfrac{2(t + 1)}{t + 2}$

c. $\dfrac{3x^2 + 2x - 1}{3x^2 - 4x + 1} = \dfrac{(3x - 1)(x + 1)}{(3x - 1)(x - 1)}$

$= \dfrac{(\overset{1}{\cancel{3x - 1}})(x + 1)}{(\underset{1}{\cancel{3x - 1}})(x - 1)}$

$= \dfrac{x + 1}{x - 1}$

The following examples involve factors such as $a - b$ and $b - a$ that are opposites of each other; that is, they differ only in sign. Recall that since

$(-1)(a - b) = b - a$, it follows that $\dfrac{a - b}{b - a} = -1$ because

$\dfrac{a - b}{b - a} = \dfrac{\overset{1}{\cancel{(a - b)}}}{-1\underset{1}{\cancel{(a - b)}}} = \dfrac{1}{-1} = -1.$

EXAMPLE 6	PRACTICE 6
Write in lowest terms.	Simplify.

EXAMPLE 6

Write in lowest terms.

a. $\dfrac{s - 5}{5 - s}$

b. $\dfrac{2p - 10}{-p + 5}$

c. $\dfrac{3x - 6}{4 - x^2}$

d. $\dfrac{1 - x^2}{x^2 - 3x + 2}$

SOLUTION

a. $\dfrac{s - 5}{5 - s} = \dfrac{s - 5}{-1(s - 5)}$ Write $5 - s$ as $-1(s - 5)$.

$= \dfrac{\overset{1}{\cancel{s - 5}}}{-1(\underset{1}{\cancel{s - 5}})}$ Divide out the common factor $s - 5$.

$= \dfrac{1}{-1}$ Simplify.

$= -1$

b. $\dfrac{2p - 10}{-p + 5} = \dfrac{2(p - 5)}{-1(p - 5)} = \dfrac{2(\overset{1}{\cancel{p - 5}})}{-1(\underset{1}{\cancel{p - 5}})} = \dfrac{2}{-1} = -2$

PRACTICE 6

Simplify.

a. $\dfrac{-y - 1}{1 + y}$

b. $\dfrac{3x - 12}{-x + 4}$

c. $\dfrac{3n - 15}{25 - n^2}$

d. $\dfrac{4 - 9s^2}{3s^2 + s - 2}$

c. $\dfrac{3x - 6}{4 - x^2} = \dfrac{3(x - 2)}{(2 - x)(2 + x)}$ Factor the numerator and denominator.

$= \dfrac{3(x - 2)}{-1(x - 2)(2 + x)}$ Write $(2 - x)$ as $-1(x - 2)$.

$= \dfrac{3(\overset{1}{\cancel{x - 2}})}{-\cancel{(x - 2)}(2 + x)}$ Divide out the common factor $(x - 2)$

$= -\dfrac{3}{x + 2}$ Simplify.

d. $\dfrac{1 - x^2}{x^2 - 3x + 2} = \dfrac{(1 + x)(1 - x)}{(x - 2)(x - 1)} = \dfrac{-(x + 1)(x - 1)}{(x - 2)(x - 1)}$

$= \dfrac{-(x + 1)(\overset{1}{\cancel{x - 1}})}{(x - 2)\cancel{(x - 1)}} = -\dfrac{x + 1}{x - 2}$

EXAMPLE 7

It costs a television manufacturer $\dfrac{95x + 10,000}{x}$ dollars per televisions to produce x televisions.

a. For which value of x is this rational expression undefined?

b. Explain in a sentence or two why you think that it makes sense for the cost per television to be undefined for the value of x found in part (a).

SOLUTION

a. A rational expression is undefined when its denominator is equal to 0. For the expression $\dfrac{95x + 10,000}{x}$, the denominator is 0 when $x = 0$.

b. When $x = 0$, the manufacturer is producing *no* television sets. So it makes no sense to speak of the cost per machine.

PRACTICE 7

For a circle of radius r, the ratio of its area to its circumference is given by the expression $\dfrac{\pi r^2}{2 \pi r}$.

a. Simplify this expression.

b. For which value of r is the original rational expression undefined?

Exercises 7.1

FOR EXTRA HELP

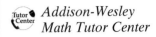

Student's Solutions Manual

Addison-Wesley Math Tutor Center

MyMathLab

Videotape 7/DVT 7

Identify the values for which the given rational expression is undefined.

1. $\dfrac{7}{x}$

2. $\dfrac{-2}{c}$

3. $\dfrac{8}{y-2}$

4. $\dfrac{4}{x+2}$

5. $\dfrac{x-3}{x+5}$

6. $\dfrac{y-6}{y-1}$

7. $\dfrac{n+11}{2n-1}$

8. $\dfrac{x-4}{3x-2}$

9. $\dfrac{x^2+1}{x^2-1}$

10. $\dfrac{n+2}{n^2-16}$

11. $\dfrac{x^2+x+1}{x^2-x-20}$

12. $\dfrac{p^2+7}{p^2-4p-21}$

Indicate whether each pair of rational expressions is equivalent.

13. $\dfrac{p}{q}$ and $\dfrac{pr}{qr}$

14. $\dfrac{8}{3y}$ and $\dfrac{16}{6y}$

15. $\dfrac{3t+5}{t+1}$ and $\dfrac{3t^2+5t}{t^2+t}$

16. $\dfrac{2x-1}{x-4}$ and $\dfrac{14x-7}{7x-28}$

17. $\dfrac{x-1}{x+3}$ and $-\dfrac{1}{3}$

18. $\dfrac{n+4}{2n+4}$ and $\dfrac{1}{2}$

19. $\dfrac{x-2}{2-x}$ and $\dfrac{2-x}{x-2}$

20. $\dfrac{y-x}{y+x}$ and $\dfrac{y+x}{y-x}$

21. $\dfrac{x^2+4}{x+2}$ and $x+2$

22. $\dfrac{(y+5)^2}{y+5}$ and $y+5$

Simplify.

23. $\dfrac{10a^4}{12a}$

24. $\dfrac{4b}{6b^3}$

25. $\dfrac{3x^2}{12x^5}$

26. $\dfrac{-2y^6}{2y^4}$

27. $\dfrac{9s^3t^2}{6s^5t}$

28. $\dfrac{10r^3s^4}{5r^3s^4}$

29. $\dfrac{24a^4b^5}{3ab^2}$

30. $\dfrac{14yz^2}{21y^2z^2}$

31. $\dfrac{-2p^2q^3}{-10pq^4}$

32. $\dfrac{-3t^4s^5}{t^2s}$

33. $\dfrac{5x(x+8)}{4x(x+8)}$

34. $\dfrac{7n(n-1)}{2n(n-1)}$

35. $\dfrac{8x^2(5-2x)}{3x(2x-5)}$

36. $\dfrac{(a-b)ab^2}{3a^3(b-a)}$

37. $\dfrac{5x-10}{5}$

38. $\dfrac{3y+12}{3}$

39. $\dfrac{2x^2+2x}{4x^2+6x}$

40. $\dfrac{7y^3-5y^2}{3y^2+y}$

41. $\dfrac{a^2-4a}{ab-4b}$

42. $\dfrac{a^2+2b}{4b+2a^2}$

43. $\dfrac{6x-4y}{9x-6y}$

44. $\dfrac{10m-2n}{n-5m}$

45. $\dfrac{t^2-1}{t+1}$

46. $\dfrac{b^2-1}{b-1}$

47. $\dfrac{p^2-q^2}{q^2-p^2}$

48. $\dfrac{y^2-4x^2}{4x^2-y^2}$

49. $\dfrac{n-1}{2-2n}$

50. $\dfrac{x-3}{3-x}$

51. $\dfrac{(b-4)^2}{b^2-16}$

52. $\dfrac{m^2-1}{(m+1)^2}$

53. $\dfrac{2x^2+5x-3}{10x-5}$

54. $\dfrac{6p+12}{p^2-p-6}$

55. $\dfrac{a^3+9a^2+14a}{a^2-10a-24}$

56. $\dfrac{x^2+3x-4}{x^2+2x-3}$

57. $\dfrac{t^2-4t-5}{t^2-3t-10}$

58. $\dfrac{y^2+8y+15}{y^2-2y-15}$

59. $\dfrac{9-16d^2}{16d^2-24d+9}$

60. $\dfrac{6n^2+7n-10}{25-36n^2}$

61. $\dfrac{8s-2s^2}{2s^2-11s+12}$

62. $\dfrac{3x^2+2x-1}{12x^2-4x}$

63. $\dfrac{6x^2+5x+1}{6x^2-x-1}$

64. $\dfrac{2n^3+2n^2-4n}{n^3+2n^2-3n}$

65. $\dfrac{6y^2-7y+2}{6y^3+5y^2-6y}$

66. $\dfrac{3x^2+xy}{3x^2+7xy+2y^2}$

67. $\dfrac{2ab^2+4a^2b}{2b^2+5ab+2a^2}$

68. $\dfrac{p^2-4pq-12q^2}{2p^2-15pq+18q^2}$

69. $\dfrac{m^2+3mn-28n^2}{2m^2+4mn-48n^2}$

70. $\dfrac{3a^2+5ab-2b^2}{3a^2+8ab-3b^2}$

Applications

Solve.

71. An expression important in the study of nuclear energy is $\dfrac{mu^2 - mv^2}{mu - mv}$, where m represents mass and u and v represent velocities. Write this expression in simplified form.

72. The force of gravity between two planets is given by the expression $\dfrac{kMm}{d^2}$, where m and M are the masses of the planets, d is the distance between the planets, and k is a fixed constant. Under what circumstances is this force of gravity undefined?

73. When a mathematics department had more faculty and staff members, each had an office with dimensions x ft by x ft. Now that the department has gotten smaller, its offices are being enlarged. Each faculty and each staff office will be made 2 ft wider, whereas each faculty office will also be made 5 ft longer.

    a. Write an expression for the area of an enlarged faculty office.

    b. Write an expression for the area of an enlarged staff office.

    c. Write an expression for the ratio of the area of an enlarged faculty office to the area of an enlarged staff office. Simplify.

    d. Find the value of the expression in part (c) if the length of each office had been 8 ft.

74. The baking time for bread is the ratio of its volume V to its surface area S. For each of the following types of bread, express the ratio $\dfrac{V}{S}$ in simplest form.

    a. A rectangular loaf of bread

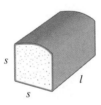

$$V = s^2 l$$
$$S = 2s^2 + 4sl$$

    b. A cylindrical bread stick

$$V = \pi r^2 h$$
$$S = 2\pi r^2 + 2\pi rh$$

75. An archer shoots an arrow at the target shown.

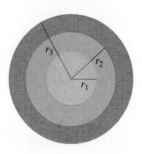

    a. Find and simplify the ratio of the area of the inner circle to the area of the adjacent ring.

    b. Find and simplify the ratio of the area of the smaller ring to the area of the larger ring.

76. A sphere with radius r is packed in a cubic box with side $2r$. The volume of the sphere is $\frac{4}{3}\pi r^3$ and the volume of the box is $(2r)^3$.

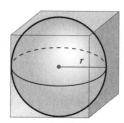

    a. The smaller volume is what fraction of the larger volume? Simplify your answer.

    b. Does the answer to part (a) depend on the value of r?

• *Check your answers on page A-27.*

Mindstretchers

TECHNOLOGY

1. Using a grapher, display the graphs of $y = \dfrac{x^2 - 1}{x - 1}$ and $y = x + 1$ on the same screen. Compare the two graphs. What conclusion can you draw from this comparison?

PATTERNS

2. Some rational expressions, when simplified, are equivalent to polynomials. Check the simplifications of the following rational expressions:

a. $\dfrac{x^2 - 1}{x - 1} = 1 + x$

b. $\dfrac{x^3 - 1}{x - 1} = 1 + x + x^2$

c. $\dfrac{x^4 - 1}{x - 1} = 1 + x + x^2 + x^3$

Identify this pattern and extend it.

WRITING

3. Sometimes, arithmetic fractions are written with a slanted fraction line, as in 3/4, rather than a horizontal fraction line, as in $\dfrac{3}{4}$. In a sentence or two, explain the disadvantage of writing a rational expression such as $\dfrac{x + 2}{x - 3}$ with a slanted fraction line.

_____

_____

_____

_____

7.2 Multiplication and Division of Rational Expressions

Multiplying Rational Expressions

OBJECTIVES

- *To multiply rational expressions*
- *To divide rational expressions*
- *To solve applied problems involving the multiplication or division of rational expressions*

Operations on rational expressions in algebra are similar to those on fractions in arithmetic. For instance, to multiply arithmetic fractions, we multiply their numerators to get the numerator of the product and multiply their denominators to get the denominator of the product.

$$\frac{2}{3} \cdot \frac{5}{7} = \frac{2 \cdot 5}{3 \cdot 7} = \frac{10}{21}$$

In algebra, rational expressions are multiplied in the same way.

$$\frac{2}{a} \cdot \frac{b}{y} = \frac{2b}{ay}$$

Recall from arithmetic that it is often easier to first divide out any common factors and then to multiply the numerators and denominators:

$$\frac{2}{9} \cdot \frac{3}{10} = \frac{\overset{1}{\cancel{2}}}{\underset{3}{\cancel{9}}} \cdot \frac{\overset{1}{\cancel{3}}}{\underset{5}{\cancel{10}}} = \frac{1}{15}$$

Similarly, in algebra:

$$\frac{5a}{b} \cdot \frac{b}{2a^2} = \frac{5\overset{1}{\cancel{a}}}{\cancel{b}} \cdot \frac{\overset{1}{\cancel{b}}}{2\underset{a}{\cancel{a^2}}} = \frac{5}{2a}$$

EXAMPLE 1

Multiply.

a. $\dfrac{3}{x} \cdot \dfrac{5}{x}$

b. $\dfrac{4x^2}{7y^3} \cdot \dfrac{3y}{8x}$

SOLUTION

a. There are no common factors in the numerators and denominators.

$$\frac{3}{x} \cdot \frac{5}{x} = \frac{3 \cdot 5}{x \cdot x} \quad \text{Multiply the numerators and multiply the denominators.}$$

$$= \frac{15}{x^2} \quad \text{Simplify.}$$

b. $\dfrac{4x^2}{7y^3} \cdot \dfrac{3y}{8x} = \dfrac{\overset{1}{\cancel{4}}\overset{x}{\cancel{x^2}}}{7\cancel{y^3}} \cdot \dfrac{\overset{1}{\cancel{3}}\cancel{y}}{\underset{2}{\cancel{8}}\cancel{x}}$ Divide out all common factors in the numerators and denominators.

$$= \frac{x \cdot 3}{7y^2 \cdot 2} \quad \text{Multiply the numerators and multiply the denominators.}$$

$$= \frac{3x}{14y^2} \quad \text{Simplify.}$$

PRACTICE 1

Multiply.

a. $\dfrac{n}{7} \cdot \dfrac{2}{m}$

b. $\dfrac{p^2}{6q^2} \cdot \dfrac{2q}{5p}$

The following rule describes how we multiply rational expressions such as
$$\frac{2n}{n^2 - 5n} \cdot \frac{3n - 15}{4n}.$$

To Multiply Rational Expressions

- Factor the numerators and denominators.
- Divide the numerators and denominators by all common factors.
- Multiply the remaining factors in the numerators and the remaining factors in the denominators.

EXAMPLE 2

Multiply.

a. $\dfrac{2n}{n^2 - 5n} \cdot \dfrac{3n - 15}{4n}$

b. $\dfrac{10}{9 - x^2} \cdot \dfrac{6 + 2x}{5}$

SOLUTION

a. $\dfrac{2n}{n^2 - 5n} \cdot \dfrac{3n - 15}{4n} = \dfrac{2n}{n(n - 5)} \cdot \dfrac{3(n - 5)}{4n}$ Factor the numerator and the denominator.

$$= \frac{\overset{1}{\cancel{2}}\overset{1}{\cancel{n}}}{\underset{1}{\cancel{n}}(\underset{1}{\cancel{n - 5}})} \cdot \frac{3(\overset{1}{\cancel{n - 5}})}{\underset{2}{\cancel{4}n}}$$ Divide out common factors.

$$= \frac{3}{2n}$$ Multiply the factors in the numerators and in the denominators.

b. $\dfrac{10}{9 - x^2} \cdot \dfrac{6 + 2x}{5} = \dfrac{10}{(3 - x)(3 + x)} \cdot \dfrac{2(3 + x)}{5}$

$$= \frac{\overset{2}{\cancel{10}}}{(3 - x)\cancel{(3 + x)}} \cdot \frac{2(3 \overset{1}{\cancel{+ x}})}{\underset{1}{\cancel{5}}} = \frac{4}{3 - x}$$

PRACTICE 2

Multiply.

a. $\dfrac{3t}{t^2 + 5t} \cdot \dfrac{3t + 15}{6t}$

b. $\dfrac{8}{36g^2 - 1} \cdot \dfrac{1 + 6g}{4}$

EXAMPLE 3

Find the product.

a. $\dfrac{x^2 - x - 20}{5x + 5} \cdot \dfrac{15x^2 - 15}{2x + 8}$

b. $\dfrac{16 + 6a - a^2}{a^2 - 10a - 24} \cdot \dfrac{a^2 - 6a - 27}{a^2 - 17a + 72}$

PRACTICE 3

Find the product.

a. $\dfrac{y^2 + 4y - 21}{3y - 9} \cdot \dfrac{6y^2 - 24}{y + 2}$

b. $\dfrac{x^2 - x - 30}{x^2 + 10x + 9} \cdot \dfrac{18 - 7x - x^2}{x^2 - 8x + 12}$

SOLUTION

a. $\dfrac{x^2 - x - 20}{5x + 5} \cdot \dfrac{15x^2 - 15}{2x + 8}$

$= \dfrac{(x - 5)(x + 4)}{5(x + 1)} \cdot \dfrac{15(x^2 - 1)}{2(x + 4)}$

$= \dfrac{(x - 5)(x + 4)}{5(x + 1)} \cdot \dfrac{15(x - 1)(x + 1)}{2(x + 4)}$

$= \dfrac{(x - 5)\cancel{(x + 4)}}{\cancel{5}\cancel{(x + 1)}} \cdot \dfrac{\overset{3}{\cancel{15}}(x - 1)\cancel{(x + 1)}}{2\cancel{(x + 4)}}$

$= \dfrac{3(x - 5)(x - 1)}{2}$

b. $\dfrac{16 + 6a - a^2}{a^2 - 10a - 24} \cdot \dfrac{a^2 - 6a - 27}{a^2 - 17a + 72}$

$= \dfrac{(8 - a)(2 + a)}{(a - 12)(a + 2)} \cdot \dfrac{(a - 9)(a + 3)}{(a - 8)(a - 9)}$

$= \dfrac{(8 - a)\cancel{(2 + a)}}{(a - 12)\cancel{(a + 2)}} \cdot \dfrac{\cancel{(a - 9)}(a + 3)}{(a - 8)\cancel{(a - 9)}}$

$= \dfrac{-1(a - 8)}{a - 12} \cdot \dfrac{a + 3}{a - 8}$

$= \dfrac{-\cancel{(a - 8)}}{a - 12} \cdot \dfrac{a + 3}{\cancel{a - 8}}$

$= \dfrac{-(a + 3)}{a - 12}$

$= -\dfrac{a + 3}{a - 12}$

Dividing Rational Expressions

In dividing arithmetic fractions, we take the reciprocal of the divisor and change the operation to multiplication. Recall that the reciprocal of a fraction is formed by interchanging its numerator and denominator.

The divisor → ↓   The reciprocal of the divisor → ↓

$$\dfrac{2}{3} \div \dfrac{3}{4} = \dfrac{2}{3} \cdot \dfrac{4}{3} = \dfrac{2 \cdot 4}{3 \cdot 3} = \dfrac{8}{9}$$

↑ Division   ↑ Multiplication

Rational expressions are divided in the same way.

The divisor → ↓   The reciprocal of the divisor → ↓

$$\dfrac{p}{q} \div \dfrac{r}{s} = \dfrac{p}{q} \cdot \dfrac{s}{r} = \dfrac{p \cdot s}{q \cdot r} = \dfrac{ps}{qr}$$

↑ Division   ↑ Multiplication

In general, to divide rational expressions, we apply the following rule.

To Divide Rational Expressions

- Take the reciprocal of the divisor and change the operation to multiplication.
- Follow the rule for multiplying rational expressions.

EXAMPLE 4

Divide.

a. $\dfrac{3}{x} \div \dfrac{y}{2}$

b. $\dfrac{6ab^2}{4a^3b} \div \dfrac{3a^4}{2b^5}$

SOLUTION

a. $\dfrac{3}{x} \div \dfrac{y}{2} = \dfrac{3}{x} \cdot \dfrac{2}{y}$ Take the reciprocal of the divisor and change the operation to multiplication.

$\qquad = \dfrac{6}{xy}$ Multiply.

b. $\dfrac{6ab^2}{4a^3b} \div \dfrac{3a^4}{2b^5} = \dfrac{6ab^2}{4a^3b} \cdot \dfrac{2b^5}{3a^4}$

$\qquad = \dfrac{\overset{2}{\overset{}{\cancel{6}}}\, \overset{1}{\cancel{a}}\, \overset{b}{\cancel{b^2}}}{\underset{\underset{1}{2}}{\cancel{4}}\, \underset{a^2}{\cancel{a^3}}\, \underset{1}{\cancel{b}}} \cdot \dfrac{\overset{1}{\cancel{2}}\, b^5}{\overset{}{\underset{1}{\cancel{3}}}\, a^4}$

$\qquad = \dfrac{b \cdot b^5}{a^2 \cdot a^4}$

$\qquad = \dfrac{b^6}{a^6}$

PRACTICE 4

Find the quotient.

a. $\dfrac{a}{4} \div \dfrac{b}{6}$

b. $\dfrac{5pq}{7p^2q^4} \div \dfrac{p^3}{3q^2}$

EXAMPLE 5

Find the quotient.

a. $\dfrac{a+1}{a-2} \div \dfrac{a+2}{a-1}$

b. $\dfrac{6x+3y}{4x-12y} \div \dfrac{10x+5y}{2x-6y}$

c. $\dfrac{x^2+3x+2}{3x+12} \div \dfrac{x^2-1}{7x}$

SOLUTION

a. $\dfrac{a+1}{a-2} \div \dfrac{a+2}{a-1} = \dfrac{a+1}{a-2} \cdot \dfrac{a-1}{a+2}$ Take the reciprocal and change the operation to multiplication.

$\qquad = \dfrac{(a+1)(a-1)}{(a-2)(a+2)}$ Multiply.

PRACTICE 5

Find the quotient.

a. $\dfrac{x+3}{x-10} \div \dfrac{x+1}{x+3}$

b. $\dfrac{p+4q}{3p-6q} \div \dfrac{2p+8q}{2p-4q}$

c. $\dfrac{y^2+4y+3}{5y+10} \div \dfrac{y^2-1}{y}$

b. $\dfrac{6x + 3y}{4x - 12y} \div \dfrac{10x + 5y}{2x - 6y}$

Take the reciprocal and change the operation to multiplication.

$= \dfrac{6x + 3y}{4x - 12y} \cdot \dfrac{2x - 6y}{10x + 5y}$

$= \dfrac{3(2x + y)}{4(x - 3y)} \cdot \dfrac{2(x - 3y)}{5(2x + y)}$

Factor the numerators and denominators.

$= \dfrac{\overset{1}{3(2x + y)}}{\underset{2}{4(x - 3y)}} \cdot \dfrac{\overset{1}{2}(x - 3y)}{\underset{1}{5(2x + y)}}$

Divide out the common factors.

$= \dfrac{3}{10}$

Multiply.

c. $\dfrac{x^2 + 3x + 2}{3x + 12} \div \dfrac{x^2 - 1}{7x} = \dfrac{x^2 + 3x + 2}{3x + 12} \cdot \dfrac{7x}{x^2 - 1}$

$= \dfrac{(x + 1)(x + 2)}{3(x + 4)} \cdot \dfrac{7x}{(x + 1)(x - 1)}$

$= \dfrac{\overset{1}{(x + 1)}(x + 2)}{3(x + 4)} \cdot \dfrac{7x}{\underset{1}{(x + 1)}(x - 1)}$

$= \dfrac{7x(x + 2)}{3(x + 4)(x - 1)}$

EXAMPLE 6

According to the physicist Isaac Newton, the force of gravitation between two objects with mass m and M is given by the expression $G \cdot \dfrac{m}{d} \cdot \dfrac{M}{d}$, where d is the distance between them and G is the gravitational constant. Simplify this expression.

SOLUTION

$$G \cdot \dfrac{m}{d} \cdot \dfrac{M}{d} = \dfrac{G}{1} \cdot \dfrac{m}{d} \cdot \dfrac{M}{d} = \dfrac{GmM}{d^2}$$

PRACTICE 6

When a body moves in a circular path, a force called the centripetal force is directed toward the center of the circle. This force has magnitude equal to the product of the object's mass m and its acceleration a. If $m = \dfrac{W}{g}$ and $a = \dfrac{v^2}{r}$, find the centripetal force in terms of W, g, v, and r, which represent the weight of the object, a constant due to gravity, the velocity of the object, and the radius of the circle, respectively.

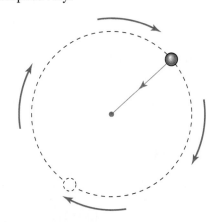

Exercises 7.2

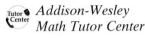

Multiply. Express products in lowest terms.

1. $\dfrac{1}{t^2} \cdot \dfrac{t}{4}$

2. $-\dfrac{y}{8} \cdot \dfrac{10}{y^3}$

3. $\dfrac{2}{a} \cdot \dfrac{3}{b}$

4. $\dfrac{5x}{2} \cdot \dfrac{2y}{3}$

5. $\dfrac{2x^4}{3x^5} \cdot \dfrac{5}{x^8}$

6. $\dfrac{4c}{d^3} \cdot \dfrac{3d}{8c^4}$

7. $-\dfrac{7x^2y}{3} \cdot \dfrac{6}{x^3y}$

8. $-\dfrac{5p^2}{10pq^2} \cdot \left(-\dfrac{6pq}{5p^3q}\right)$

9. $\dfrac{x}{x-2} \cdot \dfrac{5x-10}{x^4}$

10. $\dfrac{t}{t+3} \cdot \dfrac{4t+12}{t}$

11. $\dfrac{8n-3}{n^2} \cdot n$

12. $\dfrac{s+1}{s} \cdot s^2$

13. $\dfrac{8x-6}{5x+20} \cdot \dfrac{2x+8}{4x-3}$

14. $\dfrac{10y-1}{3y-6} \cdot \dfrac{5y-10}{10y-1}$

15. $\dfrac{x^2-4y^2}{x+y} \cdot \dfrac{3x+3y}{4x-8y}$

16. $\dfrac{a^2-4b^2}{6a-6b} \cdot \dfrac{10a-10b}{3a+6b}$

17. $\dfrac{p^4-1}{p^4-16} \cdot \dfrac{p^2+4}{p^2+1}$

18. $\dfrac{x^4-81}{x^2-x-12} \cdot \dfrac{x^2-16}{x^2+9}$

19. $\dfrac{n^2-2n-24}{n^2+6n+8} \cdot \dfrac{n^2+5n+6}{n^2-5n-6}$

20. $\dfrac{t^2+4t-21}{t^2+2t-15} \cdot \dfrac{t^2+t-20}{t^2+3t-28}$

21. $\dfrac{2y^2-y-6}{2y^2+y-3} \cdot \dfrac{2y^2-3y+1}{2y^2-9y+10}$

22. $\dfrac{2m+1}{2m^2+7m+3} \cdot \dfrac{m^2+2m-3}{2m+4m^2}$

23. $\dfrac{2}{x^3} \cdot \dfrac{4x}{5} \cdot \dfrac{10}{x^2}$

24. $\dfrac{a-3}{a^2} \cdot \dfrac{2a}{5} \cdot \dfrac{10a}{3}$

25. $\dfrac{x^2-7x+10}{2x-2} \cdot \dfrac{6x}{x^2-2x-15} \cdot \dfrac{x^2+2x-3}{x-2}$

26. $\dfrac{p^2-q^2}{p^2-pq} \cdot \dfrac{q}{2p^2-pq-q^2} \cdot \dfrac{6p+3q}{p}$

Divide. Express the quotient in lowest terms.

27. $\dfrac{7}{a} \div \dfrac{14}{a}$

28. $\dfrac{-5}{n} \div \dfrac{n}{2}$

29. $\dfrac{p^3}{10} \div \dfrac{p^3}{20}$

30. $\dfrac{-s}{v^2} \div \dfrac{s^2}{v}$

31. $\dfrac{12}{x^3} \div \dfrac{6}{5x^2}$

32. $\dfrac{1}{a^2} \div \dfrac{2}{3a}$

33. $-\dfrac{3}{t} \div t$

34. $\dfrac{5}{s} \div s$

35. $\dfrac{9xy^2}{2x^3} \div \dfrac{3x^2y}{4y}$

36. $\dfrac{10a^3}{7ab^2} \div \dfrac{-6a^2b^2}{14ab}$

37. $\dfrac{c+3}{c-5} \div \dfrac{c+9}{c-7}$

38. $\dfrac{t+4}{t-6} \div \dfrac{2t-8}{2t-4}$

39. $\dfrac{6a-12}{8a+32} \div \dfrac{9a-18}{5a+20}$

40. $\dfrac{3x+6}{6x+18} \div \dfrac{2x+4}{x+3}$

41. $\dfrac{x+1}{10} \div \dfrac{1-x^2}{5}$

42. $\dfrac{4x+8}{8} \div \dfrac{4-x^2}{4}$

43. $\dfrac{p^2-1}{1-p} \div \dfrac{p+1}{p}$

44. $\dfrac{y+6}{3y} \div \dfrac{y^2-36}{6-y}$

45. $\dfrac{x^2y+3xy^2}{x^2-9y^2} \div \dfrac{5x^2y}{x^2-2xy-3y^2}$

46. $\dfrac{2x+1}{2x^2+7x+3} \div \dfrac{2x+4x^2}{x^2+2x-3}$

47. $\dfrac{2t^2-3t-2}{2t+1} \div (4-t^2)$

48. $(y-x) \div \dfrac{x^2-y^2}{x^2+xy}$

49. $\dfrac{x^2-11x+28}{x^2-x-42} \div \dfrac{x^2-2x-8}{x^2+7x+10}$

50. $\dfrac{a^2-a-56}{a^2+8a+7} \div \dfrac{a^2-13a+40}{a^2-4a-5}$

51. $\dfrac{3p^2-3p-18}{p^2+2p-15} \div \dfrac{2p^2+6p-20}{2p^2-12p+16}$

52. $\dfrac{3y^2+13y+4}{16-y^2} \div \dfrac{3y^2-5y-2}{3y-12}$

Applications

Solve.

53. An investment of p dollars is growing at the annual simple interest rate r. The number of years that it will take the investment to be worth A dollars is given by the expression

$$\left(\dfrac{A-p}{p}\right) \div r$$

Simplify this expression.

54. A store is having a sale, with each item selling at a discount of $x\%$.

    a. With this discount, what percent of the normal price is a customer paying on each item?

    b. What is the sale price of 10 items that normally sell for z dollars each?

55. A company has annual expenses totaling B dollars, of which $p\%$ goes toward rents. Of the rental expenses, $q\%$ goes toward the head office. Write as a rational expression the annual cost of the head office rental.

56. Physicists studying momentum may use the expression

$$\frac{W}{g} \cdot \frac{1}{t} \cdot (v_2 - v_1),$$

where W is the weight of an object, g is a constant, t is time, v_2 is the final velocity of the object, and v_1 is the initial velocity of the object. Rewrite as a single rational expression.

57. Electricians use the following formula when studying the resistance in a heating element:

$$P = \frac{V^2}{R + r} \cdot \frac{r}{R + r}$$

Multiply out the right-hand side of this formula.

58. Suppose that the chance that one event occurs is $\dfrac{a}{b}$ and the chance that an independent (or unrelated) event occurs is $\dfrac{c}{d}$.

    a. The chance that both events will occur is the product of their individual chances. Write this product as a rational expression.

    b. The chance that neither event will occur can be represented by $\left(1 - \dfrac{a}{b}\right)\left(1 - \dfrac{c}{d}\right)$. Write this product as a single rational expression.

59. The following diagram shows a cylinder and its inscribed sphere, where the radius of the sphere is r and the height of the cylinder is h.

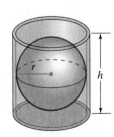

    Volume of a sphere $= \dfrac{4}{3}\pi r^3$

    Volume of a cylinder $= \pi r^2 h$

    Surface area of a sphere $= 4\pi r^2$

    Surface area of a cylinder $= 2\pi rh + 2\pi r^2$

Use these formulas to answer the following questions.

a. Find the ratio of the volume of the sphere to the volume of the cylinder.

b. Find the ratio of the surface area of the sphere to the surface area of the cylinder.

c. Divide the expression in part (a) by the expression in part (b).

d. In the diagram, note that $h = 2r$. Substitute $2r$ for h in the expression in part (c) and simplify.

60. In 1934, Harold Urey won the Nobel Prize in chemistry for discovering deuterium (also called heavy hydrogen). This discovery involved reducing the mass of an electron in an atom of deuterium.

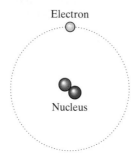

If m stands for the mass of an electron, then the reduced mass r can be represented by

$$r = \frac{mM}{M + m},$$

where M is the mass of the atom's nucleus. Find an expression for the quotient r divided by m in terms of m and M, and simplify.

● *Check your answers on page A-28.*

Mindstretchers

CRITICAL THINKING

1. Even though the operation of division is not commutative, can you find four different polynomials P, Q, R, and S for which $\dfrac{P}{Q} \div \dfrac{R}{S} = \dfrac{R}{S} \div \dfrac{P}{Q}$? Explain.

MATHEMATICAL REASONING

2. True or false, the expressions $\dfrac{\left(\dfrac{a}{b}\right)}{c}$ and $\dfrac{a}{\left(\dfrac{b}{c}\right)}$ are equivalent. Explain.

GROUPWORK

3. Working with a partner, find the following.

a. Two different pairs of rational expressions whose quotient is $\dfrac{x + 4}{x + 6}$.

b. Two different pairs of rational expressions whose product is $\dfrac{x^2 - x - 6}{2x^2 + 5x - 3}$.

7.3 Addition and Subtraction of Rational Expressions

Adding and Subtracting Rational Expressions with the Same Denominator

OBJECTIVES

- *To add and subtract rational expressions with the same denominator*
- *To find the least common denominator (LCD) of two or more rational expressions*
- *To add and subtract rational expressions with different denominators*
- *To solve applied problems involving the addition or subtraction of rational expressions*

Recall from arithmetic that to add like fractions, we add the numerators and keep the same denominator.

$$\frac{3}{5} + \frac{1}{5} = \frac{3+1}{5} = \frac{4}{5}$$

To subtract like fractions, we subtract the numerators and keep the same denominator.

$$\frac{3}{5} - \frac{1}{5} = \frac{3-1}{5} = \frac{2}{5}$$

In algebra, adding and subtracting rational expressions with the same denominator is similar:

$$\frac{3}{x} + \frac{1}{x} = \frac{3+1}{x} = \frac{4}{x} \qquad \text{and} \qquad \frac{3}{x} - \frac{1}{x} = \frac{3-1}{x} = \frac{2}{x}$$

To Add (or Subtract) Rational Expressions with the Same Denominator
- Add (or subtract) the numerators and keep the same denominator.
- Simplify, if possible.

EXAMPLE 1

Add.

a. $\dfrac{3}{x-1} + \dfrac{8}{x-1}$

b. $\dfrac{3x}{4y} + \dfrac{x}{4y}$

c. $\dfrac{3x}{x+1} + \dfrac{3}{x+1}$

d. $\dfrac{2t^2 + 5t - 7}{3t - 1} + \dfrac{7t^2 - 5t + 6}{3t - 1}$

SOLUTION

a. $\dfrac{3}{x-1} + \dfrac{8}{x-1} = \dfrac{3+8}{x-1}$ Add the numerators and keep the same denominator.

$\qquad = \dfrac{11}{x-1}$ Simplify.

PRACTICE 1

Add.

a. $\dfrac{9}{y+2} + \dfrac{1}{y+2}$

b. $\dfrac{10r}{3s} + \dfrac{5r}{3s}$

c. $\dfrac{6t - 7}{t - 1} + \dfrac{1}{t - 1}$

d. $\dfrac{n^2 + 10n + 1}{n + 5} + \dfrac{2n^2 + 4n - 6}{n + 5}$

b. $\dfrac{3x}{4y} + \dfrac{x}{4y} = \dfrac{4x}{4y}$ Add the numerators and keep the
same denominator.

$= \dfrac{\overset{1}{\cancel{4}}x}{\underset{1}{\cancel{4}}y}$ Divide out the common factor.

$= \dfrac{x}{y}$ Simplify.

c. $\dfrac{3x}{x+1} + \dfrac{3}{x+1} = \dfrac{3x+3}{x+1}$ Add the numerators and keep the same
denominator.

$= \dfrac{3\overset{1}{\cancel{(x+1)}}}{\underset{1}{\cancel{x+1}}}$ Factor the numerator and divide
out the common factor.

$= 3$ Simplify.

d. $\dfrac{2t^2+5t-7}{3t-1} + \dfrac{7t^2-5t+6}{3t-1} = \dfrac{(2t^2+5t-7)+(7t^2-5t+6)}{3t-1}$

$= \dfrac{9t^2-1}{3t-1}$ Combine like terms in the
numerator.

$= \dfrac{\overset{1}{\cancel{(3t-1)}}(3t+1)}{\underset{1}{\cancel{3t-1}}}$

$= 3t + 1$

EXAMPLE 2

Subtract.

a. $\dfrac{6}{z} - \dfrac{4}{z}$

b. $\dfrac{5y}{8} - \dfrac{3y}{8}$

c. $\dfrac{x}{3y} - \dfrac{2x}{3y}$

SOLUTION

a. $\dfrac{6}{z} - \dfrac{4}{z} = \dfrac{6-4}{z}$ Subtract the numerators and keep the same
denominator.

$= \dfrac{2}{z}$ Simplify.

b. $\dfrac{5y}{8} - \dfrac{3y}{8} = \dfrac{5y-3y}{8} = \dfrac{\overset{1}{\cancel{2}}y}{\underset{4}{\cancel{8}}} = \dfrac{y}{4}$

c. $\dfrac{x}{3y} - \dfrac{2x}{3y} = \dfrac{x-2x}{3y} = \dfrac{-x}{3y} = -\dfrac{x}{3y}$

PRACTICE 2

Find the difference.

a. $\dfrac{12}{v} - \dfrac{7}{v}$

b. $\dfrac{7t}{10} - \dfrac{t}{10}$

c. $\dfrac{7p}{3q} - \dfrac{8p}{3q}$

EXAMPLE 3

Find the difference.

a. $\dfrac{x + 5y}{2y} - \dfrac{x - 11y}{2y}$

b. $\dfrac{3ax + bx}{a + 2b} - \dfrac{2ax - bx}{a + 2b}$

c. $\dfrac{6x + 12}{x^2 - x - 6} - \dfrac{x + 2}{x^2 - x - 6}$

SOLUTION

a. $\dfrac{x + 5y}{2y} - \dfrac{x - 11y}{2y}$

$= \dfrac{(x + 5y) - (x - 11y)}{2y}$ Subtract the numerators and keep the same denominator.

$= \dfrac{x + 5y - x + 11y}{2y}$ Remove the parentheses.

$= \dfrac{16y}{2y}$ Combine like terms.

$= \dfrac{\overset{8}{\cancel{16y}}}{\underset{1}{\cancel{2y}}}\overset{1}{}$ Divide out the common factors.

$= 8$ Simplify.

b. $\dfrac{3ax + bx}{a + 2b} - \dfrac{2ax - bx}{a + 2b} = \dfrac{(3ax + bx) - (2ax - bx)}{a + 2b}$

$= \dfrac{3ax + bx - 2ax + bx}{a + 2b}$

$= \dfrac{ax + 2bx}{a + 2b}$

$= \dfrac{x(a + 2b)}{a + 2b}$

$= \dfrac{x(\cancel{a + 2b})^{1}}{\cancel{a + 2b}_{1}}$

$= x$

c. $\dfrac{6x + 12}{x^2 - x - 6} - \dfrac{x + 2}{x^2 - x - 6} = \dfrac{(6x + 12) - (x + 2)}{x^2 - x - 6}$

$= \dfrac{6x + 12 - x - 2}{x^2 - x - 6}$

$= \dfrac{5x + 10}{x^2 - x - 6}$

$= \dfrac{5(x + 2)}{(x - 3)(x + 2)}$

$= \dfrac{5(\cancel{x + 2})^{1}}{(x - 3)(\cancel{x + 2})_{1}}$

$= \dfrac{5}{x - 3}$

PRACTICE 3

Subtract.

a. $\dfrac{7a - 4b}{3a} - \dfrac{a - 4b}{3a}$

b. $\dfrac{9xy - 5xz}{4y - z} - \dfrac{xy - 3xz}{4y - z}$

c. $\dfrac{2x + 13}{x^2 - 7x + 10} - \dfrac{5x + 7}{x^2 - 7x + 10}$

The Least Common Denominator of Rational Expressions

Recall that combining unlike arithmetic fractions involves finding the least common denominator (LCD). We rewrite the fractions in terms of their LCD, and then add these like factions.

$$\frac{1}{2} + \frac{4}{5} = \frac{1}{2} \cdot \frac{5}{5} + \frac{4}{5} \cdot \frac{2}{2} = \frac{5}{10} + \frac{8}{10} = \frac{13}{10}$$

10 is the LCD of $\frac{1}{2}$ and $\frac{4}{5}$.

To find the LCD of rational expressions, we begin by factoring their denominators completely. For instance, consider the rational expressions $\dfrac{8x}{x^2 + 3x + 2}$ and $\dfrac{5x - 6}{x^2 + 2x + 1}$, which we can write as

$$\frac{8x}{(x + 1)(x + 2)} \quad \text{and} \quad \frac{5x - 6}{(x + 1)(x + 1)}.$$

Denominators in factored form.

The LCD is the product of the different factors in the denominators, where the power of each factor is the greatest number of times that it occurs in any single denominator.

The highest power of this factor
in any denominator

$$\text{LCD} = (x + 1)(x + 1)(x + 2) = (x + 1)^2 (x + 2)$$

To Find the LCD of Rational Expressions
- Factor each denominator completely.
- Multiply these factors, using for the power of each factor the greatest number of times that it occurs in any of the denominators. The product of all these factors is the LCD.

EXAMPLE 4

Find the LCD of each group of rational expressions.

a. $\dfrac{1}{6}$ and $\dfrac{2}{n}$

b. $\dfrac{1}{10x}$ and $\dfrac{7}{12x^2}$

c. $\dfrac{3}{8p}$, $\dfrac{7}{10p^2q}$, and $\dfrac{1}{4pqr}$

PRACTICE 4

For each group of rational expressions, determine the least common denominator.

a. $\dfrac{8}{y}$ and $\dfrac{x}{20}$

b. $\dfrac{1}{6t}$ and $\dfrac{4}{3t^2}$

SOLUTION

a. We begin by factoring the denominators of $\dfrac{1}{6}$ and $\dfrac{2}{n}$.

$$\text{Factor 6:} \quad 2 \cdot 3$$
$$\text{Factor } n: \quad n$$

No factor is repeated more than once in any denominator. So the LCD is the product of the factors.

$$\text{LCD} = 2 \cdot 3 \cdot n = 6n$$

b. $\dfrac{1}{10x}$ and $\dfrac{7}{12x^2}$

$$\text{Factor } 10x: \quad 2 \cdot 5 \cdot x$$
$$\text{Factor } 12x^2: \quad 2^2 \cdot 3 \cdot x^2$$

The factors 2 and x each appear at most twice in any denominator. The factors 3 and 5 each appear at most once in any denominator. So

$$\text{LCD} = 2^2 \cdot 3 \cdot 5 \cdot x^2 = 60x^2.$$

c. $\dfrac{3}{8p}, \dfrac{7}{10p^2q},$ and $\dfrac{1}{4pqr}$

$$\text{Factor } 8p: \quad 2^3 \cdot p$$
$$\text{Factor } 10p^2q: \quad 2 \cdot 5 \cdot p^2 \cdot q$$
$$\text{Factor } 4pqr: \quad 2^2 \cdot p \cdot q \cdot r$$
$$\text{LCD} = 2^3 \cdot 5 \cdot p^2 \cdot q \cdot r = 40p^2qr$$

c. $\dfrac{1}{5x}, \dfrac{7}{15xy^3},$ and $\dfrac{x+y}{2x^2}$

EXAMPLE 5

Find the LCD of each group of rational expressions.

a. $\dfrac{4x+3}{3x^2-3x}$ and $\dfrac{x-6}{x^2-2x+1}$

b. $\dfrac{x+4}{x+7}, \dfrac{3}{x-4},$ and $\dfrac{8x-1}{x+9}$

c. $\dfrac{2y}{x^2-2xy+y^2}, \dfrac{x}{x^2-y^2},$ and $\dfrac{x-y}{x^2+2xy+y^2}$

SOLUTION

a. First we factor the denominators of $\dfrac{4x+3}{3x^2-3x}$ and $\dfrac{x-6}{x^2-2x+1}$.

$$\text{Factor } 3x^2-3x: \quad 3x(x-1)$$
$$\text{Factor } x^2-2x+1: \quad (x-1)(x-1) = (x-1)^2$$

The factor $3x$ appears at most once and the factor $(x-1)$ appears at most twice, so

$$\text{LCD} = 3x(x-1)^2.$$

PRACTICE 5

Determine the LCD for each group of rational expressions.

a. $\dfrac{9n+1}{2n^2+2n}$ and $\dfrac{n-5}{n^2+2n+1}$

b. $\dfrac{7p+1}{p+2}, \dfrac{5p}{p-1},$ and $\dfrac{3p+1}{p+5}$

c. $\dfrac{s-t}{s^2+4st+4t^2}, \dfrac{3t}{s^2-4t^2},$ and $\dfrac{6s}{s^2-4st+4t^2}$

b. $\dfrac{x + 4}{x + 7}$, $\dfrac{3}{x - 4}$, and $\dfrac{8x - 1}{x + 9}$

Factor $x + 7$: $x + 7$

Factor $x - 4$: $x - 4$

Factor $x + 9$: $x + 9$

No factor is repeated more than once in any denominator, so

$$\text{LCD} = (x + 7)(x - 4)(x + 9).$$

c. $\dfrac{2y}{x^2 - 2xy + y^2}$, $\dfrac{x}{x^2 - y^2}$, and $\dfrac{x - y}{x^2 + 2xy + y^2}$

Factor $x^2 - 2xy + y^2$: $(x - y)(x - y) = (x - y)^2$

Factor $x^2 - y^2$: $(x - y)(x + y)$

Factor $x^2 + 2xy + y^2$: $(x + y)(x + y) = (x + y)^2$

$\text{LCD} = (x - y)^2(x + y)^2$

Adding and Subtracting Rational Expressions with Different Denominators

In order to add or subtract rational expressions with different denominators, we will need to change each expression to an equivalent rational expression whose denominator is the LCD.

EXAMPLE 6

Rewrite the following rational expressions in terms of their LCD.

a. $\dfrac{3}{5x^2}$ and $\dfrac{x + 1}{6xy}$

b. $\dfrac{6x + 1}{x^2 - 4}$ and $\dfrac{x}{x^2 + 5x + 6}$

SOLUTION

a. The LCD of $\dfrac{3}{5x^2}$ and $\dfrac{x + 1}{6xy}$ is $30x^2y$.

Since $5x^2 \cdot 6y = 30x^2y$, we multiply the numerator and denominator of $\dfrac{3}{5x^2}$ by $6y$ so that the denominator becomes the LCD.

$$\frac{3}{5x^2} = \frac{3 \cdot 6y}{5x^2 \cdot 6y} = \frac{18y}{30x^2y}$$

Note that multiplying the numerator and the denominator by $6y$ is the same as multiplying the expression by 1. So $\dfrac{3}{5x^2}$ and $\dfrac{18y}{30x^2y}$ are equivalent expressions.

PRACTICE 6

Express each pair of rational expressions in terms of their LCD.

a. $\dfrac{2}{7p^3}$ and $\dfrac{p + 3}{2p}$

b. $\dfrac{3y - 2}{y^2 - 9}$ and $\dfrac{y}{y^2 - 6y + 9}$

Since $6xy \cdot 5x = 30x^2y$, we multiply the numerator and denominator of $\dfrac{x+1}{6xy}$ by $5x$ so that the denominator becomes the LCD.

$$\frac{x+1}{6xy} = \frac{(x+1) \cdot 5x}{6xy \cdot 5x} = \frac{5x(x+1)}{30x^2y}$$

b. To find the LCD, we begin by factoring the denominators of the expressions.

$$\text{Factor } x^2 - 4: \quad (x+2)(x-2)$$
$$\text{Factor } x^2 + 5x + 6: \quad (x+2)(x+3)$$

The LCD of $\dfrac{6x+1}{x^2-4}$ and $\dfrac{x}{x^2+5x+6}$ is $(x+2)(x-2)(x+3)$.

Since $(x^2 - 4)(x+3) = (x+2)(x-2)(x+3)$, we multiply the numerator and denominator of $\dfrac{6x+1}{x^2-4}$ by $(x+3)$ so that the denominator becomes the LCD.

$$\frac{6x+1}{x^2-4} = \frac{(6x+1)(x+3)}{(x+2)(x-2)(x+3)}$$

Since $(x^2 + 5x + 6)(x-2) = (x+2)(x+3)(x-2)$, we multiply the numerator and denominator of $\dfrac{x}{x^2+5x+6}$ by $(x-2)$ so that the denominator becomes the LCD.

$$\frac{x}{x^2+5x+6} = \frac{x(x-2)}{(x+2)(x+3)(x-2)}$$

Now let's look at how to add and subtract rational expressions with different denominators using the concept of equivalent rational expressions.

To Add (or Subtract) Rational Expressions with Different Denominators

- Find the LCD of the rational expressions.
- Write each rational expression with a common denominator, usually the LCD.
- Add (or subtract) the numerators.
- Simplify, if possible.

EXAMPLE 7

Perform the indicated operation.

a. $\dfrac{1}{2n} - \dfrac{3}{5n}$

b. $\dfrac{2}{3x^2} + \dfrac{5}{9x}$

PRACTICE 7

Combine.

a. $\dfrac{3}{4p} + \dfrac{1}{6p}$

b. $\dfrac{1}{5y} - \dfrac{2}{15y^2}$

SOLUTION

a. The LCD of the rational expressions is $10n$.

$$\frac{1}{2n} - \frac{3}{5n} = \frac{1 \cdot 5}{2n \cdot 5} - \frac{3 \cdot 2}{5n \cdot 2}$$ Write as equivalent rational expressions with the LCD as the denominator.

$$= \frac{5}{10n} - \frac{6}{10n}$$ Simplify.

$$= \frac{-1}{10n}$$ Subtract the numerators.

$$= -\frac{1}{10n}$$ Simplify.

b. The LCD of the rational expressions is $9x^2$.

$$\frac{2}{3x^2} + \frac{5}{9x} = \frac{2 \cdot 3}{3x^2 \cdot 3} + \frac{5 \cdot x}{9x \cdot x}$$ Write as equivalent rational expressions with the LCD as the denominator.

$$= \frac{6}{9x^2} + \frac{5x}{9x^2}$$ Simplify.

$$= \frac{5x + 6}{9x^2}$$ Add the numerators.

EXAMPLE 8

Combine.

a. $\dfrac{y + 5}{y - 2} - \dfrac{y - 3}{y}$

b. $\dfrac{7a + 5}{a - 1} - \dfrac{a}{1 - a}$

SOLUTION

a. The LCD of the rational expression is $y(y - 2)$.

$$\frac{y + 5}{y - 2} - \frac{y - 3}{y}$$

$$= \frac{(y + 5) \cdot y}{(y - 2) \cdot y} - \frac{(y - 3) \cdot (y - 2)}{y \cdot (y - 2)}$$ Write in terms of the LCD.

$$= \frac{y^2 + 5y}{y(y - 2)} - \frac{y^2 - 5y + 6}{y(y - 2)}$$ Multiply.

$$= \frac{(y^2 + 5y) - (y^2 - 5y + 6)}{y(y - 2)}$$ Subtract the numerators.

$$= \frac{y^2 + 5y - y^2 + 5y - 6}{y(y - 2)}$$ Remove the parentheses.

$$= \frac{10y - 6}{y(y - 2)}$$ Simplify.

$$= \frac{2(5y - 3)}{y(y - 2)}$$ Factor the numerator.

PRACTICE 8

Combine.

a. $\dfrac{x + 2}{x} - \dfrac{x - 4}{x + 3}$

b. $\dfrac{3x - 4}{x - 1} + \dfrac{x + 1}{1 - x}$

b. The LCD of the rational expressions can be either $a - 1$ or $1 - a$, since $1 - a = -(a - 1)$. To get the LCD $(a - 1)$, we factor out -1 in the denominator of the expression $\dfrac{a}{1 - a}$.

$$\frac{7a + 5}{a - 1} - \frac{a}{1 - a}$$

$$= \frac{7a + 5}{a - 1} - \frac{a}{-(a - 1)} \qquad \text{Write } 1 - a \text{ as } -(a - 1).$$

$$= \frac{7a + 5}{a - 1} - \left(-\frac{a}{a - 1}\right) \qquad \text{Write } \frac{a}{-(a - 1)} \text{ as } -\frac{a}{(a - 1)}.$$

$$= \frac{7a + 5}{a - 1} + \frac{a}{a - 1} \qquad \text{Simplify.}$$

$$= \frac{7a + 5 + a}{a - 1} \qquad \text{Add the numerators.}$$

$$= \frac{8a + 5}{a - 1} \qquad \text{Simplify.}$$

EXAMPLE 9	**PRACTICE 9**

EXAMPLE 9

Combine.

a. $\dfrac{9}{2x + 4} + \dfrac{x}{x^2 - 4}$

b. $\dfrac{2}{x - 3} - \dfrac{x - 1}{9 - x^2}$

SOLUTION

a. $\dfrac{9}{2x + 4} + \dfrac{x}{x^2 - 4}$

$$= \frac{9}{2(x + 2)} + \frac{x}{(x + 2)(x - 2)} \qquad \text{Factor the denominators.}$$

$$= \frac{9 \cdot (x - 2)}{2(x + 2) \cdot (x - 2)} + \frac{x \cdot 2}{(x + 2)(x - 2) \cdot 2} \qquad \begin{array}{l}\text{Write in terms of the}\\ \text{LCD } 2(x + 2)(x - 2).\end{array}$$

$$= \frac{9x - 18}{2(x + 2)(x - 2)} + \frac{2x}{2(x + 2)(x - 2)} \qquad \text{Multiply.}$$

$$= \frac{11x - 18}{2(x + 2)(x - 2)} \qquad \begin{array}{l}\text{Add the numerators}\\ \text{and combine like terms.}\end{array}$$

PRACTICE 9

Combine.

a. $\dfrac{1}{4x - 16} + \dfrac{2x}{x^2 - 16}$

b. $\dfrac{3x - 7}{x^2 - 1} + \dfrac{2}{1 - x}$

b. $\dfrac{2}{x-3} - \dfrac{x-1}{9-x^2}$

$= \dfrac{2}{x-3} - \dfrac{x-1}{(3-x)(3+x)}$

$= \dfrac{2}{x-3} - \dfrac{x-1}{-(x-3)(x+3)}$ Write $3-x$ as $-(x-3)$.

$= \dfrac{2}{x-3} - \left[-\dfrac{x-1}{(x-3)(x+3)} \right]$

$= \dfrac{2}{x-3} + \dfrac{x-1}{(x-3)(x+3)}$

$= \dfrac{2 \cdot (x+3)}{(x-3) \cdot (x+3)} + \dfrac{x-1}{(x-3)(x+3)}$ Write in terms of the LCD $(x-3)(x+3)$.

$= \dfrac{2x+6}{(x-3)(x+3)} + \dfrac{x-1}{(x-3)(x+3)}$ Add the numerators and combine like terms.

$= \dfrac{(2x+6) + (x-1)}{(x-3)(x+3)}$

$= \dfrac{3x+5}{(x-3)(x+3)}$

EXAMPLE 10

Perform the indicated operations.

a. $\dfrac{7n}{n^2+4n+3} - \dfrac{3n-2}{n^2+2n+1}$

b. $\dfrac{y}{y-1} - \dfrac{y}{3} - \dfrac{4}{y+2}$

SOLUTION

a. $\dfrac{7n}{n^2+4n+3} - \dfrac{3n-2}{n^2+2n+1}$

$= \dfrac{7n}{(n+3)(n+1)} - \dfrac{3n-2}{(n+1)^2}$ Factor the denominators.

$= \dfrac{7n \cdot (n+1)}{(n+3)(n+1) \cdot (n+1)}$

$\quad - \dfrac{(3n-2) \cdot (n+3)}{(n+1)^2 \cdot (n+3)}$ Write in terms of the LCD $(n+3)(n+1)^2$.

$= \dfrac{7n^2+7n}{(n+3)(n+1)^2} - \dfrac{3n^2+7n-6}{(n+3)(n+1)^2}$ Multiply.

$= \dfrac{(7n^2+7n) - (3n^2+7n-6)}{(n+3)(n+1)^2}$ Subtract the numerators.

$= \dfrac{7n^2+7n-3n^2-7n+6}{(n+3)(n+1)^2}$ Remove the parentheses.

$= \dfrac{4n^2+6}{(n+3)(n+1)^2}$ Combine like terms.

$= \dfrac{2(n^2+3)}{(n+3)(n+1)^2}$ Factor the numerator.

PRACTICE 10

Perform the indicated operation.

a. $\dfrac{y}{y^2+5y+6} - \dfrac{4y+1}{y^2+3y+2}$

b. $\dfrac{2x}{5} - \dfrac{1}{x+1} - \dfrac{x-1}{4x}$

b. The LCD is $3(y - 1)(y + 2)$.

$$\frac{y}{y - 1} - \frac{y}{3} - \frac{4}{y + 2}$$

$$= \frac{y \cdot 3(y + 2)}{(y - 1) \cdot 3(y + 2)} - \frac{y \cdot (y - 1)(y + 2)}{3 \cdot (y - 1)(y + 2)} - \frac{4 \cdot 3(y - 1)}{(y + 2) \cdot 3(y - 1)}$$

$$= \frac{3y^2 + 6y}{3(y - 1)(y + 2)} - \frac{y^3 + y^2 - 2y}{3(y - 1)(y + 2)} - \frac{12y - 12}{3(y - 1)(y + 2)}$$

$$= \frac{(3y^2 + 6y) - (y^3 + y^2 - 2y) - (12y - 12)}{3(y - 1)(y + 2)}$$

$$= \frac{3y^2 + 6y - y^3 - y^2 + 2y - 12y + 12}{3(y - 1)(y + 2)}$$

$$= \frac{-y^3 + 2y^2 - 4y + 12}{3(y - 1)(y + 2)}$$

EXAMPLE 11

An expression used in the design of electric motors is $\frac{V}{kp} - \frac{RT}{k^2p^2}$. Rewrite this difference as a single rational expression.

SOLUTION The LCD is k^2p^2.

$$\frac{V}{kp} - \frac{RT}{k^2p^2} = \frac{V \cdot kp}{kp \cdot kp} - \frac{RT}{k^2p^2} = \frac{Vkp}{k^2p^2} - \frac{RT}{k^2p^2} = \frac{Vkp - RT}{k^2p^2}$$

PRACTICE 11

To find the percent change for the cost of an item, retailers can use the expression

$$100\left(\frac{C_1}{C_0} - 1\right),$$

where C_1 is the new cost and C_0 is the old cost. Write as a single rational expression.

Exercises 7.3

FOR EXTRA HELP

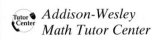

Student's Solutions Manual

Addison-Wesley Math Tutor Center

MyMathLab

Videotape 7/DVT 7

Perform the indicated operation. Simplify, if possible.

1. $\dfrac{5a}{12} + \dfrac{11a}{12}$

2. $\dfrac{y}{5} + \dfrac{4y}{5}$

3. $\dfrac{5t}{3} - \dfrac{2t}{3}$

4. $\dfrac{2x}{15} - \dfrac{8x}{15}$

5. $\dfrac{10}{x} + \dfrac{1}{x}$

6. $\dfrac{4}{a} - \dfrac{3}{a}$

7. $\dfrac{6}{7y} - \dfrac{1}{7y}$

8. $\dfrac{-7}{8x} + \dfrac{3}{8x}$

9. $\dfrac{5x}{2y} + \dfrac{x}{2y}$

10. $\dfrac{4a}{3b} + \dfrac{8a}{3b}$

11. $\dfrac{2p}{5q} - \dfrac{3p}{5q}$

12. $\dfrac{x}{6y} - \dfrac{11x}{6y}$

13. $\dfrac{2}{x+1} + \dfrac{7}{x+1}$

14. $\dfrac{8}{p+q} + \dfrac{1}{q+p}$

15. $\dfrac{5}{x+2} - \dfrac{9}{2+x}$

16. $\dfrac{10}{r+s} - \dfrac{14}{s+r}$

17. $\dfrac{a}{a+3} + \dfrac{1}{a+3}$

18. $\dfrac{p}{p-1} + \dfrac{3}{p-1}$

19. $\dfrac{3x}{x-8} + \dfrac{2x+1}{x-8}$

20. $\dfrac{4p}{p-5} + \dfrac{p-2}{p-5}$

21. $\dfrac{7x+1}{5x+2} - \dfrac{3x}{5x+2}$

22. $\dfrac{2x}{2x-1} - \dfrac{x+1}{2x-1}$

23. $\dfrac{9x+17}{2x+5} - \dfrac{3x+2}{2x+5}$

24. $\dfrac{5a+1}{2a+3} - \dfrac{a-5}{2a+3}$

25. $\dfrac{-7+5n}{3n-1} + \dfrac{7n+3}{3n-1}$

26. $\dfrac{-5+8x}{5x-1} + \dfrac{4-3x}{5x-1}$

27. $\dfrac{x^2-1}{x^2-4x-2} - \dfrac{x^2-x+3}{x^2-4x-2}$

28. $\dfrac{9+3x-x^2}{x^2+x+1} + \dfrac{x^2-5}{x^2+x+1}$

29. $\dfrac{x}{x^2-3x+2} + \dfrac{2}{x^2-3x+2} + \dfrac{x^2-4x}{x^2-3x+2}$

30. $\dfrac{a}{a^2-5a+4} + \dfrac{2}{a^2-5a+4} + \dfrac{a^2-4a}{a^2-5a+4}$

31. $\dfrac{2x-1}{3x^2-x+2} + \dfrac{8}{3x^2-x+2} - \dfrac{3x}{3x^2-x+2}$

32. $\dfrac{4y-3}{y^2+7y+1} - \dfrac{y}{y^2+7y+1} + \dfrac{6-y}{y^2+7y+1}$

The following expressions represent denominators of rational expressions. Find their LCD.

33. $5(x + 2)$ and $3(x + 2)$

34. $9(4c - 1)$ and $6(4c - 1)$

35. $(p - 3)(p + 8)$ and $(p - 3)(p - 8)$

36. $(b + c)(5b)$ and $(b + c)(2b)$

37. $t, t + 3$, and $t - 3$

38. $s, 4s$, and $s + 5$

39. $t^2 + 7t + 10$ and $t^2 - 25$

40. $n^2 - 1$ and $n^2 + 6n - 7$

41. $3s^2 - 11s + 6$ and $3s^2 + 4s - 4$

42. $2x^2 + x - 15$ and $-2x^2 + 9x - 10$

Write each pair of rational expressions in terms of their LCD.

43. $\dfrac{1}{3x}$ and $\dfrac{5}{4x^2}$

44. $\dfrac{2}{5y^3}$ and $\dfrac{3}{y^2}$

45. $\dfrac{5}{2a^2}$ and $\dfrac{a - 3}{7ab}$

46. $\dfrac{x + 2}{4xy}$ and $\dfrac{7}{6x^2}$

47. $\dfrac{8}{n(n + 1)}$ and $\dfrac{5}{(n + 1)^2}$

48. $\dfrac{2}{c(c - 3)^2}$ and $\dfrac{4}{(c - 3)}$

49. $\dfrac{3n}{4n + 4}$ and $\dfrac{2n}{n^2 - 1}$

50. $\dfrac{4y}{y^2 - 1}$ and $\dfrac{y}{2y + 2}$

51. $\dfrac{2n}{n^2 + 6n + 5}$ and $\dfrac{3n}{n^2 + 2n - 15}$

52. $\dfrac{7t}{t^2 - 2t + 1}$ and $\dfrac{4t}{t^2 - 5t + 4}$

Perform the indicated operations. Simplify, if possible.

53. $\dfrac{5}{3x} + \dfrac{1}{2x}$

54. $\dfrac{3}{4a} + \dfrac{2}{5a}$

55. $\dfrac{2}{3x^2} - \dfrac{5}{6x}$

56. $\dfrac{9}{7c^2} - \dfrac{3}{5c^3}$

57. $\dfrac{-2}{3x^2y} + \dfrac{4}{3xy^2}$

58. $\dfrac{6}{p^2q} + \dfrac{8}{pq^2}$

59. $\dfrac{1}{x + 1} + \dfrac{1}{x - 1}$

60. $\dfrac{2}{a + b} + \dfrac{2}{a - b}$

61. $\dfrac{p + 6}{3} - \dfrac{2p + 1}{7}$

62. $\dfrac{b + 9}{5} - \dfrac{5 - 7b}{2}$

63. $x - \dfrac{10 - 4x}{2}$

64. $\dfrac{-2t + 1}{8} - 3t$

65. $\dfrac{3a + 1}{6a} - \dfrac{a^2 - 2}{2a^2}$

66. $\dfrac{y^2 - 2}{2y^2} - \dfrac{2y - 7}{4y}$

67. $\dfrac{a^2}{a - 1} - \dfrac{1}{1 - a}$

68. $\dfrac{6}{x - 4} - \dfrac{x}{4 - x}$

69. $\dfrac{4}{c - 4} + \dfrac{c}{4 - c}$

70. $\dfrac{a}{a - b} + \dfrac{b}{b - a}$

71. $\dfrac{x - 5}{x + 1} - \dfrac{x + 2}{x}$

72. $\dfrac{p + 4}{p} - \dfrac{p + 3}{p - 1}$

73. $\dfrac{4x - 5}{x - 4} + \dfrac{1 - 3x}{4 - x}$

74. $\dfrac{5n}{1 - n} + \dfrac{3n - 2}{n - 1}$

75. $\dfrac{5x}{x^2 + x - 2} + \dfrac{6}{x + 2}$

76. $\dfrac{p}{p^2 - 3p + 2} + \dfrac{4}{p - 1}$

77. $\dfrac{4}{3n - 9} - \dfrac{n}{n^2 + 2n - 15}$

78. $\dfrac{-2x}{x^2 + 7x + 12} + \dfrac{5}{4x + 16}$

79. $\dfrac{2}{t + 5} - \dfrac{t + 6}{25 - t^2}$

80. $\dfrac{4}{x-2} - \dfrac{x-1}{4-x^2}$

81. $\dfrac{4x}{x^2+2x+1} - \dfrac{2x+5}{x^2+4x+3}$

82. $\dfrac{y-1}{y^2-4y+4} + \dfrac{3y}{y^2-y-2}$

83. $\dfrac{2t-1}{2t^2+t-3} + \dfrac{2}{t-1}$

84. $\dfrac{4}{y-2} + \dfrac{3y-1}{y^2-6y+8}$

85. $\dfrac{4x}{x-1} + \dfrac{2}{3x} + \dfrac{x}{x^2-1}$

86. $\dfrac{c}{c+2} + \dfrac{3}{4c} + \dfrac{2c}{c^2-4}$

87. $\dfrac{5y}{3y-1} - \dfrac{3}{y-4} + \dfrac{y+1}{3y^2-13y+4}$

88. $\dfrac{6x-1}{2x+1} + \dfrac{x}{x-1} - \dfrac{4x}{2x^2-x-1}$

89. $\dfrac{a-1}{(a+3)^2} - \dfrac{2a-3}{a+3} - \dfrac{a}{4a+12}$

90. $\dfrac{y}{8y-16} + \dfrac{3y+4}{y-2} - \dfrac{y-3}{(y-2)^2}$

Applications

Solve.

91. The distance that an object falls is given by the expression $vt + \dfrac{at^2}{2}$. Write this expression as a single rational expression.

92. The chances of an event happening can be represented by the rational expression $\dfrac{f}{t}$, whereas $\dfrac{t-f}{t}$ represents the chances of the event *not* happening. What is the sum of these two expressions?

93. Your bank pays an interest rate r compounded annually on all account balances. If you wanted the balance in an account to be $1000 at the end of one year, you would need to have a current balance of $\dfrac{1000}{1+r}$ dollars. However, if you were willing to wait two years for the balance to reach $1000, then your current balance would need to be only $\dfrac{1000}{(1+r)^2}$ dollars. Express the difference between the quantities $\dfrac{1000}{1+r}$ dollars and $\dfrac{1000}{(1+r)^2}$ dollars as a single rational expression.

94. An expression to find the length of base b of a trapezoid is $\dfrac{2A}{h} - a$. Another expression is $\dfrac{2A - ah}{h}$. Explain whether these two expressions are equivalent.

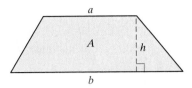

95. A trucker drove 20 mi at a speed r mph and then returned at double the speed. How long did the whole trip take? Write the answer as a single rational expression.

96. A train traveled m mi at a speed of s mph. A bus following the same route traveled 5 mph slower. How much longer did the bus take than the train to make this trip? Write the answer as a single rational expression.

97. To maintain a checking account, a bank charges a customer $3 per month and $0.10 per check. For x checks, the cost per check is $\left(\dfrac{3}{x} + 0.1\right)$ dollars. Write this cost as a single rational expression.

98. In baseball, an expression for *runners per inning* is $\dfrac{H}{I} + \dfrac{W}{I}$, where H represents the number of hits, W the number of walks, and I the number of innings pitched. Explain whether the expression $\dfrac{H + W}{2I}$ is equivalent to $\dfrac{H}{I} + \dfrac{W}{I}$.

● *Check your answers on page A-28.*

Mindstretchers

GROUPWORK

1. When we break a given rational expression into *partial fractions*, we are expressing it as the sum of two other rational expressions. For instance, we could write the rational expression $\dfrac{4x + 1}{x^2 + x}$ as $\dfrac{3}{x + 1} + \dfrac{1}{x}$.

a. Confirm that $\dfrac{4x + 1}{x^2 + x} = \dfrac{3}{x + 1} + \dfrac{1}{x}$.

b. Find the missing numerators so that $\dfrac{5x + 1}{x^2 - 1} = \dfrac{?}{x - 1} + \dfrac{?}{x + 1}$.

CRITICAL THINKING

2. Find the following product.

$$\left(1 + \frac{1}{n}\right)\left(1 + \frac{1}{n + 1}\right)\left(1 + \frac{1}{n + 2}\right)\left(1 + \frac{1}{n + 3}\right)\cdots\left(1 + \frac{1}{n + 99}\right)\left(1 + \frac{1}{n + 100}\right)$$

MATHEMATICAL REASONING

3. A formula sometimes used to add arithmetic fractions is:

$$\frac{p}{q} + \frac{r}{s} = \frac{ps + qr}{qs}$$

a. Working with a pair of arithmetic fractions of your choice, confirm that this formula gives the correct sum by comparing it to the answer derived using an alternative method.

b. Consider the left side of this formula as a sum of rational expressions. Explain why the right side of the formula is correct.

Cultural Note

(**Source:** Jan Gullberg, *From the Birth of Numbers*, W. W. Norton & Company, New York, 1997)

The ancient Egyptians expressed most fractions as the sum of *unit fractions* (fractions whose numerators are 1). For instance, they would write the fraction $\frac{2}{5}$ as $\frac{1}{3} + \frac{1}{15}$. More generally, the rational expression $\frac{x + y}{xy}$ can be written as the sum of the unit fractions $\frac{1}{x}$ and $\frac{1}{y}$.

7.4 Complex Rational Expressions

Recall that a *complex fraction* in arithmetic is a fraction that in turn contains one or more fractions in its numerator, denominator, or both:

$$\text{Main fraction line} \longrightarrow \cfrac{\dfrac{1}{3} \longleftarrow \text{Fraction in the numerator}}{\dfrac{4}{5} \longleftarrow \text{Fraction in the denominator}}$$

Such fractions can be put in standard form as the quotient of two integers by recalling that the main fraction line represents division:

$$\cfrac{\dfrac{1}{3}}{\dfrac{4}{5}} = \dfrac{1}{3} \div \dfrac{4}{5} = \dfrac{1}{3} \cdot \dfrac{5}{4} = \dfrac{5}{12}$$

A comparable expression in algebra is called a *complex rational expression* (or a *complex algebraic fraction*). Such an expression contains a rational expression in its numerator, denominator, or both. Here are some examples.

$$\cfrac{x^2 + 5x - 2}{\dfrac{3}{4}} \qquad \cfrac{7}{\dfrac{a + b}{2}} \qquad \cfrac{\dfrac{3n}{2} + \dfrac{1}{n}}{\dfrac{n - 4}{n^2}}$$

As in the case of an arithmetic complex fraction, a complex rational expression is usually simplified, that is, written as the quotient of two polynomials with no common factors.

We consider two methods of simplifying a complex rational expression: the *division method* and the *LCD method*.

In the division method, we begin by writing the numerator and denominator as single rational expressions, simplifying if necessary. Then we divide.

For instance, suppose we want to simplify the complex rational expression

$$\cfrac{\dfrac{x}{2} + \dfrac{1}{2}}{\dfrac{x^2}{3} + \dfrac{x}{3}}.$$

We first write the numerator and denominator as single rational expressions.

Add the rational expressions in the numerator.

Add the rational expressions in the denominator.

$$\cfrac{\dfrac{x}{2} + \dfrac{1}{2}}{\dfrac{x^2}{3} + \dfrac{x}{3}} = \cfrac{\dfrac{x + 1}{2}}{\dfrac{x^2 + x}{3}}$$

$$= \dfrac{x + 1}{2} \div \dfrac{x^2 + x}{3} \qquad \text{Write the expression as the numerator divided by the denominator.}$$

$$= \dfrac{x + 1}{2} \cdot \dfrac{3}{x^2 + x} \qquad \text{Take the reciprocal of the divisor and change the operation to multiplication.}$$

$$= \frac{\overset{1}{\cancel{x+1}}}{2} \cdot \frac{3}{x(\cancel{x+1})}$$ Factor and divide out the common factor.

$$= \frac{3}{2x}$$ Simplify.

So we can conclude that the original complex rational expression

$$\frac{\dfrac{x}{2} + \dfrac{1}{2}}{\dfrac{x^2}{3} + \dfrac{x}{3}} \text{ is equivalent to the rational expression } \frac{3}{2x}.$$

To Simplify a Complex Rational Expression: Division Method

- Write the numerator and denominator as single rational expressions in simplified form.
- Write the expression as the numerator divided by the denominator.
- Divide.
- Simplify, if possible.

Let's use the division method in the following examples.

EXAMPLE 1

Simplify.

a. $\dfrac{\dfrac{2}{x}}{\dfrac{6}{x^3}}$

b. $\dfrac{\dfrac{y}{y}}{\dfrac{y}{2} + \dfrac{y^2}{3}}$

SOLUTION

a. Neither the numerator nor the denominator of the complex rational expression can be simplified. So we write the expression as the numerator divided by the denominator.

$$\frac{\dfrac{2}{x}}{\dfrac{6}{x^3}} = \frac{2}{x} \div \frac{6}{x^3}$$

$$= \frac{2}{x} \cdot \frac{x^3}{6}$$ Take the reciprocal of the divisor and change the operation to multiplication.

$$= \frac{\overset{1}{\cancel{2}}}{\cancel{x}} \cdot \frac{\overset{x^2}{\cancel{x^3}}}{\cancel{6}}$$ Divide out the common factors.

$$= \frac{x^2}{3}$$ Simplify.

PRACTICE 1

Simplify.

a. $\dfrac{\dfrac{3}{x^4}}{\dfrac{5}{x}}$

b. $\dfrac{\dfrac{2x}{x^2}}{\dfrac{x^2}{4} + \dfrac{x}{2}}$

b. First we express the denominator as a single rational expression.

$$\frac{y}{\dfrac{y}{2} + \dfrac{y^2}{3}} = \frac{y}{\dfrac{y \cdot 3}{2 \cdot 3} + \dfrac{y^2 \cdot 2}{3 \cdot 2}}$$

Add the rational expressions in the denominator. The LCD is 6.

$$= \frac{y}{\dfrac{3y + 2y^2}{6}}$$

$$= y \div \frac{3y + 2y^2}{6}$$

Write the expression as the numerator divided by the denominator.

$$= y \cdot \frac{6}{3y + 2y^2}$$

Take the reciprocal of the divisor and change the operation to multiplication.

$$= \overset{1}{y} \cdot \frac{6}{\underset{1}{y}(3 + 2y)}$$

Factor and divide out the common factor.

$$= \frac{6}{3 + 2y}$$

Simplify.

EXAMPLE 2

Simplify: $\dfrac{1 + \dfrac{1}{x}}{1 - \dfrac{1}{x}}$

SOLUTION First we simplify the numerator and denominator so that each is a single rational expression.

$$\frac{1 + \dfrac{1}{x}}{1 - \dfrac{1}{x}} = \frac{\dfrac{x + 1}{x}}{\dfrac{x - 1}{x}}$$

$$= \frac{x + 1}{x} \div \frac{x - 1}{x}$$

$$= \frac{x + 1}{x} \cdot \frac{x}{x - 1}$$

$$= \frac{x + 1}{\underset{1}{\cancel{x}}} \cdot \frac{\overset{1}{\cancel{x}}}{x - 1}$$

$$= \frac{x + 1}{x - 1}$$

PRACTICE 2

Simplify: $\dfrac{2 - \dfrac{1}{n}}{2 + \dfrac{1}{n}}$

Now we consider the LCD method of simplifying a complex rational expression. In this method, we multiply the numerator and denominator of the complex rational expression by the LCD of all rational expressions that appear within it.

Let's simplify the complex rational expression on page 572 using the LCD method. First, we must find the LCD of all the rational expressions in the numerator and denominator. The denominators within the complex rational expression are 2 and 3, so the LCD is 6.

$$\frac{\dfrac{x}{2}+\dfrac{1}{2}}{\dfrac{x^2}{3}+\dfrac{x}{3}}=\frac{\left(\dfrac{x}{2}+\dfrac{1}{2}\right)\cdot 6}{\left(\dfrac{x^2}{3}+\dfrac{x}{3}\right)\cdot 6}$$

Multiply the numerator and denominator by the LCD 6.

$$=\frac{\dfrac{x}{2}\cdot 6+\dfrac{1}{2}\cdot 6}{\dfrac{x^2}{3}\cdot 6+\dfrac{x}{3}\cdot 6}$$

Use the distributive property.

$$=\frac{3x+3}{2x^2+2x}$$

Simplify.

$$=\frac{3(x+1)}{2x(x+1)}$$

Factor and divide out the common factor.

$$=\frac{3}{2x}$$

Simplify.

Note that the division method and the LCD method result in the same answer.

To Simplify a Complex Rational Expression: LCD Method

- Find the LCD of all the rational expressions *within* both the numerator and denominator.
- Multiply the numerator and denominator of the complex rational expression by this LCD.
- Simplify, if possible.

EXAMPLE 3

Simplify.

a. $\dfrac{\dfrac{3}{y^2}}{\dfrac{1}{y}}$

b. $\dfrac{n^2}{\dfrac{1}{n}+\dfrac{2}{n^2}}$

SOLUTION

a. $\dfrac{\dfrac{3}{y^2}}{\dfrac{1}{y}}=\dfrac{\dfrac{3}{y^2}\cdot y^2}{\dfrac{1}{y}\cdot y^2}$ Multiply by the LCD y^2.

$=\dfrac{3}{y}$ Simplify.

PRACTICE 3

Simplify.

a. $\dfrac{\dfrac{4}{x}}{\dfrac{2}{x^3}}$

b. $\dfrac{\dfrac{1}{y}+\dfrac{3}{y^2}}{2y}$

b. $\dfrac{n^2}{\dfrac{1}{n} + \dfrac{2}{n^2}} = \dfrac{n^2 \cdot n^2}{\left(\dfrac{1}{n} + \dfrac{2}{n^2}\right) \cdot n^2}$ Multiply by the LCD n^2.

$\qquad = \dfrac{n^2 \cdot n^2}{\dfrac{1}{n} \cdot n^2 + \dfrac{2}{n^2} \cdot n^2}$ Use the distributive property.

$\qquad = \dfrac{n^4}{n + 2}$ Simplify.

EXAMPLE 4

Simplify.

a. $\dfrac{3 + \dfrac{1}{x^2}}{3 - \dfrac{1}{x}}$ **b.** $\dfrac{\dfrac{1}{x^2} - \dfrac{1}{y^2}}{\dfrac{3}{x} - \dfrac{3}{y}}$

SOLUTION

a. Multiply the numerator and denominator by the LCD x^2.

$$\frac{3 + \dfrac{1}{x^2}}{3 - \dfrac{1}{x}} = \frac{\left(3 + \dfrac{1}{x^2}\right) \cdot x^2}{\left(3 - \dfrac{1}{x}\right) \cdot x^2}$$

$$= \frac{3 \cdot x^2 + \dfrac{1}{x^2} \cdot x^2}{3 \cdot x^2 - \dfrac{1}{x} \cdot x^2}$$

$$= \frac{3x^2 + 1}{3x^2 - x}$$

b. Multiply the numerator and denominator by the LCD $x^2 y^2$.

$$\frac{\dfrac{1}{x^2} - \dfrac{1}{y^2}}{\dfrac{3}{x} - \dfrac{3}{y}} = \frac{\left(\dfrac{1}{x^2} - \dfrac{1}{y^2}\right) \cdot x^2 y^2}{\left(\dfrac{3}{x} - \dfrac{3}{y}\right) \cdot x^2 y^2}$$

$$= \frac{\dfrac{1}{x^2}(x^2 y^2) - \dfrac{1}{y^2}(x^2 y^2)}{\dfrac{3}{x}(x^2 y^2) - \dfrac{3}{y}(x^2 y^2)}$$

$$= \frac{y^2 - x^2}{3xy^2 - 3x^2 y}$$

$$= \frac{\overset{1}{\cancel{(y - x)}}(y + x)}{3xy\underset{1}{\cancel{(y - x)}}}$$

$$= \frac{y + x}{3xy}$$

PRACTICE 4

Express in simplest terms.

a. $\dfrac{4 + \dfrac{1}{y}}{4 - \dfrac{1}{y^2}}$

b. $\dfrac{\dfrac{1}{2a^2} - \dfrac{1}{2b^2}}{\dfrac{5}{a} + \dfrac{5}{b}}$

EXAMPLE 5

A resistor is an electrical device such as a lightbulb that offers resistance to the flow of electricity. When two lightbulbs with resistance R_1 and R_2 are connected in a certain kind of circuit, the combined resistance is given by the expression

$$\frac{1}{\dfrac{1}{R_1} + \dfrac{1}{R_2}}$$

Simplify this expression for the combined resistance.

SOLUTION

$$\frac{1}{\dfrac{1}{R_1} + \dfrac{1}{R_2}} = \frac{1 \cdot R_1 R_2}{\left(\dfrac{1}{R_1} + \dfrac{1}{R_2}\right) \cdot R_1 R_2}$$

$$= \frac{1 \cdot R_1 R_2}{\dfrac{1}{R_1} \cdot R_1 R_2 + \dfrac{1}{R_2} \cdot R_1 R_2} = \frac{R_1 R_2}{R_2 + R_1}$$

PRACTICE 5

The harmonic mean is a kind of average. The harmonic mean of the three numbers a, b, and c is given by the expression $\dfrac{3}{\dfrac{1}{a} + \dfrac{1}{b} + \dfrac{1}{c}}$. Simplify this complex rational expression.

Exercises 7.4

Simplify.

1. $\dfrac{\dfrac{x}{5}}{\dfrac{x^2}{10}}$

2. $\dfrac{\dfrac{3}{s^2}}{\dfrac{s^3}{2}}$

3. $\dfrac{\dfrac{a+1}{2}}{\dfrac{a-1}{2}}$

4. $\dfrac{\dfrac{n-1}{n}}{\dfrac{n+1}{2n}}$

5. $\dfrac{3+\dfrac{1}{x}}{3-\dfrac{1}{x^2}}$

6. $\dfrac{1+\dfrac{1}{y^2}}{8-\dfrac{1}{y}}$

7. $\dfrac{\dfrac{1}{3d}-\dfrac{1}{d^2}}{d-\dfrac{9}{d}}$

8. $\dfrac{a-\dfrac{4}{a}}{\dfrac{1}{a^2}+\dfrac{1}{2a}}$

9. $\dfrac{1-\dfrac{4y^2}{x^2}}{3+\dfrac{6y}{x}}$

10. $\dfrac{\dfrac{p}{q}+2}{\dfrac{p^2}{q^2}-4}$

11. $\dfrac{\dfrac{2}{y}-\dfrac{1}{5}}{\dfrac{5}{y}-1}$

12. $\dfrac{\dfrac{2}{t}-\dfrac{3}{t^2}}{10+\dfrac{2}{t}}$

13. $\dfrac{1+\dfrac{4}{x}+\dfrac{4}{x^2}}{1+\dfrac{5}{x}+\dfrac{6}{x^2}}$

14. $\dfrac{1-\dfrac{1}{a^2}}{4-\dfrac{5}{a}+\dfrac{1}{a^2}}$

15. $\dfrac{3+\dfrac{1}{y+1}}{5-\dfrac{1}{y+1}}$

16. $\dfrac{2+\dfrac{1}{b-1}}{2-\dfrac{1}{b-1}}$

17. $\dfrac{\dfrac{x}{4}-\dfrac{x}{8}}{\dfrac{2}{y^2}+\dfrac{2}{y}}$

18. $\dfrac{\dfrac{n}{2}+\dfrac{n}{3}}{\dfrac{1}{m}-\dfrac{1}{m^2}}$

19. $\dfrac{\dfrac{x}{x+1}-\dfrac{2}{x}}{\dfrac{x}{3}}$

20. $\dfrac{\dfrac{y}{5}}{\dfrac{y}{y+2}+\dfrac{3}{y}}$

Applications

Solve.

21. An expression from the study of electricity is

$$\frac{V}{\dfrac{1}{2R} + \dfrac{1}{2R + 2}},$$

where V represents voltage and R represents resistance. Simplify this expression.

22. The expression

$$\frac{\dfrac{m}{c}}{1 - \dfrac{p^2}{c^2}}$$

is important in the design of airplanes. Write this expression in simplified form.

23. The earned run average (ERA) is a statistic used in baseball to represent the average number of earned runs that a pitcher allows. A pitcher's ERA can be calculated using the expression

$$\frac{E}{\dfrac{I}{9}},$$

where E stands for the number of earned runs a pitcher gave up after pitching I innings. Simplify this complex rational expression.

24. The ratio of the volume of a cube with side s to the volume of its inscribed sphere is

$$\frac{s^3}{\dfrac{1}{6}\pi s^3}.$$

Simplify this ratio.

25. On a trip, an airplane flew at an average speed of a mph, returning on the same route at an average speed of b mph. The plane's average speed for the round trip is given by the complex rational expression

$$\frac{2}{\dfrac{1}{a} + \dfrac{1}{b}}.$$

Simplify.

26. An object travels at speed s for a distance d and later travels at speed S for distance D. The following expression represents the average speed for the entire trip.

$$\frac{d + D}{\dfrac{d}{s} + \dfrac{D}{S}}$$

Simplify this expression.

27. The weight of an object decreases as its distance from the Earth's surface increases. Suppose an object weighs w kilograms at sea level. Then at a height of h km above sea level, it will weigh

$$\frac{w}{\left(1 + \dfrac{h}{6400}\right)^2}.$$

Show that $\dfrac{w}{\left(1 + \dfrac{h}{6400}\right)^2}$ and $\dfrac{6400^2 w}{(6400 + h)^2}$ are equivalent expressions.

28. The sound from a car horn as it approaches an observer seems to change its frequency. This is an example of the Doppler effect, which is studied in physics. The observer will hear a sound with frequency

$$\frac{S}{\dfrac{S - v}{f}},$$

where f is the actual frequency of the sound, S is the speed of sound, and v is the speed of the approaching object. Simplify the expression.

● *Check your answers on page A-28.*

Mindstretchers

RESEARCH

1. The harmonic mean (see Practice 5, page 577) is related to musical harmony. Either in your college library or on the Web, investigate the relationship between music and the harmonic mean. Summarize your findings in a few sentences.

_____

WRITING

2. Select a complex rational expression of your choice and simplify it using (a) the division method and (b) the LCD method. Which method do you prefer? Explain why.

_____

_____

_____

GROUPWORK

3. Find a complex rational expression with numerator $\dfrac{4}{y}$ that simplifies to $\dfrac{3}{x+5}$.

7.5 Solving Rational Equations

What Rational Equations Are and Why They Are Important

So far in this chapter, we have discussed rational expressions. Now let's consider *rational* or *fractional equations*, that is, equations that contain one or more rational expressions. Here are some examples:

$$\frac{n}{2} - 3 = \frac{n}{5} \qquad \frac{1}{t} + \frac{1}{3} = \frac{1}{2} \qquad \frac{3}{x+1} - \frac{1}{8} = \frac{5}{x^2-1}$$

Many situations involving rates of work, motion, and proportions can be modeled by rational equations.

Solving Rational Equations

In solving rational equations, it is important not to confuse a rational expression with a rational equation.

$$\frac{4x}{3} + \frac{x}{3} \qquad\qquad \frac{4x}{3} + \frac{x}{3} = 5$$

Rational *expression*   Rational *equation*

The key to solving a rational equation is to *clear the equation of rational expressions.* We do this by first determining their *least common denominator*, and then by multiplying both sides of the equation by the LCD.

EXAMPLE 1

Solve and check: $\dfrac{x}{2} + \dfrac{x}{6} = \dfrac{2}{3}$

SOLUTION The rational expressions in this equation are $\dfrac{x}{2}, \dfrac{x}{6}$, and $\dfrac{2}{3}$. The denominators of these expressions are 2, 6, and 3, so the LCD is 6. To clear the equation of rational expressions, we multiply each side of the equation by 6.

$$\frac{x}{2} + \frac{x}{6} = \frac{2}{3}$$

$$6 \cdot \left(\frac{x}{2} + \frac{x}{6}\right) = 6 \cdot \frac{2}{3} \qquad \text{Multiply each side of the equation by the LCD.}$$

$$6 \cdot \frac{x}{2} + 6 \cdot \frac{x}{6} = 6 \cdot \frac{2}{3} \qquad \text{Use the distributive property.}$$

$$3x + x = 4 \qquad \text{Simplify.}$$

$$4x = 4 \qquad \text{Combine like terms.}$$

$$x = 1 \qquad \text{Divide each side by 4.}$$

PRACTICE 1

Solve and check: $\dfrac{y}{2} - \dfrac{y}{3} = \dfrac{1}{12}$

CHECK

$$\frac{x}{2} + \frac{x}{6} = \frac{2}{3}$$

$$\frac{1}{2} + \frac{1}{6} \overset{?}{=} \frac{2}{3} \qquad \text{Substitute 1 for } x.$$

$$\frac{3}{6} + \frac{1}{6} \overset{?}{=} \frac{2}{3}$$

$$\frac{4}{6} \overset{?}{=} \frac{2}{3}$$

$$\frac{2}{3} = \frac{2}{3} \qquad \text{True.}$$

So the solution to the given equation is 1.

The following rule describes the general procedure for solving equations of this type.

To Solve a Rational Equation

- Find the LCD of all rational expressions in the equation.
- Multiply each side of the equation by the LCD.
- Solve the equation.
- Check the solution(s) in the original equation.

EXAMPLE 2

Solve and check: $\dfrac{4}{n} - \dfrac{n+1}{3} = 1$

SOLUTION The LCD of the rational expressions in the equation is $3n$.

$$\frac{4}{n} - \frac{n+1}{3} = 1$$

$$3n \cdot \left(\frac{4}{n} - \frac{n+1}{3} \right) = 3n \cdot 1 \qquad \begin{array}{l}\text{Multiply each side of the equation} \\ \text{by the LCD.}\end{array}$$

$$3n \cdot \frac{4}{n} - 3n \cdot \frac{n+1}{3} = 3n \cdot 1 \qquad \begin{array}{l}\text{Distribute } 3n \text{ on the left side} \\ \text{of the equation.}\end{array}$$

$$3\overset{1}{\cancel{n}} \cdot \frac{4}{\cancel{n}} - \cancel{3}n \cdot \frac{n+1}{\cancel{3}} = 3n \cdot 1$$

$$12 - n(n+1) = 3n \qquad \text{Simplify.}$$

$$12 - n^2 - n = 3n \qquad \text{Use the distributive property.}$$

$$n^2 + n + 3n - 12 = 0$$

$$n^2 + 4n - 12 = 0 \qquad \text{Write in standard form.}$$

$$(n + 6)(n - 2) = 0 \qquad \text{Factor the left side of the equation.}$$

$$n + 6 = 0 \quad \text{or} \quad n - 2 = 0 \qquad \text{Set each factor equal to 0.}$$

$$n = -6 \qquad\qquad n = 2$$

PRACTICE 2

Solve and check: $\dfrac{x-2}{5} - 1 = -\dfrac{2}{x}$

CHECK

Substitute −6 for n.

$$\frac{4}{n} - \frac{n+1}{3} = 1$$

$$\frac{4}{-6} - \frac{-6+1}{3} \overset{?}{=} 1$$

$$-\frac{2}{3} - \left(-\frac{5}{3}\right) \overset{?}{=} 1$$

$$-\frac{2}{3} + \frac{5}{3} \overset{?}{=} 1$$

$$\frac{3}{3} \overset{?}{=} 1$$

$$1 = 1 \qquad \text{True.}$$

Substitute 2 for n.

$$\frac{4}{n} - \frac{n+1}{3} = 1$$

$$\frac{4}{2} - \frac{2+1}{3} \overset{?}{=} 1$$

$$2 - 1 \overset{?}{=} 1$$

$$1 = 1 \qquad \text{True.}$$

Our check confirms that the solutions are −6 and 2.

EXAMPLE 3

Solve and check: $\dfrac{2}{x+3} + \dfrac{1}{x-3} = -\dfrac{6}{x^2-9}$

SOLUTION First we find the LCD of the rational expressions in this equation, which is $x^2 - 9$, or $(x+3)(x-3)$. Then we muliply each side of the equation by the LCD.

$$\frac{2}{x+3} + \frac{1}{x-3} = -\frac{6}{x^2-9}$$

$$\frac{2}{x+3} + \frac{1}{x-3} = -\frac{6}{(x+3)(x-3)}$$

$$(x+3)(x-3) \cdot \frac{2}{x+3} + (x+3)(x-3) \cdot \frac{1}{x-3} = (x+3)(x-3) \cdot \frac{-6}{(x+3)(x-3)}$$

$$(x+3)(x-3) \cdot \frac{2}{x+3} + (x+3)(x-3) \cdot \frac{1}{x-3} = (x+3)(x-3) \cdot \frac{-6}{(x+3)(x-3)}$$

$$2(x-3) + (x+3) = -6$$

$$2x - 6 + x + 3 = -6$$

$$3x - 3 = -6$$

$$3x = -3$$

$$x = -1$$

CHECK

$$\frac{2}{x+3} + \frac{1}{x-3} = -\frac{6}{x^2-9}$$

$$\frac{2}{-1+3} + \frac{1}{-1-3} \overset{?}{=} -\frac{6}{(-1)^2-9} \qquad \text{Substitute −1 for } x.$$

$$\frac{2}{2} + \frac{1}{-4} \stackrel{?}{=} -\frac{6}{-8} \qquad \text{Simplify.}$$

$$\frac{2}{2} + \left(-\frac{1}{4}\right) \stackrel{?}{=} -\left(-\frac{6}{8}\right)$$

$$1 - \frac{1}{4} \stackrel{?}{=} \frac{3}{4}$$

$$\frac{3}{4} = \frac{3}{4} \qquad \text{True.}$$

So the solution is -1.

PRACTICE 3

Solve and check: $\dfrac{4}{y + 2} + \dfrac{2}{y - 1} = \dfrac{12}{y^2 + y - 2}$

When multiplying each side of a rational equation by a variable expression, the resulting equation may have a solution that does not satisfy the original equation. If such a result makes a denominator in the original equation 0, then the rational expression is undefined. These *extraneous solutions* are *not* solutions of the original equation. So in solving rational equations, it is particularly important to check all possible solutions.

EXAMPLE 4

Solve and check: $\dfrac{x^2}{x - 2} = \dfrac{4}{x - 2}$

SOLUTION The LCD of the rational expressions is $x - 2$.

$$\frac{x^2}{x - 2} = \frac{4}{x - 2}$$

$$(x - 2) \cdot \frac{x^2}{x - 2} = (x - 2) \cdot \frac{4}{x - 2} \qquad \begin{array}{l}\text{Multiply each side of the equation} \\ \text{by the LCD.}\end{array}$$

$$(x - 2) \cdot \frac{x^2}{x - 2} = (x - 2) \cdot \frac{4}{x - 2}$$

$$x^2 = 4$$

$$x^2 - 4 = 0$$

$$(x + 2)(x - 2) = 0 \qquad \text{Factor the left side of the equation.}$$

$$x + 2 = 0 \quad \text{or} \quad x - 2 = 0 \qquad \text{Set each factor equal to 0.}$$

$$x = -2 \qquad\qquad x = 2 \qquad \text{Solve for } x.$$

PRACTICE 4

Solve and check: $x = \dfrac{9}{x + 3} + \dfrac{3x}{x + 3}$

CHECK

Substitute -2 for x.　　　　　Substitute 2 for x.

$$\dfrac{x^2}{x-2} = \dfrac{4}{x-2}$$

$$\dfrac{(-2)^2}{-2-2} \overset{?}{=} \dfrac{4}{-2-2}$$

$$-\dfrac{4}{4} = -\dfrac{4}{4} \qquad \text{True.}$$

$$\dfrac{x^2}{x-2} = \dfrac{4}{x-2}$$

$$\dfrac{2^2}{2-2} \overset{?}{=} \dfrac{4}{2-2}$$

$$\dfrac{4}{0} = \dfrac{4}{0} \qquad \text{Undefined.}$$

Since we get undefined fractions when we substitute 2 for x in the original equation, 2 is *not* a solution. So the solution is -2. Without solving, how could we have known that 2 is *not* a solution of the original equation? Explain.

Rational equations play an important role in a kind of application known as *work problems*. In these problems, we typically want to compute how long it will take to complete a task.

The key to solving a work problem is to determine the *rate of work*, that is, the fraction of the task that is completed in one unit of time. For instance, if it takes a secretary 5 hr to type a report, then the secretary's rate of work—the fraction of the report typed in 1 hr—would be $\dfrac{1}{5}$. If it takes a painter 6 hr to paint a room, then $\dfrac{1}{6}$ of the room would be painted in an hour so that $\dfrac{1}{6}$ is the painter's rate of work.

Consider the following example.

EXAMPLE 5

Two company employees, one senior and the other junior, are responsible for carrying out a project. If the two employees had worked alone, the junior employee would have completed the project in 6 hr and the senior employee would have completed it in 4 hr. How long would it take the two employees to carry out the project working together?

SOLUTION Since this is a work problem, we can use the following equation to determine how long it will take the two employees to carry out the project working together.

Rate of work · Time worked = Part of the task completed

Using this equation, we can set up a table. Let t represent the time it takes the two employees to complete the project working together. Note here that the task to be completed is the project.

	Rate of Work ·	Time Worked =	Part of the Task Completed
Senior employee	$\dfrac{1}{4}$	t	$\dfrac{1}{4} \cdot t$
Junior employee	$\dfrac{1}{6}$	t	$\dfrac{1}{6} \cdot t$

PRACTICE 5

A town water tank has two pumps. Working alone, the less powerful pump can fill the tank in 10 hr, whereas the more powerful pump can fill it in 6 hr. How long will it take both pumps working together to fill the tank?

Since the sum of the parts of the task completed must equal one complete task, we have:

$$\frac{1}{4} \cdot t + \frac{1}{6} \cdot t = 1$$

$$\frac{t}{4} + \frac{t}{6} = 1$$

To solve this equation, we multiply each side by the LCD, 12.

$$12 \cdot \frac{t}{4} + 12 \cdot \frac{t}{6} = 12 \cdot 1$$

$$3t + 2t = 12$$

$$5t = 12$$

$$t = 2\tfrac{2}{5} = 2.4$$

So working together, it would take the two employees 2.4 hr (or 2 hr and 24 min) to complete the project. We can confirm this solution by checking.

Another application of rational equations is motion problems. Recall that in these problems, an object moves at a constant rate r for time t and travels a distance d. These three quantities are related by the following formula:

$$r \cdot t = d$$

If we solve this equation for t, we get $t = \dfrac{d}{r}$, a variation on the formula that we apply in Example 6. In this example, note that the total time that the two objects traveled is known.

EXAMPLE 6

A family on vacation drove 50 mi to a hotel and then returned home following the same route. Because of lighter traffic, the family drove at twice the speed going to the hotel as compared to returning home. If the round trip took 3 hr, at what speed did the family return home?

SOLUTION We are looking for the family's speed returning home. Let's represent this unknown quantity by r. Since the family traveled twice as fast going to the hotel as returning home, their speed going to the hotel must have been $2r$. We use the formula $\dfrac{d}{r} = t$ to find the time traveled in each direction, and set up a table.

	Distance	÷ Rate	= Time
Going to the hotel	50	$2r$	$\dfrac{50}{2r}$
Returning home	50	r	$\dfrac{50}{r}$

PRACTICE 6

A business executive traveled 1800 mi by jet, continuing the trip an additional 300 mi on a propeller plane. The speed of the jet was 3 times that of the propeller plane. If the entire trip took 6 hr, what was the speed of the propeller plane?

Since it is given that the round trip took 3 hr in all, we write:

$$\frac{50}{2r} + \frac{50}{r} = 3$$

To solve this rational equation, we multiply each side of the equation by the LCD, $2r$.

$$2r \cdot \frac{50}{2r} + 2r \cdot \frac{50}{r} = 2r \cdot 3$$

$$\overset{1}{\cancel{2r}} \cdot \frac{50}{\underset{1}{\cancel{2r}}} + 2\overset{1}{\cancel{r}} \cdot \frac{50}{\underset{1}{\cancel{r}}} = 2r \cdot 3$$

$$50 + 100 = 6r$$
$$6r = 150$$
$$r = 25$$

So the family returned home at 25 mph. We can confirm this solution by checking.

Some rational equations are formulas that relate two or more variables. Consider the following example.

EXAMPLE 7	PRACTICE 7

EXAMPLE 7

The formula $\dfrac{1}{f} = \dfrac{1}{p} + \dfrac{1}{q}$ gives the focal length f of a lens, where p is the distance between the lens and an object and q is the distance between the image and the lens.

a. Solve this equation for f.

b. Use the formula found in part (a) to find the value of f when $p = 40$ cm and $q = 10$ cm.

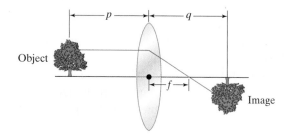

SOLUTION

a. Our task is to solve the equation for f.

$$\frac{1}{f} = \frac{1}{p} + \frac{1}{q}$$

$$fpq \cdot \frac{1}{f} = fpq \cdot \left(\frac{1}{p} + \frac{1}{q} \right)$$

$$fpq \cdot \frac{1}{f} = fpq \cdot \frac{1}{p} + fpq \cdot \frac{1}{q}$$

$$\overset{1}{\cancel{f}}pq \cdot \frac{1}{\underset{1}{\cancel{f}}} = f\overset{1}{\cancel{p}}q \cdot \frac{1}{\underset{1}{\cancel{p}}} + fp\overset{1}{\cancel{q}} \cdot \frac{1}{\underset{1}{\cancel{q}}}$$

$$pq = fq + fp$$

PRACTICE 7

Economists are interested in how the free market works. Suppose that a commodity sells at the price x dollars per unit. A formula that might represent the number of units sold, called the demand D, is:

$$D = \frac{500}{x} + 50$$

a. Solve for x in terms of D.

b. Find the value of x when the demand is 450 units.

Since we are solving for f, we factor it out on the right side of the equation.

$$pq = f(q + p)$$

$$f = \frac{pq}{p + q}$$

b. Substituting 40 for p and 10 for q in the formula $f = \dfrac{pq}{p + q}$

we get:

$$f = \frac{40 \cdot 10}{40 + 10}$$

$$= \frac{400}{50}$$

$$= 8$$

So the focal length of the lens is 8 cm.

Exercises 7.5

FOR EXTRA HELP

📖 *Student's Solutions Manual*

📞 *Addison-Wesley Math Tutor Center*

🚪 *MyMathLab*

📼 *Videotape 7/DVT 7*

Solve and check.

1. $\dfrac{y}{2} + \dfrac{7}{10} = -\dfrac{4}{5}$

2. $\dfrac{x}{6} - \dfrac{1}{10} = \dfrac{2}{5}$

3. $\dfrac{1}{t} - \dfrac{7}{3} = -\dfrac{1}{3}$

4. $\dfrac{5}{p} + \dfrac{1}{3} = \dfrac{6}{p}$

5. $x + \dfrac{1}{x} = 2$

6. $y + \dfrac{2}{y} = 3$

7. $\dfrac{t+1}{2t-1} - \dfrac{5}{7} = 0$

8. $\dfrac{b-3}{3b-2} - \dfrac{4}{5} = 0$

9. $\dfrac{t-2}{3} = 4$

10. $\dfrac{4}{x+1} = 3$

11. $\dfrac{4}{s-3} - \dfrac{3s}{s-3} = 2$

12. $\dfrac{2n}{n+1} = \dfrac{-2}{n+1} + 1$

13. $\dfrac{5x}{x+1} = \dfrac{x^2}{x+1} + 2$

14. $\dfrac{x^2}{x-2} = \dfrac{2x}{x-2} + 3$

15. $\dfrac{x}{x-3} - \dfrac{6}{x} = 1$

16. $\dfrac{2}{t} + \dfrac{t}{t+1} = 1$

17. $1 + \dfrac{4}{x^2} = \dfrac{4}{x}$

18. $\dfrac{1}{2x} + \dfrac{3}{x^2} = 1$

19. $\dfrac{2}{p+1} - \dfrac{1}{p-1} = \dfrac{2p}{p^2-1}$

20. $\dfrac{2}{y+2} - \dfrac{5}{2-y} = \dfrac{3y}{y^2-4}$

21. $\dfrac{3}{x} - \dfrac{1}{x+4} = \dfrac{5}{x^2+4x}$

22. $\dfrac{2}{y-2} + \dfrac{3}{y} = \dfrac{4}{-2y+y^2}$

23. $1 - \dfrac{6x}{(x-4)^2} = \dfrac{2x}{x-4}$

24. $\dfrac{4x}{x+1} - 2 = -\dfrac{3x}{(x+1)^2}$

25. $\dfrac{n+1}{n^2+2n-3} = \dfrac{n}{n+3} - \dfrac{1}{n-1}$

26. $\dfrac{7}{x-5} - \dfrac{5x+6}{x^2-3x-10} = \dfrac{x}{x+2}$

Applications

Solve.

27. Two brothers share a house. It would take the younger brother working alone 45 min to clean the attic, whereas it would take the older brother only 30 min. If the two brothers worked together, how long would it take them to clean the attic?

28. One crew can pave a road in 24 hr and a second crew can do the same job in 16 hr. How long would it take for the two crews working together to pave the road?

29. A clerical worker takes 4 times as long to finish a job as it does an executive secretary. Working together, it takes them 3 hr to finish the job. How long would it take the clerical worker, working alone, to finish the job?

30. One pipe can fill a tank in 1 min. A second pipe takes 2 min to fill the same tank. Working together, how long will it take both pipes to fill the tank?

31. A car traveled twice as fast on a dry road as it did making the return trip on a slippery road. The trip was 60 mi each way, and the round trip took 3 hr. What was the speed of the car on the dry road?

32. A cyclist rode uphill and then turned around and made the same trip downhill. The downhill speed was 3 times the uphill speed. If the trip each way was 18 mi and the entire trip lasted 2 hr, at what speed was the cyclist going uphill?

33. Steam exerts pressure on a pipe. In the formula

$$p = \frac{P}{LD},$$

p represents the pressure per square inch in the pipe, P stands for the total pressure in the pipe, L is the pipe's length, and D is the pipe's diameter. Solve this formula for D.

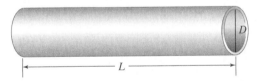

34. To approximate the appropriate dosage of medicine for a child, doctors sometimes use Young's rule:

$$C = \frac{aA}{a + 12},$$

where C represents the child's dosage, a stands for the child's age, and A is the adult dosage. Solve this formula for a.

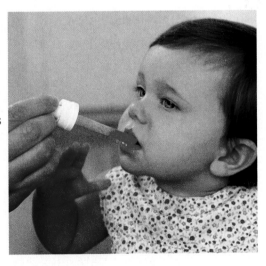

• *Check your answers on page A-28.*

Mindstretchers

GROUPWORK

1. Working with a partner, show that there are no positive real numbers a and b for which the equation $\dfrac{1}{a} + \dfrac{1}{b} = \dfrac{1}{a + b}$ is true.

MATHEMATICAL REASONING

2. Use your knowledge of systems of equations to solve the following system:

$$\textbf{(1)} \quad \frac{1}{x} + \frac{3}{y} = 1$$

$$\textbf{(2)} \quad -\frac{4}{x} + \frac{3}{y} = -3$$

TECHNOLOGY

3. Consider the rational equation $y = \dfrac{100}{x}$.

a. Graph this equation by plotting points whose coordinates satisfy the equation on the following grid.

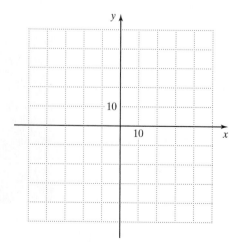

b. Graph this equation by using a grapher.

c. Using the graph found in either part (a) or part (b), describe what happens to the graph at $x = 0$.

_____

_____

7.6 Ratio and Proportion

Recall in Section 7.5 that to solve rational equations we multiplied every term by the LCD in order to clear the denominators. However, rational equations of a particular form, where one rational expression equals another, lend themselves to an alternative method for clearing denominators. Here are some examples of equations of that form:

$$\frac{x}{12} = \frac{2}{3} \qquad \frac{5}{6} = \frac{10}{n} \qquad \frac{1}{n+1} = \frac{3}{n-1}$$

Note that in each of these equations, two rational expressions are equal to one another.

Two rational expressions are equal to one another when their *cross products* are equal. So rather than multiplying by the LCD, we can simply *set the cross products equal*. Let's apply each method to the first equation.

LCD Method		**Cross-Product Method**	
$\dfrac{x}{12} = \dfrac{2}{3}$		$\dfrac{x}{12} = \dfrac{2}{3}$	
$12 \cdot \dfrac{x}{12} = 12 \cdot \dfrac{2}{3}$	Multiply each side of the equation by the LCD, 12.		Cross products
$\overset{1}{\cancel{12}} \cdot \dfrac{x}{\cancel{12}} = \overset{4}{\cancel{12}} \cdot \dfrac{2}{\cancel{3}}$	Divide out common factors.	$3 \cdot x = 12 \cdot 2$	Cross multiply.
$1 \cdot x = 4 \cdot 2$	Simplify.	$3x = 24$	Simplify.
$x = 8$		$\dfrac{3x}{3} = \dfrac{24}{3}$	Divide each side of the equation by 3.
		$x = 8$	

So in both methods, our solution appears to be 8, but is it correct? We can check by substituting in the original equation:

$$\frac{x}{12} = \frac{2}{3}$$

$$\frac{8}{12} \overset{?}{=} \frac{2}{3}$$

$$\frac{2}{3} = \frac{2}{3} \qquad \text{True.}$$

We conclude that when two rational expressions are equal to one another, we can solve the equation by either the LCD method or the cross-product method. In this section, we solve these types of equations using the cross-product method.

EXAMPLE 1

Solve: $\dfrac{5}{6} = \dfrac{10}{n}$

SOLUTION We clear the denominators by cross multiplying.

$$\dfrac{5}{6} = \dfrac{10}{n} \qquad \textbf{Cross multiply.}$$

$$5n = 60$$

$$\dfrac{5n}{5} = \dfrac{60}{5} \qquad \textbf{Divide both sides by 5.}$$

$$n = 12$$

CHECK

$$\dfrac{5}{6} = \dfrac{10}{n}$$

$$\dfrac{5}{6} \overset{?}{=} \dfrac{10}{12} \qquad \textbf{Substitute 12 for } n.$$

$$\dfrac{5}{6} = \dfrac{5}{6} \qquad \textbf{True.}$$

PRACTICE 1

Solve: $\dfrac{4}{5} = \dfrac{p}{10}$

Equations of the type shown in Example 1 commonly arise from *ratio and proportion* problems.

A *ratio* is a comparison of two numbers, expressed as a quotient. For instance, if we compare the numbers 5 and 8, their ratio would be 5 to 8, written as $\dfrac{5}{8}$ or 5:8. Here are some other ratios.

- A ratio of 6 women to 4 men, written as $\dfrac{6}{4}$, or in simplest terms, $\dfrac{3}{2}$

- A ratio of 230 congressmen voting for a bill to 180 congressmen voting against the same bill, written as $\dfrac{230}{180}$, or $\dfrac{23}{18}$

A ratio of quantities with different units is called a *rate*. Here are some examples.

- A basketball team's record of 8 wins and 2 losses, written as $\dfrac{8 \text{ wins}}{2 \text{ losses}}$

- A wage of $20 per hour, written as $\dfrac{20 \text{ dollars}}{1 \text{ hour}}$

When two ratios (or rates) are equal, we say that they are *in proportion*. For instance, the ratios $\dfrac{1}{2}$ and $\dfrac{4}{8}$ are in proportion. The equation $\dfrac{1}{2} = \dfrac{4}{8}$ is called *a proportion*.

Definition

A **proportion** is a statement that two ratios $\frac{a}{b}$ and $\frac{c}{d}$ are equal, written $\frac{a}{b} = \frac{c}{d}$, where $b \neq 0$ and $d \neq 0$.

Now let's consider an example of *solving a proportion problem*. Suppose that you saved $500 in 4 months. At this rate, how long would it take you to save for a computer that costs $750? To answer this question, we can write a proportion in which the rates compare the amount of savings in a given amount of time. We want to find the amount of time corresponding to a savings of $750. Let's call this missing value x.

$$\text{Savings in dollars} \longrightarrow \frac{500}{4} = \frac{750}{x} \longleftarrow \text{Savings in dollars}$$
$$\text{Time in months} \qquad\qquad\qquad \longleftarrow \text{Time in months}$$

We then set the cross products equal in order to find the missing value.

$$\frac{500}{4} = \frac{750}{x}$$
$$500 \cdot x = 4 \cdot 750 \qquad \text{Cross multiply.}$$
$$500x = 3000$$
$$x = \frac{3000}{500}$$
$$x = 6$$

So it will take you 6 months to save for the computer.

To Solve a Proportion

- Find the cross products and set them equal.
- Solve the resulting equation.
- Check the solution in the original equation.

EXAMPLE 2

The actual length of the bedroom shown in the floor plan below is 15 ft. What is the actual width of the room?

$l = 2$ inches

$w = 1.5$ inches

SOLUTION The actual measurements and the floor plan measurements are in proportion.

$$\text{The actual width in feet} \longrightarrow \frac{w}{15} = \frac{1.5}{2} \longleftarrow \text{The floor plan width in inches}$$
$$\text{The actual length in feet} \qquad\qquad\qquad \longleftarrow \text{The floor plan length in inches}$$
$$2w = (15)(1.5) \qquad \text{Cross multiply.}$$
$$\frac{2w}{2} = \frac{22.5}{2} \qquad \begin{array}{l}\text{Divide each side of the} \\ \text{equation by 2.}\end{array}$$
$$w = 11.25$$

PRACTICE 2

It takes 80 lb of sodium hydroxide to neutralize 98 lb of sulfuric acid. At this rate, how many pounds of sodium hydroxide are needed to neutralize 49 lb of sulfuric acid?

CHECK

$$\frac{w}{15} = \frac{1.5}{2}$$

$$\frac{11.25}{15} \stackrel{?}{=} \frac{1.5}{2}$$

$$0.75 = 0.75 \qquad \text{True.}$$

Since our answer checks, we can conclude that the bedroom is actually 11.25 ft wide.

Would we get the same answer if we had set up the proportion in Example 2 as $\frac{w}{1.5} = \frac{15}{2}$? Explain.

EXAMPLE 3	**PRACTICE 3**
A 125-lb adult gets a dosage of 2 ml of a particular drug. At this rate, how much additional drug does a 175-lb adult require?	A homeowner pays $900 a month on a $100,000 mortgage. If instead she had a $75,000 mortgage, how much less money would she be paying per month at the same interest rate?

SOLUTION We begin by writing a proportion in which we use x to represent the amount of additional drug required.

$$\frac{2}{125} = \frac{2 + x}{175} \qquad \begin{array}{l} \leftarrow \text{Amount of drug in milliliters} \\ \leftarrow \text{Weight in pounds} \end{array}$$

$$2 \cdot 175 = 125(2 + x) \qquad \text{Cross multiply.}$$

$$350 = 250 + 125x \qquad \text{Use the distributive property.}$$

$$125x = 100 \qquad \text{Combine like terms.}$$

$$x = \frac{100}{125} \qquad \text{Divide each side of the equation by 125.}$$

$$x = 0.8$$

CHECK

$$\frac{2}{125} = \frac{2 + x}{175}$$

$$\frac{2}{125} \stackrel{?}{=} \frac{2 + 0.8}{175} \qquad \text{Substitute 0.8 for } x.$$

$$\frac{2}{125} \stackrel{?}{=} \frac{2.8}{175} \qquad \text{Simplify.}$$

$$0.016 = 0.016 \qquad \text{True.}$$

So an additional 0.8 ml of the drug is required for a 175-lb adult.

Another application of ratio and proportion is the geometric topic of *similar triangles*. These are triangles with the same shape but not necessarily the same size.

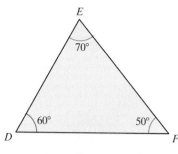

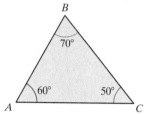

In the diagram to the left, $\triangle ABC$ and $\triangle DEF$ are similar. These triangles have corresponding angles that have equal measures, that is:

$$m\angle A = m\angle D$$
$$m\angle B = m\angle E$$
$$m\angle C = m\angle F$$

Note that in similar triangles, corresponding sides are opposite equal angles. Each side of $\triangle ABC$ corresponds to a side of $\triangle DEF$.

$\overline{AB}$ corresponds to $\overline{DE}$.
$\overline{BC}$ corresponds to $\overline{EF}$.
$\overline{AC}$ corresponds to $\overline{DF}$.

It can be shown that the lengths of the corresponding sides of similar triangles are in proportion:

$$\frac{AB}{DE} = \frac{BC}{EF} = \frac{AC}{DF} \quad \begin{array}{l} \leftarrow \triangle ABC \\ \leftarrow \triangle DEF \end{array}$$

We can use this relationship to find missing sides of similar triangles, as the following example illustrates.

EXAMPLE 4

In the following diagram, $\triangle PQR$ and $\triangle STU$ are similar. Find x, the length of side $\overline{SU}$.

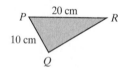
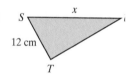

SOLUTION Corresponding sides are in proportion. To solve for x, let's set up a proportion involving the lengths of sides $\overline{PQ}$, $\overline{ST}$, $\overline{PR}$, and $\overline{SU}$.

$$\frac{PQ}{ST} = \frac{PR}{SU}$$

$$\frac{10}{12} = \frac{20}{x} \qquad \text{Substitute the given values.}$$

$$10x = 240 \qquad \text{Cross multiply.}$$

$$x = \frac{240}{10}$$

$$x = 24$$

So the length of $\overline{SU}$ is 24 cm.

PRACTICE 4

Triangle ABC and triangle DEC are similar. Find x, the length of side $\overline{DE}$.

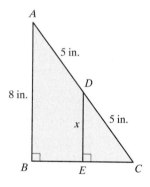

In Section 7.5, we discussed motion problems involving rational equations. Here we continue the discussion of these types of problems. In this case, we use $t = \dfrac{d}{r}$ because we must set two travel times equal to one another.

EXAMPLE 5

A boat travels 60 mph in still water. Find the speed of the river's current if the boat traveled 80 mi down the river in the same time that it took to travel 70 mi up the river.

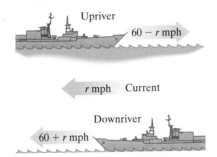

Upriver

60 − r mph

r mph   Current

Downriver

60 + r mph

SOLUTION Let r represent the speed of the river's current. When traveling downriver, the speed of the current is added to that of the boat. When traveling upriver, the speed of the river is subtracted from that of the boat. Applying the formula $t = \dfrac{d}{r}$, we can set up the following table:

	d	÷	r	=	t
	Distance		Rate		Time
Downriver	80		$60 + r$		$\dfrac{80}{60 + r}$
Upriver	70		$60 - r$		$\dfrac{70}{60 - r}$

We are told that these two times are equal, so we write the following proportion and solve for r.

$$\frac{80}{60 + r} = \frac{70}{60 - r}$$
$$80(60 - r) = 70(60 + r) \qquad \text{Cross multiply.}$$
$$4800 - 80r = 4200 + 70r$$
$$600 = 150r$$
$$r = 4$$

The speed of the river's current was 4 mph. We leave the check to you.

PRACTICE 5

The speed of the jet stream was 300 mph. When flying in the direction of the jet stream, a plane flies 1000 mi in the same time that it takes to fly 250 mph against the jet stream. Find the speed of the plane in still air.

Exercises 7.6

FOR EXTRA HELP

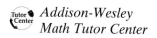

📖 *Student's Solutions Manual*

Tutor Center *Addison-Wesley Math Tutor Center*

🚪 *MyMathLab*

📼 *Videotape 7/DVT 7*

Solve and check.

1. $\dfrac{x}{10} = \dfrac{4}{5}$

2. $\dfrac{2}{9} = \dfrac{x}{27}$

3. $\dfrac{n}{100} = \dfrac{4}{5}$

4. $\dfrac{22}{35} = \dfrac{44}{x}$

5. $\dfrac{8}{7} = \dfrac{s}{21}$

6. $\dfrac{1}{v} = \dfrac{10}{3}$

7. $\dfrac{8 + x}{12} = \dfrac{22}{36}$

8. $\dfrac{75}{20} = \dfrac{30}{p - 1}$

9. $\dfrac{y + 3}{14} = \dfrac{y}{7}$

10. $\dfrac{n - 6}{3} = \dfrac{n}{5}$

11. $\dfrac{x - 1}{8} = \dfrac{x + 1}{12}$

12. $\dfrac{3}{t - 2} = \dfrac{9}{t + 2}$

13. $\dfrac{x}{8} = \dfrac{2}{x}$

14. $\dfrac{4}{n} = \dfrac{n}{16}$

15. $\dfrac{2}{y} = \dfrac{y - 4}{16}$

16. $\dfrac{5}{x + 2} = \dfrac{x}{7}$

17. $\dfrac{a}{a + 3} = \dfrac{4}{5a}$

18. $\dfrac{1}{3n} = \dfrac{n}{n + 2}$

19. $\dfrac{y + 1}{y + 6} = \dfrac{y}{y + 6}$

20. $\dfrac{2x + 4}{x - 3} = \dfrac{3x}{x - 3}$

Applications

Solve.

21. The owner of a small business is considering the purchase of a laser printer that can print 6 pages in 2 min. How long would it take to print a 25-page report?

22. In a mayoral election, 48 out of every 100 voters voted for a certain candidate. How many of the 200,000 voters chose the candidate?

23. A trucker drives 60 mi on 8 gal of gas. At the same rate, how many gallons of gas will it take him to drive 120 mi?

24. A chauffeur took 2 hr longer to drive 275 mi than he took to drive 165 mi. If his speed was the same on both trips, at what speed was he driving?

25. A runner traveled 3 mi in the same time that a cyclist traveled 10 mi. The speed of the cyclist was 14 mph greater than that of the runner. What was the cyclist's speed?

26. A train travels 225 mi in the same time that a bus travels 200 mi. If the speed of the train is 5 mph greater than that of the bus, find the speed of the bus.

27. A train goes 30 mph faster than a bus. The train travels 400 mi in the same time as the bus goes 250 mi. What are their speeds?

28. A pilot flies 600 mi with a tailwind of 20 mph. Against the wind, he flies only 500 mi in the same amount of time. What is the speed of the plane in still air?

29. △ABC and △DEF are similar. Find y, the length of side $\overline{AB}$.

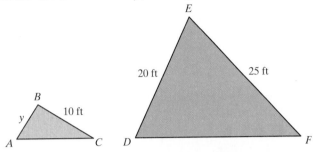

30. In the following map of Kansas, the two triangles shown are similar. Find the distance between Dodge City and Great Bend, rounded to the nearest 10 miles.

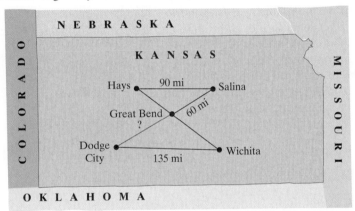

31. When a 6-ft tall man is 8 ft away from a tree, the tip of his shadow and the tip of the tree's shadow meet 4 ft behind him. The two right triangles shown are similar. Find the height of the tree.

32. Similar triangles can be used to find how far a ship is from the shore. Find the value of x in the diagram.

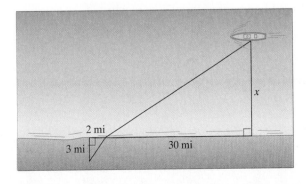

33. There are 20 guests at a party. If 4 more women were to arrive at the party, then 50% of the guests would be women. How many women are there at the party?

34. At a local bank, the simple interest rate on a savings account is 2% higher than the interest rate for a checking account. After one year, a deposit in the checking account would earn interest of $60, whereas the same deposit would earn interest of $120 in the savings account. Find the interest rate on each account.

● *Check your answers on page A-28.*

Mindstretchers

RESEARCH

1. Eratosthenes headed the great library at Alexandria in Egypt more than 2000 years ago. In addition to his work on prime numbers, Eratosthenes used the method of ratio and proportion to approximate the circumference of the Earth. Either in your college library or on the Web, investigate how he did this and how successful he was. Summarize your findings.

MATHEMATICAL REASONING

2. If $\dfrac{a}{b} = \dfrac{c}{d}$, can you show that $\dfrac{a+b}{b} = \dfrac{c+d}{d}$? Explain.

GROUPWORK

3. Working with a partner, make up an equation where one rational expression equals another.

a. Solve the equation using the LCD method.

b. Solve the same equation using the cross-product method.

c. Which method do you prefer? Explain why.

CONCEPT/SKILL	DESCRIPTION	EXAMPLE
[7.1] Rational Expression	An algebraic expression $\frac{P}{Q}$ that can be written as the quotient of two polynomials, P and Q, where $Q \neq 0$.	$\frac{2x}{x + 5}$, where $x + 5 \neq 0$.
[7.1] To Find an Equivalent Rational Expression	Multiply the numerator and denominator of $\frac{P}{Q}$ by the same polynomial R. $$\frac{P}{Q} = \frac{PR}{QR},$$ where $Q \neq 0$ and $R \neq 0$.	$\frac{3}{5y + 1} \cdot \frac{y}{y} = \frac{3y}{5y^2 + y}$
[7.1] To Simplify a Rational Expression	• Factor the numerator and denominator. • Divide out any common factors.	$\frac{3n^2 - 3}{n^2 + n - 2}$ $= \frac{3(\overset{1}{\cancel{n - 1}})(n + 1)}{(\underset{1}{\cancel{n - 1}})(n + 2)} = \frac{3(n + 1)}{n + 2}$
[7.2] To Multiply Rational Expressions	• Factor the numerators and denominators. • Divide the numerators and denominators by all common factors. • Multiply the remaining factors in the numerators and the remaining factors in the denominators.	$\frac{6x}{x^2 - 4x} \cdot \frac{x^2 - 16}{3x}$ $= \frac{6x}{x(x - 4)} \cdot \frac{(x - 4)(x + 4)}{3x}$ $= \frac{\overset{2}{\overset{1}{\cancel{6x}}}}{\underset{1}{x}(\underset{1}{\cancel{x - 4}})} \cdot \frac{(x + 4)(\overset{1}{\cancel{x - 4}})}{\underset{1}{3x}}$ $= \frac{2(x + 4)}{x}$
[7.2] To Divide Rational Expressions	• Take the reciprocal of the divisor and change the operation to multiplication. • Follow the rule for multiplying rational expressions.	$\frac{x^2 - x - 6}{3x - 9} \div \frac{4x + 8}{5x}$ $= \frac{x^2 - x - 6}{3x - 9} \cdot \frac{5x}{4x + 8}$ $= \frac{(\overset{1}{\cancel{x + 2}})(\overset{1}{\cancel{x - 3}})}{3(\underset{1}{\cancel{x - 3}})} \cdot \frac{5x}{4(\underset{1}{\cancel{x + 2}})}$ $= \frac{5x}{12}$

continued

☐ = CONCEPT   ☐ = SKILL

CONCEPT/SKILL	DESCRIPTION	EXAMPLE
[7.3] To Add (or Subtract) Rational Expressions with the Same Denominator	• Add (or subtract) the numerators and keep the same denominator. • Simplify, if possible.	$\dfrac{3n - 5}{n + 1} + \dfrac{n + 6}{n + 1}$ $= \dfrac{(3n - 5) + (n + 6)}{n + 1}$ $= \dfrac{3n - 5 + n + 6}{n + 1} = \dfrac{4n + 1}{n + 1}$ $\dfrac{2n^2 + 4n + 6}{n - 5} - \dfrac{n^2 + 10n + 1}{n - 5}$ $= \dfrac{(2n^2 + 4n + 6) - (n^2 + 10n + 1)}{n - 5}$ $= \dfrac{2n^2 + 4n + 6 - n^2 - 10n - 1}{n - 5}$ $= \dfrac{n^2 - 6n + 5}{n - 5}$ $= \dfrac{(n - 1)\overset{1}{\cancel{(n - 5)}}}{\underset{1}{\cancel{(n - 5)}}} = n - 1$
[7.3] To Find the LCD of Rational Expressions	• Factor each denominator completely. • Multiply these factors, using for the power of each factor the greatest number of times that it occurs in any of the denominators. The product of all these factors is the LCD.	$\dfrac{x}{x^2 - 4x + 3}$ and $\dfrac{x + 5}{2x - 2}$ Factor $x^2 - 4x + 3$: $(x - 1)(x - 3)$ Factor $2x - 2$: $2(x - 1)$ LCD $= 2(x - 1)(x - 3)$
[7.3] To Add (or Subtract) Rational Expressions with Different Denominators	• Find the LCD of the rational expressions. • Write each rational expression with a common denominator, usually the LCD. • Add (or subtract) the numerators. • Simplify, if possible.	$\dfrac{n}{n^2 + 3n + 2} + \dfrac{3}{2n + 2}$ $= \dfrac{n}{(n + 1)(n + 2)} + \dfrac{3}{2(n + 1)}$ $= \dfrac{n \cdot 2}{(n + 1)(n + 2) \cdot 2}$ $\quad + \dfrac{3 \cdot (n + 2)}{2(n + 1) \cdot (n + 2)}$ $= \dfrac{2n}{2(n + 1)(n + 2)} + \dfrac{3n + 6}{2(n + 1)(n + 2)}$ $= \dfrac{5n + 6}{2(n + 1)(n + 2)}$ $\dfrac{5y}{y^2 - 9} - \dfrac{2}{y + 3}$ $= \dfrac{5y}{(y + 3)(y - 3)} - \dfrac{2}{y + 3}$ $= \dfrac{5y}{(y + 3)(y - 3)} - \dfrac{2 \cdot (y - 3)}{(y + 3) \cdot (y - 3)}$ $= \dfrac{5y}{(y + 3)(y - 3)} - \dfrac{2y - 6}{(y + 3)(y - 3)}$ $= \dfrac{5y - (2y - 6)}{(y + 3)(y - 3)}$ $= \dfrac{3y + 6}{(y + 3)(y - 3)} = \dfrac{3(y + 2)}{(y + 3)(y - 3)}$

| = CONCEPT | = SKILL |

CONCEPT/SKILL	DESCRIPTION	EXAMPLE
[7.4] To Simplify a Complex Rational Expression: Division Method	• Write the numerator and denominator as single rational expressions in simplified form. • Write the expression as the numerator divided by the denominator. • Divide. • Simplify, if possible.	$$\dfrac{\dfrac{x}{4}}{\dfrac{x^2}{3}+\dfrac{x}{2}}=\dfrac{\dfrac{x}{4}}{\dfrac{x^2}{3}\cdot\dfrac{2}{2}+\dfrac{x}{2}\cdot\dfrac{3}{3}}$$ $$=\dfrac{\dfrac{x}{4}}{\dfrac{2x^2+3x}{6}}$$ $$=\dfrac{x}{4}\div\dfrac{2x^2+3x}{6}$$ $$=\dfrac{x}{4}\cdot\dfrac{6}{2x^2+3x}$$ $$=\dfrac{\overset{1}{x}}{\underset{2}{4}}\cdot\dfrac{\overset{3}{6}}{\underset{1}{x(2x+3)}}$$ $$=\dfrac{3}{2(2x+3)}$$
[7.4] To Simplify a Complex Rational Expression: LCD Method	• Find the LCD of all the rational expressions *within* both the numerator and denominator. • Multiply the numerator and denominator of the complex rational expression by this LCD. • Simplify, if possible.	$$\dfrac{1-\dfrac{1}{y}}{1-\dfrac{1}{y^2}}=\dfrac{\left(1-\dfrac{1}{y}\right)\cdot y^2}{\left(1-\dfrac{1}{y^2}\right)\cdot y^2}$$ $$=\dfrac{1\cdot y^2-\dfrac{1}{\underset{1}{y}}\cdot\overset{y}{y^2}}{1\cdot y^2-\dfrac{1}{\underset{1}{y^2}}\cdot\overset{1}{y^2}}$$ $$=\dfrac{y^2-y}{y^2-1}$$ $$=\dfrac{y\overset{1}{(y-1)}}{(y+1)\underset{1}{(y-1)}}$$ $$=\dfrac{y}{y+1}$$

continued

CONCEPT/SKILL	DESCRIPTION	EXAMPLE
[7.5] To Solve a Rational Equation	• Find the LCD of all rational expressions in the equation. • Multiply each side of the equation by the LCD. • Solve the equation. • Check your solution(s) in the original equation.	$\dfrac{1}{x+3} + \dfrac{1}{x-3} = \dfrac{2}{x^2-9}$ $\dfrac{1}{x+3} + \dfrac{1}{x-3} = \dfrac{2}{(x+3)(x-3)}$ $\overset{1}{\cancel{(x+3)}}(x-3) \cdot \dfrac{1}{\underset{1}{x+3}}$ $+ (x+3)\overset{1}{\cancel{(x-3)}}\dfrac{1}{\underset{1}{x-3}}$ $= \overset{1}{\cancel{(x+3)}}\,\overset{1}{\cancel{(x-3)}}$ $\cdot \dfrac{2}{\underset{1}{\cancel{(x+3)}}\,\underset{1}{\cancel{(x-3)}}}$ $x - 3 + x + 3 = 2$ $2x = 2$ $x = 1$ **CHECK** Substitute 1 for x. $\dfrac{1}{x+3} + \dfrac{1}{x-3} = \dfrac{2}{x^2-9}$ $\dfrac{1}{\mathbf{1}+3} + \dfrac{1}{\mathbf{1}-3} \overset{?}{=} \dfrac{2}{\mathbf{1}^2-9}$ $\dfrac{1}{4} - \dfrac{1}{2} \overset{?}{=} -\dfrac{2}{8}$ $-\dfrac{1}{4} = -\dfrac{1}{4}$ **True.**
[7.6] Proportion	A statement that two ratios $\dfrac{a}{b}$ and $\dfrac{c}{d}$ are equal, written $\dfrac{a}{b} = \dfrac{c}{d}$, where $b \neq 0$ and $d \neq 0$.	The equation $\dfrac{3}{4} = \dfrac{10}{x}$ is a proportion, where $\dfrac{3}{4}$ and $\dfrac{10}{x}$ are ratios.
[7.6] To Solve a Proportion	• Find the cross products and set them equal. • Solve the resulting equation. • Check the solution in the original equation.	$\dfrac{8}{x-3} = \dfrac{6}{x+4}$ $6(x-3) = 8(x+4)$ $6x - 18 = 8x + 32$ $-2x = 50$ $x = -25$ **CHECK** Substitute -25 for x. $\dfrac{8}{x-3} = \dfrac{6}{x+4}$ $\dfrac{8}{\mathbf{-25}-3} \overset{?}{=} \dfrac{6}{\mathbf{-25}+4}$ $\dfrac{8}{-28} \overset{?}{=} \dfrac{6}{-21}$ $-\dfrac{2}{7} = -\dfrac{2}{7}$ **True.**

Chapter 7 Review Exercises

To help you review this chapter, solve these problems.

[7.1]

1. Identify the values for which the given rational expression is undefined.

a. $\dfrac{4}{x + 1}$

b. $\dfrac{6x + 12}{x^2 - x - 6}$

2. Determine whether each pair of rational expressions is equivalent.

a. $\dfrac{2x}{y} \stackrel{?}{=} \dfrac{10x^2 y}{5xy^2}$

b. $\dfrac{x^2 - 9}{x^2 + 6x + 9} \stackrel{?}{=} \dfrac{x - 3}{x + 3}$

Simplify.

3. $\dfrac{12m}{20m^2}$

4. $\dfrac{15n - 18}{9n + 6}$

5. $\dfrac{x^2 + 2x - 8}{4 - x^2}$

6. $\dfrac{2x^2 - 3x - 20}{3x^2 - 13x + 4}$

[7.2]

Perform the indicated operation.

7. $\dfrac{10mn}{3p^2} \cdot \dfrac{9np}{5m^2}$

8. $\dfrac{y - 5}{4y + 6} \cdot \dfrac{6y + 9}{3y - 15}$

9. $\dfrac{x + 6}{x^2 + x - 30} \cdot \dfrac{x^2 - 10x + 25}{2x + 5}$

10. $\dfrac{2a^2 - 2a - 4}{4 - a^2} \cdot \dfrac{2a^2 + a - 6}{4a^2 - 2a - 6}$

11. $\dfrac{x^2 y}{2x} \div xy^2$

12. $\dfrac{5m + 10}{2m - 20} \div \dfrac{7m + 14}{14m - 20}$

13. $\dfrac{5y^2}{x^2 - 36} \div \dfrac{25xy - 25y}{x^2 - 7x + 6}$

14. $\dfrac{2x^2 + x - 1}{x^2 + 8x + 7} \div \dfrac{6x^2 + x - 2}{x^2 + 14x + 49}$

[7.3]

Write each pair of rational expressions in terms of their LCD.

15. $\dfrac{1}{5x}$ and $\dfrac{3}{20x^2}$

16. $\dfrac{4}{n - 1}$ and $\dfrac{n}{n + 4}$

17. $\dfrac{1}{3x + 9}$ and $\dfrac{x}{x^2 + 4x + 3}$

18. $\dfrac{2}{3x^2 - 5x - 2}$ and $\dfrac{1}{4 - x^2}$

Perform the indicated operation.

19. $\dfrac{3t + 1}{2t} + \dfrac{t - 1}{2t}$

20. $\dfrac{5y}{y + 7} - \dfrac{y - 28}{y + 7}$

21. $\dfrac{5y + 4}{4y^2 - 2y} - \dfrac{2}{2y - 1}$

22. $\dfrac{n}{3n + 15} + \dfrac{n - 2}{n^2 + 5n}$

23. $\dfrac{4}{x - 3} - \dfrac{4x + 1}{9 - x^2}$

24. $\dfrac{y + 3}{4 - y^2} + \dfrac{1}{2 - y}$

25. $\dfrac{2}{m + 1} + \dfrac{6m - 2}{m^2 - 2m - 3}$

26. $\dfrac{3x - 2}{x^2 - x - 12} - \dfrac{x + 3}{x - 4}$

27. $\dfrac{2x}{x^2 + 4x + 4} - \dfrac{x - 1}{x^2 - 2x - 8}$

28. $\dfrac{n + 4}{2n^2 - 3n + 1} + \dfrac{n + 1}{2n^2 + 5n - 3}$

[7.4]

Simplify.

29. $\dfrac{\dfrac{x}{2}}{\dfrac{3x^2}{7}}$

30. $\dfrac{1 - \dfrac{9}{y}}{1 - \dfrac{81}{y^2}}$

31. $\dfrac{\dfrac{1}{x} + \dfrac{1}{y}}{\dfrac{1}{2x} + \dfrac{1}{2y}}$

32. $\dfrac{4 - \dfrac{3}{x} - \dfrac{1}{x^2}}{2 - \dfrac{5}{x} + \dfrac{3}{x^2}}$

[7.5]

Solve and check.

33. $\dfrac{2x}{x - 4} = 5 - \dfrac{1}{x - 4}$

34. $\dfrac{y + 1}{y} + \dfrac{1}{2y} = 4$

35. $\dfrac{5}{2x} + \dfrac{3}{x + 1} = \dfrac{7}{x}$

36. $\dfrac{y - 2}{y - 4} = \dfrac{1}{y + 2} + \dfrac{y + 3}{y^2 - 2y - 8}$

37. $\dfrac{x}{x + 2} - \dfrac{2}{2 - x} = \dfrac{x + 6}{x^2 - 4}$

38. $\dfrac{3}{n^2 - 5n + 4} - \dfrac{1}{n^2 - 4n + 3} = \dfrac{n - 3}{n^2 - 7n + 12}$

[7.6]

Solve and check.

39. $\dfrac{8}{5} = \dfrac{72}{x}$

40. $\dfrac{28}{x + 3} = \dfrac{7}{9}$

41. $\dfrac{5}{3 + y} = \dfrac{3}{7y + 1}$

42. $\dfrac{11}{x - 2} = \dfrac{x + 7}{2}$

Mixed Applications

Solve.

43. A company found that the cost per booklet for printing x booklets can be represented by $0.72 + \dfrac{200}{x}$. Write this cost as a single rational expression.

44. Four friends decide to split the cost of renting a car equally. They discover that if they let one more friend share in the rental, the cost for each of the original four friends will be reduced by $10. What is the total cost of the car rental?

45. A hiker walks a distance d at a speed of r mph, and then returns on the same path at a speed of s mph. The hiker's average speed for the entire trip can be represented by

$$\dfrac{2d}{\dfrac{d}{r} + \dfrac{d}{s}}.$$

Simplify this expression.

46. With the water running at full force, it takes 10 min to fill a bathtub. It then takes 15 min for the bathtub to drain. If by mistake the water is running at full force while the tub is draining, how long will it take the tub to fill?

47. A family on vacation drove 400 mi at two different speeds, 50 mph and 60 mph. The total driving time was 7 hr. How many miles did the family drive at 50 mph?

48. One student takes x hours to design a Web page. Another student takes an hour longer. What part of the job will be finished in an hour if the two students work together?

49. The director of a college cafeteria knows that it cost $31,000 to serve 15,000 meals in September. She expects to serve about 20,000 meals in October. How much should she expect to spend on the October meals?

50. Find a rational expression equal to the sum of the reciprocals of three consecutive integers, starting with n.

● *Check your answers on page A-28.*

To see if you have mastered the topics in this chapter, take this test.

1. Identify the values for which the rational expression $\dfrac{3x}{x-8}$ is undefined.

2. Show that $\dfrac{y-3}{y}$ is equivalent to $-\dfrac{3y-y^2}{y^2}$.

Simplify.

3. $\dfrac{15a^3b}{12ab^2}$

4. $\dfrac{x^2-4x}{xy-4y}$

5. $\dfrac{3b^2-27}{b^2-4b-21}$

6. $\dfrac{\dfrac{3}{x^2}-\dfrac{1}{x}}{\dfrac{9}{x^2}-1}$

7. Write $\dfrac{4n-1}{n^2+6n-16}, \dfrac{2}{n+8}$, and $\dfrac{n}{4n-8}$ in terms of their LCD.

Perform the indicated operation.

8. $\dfrac{7x-10}{x+6}-\dfrac{5x-22}{x+6}$

9. $\dfrac{3}{2y-8}+\dfrac{2}{4y^2-16y}$

10. $\dfrac{5}{d-3}-\dfrac{d-4}{d^2-d-6}$

11. $\dfrac{5}{2x^2-3x-2}-\dfrac{x}{4-x^2}$

12. $\dfrac{n+1}{3n-18}\cdot\dfrac{n-6}{6n^3-6n}$

13. $\dfrac{a^2-25}{a^2-2a-24}\div\dfrac{a^2+a-30}{a^2-36}$

14. $\dfrac{x^2+6x+8}{x^2+x-2}\div\dfrac{x+4}{2x^2+12x+16}$

Solve and check.

15. $\dfrac{1}{y-5} + \dfrac{y+4}{25-y^2} = \dfrac{1}{y+5}$

16. $\dfrac{2y}{y-4} - 2 = \dfrac{4}{y+5}$

17. $\dfrac{x}{x+6} = \dfrac{1}{x+2}$

Solve.

18. When a circuit connected in parallel contains two resistors with resistances R_1 and R_2 ohms, electricians use the formula $\dfrac{1}{R} = \dfrac{1}{R_1} + \dfrac{1}{R_2}$ to find the total resistance R (in ohms) of the circuit. Solve the formula for R_1.

19. A company owns two electronic mail processors. The newer machine works twice as fast as the older one. Together, the two machines process 1000 pieces of mail in 20 min. How long does it take each machine, working alone, to process 1000 pieces of mail?

20. In the diagram shown, the heights and shadows of the woman and of the tree are in proportion. Find the height of the tree in meters (m).

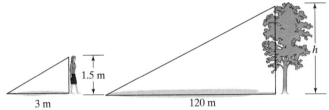

1.5 m

h

3 m

120 m

● *Check your answers on page A-29.*

Cumulative Review Exercises

To help you review, solve the following.

1. Simplify: $y - [2y - 3(y - 1)]$

2. Solve $4n - 5(n + 2) < -7$. Graph the solution on the number line.

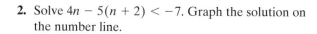

3. Graph the inequality $y \geq 2$ on the coordinate plane.

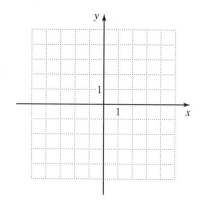

4. Solve by substitution and then check.

$$x + y = 8$$
$$y = 2x - 1$$

5. Solve: $(n + 5)(n - 2) = 0$

6. Factor: $100y^2 - 81$

7. Solve and check: $\dfrac{c}{c + 6} = \dfrac{1}{c + 2}$

8. A business woman wants to invest twice as much money in a fund that has a guaranteed return of 6% as in a fund that has a guaranteed return of 4%. What is the minimum amount that should be invested in each fund if she wants to have a return of at least $1200?

9. Two buses following the same route leave from the same station at different times. The Reston bus leaves 2 hr later than the Arlington bus. The Arlington bus is traveling at 40 mph and the Reston bus is traveling at 60 mph. How long will it take the Reston bus to overtake the Arlington bus?

10. A laser printer prints 7 pages every 3 min. At this rate, how long would it take to print a 20-page report, to the nearest minute?

• Check your answers on page A-29.

Chapter 8

Radical Expressions and Equations

Square Roots and Lighting

A theatrical lighting designer focuses the audience's attention on what is lit: actors, costumes, props, and scenery. In planning a production for the stage, the designer must take into account how much illumination a lighting fixture will deliver from a particular distance. An actor further from the fixture seems more dimly lit than one close.

In general, the distance d associated with an illumination of I on a person or object is given by the equation

$$d = \sqrt{\frac{k}{I}},$$

where k is a constant that depends on the fixture, d is in feet, and I is in footcandles. It follows from this formula that if a lighting designer wants to increase the illumination on someone by a factor of four, the distance to the light source must be divided by the square root of 4, that is, by 2.

Source: J. Michael Gillette, *Theatrical Design and Production*, (New York: McGraw-Hill, 1999)

Chapter 8 Pretest

To see if you have already mastered the topics in this chapter, take this test.

Assume all variables and radicands represent nonnegative real numbers.

Simplify.

1. $\sqrt{81}$
2. $-\sqrt{27}$
3. $\sqrt{45a^2}$
4. $\sqrt{\dfrac{x}{64}}$

5. $6\sqrt{2} + \sqrt{2} - 3\sqrt{2}$
6. $\sqrt{12} + 2\sqrt{75}$
7. $\sqrt{9x^3} - 4x\sqrt{x} + x\sqrt{36x}$

Multiply or divide. Simplify, if possible.

8. $\sqrt{6} \cdot \sqrt{3}$
9. $\sqrt{2xy} \cdot \sqrt{10xy^3}$
10. $\dfrac{\sqrt{30}}{\sqrt{5}}$

11. $\sqrt{n}(\sqrt{n} + 2)$
12. $(\sqrt{3} - 1)(\sqrt{3} + 4)$

Simplify.

13. $\sqrt{\dfrac{5x}{6}}$
14. $\dfrac{\sqrt{40x^3}}{\sqrt{2x}}$
15. Rationalize the denominator:

$$\dfrac{8 + \sqrt{7}}{\sqrt{2}}$$

Solve and check.

16. $\sqrt{x} - 1 = 5$
17. $y = \sqrt{4y - 3}$

18. The velocity of a car in meters per second that starts from rest with a constant acceleration of a m/sec² can be found using the expression $\sqrt{2as}$, where s is the distance traveled in meters. If the acceleration of the car is 2 m/sec², find its velocity after it has traveled 100 m.

19. An Olympic gymnast is practicing her floor exercise routine. The floor is a square whose sides measure 12 m. In the routine, she uses the diagonal of the square surface to complete a tumbling sequence. Find the distance the gymnast covers in the tumbling sequence. Express this distance as both a radical in simplest form and as a decimal rounded to the nearest tenth of a meter.

12 m

12 m

20. Traffic accident investigators use the lengths of skid marks to determine the minimum speed a car was traveling before it skids to a stop. The minimum speed, S, in miles per hour can be approximated by the formula

$$S = \sqrt{30fL},$$

where f is the drag factor (or coefficient of friction) for the road surface and L is the length in feet of the skid marks. Solve this formula for L in terms of S and f.

● *Check your answers on page A-29.*

8.1 Introduction to Radical Expressions

OBJECTIVES

- *To evaluate and simplify radical expressions*

- *To solve applied problems involving the simplification of radical expressions*

What Radicals Are and Why They Are Important

So far, we have considered two types of algebraic expressions, namely, polynomials and rational expressions. In this chapter, we extend the discussion to a third type, called *radical expressions*. **Radical expressions** such as $4\sqrt{y}$ or $5 - \sqrt{x}$ are algebraic expressions that involve *square roots.* Note that in this text we use the terms *radical* and *square root* interchangeably.

When we find a square root of a number, we ask ourselves: What number multiplied by itself gives the original number? This question arises naturally in many situations, notably in geometry. For instance, recall the formula for the area A of a square with side s.

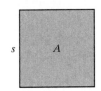

The formula $A = s^2$ says that to find the area of a square, we square the length of a side. If we know the value of A and wish to determine the value of s, we find the square root of A, that is, $s = \sqrt{A}$.

In this chapter, we discuss evaluating and simplifying radical expressions, as well as carrying out the usual operations on them—adding, subtracting, multiplying, and dividing. Then we consider how to solve equations involving radical expressions.

Introduction to Radicals

Let's begin with the definition of square root.

> **Definition**
>
> The **square root** of a nonnegative real number a is a number that when squared is a.

Actually, every positive number has *two* square roots, one positive and the other negative. For example, the square roots of 4 are $+2$ and -2 because $(+2)^2 = 4$ and $(-2)^2 = 4$. The symbol $\sqrt{}$, called the **radical sign**, stands for the positive or *principal square root,* but is commonly referred to as "**the** square root." For instance, $\sqrt{9}$ is read "the square root of 9", or "radical 9", and represents $+3$, or 3. By contrast, the negative square root of 9, namely, -3, is represented by $-\sqrt{9}$. Throughout the remainder of this text, when we speak of the square root of a number we mean its principal square root.

The number under the radical sign is called the **radicand.**

The radical sign   The radicand

We read $\sqrt{n}$ as "the square root of n."

This chapter deals with radicals with nonnegative radicands, such as $\sqrt{0}$ and $\sqrt{3}$. We will not discuss radicals with a negative radicand, say, $\sqrt{-4}$. Can you explain why such radicals do not represent real numbers?

Evaluating Radicals

Let's continue our discussion of radicals by finding the value of radicals with radicands that are whole numbers. A whole number is said to be a **perfect square** if it is the square of another whole number. For instance, 9 is a perfect square, since $9 = 3^2$. On the other hand, 8 is not a perfect square, since it is not the square of any whole number. Perfect squares play a special role in finding the value of square roots.

The square root of a perfect square is always a whole number.

$$\sqrt{9} = 3, \text{ since } 3^2 = 9.$$

EXAMPLE 1	PRACTICE 1
Find the value of the following radical expressions.	Evaluate the following radical expressions.
a. $\sqrt{16}$	**a.** $\sqrt{4}$
b. $3\sqrt{25}$	**b.** $-5\sqrt{49}$
SOLUTION	
a. $\sqrt{16} = 4$ since $4^2 = 16$	
b. $3\sqrt{25} = 3 \cdot 5 = 15$	

TIP In evaluating radicals, remember that squaring, doubling, and halving a number are *not* the same as finding its square root.

The square root of a whole number that is not a perfect square is an *irrational number*. Irrational numbers have decimal representations that neither terminate nor repeat. For example, $\sqrt{2}$ and $\sqrt{3}$ are irrational numbers.

$$\sqrt{2} = 1.4142135 \ldots, \text{ which is approximately } 1.414.$$
$$\sqrt{3} = 1.7320508 \ldots, \text{ which is approximately } 1.732.$$

We can use a calculator to approximate the value of these square roots by decimals rounded to a specific place value.

EXAMPLE 2	PRACTICE 2
Evaluate $\sqrt{7}$, rounded to the nearest thousandth.	Find the value of $\sqrt{10}$, rounded to the nearest thousandth.
SOLUTION Since the radicand 7 is not a perfect square, its square root is an irrational number. Using a calculator, we see that $\sqrt{7} = 2.645751311\ldots$. Rounding to the nearest thousandth gives us 2.646.	

Simplifying Radicals

The operations of squaring and taking a square root undo each other. They are opposite operations in the same way that adding a number is the opposite of subtracting that number. The following two properties of radicals stem from this relationship.

Squaring a Square Root

For any nonnegative real number a,

$$(\sqrt{a})^2 = a.$$

This property states that when we take the square root of a nonnegative number and then square the result, we get the original number. For instance, $(\sqrt{9})^2 = 9$ and $(\sqrt{8})^2 = 8$.

Taking the Square Root of a Square

For any nonnegative real number a,

$$\sqrt{a^2} = a.$$

According to this property, when we square a nonnegative number and then take the square root, the result is the original number. For example, $\sqrt{3^2} = 3$.

We will use both of these properties repeatedly throughout this chapter. Do you see the difference between the two properties? Explain.

EXAMPLE 3	PRACTICE 3
Simplify each radical expression.	Simplify.
a. $(\sqrt{25})^2$ **b.** $(\sqrt{2})^2$	**a.** $(\sqrt{6})^2$
c. $\sqrt{4^2}$ **d.** $\sqrt{9^2}$	**b.** $(\sqrt{5})^2$
	c. $\sqrt{7^2}$
SOLUTION	**d.** $\sqrt{1^2}$
a. $(\sqrt{25})^2 = 25$ Use the property of squaring a square root.	
b. $(\sqrt{2})^2 = 2$	
c. $\sqrt{4^2} = 4$ Use the property of taking the square root of a square.	
d. $\sqrt{9^2} = 9$	

Some radicands contain variables. Consider, for instance, the expression $\sqrt{x}$. For negative values of x, the radicand is negative and so $\sqrt{x}$ is not a real number. For purposes of simplicity, we will assume throughout the remainder of this text that all radicands and all variables are nonnegative.

Let's look at some radicals that are perfect squares involving variables. For instance, the radicands for $\sqrt{x^8}$, $\sqrt{49y^6}$, and $\sqrt{25a^2b^4}$ are all perfect squares.

$$\sqrt{x^8} = \sqrt{(x^4)^2} = x^4$$
$$\sqrt{49y^6} = \sqrt{(7y^3)^2} = 7y^3$$
$$\sqrt{25a^2b^4} = \sqrt{(5ab^2)^2} = 5ab^2$$

Note that the exponent of the variable(s) in any perfect square is always an even number, such as 8 or 10. Note that to find the square root of an *even* power we can simply take half of the exponent. For example,

$$\sqrt{x^8} = x^4 \quad \leftarrow \frac{8}{2} = 4$$

EXAMPLE 4

Simplify each radical expression.

a. $\sqrt{n^6}$

b. $-\sqrt{16x^8}$

c. $\sqrt{100a^4b^2}$

SOLUTION

a. The radicand n^6 is a perfect square, so we can use the property of taking the square root of a square:

$$\sqrt{n^6} = \sqrt{(n^3)^2} = n^3$$

b. $-\sqrt{16x^8} = -\sqrt{(4x^4)^2} = -4x^4$

c. $\sqrt{100a^4b^2} = \sqrt{(10a^2b)^2} = 10a^2b$

PRACTICE 4

Simplify.

a. $\sqrt{x^4}$

b. $\sqrt{64t^{10}}$

c. $-\sqrt{121x^2y^2}$

Just as we simplify fractions to express them in lowest terms, so we put radical expressions *in simplified form*. In this way, we can recognize that expressions that appear to be different are really the same. Also, simplified radical expressions are often easier to work with.

But what exactly does it mean to simplify a radical? It is easier to say when a radical expression is *not* simplified than to say when it *is* simplified. *A radical is not considered to be in simplified form if its radicand is divisible by a perfect square.* For instance, the radical $\sqrt{8}$ is not in simplified form because the perfect square 4 is a factor of the radicand 8. To simplify such a radical, we apply the *product rule of radicals*.

The Product Rule of Radicals

If a and b are any nonnegative real numbers, then

$$\sqrt{ab} = \sqrt{a} \cdot \sqrt{b}.$$

In words, this rule states that the square root of a product is the product of the square roots.

To check that the product rule works in a particular example, we consider the radical $\sqrt{4 \cdot 9}$.

$$\sqrt{4 \cdot 9} \overset{?}{=} \sqrt{4} \cdot \sqrt{9}$$
$$\sqrt{36} \overset{?}{=} 2 \cdot 3$$
$$6 = 2 \cdot 3 \quad \text{True.}$$

So $\sqrt{4 \cdot 9} = \sqrt{4} \cdot \sqrt{9}$, as the product rule implies.

Now let's use this rule to simplify $\sqrt{8}$.

$$\sqrt{8} = \sqrt{4 \cdot 2} \qquad \text{Factor out the perfect square 4 from the radicand.}$$
$$= \sqrt{4} \cdot \sqrt{2} \qquad \text{Use the product rule of radicals.}$$
$$= 2\sqrt{2} \qquad \sqrt{4} = 2.$$

So $2\sqrt{2}$ is the simplified form of $\sqrt{8}$.

Some radicals contain radicands that have more than one possible perfect square factor. To simplify these radicals, we generally factor out the *largest* perfect square factor of the radicand, as shown in Example 5a.

EXAMPLE 5	PRACTICE 5
Simplify.	Express in simplified form.

EXAMPLE 5

Simplify.

a. $\sqrt{48}$ **b.** $-4\sqrt{27}$ **c.** $\dfrac{\sqrt{24}}{6}$

SOLUTION

a. $\sqrt{48} = \sqrt{16 \cdot 3}$ Factor out the perfect square 16.

$\phantom{\sqrt{48}} = \sqrt{16} \cdot \sqrt{3}$ Use the product rule of radicals.

$\phantom{\sqrt{48}} = 4\sqrt{3}$ Take the square root of the perfect square.

b. $-4\sqrt{27} = -4\sqrt{9 \cdot 3}$

$\phantom{-4\sqrt{27}} = -4\sqrt{9} \cdot \sqrt{3}$ Use the product rule of radicals.

$\phantom{-4\sqrt{27}} = -4 \cdot 3\sqrt{3}$ Take the square root.

$\phantom{-4\sqrt{27}} = -12\sqrt{3}$ Simplify.

c. $\dfrac{\sqrt{24}}{6} = \dfrac{\sqrt{4 \cdot 6}}{6}$

$\phantom{\dfrac{\sqrt{24}}{6}} = \dfrac{\sqrt{4} \cdot \sqrt{6}}{6}$ Use the product rule of radicals.

$\phantom{\dfrac{\sqrt{24}}{6}} = \dfrac{2\sqrt{6}}{6}$ Take the square root of the perfect square.

$\phantom{\dfrac{\sqrt{24}}{6}} = \dfrac{\overset{1}{\cancel{2}}\sqrt{6}}{\underset{3}{\cancel{6}}}$ Divide out the common factor.

$\phantom{\dfrac{\sqrt{24}}{6}} = \dfrac{\sqrt{6}}{3}$ Simplify.

PRACTICE 5

Express in simplified form.

a. $\sqrt{72}$

b. $2\sqrt{40}$

c. $\dfrac{\sqrt{75}}{15}$

Note that in Example 5(c), we cannot divide out the 6 in the numerator with the 6 in the denominator, since one is under a radical sign and the other is not.

TIP Be careful when dividing out common factors in radical expressions.

$$\frac{\sqrt{3}}{3} \neq \frac{\sqrt{\cancel{3}}}{\cancel{3}} \qquad \text{but} \qquad \frac{3\sqrt{3}}{3} = \frac{\cancel{3}\sqrt{3}}{\cancel{3}}$$

Now let's apply the product rule to radical expressions involving variables. The key here is to factor out the largest possible even power of each variable. Note that these problems test our knowledge of exponents as well as of radicals.

EXAMPLE 6

Simplify.

a. $\sqrt{y^5}$ **b.** $\sqrt{20a^6}$ **c.** $\sqrt{60x^5y}$

SOLUTION

a. $\sqrt{y^5} = \sqrt{y^4 \cdot y}$ Factor out the perfect square y^4, using the product rule of exponents.

$\qquad = \sqrt{y^4} \cdot \sqrt{y}$ Use the product rule of radicals.

$\qquad = y^2\sqrt{y}$ Take the square root of the perfect square.

b. $\sqrt{20a^6} = \sqrt{4 \cdot 5 \cdot a^6}$

$\qquad = \sqrt{4} \cdot \sqrt{a^6} \cdot \sqrt{5}$ Use the product rule of radicals.

$\qquad = 2a^3\sqrt{5}$ Take the square root of the perfect squares.

c. $\sqrt{60x^5y} = \sqrt{4 \cdot 15 \cdot x^4 \cdot x \cdot y}$ Factor out the perfect squares.

$\qquad = \sqrt{4} \cdot \sqrt{x^4} \cdot \sqrt{15xy}$ Use the product rule of radicals.

$\qquad = 2x^2\sqrt{15xy}$ Simplify.

PRACTICE 6

Express in simplified form.

a. $\sqrt{x^3}$

b. $\sqrt{18n^4}$

c. $-\sqrt{50ab^2}$

Some radical expressions involve quotients. If the radicand is a perfect square, we can take the square root directly.

EXAMPLE 7

Find the square root.

a. $\sqrt{\dfrac{1}{4}}$

b. $\sqrt{\dfrac{x^2}{49}}$

c. $\sqrt{\dfrac{a^2}{b^8}}$

SOLUTION

a. $\sqrt{\dfrac{1}{4}} = \dfrac{1}{2}$ since $\left(\dfrac{1}{2}\right)^2 = \dfrac{1}{4}$.

b. $\sqrt{\dfrac{x^2}{49}} = \dfrac{x}{7}$ since $\left(\dfrac{x}{7}\right)^2 = \dfrac{x^2}{49}$.

c. $\sqrt{\dfrac{a^2}{b^8}} = \dfrac{a}{b^4}$ since $\left(\dfrac{a}{b^4}\right)^2 = \dfrac{a^2}{b^8}$.

PRACTICE 7

Find the square root.

a. $\sqrt{\dfrac{1}{16}}$

b. $\sqrt{\dfrac{y^2}{4}}$

c. $\sqrt{\dfrac{x^4}{y^6}}$

Some radical expressions contain quotients that are not perfect squares. To simplify these radicals, we use the following rule.

The Quotient Rule of Radicals

If a is a nonnegative real number and b is a positive real number, then

$$\sqrt{\frac{a}{b}} = \frac{\sqrt{a}}{\sqrt{b}}.$$

In words, this rule states that the square root of a quotient is the quotient of the square roots.

To check that the quotient rule works in a particular example, let's consider the radical $\sqrt{\frac{4}{9}}$.

$$\sqrt{\frac{4}{9}} \stackrel{?}{=} \frac{\sqrt{4}}{\sqrt{9}}$$

$$\sqrt{\left(\frac{2}{3}\right)^2} \stackrel{?}{=} \frac{2}{3}$$

$$\frac{2}{3} = \frac{2}{3} \qquad \text{True.}$$

So $\sqrt{\frac{4}{9}} = \frac{\sqrt{4}}{\sqrt{9}}$, which is in agreement with the quotient rule.

EXAMPLE 8	PRACTICE 8
Simplify.	Simplify.
a. $\sqrt{\dfrac{7}{4}}$	**a.** $\sqrt{\dfrac{3}{16}}$
b. $\sqrt{\dfrac{3x}{25}}$	**b.** $\sqrt{\dfrac{2y}{49}}$
c. $\sqrt{\dfrac{2a^5b^{10}}{9}}$	**c.** $\sqrt{\dfrac{5x^7y^2}{4}}$

SOLUTION

a. $\sqrt{\dfrac{7}{4}} = \dfrac{\sqrt{7}}{\sqrt{4}}$ Use the quotient rule of radicals.

$\quad = \dfrac{\sqrt{7}}{2}$ Take the square root of the perfect square.

b. $\sqrt{\dfrac{3x}{25}} = \dfrac{\sqrt{3x}}{\sqrt{25}}$ Use the quotient rule of radicals.

$\quad = \dfrac{\sqrt{3x}}{5}$ Take the square root of the perfect square.

c. $\sqrt{\dfrac{2a^5b^{10}}{9}} = \dfrac{\sqrt{2a^5b^{10}}}{\sqrt{9}}$ Use the quotient rule of radicals.

$= \dfrac{\sqrt{a^4b^{10}} \cdot \sqrt{2a}}{\sqrt{9}}$ Use the product rule of radicals.

$= \dfrac{a^2b^5\sqrt{2a}}{3}$ Take the square root of the perfect squares.

Now let's see if we can apply our knowledge of radicals to some word problems. The following problem deals with the Pythagorean theorem, a topic that we discussed in Section 6.5. Recall that this theorem describes the relationship between the lengths of the three sides of a right triangle, which is expressed as $c^2 = a^2 + b^2$. We can rewrite the theorem as

$$c = \sqrt{a^2 + b^2},$$

where c is the length of the hypotenuse, and a and b are the lengths of the other two sides. Note that in evaluating a radical such as $\sqrt{a^2 + b^2}$ with arithmetic operations in the radicand, parentheses are understood around the radicand. So in evaluating $\sqrt{a^2 + b^2}$, we compute $a^2 + b^2$, take the square root, and then simplify, if possible.

EXAMPLE 9

A flat panel television is rectangular in shape, with dimensions 25 in. by 15 in. Find the length of the panel's diagonal, both as a radical and as a decimal rounded to the nearest inch.

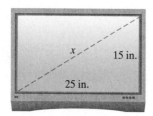

SOLUTION Let x represent the length of the diagonal of the panel. The lengths of the other two sides of the triangle shown are 15 in. and 25 in. Using the Pythagorean theorem, we get:

$$x = \sqrt{a^2 + b^2}$$
$$= \sqrt{15^2 + 25^2}$$
$$= \sqrt{225 + 625}$$
$$= \sqrt{850}$$
$$= \sqrt{25 \cdot 34}$$
$$= \sqrt{25} \cdot \sqrt{34}$$
$$= 5\sqrt{34}$$

So the length of the diagonal of the panel is $5\sqrt{34}$ in., or approximately 29 in.

PRACTICE 9

Two Jeeps try to pull a car out of the snow, tugging at a 90° angle to each other.

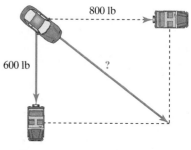

If one Jeep exerts a force of 600 lb and the other a force of 800 lb, the magnitude of the resulting force on the car (in pounds) can be found by computing $\sqrt{600^2 + 800^2}$. Calculate this force.

Exercises 8.1

FOR EXTRA HELP

📖 *Student's Solutions Manual*

Addison-Wesley Math Tutor Center

🚪 *MyMathLab*

📼 *Videotape 8/DVT 8*

Find the value of each radical. When a radicand is not a perfect square, use a calculator to evaluate, rounding to the nearest thousandth.

1. $\sqrt{36}$ **2.** $\sqrt{25}$ **3.** $\sqrt{1}$

4. $\sqrt{9}$ **5.** $-\sqrt{100}$ **6.** $-\sqrt{64}$

7. $3\sqrt{49}$ **8.** $2\sqrt{81}$ **9.** $\sqrt{5}$

10. $\sqrt{6}$ **11.** $3\sqrt{2}$ **12.** $4\sqrt{3}$

Simplify.

13. $(\sqrt{16})^2$ **14.** $(\sqrt{5})^2$ **15.** $(\sqrt{11})^2$ **16.** $(\sqrt{10})^2$

17. $(\sqrt{5x})^2$ **18.** $(\sqrt{8y})^2$ **19.** $\sqrt{2^2}$ **20.** $\sqrt{3^2}$

21. $\sqrt{9^2}$ **22.** $\sqrt{14^2}$ **23.** $\sqrt{n^8}$ **24.** $\sqrt{s^2}$

25. $\sqrt{49y^2}$ **26.** $\sqrt{16t^4}$ **27.** $\sqrt{9x^4}$ **28.** $\sqrt{100y^6}$

29. $\sqrt{25x^2y^{10}}$ **30.** $\sqrt{49p^{12}q^4}$

Simplify each expression, factoring out any perfect square.

31. $\sqrt{32}$ **32.** $\sqrt{75}$ **33.** $-\sqrt{108}$ **34.** $-\sqrt{98}$

35. $6\sqrt{27}$ **36.** $3\sqrt{20}$ **37.** $\dfrac{\sqrt{48}}{12}$ **38.** $\dfrac{\sqrt{50}}{10}$

39. $\sqrt{11x^2}$ **40.** $\sqrt{7n^4}$ **41.** $\sqrt{n^5}$ **42.** $\sqrt{t^7}$

43. $\sqrt{20x^3}$ **44.** $-\sqrt{32y^9}$ **45.** $\sqrt{12p^2q}$ **46.** $-\sqrt{24a^3b^4}$

47. $9\sqrt{10x^3y^4}$ **48.** $-2\sqrt{25a^7b^6}$

Simplify.

49. $\sqrt{\dfrac{4}{25}}$

50. $\sqrt{\dfrac{1}{36}}$

51. $-\sqrt{\dfrac{1}{4}}$

52. $-\sqrt{\dfrac{49}{9}}$

53. $\sqrt{\dfrac{81}{n^6}}$

54. $\sqrt{\dfrac{121}{x^8}}$

55. $\sqrt{\dfrac{x^4}{y^2}}$

56. $\sqrt{\dfrac{a^2}{b^6}}$

57. $\sqrt{\dfrac{3}{4}}$

58. $-\sqrt{\dfrac{2}{9}}$

59. $\sqrt{\dfrac{5n}{16}}$

60. $-\sqrt{\dfrac{3t}{25}}$

61. $\sqrt{\dfrac{3x^2y^6}{4}}$

62. $\sqrt{\dfrac{5a^4b^2}{9}}$

63. $\sqrt{\dfrac{27x^6y}{16}}$

64. $\sqrt{\dfrac{32ab^8}{25}}$

Applications

Solve.

65. The *geometric mean m* of two numbers *a* and *b* is the square root of their product. The geometric mean can be thought of as a kind of average.

    a. Express this relationship as a formula.

    b. Find the geometric mean of 2 and 8.

66. Sailors approximate the maximum speed *s* (in knots) of a sailboat by multiplying 1.3 by the square root of the length of the boat's waterline *w* (in feet).

    a. Express this relationship as a formula.

    b. Use this formula to approximate the maximum speed, to the nearest knot, of a sailboat with a 16-ft waterline.

67. When an object is dropped from a height *h* (in meters), it takes approximately $\sqrt{\dfrac{h}{5}}$ sec to reach the ground.

    a. Find the time it takes for an object dropped from a height of 20 m to reach the ground.

    b. If the same object is dropped from double the height, will it take twice as long to reach the ground? Explain.

68. The expression $2\pi\sqrt{\dfrac{L}{32}}$ approximates the time (in seconds) that a pendulum of length L (in feet) takes to make one complete swing back and forth.

    a. How long does it take the pendulum shown to make one complete swing? Use 3.14 for π, and round to the nearest second.

8 ft

    b. How long would it take a pendulum 4 times the length of that in part (a) to make a complete swing? Is this answer 4 times the answer to part (a)?

69. Under certain conditions, the expression $2\sqrt{5L}$ can be used to approximate the speed of a car (in miles per hour) that has left a skid mark of length L (in ft). If an investigating officer arrives at the scene of an accident where these conditions apply and finds a skid mark 180 ft long, at what speed was the car traveling at the time of the accident?

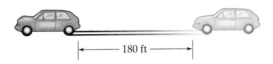

180 ft

70. Firefighters can approximate the speed S at which water leaves a typical nozzle by using the formula

$$S = 12\sqrt{P},$$

where the pressure P is measured in pounds per square inch (psi) and the speed is in feet per second. Find the speed of the water if the pressure is 50 psi. Express your answer both as a simplified radical and as a decimal rounded to the nearest whole number. (***Source:*** Jim Cottrell, "Fire Stream Physics," *Firefighter's News*, 1995)

71. A surveyor wishes to find the distance between the towns B and C across from one another on a lake, as shown in the illustration. Find this distance expressed both as a radical in simplified form and as a decimal rounded to the nearest mile.

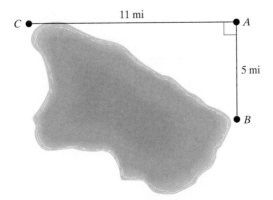

11 mi

C A

5 mi

B

72. A plane is about to land at an airport. The flight path of the plane's descent is shown in the following diagram. What is the distance from the plane to the airport? Express this distance both as a radical and as a decimal rounded to the nearest multiple of 100 ft.

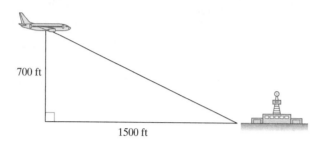

700 ft

1500 ft

● *Check your answers on page A-29.*

Mindstretchers

RESEARCH

1. Using your college library or the Web, investigate whether there is a connection between the radical symbol and the symbol for a drugstore prescription.

Describe the results of your research.

_____

WRITING

2. Consider the following statement: *Just as with adding and subtracting, the operations of* **squaring** *and* **taking a square root** *are opposites.* In a few sentences, support or refute this statement.

_____

_____

_____

_____

_____

_____

_____

INVESTIGATION

3. Consider the statement: For any positive numbers, the larger the number, the larger its square root.

a. Use a calculator either to support this assertion with many examples or to give a counterexample. Sum up your findings.

_____

b. If you supported this assertion, do your examples prove the assertion true? If you gave a counterexample, does the counterexample prove the assertion false? Explain.

_____

_____

_____

Cultural Note

The square root is related to one of the most revolutionary experiments in the history of science. Working some 500 years ago, Galileo Galilei discovered that contrary to ancient authority the speed of falling objects dropped from an Italian cathedral tower was proportional to the square root of the height from which they were dropped. Because of such experiments, Galileo is considered to be the founder of modern physics.

Source: Jeanne Bendick, _Along came_

Galileo (Beautiful Feat Books, Sandwich, MA, 1999)

8.2 Addition and Subtraction of Radical Expressions

- *To add and subtract radical expressions*
- *To solve applied problems involving the addition or subtraction of radical expressions*

Sums and differences of many radicals, in contrast to other kinds of numbers such as fractions and decimals, cannot be simplified. For instance, there is no way to combine $\sqrt{2}$ and $\sqrt{3}$, so we cannot simplify the expression $\sqrt{2}+\sqrt{3}$. Similarly, we cannot simplify the expression $\sqrt{5} - 1$. However, we can approximate the value of these expressions using a calculator.

Some other radicals can be combined. In this section, we discuss such radicals.

Adding and Subtracting Like Radicals

When adding or subtracting *like* radicals, we can simplify the result. **Like radicals** are radical expressions that have the same radicand. For instance, $4\sqrt{2}$ and $3\sqrt{2}$ are like radicals. The radicals $7\sqrt{2}$ and $\sqrt{3}$ are *unlike*.

We use the distributive property to add or subtract like radicals, just as we do for adding and subtracting like terms.

Adding Like Terms

$4x + 3x = (4 + 3)x = 7x$

Like terms

Adding Like Radicals

$4\sqrt{2} + 3\sqrt{2} = (4 + 3)\sqrt{2} = 7\sqrt{2}$

Like radicals

Subtracting Like Terms

$4x - 3x = (4 - 3)x = x$

Like terms

Subtracting Like Radicals

$4\sqrt{2} - 3\sqrt{2} = (4 - 3)\sqrt{2} = \sqrt{2}$

Like radicals

EXAMPLE 1

Add or subtract.

a. $5\sqrt{3} + 2\sqrt{3}$ **b.** $7\sqrt{x} - 2\sqrt{x} - 4\sqrt{x}$

c. $4\sqrt{2y + 1} - \sqrt{2y + 1}$ **d.** $5\sqrt{3} + 3\sqrt{5}$

SOLUTION

a. $5\sqrt{3} + 2\sqrt{3} = (5 + 2)\sqrt{3}$ Combine the coefficients using the distributive property.

$\qquad = 7\sqrt{3}$ Simplify.

b. $7\sqrt{x} - 2\sqrt{x} - 4\sqrt{x} = (7 - 2 - 4)\sqrt{x}$ Use the distributive property.

$\qquad = 1\sqrt{x}$ Simplify.

$\qquad = \sqrt{x}$

c. $4\sqrt{2y + 1} - \sqrt{2y + 1} = (4 - 1)\sqrt{2y + 1}$

$\qquad = 3\sqrt{2y + 1}$

d. $5\sqrt{3} + 3\sqrt{5}$ cannot be combined because they are not like radicals.

PRACTICE 1

Add or subtract.

a. $8\sqrt{5} - 2\sqrt{5}$

b. $3\sqrt{n} + \sqrt{n} + 7\sqrt{n}$

c. $10\sqrt{t^2 - 3} + \sqrt{t^2 - 3}$

d. $4\sqrt{6} - 2\sqrt{2}$

Adding and Subtracting Unlike Radicals

Some *unlike* radicals become *like* when they are simplified. When this happens, they can be combined.

EXAMPLE 2	PRACTICE 2
Combine. Simplify, if possible.	Combine. Simplify, if possible.

EXAMPLE 2

Combine. Simplify, if possible.

a. $\sqrt{12} + \sqrt{27}$

b. $7\sqrt{50} - \sqrt{72} + \sqrt{32}$

c. $-\sqrt{4x} + 3\sqrt{x}$

d. $a\sqrt{a^2b} - 5b\sqrt{b}$

SOLUTION

a. $\sqrt{12} + \sqrt{27} = \sqrt{4 \cdot 3} + \sqrt{9 \cdot 3}$ Factor out perfect squares.

$\qquad\qquad = \sqrt{4} \cdot \sqrt{3} + \sqrt{9} \cdot \sqrt{3}$ Use the product rule of radicals.

$\qquad\qquad = 2\sqrt{3} + 3\sqrt{3}$ Take the square root of a perfect square.

$\qquad\qquad = (2 + 3)\sqrt{3}$ Use the distributive property.

$\qquad\qquad = 5\sqrt{3}$ Simplify.

b. $7\sqrt{50} - \sqrt{72} + \sqrt{32}$

$\qquad = 7\sqrt{25 \cdot 2} - \sqrt{36 \cdot 2} + \sqrt{16 \cdot 2}$ Factor out perfect squares.

$\qquad = 7 \cdot \sqrt{25} \cdot \sqrt{2} - \sqrt{36} \cdot \sqrt{2} + \sqrt{16} \cdot \sqrt{2}$ Use the product rule of radicals.

$\qquad = 7 \cdot 5\sqrt{2} - 6\sqrt{2} + 4\sqrt{2}$ Take the square roots.

$\qquad = 35\sqrt{2} - 6\sqrt{2} + 4\sqrt{2}$ Simplify.

$\qquad = (35 - 6 + 4)\sqrt{2}$ Use the distributive property.

$\qquad = 33\sqrt{2}$ Simplify.

c. $-\sqrt{4x} + 3\sqrt{x} = -2\sqrt{x} + 3\sqrt{x} = (-2 + 3)\sqrt{x} = \sqrt{x}$

d. $a\sqrt{a^2b} - 5b\sqrt{b} = a \cdot a\sqrt{b} - 5b\sqrt{b}$

$\qquad\qquad\qquad = a^2\sqrt{b} - 5b\sqrt{b}$

$\qquad\qquad\qquad = (a^2 - 5b)\sqrt{b}$

PRACTICE 2

Combine. Simplify, if possible.

a. $\sqrt{50} + \sqrt{98}$

b. $\sqrt{12} + 2\sqrt{75} - 6\sqrt{27}$

c. $-3\sqrt{16t} + \sqrt{9t}$

d. $\sqrt{25ab^4} + 7b^2\sqrt{a}$

EXAMPLE 3

It takes $\sqrt{20}$ sec for an object to fall 320 ft, and $\sqrt{5}$ sec for the object to fall 80 ft. How much longer will it take an object to fall 320 ft than 80 ft? Express your answer both in radical form and as a decimal rounded to the nearest second.

SOLUTION We need to find the difference between $\sqrt{20}$ sec and $\sqrt{5}$ sec.

$$
\begin{aligned}
\sqrt{20} - \sqrt{5} &= \sqrt{4 \cdot 5} - \sqrt{5} \\
&= \sqrt{4} \cdot \sqrt{5} - \sqrt{5} \\
&= 2\sqrt{5} - \sqrt{5}
\end{aligned}
$$

So it takes an object $\sqrt{5}$ sec, or approximately 2 sec, longer for the object to fall 320 ft than 80 ft.

PRACTICE 3

A young couple wants to build a square cabin with an area of 200 sq m on the corner of a square plot of land with area 1800 sq m. Find the length of the front yard shown in the illustration. Express this length as a decimal rounded to the nearest meter.

Exercises 8.2

FOR EXTRA HELP

📖 *Student's Solutions Manual*

Tutor Center *Addison-Wesley Math Tutor Center*

🚪 *MyMathLab*

📼 *Videotape 8/DVT 8*

Combine and simplify, if possible.

1. $5\sqrt{7} + 3\sqrt{7}$

2. $7\sqrt{11} + \sqrt{11}$

3. $3\sqrt{2} - 8\sqrt{2}$

4. $\sqrt{3} - 10\sqrt{3}$

5. $6\sqrt{3} - 3\sqrt{6}$

6. $2\sqrt{7} + 7\sqrt{2}$

7. $-5\sqrt{11} - 10\sqrt{11} + 2\sqrt{11}$

8. $-4\sqrt{5} + 4\sqrt{5} + 2\sqrt{5}$

9. $7t\sqrt{3} + 2t\sqrt{3}$

10. $3y\sqrt{2} + 5y\sqrt{2}$

11. $13\sqrt{x} + 10\sqrt{x}$

12. $2\sqrt{3k} + 9\sqrt{3k}$

13. $6\sqrt{x+1} - \sqrt{x+1}$

14. $\sqrt{2m-1} - 7\sqrt{2m-1}$

15. $\sqrt{8} - \sqrt{32}$

16. $\sqrt{12} - \sqrt{27}$

17. $\sqrt{50} + \sqrt{72}$

18. $\sqrt{48} + \sqrt{12}$

19. $-\sqrt{12} + 5\sqrt{3}$

20. $3\sqrt{2} - \sqrt{18}$

21. $6\sqrt{75} - 2\sqrt{12}$

22. $5\sqrt{72} - 4\sqrt{50}$

23. $5\sqrt{8} - 3\sqrt{12} + \sqrt{2}$

24. $2\sqrt{3} + \sqrt{20} + \sqrt{5}$

25. $2\sqrt{16y} + 3\sqrt{4y}$

26. $2\sqrt{9x} + 8\sqrt{4x}$

27. $\sqrt{9x} - \sqrt{16x^3}$

28. $2\sqrt{25a^3} - \sqrt{a}$

29. $\sqrt{25p} + \sqrt{64p} + \sqrt{p}$

30. $\sqrt{49a} - 2\sqrt{a} + 9\sqrt{a}$

31. $-5x\sqrt{2x^3y^4} + x\sqrt{2x^5y^2}$

32. $-2\sqrt{9ab^5} - 3a\sqrt{4a^3b}$

Applications

Solve. Express the answer as a radical in simplified form.

33. For the isosceles triangle shown, find

  a. the lengths of the missing sides

  b. the perimeter.

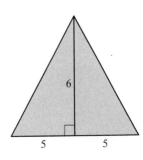

34. The size of a television set is commonly given by the length of the screen's diagonal. For the two sets pictured, find

  a. the lengths of their diagonals

  b. the difference of the diagonal lengths

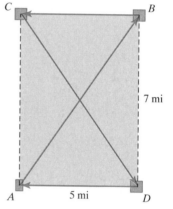

35. Two square tiles are pictured.

  Area = 90 sq in.   Area = 40 sq in.

  a. Determine the side lengths of the two tiles.

  b. How much longer is a side of the larger tile than the smaller tile?

36. The accompanying map shows the route that a college recruiter takes in calling on colleges each week. She starts at home (A), visits colleges in towns B, C, and D in that order, and then returns home.

  a. How long is the road from A to B?

  b. What is the length of the recruiter's weekly trip?

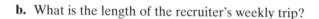

37. A manufacturer of machine parts is willing to supply a retailer n machine parts at a total price P (in dollars) following the model

$$P = 9\sqrt{n}.$$

How much more will the manufacturer charge the retailer for 4000 machine parts than for 1000 machine parts?

38. It takes $\dfrac{\sqrt{50 - h}}{4}$ sec for an object to fall from a height of 50 ft to a height of h ft above the ground. From a height of 50 ft, how much longer does it take to drop to a height of 10 ft above the ground than to drop to a height of 40 ft above the ground?

• *Check your answers on page A-29.*

Mindstretchers

GROUPWORK

1. Working with a partner, choose several arbitrary nonnegative values for the variables a and b in the two left columns of the following table.

a	b	$a + b$	$\sqrt{a}$	$\sqrt{b}$	$\sqrt{a} + \sqrt{b}$	$\sqrt{a + b}$

   a. Using a calculator, complete the table with each entry rounded to the nearest thousandth.

   b. Compare the entries in the two rightmost columns. Are the entries in one column consistently larger than the entries in the other column? State a conjecture based on this observation.

PATTERNS

2. Consider the isosceles right triangle ABC shown below.

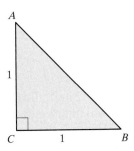

   On side $\overline{AB}$, build right triangle ABD with $AD = 1$.

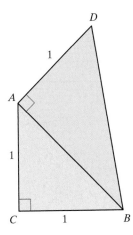

   a. Find the lengths of $\overline{AB}$ and $\overline{DB}$.

b. How much longer is $\overline{DB}$ than $\overline{AB}$?

_____

c. Now build another right triangle on $\overline{DB}$ with a leg of length 1. What is the length of $\overline{EB}$?

_____

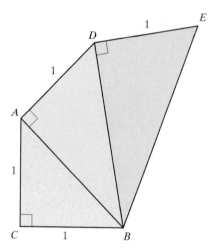

d. Describe the pattern that you observe in this *spiral* of triangles.

_____

_____

_____

WRITING

3. Recall that the radicals $\sqrt{2}$ and $5\sqrt{2}$ are called *like*, whereas the radicals $7\sqrt{2}$ and $\sqrt{3}$ are called *unlike*. List two other kinds of numbers where a distinction is made between like and unlike. Why are these distinctions made?

_____

_____

_____

_____

_____

_____

8.3 Multiplication and Division of Radical Expressions

OBJECTIVES

- *To multiply radical expressions*
- *To divide radical expressions*
- *To rationalize denominators in radical expressions*
- *To solve applied problems involving the multiplication or division of radical expressions*

In the last section, we discussed the addition and subtraction of radical expressions. In this section, we discuss how to find their products and quotients.

Multiplying Radical Expressions

In considering how to find the product of radical expressions, we begin with the simplest case—multiplying two radical expressions that are the same, that is, squaring a radical expression. Recall the property used in Section 8.1 for squaring a square root: $(\sqrt{a})^2 = a$.

EXAMPLE 1

Simplify.

a. $\sqrt{3} \cdot \sqrt{3}$

b. $(\sqrt{5x})^2$

c. $(2\sqrt{n+1})^2$

SOLUTION Here, we use the property of squaring a square root.

a. $\sqrt{3} \cdot \sqrt{3} = (\sqrt{3})^2 = 3$

b. $(\sqrt{5x})^2 = 5x$

c. $(2\sqrt{n+1})^2 = 2^2 \cdot (\sqrt{n+1})^2$ Use the rule of raising a product to a power.

$\qquad\qquad = 4(n+1)$

PRACTICE 1

Simplify:

a. $\sqrt{5} \cdot \sqrt{5}$

b. $(\sqrt{2y^3})^2$

c. $(\sqrt{t+1})^2$

Now let's look at multiplying two radical expressions that are different from one another. The key here is to apply the product rule of radicals discussed in Section 8.1. We can write this rule as

$$\sqrt{a}\sqrt{b} = \sqrt{ab},$$

where a and b are nonnegative numbers. In words, this rule states that the product of square roots is the square root of the product.

EXAMPLE 2

Multiply and simplify, if possible.

a. $\sqrt{3} \cdot \sqrt{5}$

b. $(-5\sqrt{10})(6\sqrt{2})$

c. $\sqrt{12n^3} \cdot \sqrt{3n}$

PRACTICE 2

Find the product and simplify, if possible.

a. $\sqrt{7} \cdot \sqrt{10}$

b. $(9\sqrt{6})(-4\sqrt{3})$

c. $\sqrt{8y} \cdot \sqrt{2y^5}$

SOLUTION Here, we use the product rule of radicals before simplifying.

a. $\sqrt{3} \cdot \sqrt{5} = \sqrt{3 \cdot 5} = \sqrt{15}$

b. $(-5\sqrt{10})(6\sqrt{2}) = -5 \cdot 6 \cdot \sqrt{10 \cdot 2}$

$$= -30\sqrt{20}$$
$$= -30\sqrt{4 \cdot 5}$$
$$= -30 \cdot 2\sqrt{5}$$
$$= -60\sqrt{5}$$

c. $\sqrt{12n^3} \cdot \sqrt{3n} = \sqrt{12n^3 \cdot 3n}$
$$= \sqrt{36n^4}$$
$$= 6n^2$$

Next we consider the multiplication of radical expressions that may contain more than one term. Just as with the multiplication of polynomials, the key here is to use the distributive property.

EXAMPLE 3

Find the product and simplify.

a. $\sqrt{8}(2\sqrt{3} + \sqrt{2})$ **b.** $\sqrt{x}(5\sqrt{y} - 2)$

SOLUTION

a. $\sqrt{8}(2\sqrt{3} + \sqrt{2})$

$= \sqrt{8}(2\sqrt{3}) + \sqrt{8}(\sqrt{2})$	Use the distributive property.
$= 2\sqrt{24} + \sqrt{16}$	Use the product rule of radicals.
$= 2\sqrt{4 \cdot 6} + 4$	Factor out a perfect square from the radicand.
$= 2 \cdot 2\sqrt{6} + 4$	Use the property of taking the square root of a square.
$= 4\sqrt{6} + 4$	Simplify.

b. $\sqrt{x}(5\sqrt{y} - 2)$

$= \sqrt{x}(5\sqrt{y}) - \sqrt{x}(2)$	Use the distributive property.
$= 5\sqrt{xy} - 2\sqrt{x}$	Use the product rule of radicals.

PRACTICE 3

Multiply and simplify.

a. $\sqrt{6}(3\sqrt{3} - \sqrt{8})$

b. $\sqrt{a}(\sqrt{b} + 3)$

EXAMPLE 4

Find the product and simplify.

a. $(4\sqrt{2} - 1)(7\sqrt{2} + 3)$

b. $(2\sqrt{a} + 4)(\sqrt{a} - 1)$

PRACTICE 4

Find the product and simplify.

a. $(2\sqrt{3} + 4)(\sqrt{3} - 1)$

b. $(\sqrt{x} + 2)(3\sqrt{x} - 2)$

SOLUTION

a. $(4\sqrt{2} - 1)(7\sqrt{2} + 3)$

$$= (4\sqrt{2} - 1)(7\sqrt{2} + 3)$$

$= (4\sqrt{2})(7\sqrt{2}) + (4\sqrt{2})3$ Use the FOIL method.
$\quad + (-1)(7\sqrt{2}) + (-1)(3)$

$= 4 \cdot 7 \cdot 2 + 4 \cdot 3\sqrt{2}$ Use the property of
$\quad - 7\sqrt{2} - 3$ squaring a square root.

$= 56 + 12\sqrt{2} - 7\sqrt{2} - 3$ Simplify.

$= 53 + 5\sqrt{2}$ Combine like terms.

b. $(2\sqrt{a} + 4)(\sqrt{a} - 1)$

$= (2\sqrt{a})(\sqrt{a}) + (2\sqrt{a})(-1) + 4\sqrt{a} + 4(-1)$ Use the FOIL method.

$= 2a - 2\sqrt{a} + 4\sqrt{a} - 4$

$= 2a + 2\sqrt{a} - 4$

Recall from Section 5.6 the formula for multiplying the sum and difference of the same two terms.

$$(a + b)(a - b) = a^2 - b^2$$

In some products, the binomial factors are radical expressions.

EXAMPLE 5

Find the product and simplify.

a. $(\sqrt{10} + 5)(\sqrt{10} - 5)$
b. $(\sqrt{x} - \sqrt{y})(\sqrt{x} + \sqrt{y})$

SOLUTION We apply the formula for the product of the sum and difference of two terms.

a. $(\sqrt{10} + 5)(\sqrt{10} - 5) = (\sqrt{10})^2 - (5)^2$

$$= 10 - 25$$

$$= -15$$

b. $(\sqrt{x} - \sqrt{y})(\sqrt{x} + \sqrt{y}) = (\sqrt{x})^2 - (\sqrt{y})^2 = x - y$

PRACTICE 5

Multiply and simplify:

a. $(\sqrt{7} - 3)(\sqrt{7} + 3)$

b. $(\sqrt{p} + \sqrt{q})(\sqrt{p} - \sqrt{q})$

Note that in Example 5, the products contain no radical sign. How would you explain why the radical signs drop out?

Recall from Section 5.6 that when squaring a binomial, the following formulas apply.

$$(a + b)^2 = a^2 + 2ab + b^2 \quad \text{The square of a sum}$$
$$(a - b)^2 = a^2 - 2ab + b^2 \quad \text{The square of a difference}$$

EXAMPLE 6

Simplify.

a. $(\sqrt{3} + 5x)^2$ **b.** $(\sqrt{p} - 2)^2$

SOLUTION

a. $(\sqrt{3} + 5x)^2 = (\sqrt{3})^2 + 2(\sqrt{3})(5x) + (5x)^2$ Use the formula for squaring a binomial sum.

$\qquad = (\sqrt{3})^2 + 2(5)(\sqrt{3})(x) + (5)^2 x^2$

$\qquad = 3 + 10\sqrt{3}x + 25x^2$

$\qquad = 25x^2 + 10\sqrt{3}x + 3$

b. $(\sqrt{p} - 2)^2 = (\sqrt{p})^2 - 2(\sqrt{p})(2) + 2^2$ Use the formula for squaring a binomial difference.

$\qquad = p - 2(\sqrt{p})(2) + 4$

$\qquad = p - 4(\sqrt{p}) + 4$

PRACTICE 6

Simplify.

a. $(\sqrt{2} + b)^2$

b. $(\sqrt{x} - 6)^2$

EXAMPLE 7

In an *equilateral* triangle, all three sides are equal in length. The height h of this kind of triangle is given by the expression $\dfrac{s\sqrt{3}}{2}$, where s is the length of each side of the triangle. What is the height of the triangle shown?

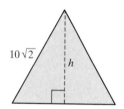

SOLUTION In the triangle shown, $s = 10\sqrt{2}$. So we get:

$$h = \frac{s\sqrt{3}}{2}$$

$$= \frac{10\sqrt{2} \cdot \sqrt{3}}{2}$$

$$= \frac{10\sqrt{6}}{2}$$

$$= 5\sqrt{6}$$

PRACTICE 7

The number of 24-hr days that it takes a planet in our solar system to revolve once around the Sun is approximated by the expression $0.2(\sqrt{R})^3$, where R is the average distance of the planet from the Sun in millions of kilometers. For the planet Mercury, the average distance is about 60 million km. How many 24-hr days does it take Mercury to revolve around the Sun, to the nearest whole day?

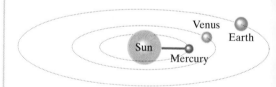

Dividing Radical Expressions

Now let's consider dividing radical expressions. Here, we use the quotient rule of radicals discussed in Section 8.1. We can write this rule as

$$\frac{\sqrt{a}}{\sqrt{b}} = \sqrt{\frac{a}{b}},$$

where a is nonnegative and b is positive. This rule allows us, in dividing two square roots, to bring the radicands under a single radical sign. We can then divide the radicands. This is particularly useful if their quotient happens to be a perfect square.

EXAMPLE 8	**PRACTICE 8**

EXAMPLE 8

Find the quotient and simplify, if possible.

a. $\dfrac{\sqrt{26}}{\sqrt{2}}$

b. $\dfrac{\sqrt{16y^7}}{\sqrt{y}}$

c. $\dfrac{5\sqrt{10t}}{\sqrt{90t^3}}$

SOLUTION Here, we use the quotient rule of radicals before simplifying.

a. $\dfrac{\sqrt{26}}{\sqrt{2}} = \sqrt{\dfrac{26}{2}} = \sqrt{13}$

b. $\dfrac{\sqrt{16y^7}}{\sqrt{y}} = \sqrt{\dfrac{16y^7}{y}} = \sqrt{16y^6} = 4y^3$

c. $\dfrac{5\sqrt{10t}}{\sqrt{90t^3}} = 5\sqrt{\dfrac{10t}{90t^3}}$

$\qquad = 5\sqrt{\dfrac{1}{9t^2}}$

$\qquad = 5 \cdot \dfrac{1}{3t}$ **Use the property of taking the square root of a square.**

$\qquad = \dfrac{5}{3t}$

PRACTICE 8

Divide. Simplify, if possible.

a. $\dfrac{\sqrt{21}}{\sqrt{3}}$

b. $\dfrac{\sqrt{4x^5}}{\sqrt{x}}$

c. $\dfrac{\sqrt{2y}}{10\sqrt{8y^5}}$

When the radicand of a radical expression is a fraction, the expression is not considered to be simplified. To simplify, we can apply the quotient rule of radicals:

$$\sqrt{\dfrac{a}{b}} = \dfrac{\sqrt{a}}{\sqrt{b}},$$

where a is nonnegative and b is positive. In words, this rule states that the square root of a quotient is the quotient of the square roots. Radicands with perfect squares in the denominator lend themselves to this approach.

EXAMPLE 9

Simplify.

a. $\sqrt{\dfrac{x^3}{y^8}}$

b. $\sqrt{\dfrac{9p^4}{q^{10}}}$

c. $\sqrt{\dfrac{7x^2}{4}}$

PRACTICE 9

Simplify.

a. $\sqrt{\dfrac{m^5}{n^4}}$

b. $\sqrt{\dfrac{y^6}{25x^2}}$

c. $\sqrt{\dfrac{5a^2}{9}}$

SOLUTION Using the quotient rule of radicals, we get:

a. $\sqrt{\dfrac{x^3}{y^8}} = \dfrac{\sqrt{x^2 \cdot x}}{\sqrt{y^8}} = \dfrac{x\sqrt{x}}{y^4}$

b. $\sqrt{\dfrac{9p^4}{q^{10}}} = \dfrac{\sqrt{9p^4}}{\sqrt{q^{10}}} = \dfrac{3p^2}{q^5}$

c. $\sqrt{\dfrac{7x^2}{4}} = \dfrac{\sqrt{7x^2}}{\sqrt{4}} = \dfrac{x\sqrt{7}}{2}$

Rationalizing the Denominator

Some radical expressions are written as fractions with radicals in their denominators:

$$\dfrac{5}{\sqrt{2}} \qquad \dfrac{3x}{\sqrt{x-1}} \qquad \dfrac{v}{\sqrt{1-m^2}}$$

This type of expression, which can be difficult to evaluate without a calculator, is not considered to be simplified. However, we can always *rationalize the denominator* of such an expression, that is, rewrite the expression in an equivalent form that contains no radical in its denominator. To do this, we multiply the numerator and denominator by a square root that will make the radicand in the denominator a perfect square.

EXAMPLE 10

Rationalize the denominator.

a. $\dfrac{3}{\sqrt{5}}$

b. $\dfrac{\sqrt{6}}{\sqrt{x}}$

c. $\dfrac{\sqrt{25y^6}}{\sqrt{8}}$

SOLUTION To rationalize the denominators, we multiply the numerator and denominator by a square root that makes the radicand in the denominator a perfect square.

a. $\dfrac{3}{\sqrt{5}} = \dfrac{3}{\sqrt{5}} \cdot \dfrac{\sqrt{5}}{\sqrt{5}}$ **Multiply the numerator and denominator by** $\sqrt{5}$.

$\qquad = \dfrac{3\sqrt{5}}{\sqrt{5^2}}$

$\qquad = \dfrac{3\sqrt{5}}{5}$

b. $\dfrac{\sqrt{6}}{\sqrt{x}} = \dfrac{\sqrt{6}}{\sqrt{x}} \cdot \dfrac{\sqrt{x}}{\sqrt{x}} = \dfrac{\sqrt{6x}}{x}$

PRACTICE 10

Rationalize the denominator.

a. $\dfrac{1}{\sqrt{2}}$

b. $\dfrac{\sqrt{5}}{\sqrt{s}}$

c. $\dfrac{\sqrt{49r^4}}{\sqrt{12}}$

c. $\dfrac{\sqrt{25y^6}}{\sqrt{8}} = \dfrac{5y^3}{\sqrt{8}}$ **Take the square root in the numerator.**

$$= \dfrac{5y^3}{\sqrt{8}} \cdot \dfrac{\sqrt{8}}{\sqrt{8}}$$

$$= \dfrac{5y^3\sqrt{8}}{8}$$

$$= \dfrac{5y^3(2\sqrt{2})}{8}$$

$$= \dfrac{5y^3\sqrt{2}}{4}$$

When the radicand of a radical expression is a fraction, we can simplify the radical by first applying the quotient rule and then rationalizing the denominator.

EXAMPLE 11	PRACTICE 11
Simplify.	Simplify.
a. $\sqrt{\dfrac{3}{5}}$	**a.** $\sqrt{\dfrac{1}{6}}$
b. $\sqrt{\dfrac{x}{12}}$	
SOLUTION	**b.** $\sqrt{\dfrac{n}{20}}$
a. $\sqrt{\dfrac{3}{5}} = \dfrac{\sqrt{3}}{\sqrt{5}} = \dfrac{\sqrt{3}}{\sqrt{5}} \cdot \dfrac{\sqrt{5}}{\sqrt{5}} = \dfrac{\sqrt{15}}{5}$	
b. $\sqrt{\dfrac{x}{12}} = \dfrac{\sqrt{x}}{\sqrt{12}}$	
$\phantom{b.\sqrt{\dfrac{x}{12}}} = \dfrac{\sqrt{x}}{\sqrt{12}} \cdot \dfrac{\sqrt{3}}{\sqrt{3}}$	
$\phantom{b.\sqrt{\dfrac{x}{12}}} = \dfrac{\sqrt{3x}}{\sqrt{36}}$	
$\phantom{b.\sqrt{\dfrac{x}{12}}} = \dfrac{\sqrt{3x}}{6}$	

To review, a radical expression is considered simplified if the following conditions are all met.

	Simplified	Not Simplified
• The radicand has no factor that is a perfect square.	$5\sqrt{2}$	$\sqrt{50} = \sqrt{25 \cdot 2}$
• There are no fractions under the radical sign.	$\dfrac{\sqrt{3}}{2}$	$\sqrt{\dfrac{3}{4}}$
• There are no radicals in the denominator.	$\dfrac{\sqrt{6}}{3}$	$\dfrac{2}{\sqrt{6}}$

Some radical expressions are in the form of fractions, with more than one term in the numerator. We may need to rationalize the denominator of such an expression.

EXAMPLE 12	PRACTICE 12
Rationalize the denominator.	Rationalize the denominator.

EXAMPLE 12

Rationalize the denominator.

a. $\dfrac{\sqrt{2}+3}{\sqrt{5}}$

b. $\dfrac{\sqrt{x}-1}{\sqrt{y}}$

SOLUTION

a. $\dfrac{\sqrt{2}+3}{\sqrt{5}} = \dfrac{(\sqrt{2}+3)}{\sqrt{5}} \cdot \dfrac{\sqrt{5}}{\sqrt{5}}$

$= \dfrac{(\sqrt{2}+3)\sqrt{5}}{5}$

$= \dfrac{(\sqrt{2})(\sqrt{5})+3\sqrt{5}}{5}$

$= \dfrac{\sqrt{10}+3\sqrt{5}}{5}$

b. $\dfrac{\sqrt{x}-1}{\sqrt{y}} = \dfrac{\sqrt{x}-1}{\sqrt{y}} \cdot \dfrac{\sqrt{y}}{\sqrt{y}}$

$= \dfrac{(\sqrt{x}-1)\sqrt{y}}{y}$

$= \dfrac{(\sqrt{x})(\sqrt{y})-\sqrt{y}}{y}$

$= \dfrac{\sqrt{xy}-\sqrt{y}}{y}$

PRACTICE 12

Rationalize the denominator.

a. $\dfrac{\sqrt{5}-1}{\sqrt{3}}$

b. $\dfrac{\sqrt{c}+2}{\sqrt{b}}$

Thus far, we have rationalized denominators containing a single radical term. But suppose that there are two radical terms in a denominator. In this case, the key is to identify the *conjugate* of the denominator. The expressions $a+b$ and $a-b$ are called conjugates of one another. Note that conjugates come in pairs, since they are the sum and difference of the same two terms. When we multiply conjugates, the formula for finding the product of the sum and difference of two terms applies.

$$(a+b)(a-b) = a^2 - b^2$$

Recall that in Example 5(a) we multiplied two conjugates, $(\sqrt{10}+5)$ and $(\sqrt{10}-5)$. The product, -15, contains no radical sign because both terms in the right-hand side are perfect squares. The elimination of radical signs suggests a procedure for rationalizing a denominator with two terms, namely, *multiplying both the numerator and the denominator by the conjugate of the denominator.*

EXAMPLE 13

Rationalize the denominator.

a. $\dfrac{4}{1 + \sqrt{3}}$

b. $\dfrac{x}{\sqrt{y} - \sqrt{2}}$

SOLUTION

a. $\dfrac{4}{1 + \sqrt{3}} = \dfrac{4}{1 + \sqrt{3}} \cdot \dfrac{1 - \sqrt{3}}{1 - \sqrt{3}}$ Multiply the numerator and the denominator by the conjugate of the denominator.

$= \dfrac{4(1 - \sqrt{3})}{(1 + \sqrt{3})(1 - \sqrt{3})}$

$= \dfrac{4 - 4\sqrt{3}}{1^2 - (\sqrt{3})^2}$ Use the formula for finding the product of the sum and difference of two terms.

$= \dfrac{4 - 4\sqrt{3}}{1 - 3}$

$= \dfrac{2(2 - 2\sqrt{3})}{-2}$

$= \dfrac{\overset{1}{\cancel{2}}(2 - 2\sqrt{3})}{\underset{1}{-\cancel{2}}}$

$= -2 + 2\sqrt{3}$

b. $\dfrac{x}{\sqrt{y} - \sqrt{2}} = \dfrac{x}{\sqrt{y} - \sqrt{2}} \cdot \dfrac{\sqrt{y} + \sqrt{2}}{\sqrt{y} + \sqrt{2}}$ Multiply the numerator and the denominator by the conjugate of the denominator.

$= \dfrac{x(\sqrt{y} + \sqrt{2})}{(\sqrt{y} - \sqrt{2})(\sqrt{y} + \sqrt{2})}$

$= \dfrac{x\sqrt{y} + x\sqrt{2}}{y - 2}$ Use the formula for finding the product of the sum and difference of two terms.

PRACTICE 13

Rationalize the denominator.

a. $\dfrac{8}{3 - \sqrt{2}}$

b. $\dfrac{a}{\sqrt{b} + \sqrt{5}}$

In Examples 13(a) and (b), note that when we multipied the numerator and denominator by the conjugate of the denominator, the radical sign is eliminated in the denominator, as expected.

EXAMPLE 14

The velocity v (in kilometers per second) of a meteor streaking toward the Earth can be approximated by the expression $\dfrac{450}{\sqrt{d}}$, where d is its distance from the center of the Earth (in kilometers). Find the velocity of this meteor when it is 20,000 km from the Earth's center, written as a radical in simplified form. Using a calculator, also express the answer as a decimal rounded to the nearest km per second.

SOLUTION We substitute 20,000 for d in $v = \dfrac{450}{\sqrt{d}}$

$$v = \frac{450}{\sqrt{20{,}000}} = \frac{450}{\sqrt{10{,}000 \cdot 2}} = \frac{450}{\sqrt{10{,}000} \cdot \sqrt{2}}$$

$$= \frac{\overset{9}{\cancel{450}}}{\underset{2}{\cancel{100}}\sqrt{2}} = \frac{9}{2\sqrt{2}} = \frac{9}{2\sqrt{2}} \cdot \frac{\sqrt{2}}{\sqrt{2}} = \frac{9\sqrt{2}}{2 \cdot 2} = \frac{9\sqrt{2}}{4}$$

So the velocity of the meteor is $\dfrac{9\sqrt{2}}{4}$ km per sec, or approximately 3 km per sec.

PRACTICE 14

The formula $P = \dfrac{590}{\sqrt{t}}$ approximates the pulse rate (in beats per minute) for an adult who is t in. tall. Find the pulse rate of an adult 72 in. tall, written as a radical expression in simplified form. Using a calculator, also express this pulse rate rounded to the nearest whole number of beats per minute.

Exercises 8.3

FOR EXTRA HELP

📖 *Student's Solutions Manual*

📞 *Addison-Wesley Math Tutor Center*

🚪 *MyMathLab*

📼 *Videotape 8/DVT 8*

Multiply and simplify, if possible.

1. $\sqrt{21} \cdot \sqrt{21}$

2. $\sqrt{15} \cdot \sqrt{15}$

3. $(\sqrt{3n})^2$

4. $(\sqrt{5y})^2$

5. $(4\sqrt{x-1})^2$

6. $(2\sqrt{t+5})^2$

7. $\sqrt{18} \cdot \sqrt{3}$

8. $\sqrt{6} \cdot \sqrt{15}$

9. $(-2\sqrt{5})(7\sqrt{10})$

10. $(3\sqrt{24})(-5\sqrt{2})$

11. $\sqrt{8x^3} \cdot \sqrt{2x}$

12. $\sqrt{3x} \cdot \sqrt{12x}$

13. $\sqrt{3r} \cdot \sqrt{5r}$

14. $\sqrt{2n} \cdot \sqrt{7n}$

15. $\sqrt{2x} \cdot \sqrt{5} \cdot \sqrt{10y}$

16. $\sqrt{6y} \cdot \sqrt{7xy} \cdot \sqrt{2x}$

17. $\sqrt{3}(\sqrt{3} - 1)$

18. $\sqrt{2}(\sqrt{2} + 10)$

19. $\sqrt{x}(\sqrt{x} - 7)$

20. $\sqrt{y}(8 + \sqrt{y})$

21. $\sqrt{a}(4\sqrt{b} + 1)$

22. $\sqrt{p}(3\sqrt{q} - 5)$

23. $(\sqrt{5} + 3)(\sqrt{5} + 2)$

24. $(4 - \sqrt{7})(3 + \sqrt{7})$

25. $(8\sqrt{3} + 1)(5\sqrt{3} - 2)$

26. $(4\sqrt{2} + 1)(5\sqrt{2} - 3)$

27. $(\sqrt{n} + 5)(3\sqrt{n} - 1)$

28. $(2 - 5\sqrt{t})(4 + \sqrt{t})$

29. $(6 - \sqrt{3})(6 + \sqrt{3})$

30. $(\sqrt{2} - 1)(\sqrt{2} + 1)$

31. $(5 + 2\sqrt{3})(5 - 2\sqrt{3})$

32. $(4\sqrt{10} - 3)(4\sqrt{10} + 3)$

33. $(\sqrt{x} + 2)(\sqrt{x} - 2)$

34. $(5 - \sqrt{y})(5 + \sqrt{y})$

35. $(\sqrt{a} + \sqrt{b})(\sqrt{a} - \sqrt{b})$

36. $(\sqrt{m} - \sqrt{n})(\sqrt{m} + \sqrt{n})$

37. $(\sqrt{3x} - \sqrt{y})(\sqrt{3x} + \sqrt{y})$

38. $(\sqrt{q} + \sqrt{5p})(\sqrt{q} - \sqrt{5p})$

39. $(\sqrt{2} - x)^2$

40. $(4y + \sqrt{3})^2$

41. $(\sqrt{x} - 1)^2$

42. $(2 + \sqrt{n})^2$

Find the quotient and simplify, if possible.

43. $\dfrac{\sqrt{15}}{\sqrt{3}}$

44. $\dfrac{\sqrt{10}}{\sqrt{2}}$

45. $\dfrac{\sqrt{5}}{\sqrt{125}}$

46. $\dfrac{\sqrt{6}}{\sqrt{24}}$

47. $\dfrac{\sqrt{4a^3}}{\sqrt{a}}$

48. $\dfrac{\sqrt{9d^7}}{\sqrt{d^3}}$

49. $\dfrac{4\sqrt{5y}}{\sqrt{45y^5}}$

50. $\dfrac{\sqrt{3x^4}}{5\sqrt{48x^8}}$

51. $\sqrt{\dfrac{a^4}{b^6}}$

52. $\sqrt{\dfrac{m^8}{n^2}}$

53. $\sqrt{\dfrac{16x^{12}}{y^8}}$

54. $\sqrt{\dfrac{49p^6}{q^{10}}}$

55. $\sqrt{\dfrac{5x^{10}}{36}}$

56. $\sqrt{\dfrac{7y^2}{100}}$

Simplify.

57. $\dfrac{2}{\sqrt{3}}$

58. $\dfrac{1}{\sqrt{2}}$

59. $\dfrac{\sqrt{5}}{\sqrt{y}}$

60. $\dfrac{\sqrt{7}}{\sqrt{a}}$

61. $\sqrt{\dfrac{2}{11}}$

62. $\sqrt{\dfrac{3}{7}}$

63. $\sqrt{\dfrac{x^2}{5}}$

64. $\sqrt{\dfrac{n^4}{3}}$

65. $\sqrt{\dfrac{t}{50}}$

66. $\sqrt{\dfrac{y}{32}}$

67. $\sqrt{\dfrac{a}{2}}$

68. $\sqrt{\dfrac{6y}{5}}$

Rationalize the denominator.

69. $\dfrac{\sqrt{5}+2}{\sqrt{3}}$

70. $\dfrac{6-\sqrt{2}}{\sqrt{10}}$

71. $\dfrac{\sqrt{n}-1}{\sqrt{m}}$

72. $\dfrac{4-\sqrt{a}}{\sqrt{b}}$

73. $\dfrac{15}{4+\sqrt{6}}$

74. $\dfrac{10}{\sqrt{7}-2}$

75. $\dfrac{11}{4-\sqrt{5}}$

76. $\dfrac{8}{\sqrt{3}+1}$

77. $\dfrac{4}{\sqrt{5}-\sqrt{3}}$

78. $\dfrac{5}{\sqrt{6}+\sqrt{2}}$

79. $\dfrac{a}{\sqrt{b}-\sqrt{3}}$

80. $\dfrac{x}{\sqrt{5}+\sqrt{y}}$

Applications

Solve.

81. Find the area of the square envelope shown.

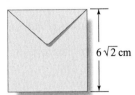

$6\sqrt{2}$ cm

82. What is the area of the cross section of the pyramid pictured?

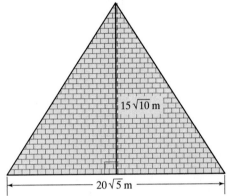

$15\sqrt{10}$ m

$20\sqrt{5}$ m

83. The distance d between two points (x_1, y_1) and (x_2, y_2) on the coordinate plane is given by the formula

$$d = \sqrt{(x_2 - x_1)^2 + (y_2 - y_1)^2}.$$

Check that point $(6, 10)$ is twice as far from the origin as the point $(3, 5)$.

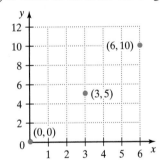

84. The expression $\sqrt{2gh}$ can be used to determine the velocity of a free-falling object in feet per second, where $g = 32$ ft/sec, and the object has fallen h ft. If a ball has fallen 60 ft, is the ball's velocity double that of a ball that has fallen 30 ft?

85. A hailstone will take t sec to drop d ft, where

$$t = \sqrt{\frac{d}{16}}.$$

How much time will it take a hailstone to drop 500 ft?

86. Chemists study the motion of gas molecules, called *diffusion*. The rates of diffusion (r_1 and r_2) of two gases are related by the formula

$$\frac{r_1}{r_2} = \frac{\sqrt{m_1}}{\sqrt{m_2}},$$

where m_1 and m_2 are the masses of the molecules of the gases. Find the ratio $\frac{r_1}{r_2}$, if $m_1 = 44$ units and $m_2 = 4$ units. Express the answer as a simplified radical.

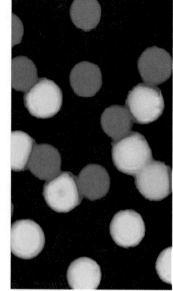

87. An expression for finding the radius r of a cylinder is $\sqrt{\dfrac{V}{\pi h}}$, where V is the volume of the cylinder, and h is the cylinder's height. Simplify this expression, rationalizing the denominator.

88. Suppose that an investment of P dollars grows at a fixed annual rate of return r. If at the end of two years the investment is worth A dollars, then the rate of return can be found from the formula

$$r = \frac{\sqrt{A} - \sqrt{P}}{\sqrt{P}}.$$

Rewrite this expression, rationalizing the denominator.

• Check your answers on page A-30.

Mindstretchers

WRITING

1. Explain why each of the following radical expressions is *not* simplified.

a. $\sqrt{x^2 - 2ax + a^2}$

_____

b. $\sqrt{\dfrac{x}{y}}$

_____

c. $\dfrac{p}{\sqrt{q}}$

_____

MATHEMATICAL REASONING

2. Many quadratic equations have solutions that involve radical expressions. Determine whether $x = 1 - \sqrt{2}$ is a solution of the equation $x^2 - 2x = 1$.

GROUPWORK

3. Heron's formula states that the area of any triangle is equal to

$\sqrt{s(s - a)(s - b)(s - c)}$, where the side lengths of the triangle are a, b, and c, and s is *half* the sum of the three side lengths, that is, $s = \dfrac{a + b + c}{2}$.

a. Working with a partner, apply Heron's formula to three triangles of your choice, filling in the four left columns in the following table.

Side Length a	Side Length b	Side Length c	Area of the Triangle	Area of the Triangle with Doubled Sides

continued

b. For each of these triangles, form a new triangle whose sides are double the length of the sides of the original triangle. Use Heron's formula to compute the area of these new triangles and enter the results in the right column of the previous table.

_____

c. In your three examples, does doubling all the side lengths of a triangle double its area?

_____

_____

8.4 Solving Radical Equations

OBJECTIVES

- *To solve radical equations*
- *To solve applied problems involving radical equations*

Now let's turn our attention to solving *radical equations*.

> **Definition**
>
> A **radical equation** is an equation in which a variable appears in one or more radicands.

Some examples of radical equations are:

$$\sqrt{3x} = 18 \qquad \sqrt{2n} = \sqrt{3n + 1} \qquad y - 2 = \sqrt{y} + 1$$

Can you explain why the equation $x + 3 = \sqrt{5}$ is not a radical equation?

The key to solving a radical equation is to find an equivalent equation with no square root. To do this, we can use the *squaring property of equality*.

> **The Squaring Property of Equality**
>
> For any real numbers a and b, if $a = b$, then $a^2 = b^2$.

This property states that if two numbers are equal, then their squares are equal.

In solving a radical equation, we begin by *isolating the radical*. Applying the squaring property of equality, we then square each side of the equation. Squaring eliminates the radical and makes the equation easier to solve. However, the resulting equation may have solutions that are not solutions to the original equation. Such "solutions" are called **extraneous solutions**. So when solving a radical equation, it is particularly important to check all possible solutions in the original equation.

EXAMPLE 1

Solve and check: $\sqrt{x} - 2 = 5$

SOLUTION

$$\sqrt{x} - 2 = 5$$
$$\sqrt{x} - 2 + 2 = 5 + 2 \qquad \text{Add 2 to each side of the equation.}$$
$$\sqrt{x} = 7 \qquad \text{Simplify.}$$
$$(\sqrt{x})^2 = (7)^2 \qquad \text{Use the squaring property of equality.}$$
$$x = 49$$

CHECK

$$\sqrt{x} - 2 = 5$$
$$\sqrt{49} - 2 \overset{?}{=} 5 \qquad \text{Substitute 49 for } x \text{ in the original equation.}$$
$$7 - 2 \overset{?}{=} 5$$
$$5 = 5 \qquad \text{True.}$$

So 49 is the solution.

PRACTICE 1

Solve and check: $\sqrt{y} + 3 = 7$

EXAMPLE 2

Solve and check: $\sqrt{x+1} + 3 = 0$

SOLUTION

$$\sqrt{x+1} + 3 = 0$$
$$\sqrt{x+1} = -3$$
$$(\sqrt{x+1})^2 = (-3)^2$$
$$x + 1 = 9$$
$$x = 8$$

CHECK

$$\sqrt{x+1} + 3 = 0$$
$$\sqrt{8+1} + 3 \overset{?}{=} 0 \qquad \text{Substitute 8 for } x \text{ in the original equation.}$$
$$\sqrt{9} + 3 \overset{?}{=} 0$$
$$3 + 3 \overset{?}{=} 0$$
$$6 \neq 0 \qquad \text{False.}$$

Our check fails, so 8 is *not* a solution to the original equation. Since 8 is the only possible solution, the equation has no solution.

PRACTICE 2

Solve and check: $\sqrt{2t-5} + 7 = 0$

Some radical equations involve more than one square root.

EXAMPLE 3

Solve and check: $\sqrt{2n+1} = \sqrt{5n-2}$

SOLUTION In this equation, the radicals are already isolated, so we begin by using the squaring property of equality to square each side of the equation.

$$\sqrt{2n+1} = \sqrt{5n-2}$$
$$(\sqrt{2n+1})^2 = (\sqrt{5n-2})^2$$
$$2n + 1 = 5n - 2$$
$$1 = 3n - 2$$
$$3 = 3n$$
$$n = 1$$

CHECK

$$\sqrt{2n+1} = \sqrt{5n-2}$$
$$\sqrt{2 \cdot 1 + 1} \overset{?}{=} \sqrt{5 \cdot 1 - 2} \qquad \text{Substitute 1 for } n \text{ in the original equation.}$$
$$\sqrt{3} = \sqrt{3} \qquad \text{True.}$$

So 1 is the solution.

PRACTICE 3

Solve and check:

$$\sqrt{4x+7} = \sqrt{6x-11}$$

To Solve a Radical Equation

● Isolate a term with a radical.

● Square each side of the equation.

● Where possible, combine like terms.

● Solve the resulting equation.

● Check the possible solution(s) in the original equation.

Some radical equations are equivalent to quadratic equations with more than one solution.

EXAMPLE 4

Solve and check: $1 + \sqrt{1 - x} = x$

SOLUTION

$$1 + \sqrt{1 - x} = x$$
$$\sqrt{1 - x} = x - 1 \qquad \text{Isolate the radical.}$$
$$(\sqrt{1 - x})^2 = (x - 1)^2 \qquad \text{Square each side of the equation.}$$
$$1 - x = x^2 - 2x + 1$$
$$0 = x^2 - x$$
$$x(x - 1) = 0 \qquad \text{Factor.}$$
$$x = 0 \quad \text{or} \quad x - 1 = 0 \qquad \text{Set each factor equal to 0.}$$
$$x = 1$$

CHECK

Substitute 0 for x.

$$1 + \sqrt{1 - x} = x$$
$$1 + \sqrt{1 - 0} \stackrel{?}{=} 0$$
$$1 + 1 \stackrel{?}{=} 0$$
$$2 \neq 0 \qquad \text{False.}$$

Substitute 1 for x.

$$1 + \sqrt{1 - x} = x$$
$$1 + \sqrt{1 - 1} \stackrel{?}{=} 1$$
$$1 + 0 \stackrel{?}{=} 1$$
$$1 = 1 \qquad \text{True.}$$

We see that $x = 1$ is a solution, whereas $x = 0$ is not. So the only solution to the original equation is 1.

EXAMPLE 5

Solve and check: $2\sqrt{x + 6} = \sqrt{x^2 + 19}$

SOLUTION

$$2\sqrt{x + 6} = \sqrt{x^2 + 19}$$
$$(2\sqrt{x + 6})^2 = (\sqrt{x^2 + 19})^2 \qquad \text{Square each side of the equation.}$$
$$4(x + 6) = x^2 + 19$$
$$4x + 24 = x^2 + 19$$
$$0 = x^2 - 4x - 5$$
$$(x + 1)(x - 5) = 0$$
$$x + 1 = 0 \quad \text{or} \quad x - 5 = 0$$
$$x = -1 \qquad\qquad x = 5$$

PRACTICE 4

Solve and check: $y - \sqrt{y - 2} = 2$

PRACTICE 5

Solve and check:

$$\sqrt{n^2 + 11} = 3\sqrt{n - 1}$$

CHECK

Substitute -1 for x.

$$2\sqrt{x + 6} = \sqrt{x^2 + 19}$$
$$2\sqrt{(-1) + 6} \stackrel{?}{=} \sqrt{(-1)^2 + 19}$$
$$2\sqrt{5} \stackrel{?}{=} \sqrt{20}$$
$$2\sqrt{5} = 2\sqrt{5} \quad \text{True.}$$

Substitute 5 for x.

$$2\sqrt{x + 6} = \sqrt{x^2 + 19}$$
$$2\sqrt{5 + 6} \stackrel{?}{=} \sqrt{5^2 + 19}$$
$$2\sqrt{11} \stackrel{?}{=} \sqrt{44}$$
$$2\sqrt{11} = 2\sqrt{11} \quad \text{True.}$$

So -1 and 5 both are solutions.

EXAMPLE 6

The approximate time t (in seconds) that it takes an object to fall a distance d (in feet) is given by the formula

$$t = \sqrt{\frac{d}{16}}.$$

If a bungee jumper had 3 sec of free fall, from what height did he leap?

SOLUTION

$$t = \sqrt{\frac{d}{16}}$$

$$3 = \sqrt{\frac{d}{16}}$$

$$(3)^2 = \left(\sqrt{\frac{d}{16}}\right)^2$$

$$9 = \frac{d}{16}$$

$$144 = d, \text{ or } d = 144$$

CHECK

$$t = \sqrt{\frac{d}{16}}$$

$$3 \stackrel{?}{=} \sqrt{\frac{144}{16}}$$

$$3 \stackrel{?}{=} \sqrt{9}$$

$$3 = 3 \quad \text{True.}$$

So the bungee jumper must have leaped from a height of 144 ft.

PRACTICE 6

The sharper a road turns, the lower the speed a car can safely travel on the road without skidding. A formula used to find the maximum safe speed on a road is

$$s = \sqrt{2.5r},$$

where r is the radius of the road's curve (in feet) and s is the maximum safe speed of the car (in miles per hour). Find the radius r that will permit a maximum safe speed of 50 mph.

Recall from Section 2.4 that formulas state a relationship between two or more variables. Some of these formulas contain radicals.

EXAMPLE 7

To escape a planet's gravity, a spacecraft must achieve an initial velocity v (in meters per second) given by the formula

$$v = \sqrt{2gR},$$

where g is the planet's force of gravity and R is the planet's radius in meters. Write this formula solving for R.

SOLUTION

$$v = \sqrt{2gR}$$

$$v^2 = 2gR$$

$$\frac{v^2}{2g} = R$$

$$R = \frac{v^2}{2g}$$

PRACTICE 7

The distance d (in miles) that a passenger can see from an airplane at altitude h (in feet) on a clear day can be approximated using the formula

$$d = \sqrt{\frac{3h}{2}}.$$

Solve this formula for h.

Exercises 8.4

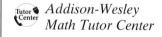
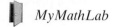
Solve and check.

1. $\sqrt{x} = 3$

2. $\sqrt{n} = 7$

3. $\sqrt{2x} = 8$

4. $\sqrt{4s} = -1$

5. $\sqrt{x} + 6 = 0$

6. $\sqrt{t} - 5 = 0$

7. $\sqrt{a} - 4 = 4$

8. $\sqrt{y} - 10 = -1$

9. $\sqrt{x + 3} = 3$

10. $\sqrt{n - 2} = 7$

11. $\sqrt{3t + 7} = 4$

12. $\sqrt{2t + 1} = 1$

13. $\sqrt{9t - 14} = \sqrt{2t}$

14. $\sqrt{3y + 2} = \sqrt{5y}$

15. $\sqrt{4x + 1} = \sqrt{2x + 7}$

16. $\sqrt{7x - 5} = \sqrt{4x + 13}$

17. $-2\sqrt{n - 2} = \sqrt{3n + 4}$

18. $\sqrt{5y + 2} = 3\sqrt{y - 2}$

19. $\sqrt{y - 1} + 4 = 6$

20. $1 + \sqrt{n + 4} = 11$

21. $3 - \sqrt{3x + 1} = 2$

22. $12 - \sqrt{2y - 1} = 7$

23. $\sqrt{x + 6} - x = 4$

24. $\sqrt{n + 8} - n = 2$

25. $7 + \sqrt{2x + 9} = x + 4$

26. $\sqrt{4 - 3x} + 10 = x + 8$

27. $7\sqrt{v} + v = -10$

28. $x + 6\sqrt{x} = -8$

29. $n - 3\sqrt{n + 2} = -4$

30. $y - 2\sqrt{y + 5} = -2$

31. $5\sqrt{y - 6} = \sqrt{y^2 - 14}$

32. $\sqrt{x^2 - 9} = 4\sqrt{x - 3}$

33. $\sqrt{2n^2 - 7} + 3 = n$

34. $\sqrt{4y^2 + 5} = y + 4$

35. $\sqrt{4x + 13} - 2x = -1$

36. $\sqrt{3x + 7} + 5 = 3x$

Applications

Solve.

37. An electrical appliance with resistance R (in ohms) draws current I (in amps) and has power P (in watts). These quantities are related by the following formula.

$$I = \sqrt{\frac{P}{R}}$$

If an appliance has a resistance of 25 ohms and draws 10 amps, find its power.

38. For a sphere, the formula $r = \sqrt{\dfrac{S}{4\pi}}$ relates the
radius r and the surface area S of the sphere.
Find the surface area of a sphere with radius
8 in. Write your answer in terms of π.

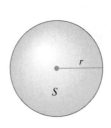

39. The period of a spring is the time it takes for the spring to stretch from one
position, down, and then back again to its original position. The formula
$T = 2\pi\sqrt{\dfrac{m}{k}}$, known as Hooke's law, expresses the period T (in seconds) in terms
of the mass m (in grams) bobbing on the spring, where k is a constant. If $k = 8$,
what mass will produce a period of 2 sec?

40. On a clear day, the distance d (in miles) that a lookout on a ship can see to the
horizon from height h (in feet) can be approximated by the formula $d = 1.2\sqrt{h}$.
How high must a lookout climb to see a ship 6 mi away?

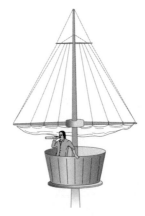

41. When firefighters are putting out a fire, the rate at which they spray
water on the fire is very important. For a hose with a nozzle 2 in. in
diameter, the flow rate f in gallons/minute is modeled by the formula
$$f = 120\sqrt{p},$$
where p is the nozzle pressure in pounds per square inch. Solve this
formula for p.

42. Suppose that an investment pays an annual rate of return r on a principal of P dollars. The value V of the investment after 2 years is related to
the rate of return and the principal as follows:
$$r = \frac{\sqrt{V}}{\sqrt{P}} - 1$$

a. Solve this formula for V.

b. If the principal was $100 and the rate of return was 0.05, what is the value of
the investment?

● *Check your answers on page A-30.*

Mindstretchers

1. In general, $\sqrt{a} + \sqrt{b} \neq \sqrt{a + b}$. Working with a partner, determine if there are any positive numbers a and b for which $\sqrt{a} + \sqrt{b} = \sqrt{a + b}$. Justify your answer.

_____

_____

_____

MATHEMATICAL REASONING

2. Using your knowledge of radical equations, show how you would solve the following equation.

$$\sqrt{x - 16} + \sqrt{x + 11} = 9$$

TECHNOLOGY

3. On a coordinate plane, graph the radical equation $y = \sqrt{x}$

a. by using the table method.

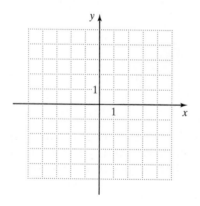

b. by using a grapher.

CONCEPT/SKILL	DESCRIPTION	EXAMPLE
[8.1] (Principal) Square Root (of a Nonnegative Real Number a)	The positive number that when squared is a.	$\sqrt{9}$, read "the square root of 9" or "radical 9," represents 3, since $3^2 = 9$.
[8.1] Radicand	The number under a radical sign.	The radicand of $\sqrt{5}$ is 5.
[8.1] Perfect Square	A whole number that is the square of another whole number.	9 is a perfect square because $$9 = 3^2.$$
[8.1] Squaring a Square Root	For any nonnegative real number a, $$(\sqrt{a})^2 = a.$$	$(\sqrt{8})^2 = 8$
[8.1] Taking the Square Root of a Square	For any nonnegative real number a, $$\sqrt{a^2} = a.$$	$\sqrt{3^2} = 3$
[8.1] The Product Rule of Radicals	If a and b are any nonnegative real numbers, then $$\sqrt{ab} = \sqrt{a} \cdot \sqrt{b}.$$	$\sqrt{4 \cdot 9} = \sqrt{4} \cdot \sqrt{9}$
[8.1] The Quotient Rule of Radicals	If a is a nonnegative real number and b is a positive real number, then $$\sqrt{\frac{a}{b}} = \frac{\sqrt{a}}{\sqrt{b}}.$$	$\sqrt{\frac{4}{9}} = \frac{\sqrt{4}}{\sqrt{9}}$
[8.2] Like Radicals	Radical expressions that have the same radicand.	$\sqrt{2}$ and $5\sqrt{2}$ are *like* radicals, whereas $7\sqrt{2}$ and $\sqrt{3}$ are *unlike* radicals.
[8.2] To Add or Subtract *Like* Radicals	• Use the distributive property. • Then simplify.	$4\sqrt{2} + 3\sqrt{2}$ $= (4 + 3)\sqrt{2} = 7\sqrt{2}$
[8.2] To Add or Subtract *Unlike* Radicals	• Simplify the unlike radicals, if possible. • If like radicals, then add or subtract.	$\sqrt{12} + \sqrt{27}$ $= \sqrt{4 \cdot 3} + \sqrt{9 \cdot 3}$ $= 2\sqrt{3} + 3\sqrt{3}$ $= 5\sqrt{3}$
[8.3] To Multiply Radicals	• Apply the product rule of radicals. • Simplify, if possible.	$(\sqrt{10})(2\sqrt{2})$ $= 2 \cdot \sqrt{10 \cdot 2}$ $= 2\sqrt{20}$ $= 2 \cdot 2\sqrt{5}$ $= 4\sqrt{5}$

continued

☐ = CONCEPT   ☐ = SKILL

CONCEPT/SKILL	DESCRIPTION	EXAMPLE
[8.3] To Divide Radicals	• Apply the quotient rule of radicals. • Simplify, if possible.	$\dfrac{\sqrt{20x^4}}{\sqrt{5x^2}} = \sqrt{\dfrac{20x^4}{5x^2}}$ $= \sqrt{4x^2}$ $= 2x$
[8.3] To Rationalize a Denominator	• If the denominator is a radical term, then multiply the numerator and denominator by the denominator. • If the denominator is a binomial with a radical term, then multiply the numerator and denominator by the conjugate of the denominator.	$\dfrac{\sqrt{x}}{\sqrt{8}} = \dfrac{\sqrt{x}}{\sqrt{8}} \cdot \dfrac{\sqrt{8}}{\sqrt{8}}$ $= \dfrac{\sqrt{8x}}{\sqrt{8^2}}$ $= \dfrac{\sqrt{4 \cdot 2x}}{8}$ $= \dfrac{2\sqrt{2x}}{8} = \dfrac{\sqrt{2x}}{4}$ $\dfrac{4}{1 - \sqrt{3}}$ $= \dfrac{4}{1 - \sqrt{3}} \cdot \dfrac{1 + \sqrt{3}}{1 + \sqrt{3}}$ $= \dfrac{4(1 + \sqrt{3})}{(1 - \sqrt{3})(1 + \sqrt{3})}$ $= \dfrac{4(1 + \sqrt{3})}{1^2 - (\sqrt{3})^2}$ $= \dfrac{4(1 + \sqrt{3})}{1 - 3}$ $= \dfrac{4(1 + \sqrt{3})}{-2}$ $= -2(1 + \sqrt{3})$ $= -2 - 2\sqrt{3}$
[8.4] Radical Equation	An equation in which a variable appears in one or more radicands.	$\sqrt{3x} = 18$
[8.4] The Squaring Property of Equality	For any real numbers a and b, if $a = b$, then $a^2 = b^2$.	If $\sqrt{x} = 7$, then $(\sqrt{x})^2 = (7)^2$.
[8.4] To Solve a Radical Equation	• Isolate a term with a radical. • Square each side of the equation. • Where possible, combine like terms. • Solve the resulting equation. • Check the possible solution(s) in the original equation.	$\sqrt{x} + 1 = 5$ $\sqrt{x} = 4$ $(\sqrt{x})^2 = 4^2$ $x = 16$ **CHECK** $\sqrt{x} + 1 = 5$ $\sqrt{16} + 1 \overset{?}{=} 5$ $4 + 1 \overset{?}{=} 5$ $5 = 5$ True.

Chapter 8 Review Exercises

To help you review this chapter, solve these problems. Assume that all variables represent nonnegative real numbers.

[8.1]

Simplify.

1. $-\sqrt{49}$

2. $\sqrt{6^2}$

3. $(\sqrt{7x})^2$

4. $\sqrt{28}$

5. $-3\sqrt{18}$

6. $\sqrt{32x^3}$

7. $\sqrt{\dfrac{9}{25}}$

8. $-\sqrt{\dfrac{3t}{16}}$

9. $\sqrt{\dfrac{144}{x^{100}}}$

10. $2\sqrt{25a^5b^3}$

[8.2]

Combine.

11. $2\sqrt{5} + \sqrt{5}$

12. $\sqrt{n} + 7\sqrt{n}$

13. $4x\sqrt{3} - 3x\sqrt{3}$

14. $\sqrt{27} - 2\sqrt{75}$

15. $x\sqrt{4x} + \sqrt{9x^3}$

16. $\sqrt{50a} - 3\sqrt{8a} + 8\sqrt{2a}$

[8.3]

Simplify.

17. $\sqrt{5} \cdot \sqrt{3}$

18. $\sqrt{8n} \cdot \sqrt{2n}$

19. $\sqrt{5a^2b^3} \cdot \sqrt{10ab^3}$

20. $\sqrt{x}(\sqrt{x} - 4)$

21. $(\sqrt{7} - 1)(\sqrt{7} + 1)$

22. $(\sqrt{y} + 1)(2\sqrt{y} - 3)$

23. $(\sqrt{y} + 5)^2$

Divide and simplify.

24. $\dfrac{\sqrt{54}}{\sqrt{6}}$

25. $\dfrac{\sqrt{3}}{\sqrt{12}}$

26. $\dfrac{\sqrt{48x}}{\sqrt{3x}}$

27. $\dfrac{\sqrt{24a^6}}{\sqrt{2a^3}}$

Rationalize the denominator.

28. $\dfrac{2}{\sqrt{11}}$

29. $\dfrac{\sqrt{3x^2}}{\sqrt{6x}}$

30. $\dfrac{4\sqrt{8} + \sqrt{2}}{\sqrt{2}}$

31. $\dfrac{10}{\sqrt{7} - 1}$

[8.4]

Solve and check.

32. $\sqrt{n} - 3 = 5$

33. $\sqrt{2x + 1} = 4$

34. $\sqrt{4n - 5} = \sqrt{n + 10}$

35. $x - \sqrt{3x + 1} = 3$

Mixed Applications

Solve.

36. The length of one side of a square city block is $50\sqrt{2}$ ft. Find the area of the lot.

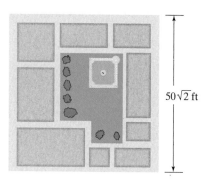

$50\sqrt{2}$ ft

37. The formula for the distance in miles that you can see on any planet is $d = \sqrt{\dfrac{rh}{2640}}$ where h is your height in feet and r is the radius of the planet (in miles). If you are 6 ft tall and the radius of Mars is about 2100 mi, how far can you see on Mars? Round the answer to the nearest mile.

38. The length of the diagonal of the metal box shown in the figure below is modeled by the expression $\sqrt{l^2 + w^2 + h^2}$, where l, w, and h represent the length, width, and height of the box, respectively. If the box is 5 in. wide, 4 in. deep, and 3 in. high, will a screwdriver 8 in. long fit diagonally in the box?

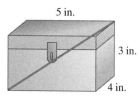

5 in.

3 in.

4 in.

39. Find the area of the square shown.

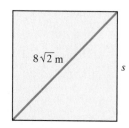

$8\sqrt{2}$ m

s

40. A formula for the radius of a sphere r is

$$r = \sqrt{\frac{S}{4\pi}},$$

where S is the surface area of the sphere. Write this formula, rationalizing the denominator.

41. Scientists who study lakes are concerned with their shape. These scientists have grouped lakes according to the concept of *shoreline development*, a measure of how closely a lake resembles a circle. Shoreline development D is defined by the formula

$$D = \frac{L}{2\sqrt{\pi A}},$$

where L is the length of the lake's shoreline and A is the area of the lake.
(**Source:** David G. Frey, Ed., *Limnology in North America*, 1966)

a. Check that if a lake is perfectly circular, the shoreline development is equal to 1.

b. Rationalize the denominator in the formula.

c. Goslute Lake, which existed in the American southwest some 50 million years ago, had a shoreline development equal to 1.58. Solve for its area in terms of the length of its shoreline.

42. For the box shown with volume V, the length of a side x of the square base is $\sqrt{\dfrac{V}{15}}$. Simplify this expression.

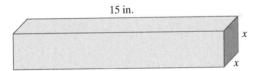

15 in.

x

x

● *Check your answers on page A-30.*

To see if you have mastered the topics in this chapter, take this test.

Assume all variables represent nonnegative real numbers.

Simplify.

1. $2\sqrt{36}$

2. $-3\sqrt{18}$

3. $\sqrt{32x^3y}$

4. $\sqrt{\dfrac{5n}{16}}$

5. $\sqrt{x} - 3\sqrt{x} + 5\sqrt{x}$

6. $\sqrt{8} - 4\sqrt{50} + \sqrt{18}$

7. $t\sqrt{4t} + 2\sqrt{16t^3}$

Multiply or divide. Simplify, if possible.

8. $(\sqrt{12})(\sqrt{2})$

9. $(\sqrt{5x^3y})(\sqrt{5x^2y})$

10. $\dfrac{\sqrt{75}}{\sqrt{3}}$

11. $\sqrt{y}(5\sqrt{y} - 1)$

12. $(\sqrt{3} + 4)^2$

Simplify.

13. $\sqrt{\dfrac{2p}{5}}$

14. $\dfrac{\sqrt{48x^4}}{\sqrt{2x}}$

15. Rationalize the denominator: $\dfrac{\sqrt{4} - 3\sqrt{10}}{\sqrt{2}}$

Solve and check.

16. $\sqrt{5x + 1} - 2 = 4$

17. $\sqrt{x + 11} = \sqrt{7x - 1}$

18. One of several expressions for the windchill temperature (WCT) is

$$91 + 0.08(3.7\sqrt{V} + 6 - 0.3V)(T - 91),$$

where T is the temperature in degrees Fahrenheit and V is the wind speed in miles per hour. Find the WCT, rounded to the nearest whole number, if the temperature is 42°F and the wind speed is 16 mph.

19. Find the length of the ladder shown, expressed as a simplified radical.

24 ft

6 ft

20. The formula for the diagonal of a rectangle d in terms of its length l and width w is:

$$d = \sqrt{l^2 + w^2}$$

Find the length of a rectangle if its width is 12 in. and its diagonal is 20 in.

• Check your answers on page A-30.

To help you review, solve the following.

1. Solve and check: $c = -2(c - 1)$

2. Compute the slope m of the line that passes through the points $(4, 0)$ and $(3, 5)$. Plot these points on the coordinate plane and draw the line.

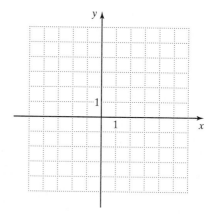

3. For the system of equations graphed, determine the number of solutions.

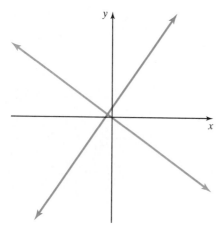

4. Find the product: $(4x^2 - 3)(4x - 1)$

5. Factor: $y^2 - 12y + 32$

6. Add: $\dfrac{9}{c - 2} + \dfrac{c - 3}{c^2 - c - 2}$

7. Solve: $\sqrt{n + 6} + 7 = 9$

8. The speed s of sound in air is modeled by the formula

$$s = 0.6t + 331,$$

where the speed is in meters per second and the temperature t is in degrees Celsius. At what temperature is this speed equal to 343 m per sec? (*Source:* Peter J. Nolan, *Fundamentals of College Physics,* Wm. C. Brown Publishers, 1993)

9. A country's balance of payments can be found by subtracting its imports from its exports. If x is the number of years since 1991, then the total exports of the United States can be approximated by the polynomial $-x^2 + 47x + 396$, and the total U.S. imports can be approximated by $x^2 + 58x + 483$ (both in billions of dollars). Find a polynomial to model the U.S. balance of payments. (*Source:* U.S. Department of Commerce)

10. Two hikers start a trip by walking due west from a campsite, as shown below. They then turn due north and walk to a waterfall. What is the distance d from the camp to the waterfall expressed in radical form? Also express this distance as a decimal, rounded to the nearest meter.

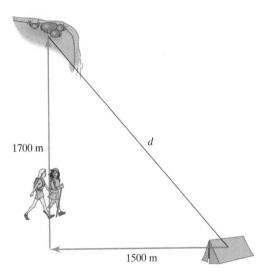

1700 m

d

1500 m

Check your answers on page A-30.

This introduction to calculators covers the basic functions of a scientific calculator that will be used in this text. The keystrokes that are covered in this introduction apply to most scientific calculators, although there are slight differences from one model to the next. Refer to your manual for specific instructions about your particular model.

Topics

- Basic Keystrokes
- Order of Operations
- Decimals and Rounding
- Memory Function
- Signed Numbers
- Exponents and Radicals
- Scientific Notation
- Other Calculator Functions

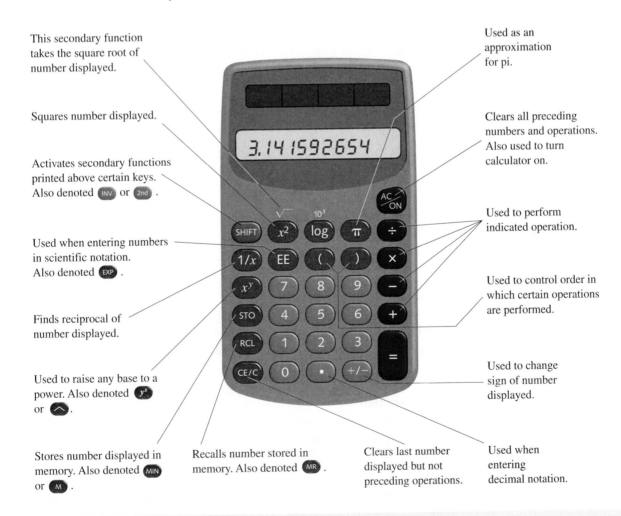

This secondary function takes the square root of number displayed.

Squares number displayed.

Activates secondary functions printed above certain keys. Also denoted INV or 2nd.

Used when entering numbers in scientific notation. Also denoted EXP.

Finds reciprocal of number displayed.

Used to raise any base to a power. Also denoted y^x or ∧.

Stores number displayed in memory. Also denoted MIN or M.

Recalls number stored in memory. Also denoted MR.

Clears last number displayed but not preceding operations.

Used when entering decimal notation.

Used as an approximation for pi.

Clears all preceding numbers and operations. Also used to turn calculator on.

Used to perform indicated operation.

Used to control order in which certain operations are performed.

Used to change sign of number displayed.

Basic Keystrokes

Most scientific calculators allow you to enter problems in the same order they appear on paper. For example, the problem $1{,}226 + 6{,}321 - 412$ is entered as follows:

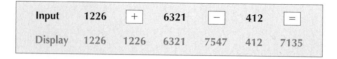

Input	1226	+	6321	−	412	=
Display	1226	1226	6321	7547	412	7135

Note that numbers do not include commas when you use a calculator.

Press the $\boxed{\text{CE/C}}$ key if the most recent entry needs to be changed. In the last example, if the number 6312 were accidentally entered instead of 6321, it can be corrected as follows:

Input	1226	+	6312	CE/C	6321	−	412	=
Display	1226	1226	6312	0	6321	7547	412	7135

The $\boxed{\text{AC/ON}}$ key clears everything in the calculator and allows you to perform a new calculation.

Order of Operations

Most scientific calculators follow the accepted order of operations. Check by evaluating $3 + 5 \times 4$ as follows:

Input	3	+	5	×	4	=
Display	3	3	5	5	4	23

The correct answer is 23. If your calculator returns the answer 32, then it *does not* follow the order of operations. Do not assume that order of operations is always followed. For example, the expression $\dfrac{10 - 8}{4 \div 2}$ must be entered using parentheses, regardless of the type of calculator used. This expression is evaluated as follows:

Input	(	10	−	8	)	÷	(	4	÷	2	)	=
Display	(	10	10	8	2	2	(	4	4	2	2	1

Decimals and Rounding

When entering decimal numbers, press the $\boxed{\cdot}$ key. The calculator will automatically add a decimal point if an answer is a decimal. Most scientific calculators can display between 8 and 10 digits. Answers will be rounded automatically to the place value of the last digit displayed.

Memory Function

Memory functions vary considerably depending on the calculator model. Most have a $\boxed{\text{STO}}$ (or $\boxed{\text{M}}$) key that, when pressed, stores the number on the display in memory. The $\boxed{\text{RCL}}$ (or $\boxed{\text{MR}}$) key recalls a stored number to the screen, and the $\boxed{\text{MC}}$ key clears the contents of memory.

- The $\boxed{\text{M−}}$ key evaluates the difference of a stored number and the number currently displayed on the screen. The new result is stored in memory.

- The $\boxed{\text{M+}}$ key evaluates the sum of a stored number and the number currently displayed on the screen. The new result is stored in memory.

Signed Numbers

Signed numbers are entered using the $\boxed{+/-}$ key. (Do not confuse this key with the $\boxed{-}$ key, which is used for subtraction.) The following keystrokes are used to evaluate $325 + (-428)$:

Input	325	$+$	428	$+/-$	$=$
Display	325	325	428	−428	−103

Basically, the $\boxed{+/-}$ key changes the sign of the number displayed.

Exponents and Radicals

Different keys can be used to evaluate a number raised to a power. Use the $\boxed{x^2}$ key when squaring a number. Use the $\boxed{x^y}$ (or $\boxed{\wedge}$) key when evaluating a number raised to any power. To evaluate 6^2, press 6 and the $\boxed{x^2}$ key. To evaluate 6^4, use the following keystrokes:

Input	6	x^y	4	$=$
Display	6	6	4	1296

To find the square root of a number, enter the number, and then press the $\boxed{\sqrt{}}$ key. For example, $\sqrt{144}$ can be found as follows:

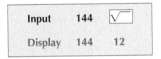

Input	144	$\sqrt{}$
Display	144	12

Scientific Notation

Use scientific notation to express numbers in the form $a \times 10^n$, where n is an integer and $1 \le a < 10$. For example, to express 8,000,000 as 8×10^6 press 8, the $\boxed{EE}$ (or $\boxed{EXP}$) key, and then 6. Some scientific calculators will automatically put answers in scientific notation if they are too large or too small to fit on the screen. This can be checked by multiplying $50,000,000 \times 50,000,000 = 2.5 \times 10^{15}$. Check to see if your calculator displays the answer as 2.5 E15.

Other Calculator Functions

- The $\boxed{\pi}$ key displays an approximation for the number pi to as many digits as are allowed on the screen.

- The $\boxed{1/x}$ key displays the reciprocal of a number.

- The $\boxed{SHIFT}$ (or $\boxed{2nd}$) key accesses any secondary functions located above certain keys.

A.2 Table of Symbols

$+$	add
$-$	subtract
$\cdot,\ \times,\ (a)(b),\ 2y$	multiply
$\dfrac{a}{b},\ \div,\ x+1\overline{)x^2-1}$	divide
x^n	x raised to the power n
$(\quad)$	parentheses (a grouping symbol)
$[\quad]$	brackets (a grouping symbol)
π	pi (a number approximately equal to $\dfrac{22}{7}$ or 3.14)
$-a$	the opposite, or additive inverse, of a
$\dfrac{1}{a}$	the reciprocal, or multiplicative inverse, of a
$=$	is equal to
$\approx$	is approximately equal to
$\neq$	is not equal to
$<$	is less than
$\leq$	is less than or equal to
$>$	is greater than
$\geq$	is greater than or equal to
(x, y)	an ordered pair whose first coordinate is a and whose second coordinate is b
$\circ$	degree (for angles)
$\sqrt{a}$	the principal square root of a
$\lvert a \rvert$	the absolute value of a

A.3 Factoring the Sum of Cubes and the Difference of Cubes

As we discussed in Section 6.4, there are formulas that make it easier to factor polynomials having a special form. Two formulas not covered in that section deal with the *sum of cubes* and the *difference of cubes*. These formulas provide a shortcut for factoring a binomial that is in the form of the cube of one term plus or minus the cube of another term. To state the formulas, we let the terms be a and b, with corresponding cubes a^3 and b^3.

Factoring the Sum of Cubes
$$a^3 + b^3 = (a + b)(a^2 - ab + b^2)$$

Factoring the Difference of Cubes
$$a^3 - b^3 = (a - b)(a^2 + ab + b^2)$$

TIP In these two formulas, the sign of b^3 on the left side of the equation is

- the *same* as that of b in the binomial factor on the right.
- the *opposite* of that of the middle term of the trinomial on the right.

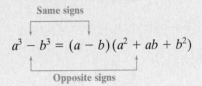

Same signs

$$a^3 + b^3 = (a + b)(a^2 - ab + b^2)$$

Opposite signs

Same signs

$$a^3 - b^3 = (a - b)(a^2 + ab + b^2)$$

Opposite signs

EXAMPLE 1

Indicate whether each binomial is a sum or difference of cubes.

a. $x^3 - 8$

b. $x^3 + y^3$

c. $27p^3 - q^6$

d. $x^2 + x^3$

SOLUTION

a. In the expression $x^3 - 8$, both x^3 and 8 (or 2^3) are perfect cubes, where x corresponds to a and 2 to b.

$$x^3 - 8 = x^3 - 2^3$$
$$\qquad\quad\; a^3 \; - \; b^3$$

So $x^3 - 8$ is a *difference of cubes*.

PRACTICE 1

Indicate whether each binomial is a sum or difference of cubes.

a. $n^3 - 1$

b. $p^3 + q^4$

c. $x^3 + y^9$

d. $8x^6 - x^3$

b. In $x^3 + y^3$, both x^3 and y^3 are *perfect cubes* and correspond to a^3 and b^3, respectively in our formula. So $x^3 + y^3$ is a *sum of cubes*.

c. For $27p^3 - q^6$, both $27p^3$ and q^6 are perfect cubes because $27p^3 = (3p)^3$ and $q^6 = (q^2)^3$. So $27p^3 - q^6$ is a *difference of cubes*.

d. In $x^2 + x^3$, the first term x^2 is not a perfect cube. So the expression is *neither a sum of cubes nor a difference of cubes*.

EXAMPLE 2

Factor:

a. $x^3 - y^3$

b. $y^3 + 8$

SOLUTION

a. The expression $x^3 - y^3$ is a difference of cubes, so we can apply that formula.

$$x^3 - y^3 = (x)^3 - (y)^3 = (x - y)(x^2 + xy + y^2)$$

$$a^3 \quad - \quad b^3 \qquad (a - b) \ (a^2 + ab + b^2)$$

So the factorization of $x^3 - y^3$ is $(x - y)(x^2 + xy + y^2)$. We can check that this factorization is correct by multiplying, which we leave for you to do on your own.

b. The expression $y^3 + 8$ is a sum of cubes.

$$y^3 + 8 = (y)^3 + (2)^3 = (y + 2)[y^2 - (y)(2) + (2)^2]$$

$$a^3 \quad + \quad b^3 \qquad (a + b) \ (a^2 - ab \quad + b^2)$$

We conclude that the factorization of $y^3 + 8$ is $(y + 2)(y^2 - 2y + 4)$.

EXAMPLE 3

Factor:

a. $x^3 + 27$

b. $2x^3 + 2$

c. $64n^3 - n^6$

SOLUTION

a. Since $27 = 3^3$, $x^3 + 27$ is a sum of cubes.

$$x^3 + 27 = x^3 + 3^3$$

Use the sum-of-cubes formula.

$$= (x + 3)(x^2 - x \cdot 3 + 3^2)$$

$$= (x + 3)(x^2 - 3x + 9)$$

So the factorization of $x^3 + 27$ is $(x + 3)(x^2 - 3x + 9)$.

PRACTICE 2

Factor:

a. $r^3 + s^3$

b. $y^3 - 64$

PRACTICE 3

Factor:

a. $125 - x^3$

b. $5n^3 - 40$

c. $2n + 54n^4$

b. We note that the two terms $2x^3$ and 2 of the binomial $2x^3 + 2$ have 2 as the greatest common factor.

$$2x^3 + 2 = 2(x^3 + 1)$$ Factor out the GCF.

$$= 2(x + 1)(x^2 - x + 1)$$ Use the sum of cubes formula.

So the factorization of $2x^3 + 2$ is $2(x + 1)(x^2 - x + 1)$.

c. We see that the two terms of the binomial $64n^3 - n^6$ have n^3 as the greatest common factor.

$$64n^3 - n^6 = n^3(64 - n^3)$$ Factor out the GCF.

$$= n^3(4 - n)(16 + 4n + n^2)$$ Use the difference-of-cubes formula.

So the factorization of $64n^3 - n^6$ is

$n^3(4 - n)(16 + 4n + n^2)$.

Summary

Sum of squares:	Cannot be factored.
Difference of squares:	$a^2 - b^2 = (a + b)(a - b)$
Sum of cubes:	$a^3 + b^3 = (a + b)(a^2 - ab + b^2)$
Difference of cubes:	$a^3 - b^3 = (a - b)(a^2 + ab + b^2)$

Exercises A.3

Factor, if possible.

1. $y^3 - 1$

2. $t^3 - 8$

3. $p^3 + q^3$

4. $p^2 + q^2$

5. $x^3 + y^6$

6. $a^3 - b^3$

7. $n^3 + 8$

8. $x^3 + 27$

9. $8 - x^5$

10. $8 - x^6$

11. $27n^3 + 1$

12. $8 + n^4$

13. $5x^3 - 5$

14. $3x^3 - 24$

15. $2p^3 + 54$

16. $128n^3 + 2n^6$

17. $x^6 - 125x^3$

18. $8x^3 + x^6$

• *Check your answers on page A-34.*

Answers

Chapter R

Pretest: Chapter R, *p. 2*

1. 7^3 **2.** 400 **3.** 8 **4.** 16 **5.** 1, 2, 3, 4, 6, 12
6. $2^2 \cdot 5$ **7.** $\frac{2}{3}$ **8.** $\frac{4}{10} = \frac{2}{5}$ **9.** $7\frac{3}{6} = 7\frac{1}{2}$ **10.** $\frac{4}{27}$
11. $\frac{8}{3} = 2\frac{2}{3}$ **12.** Nine and thirteen thousandths
13. 3.1 **14.** 20.3103 **15.** 5.66 **16.** 37.843
17. 23.5 **18.** 0.18 **19.** 0.0031 **20.** 0.07
21. \$2 million **22.** $\frac{1}{3}$ mi **23.** 2 times **24.** 10%
25. 0.95

Practices: Section R.1 *pp. 3–6*

1, *p. 3:* 2^5 **2,** *p. 3:* 784 **3,** *p. 4:* 10^9 **4,** *p. 5:* 16
5, *p. 5:* 1 **6,** *p. 6:* No; the average monthly bill this year was \$100.

Practices: Section R.2 *pp. 7–8*

1, *p. 7:* 50 **2,** *p. 8:* 180 **3,** *p. 8:* 24 hours

Practices: Section R.3 *pp. 9–15*

1, *p. 9:* $\frac{29}{9}$ **2,** *p. 10:* $2\frac{2}{3}$ **3,** *p. 10:* $\frac{4}{5}$ **4,** *p. 11:* $\frac{10}{15} = \frac{2}{3}$
5, *p. 11:* $\frac{8}{20} = \frac{2}{5}$ **6,** *p. 11:* $\frac{20}{12} = \frac{5}{3}$, or $1\frac{2}{3}$ **7,** *p. 12:* $\frac{3}{10}$
8, *p. 12:* $7\frac{9}{8} = 8\frac{1}{8}$ **9,** *p. 13:* $5\frac{2}{12} = 5\frac{1}{6}$ **10,** *p. 13:* $\frac{3}{8}$
11, *p. 14:* $\frac{7}{22}$ **12,** *p. 14:* $\frac{63}{8}$, or $7\frac{7}{8}$ **13,** *p. 14:* 6
14, *p. 15:* $\frac{8}{5}$, or $1\frac{3}{5}$ **15,** *p. 15:* 400 students

Practices: Section R.4 *pp. 16–21*

1, *p. 17:* a. $\frac{5}{10} = \frac{1}{2}$ b. $2\frac{73}{1000}$ **2,** *p. 17:* Four and three
thousandths **3,** *p. 18:* 748.08 **4,** *p. 18:* 42.092
5, *p. 18:* 1.179 **6,** *p. 19:* 9.835 **7,** *p. 19:* 327,000
8, *p. 20:* 18.04 **9,** *p. 20:* 0.00086 **10,** *p. 21:* 6.4

Practices: Section R.5 *pp. 22–23*

1, *p. 22:* $\frac{7}{100}$ **2,** *p. 22:* 0.05 **3,** *p. 22:* 2.5%
4, *p. 23:* 25% **5,** *p. 23:* 0.40, or 0.4

Review Exercises: Chapter R, *p. 24*

1. 6^5 **2.** 7^8 **3.** $2^2 \cdot 10^3$ **4.** $5^4 \cdot 4^3$ **5.** 25,000 **6.** 576
7. 15 **8.** 0 **9.** 14 **10.** 123 **11.** 4 **12.** 2 **13.** 1, 2, 3,
5, 6, 10, 15, 25, 30, 50, 75, 150 **14.** 1, 3, 19, 57
15. Prime **16.** Composite **17.** Composite **18.** Prime
19. $2 \cdot 3 \cdot 7$ **20.** $2 \cdot 3^3$ **21.** $2^4 \cdot 3$ **22.** $2^2 \cdot 5^2$ **23.** 24
24. 60 **25.** 72 **26.** 84 **27.** $\frac{19}{5}$ **28.** $\frac{73}{10}$ **29.** $5\frac{3}{4}$ **30.** $3\frac{4}{9}$
31. $\frac{1}{2}$ **32.** $\frac{2}{3}$ **33.** $5\frac{1}{2}$ **34.** $6\frac{2}{7}$ **35.** $\frac{5}{9}$ **36.** $\frac{10}{10} = 1$

37. $\frac{2}{8} = \frac{1}{4}$ **38.** $\frac{3}{3} = 1$ **39.** $\frac{34}{35}$ **40.** $\frac{25}{18} = 1\frac{7}{18}$ **41.** $\frac{5}{20} = \frac{1}{4}$
42. $\frac{7}{20}$ **43.** $6\frac{4}{8} = 6\frac{1}{2}$ **44.** $7\frac{2}{5}$ **45.** $9\frac{16}{10} = 10\frac{3}{5}$ **46.** $7\frac{6}{8} = 8$
47. $3\frac{4}{12} = 3\frac{1}{3}$ **48.** $2\frac{2}{4} = 2\frac{1}{2}$ **49.** $1\frac{8}{10} = 1\frac{4}{5}$ **50.** $2\frac{4}{8} = 2\frac{1}{2}$
51. $6\frac{1}{2}$ **52.** $1\frac{1}{5}$ **53.** $2\frac{7}{8}$ **54.** $9\frac{7}{12}$ **55.** $\frac{2}{15}$ **56.** $\frac{2}{3}$ **57.** 14
58. $\frac{110}{3} = 36\frac{2}{3}$ **59.** $\frac{91}{6} = 15\frac{1}{6}$ **60.** 3 **61.** $\frac{17}{3} = 5\frac{2}{3}$
62. $\frac{5}{3} = 1\frac{2}{3}$ **63.** $\frac{1}{9}$ **64.** $\frac{1}{40}$ **65.** $\frac{24}{7} = 3\frac{3}{7}$ **66.** $\frac{9}{15} = 1\frac{4}{5}$
67. $\frac{8}{16} = \frac{1}{2}$ **68.** $\frac{102}{5} = 20\frac{2}{5}$ **69.** $\frac{875}{1000} = \frac{7}{8}$ **70.** $2\frac{6}{1000} = 2\frac{3}{500}$
71. hundredths **72.** tenths **73.** Seventy-two hundredths
74. Five hundredths **75.** Three and nine thousandths
76. Twelve and two hundred thirty-five thousandths **77.** 7.3
78. 0.039 **79.** 4.39 **80.** \$899 **81.** 18.11 **82.** 24.13
83. 1.873 **84.** 0.9 **85.** 2.912 **86.** 0.000010, or
0.00001 **87.** 2710 **88.** 530 **89.** 0.0015 **90.** 3.19
91. 5 **92.** 23.7 **93.** 7.35 **94.** 14.5 **95.** $\frac{75}{100} = \frac{3}{4}$
96. $\frac{4}{100} = \frac{1}{25}$ **97.** $1\frac{6}{100} = 1\frac{3}{50}$ **98.** $2\frac{50}{100} = 2\frac{1}{2}$ **99.** 0.06
100. 0.29 **101.** 1.5 **102.** 0.002 **103.** 31% **104.** 5%
105. 1.45% **106.** 200% **107.** 10% **108.** 37.5%
109. 80% **110.** 35% **111.** 73°F **112.** 8:10 A.M.
113. $\frac{3}{4}$ mi **114.** 7 lb **115.** \$18 **116.** 1.66 m
117. \$1.30 **118.** 14.42 in. **119.** $\frac{15}{100} = \frac{3}{20}$

Posttest: Chapter R, *p. 29*

1. 512 **2.** 37 **3.** 1, 2, 4, 5, 10, 20 **4.** $\frac{13}{4}$ **5.** $\frac{5}{18}$
6. $\frac{12}{8} = 1\frac{1}{2}$ **7.** $11\frac{25}{24} = 12\frac{1}{24}$ **8.** $\frac{13}{90}$ **9.** $3\frac{19}{20}$ **10.** $\frac{3}{5}$ **11.** 2
12. $\frac{35}{16} = 2\frac{3}{16}$ **13.** Two and three hundred ninety-six thou-
sandths **14.** 16.202 **15.** 6.99 **16.** 44.678 **17.** 2070
18. 0.0005 **19.** 0.125; 12.5% **20.** 70%; $\frac{7}{10}$ **21.** 6 times
22. 1.8 **23.** 625.3 sq m **24.** 15 times **25.** 0.78

Chapter 1

Pretest: Chapter 1, *p.32*

1. +\$2000 **2.** yes **3.**

4. 5

5. $\frac{2}{3}$ **6.** < **7.** −13 **8.** −2 **9.** −26 **10.** $\frac{4}{1}$ or 4
11. 9 **12.** Ten less than the product of three and n
(Answers may vary.) **13.** -6^4 **14.** −8 **15.** $4n − 7$
16. $14x − 10$ **17.** 6051 m **18.** $\frac{L}{3}$ or $\frac{1}{3}L$ **19.** 30 cm
20. The net debit is \$800 (−\$800).

Practices: Section 1.1 *pp. 33–41*

1, *p. 34:* −5°F **2,** *p. 36:*

3, *p. 37:* **a.** 41 **b.** $\frac{8}{9}$ **c.** -1.7 **d.** $\frac{2}{5}$ **4, *p. 38:*** **a.** $\frac{1}{2}$ **b.** 0
c. 9 **d.** -3 **5, *p. 39:*** **a.** True **b.** False **c.** True **d.** True
e. False **6, *p. 39:*** ; $3, -\frac{1}{2}, -1.6,$

and -2.4 **7, *p. 40:*** Your house; $-15 < -10$ **8, *p. 41:***
a.

b. A, B, D, C, F, E, and G

Exercises 1.1, *p. 42*

1. -5 km **3.** $-22.5°$C **5.** $-\$160$
7.
9.
11.
13.

	Whole Numbers	**Integers**	**Rational Numbers**	**Real Numbers**
15. -7		✓	✓	✓
17. -1.9			✓	✓
19. 10	✓	✓	✓	✓

21. 3 **23.** 0 **25.** 3.5 **27.** 4 **29.** 0 **31.** 4.6
33. $-\frac{1}{2}$ **35.** 4 and -4 **37.** Impossible; absolute
value is always positive or zero. **39.** True **41.** True
43. True **45.** $>$ **47.** $>$ **49.** $=$ **51.** $<$
53. ; $3\frac{1}{2}, 0, -\frac{1}{2}, -1\frac{1}{2}$

55. ; $3.5, 3, -3, -3.5$

57. Today **59.** $-64.8°$C **61. a.** Sirius **b.** -13
c.

Practices: Section 1.2 *pp. 47–52*

1, *p. 47:* -1;

2, *p. 48:* 0;

3, *p. 48:* 0.5;

4, *p. 49:* -31 **5, *p. 49:*** 3.5 **6, *p. 50:*** 0 **7, *p. 51:*** -10
8, *p. 51:* $\$36.50$ **9, *p. 52:*** -3.588

Exercises 1.2, *p. 53*

1. 1 **3.** 0 **5.** 5 **7.** Additive inverse property
9. Commutative property of addition
11. Additive inverse property **13.** Commutative property
of addition **15.** Additive identity property **17.** 23
19. -5 **21.** 4 **23.** -80 **25.** -8 **27.** 0 **29.** 4.3
31. 0.6 **33.** -0.3 **35.** -5.7 **37.** -16.3 **39.** -1
41. $\frac{2}{5}$ **43.** -88 **45.** 0 **47.** -7 **49.** 10.48 **51.** -12
53. 1.245 **55.** 5° above 0° $(+5)$ **57.** Lost $\$16,000$
$(-\$16,000)$ **59.** 30 B.C. (-30) **61.** Yes; you will have
$\$283.26$ in the account. **63.** 31,000 ft

Practices: Section 1.3 *pp. 57–59*

1, *p. 57:* 5 **2, *p. 58:*** 3 **3, *p. 58:*** -4 **4, *p. 58:*** -15.7
5, *p. 58:* 28 **6, *p. 59:*** 17 **7, *p. 59:*** 870 years older

Exercises 1.3, *p. 60*

1. 17 **3.** -31 **5.** -44 **7.** 71 **9.** -35 **11.** -32 **13.** 32
15. -45 **17.** -62 **19.** 44 **21.** 1000 **23.** -1.42 **25.** -7.8
27. 0 **29.** 10.3 **31.** $-\frac{7}{6} = -1\frac{1}{6}$ **33.** $-12\frac{1}{4}$ **35.** $5\frac{11}{10} = 6\frac{1}{10}$
37. 12 **39.** -7 **41.** -18 **43.** -21 **45.** -26.487
47. 28 centuries **49.** 9000 ft **51.** $\$276,039$ **53.** 10,336 ft
55. a. radon: 9.2° neon: 2.7° bromine: 66° **b.** bromine
c. bromine

Practices: Section 1.4 *pp. 64–68*

1, *p. 64:* 100 **2, *p. 65:*** -15 **3, *p. 66:* a.** 8 **b.** $-\frac{5}{27}$
c. 0.12 **d.** -4.75 **e.** 0 **f.** $\frac{2}{3}$ **4, *p. 66:*** 64 **5, *p. 67:*** -240
6, *p. 67:* -28 **7, *p. 68:*** -30 **8, *p. 68:*** -59; the object is
moving downward at a velocity of 59 ft/sec.

Exercises 1.4, *p. 69*

1. Commutative property of multiplication **3.** Associative
property of multiplication **5.** Multiplicative identity
property **7.** Multiplication property of zero **9.** -12
11. 21 **13.** -3 **15.** $\frac{5}{21}$ **17.** 0.9 **19.** -60 **21.** 120
23. 0 **25.** 144 **27.** 120 **29.** $-\frac{1}{27}$ **31.** 0.98 **33.** -23
35. 0 **37.** 27 **39.** -15 **41.** -5

43.

	Input	**Output**
a.	-2	$-4(-2) - 3 = 5$
b.	-1	$-4(-1) - 3 = 1$
c.	0	$-4(0) - 3 = -3$
d.	1	$-4(1) - 3 = -7$
e.	2	$-4(2) - 3 = -11$

45. $-\$10$ (lost $\$10$) **47.** The team scored 2 more points
than its opponents $(+2)$. **49.** -15 in. (dropped 15 in.)
51. a. -135 calories **b.** $+106$ calories **c.** -852 calories

Practices: Section 1.5 *pp. 73–77*

1, *p. 73:* **a.** -8 **b.** 7 **c.** -0.7 **d.** 60 **2,** *p. 75:*
a. $\frac{1}{-5}$ or $-\frac{1}{5}$ **b.** $\frac{-8}{1}$ or -8 **c.** $\frac{3}{4}$ **d.** $-\frac{5}{8}$ **3,** *p. 76:*
a. $-\frac{4}{3}$ or $-1\frac{1}{3}$ **b.** 25 **4,** *p. 76:* **a.** -12 **b.** -3
5, *p. 77:* $-\$125$ (Down \$125)

Exercises 1.5, *p. 78*

1. a. $-\frac{2}{1}$ or -2 **b.** $\frac{1}{5}$ **c.** $-\frac{4}{3}$ or $-1\frac{1}{3}$ **d.** $\frac{5}{16}$ **e.** $\frac{1}{-1}$ or -1
3. 8 **5.** -9 **7.** 0 **9.** -25 **11.** 25 **13.** 4 **15.** 5
17. $-\frac{1}{8}$ or -0.125 **19.** $-\frac{1}{2}$ or -0.5 **21.** $-\frac{6}{5} = -1\frac{1}{5}$
23. -32 **25.** $-\frac{1}{8}$ **27.** -0.5 **29.** -20 **31.** -8
33. 10 **35.** 2.54 **37.** -1.17 **39.** -16 **41.** 1
43. 2 **45.** $\frac{1}{2}$ **47.** 4 **49.** -26 **51.** A decrease of about
4736 people per year (-4735.5) **53.** An average loss of 4
yd (-4 yd) **55.** Expenses averaged \$6000 per month
($-\$6000$). **57.** Yes.

Practices: Section 1.6 *pp. 81–87*

1, *p. 81:* **a.** 3 **b.** 1 **2,** *p. 82:* Answers may vary.
a. one-third of p **b.** the difference between 9 and x
c. s divided by -8 **d.** n plus -6 **e.** the product of $\frac{3}{8}$ and m
3, *p. 83:* **a.** twice x minus the product of 3 and y **b.** four
plus $3m$ **c.** five times the difference between a and b **d.** the
difference between r and s divided by the sum of r and s
4, *p. 83:* **a.** $\frac{1}{6}n$ **b.** $n + (-5)$ **c.** $m - (-4)$ **d.** $\frac{100}{x}$ **e.** $-2y$
5, *p. 84:* **a.** $m + (-n)$ **b.** $5y - 11$ **c.** $\frac{m + n}{mn}$ **d.** $-6(x + y)$
6, *p. 84:* $60(m + 1)$ words **7,** *p. 86:* **a.** -36 **b.** 324
8, *p. 86:* $2^4(-5)^2$ **9,** *p. 86:* **a.** $-x^5$ **b.** $2m^3n^4$
10, *p. 87:* The population after 10 hr was $243x$, or $3^5 \cdot x$.

Exercises 1.6, *p. 88*

1. 1 **3.** 3 **5.** 2 **7.** three plus t **9.** four less than x
11. seven times r **13.** the quotient of a and four
15. the product of four-fifths and w **17.** the sum of negative three and z **19.** twice n plus one **21.** four times the
quantity x minus y **23.** one minus three times x
25. the product of a and b divided by the sum of a and b
27. twice x minus five times y **29.** $x + 5$ **31.** $d - 4$
33. $-6a$ **35.** $y + (-15)$ **37.** $\frac{1}{8}k$ **39.** $\frac{m}{n}$ **41.** $a - 2b$
43. $4z + 5$ **45.** $12(x - y)$ **47.** $\frac{b}{a - b}$ **49.** -9
51. -432 **53.** $(-2)^3 \cdot (4)^2$ **55.** $6^2 \cdot (-3)^3$ **57.** $3n^3$
59. $-4a^3b^2$ **61.** $-y^3$ **63.** $10a^3b^2c$ **65.** $-x^2y^3$
67. $90° + x° + y°$ **69.** $\frac{30,000}{9}$ dollars **71.** $(t + x)$ dollars
73. $(2^3 \cdot 5000)$ dollars **75.** s^2
77. $10,000\left(\frac{1}{20}\right)(20 - n)$ dollars or $500(20 - n)$ dollars
79. $(ab - cd)$ sq ft

Practices: Section 1.7 *pp. 93–96*

1, *p. 93:* **a.** 15 **b.** 30 **2,** *p. 93:* **a.** 18 **b.** 16 **c.** -300
d. 52 **3,** *p. 94:* **a.** $\frac{7}{3}$, or $2\frac{1}{3}$ **b.** $\frac{3}{4}$ **c.** 81 **d.** -81
4, *p. 94:* 0.1 **5,** *p. 95:* $F = \frac{9}{5}C + 32$ **6,** *p. 96:* The dis-
tance d is 80 mi. **7,** *p. 96:* **a.** $K = C + 273$ **b.** K is 267.

Exercises 1.7, *p. 97*

1. -2 **3.** 16 **5.** -32 **7.** -7 **9.** 0 **11.** 12 **13.** 5
15. 56 **17.** -7 **19.** 15 **21.** -14.5 **23.** -16 **25.** 15

27.

x	$2x + 5$
0	5
1	7
2	9
−1	3
−2	1

29.

y	$y - 0.5$
0	−0.5
1	0.5
2	1.5
3	2.5
4	3.5

31.

x	$-\frac{1}{2}x$
0	0
2	−1
4	−2
−2	1
−4	2

33.

n	$\frac{n}{2}$
2	1
4	2
6	3
−2	−1
−4	−2

35.

g	$-g^2$
0	0
1	−1
2	−4
−1	−1
−2	−4

37.

a	$a^2 + 2a - 2$
0	−2
1	1
2	6
−1	−3
−2	−2

39. $-20°$ **41.** $7\frac{1}{2}$ ft **43.** 314 m **45.** 13.5 cm^2
47. $A = \frac{a + b + c}{3}$ **49.** $P = 2(l + w)$ **51.** $E = mc^2$
53. $l = 0.4w + 25$ **55.** The object falls 64 ft.
57. a. $m = \frac{100(s - c)}{c}$ **b.** 40% (40)

Practices: Section 1.8 *pp. 102–106*

1, *p. 102:* **a.** Terms: m and $-3m$; Like **b.** Terms: $5x$ and 7;
Unlike **c.** Terms: $2x^2y$ and $-3xy^2$; Unlike **d.** Terms: m, $2m$,
and $-4m$, Like **2,** *p. 103:* **a.** $-40r - 10s$ **b.** $5w + w$
c. $3g - 9h$ **d.** $1.5y + 3$ **3,** *p. 103:* **a.** $6x$ **b.** $-6y$
c. $-2a + b$ **d.** 0 **4,** *p. 104:* **a.** $-2y^2$
b. Cannot be simplified **c.** $3xy^2$ **5,** *p. 104:* $3y - 10$
6, *p. 104:* $-2a + 3b$ **7,** *p. 105:* $4y - 1$
8, *p. 105:* $-2y - 18$ **9,** *p. 105:* $-10y + 13$
10, *p. 106:* $5c + 12(c - 40)$; $17c - 480$ dollars

Exercises 1.8, *p. 107*

1. 7 **3.** 1 **5.** -0.1 **7.** Terms; $2a$ and $-a$; Like
9. Terms; $5p$ and 3; Unlike **11.** Terms; $4x^2$ and $-6x^2$; Like
13. Terms; x^2 and $7x^3$; Unlike **15.** $-7x + 7y$

17. $a - 10a$ **19.** $-0.5r - 1.5$ **21.** $10x$ **23.** $-11n$
25. $14a$ **27.** $2y + 2$ **29.** 0 **31.** Cannot be simplified
33. $4r^2t^2$ **35.** Cannot be simplified **37.** $2x + 2$ **39.** $9x$
41. $-3y + 10$ **43.** $4x - 9$ **45.** $-n + 39$ **47.** $5x + 1$
49. $-3x + 13$ **51.** $-3a - 14$ **53.** $x° + x° + 40°$;
$2x° + 40°$ **55.** $d + 2(d + 4)$; $(3d + 8)$ dollars
57. $n + (n + 1) + (n + 2)$; $3n + 3$
59. $0.05x + 0.04(1000 - x)$; $(0.01x + 40)$ dollars

Review Exercises: Chapter 1, *p. 113*

1. $+3$ mi **2.** $-\$160$ **3.**
4.
5.
6.
7. 4 **8.** -6.5 **9.** $-\frac{2}{3}$ **10.** 0.7 **11.** 4 **12.** 0 **13.** 2.6
14. $\frac{5}{9}$ **15.** True **16.** False **17.** -5 **18.** -4
19. Commutative property of addition **20.** Additive
identity property **21.** Associative property of addition
22. Additive inverse property **23.** 0 **24.** 2 **25.** 2
26. -15 **27.** -5 **28.** -85 **29.** -8.1 **30.** 15.3
31. 9 **32.** -11 **33.** -55 **34.** -3 **35.** -27 **36.** 27
37. 16 **38.** -5 **39.** -1.42 **40.** $-8\frac{5}{8}$ **41.** 5 **42.** 10
43. Commutative property of multiplication **44.** Associa-
tive property of multiplication **45.** Multiplicative identity
property **46.** Multiplication property of zero **47.** -10
48. -21 **49.** -5400 **50.** 2400 **51.** 27 **52.** $-\frac{1}{4}$
53. 6000 **54.** 36 **55.** -23 **56.** 14 **57.** 26 **58.** 38
59. -12 **60.** 6 **61.** $-\frac{3}{2}$ **62.** $\frac{1}{8}$ **63.** 3 **64.** -6
65. $-2\frac{1}{5}$ **66.** $-\frac{6}{5} = -1\frac{1}{5}$ **67.** 32 **68.** 2 **69.** -1
70. -2 **71.** 13 **72.** -20 **73.** 3 **74.** 2 **75.** 1 **76.** 4
For Exs. 77–86, answers may vary. **77.** the sum of nega-
tive six and w **78.** the product of negative one-third and x
79. six more than negative three times n **80.** five times the
quantity p minus q **81.** $x - 10$
82. $\frac{1}{2}s$ **83.** $\frac{p}{q}$ **84.** $R - 2V$ **85.** $6(4n - 2)$ **86.** $\frac{-4a}{5b + c}$
87. $(-3)^4$ **88.** $(-5)^3 3^2$ **89.** $4x^3$ **90.** $-5a^2b^3c$
91. 29 **92.** $-\frac{20}{9}$ **93.** -20 **94.** 60 **95.** 1
96. 1 **97.** $-5x + 5y$ **98.** $14x - 2y$
99. $-2x^2$ **100.** r^2t^2 **101.** $2a - 9$ **102.** $-3x - 2$
103. $-4x - 15$ **104.** $a - 17$ **105.** $+\$700$
106. $-\$7000$ **107.** -2 dollars **108.** Exothermic $(+3°C)$
109. $I - 0.5h$ degrees **110.** $14°F$ **111.** $6w$ **112.** $-4°$
113. The boiling point is $9.2°$ higher. **114.** The price per
share on Tuesday was $\$11.91$. **115.** $3^3 \cdot 10$
116. 71 ft **117.** 406 B.C. **118.** The first loss is 3 times
the second loss. **119.** 20 amperes **120.** The account is
overdrawn by $\$10$ (-10). **121.** $(x + 12y)$ dollars
122. $(f + 4s)$ students

Posttest: Chapter 1, *p. 118*

1. $-10,000$ **2.** Yes **3.**
4. -7 **5.** 3.5 **6.** True **7.** 7 **8.** 3 **9.** 10
10. $\frac{1}{12}$ **11.** -50 **12.** $x + 2y$ **13.** $(-6)^3$ **14.** -5
15. $7y + 4$ **16.** $2t + 3$ **17.** $2°$ **18.** $1.05d$ dollars
19. An improvement of $\$70,000$ **20.** $(40 - 0.02x)$ dollars

Chapter 2

Pretest: Chapter 2, *p. 120*

1. No **2.** $n = -8$ **3.** $y = -5$ **4.** $n = -8$ **5.** $x = -9$
6. $x = -\frac{1}{2}$ **7.** $y = 11$ **8.** $x = 3$ **9.** $n = -2$
10. $x = \frac{5}{3}$ **11.** $v = w + 5u$ **12.** 25% **13.** 20
14.
15.
16. 12 min **17.** 20 centerpieces
18. $m = \frac{2E}{v^2}$ **19.** $\$4000$ was invested at 8%, and $\$2000$
was invested at 5%. **20.** Option A is a better deal if you
use the gym more than 15 hours per month $(x > 15)$.

Practices: Section 2.1 pp. 121–126

1, *p. 122:* No, 4 is not a solution. **2,** *p. 122:* Yes, -8 is a
solution. **3,** *p. 124:* $y = 5$ **4,** *p. 124:* $n = -17$
5, *p. 125:* $x = 0.1$ **6,** *p. 126:* 14.88

Exercises 2.1, *p. 127*

1. **a.** True **b.** False **c.** True **d.** True
3. Subtract 4 (or add -4). **5.** Add 1. **7.** Subtract 3.5
(or add -3.5). **9.** Add $2\frac{1}{5}$. **11.** $y = -23$ **13.** $t = 0$
15. $a = -12$ **17.** $z = -6$ **19.** $x = 0$ **21.** $t = 6$
23. $r = 6$ **25.** $n = 13$ **27.** $x = -1$ **29.** $y = -3\frac{1}{2}$
31. $m = 2.9$ **33.** $t = -3.6$ **35.** $a = -5$ **37.** $m = -\frac{1}{2}$
39. $y = 1.88$ **41.** $x + 2 = 12$; $x = 10$ **43.** $n - 4 = 21$;
$n = 25$ **45.** $x + (-3) = -1$; $x = 2$ **47.** $n + 7 = 11$;
$n = 4$ **49.** d **51.** a **53.** $x + 10 = 44$; $x = 34$ mph
55. $x - 130 = 220$; $x = 350$ calories **57.** $h - 170 = 215$;
$h = 385$ m **59.** $x + 118.5 = 180$; $x = 61.5°$

Practices: Section 2.2 pp. 132–136

1, *p. 132:* $y = 63$ **2,** *p. 133:* $y = 9$ **3,** *p. 133:* $x = -10$
4, *p. 134:* $z = 13$ **5,** *p. 134:* $y = -14$ **6,** *p. 135:* The
total bill was $\$758$. **7,** *p. 136:* It will take about 2.2 hr

Exercises 2.2, *p. 137*

1. Multiply by 3. **3.** Divide by -5. **5.** Divide by -2.2.
7. Multiply by $\frac{4}{3}$ **9.** $x = -5$ **11.** $n = 18$ **13.** $a = 4.8$
15. $x = -0.5$ **17.** $c = -7$ **19.** $r = -22$ **21.** $x = 12$
23. $y = -\frac{5}{2}$ **25.** $n = 8$ **27.** $c = -3$ **29.** $x = -2.88$
31. $a = -2$ **33.** $y = \frac{2}{3}$ **35.** $x = -2.30$ **37.** $x = -6.82$
39. $-4x = 56$; $x = -14$ **41.** $\frac{n}{0.2} = 1.1$; $n = 0.22$
43. $\frac{x}{-3} = 20$; $x = -60$ **45.** $\frac{1}{6}x = 2\frac{4}{5}$; $x = \frac{84}{5}$
47. c **49.** a **51.** $0.02x = 10.5$; $x = 525$ yr **53.** $70r =$
3348; $r \approx 48$ mph **55.** $0.05c = 20$; $c = 400$ copies
57. $\frac{2}{3}x = 800,000$; $x = \$1,200,000$ **59.** $\frac{1}{5}d = 1000$;
$d = 5000$ m **61.** $7.50t = 187.50$; $t = 25$ hr
63. $12x = 10,020$; $x = \$835$ per month

Practices: Section 2.3 pp. 142–149

1, *p. 142:* $y = 4$ **2,** *p. 143:* $c = 45$ **3,** *p. 143:* $b = -3$
4, *p. 144:* $t = 3$ **5,** *p. 144:* $f = -\frac{3}{4}$ **6,** *p. 145:* $z = -5$
7, *p. 145:* $t = -4$ **8,** *p. 146:* $y = -2$ **9,** *p. 146:* The car
will have a value of $\$6500$ in 5 years. **10,** *p. 147:* The ex-
press train will catch up with the local train in 2.5 hr or
$2\frac{1}{2}$ hr. **11,** *p. 148:* 75 mi **12,** *p. 149:* 20 mph

Exercises 2.3, *p. 150*

1. $x = 3$ **3.** $t = -2$ **5.** $m = -5$ **7.** $n = 12$
9. $x = -75$ **11.** $t = 2$ **13.** $b = -19$ **15.** $x = 39$
17. $r = -50$ **19.** $y = -2$ **21.** $z = -6$ **23.** $a = -7$
25. $t = 0$ **27.** $y = -1$ **29.** $r = \frac{10}{3}$ **31.** $x = -7$
33. $y = 2$ **35.** $a = 14$ **37.** $t = \frac{3}{2}$ **39.** $y = 0$ **41.** $z = 2$ **43.** $m = -2$ **45.** $y = 1.32$ **47.** $n = 0.27$ **49.** a
51. d **53.** $50 + 120x = 1010$; $x = 8$; The student is carrying 8 credits. **55.** $x + 2x = 3690$; $x = 1230$; One candidate received 1230 votes, the other candidate received 2460 votes. **57.** $3 + 2(t - 1) = 9$; $t = 4$; The car was parked in the garage for 4 hr. **59.** $0.02x + 0.01(5000 - x) = 85$; $x = 3500$; 3500 large postcards and 1500 small postcards can be printed.
61. $24\left(t + \frac{1}{3}\right) = 36t$; $t = \frac{2}{3}$; It will take $\frac{2}{3}$ hr, or 40 min, to catch the bus. **63.** $27r + 27(r + 2) = 432$; $r = 7$; One snail is crawling at a rate of 7 cm/min, the other is crawling at a rate of 9 cm/min. **65.** $2r + 2(r + 4) = 212$; $r = 51$; The speed of the slower truck is 51 mph.

Practices: Section 2.4 *pp. 155–158*

1, *p. 155:* $r = \frac{t + s}{3}$ **2,** *p. 156:* $x = \frac{5ac}{4}$
3, *p. 156:* **a.** $x = \frac{y - b}{m}$ **b.** $x = -1$
4, *p. 157:* **a.** $r = \frac{A - P}{Pt}$ **b.** $r = 0.025$, or 2.5%
5, *p. 157:* **a.** $w = \frac{A}{l}$ **b.** $w = 7$ in.
6, *p. 158:* **a.** $A = \frac{1}{2}h(b + B)$
b. $b = \frac{2A - hB}{h}$ **c.** $b = 5$ cm

Exercises 2.4, *p. 159*

1. $y = x - 10$ **3.** $d = c + 4$
5. $d = \frac{-3y}{a}$ **7.** $n = 4p$
9. $z = \frac{2a}{xy}$ **11.** $x = \frac{7 - y}{3}$ **13.** $y = \frac{12 - 3x}{4}$
15. $y = 4t$ **17.** $b = \frac{p - r}{5}$
19. $l = \frac{2m - h}{4}$ **21.** $r = \frac{I}{pt}$
23. $r = \frac{d}{t}$ **25.** $b = P - a - c$ **27.** $d = \frac{C}{\pi}$
29. $R = \frac{P}{I^2}$ **31.** $a = 3A - b - c$ **33.** $a = S - dn + d$
35. $y = 6 - 3x$; $y = 42$ **37.** $x = \frac{y + 7}{3}$; $x = 4$
39. $y = -3x$; $y = -\frac{3}{2}$
41. $x = \frac{C - by}{a}$; $x = 14$ **43.** **a.** $K = \frac{V}{T}$ **b.** $V = KT$
45. **a.** $C = \frac{W}{150} \cdot A$ **b.** $A = \frac{150C}{W}$ **47.** **a.** $m = \frac{t}{5}$
b. $t = 5$ m **c.** You will hear the thunder in 12.5 sec ($t = 12.5$). **49.** **a.** $C = 2\pi r$ **b.** $r = \frac{C}{2\pi}$ **c.** $r \approx 0.8$ ft

Practices: Section 2.5 *pp. 163–168*

1, *p. 163:* 20 **2,** *p. 163:* \$25 million **3,** *p. 164:* 10.35 m
4, *p. 164:* \$37.28 **5,** *p. 165:* $87\frac{1}{2}\%$ **6,** *p. 165:* 31% of the presidents had been vice president. **7,** *p. 166:* The number of nursing homes increased by 20.3%. **8,** *p. 166:* The stock index dropped more in 1929. **9,** *p. 167:* 6.5% ($r = 0.065$) **10,** *p. 167:* She invested \$7000 in a mutual fund and \$14,000 in bonds **11,** *p. 168:* 2 g

Exercises 2.5, *p. 169*

1. 6 **3.** 23 **5.** 2.87 kg **7.** \$40 **9.** 4 **11.** 32 sq in.
13. \$120 **15.** \$200 **17.** 1.75 **19.** 4600 m
21. $62\frac{1}{2}\%$, or 62.5% **23.** $33\frac{1}{3}\%$ **25.** 125%
27. 10% **29.** $62\frac{1}{2}\%$, or 62.5% **31.** \$140 **33.** 40%
35. 20 **37.** 0.035 **39.** $3\frac{1}{3}\%$ **41.** 15 oz **43.** There are 16 more women than men. **45.** 18.75%
47. There are 32 employees. **49.** 20% **51.** The workforce is 18.75 million people. **53.** 54 tables **55.** No
57. \$100 **59.** \$250 **61.** \$20,000 was invested at 8% and \$14,000 was invested at 10%. **63.** \$10,000 was invested at 5%. **65.** 8 cups **67.** 6 oz

Practices: Section 2.6 *pp. 173–181*

1, *p. 174:* No, 4 is not a solution.
2, *p. 174:*
3, *p. 174:*
4, *p.175:*
5, *p.176:* $n > -1$;
6, *p.177:* $x \leq 5\frac{1}{2}$;
7, *p.177:* $x \geq -7$;
8, *p.178:* $x \leq 3$;
9, *p.178:* $x < -5$;
10, *p. 179:* $x > -5$;
11, *p. 179:* $z \leq -5$ **12,** *p. 179:* $x < 2$
13, *p. 180:* $(x + 3) + (x + 2) + x \geq 14$; $x \geq 3$. The perimeter will be greater than or equal to 14 in. for any value of x greater than or equal to 3.
14, *p. 181:* $15(8.50) + 7.5t \geq 300$; $t \geq 23$. You should work at least 23 hr on the second job.

Exercises 2.6, *p. 182*

1. **a.** False **b.** True **c.** False **d.** False
3.
5.
7.
9.
11.
13.
15.
17. $v < -7$;
19. $y > 0$;
21. $y \leq 3.5$;

23. $v \le 2$;
  -5 -4 -3 -2 -1 0 1 2 3 4 5

25. $2 \ge x$, or $x \le 2$;
  -5 -4 -3 -2 -1 0 1 2 3 4 5

27. $a < -3$;
  -10 -9 -8 -7 -6 -5 -4 -3 -2 -1 0

29. $y < -2$;
  -10 -9 -8 -7 -6 -5 -4 -3 -2 -1 0

31. $x \ge 0$;
  -5 -4 -3 -2 -1 0 1 2 3 4 5

33. $a \le -4$;
  -12 -11 -10 -9 -8 -7 -6 -5 -4 -3 -2

35. $9 \ge n$, or $n \le -9$;
  -18 -17 -16 -15 -14 -13 -12 -11 -10 -9 -8

37. $n > 3$ **39.** $x \le 6$ **41.** $y < -7$ **43.** $n \ge 13$
45. $m \ge 7$ **47.** $x > 7$ **49.** $z < 0$ **51.** $x \le 0.25$
53. $x \le -3$ **55.** $y > -3$ **57.** $x \le 0.4$ **59.** $x < \frac{1}{2}$
61. $n \ge 4.5$ **63.** $x < -6$ **65.** $y < -625$ **67.** d   **69.** d
71. $\frac{81 + 85 + 91 + x}{4} > 85; x > 83$. The student must score above 83.   **73.** $\frac{250 + 250 + 150 + 130 + 180 + x}{6} \ge 200; x \ge 240$. The store must make at least $240.   **75.** $0.50 + 0.10x \ge 2$; $x \ge 15$. Each call lasts at least 15 min.
77. $1000 + 1500h > 1500 + 1200h; h > \frac{5}{3}$, or $1\frac{2}{3}$. He should accept the deal if he sells 2 or more houses each month.   **79.** $200 - 2.5x < 180; x > 8$. He will weigh less than 180 lb after 8 months.

Review Exercises: Chapter 2, *p. 190*

1. No.   **2.** 0 is a solution.   **3.** $x = -9$ **4.** $t = -2$
5. $a = -14$ **6.** $n = 11$ **7.** $y = 7.9$ **8.** $r = 15.2$
9. $x = -6$ **10.** $z = -10$ **11.** $x = -10$ **12.** $d = -3$
13. $y = 4$ **14.** $x = -3$ **15.** $n = 41$ **16.** $r = -150$
17. $t = -9$ **18.** $y = -12$ **19.** $x = 3$ **20.** $t = -9$
21. $a = -14$ **22.** $r = 54$ **23.** $y = 9$ **24.** $t = 1$
25. $x = 6$ **26.** $y = -3$ **27.** $z = 3$ **28.** $n = 5$
29. $c = -\frac{2}{3}$ **30.** $p = \frac{5}{2}$ **31.** $x = -5$ **32.** $x = -\frac{2}{3}$
33. $x = \frac{8}{5}$ **34.** $x = -1$ **35.** $a = 2c + 5b$ **36.** $a = \frac{bn}{2}$
37. a. $x = \frac{C - By}{A}$ **b.** $x = \frac{5}{2}$ **38. a.** $h = \frac{2A}{b}$ **b.** $h = 6$ cm
39. 40   **40.** 4   **41.** 160%   **42.** $62\frac{1}{2}$%
43. 25.5   **44.** 70   **45.**
  -4 -3 -2 -1 0 1 2 3 4

46.
  -6 -5 -4 -3 -2 -1 0 1 2

47.
  -2 -1 0 1 2 3 4 5 6

48.
  -2 -1 0 1 2 3 4 5 6

49. $y > 5$;
  4 5 6 7 8 9 10

50. $t \ge 0$;
  -1 0 1 2 3 4 5

51. $y \le 2$;
  -3 -2 -1 0 1 2 3

52. $x \ge 2$;
  0 1 2 3 4 5 6

53. $n < 5$;   **54.** 16,000 Btu
  1 2 3 4 5 6 7

55. $60°$ **56.** 140 guests   **57.** 5 sides   **58.** One candidate received 11,925 votes; the other received 27,285 votes.
59. a. $C = 2 + 16y$ **b.** $y = \frac{C - 2}{16}$ **60.** The trucks will meet 4 hr after departure.   **61.** 10:15 P.M.   **62.** 1000 mi

63. Seaver received 99% of the votes cast.   **64.** 35%
65. 28 students   **66.** $30   **67.** Van Buren's electoral vote count dropped 65%.   **68.** 2 L   **69.** 5 pt   **70. a.** $p = 2.2k$
b. $k = \frac{p}{2.2}$ **71.** 4000 books   **72.** You can surf the Web 22 hr or less.

Posttest: Chapter 2, *p. 194*

1. -2 is not a solution.   **2.** $x = -9$ **3.** $n = -6$
4. $y = 11$ **5.** $y = 8$ **6.** $x = 3$ **7.** $s = 2$ **8.** $x = 2$
9. $a = 1$ **10.** $x = \frac{5}{6}$ **11.** $p = t - 5n$ **12.** 20
13. 200%   **14.**
  -3 -2 -1 0 1 2 3

15. $z \ge -3$;   **16.** 10 mi
  -3 -2 -1 0 1 2 3

17. $L = \frac{S + 21}{3}$ **18.** 23,000,000 operations   **19.** 10 mph and 12 mph   **20.** The monthly cost of Plan A exceeds the monthly cost of Plan B if more than 75 min of calls are made outside the network.

Cumulative Review: Chapter 2, *p. 195*

1. -6 yd   **2.**
  -3 -2 -1 0 1 2 3
   3. 2   **4.** True
5. 1   **6.** 5   **7.** $-11x + 36$ **8.** -2 lb   **9.** $3^4 \cdot \$1000$
10. a. $A = 50 + 25(t - 1)$ **b.** $t = \frac{A - 25}{25}$ **c.** 4 hr

Chapter 3

Pretest: Chapter 3, *p. 198*

1.   **2.** IV   **3.** $m = \frac{1}{2}$

4. $\overleftrightarrow{AB}$ is parallel to $\overleftrightarrow{CD}$, since they have the same slope: -2.   **5.** The slope of $\overleftrightarrow{PQ}$ is -1 and the slope of $\overleftrightarrow{RS}$ is 1. $\overleftrightarrow{PQ}$ is perpendicular to $\overleftrightarrow{RS}$, since the product of their slopes is -1.   **6.** x-intercept: $(3, 0)$; y-intercept: $(0, 4)$
7. The slope of the line is positive. As the population of a state increases, the number of representatives in Congress from that state increases.   **8.** Variety A grows faster.

9.

x	y
4	3
7	9
$\frac{5}{2}$	0
2	-1

10.

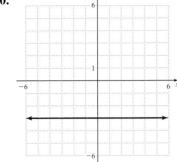

11.

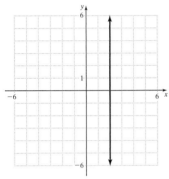

12.

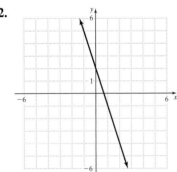

13.

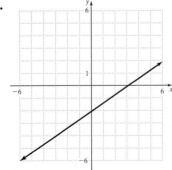

14. Slope is 2; y-intercept is $(0, -5)$ **15.** $y = 5x - 8$
16. Slope-intercept form: $y = 2x + 8$; point-slope form:
$y - 8 = 2(x - 0)$ **17.** Slope-intercept form: $y = x - 3$;
Point-slope form: $y - 1 = (x - 4)$

18.

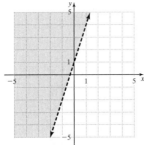

19. a. $c = 2.5x$ **b.**

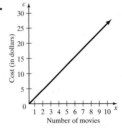

c. The slope of the line is 2.5. It represents the cost of
renting a movie.   **20. a.** $d = 50t$ **b.**

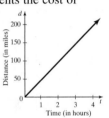

c. The slope of the graph is 50. It represents the speed the
sales representative is driving.

Practices: Section 3.1 *pp. 202–207*

1, *p. 204:*

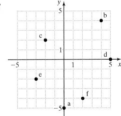

2, *p. 205:*

Point	Quadrant
$\left(-\frac{1}{2}, 3\right)$	II
$(6, -7)$	IV
$(-1, -4)$	III
$(2, 9)$	I

3, p. 206:

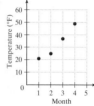

4, p. 207: The value of the car decreases as the number of years increases. **5, p. 207:** From A to B and B to C, the line segment slants up to the right, indicating that the runner's heartbeats per minute increase over this period of time. From C to D, the line segment slants downward, to the right, indicating that the runner's heartbeats per minute decrease. Possible scenario: The runner starts out warming up by jogging slowly for a certain length of time (A to B), then the runner jogs more quickly for some time (B to C), and finally, the runner jogs more slowly (C to D), resting at D.

Exercises 3.1, p. 208

1.

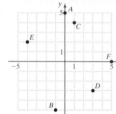

3.

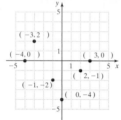

5. III   **7.** IV   **9.** I   **11.** II   **13. a.** $A(20, 40)$, $B(52, 90)$, $C(76, 80)$, and $D(90, 28)$ **b.** Students A, B, and C scored higher in English than in mathematics.

15.

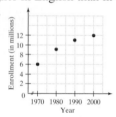

17. a.

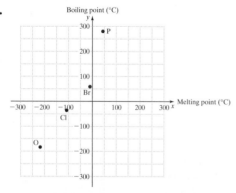

b. The y-coordinate is larger. The pattern shows that for each substance its boiling point is higher than its melting point.   **19.** The number of senators from a state (2) is the same regardless of the size of the state's population.
21. The graph in (a) could describe this motion. As the child

moves away from the wall, the distance from the wall increases (line segment slants upward to the right). When the child stands still, the distance from the wall does not change (horizontal line segment). Finally, as the child moves toward the wall, the child's distance from the wall decreases (line segment slants downward to the right).

Practices: Section 3.2 pp. 217–228

1, p. 218: $m = \frac{1}{3}$

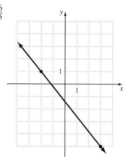

2, p. 219: $m = -\frac{6}{5}$

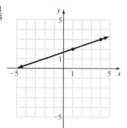

3, p. 220: $m = 0$

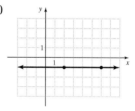

4, p. 220: The slope is undefined.

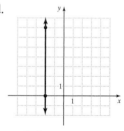

5, p. 222: Slope of $\overleftrightarrow{PQ}$: $-\frac{2}{3}$; slope of $\overleftrightarrow{RS}$: $-\frac{1}{2}$ **6, p. 222:** Scenario A is most desirable. The slope of the line is negative, which indicates a decrease in the number of people ill over time.   **7, p. 223:**

8, *p. 224:* a.

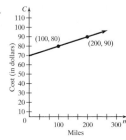

b. $m = 0.1$

c. The slope represents the cost per mile for renting a car.
9, *p. 225:* The slope of $\overleftrightarrow{EF}$ is $-\frac{5}{4}$ and the slope of $\overleftrightarrow{GH}$ is $-\frac{5}{4}$. Since their slopes are equal, the lines are parallel.
10, *p. 226:* a. Yes, the lines are parallel since their slopes are both $\frac{15}{4}$. **b.** Yes; the lines on the graph appear to be parallel. **c.** The salaries increased at the same rate.
d. The starting salary of the computer lab technician was about \$57,000. **11, *p. 227:*** The slope of $\overleftrightarrow{AB}$ is 2 and the slope of $\overleftrightarrow{AC}$ is $\frac{1}{2}$. Since the product of their slopes is not equal to -1, the lines are not perpendicular. **12, *p. 228:*** The slope of the diagonal from $(0, 0)$ to $(6, 6)$ is 1. The slope of the diagonal from $(0, 6)$ to $(6, 0)$ is -1. Since the product of the slopes is -1, the diagonals of the square are perpendicular.

Exercises 3.2, *p. 229*

1. $\frac{3}{4}$

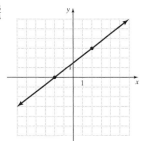

3. undefined

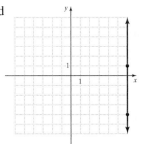

5. $-\frac{2}{5}$

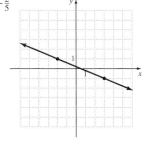

7. 0

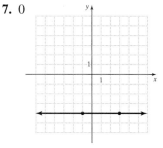

9. -7

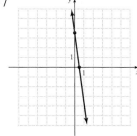

11. The slope of $\overleftrightarrow{AB}$ is -1. The slop of $\overleftrightarrow{CD}$ is 2.

13.

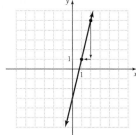

15.

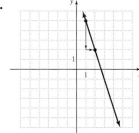

17.

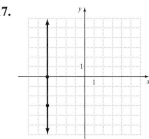

19. Positive slope; neither

21. Negative slope; neither **23.** Undefined; vertical
25. Zero slope; horizontal **27. a.** $\overleftrightarrow{PQ}: m = 4$; $\overleftrightarrow{RS}: m = 4$
The lines are parallel. **b.** $\overleftrightarrow{PQ}: m = -\frac{3}{2}$; $\overleftrightarrow{RS}: m = \frac{2}{3}$ The
lines are perpendicular. **28. a.** $\overleftrightarrow{PQ}: m = 1$; $\overleftrightarrow{RS}: m = -1$

The lines are perpendicular.　**b.** $\overleftrightarrow{PQ}: m = -\frac{1}{2}$; $\overleftrightarrow{RS}: m = -\frac{1}{2}$
The lines are parallel.　**29. a.** The slope is positive.
b. A positive slope indicates that as the temperature of the gas increases, the pressure in the tube increases.　**31. a.** Motorcycle A　**b.** Motorcycle B　**c.** The slope is the change in distance over time, or the average speed of the motorcycles.
33. The slope of each line is 1. Since the slopes of the lines are equal, the landfills are growing at the same rate.
35. a.

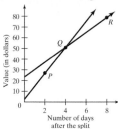

b. The slopes are 12 and 17. Since the slopes are not equal, the rate of increase did change over time.　**37.** The product of the slopes of the two lines is $-5 \cdot \frac{1}{3}$, which is not equal to -1, so $\overleftrightarrow{AD}$ is not the shortest route.　**39. a.** Graph II; As the car travels, its distance increases with time. This implies a positive slope.　**b.** Graph I; The car is set for a constant speed. The speed of the car does not change over time. This implies a 0 slope.

Practices: Section 3.3 pp. 240–251

1, p. 241:

x	y
0	1
5	11
-3	-5
$-\frac{1}{2}$	0
-2	-3

2, p. 244:

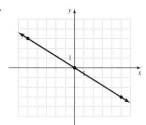

3, p. 245: a.

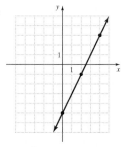

b. $m = 2$　**4, p. 247:** x-intercept: $(4, 0)$; y-intercept: $(0, -2)$;

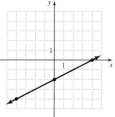

5, p. 248:

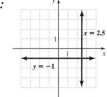

6, p. 249: a. $C = 0.03s + 40$
b.

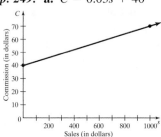

c. $m = 0.03$; for every sale, the commission increases by 0.03 times the value of the sale.

d. \$55.　**7, p. 251: a.** $w + 2t = 10$
b.

c. For each year the athlete is paid \$2 million, the number of years that she could be paid \$1 million decreases by 2 years.
d. The t-intercept is the number of years of the contract if she was paid \$2 million in each year of the contract. The w-intercept is the number of years of the contract if she was paid \$1 million in each year of the contract.

Exercises 3.3, p. 252

1.

x	y
4	4
7	13
$\frac{8}{3}$	0

3.

x	y
3.5	17.5
6	30
$\frac{1}{10}$	$\frac{1}{2}$
$-\frac{8}{5}$	-8

5.

x	y
0	3
−4	6
8	−3
4	0

7.

x	y
3	0
6	1
−3	−2
0	−1

9.

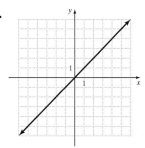

11.

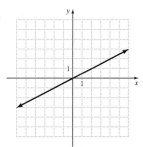

13.

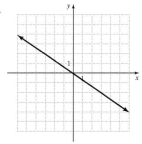

15.

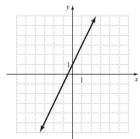

17.

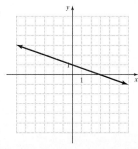

19.

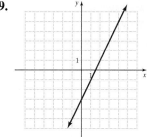

21.

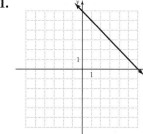

23.

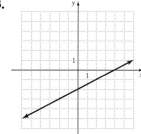

25.

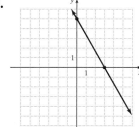

x-intercept: (3, 0)
y-intercept: (0, 5)

27.

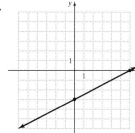

x-intercept: (6, 0)
y-intercept: (0, −3)

29.

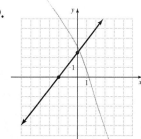

x-intercept: (−2, 0)
y-intercept: $(0, \frac{5}{2})$

31.

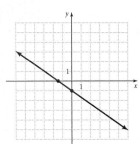

x-intercept: $\left(-\frac{3}{2}, 0\right)$
y-intercept: $(0, -1)$

33.

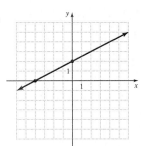

x-intercept: $(-4, 0)$
y-intercept: $(0, 2)$

35.

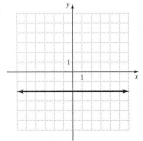

37.

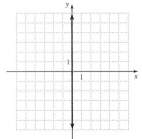

39.

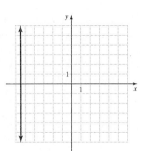

41.

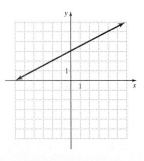

43.

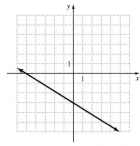

45.

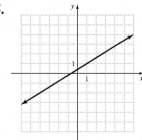

47. a.

t	v
0	10
0.5	−6
1	−22
1.5	−38
2	−54

A positive value of v means that the object is moving upward. A negative value of v means that the object is moving downward. **b.**

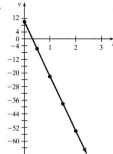

c. The v-intercept is the initial velocity of the object.
d. The t-intercept represents the time when the object changes from an upward motion to a downward motion.
49. a. $P = 100m + 500$
b.

m	P
1	600
2	700
3	800

c.

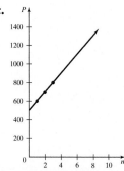

51. a. $0.05n + 0.1d = 2$ **b.**

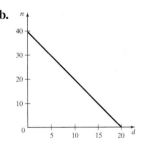

c. Only positive integer values make sense, since you cannot have fractions of nickels or dimes.

53. a. $F = 5d + 40$ **b.**

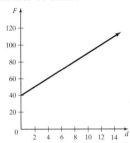

c. The F-intercept represents the cost of renting the computer for 0 days.

Practices: Section 3.4 *pp. 265–272*

1, p. 265: Slope is -2; y-intercept is $(0, 3)$.

2, p. 266: $y = \frac{3}{2}x - 2$ **3, p. 266:** $y = 4x + 6$

4, p. 266: Slope is -1; y-intercept is $(0, 0)$.

5, p. 267:

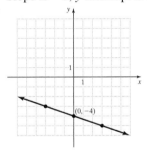

6, p. 268: $y = 1x + 2$, or $y = x + 2$

7, p. 268: $y = -2x - 1$ **8, p. 269:** $y = -\frac{1}{2}x - 2$

9, p. 279: $w = 45 - 3t$ **10, p. 270:** $y - 0 = 2(x - 7)$

11, p. 270: $y - 7 = 1(x - 7)$ or $y - 0 = 1(x - 0)$

12, p. 270: Point-slope form: $w - 27 = 5(b - 4)$; slope-intercept form: $w = 5b + 7$ **13, p. 271:**

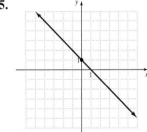

The displayed coordinates of the y-intercept are $x = 0$ and $y = 1.5$

Exercises 3.4, *p. 273*

1. For $y = 3x - 5$: 3, $(0, -5)$, ╱, $\left(\frac{5}{3}, 0\right)$; for $y = -2x$: -2, $(0, 0)$, ╲, $(0, 0)$; for $y = 0.7x + 3.5$: 0.7, $(0, 3.5)$, ╱, $(-5, 0)$; for $y = \frac{3}{4}x - \frac{1}{2}$: $\frac{3}{4}$, $\left(0, -\frac{1}{2}\right)$, ╱, $\left(\frac{2}{3}, 0\right)$; for $6x + 3y = 12$: -2, $(0, 4)$; ╲, $(2, 0)$; for $y = -5$: 0, $(0, -5)$, —, no x-intercept; for $x = -2$: undefined, no y-intercept, |, $(-2, 0)$

3. Slope: -1; y-intercept: $(0, 2)$ **5.** Slope: $-\frac{1}{2}$; y-intercept: $(0, 0)$ **7.** $y = x - 10$ **9.** $y = -\frac{1}{10}x + 1$

11. $y = -\frac{3}{2}x + \frac{1}{4}$ **13.** $y = \frac{2}{5}x - 2$ **15.** $y = 3x + 14$

17. b **19.** a

21.

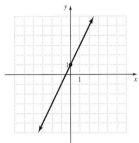

23.

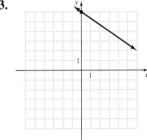

25.

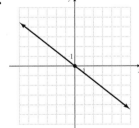

27.

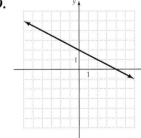

29.

31.

33. $y = 3x + 7$ **35.** $y = 5x - 20$ **37.** $y = -\frac{1}{2}x + 4$

39. $x = -3$ **41.** $y = 0$ **43.** $y = -x + 3$

45. $y = \frac{3}{4}x + 3$ **47.** $y = 2$ **49.** $y = -x - 2$

51. a. $\frac{9}{5}$ **b.** $F = \frac{9}{5}C + 32$ **c.** Water boils at $100°C$.

53. a. $y - 3500 = 4(x - 500)$ **b.** $y = 4x + 1500$

c. The *y*-intercept represents the monthly flat fee the utility company charges its residential customers.

55. a. $t - 1 = \frac{1}{5}(L - 5)$, or $L - 5 = 5(t - 1)$
b. $t = \frac{1}{5}L$, or $L = 5t$ **57. a.** $I = 0.03S + 1500$
b.   **c.** \$1686   **59.** $P = \frac{1}{33}d + 1$

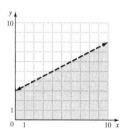

61. $L = \frac{5}{6}F + 10$

Practices: Section 3.5 *pp. 283–287*

1, p. 284: No, (1, 3) is not a solution to the inequality.
2, p. 285:

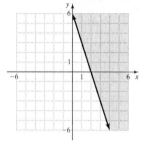

3, p. 286:

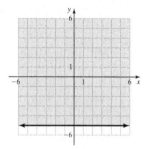

4, p. 286:

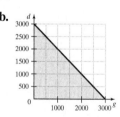

5, p. 287: a. $d + g \leq 3000$ **b.**

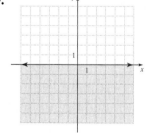

c. The *d*-intercept represents the maximum number of gallons of diesel fuel the refinery produces if no gasoline is produced. The *g*-intercept represents the maximum number

of gallons of gasoline the refinery produces if no diesel fuel is produced.

Exercises 3.5, *p. 288*

1. No, not a solution   **3.** Yes, a solution   **5.** No, not a solution   **7.**

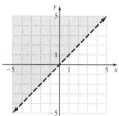

9.

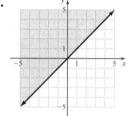

11.   **13.** d   **15.** b

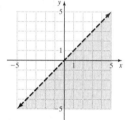

17.

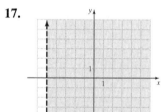

19.

21.

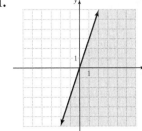

23.

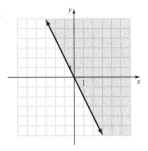

25.

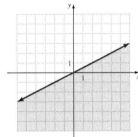

27.

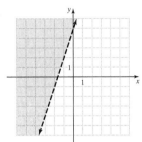

29.

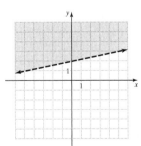

31.

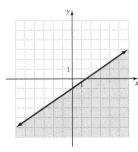

33. a. $h < \frac{1}{4}i$ **b.**

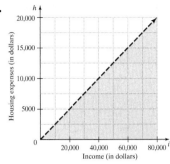

c. Choice of point may vary. Possible point: (20,000, 2500). The guideline holds since the inequality is true when the values are substituted into the original inequality.

35. a. $x + y \geq 200$ **b.**

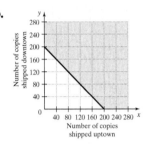

c. Choice of point may vary. Possible point: (200, 60). Check: $200 + 60 \geq 200$, $260 \geq 200$, True. At least 200 copies are shipped.

37. a. $30x + 75y \geq 1500$ **b.**

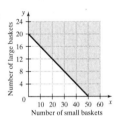

c. Since the point (20, 20) lies in the solution region, selling 20 small and 20 large gift baskets will generate the desired revenue. **39.**

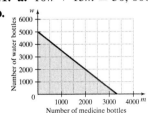

41. a. $10w + 15m \leq 50,000$

b.

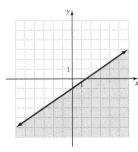

c. Answers may vary. Possible answers: 1500 medicine containers and 1000 bottles of water: (1500, 1000); 300 medicine containers and 500 bottles of water: (300, 500);

1200 medicine containers and 2000 bottles of water: (1200, 2000)   **43. a.** $8x + 10y \geq 200$

b.
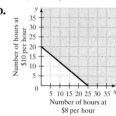

c. Answers may vary. Possible answers: 20 hr at the job paying \$8 per hr and 6 hr at the job paying \$10 per hr 10 hr at the job paying \$8 per hr and 15 hr at the job paying \$10 per hr

Review Exercises: Chapter 3, *p. 303*

1.
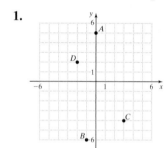

2.
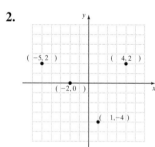

3. IV   **4.** III

5. 5;
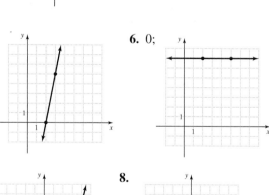

6. 0;

7.

8.

9. Positive slope   **10.** Undefined slope   **11.** Negative slope   **12.** Zero slope   **13.** Parallel   **14.** Perpendicular
15. (30, 0)   **16.** (0, 50)

17.

x	y
0	−5
1	−3
$\frac{5}{2}$	0
3	1

18.

x	y
2	1
5	−2
−4	7
8	−5

19.
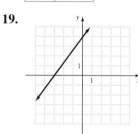

20.
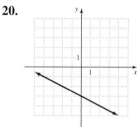

21.

22.

23. $y = x - 10$ **24.** $y = -\frac{1}{2}x - \frac{1}{2}$ **25.** 4,   (0, −16),
╱,   (4, 0)   **26.** $-\frac{1}{3}$,   (0, 0),   ╲,   (0, 0)   **27.** The slope of a line perpendicular to this line is −2.   **28.** The slope of a line parallel to this line is 3.   **29.** Point-slope form: $y - 5 = -(x - 3)$; slope-intercept form: $y = -x + 8$
30. $y = 0$ **31.** Point-slope form: $y - 5 = -5(x - 1)$; slope-intercept form: $y = -5x + 10$ **32.** Point-slope form: $y - 1 = \frac{1}{5}(x - 3)$; slope-intercept form: $y = \frac{1}{5}x + \frac{2}{5}$
33. $y = -\frac{3}{2}x + 3$ **34.** $y = \frac{3}{2}x - 3$ **35.** No, it is not a solution   **36.** Yes, it is a solution

37.
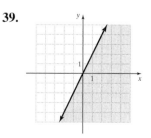

38.
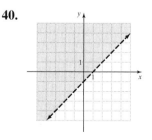

39.
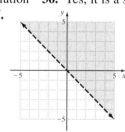

40.
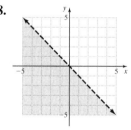

41. a.

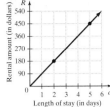

b. The R-intercept is $(0, 0)$. The R-intercept means that the cost for renting a room for 0 days is $0.

42. a.

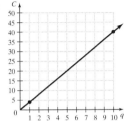

b. The slope of the line is 4. The slope represents the rate the print shop charges for each flyer, which is 4 cents.

43. The graph in part (a) could describe this motion. As the child walks toward the wall, the distance between the child and the wall decreases implying a negative slope. When the child stands still, the distance between the child and the wall remains the same, as indicated by the horizontal line segment. When the child moves toward the wall again, the distance again decreases, implying a negative slope.

44. In the first part of the flight, the airplane takes off and ascends to a particular altitude (line segment slanting up to the right), then it flies at that same altitude during the second and longest part of the flight (horizontal line segment), and finally in the last part of the flight, it descends and lands (line segment slanting down to the right).

45. a. $i = 20,000 + 0.09s$ **b.**

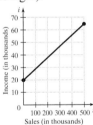

46. a.

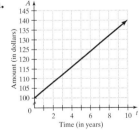

b. The A-intercept of the graph is $(0, 100)$. The A-intercept represents the initial balance in the bank account.

47. a.

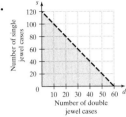

b. Answers may vary. Possible answer: 20 double jewel cases and 30 single jewel cases.

48. a.

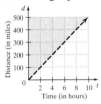

b. Choice of point may vary. Possible answer: $(2, 110)$; the coordinates mean that you would catch up to your friend if you covered a distance of 110 mi in 2 hr.

Posttest: Chapter 3, *p. 311*

1.

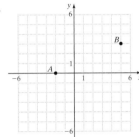

2. II **3.** $m = 1$

4. The graphs are parallel. The slope of $y = 3x + 1$ is 3 and the slope of $y = 3x - 2$ is 3. Since the slopes of the two lines are equal, their graphs are parallel. **5.** The slope of $\overleftrightarrow{AB}$ is $\frac{7}{2}$. The slope of $\overleftrightarrow{CD}$ is $-\frac{2}{7}$. $\overleftrightarrow{AB}$ is perpendicular to $\overleftrightarrow{CD}$, since the product of their slopes is -1. **6.** x-intercept: $(-5, 0)$, y-intercept: $(0, 2)$ **7.** The slope is positive. As the number of miles driven increases, the rental cost increases. **8.** Yes, the points do lie on the same line. The line containing $(0, 0)$ and $(-2, -4)$ is $y = 2x$. The line containing $(0, 0)$ and $(1, 2)$ is $y = 2x$.

9.

x	y
-3	10
5	-14
$\frac{1}{3}$	0
1	-2

10. 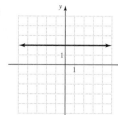 **11.**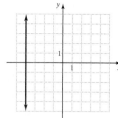

12. 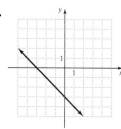 **13.**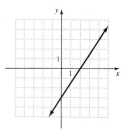

14. Slope: 3; y-intercept: $(0, 1)$ **15.** $y = 2x - 5$
16. $y = -x - 3$ **17.** Point-slope form:
$y - 5 = \frac{3}{7}(x - 3)$; slope-intercept form: $y = \frac{3}{7}x + \frac{26}{7}$
18.

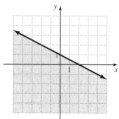

19. $C = 1000 + 30b$

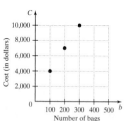

20. $0.04x + 0.08y \geq 500$

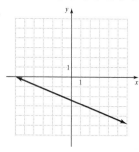

Cumulative Review: Chapter 3, *p. 214*

1. -24 **2.** 22 **3.** -4 **4.** 17
5. $x > 2$

6.

7. The assets of NY Bank are 40% of those of VA Bank
$(x = 0.4)$. **8.** There are 20 years in a score.
9. $l = \frac{P - 2w}{2}$ **10. a.** $y = 6x$
b.

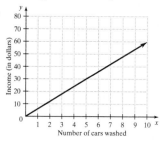

c. x-intercept: $(0, 0)$, y-intercept: $(0, 0)$

Chapter 4

Pretest: Chapter 4, *p. 316*

1. a. Not a solution **b.** A solution **c.** Not a solution
2. One solution
3. The solution is $(-3, 1)$.

4. The solution is $(5, 2)$.

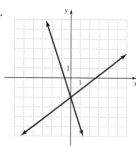

5. The solution is $(0, -2)$.

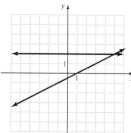

6. $(-5, -6)$ **7.** $(2, 1)$ **8.** $a = -5, b = 1$ **9.** $(1, -3)$
10. Infinitely many solutions **11.** $(-4, 1)$ **12.** $(-1, 4)$
13. $n = -15, m = -7$ **14.** No solution **15.** $(2, 0)$
16. The college awarded 2476 bachelor's degrees and 619
associate's degrees. **17.** 600 tickets were sold before 5:00
P.M. and 1375 tickets were sold after 5:00 P.M. **18.** Fifty $5
tickets were printed. **19.** $80,000 was invested in the fund
at 5% interest, and $120,000 was invested in the fund at 6%.
20. The speed of the boat was 6 mph, and the speed of the
current was 0.5 mph.

Practices: Section 4.1 *pp. 318–328*

1, *p. 319:* **a.** Yes, it is a solution of the system. **b.** No, it is not a solution of the system. **2,** *p. 321:* **a.** One solution **b.** Infinitely many solutions **c.** No solution

3, *p. 322:* The solution is $(3, -1)$.

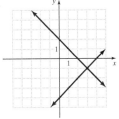

4, *p. 324:* The system has no solution.

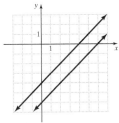

5, *p. 324:* The system has infinitely many solutions.

6, *p. 325:* **a.** $\begin{cases} m + v = 1150 \\ v = m - 100 \end{cases}$

b.

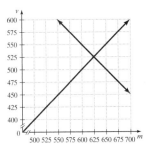

c. $(625, 525)$ **d.** The point of intersection indicates that she got a score of 625 on her test of math skills and a score of 525 on her test of verbal skills. **7,** *p. 326:* **a.** $y = 1.50x + 450$ **b.** $y = 3x$

c.

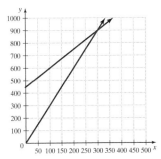

d. The break-even point is $(300, 900)$. So when 300 newsletters are printed, the cost of printing the newsletter and the income from sales will be the same, \$900.

8, *p. 327:*

The approximate solution is $(0.857, 5.857)$.

Exercises 4.1, *p. 329*

1. a. Not a solution; **b.** Not a solution; **c.** A solution
3. a. Not a solution; **b.** Not a solution; **c.** A solution
5. a. III **b.** IV **c.** II **d.** II

7. The solution is $(3, 1)$.

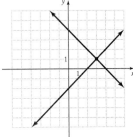

9. The solution is $(0, 4)$.

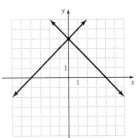

11. The solution is $(1, 5)$.

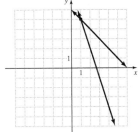

13. The solution is $(0, 1)$.

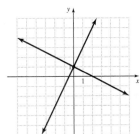

15. The solution is $(-2, -1)$.

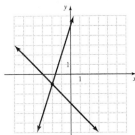

17.

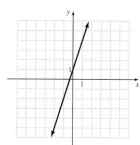

Infinitely many solutions

19.

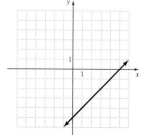

No solution

21.

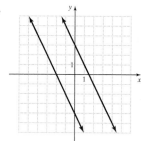

Infinitely many solutions

23.

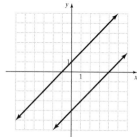

No solution

25.

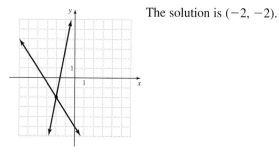

The solution is $(-2, -2)$.

27.

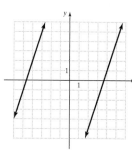

No solution

29.

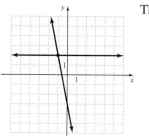

The solution is $(-1, 2)$.

31.

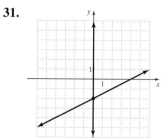

The solution is $(0, -2)$.

33.

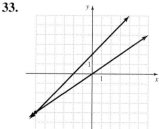

The solution is $(-6, -4)$.

35. a. $x + y = 57{,}000$

$y = x + 3000$

b.

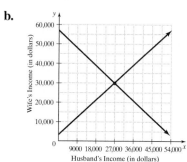

c. The husband made \$27,000 and the wife made \$30,000.

37. a. $y = 40x + 75$ (Mike)

$y = 30x + 100$ (Sally)

b.

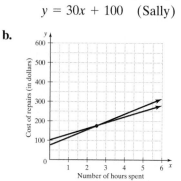

c. The plumbers would charge the same amount for 2.5 hr of work. **d.** Sally charges less.

39.

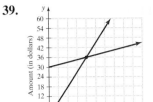

The break-even point for duplicating DVDs is (24, 36).

41.

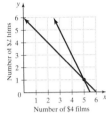

Five $4 films were rented.

43.

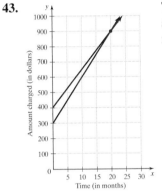

The health clubs charge the same amount ($900) for 20 months.

Practices: Section 4.2 pp. 341–348

1, p. 341: (4, −3) **2, p. 342:** $m = \frac{32}{7}, n = -\frac{5}{7}$
3, p. 343: (0, −1) **4, p. 344:** No solution
5, p. 344: Infinitely many solutions **6, p. 345:**
a. $c = 35n + 20$ (TV Deal), $c = 25n + 30$ (Movie Deal)
b. $n = 1$ and $c = 55$ **c.** The cost is the same ($55) for both cable deals if you sign up for one month. **7, p. 346:**
12.5 ounces of the 20% copper alloy and 2.5 ounces of the 50% copper alloy are required. **8, p. 347:** The manager put $110,000 in the investment that pays 4% and $88,000 in the investment that pays 5%.

Exercises 4.2, p. 349

1. (3, 7) **3.** (−4, −3) **5.** (−12, 4) **7.** (2, 1) **9.** (0, 0)
11. (−1, 2) **13.** (6, −6) **15.** $(\frac{7}{2}, -\frac{1}{2})$ **17.** No solution
19. Infinitely many solutions **21.** $p = 3, q = 5$
23. $s = -2, t = 1$ **25. a.** $c = 1.25m + 3, c = 1.50m + 2$
b. $m = 4, c = 8$. The solution indicates that both companies charge the same amount ($8) for a 4-mi taxi ride.
27. 80 full-price tickets were sold. **29.** She can combine 2.5 L of the antiseptic that is 30% alcohol with 7.5 L of the antiseptic that is 70% alcohol to get the desired concentration. **31.** There were 3 women in one department and 72 women in the other department. **33.** The loan at 6% was

$4000 and the loan at 7% was $1000. **35.** $23,000 was invested at 7% and $17,000 was invested at 9%.

Practices: Section 4.3 pp. 363–359

1, p. 353: (−2, 8) **2, p. 354:** (2, −5) **3, p. 354:** (0, 6)
4, p. 355: (2, −2) **5, p. 356:** (10, 8) **6, p. 356:** Infinitely many solutions **7, p. 357:** The whale's speed in calm water is 30 mph and the speed of the current is 10 mph.
8, p. 358: 100 adults and 75 children attended the game.

Exercises 4.3, p. 360

1. (5, −2) **3.** $(-\frac{3}{2}, -\frac{5}{2})$ **5.** $p = -3, q = -16$
7. (−1, 0) **9.** No solution **11.** Infinitely many solutions
13. $(-2, \frac{1}{2})$ **15.** $s = 0, d = -2$ **17.** (7, 4) **19.** (−1, 2)
21. $p = \frac{9}{2}, q = -\frac{11}{2}$ **23.** (−3.5, 2.5) **25.** (2, −2)
27. $(\frac{8}{3}, -\frac{4}{3})$ **29.** No solution **31.** The speed of the pass if there were no wind would be 13 yd per sec. **33.** The zoo collected 83 full-price admissions and 140 half-price admissions. **35.** The salary of a senator is $125,100 and the salary of a congressman is $101,900. **37.** It takes the computer 3 nanoseconds to carry out one sum and 4 nanoseconds to carry out one product. **39.** The rate for full-page ads is $950 and for half-page ads is $645.

Review Exercises: Chapter 4, p. 366

1. No, it is not a solution of the system. **2. a.** No solution
b. One solution **c.** Infinitely many solutions **3. a.** III
b. IV **c.** II **d.** I

4.

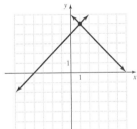

The solution is (1, 5).

5.

No solution

6.

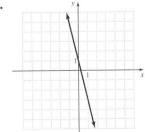

Infinitely many solutions

7.

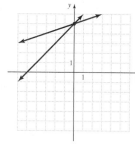

The solution is (0, 5)

8. (−1, 4)   **9.** $a = 2, b = 2$ **10.** No solution
11. Infinitely many solutions   **12.** (4, −3)   **13.** Infinitely
many solutions   **14.** (6, −3)   **15.** (2, −5)   **16. a.** $y = 0.50x + 1750, y = 5.50x$ **b.**   The student must type 350
pages in order to break even.   **17. a.** $s = 10h, s = 8h + 50$
b.   25 hr   **18.** The area of the screen is 6720 sq ft.
19. The tennis court is 31.5 ft wide and 82.5 ft long.
20. The coin box contained 200 nickels and 150 dimes.
21. One train travels at a rate of 60 mph and the other travels
at a rate of 65 mph.   **22.** The team made 818 two-point baskets and 267 three-point baskets.   **23.** The pharmacist should
mix 150 ml of the 30% solution and 50 ml of the 10% solution.   **24.** 1400 L of the 50% solution and 600 L of water are
needed to fill the tank.   **25.** The client put $40,000 in munic-
ipal bonds and $10,000 in corporate stocks.
26. $7000 was invested in the high-risk fund and $3000 was
invested in the low-risk fund.   **27.** The speed of the slower
plane was 400 mph.   **28.** The bird flies at a speed of 21
mph in calm air and the speed of the wind is 5 mph.
29. a. 57 senators   **b.**   43 senators   **30. a.** The two metals will be the same temperature after 12 min.   **b.**   The
iron will be 14° colder than the copper after 14 min.

Posttest: Chapter 4, *p. 371*

1. a. A solution   **b.**   Not a solution   **c.**   Not a solution
2. The system has no solution.
3.

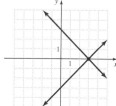

The solution is (3, 0).

4.

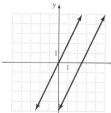

The system has no solution.

5.

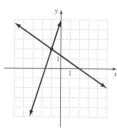

The solution is (−1, 2).

6. (−4, 1)   **7.** (1, 3)   **8.** $u = \frac{3}{4}, v = \frac{17}{4}$ **9.** (2, −5)
10. No solution   **11.** $p = 0, q = 0.5$ **12.** (27, 45)
13. Infinitely many solutions   **14.** $(\frac{1}{7}, -\frac{6}{7})$ **15.** (3, −2)
16. The winning candidate got 4204 votes.   **17.** One serv-
ing of turkey and two servings of salmon   **18.** $8000 was
invested at 7.5% and $4000 at 6%.   **19.** 1 gal of the 20%
iodine solution and 3 gal of the 60% iodine solution
20. The speed of the wind was 20 mph and the speed of the
plane was 150 mph.

Cumulative Review: Chapter 4, *p. 373*

1. −26   **2.** True   **3.** No, 5 is not a solution.   **4.** $x = -3$
5.  ; $x > 1$ **6.** The slope is $\frac{3}{4}$.
7. Slope: $m = -\frac{1}{2}$; y-intercept: (0, 2)
8.

9. The plane can fly 1554 mph ($S = 1554$).
10. The two companies charge the same amount ($95) for a
one-day rental if the car is driven 300 miles.

Chapter 5

Pretest: Chapter 5, *p. 376*

1. x^9 **2.** y^4 **3.** −3   **4.** $16x^8y^6$ **5.** $\frac{a^3}{b^{15}}$ **6.** $\frac{x^2}{25y^8}$
7. a. $6x^4, 5x^3, x^2, -7x,$ and 8   **b.** 6, 5, 1, −7, and 8   **c.** 4
d. 8   **8.** $3n^2 + n + 2$ **9.** $x^2 + x - 4$
10. $-6a^2 + 9a^2b + 3ab - 4b^2$ **11.** $3x^4 - 12x^3 + 27x^2$
12. $2n^3 + 7n^2 - 3n - 18$ **13.** $4x^2 - 3x - 27$
14. $9y^2 - 49$ **15.** $25 - 20n + 4n^2$ **16.** $t^2 - 2t - 5$
17. $4x + 5$ **18.** 200 mol of hydrogen will contain 1.2×10^{26} molecules.   **19.** The average monthly cellular telephone bill was $48.44 in 2002.   **20.** The area of the sand-
box is $(4x^2 - 25)$ sq ft.

Practices: Section 5.1 *pp. 378–385*

1, *p. 378:* **a.** 10,000   **b.** $-\frac{1}{32}$ **c.** y^6 **d.** $-y$ **2,** *p. 379:*
a. 1   **b.** 1   **c.** 1   **d.** −1   **3,** *p. 380:* **a.** 10^{12} **b.** $(-4)^6$
c. n^{10} **d.** y^5 **e.** Cannot apply the product rule because the
bases are not the same   **4,** *p. 381:* **a.** 7^5 **b.** $(-9)^1$, or −9
c. s^0, or 1   **d.** r^7 **e.** Cannot apply the quotient rule because the bases are not the same   **5,** *p. 382:* **a.** y^9 **b.** x^5y^6
c. a^2 **6,** *p. 383:* **a.** $\frac{1}{9^2} = \frac{1}{81}$ **b.** $\frac{1}{n^5}$ **c.** $-\frac{1}{3y}$ **d.** $\frac{1}{5^3} = \frac{1}{125}$
7, *p. 384:* **a.** $\frac{s}{8}$ **b.** $\frac{3}{x}$ **c.** $\frac{1}{r^6}$ **d.** $\frac{3^2}{g^3} = \frac{9}{g^3}$ **e.** x^3 **8,** *p. 384:*
a. a^3 **b.** $\frac{2x^2}{5}$ **c.** $\frac{r^3s}{2}$ **9,** *p. 385:* **a.** 2^{23} **b.** 2^{30}

Exercises 5.1, *p. 386*

1. 125   **3.** −0.25   **5.** −8   **7.** $-\frac{1}{8}$ **9.** x^4 **11.** pq
13. 1   **15.** −1   **17.** 10^{11} **19.** a^6 **21.** Cannot be simplified   **23.** n^7 **25.** Cannot be simplified   **27.** 8^2 **29.** y^1,
or y **31.** a^6 **33.** Cannot be simplified   **35.** $x^0 = 1$

37. y^6 **39.** p^7q^5 **41.** $x^3y^2z^3$ **43.** a^1, or a **45.** x^2 **47.** $\frac{1}{5}$
49. $\frac{1}{x}$ **51.** $-\frac{1}{3a}$ **53.** $\frac{1}{2^4}$ **55.** $-\frac{1}{3^4}$ **57.** $\frac{1}{(-4)^2}$ **59.** $\frac{8}{n^3}$
61. $\frac{1}{(-x)^2}$, or $\frac{1}{x^2}$ **63.** $-\frac{1}{x^2}$ **65.** $\frac{-x}{3^2}$ **67.** $\frac{y^3}{x^2}$ **69.** $\frac{q}{r}$ **71.** $\frac{4y^2}{x}$
73. $\frac{1}{p^5}$ **75.** p^3 **77.** $\frac{1}{a}$ **79.** $2n^4$ **81.** $\frac{p^5}{2}$ **83.** p^4q **85.** $\frac{1}{t^5}$
87. x^7 **89.** a^1, or a **91.** $\frac{b^3}{a^3}$ **93. a.** $35 \cdot 2^5 = 1120$ people
were ill on the sixth day of the epidemic; $35 \cdot 2^9 = 17{,}920$
people were ill on the tenth day. **b.** The number of people
ill on the tenth day was 2^4, or 16, times as great as the number ill on the sixth day. **95.** $60 \times (0.95)^{11}$ ppm
97. a. Volume of small box: $8x^3$, Volume of large box:
$125x^3$ **b.** The volume of the larger box is $15\frac{5}{8}$ times the
volume of the small box.

Practices: Section 5.2 *pp. 390–399*

1, p. 390: a. $2^6 = 64$ **b.** $\frac{1}{7^3} = \frac{1}{343}$ **c.** q^8 **d.** $\frac{-1}{p^{15}} = -\frac{1}{p^{15}}$
2, p. 391: a. $49a^2$ **b.** $-64x^3$ **c.** $-64x^3$ **3, p. 391:**
a. $36a^{18}$ **b.** $q^{16}r^{20}$ **c.** $-2a^3b^{21}$ **d.** $\frac{49}{a^2c^{10}}$ **4, p. 392: a.** $\frac{y^2}{9}$
b. $\frac{u^{10}}{v^{10}}$ **c.** $\frac{y^2}{9}$ **d.** $\frac{100a^{10}}{9b^4c^2}$ **e.** $125x^3y^6$ **5, p. 393: a.** $\frac{a^2}{25}$ **b.** $\frac{v}{4u}$
c. $\frac{b^6}{a^{10}}$ **6, p. 395:** 253.9 **7, p. 395:** 0.0000000043
8, p. 396: 8×10^{12} **9, p. 396:** 7.1×10^{-11} **10, p. 396:**
a. 2.464×10^2 **b.** 4×10^{11} **11, p. 397:** 9×10^{14}
12, p. 398: $1 \times 10^{-3} = 0.001$
13, p. 398: 2.5E $^-$17 (Answers may vary.) **14, p. 399:**
7.3E $^-$10 (Answers may vary.) **15, p. 399:** 4.6×10^8, or
460,000,000

Exercises 5.2, *p. 400*

1. $2^8 = 256$ **3.** $10^{10} = 10{,}000{,}000{,}000$ **5.** $\frac{1}{4^4} = \frac{1}{256}$
7. x^{24} **9.** y^8 **11.** $\frac{1}{x^6}$ **13.** n^4 **15.** $64x^3$ **17.** $64y^2$
19. $-64n^{15}$ **21.** $64y^8$ **23.** $\frac{1}{9a^2}$ **25.** $\frac{1}{p^7q^7}$ **27.** $r^{12}t^6$
29. $4p^{10}q^2$ **31.** $-2m^{12}n^{24}$ **33.** $-\frac{64m^{15}}{n^{30}}$
35. $\frac{1}{a^{12}b^8}$ **37.** $\frac{16y^6}{x^4}$ **39.** $\frac{125}{b^3}$ **41.** $\frac{c^2}{b^2}$ **43.** $-\frac{a^7}{b^7}$ **45.** $\frac{a^6}{27}$
47. $-\frac{p^{15}}{q^{10}}$ **49.** $\frac{4}{a}$ **51.** $\frac{8x^{15}}{y^6}$ **53.** $\frac{1}{p^5q^5}$ **55.** $81x^4y^{12}$
57. $\frac{v^4}{16u^4}$ **59.** $\frac{y^4z^{16}}{16x^8}$ **61.** $\frac{t^{12}}{r^{10}}$ **63.** $-\frac{b^6}{8a^{12}}$
65. 317,000,000 **67.** 0.000001 **69.** 6,200,000
71. 0.00004025 **73.** 4.2×10^8 **75.** 3.5×10^{-6}
77. 2.17×10^{11} **79.** 7.31×10^{-9}

81.

Standard Notation	Scientific Notation (written)	Scientific Notation (displayed on a calculator)
975,000,000	9.75×10^8	9.75E8
487,000,000	4.87×10^8	4.87E8
0.0000000001652	1.652×10^{-10}	1.652E−10
0.000000067	6.7×10^{-8}	6.7E−8
0.0000000000001	1×10^{-13}	1E−13
3,281,000,000	3.281×10^9	3.281E9

83. 9×10^7 **85.** 2.075×10^{-4} **87.** 3.784×10^{-2}
89. 1.25×10^{10} **91.** 3×10^2 **93.** 3×10^8
95. 4,000,000,000 bytes and 17,000,000,000 bytes
97. 7×10^{-7} m **99.** 2×10^{11} cells
101. 0.00000000000000000000000017 g **103.** 780,000,000
105. 1.6×10^{13} red blood cells **107. a.** 1.86×10^5 mi per
sec **b.** It will take about 8.495×10^8 sec, which is about
27 years.

Practices: Section 5.3 *pp. 404–410*

1, p. 405: (a) Terms: $-10x^2$, $4x$, and 20 (b) Coefficients:
-10, 4, and 20
2, p. 406:

Polynomial	Monomial	Binomial	Trinomial	Other Polynomial
$2x + 9$		✓		
$-4x^2$	✓			
$12p - 1$		✓		
$3x^4 - 6x^2 + 9x + 1$				✓

3, p. 407: a. Degree 1 **b.** Degree 2 **c.** Degree 3
d. Degree 0

4, p. 407:

Polynomial	Constant Term	Leading Term	Leading Coefficient
$-3x^7 + 9$	9	$-3x^7$	-3
x^5	0	x^5	1
$x^4 - 7x - 1$	-1	x^4	1
$3x + 5x^3 + 20$	20	$5x^3$	5

5, p. 408: a. $9x^5 - 7x^4 + 9x^2 - 8x - 6$ **b.** $7x^5 + x^3 - 3x^2 + 8$ **6, p. 409:** $x^2 + 6x + 20$ **7, p. 409: a.** -1
b. 19 **8, p. 410:** 356 ft

Exercises 5.3, *p. 411*

1. Polynomial **3.** Not a polynomial **5.** Polynomial
7. Not a polynomial

9.

Polynomial	Monomial	Binomial	Trinomial	Other Polynomial
$5x - 1$		✓		
$-5a^2$	✓			
$-6a + 3$		✓		
$x^3 + 4x^2 + 2$				✓

11. $-4x^3 + 3x^2 - 2x + 8$; degree 3 **13.** $-3y + 2$; degree 1 **15.** $-5x^2 + 7x$; degree 2 **17.** $-4y^5 - y^3 - 2y + 2$; degree 5 **19.** $5a^2 - a$; degree 2 **21.** $3p^3 + 9p$; degree 3

23.

Polynomial	Constant Term	Leading Term	Leading Coefficient
$-x^7 + 2$	2	$-x^7$	-1
$2x - 30$	-30	$2x$	2
$-5x + 1 + x^2$	1	x^2	1
$7x^3 - 2x - 3$	-3	$7x^3$	7

25. $10x^3 - 7x^2 + 10x + 6$ **27.** $r^3 + 3r^2 - 8r + 14$ **29.** $0x^2$ **31.** $0x$ **33.** 11; -17 **35.** 37; 79 **37.** 13.73849; -4.74751 **39.** $3x^2 - 5x - 6$ **41.** $2n^3 + 14n^2 + 20n + 10$ **43.** A polynomial in x; degree 16 **45.** 120 ft **47.** The world population in 2000 was 5,942,000,000 people (5942 million). **49.** There were about 950 U.S. radio stations with a rock music format in 2003.

Practices: Section 5.4 pp. 417–421

1, p. 417: $9x^2 + 3x - 43$ **2, p. 417:** $10p^2 + pq - 10q^2$ **3, p. 418:** $11n^2 + 2n - 3$ **4, p. 419:** $8p^3 + 2p^2q - 2pq^2 - 2q^3 + 25$ **5, p. 419: a.** $3r + 3s$ **b.** $-3q$ **6, p. 420:** $-3x^2 - 13x$ **7, p. 420:** $-5x^2 + 32x - 26$ **8, p. 421:** $-p^2 - 11pq + 17q^2$ **9, p. 421:** The polynomial 7.6 approximates how much greater the life expectancy is for females than for males.

Exercises 5.4, p. 422

1. $2x^2 + 8x + 2$ **3.** $5n^3 + 9n$ **5.** $2p^2 + 3p - 1$ **7.** $11x^2 - 3xy + 2y^2$ **9.** $3p^3 + 2p^2q - 3pq^2 - 3q^3 + 5$ **11.** $10x^2 + 17x - 5$ **13.** $5x^3 + x^2 + 9x + 2$ **15.** $-3a^3 + 6a^2 + 7ab^2$ **17.** $-x^2 - 2x + 11$ **19.** $-2x^3 + 9x^2 - 13x + 11$ **21.** $x^2 - 2x - 9$ **23.** $5x^2 - 5y^2 + 4$ **25.** $-5p^2 + 7p + 6$ **27.** $t^3 - 12t^2 + 8$ **29.** $3r^3 - 17r^2s - 2$ **31.** $-x - r$ **33.** $2p - 3q - r$ **35.** $3y^2 + 3y + 4$ **37.** $m^3 - 12m + 16$ **39.** $2x^3 - 5x^2 - 10x + 9$ **41.** $9x^2 + 4x + 7$ **43.** $-2x + 12$ **45.** $8x^2y^2 - 12xy - 14$ **47. a.** $6.28r^2 + 6.28rh$ **b.** $12.56r^2$ or $12.56h^2$ **49.** In a given year, $(32x^3 - 538x^2 + 2061x + 5862)$ million

barrels more were imported than exported. **51.** $(-5x^2 + 154x + 31)$ million more CDs than cassettes were sold in a given year.

Practices: Section 5.5 pp. 426–432

1, p. 426: $40x^5$ **2, p. 426:** $-350a^4b^5$ **3, p. 427:** $25x^2y^4$ **4, p. 427:** $70s^3 - 21s$ **5, p. 427:** $12m^6n^7 - 4m^4n^4 - 2m^3n^3$ **6, p. 427:** $-14s^5 + 34s^4 + 22s^3 + s^2$ **7, p. 428:** $2a^2 + a - 3$ **8, p. 430:** $16x^2 - 2x - 3$ **9, p. 430:** $14m^2 + 5mn - n^2$ **10, p. 431:** $8n^3 + 15n^2 + n + 6$ **11, p. 431:** $24x^4 + 56x^3 + 27x^2 + 60x - 7$ **12, p. 431:** $p^3 - 3p^2q + 3pq^2 - q^3$ **13, p. 432:** $P + 2Pr + Pr^2$

Exercises 5.5, p. 433

1. $-24x^2$ **3.** $-9t^5$ **5.** $20x^6$ **7.** $-70x^8$ **9.** $16p^3q^3r^2$ **11.** $64x^2$ **13.** $\frac{1}{8}t^{12}$ **15.** $-350a^4$ **17.** $-24a^4b^3c$ **19.** $7x^2 - 5x$ **21.** $45t^2 + 5t^3$ **23.** $24a^5 - 42a^4$ **25.** $12x^3 - 8x^2$ **27.** $x^5 - 2x^4 + 4x^3$ **29.** $15x^3 + 25x^2 + 30x$ **31.** $-45x^3 + 27x^2 + 63x$ **33.** $6x^5 + 24x^4 - 6x^3 - 6x^2$ **35.** $28pq - 4p^3$ **37.** $-7v^2 - 21vw^2$ **39.** $6a^6b^5 + 20a^3b^8$ **41.** $-6x^2 + 26x$ **43.** $8x^3 - 16x^2 + 7x$ **45.** $-23x^3 + 35x^2 - 45x$ **47.** $7x^4y - 8x^3y - 18x^2y^2$ **49.** $-45a^5b^4 + 51a^3b^6$ **51.** $y^2 + 5y + 6$ **53.** $x^2 - 8x + 15$ **55.** $a^2 - 4$ **57.** $2w^2 - w - 21$ **59.** $-10y^2 + 17y - 3$ **61.** $20p^2 - 18p + 4$ **63.** $u^2 - v^2$ **65.** $-2p^2 + 3pq - q^2$ **67.** $3a^2 - 7ab + 2b^2$ **69.** $4pq + 3p - 32q - 24$ **71.** $x^3 - 6x^2 + 10x - 3$ **73.** $2x^3 + 5x^2 - 13x + 5$ **75.** $a^3 - b^3$ **77.** $3x^3 - 6x^2 - 105x$ **79.** $x^2 + 30x$ mm^2 **81.** $(-3000x^2 + 55,000x + 1,500,000)$ dollars **83. a.** $(5000 + 15,000r + 15,000r^2 + 5000r^3)$ dollars **b.** $(5000r + 10,000r^2 + 5000r^3)$ dollars **c.** \$605

Practices: Section 5.6 pp. 438–442

1, p. 438: $p^2 + 20p + 100$ **2, p. 439:** $s^2 + 2st + t^2$ **3, p. 439:** $16p^2 + 40pq + 25q^2$ **4, p. 440:** $25x^2 - 20x + 4$ **5, p. 440:** $u^2 - 2uv + v^2$ **6, p. 440:** $4x^2 - 36xy + 81y^2$ **7, p. 441:** $t^2 - 100$ **8, p. 441: a.** $r^2 - s^2$ **b.** $64s^2 - 9t^2$ **9, p. 441:** $100 - 49k^4$ **10, p. 442:** $S^2 - s^2$

Exercises 5.6, p. 443

1. $y^2 + 4y + 4$ **3.** $x^2 + 8x + 16$ **5.** $x^2 - 22x + 121$ **7.** $36 - 12n + n^2$ **9.** $x^2 + 2xy + y^2$ **11.** $9x^2 + 6x + 1$ **13.** $16n^2 - 40n + 25$ **15.** $81x^2 + 36x + 4$ **17.** $a^2 + a + \frac{1}{4}$ **19.** $64b^2 + 16bc + c^2$ **21.** $25x^2 - 20xy + 4y^2$ **23.** $x^2 - 6xy + 9y^2$ **25.** $16x^6 + 8x^3y^4 + y^8$ **27.** $a^2 - 1$ **29.** $16x^2 - 9$ **31.** $9y^2 - 100$ **33.** $m^2 - \frac{1}{4}$ **35.** $16a^2 - b^2$ **37.** $9x^2 - 4y^2$ **39.** $1 - 25n^2$ **41.** $x^3 - 25x$ **43.** $5n^4 + 70n^3 + 245n^2$ **45.** $n^4 - m^8$ **47.** $a^4 - b^4$ **49.** $x^2 + y^2 - 10x - 2y + 26$ **51.** $A + \frac{AP}{50} + \frac{AP^2}{10,000}$ **53.** $\frac{3m^2 - 2am - 2bm - 2cm + a^2 + b^2 + c^2}{2}$

Practices: Section 5.7 pp. 447–453

1, p. 447: $-4n^5$ **2, p. 447:** $-4pr^3$ **3, p. 448:** $3x^2 - 2x$ **4, p. 448:** $-7x^5 - 5x^2 + 4$ **5, p. 448:** $-a^6b^3 + \frac{ab}{5} - 3$ **6, p. 450:** $2x + 3$ **7, p. 451:** $x^2 + 2x + 3 + \frac{2}{3x + 1}$ **8, p. 452:** $3s - 5$ **9, p. 452:** $n^2 - 4n - 3 + \frac{-13}{4n - 3}$ **10, p. 453: a.** The future value of the investment after 1 year is $10(1 + r)^1$, or $10(r + 1)$. The future value of the investment after 2 years is $10(1 + r)^2$.   **b.** $10r + 10$ and $10r^2 + 20r + 10$ **c.** The future value of the investment after 2 years is $(r + 1)$ times as great as the future value of the investment after 1 year.

Exercises 5.7, p. 454

1. $2x^2$ **3.** $-4a^7$ **5.** $-\frac{4x}{3}$ **7.** $4q^2$ **9.** $3u^2v^2$
11. $-\frac{15ab^2}{7}$ **13.** $-\frac{3u^3v^2}{2}$ **15.** $3n + 5$ **17.** $2b^3 - 1$
19. $-6a - 4$ **21.** $3 - 2x^2$ **23.** $2a^2 - 3a + 5$
25. $-\frac{n^2}{5} + 2n + 1$ **27.** $\frac{5a}{2} + \frac{b^2}{2}$ **29.** $-4xy^2 + 3 + y$
31. $2q^2 - pq^2 + \frac{3p^2}{2}$ **33.** $x - 7$ **35.** $7x - 2$
37. $3x - 1$ **39.** $5x + 3$ **41.** $7x + 2$ **43.** $x + \frac{-5}{x + 2}$
45. $2x + 1$ **47.** $2x - 3 + \frac{2}{4x + 3}$ **49.** $x^2 - 6x + 5$
51. $2x^2 - x - 3 + \frac{7}{3x - 4}$ **53.** $5x + 20 + \frac{78}{x - 4}$
55. $2x^2 + 3x + 4 + \frac{15}{2x - 3}$ **57.** $x^2 - 3x + 9$
59. a. $t = \frac{d}{r}$ **b.** It takes $(t^2 - 7t + 14)$ hr.   **61.** There are $(3x - 14)$ thousand subscribers per cell system.

Review Exercises: Chapter 5, p. 460

1. $-x^3$ **2.** -1 **3.** n^{11} **4.** x^7 **5.** n^3 **6.** p^3 **7.** y^7
8. a^3b^3 **9.** y **10.** n^2 **11.** $\frac{1}{(5x)^1}$ **12.** $-\frac{3}{n^2}$ **13.** $\frac{v^4}{8^2}$
14. y^4 **15.** $\frac{1}{x^1}$ **16.** $\frac{y^3}{5^1}$ **17.** a^{10} **18.** $\frac{1}{t^6}$ **19.** $\frac{1}{x^2y}$ **20.** x^2y^1
21. $10^8 = 100,000,000$ **22.** $-x^9$ **23.** $4x^6$
24. $-64m^{15}n^3$ **25.** $\frac{3}{x^{12}}$ **26.** $\frac{b^8}{a^6}$ **27.** $\frac{x^4}{81}$ **28.** $\frac{a^2}{b^6}$ **29.** $\frac{y^6}{x^6}$
30. $x^{10}y^5$ **31.** $\frac{16a^6}{b^8c^2}$ **32.** $\frac{v^4}{49u^{10}w^2}$ **33.** $37,000,000,000$
34. $1,630,000,000$ **35.** 0.00005022 **36.** 0.00000000006
37. 1.2×10^{12} **38.** 4.27×10^8 **39.** 4×10^{-14}
40. 5.6×10^{-7} **41.** 5.88×10^9 **42.** 6.3×10^3
43. 6×10^6 **44.** 6×10^{-10} **45.** Polynomial   **46.** Not a polynomial   **47.** Trinomial   **48.** Binomial   **49.** $-3y^3 + y^2 + 8y - 1$; degree 3, leading term: $-3y^3$, leading coefficient: -3 **50.** $n^4 - 7n^3 - 6n^2 + n$; degree 4, leading term: n^4, leading coefficient: 1   **51.** $-x^3 + x^2 + 2x + 13$
52. $3n^3 + 4n^2 - 6n + 4$ **53.** 12; 0   **54.** 0; -16
55. $x^2 - x + 13$ **56.** $-2y^3 - y^2 - y - 5$ **57.** $a^2 - 2ab - 3b^2$ **58.** $5s^3t + s^2t + 9s^2 - 6st - 3t^2$ **59.** $2x^2 - 8x - 8$ **60.** $-n^3 + 3n^2 + n$ **61.** $5y^4 - 5y^3 + 2y^2 - 6y - 3$ **62.** $2x^3 + 8x^2 - 12x + 3$ **63.** $4t^2 + 4t$
64. $-2x - y$ **65.** $2y^2 - 5y + 2$ **66.** $-5x^2 + 9$
67. $-6x^5$ **68.** $-144a^3b^5$ **69.** $8x^2y^2 - 10xy^3$
70. $-5x^4 + 15x^3 - 5x^2$ **71.** $n^2 + 10n + 21$
72. $3x^2 + 9x - 54$ **73.** $8x^2 - 6x + 1$ **74.** $9a^2 + 3ab - 2b^2$ **75.** $2x^4 + 6x^3 - 5x^2 - 13x + 6$ **76.** $y^3 - 9y^2 + 15y - 2$ **77.** $-6y^2 + 13y$ **78.** $-x^3 + 6x^2 - 6x$
79. $a^2 - 2a + 1$ **80.** $s^2 + 8s + 16$ **81.** $4x^2 + 20x + 25$
82. $9 - 24t + 16t^2$ **83.** $25a^2 - 20ab + 4b^2$
84. $u^4 + 2u^2v^2 + v^4$ **85.** $m^2 - 16$ **86.** $36 - n^2$
87. $49n^2 - 1$ **88.** $4x^2 - y^2$ **89.** $16a^2 - 9b^2$
90. $x^3 - 100x$ **91.** $-48t^4 + 120t^3 - 75t^2$ **92.** $p^4 - 2p^2q^2 + q^4$ **93.** $3x^2$ **94.** $-2a^2b^3c$ **95.** $6x^2 - 2$
96. $5x^3 + 3x^2 - 2x - 1$ **97.** $3x - 7$
98. $x^2 - 2x - 1 + \frac{12}{2x - 1}$ **99.** 1.39×10^{10} yr
100. $6,240,000,000,000,000,000$ eV   **101.** 3×10^{-5} m
102. 0.00000000011 m   **103.** There will be 36 handshakes.
104. The object is 480.4 m above the ground.

105. There were about 249,000 divorces in 1951.
106. There were about 899 two-year colleges in 1970.
107. a. $(3w^2 - 10w)$ sq ft   **b.** $(48w + 24)$ sq ft
c. The area of the concrete walk is 600 sq ft.
108. $x^2 + 4x + 4$

Posttest: Chapter 5, p. 465

1. x^7 **2.** n^6 **3.** $\frac{7}{a^1} = \frac{7}{a}$ **4.** $-27x^6y^3$ **5.** $\frac{x^8}{y^{12}}$ **6.** $\frac{y^3}{27x^6}$
7. a. $-x^3, 2x^2, 9x, -1$ **b.** $-1, 2, 9,$ and -1 **c.** 3
d. -1 **8.** $2y^2 - y + 5$ **9.** $-x^2 + x - 9$ **10.** $3x^2y^2 - 4x^2$ **11.** $10m^3n^3 - 20m^2n^3 + 2m^2n^4$ **12.** $y^4 - 3y^3 + 2y^2 + 4y - 4$ **13.** $6x^2 + 19x - 7$ **14.** $49 - 4n^2$
15. $4m^2 - 12m + 9$ **16.** $-4s^2 - 5s + 9$
17. $t^2 - t - 1 + \frac{4}{3t - 2}$ **18.** 1×10^{-7} m
19. a. First house: $(1500x + 140,000)$ dollars; second house: $(800x + 90,000)$ dollars   **b.** $(2300x + 230,000)$ dollars   **20.** The account balance is $1060.90.

Cumulative Review: Chapter 5, p. 467

1. $m = \frac{y - b}{x}$ **2.** 61   **3.** 4   **4.** Slope: $\frac{2}{3}$; y-intercept: $(0, -2)$ **5.**

6. $(2, -2)$

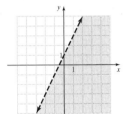

7. $m^2 - 16m + 16$ **8.** 9×10^{13} kg $\cdot$ m²/sec²   **9. a.** $x + 4, x + 8,$ and $x + 12$ **b.** Yes; $1980 - 1972 = 8$, which is a multiple of 4.   **10. a.** $0.20b$ **b.** $c = 1.20b$

Chapter 6

Pretest: Chapter 6, p. 470

1. $18a$ **2.** $4p(q + 4)$ **3.** $5xy(2x - x^2y^2 + y)$
4. $(x + 2)(3x + 2)$ **5.** $(n - 3)(n - 8)$ **6.** $(a - 3)(a + 7)$
7. $3y(y - 1)(y - 3)$ or $3y(1 - y)(3 - y)$
8. $(5a - 4b)(a + 2b)$ **9.** $-2(3n + 1)(2n - 7)$
10. $(2x - 7)^2$ **11.** $(5n + 3)(5n - 3)$
12. $y(x + 2y)(x - 2y)$ **13.** $(y^3 - 4)(y^3 - 5)$
14. 0, 6   **15.** $\frac{2}{3}, -1$ **16.** 3, -5 **17.** $h = \frac{A - 2lw}{2l + 2w}$
18. $-(16t + 1)(t - 4)$ ft   **19.** $(S + 15)(S - 15)$ sq ft
20. The length of the screen is 32 in. and the width is 24 in.

Practices: Section 6.1 pp. 471–476

1, p. 472: 24   **2, p. 472:** a **3, p. 473:** $6xy^2$ **4, p. 473:** $2y^2(5 + 4y^3)$ **5, p. 474:** $7a(3ab - 2)$ **6, p. 474:** $2ab^2(4a - 3b)$ **7, p. 474:** $12(2a^2 - 4a + 1)$
8, p. 474:: $a = \frac{s^2}{b + c}$ **9, p. 475:** $(y - 3)(4 + y)$, or $(y - 3)(y + 4)$ **10, p. 475:** $(x - 1)(3y - 2)$
11, p. 475: $(4 - 3x)(1 + 2x)$ **12, p. 476:** $(a + 2)(a - 2b)$
13, p. 476: $(y - z)(5 - y^4)$ **14, p. 476:** $t(v_0 + \frac{1}{2}at)$

Exercises 6.1, p. 477

1. 27   **3.** x^3 **5.** $4b$ **7.** $4y^3$ **9.** $3a^2b^2$ **11.** $3x - 1$
13. $x(x + 7)$ **15.** $3(x + 2)$ **17.** $8(3x^2 + 1)$
19. $9(3m + n)$ **21.** $x(2 - 7x)$ **23.** $4z^2(z^3 + 3)$

25. $5x(2x^2 - 3)$ **27.** $ab(ab - 1)$ **29.** $xy(6y + 7x)$
31. $9pq(3q + 2p)$ **33.** $2x^3y(1 - 6y^3)$ **35.** $3(c^3 + 2c^2 + 4)$
37. $b^2(9b^2 - 3b + 1)$ **39.** $2m^2(m^2 + 5m - 3)$
41. $b^2(5b^3 - 3b + 2)$ **43.** $5x(3x^3 - 2x^2 - 5)$
45. $4ab(a + 2ab - 3)$ **47.** $3cd(3cd + 4c^2 + d^2)$
49. $(x - 1)(x + 3)$ **51.** $(a - 1)(5a - 3)$
53. $(s + 7)(r - 2)$ **55.** $(x - y)(a - b)$
57. $(y + 2)(3x - 1)$ **59.** $(b - 1)(b - 5)$
61. $(y - 1)(y + 5)$ **63.** $(t - 3)(1 + t)$
65. $(b - 7)(9a - 2)$ **67.** $(r + 3)(s + t)$
69. $(x + 6)(y - 4)$ **71.** $(5x - 3z)(3y + 4z)$
73. $(z + 4)(2x + 5y)$ **75.** $P = \frac{TM}{C + L}$ **77.** $l = \frac{S - 2wh}{2w + 2h}$
79. $m(v_2 - v_1)$ **81.** $0.5n(n - 1)$ **83.** $\frac{1}{2}n(n - 3)$
85. $n = \frac{P - D}{C + T}$

Practices: Section 6.2 pp. 481–488

1, p. 482: $(x + 1)(x + 4)$, or $(x + 4)(x + 1)$
2, p. 483: $(y - 4)(y - 5)$, or $(y - 5)(y - 4)$
3, p. 483: Prime polynomial; cannot be factored
4, p. 484: $(y - 4)(y - 8)$ **5, p. 484:** $(p - q)(p - 3q)$, or
$(p - 3q)(p - q)$ **6, p. 485:** $(x - 2)(x + 3)$
7, p. 485: $(x + 2)(x - 23)$ **8, p. 486:** $(y - 4)(y + 6)$
9, p. 486: $(a + 3b)(a - 8b)$ **10, p. 487:** $y(y + 1)(y - 10)$
11, p. 487: $8x(x - 1)(x - 2)$ **12, p. 487:**
$-(x - 1)(x + 11)$, or $(-x + 1)(x + 11)$, or
$(x - 1)(-x - 11)$ **13, p. 488:** $-16(t + 1)(t - 3)$

Exercises 6.2, p. 489

1. f   **3.** e   **5.** b   **7.** $(x - 5)$ **9.** $(x + 4)$ **11.** $(x - 1)$
13. $(x + 2)(x + 4)$ **15.** $(x - 1)(x + 6)$
17. Not factorable   **19.** $(x + 1)(x + 4)$
21. $(x - 1)(x - 3)$ **23.** $(y - 4)(y - 8)$
25. $(t + 1)(t - 5)$ **27.** $(n + 3)(n - 12)$
29. $(x - 5)(x + 9)$ **31.** $(y - 4)(y - 5)$
33. $(b + 4)(b + 7)$ **35.** $(m - 4)(m - 11)$
37. $-(y + 5)(y - 10)$ **39.** $(x - 8)(x - 8)$
41. $(x - 2)(x - 8)$ **43.** $(w - 3)(w - 27)$
45. $(p - q)(p - 7q)$ **47.** $(p + q)(p - 5q)$
49. $(m - 5n)(m - 7n)$ **51.** $(x + y)(x + 8y)$
53. $5(x + 2)(x - 3)$ **55.** $2(x - 2)(x + 7)$
57. $6(t - 1)(t - 2)$ **59.** $3(x + 2)(x + 4)$
61. $y(y - 2)(y + 5)$ **63.** $a(a + 3)(a + 5)$
65. $t^2(t - 2)(t - 12)$ **67.** $4a(a - 1)(a - 2)$
69. $2x(x + 3)(x + 5)$ **71.** $4x(x - 3)(x - 4)$
73. $2s(s - 4)(s + 7)$ **75.** $2c^2(c - 5)(c + 7)$
77. $ax(x - 2)(x - 16)$ **79.** $n^2 + 11n + 30 =$
$(n + 5)(n + 6)$; the factors represent two whole numbers
that differ by 1.   **81.** $C = (x - 5)(x - 9)$

Practices: Section 6.3 pp. 492–497

1, p. 493: $(5x + 4)(x + 2)$ **2, p. 493:** $(6x - 7)(x - 3)$
3, p. 494: $(7y - 2)(y + 7)$ **4, p. 495:** $(2x - 5)(x + 2)$
5, p. 495: $3x(3x + 1)(2x - 3)$ **6, p. 496:**
$3(6c - 5d)(2c + d)$ **7, p. 496:** $(2x + 1)(x - 4)$
8, p. 497: $x(2x - 5)(2x - 7)$

Exercises 6.3, p. 498

1. e   **3.** b   **5.** c   **7.** $(3x + 1)$ **9.** $(x - 3)$ **11.** $(x - 3)$
13. $(3x + 5)(x + 1)$ **15.** $(2y - 1)(y - 5)$

17. $(3x + 2)(x + 4)$ **19.** Cannot be factored
21. $(6y + 5)(y - 1)$ **23.** $(2y - 7)(y - 2)$
25. $(3a + 2)(3a - 8)$ **27.** $(4x - 1)(x - 3)$
29. $(3y + 2)(4y + 3)$ **31.** $(2m - 3)(m - 7)$
33. $-(3a - 1)(2a + 3)$ **35.** $(8y - 11)(y + 2)$
37. Cannot be factored   **39.** $(8a + 1)(a + 8)$
41. $(3x - 1)(2x + 9)$ **43.** $(4y - 3)(2y - 5)$
45. $2(7y - 5)(y - 2)$ **47.** $4(7a - 1)(a + 1)$
49. $-2(3b + 1)(b - 7)$ **51.** $2y(3y + 2)(2y + 7)$
53. $2a^2(7a - 5)(a - 2)$ **55.** $xy(2x + 3)(x + 5)$
57. $2ab(3b - 1)(b - 7)$ **59.** $(5c - d)(4c - d)$
61. $(2x + y)(x - 3y)$ **63.** $(4a - b)(2a - b)$
65. $3(3x + 2y)(2x - y)$ **67.** $2(4c - 5d)(2c - 3d)$
69. $3(3u + v)(3u + v)$ **71.** $3x(7x - 3y)(2x + 3y)$
73. $-5x^2y(3x + y)(2x - 3y)$ **75.** $a(5x + 2y)(x - 6y)$
77. $-(5t - 4)(t + 5)$ **79.** $(2n - 5)(2n - 1)$; since the
difference of the factors is $(2n - 1) - (2n - 5) = 2n -$
$1 - 2n + 5 = 4$, the factors represent two integers that differ by 4 no matter what integer n represents.

Practices: Section 6.4 pp. 501–506

1, p. 502: a. The trinomial is a perfect square.   **b.** The trinomial is not a perfect square.   **c.** The trinomial is a perfect
square.   **d.** The trinomial is not a perfect square.
e. The trinomial is a perfect square.   **2, p. 503:** $(n + 10)^2$
3, p. 503: $(t - 2)^2$ **4, p. 503:** $(5c - 4d)^2$
5, p. 504: $(x^2 + 4)^2$ **6, p. 504: a.** The binomial is a
difference of squares.   **b.** The binomial is not a difference
of squares.   **c.** The binomial is not a difference of squares.
d. The binomial is a difference of squares.
7, p. 505: $(y + 11)(y - 11)$ **8, p. 505:** $(3x + 5y)(3x - 5y)$
9, p. 506: $(8x^4 + 9y)(8x^4 - 9y)$
10, p. 506: $16(4 + t)(4 - t)$

Exercises 6.4, p. 507

1. Perfect square trinomial   **3.** Neither   **5.** Perfect square
trinomial   **7.** Difference of squares   **9.** Difference of
squares   **11.** Perfect square trinomial   **13.** Neither
15. Neither   **17.** Neither   **19.** $(x - 6)^2$ **21.** $(y + 10)^2$
23. $(a - 2)^2$ **25.** Not factorable   **27.** $(m + 8)(m - 8)$
29. $(y + 9)(y - 9)$ **31.** $(12 + x)(12 - x)$ **33.** $(2a - 9)^2$
35. $(7x + 2)^2$ **37.** $(6 - 5x)^2$ **39.** $(10m + 9)(10m - 9)$
41. Not factorable   **43.** $(1 + 3x)(1 - 3x)$
45. $(m + 13n)^2$ **47.** $(2a + 9b)^2$ **49.** $(x + 2y)(x - 2y)$
51. $(10x + 3y)(10x - 3y)$ **53.** $(y^3 + 1)^2$ **55.** $(8x^4 + 1)^2$
57. $(10x^5 - y^5)^2$ **59.** $(5m^3 + 6)(5m^3 - 6)$
61. $(x^2 + 12y)(x^2 - 12y)$ **63.** $6(x + 1)^2$
65. $3m(3m - 2)^2$ **67.** $4s^2t(t + 10)^2$ **69.** $3(2x^3y^2 - 3)^2$
71. $3k(k + 7)(k - 7)$ **73.** $4y^2(y + 3)(y - 3)$
75. $3x^2y(3 + y)(3 - y)$ **77.** $2(ab + 7)(ab - 7)$
79. $(4b^2 + 11)(4b^2 - 11)$ **81.** $(16 + r^2)(4 + r)(4 - r)$
83. $5(x^2 + 4y^4)(x + 2y^2)(x - 2y^2)$
85. $(c - d)(x + 2)(x - 2)$ **87.** $(x - y)(4 + a)(4 - a)$
89. $4\pi(r_1 + r_2)(r_1 - r_2)$ **91.** $16{,}000(1 + r)^2$, or
$16{,}000(r + 1)^2$ **93.** $k(v_2 + v_1)(v_2 - v_1)$

Practices: Section 6.5 pp. 511–516

1, p. 512: $\frac{1}{3}, -5$ **2, p. 513:** $0, -6$ **3, p. 513:** $-\frac{1}{4}, 3$
4, p. 514: $1, -5$ **5, p. 514:** The dimensions of the frame

should be 8 in. by 10 in.   **6, *p. 516:*** The scooter going north has traveled 12 mi.

Exercises 6.5, *p. 517*

1. Quadratic   **3.** Linear   **5.** Quadratic   **7.** $-3, 4$
9. $0, -\frac{5}{3}$ **11.** $-\frac{1}{2}, 5$ **13.** $-\frac{3}{2}, \frac{3}{2}$ **15.** $0, \frac{2}{3}$ **17.** $0, 2$
19. $0, \frac{1}{5}$ **21.** $-2, -3$ **23.** $7, -8$ **25.** $-\frac{1}{2}, 3$ **27.** $\frac{2}{3}, -\frac{1}{2}$
29. $\frac{1}{6}$ **31.** $-11, 11$ **33.** $\frac{3}{2}$ **35.** $\frac{1}{2}$ **37.** $\frac{1}{3}, -2$
39. $-2, 3$ **41.** $3, 4$ **43.** $2, -4$ **45.** $-\frac{1}{3}, -1$
47. $-\frac{1}{2}, -1$ **49.** $0, -5$ **51.** $-\frac{1}{2}, \frac{1}{2}$ **53.** $-\frac{1}{2}, \frac{1}{2}$
55. -3 **57.** $-3, 4$ **59.** $-2, 3$ **61.** $4, -5$
63. $-\frac{1}{3}, -4$ **65.** $2, 4$ **67.** $1, 2$ **69.** There were 15 teams in the league.   **71.** One car traveled 6 mi and the other traveled 8 mi.   **73.** The length of the room is 16 ft and the width is 12 ft.   **75.** The diver will hit the water in $\frac{3}{2}$, or 1.5 sec.

Review Exercises: Chapter 6, *p. 522*

1. 12 **2.** $3m^2$ **3.** $3(x - 2y)$ **4.** $2pq(8p^2q + 9p - 2q)$
5. $(n - 1)(1 + n)$ **6.** $(x - 5)(b - 2)$ **7.** $r = \frac{d}{t_1 + t_2}$
8. $x = \frac{c - y}{a - b}$ **9.** Not factorable   **10.** Not factorable
11. $(y + 6)(y + 7)$ **12.** $(m - 2n)(m - 5n)$
13. $-2(x - 2)(x + 6)$ **14.** $3x(x + y)(x - 5y)$
15. $(3x - 1)(x + 2)$ **16.** $(5n + 3)(n + 2)$
17. Not factorable   **18.** $(3x + 4)(2x - 3)$
19. $(2a - 7b)(a + 5b)$ **20.** $-(2a - 3)(2a - 5)$
21. $3y(3y - 1)(y + 7)$ **22.** $q(2p + q)(p - 2q)$
23. $(b - 3)^2$ **24.** $(8 + x)(8 - x)$ **25.** $(5y - 2)^2$
26. $(3a + 4b)^2$ **27.** $(9p + 10q)(9p - 10q)$
28. $(2x^4 - 7)^2$ **29.** $3(4x^2 + y^2)(2x + y)(2x - y)$
30. $(x - 1)(x + 3)(x - 3)$ **31.** $-2, 1$ **32.** $0, 4$
33. $0, -6$ **34.** $-\frac{1}{2}$ **35.** $2, 8$ **36.** $-\frac{2}{3}, 1$ **37.** $-\frac{5}{2}, 1$
38. $3, -4$ **39.** $aL(t_2 - t_1)$
40. $(t_2 - t_1)[a - 16(t_2 + t_1)]$ **41.** The distance between the two intersections is 2500 ft.   **42.** The length of the horizontal diagonal of the kite is 32 in.   **43.** The rocket will reach a height of 18 ft above the launch in $\frac{1}{4}$ sec and $\frac{9}{2}$ sec, or in 0.25 sec and 4.5 sec.   **44.** $h = \frac{2A}{b + B}$

Posttest: Chapter 6, *p. 525*

1. $3x^2$ **2.** $2y(x - 7)$ **3.** $2p(2p - 3q)(2p - q)$
4. $(a - b)(x - y)$ **5.** $(n + 3)(n - 16)$ **6.** $(x + 2)(x - 4)$
7. $-5x(x + 1)(x - 4)$ **8.** $(4x - 3y)(x + 4y)$
9. $-3(2x - 3)^2$ **10.** $(3x + 5y)^2$ **11.** $(11 + 2x)(11 - 2x)$
12. $(pq + 1)(pq - 1)$ **13.** $(y + 2)^2(y - 2)^2$ **14.** $-8, 1$
15. $\frac{1}{3}, -2$ **16.** $-\frac{3}{2}, 2$ **17.** 8 m   **18.** $mg(y_2 - y_1)$
19. The weight reaches the ground in $\frac{3}{4}$, or 0.75 sec.
20. $2x(2x + 55)$ sq ft

Cumulative Review: Chapter 6, *p. 527*

1. -3 **2.** $8a + 7b + 2$ **3.** 8 **4.**

5. $(-1, 7)$ **6.** n **7.** $21x^2 + x - 2$ **8.** The charge is $(f + 8c)$ dollars.   **9.** The company must sell 50 shirts per day in order to break even.   **10.** $2\pi r(r + h)$

Chapter 7

Pretest: Chapter 7, *p. 530*

1. The expression is undefined when $x = -6$.
2. $\frac{n^2 - 2n}{3n} = \frac{n(n - 2)}{3n} = \frac{\not{n}(n - 2)}{3\not{n}} = \frac{n - 2}{3}$ **3.** $\frac{4x}{y^2}$ **4.** $4a$
5. $-\frac{w}{w + 6}$ **6.** $\frac{10}{n^2}$ **7.** $\frac{6(a - 2)}{9a(a - 2)}$ and $\frac{a}{9a(a - 2)}$ **8.** $\frac{5y - 2}{y + 1}$
9. $\frac{15x + 2}{12x^2}$ **10.** $\frac{2c + 12}{(c - 3)(c + 3)}$ **11.** $\frac{3x - 1}{(x - 1)^2(x + 1)}$ **12.** $\frac{4a^2}{3n^2}$
13. $\frac{y - 4}{5y(y + 4)}$ **14.** $\frac{1}{x + 4}$ **15.** 5 **16.** $-\frac{2}{3}$ **17.** $\frac{3}{2}$ and 3
18. $\frac{2x + 1500}{x}$ dollars   **19.** The average speed during the first part of the trip was 65 mph and the average speed during the second part was 55 mph.   **20.** It takes the photocopier $2\frac{1}{2}$ (or 2.5) minutes to make 30 copies.

Practices: Section 7.1 *pp. 532–538*

1, *p. 533:* a. The expression is undefined when n is equal to 3.   **b.** The expression is undefined when n is equal to -3 or 3.   **2, *p. 534:* a.** The expressions are equivalent.   **b.** The expressions are equivalent.   **3, *p. 535:* a.** $\frac{2n^2}{m}$
b. $-\frac{3x^2}{2}$ **4, *p. 536:* a.** $\frac{y - 4}{2y + 3}$ **b.** The expression cannot be simplified.   **c.** $\frac{1}{3}$ **5, *p. 536:* a.** $\frac{t - x}{z - 3g}$ **b.** $\frac{4(n - 1)}{n + 2}$
c. $\frac{y - 1}{y + 3}$ **6, *p. 537:* a.** -1 **b.** -3 **c.** $-\frac{3}{n + 5}$
d. $-\frac{3s + 2}{s + 1}$ **7, *p. 538:* a.** $\frac{r}{2}$ **b.** The expression is undefined when $r = 0$.

Exercises 7.1, *p. 539*

1. $x = 0$ **3.** $y = 2$ **5.** $x = -5$ **7.** $n = \frac{1}{2}$ **9.** $x = -1$ or $x = 1$ **11.** $x = -4$ or $x = 5$ **13.** The expressions are equivalent.   **15.** The expressions are equivalent.   **17.** The expressions are not equivalent.   **19.** The expressions are equivalent.   **21.** The expressions are not equivalent.
23. $\frac{5a^3}{6}$ **25.** $\frac{1}{4x^3}$ **27.** $\frac{3t}{2s^2}$ **29.** $8a^3b^3$ **31.** $\frac{p}{5q}$ **33.** $\frac{5}{4}$
35. $-\frac{8x}{3}$ **37.** $x - 2$ **39.** $\frac{x + 1}{2x + 3}$ **41.** $\frac{a}{b}$ **43.** $\frac{2}{3}$
45. $t - 1$ **47.** -1 **49.** $-\frac{1}{2}$ **51.** $\frac{b - 4}{b + 4}$ **53.** $\frac{x + 3}{5}$
55. $\frac{a(a + 7)}{a - 12}$ **57.** $\frac{t + 1}{t + 2}$ **59.** $-\frac{4d + 3}{4d - 3}$ **61.** $-\frac{2s}{2s - 3}$
63. $\frac{2x + 1}{2x - 1}$ **65.** $\frac{2y - 1}{y(2y + 3)}$ **67.** $\frac{2ab}{2b + a}$ **69.** $\frac{m + 7n}{2(m + 6n)}$
71. $u + v$ **73. a.** $x^2 + 7x + 10$ **b.** $x^2 + 2x$
c. $\frac{x^2 + 7x + 10}{x^2 + 2x}, \frac{x + 5}{x}$ **d.** $\frac{13}{8}$ **75. a.** $\frac{\pi r_1^2}{\pi r_2^2 - \pi r_1^2}; \frac{r_1^2}{r_2^2 - r_1^2}$
b. $\frac{\pi r_2^2 - \pi r_1^2}{\pi r_3^2 - \pi r_2^2}; \frac{r_2^2 - r_1^2}{r_3^2 - r_2^2}$

Practices: Section 7.2 *pp. 544–548*

1, *p. 544:* a. $\frac{2n}{7m}$ **b.** $\frac{p}{15q}$ **2, *p. 545:* a.** $\frac{3}{2t}$ **b.** $\frac{2}{6g - 1}$
3, *p. 545:* a. $2(y + 7)(y - 2)$ **b.** $-\frac{x + 5}{x + 1}$ **4, *p. 547:* a.** $\frac{3a}{2b}$
b. $\frac{15}{7p^4q}$ **5, *p. 547:* a.** $\frac{(x + 3)(x + 3)}{(x - 10)(x + 1)}$, or $\frac{(x + 3)^2}{(x - 10)(x + 1)}$
b. $\frac{1}{3}$ **c.** $\frac{y(y + 3)}{5(y + 2)(y - 1)}$ **6, *p. 548:* $\frac{Wv^2}{gr}$

Exercises 7.2, p. 549

1. $\frac{1}{4t}$ 3. $\frac{6}{ab}$ 5. $\frac{10}{3x^9}$ 7. $-\frac{14}{x}$ 9. $\frac{5}{x^3}$ 11. $\frac{8n-3}{n}$ 13. $\frac{4}{5}$

15. $\frac{3(x+2y)}{4}$ 17. $\frac{p^2-1}{p^2-4}$ 19. $\frac{n+3}{n+1}$ 21. $\frac{(2y-1)}{(2y-5)}$ 23. $\frac{16}{x^4}$

25. $3x$ 27. $\frac{1}{2}$ 29. 2 31. $\frac{10}{x}$ 33. $-\frac{3}{t^2}$ 35. $\frac{6y^2}{x^4}$

37. $\frac{(c+3)(c-7)}{(c-5)(c+9)}$ 39. $\frac{5}{12}$ 41. $\frac{1}{2(1-x)}$ 43. $-p$ 45. $\frac{x+y}{5x}$

47. $-\frac{1}{t+2}$ 49. $\frac{x+5}{x+6}$ 51. $\frac{3(p+2)(p-4)}{(p+5)^2}$ 53. $\frac{A-p}{pr}$

55. $\frac{pqB}{10,000}$ 57. $\frac{V^2r}{(R+r)^2}$ 59. a. $\frac{4r}{3h}$ b. $\frac{2r}{h+r}$

c. $\frac{2(h+r)}{3h}$ d. 1

Practices: Section 7.3 pp. 554–564

1, p. 554: a. $\frac{10}{y+2}$ b. $\frac{5r}{s}$ c. 6 d. $3n-1$

2, p. 555: a. $\frac{5}{v}$ b. $\frac{3t}{5}$ c. $-\frac{p}{3q}$ 3, p. 556: a. 2 b. $2x$

c. $-\frac{3}{x-5}$ 4, p. 557: a. LCD $= 20y$ b. LCD $= 6t^2$

c. LCD $= 30x^2y^3$ 5, p. 558: a. LCD $= 2n(n+1)^2$

b. LCD $= (p+2)(p-1)(p+5)$ c. LCD $=$

$(s+2t)^2(s-2t)^2$ 6, p. 559: a. $\frac{4}{14p^3}$ and $\frac{7p^2(p+3)}{14p^3}$

b. $\frac{(3y-2)(y-3)}{(y+3)(y-3)^2}$ and $\frac{y(y+3)}{(y+3)(y-3)^2}$ 7, p. 560: a. $\frac{11}{12p}$

b. $\frac{3y-2}{15y^2}$ 8, p. 561: a. $\frac{9x+6}{x(x+3)} = \frac{3(3x+2)}{x(x+3)}$ b. $\frac{2x-5}{x-1}$

9, p. 562: a. $\frac{9x+4}{4(x-4)(x+4)}$ b. $\frac{x-9}{(x+1)(x-1)}$

10, p. 563: a. $\frac{-3y^2-12y-3}{(y+3)(y+2)(y+1)} = \frac{-3(y^2+4y+1)}{(y+3)(y+2)(y+1)}$

b. $\frac{8x^3+3x^2-20x+5}{20x(x+1)}$ 11, p. 564: $\frac{100(C_1-C_0)}{C_0}$

Exercises 7.3, p. 656

1. $\frac{4a}{3}$ 3. t 5. $\frac{11}{x}$ 7. $\frac{5}{7y}$ 9. $\frac{3x}{y}$ 11. $-\frac{p}{5q}$ 13. $\frac{9}{x+1}$

15. $-\frac{4}{x+2}$ 17. $\frac{a+1}{a+3}$ 19. $\frac{5x+1}{x-8}$ 21. $\frac{4x+1}{5x+2}$ 23. 3

25. 4 27. $\frac{x-4}{x^2-4x-2}$ 29. 1 31. $\frac{-x+7}{3x^2-x+2}$

33. LCD $= 15(x+2)$ 35. LCD $= (p-3)(p+8)(p-8)$

37. LCD $= t(t+3)(t-3)$ 39. LCD $=$

$(t+2)(t+5)(t-5)$ 41. LCD $= (3s-2)(s-3)(s+2)$

43. $\frac{4x}{12x^2}$ and $\frac{15}{12x^2}$ 45. $\frac{35b}{14a^2b}$ and $\frac{2a(a-3)}{14a^2b}$ 47. $\frac{8(n+1)}{n(n+1)^2}$

and $\frac{5n}{n(n+1)^2}$ 49. $\frac{3n(n-1)}{4(n+1)(n-1)}$ and $\frac{8n}{4(n+1)(n-1)}$

51. $\frac{2n(n-3)}{(n+1)(n+5)(n-3)}$ and $\frac{3n(n+1)}{(n+1)(n+5)(n-3)}$

53. $\frac{13}{6x}$ 55. $\frac{4-5x}{6x^2}$ 57. $\frac{-2y+4x}{3x^2y^2} = \frac{-2(y-2x)}{3x^2y^2}$

59. $\frac{2x}{(x+1)(x-1)}$ 61. $\frac{p+39}{21}$ 63. $3x-5$ 65. $\frac{a+6}{6a^2}$

67. $\frac{a^2+1}{a-1}$ 69. -1 71. $\frac{-8x-2}{x(x+1)} = \frac{-2(4x+1)}{x(x+1)}$ 73. $\frac{7x-6}{x-4}$

75. $\frac{11x-6}{(x-1)(x+2)}$ 77. $\frac{n+20}{3(n-3)(n+5)}$ 79. $\frac{3t-4}{(t+5)(t-5)}$

81. $\frac{2x^2+5x-5}{(x+1)^2(x+3)}$ 83. $\frac{6t+5}{(2t+3)(t-1)}$ 85. $\frac{12x^3+17x^2-2}{3x(x-1)(x+1)}$

87. $\frac{5y^2-28y+4}{(3y-1)(y-4)}$ 89. $\frac{-9a^2-11a+32}{4(a+3)^2}$ 91. $\frac{2vt+at^2}{2}$

93. $\frac{1000r}{(1+r)^2}$ dollars 95. The trip took $\frac{30}{r}$ hr.

97. $\frac{3+0.1x}{x}$ dollars

Practices: Section 7.4 pp. 572–577

1, p. 573: a. $\frac{3}{5x^3}$ b. $\frac{8}{x+2}$ 2, p. 574: $\frac{2n-1}{2n+1}$

3, p. 575: a. $2x^2$ b. $\frac{y+3}{2y^3}$ 4, p. 576: a. $\frac{4y^2+y}{4y^2-1}$

b. $\frac{b-a}{10ab}$ 5, p. 577: $\frac{3abc}{bc+ac+ab}$

Exercises 7.4, p. 578

1. $\frac{2}{x}$ 3. $\frac{a+1}{a-1}$ 5. $\frac{x(3x+1)}{3x^2-1}$ 7. $\frac{1}{3d(d+3)}$ 9. $\frac{x-2y}{3x}$

11. $\frac{10-y}{5(5-y)}$ 13. $\frac{x+2}{x+3}$ 15. $\frac{3y+4}{5y+4}$ 17. $\frac{xy^2}{16(y+1)}$

19. $\frac{3(x^2-2x-2)}{x^2(x+1)}$ 21. $\frac{2VR(R+1)}{2R+1}$ 23. $\frac{9E}{I}$ 25. $\frac{2ab}{a+b}$ mph

27. $\frac{w}{\left(1+\frac{h}{6400}\right)^2} = \frac{w}{\left(\frac{6400+h}{6400}\right)^2} = \frac{w}{\frac{(6400+h)^2}{6400^2}} = \frac{6400^2w}{(6400+h)^2}$

Practices: Section 7.5 pp. 582–589

1, p. 582: $\frac{1}{2}$ 2, p. 583: 2, 5 3, p. 584: 2 4, p. 585: 3
5, p. 586: Working together, it will take both pumps $3\frac{3}{4}$ hr
(or 3 hr and 45 min) to fill the tank. 6, p. 587: The speed
of the propeller plane was 150 mph. 7, p. 588:
a. $x = \frac{500}{D-50}$ b. $1.25 per unit

Exercises 7.5, p. 590

1. -3 3. $\frac{1}{2}$ 5. 1 7. 4 9. 14 11. 2 13. $1, 2$
15. 6 17. 2 19. -3 21. $-\frac{7}{2}$ 23. $2, -8$ 25. $4, -1$
27. It will take them 18 min to clean the attic. 29. It
would take the clerical worker 15 hr to finish the job
working alone. 31. The speed on the dry road was
60 mph. 33. $D = \frac{P}{Lp}$

Practices: Section 7.6 pp. 594–599

1, p. 595: 8 2, p. 596: 40 lb of sodium hydroxide are
needed to neutralize 49 lb of sulfuric acid. 3, p. 597: She
would be paying $225 less if she had a $75,000 mortgage at
the same rate. 4, p. 598: The length of DE is 4 in.
5, p. 599: The speed of the plane in still air is 500 mph.

Exercises 7.6, p. 600

1. 8 3. 80 5. 24 7. $-\frac{2}{3}$ 9. 3 11. 5 13. $-4, 4$
15. $8, -4$ 17. $-\frac{6}{5}, 2$ 19. No solution 21. It would
take $8\frac{1}{3}$ min (or 8 min and 20 sec) to print a 25-page report.
23. It will take 16 gal of gas to drive 120 mi. 25. The cyclist's speed was 20 mph. 27. The speed of the bus is 50
mph and the speed of the train is 80 mph. 29. $AB = 8$ ft
31. The height of the tree is 18 feet. 33. There are 8
women at the party.

Review Exercises: Chapter 7, p. 607

1. a. $x = -1$ b. $x = 3$ and $x = -2$ 2. a. Equivalent
b. Equivalent 3. $\frac{3}{5m}$ 4. $\frac{5n-6}{3n+2}$ 5. $-\frac{x+4}{x+2}$ 6. $\frac{2x+5}{3x-1}$

7. $\frac{6n^2}{pm}$ 8. $\frac{1}{2}$ 9. $\frac{x-5}{2x+5}$ 10. -1 11. $\frac{1}{2y}$ 12. $\frac{5(7m-10)}{7(m-10)}$
13. $\frac{y}{5(x+6)}$ 14. $\frac{x+7}{3x+2}$ 15. $\frac{4x}{20x^2}$ and $\frac{3}{20x^2}$

16. $\frac{4(n+4)}{(n-1)(n+4)}$ and $\frac{n(n-1)}{(n-1)(n+4)}$

17. $\frac{x+1}{3(x+3)(x+1)}$ and $\frac{3x}{3(x+3)(x+1)}$

18. $\frac{2(x+2)}{(3x+1)(x-2)(x+2)}$ and $-\frac{3x+1}{(3x+1)(x-2)(x+2)}$ 19. 2

20. 4 21. $\frac{y+4}{2y(2y-1)}$ 22. $\frac{n^2+3n-6}{3n(n+5)}$ 23. $\frac{8x+13}{(x-3)(x+3)}$

24. $\frac{2y+5}{(2+y)(2-y)}$ 25. $\frac{8m-8}{(m+1)(m-3)}$ 26. $\frac{-x^2-3x-11}{(x+3)(x-4)}$

27. $\frac{x^2-9x+2}{(x+2)^2(x-4)}$ 28. $\frac{2n^2+7n+11}{(2n-1)(n-1)(n+3)}$ 29. $\frac{7}{6x}$

30. $\frac{y}{y+9}$ 31. 2 32. $\frac{4x+1}{2x-3}$ 33. 7 34. $\frac{1}{2}$ 35. -3
36. $3, -1$ 37. -1 38. 2 39. 45 40. 33 41. $\frac{1}{8}$

42. $4, -9$ **43.** $\frac{0.72x + 200}{x}$ dollars **44.** The total cost of the car rental is $200. **45.** $\frac{2rs}{s + r}$ **46.** It will take 30 min to fill the tub. **47.** The family drove 100 miles at 50 mph.
48. $\frac{2x + 1}{x(x + 1)}$ of the job will be done in an hour. **49.** She should expect to spend about $41,333.
50. $\frac{3n^2 + 6n + 2}{n(n + 1)(n + 2)}$

Posttest: Chapter 7, *p. 620*

1. The expression is undefined when $x = 8$.
2. $-\frac{3y - y^2}{y^2} = -\frac{y(3 - y)}{y^2} = -\frac{\overset{1}{y}(3 - y)}{\underset{y}{y^2}} = \frac{-(3 - y)}{y} = \frac{y - 3}{y}$
3. $\frac{5a^2}{4b}$ **4.** $\frac{x}{y}$ **5.** $\frac{3(b - 3)}{(b - 7)}$ **6.** $\frac{1}{x + 3}$
7. $\frac{4(4n - 1)}{4(n + 8)(n - 2)}$, $\frac{8(n - 2)}{4(n + 8)(n - 2)}$, and $\frac{n(n + 8)}{4(n + 8)(n - 2)}$ **8.** 2
9. $\frac{3y + 1}{2y(y - 4)}$ **10.** $\frac{4d + 14}{(d - 3)(d + 2)} = \frac{2(2d + 7)}{(d - 3)(d + 2)}$
11. $\frac{2x^2 + 6x + 10}{(2x + 1)(x - 2)(x + 2)} = \frac{2(x^2 + 3x + 5)}{(2x + 1)(x - 2)(x + 2)}$
12. $\frac{1}{18n(n - 1)}$ **13.** $\frac{a + 5}{a + 4}$ **14.** $\frac{2(x + 4)(x + 2)}{x - 1}$ **15.** 6
16. -14 **17.** $2, -3$ **18.** $R_1 = \frac{RR_2}{R_2 - R}$ **19.** Working alone, the newer machine can process 1000 pieces of mail in 30 min and the older machine can process 1000 pieces of mail in 60 min. **20.** The height of the tree is 60 m.

Cumulative Review: Chapter 7, *p. 612*

1. $2y - 3$ **2.** $n > -3$;
3.
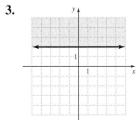
4. $(3, 5)$ **5.** $-5, 2$ **6.** $(10y + 9)(10y - 9)$ **7.** $-3, 2$
8. She should invest $7500 in the fund at 4% and $15,000 in the fund at 6% **9.** It will take the Reston bus 4 hr to overtake the Arlington bus. **10.** It would take about 9 min to print a 20-page report.

Chapter 8

Pretest: Chapter 8, *p. 614*

1. 9 **2.** $-3\sqrt{3}$ **3.** $3a\sqrt{5}$ **4.** $\frac{\sqrt{x}}{8}$ **5.** $4\sqrt{2}$
6. $12\sqrt{3}$ **7.** $5x\sqrt{x}$ **8.** $3\sqrt{2}$ **9.** $2xy^2\sqrt{5}$ **10.** $\sqrt{6}$
11. $n + 2\sqrt{n}$ **12.** $-1 + 3\sqrt{3}$ **13.** $\frac{\sqrt{30x}}{6}$ **14.** $2x\sqrt{5}$
15. $\frac{8\sqrt{2} + \sqrt{14}}{2}$ **16.** 36 **17.** $1, 3$ **18.** The velocity of the car is 20 m/sec. **19.** The gymnast covers $12\sqrt{2}$ m, or approximately 17.0 m in the tumbling sequence.
20. $L = \frac{S^2}{30f}$

Practices: Section 8.1 *pp. 615–622*

1, *p. 616:* **a.** 2 **b.** -35 **2,** *p. 616:* 3.162 **3,** *p. 617:*
a. 6 **b.** 5 **c.** 7 **d.** 1 **4,** *p. 618:* **a.** x^2 **b.** $8t^5$
c. $-11xy$ **5,** *p. 619:* **a.** $6\sqrt{2}$ **b.** $4\sqrt{10}$ **c.** $\frac{\sqrt{3}}{3}$

6, *p. 620:* **a.** $x\sqrt{x}$ **b.** $3n^2\sqrt{2}$ **c.** $-5b\sqrt{2a}$ **7,** *p. 620:*
a. $\frac{1}{4}$ **b.** $\frac{y}{2}$ **c.** $\frac{x^2}{y^3}$ **8,** *p. 621:* **a.** $\frac{\sqrt{3}}{4}$ **b.** $\frac{\sqrt{2y}}{7}$ **c.** $\frac{x^3y\sqrt{5x}}{2}$
9, *p. 622:* 1000 lb

Exercises 8.1, *p. 623*

1. 6 **3.** 1 **5.** -10 **7.** 21 **9.** 2.236 **11.** 4.243
13. 16 **15.** 11 **17.** $5x$ **19.** 2 **21.** 9 **23.** n^4 **25.** $7y$
27. $3x^2$ **29.** $5xy^5$ **31.** $4\sqrt{2}$ **33.** $-6\sqrt{3}$ **35.** $18\sqrt{3}$
37. $\frac{\sqrt{3}}{3}$ **39.** $x\sqrt{11}$ **41.** $n^2\sqrt{n}$ **43.** $2x\sqrt{5x}$
45. $2p\sqrt{3q}$ **47.** $9xy^2\sqrt{10x}$ **49.** $\frac{2}{5}$ **51.** $-\frac{1}{2}$ **53.** $\frac{9}{n^3}$
55. $\frac{x^2}{y}$ **57.** $\frac{\sqrt{3}}{2}$ **59.** $\frac{\sqrt{5n}}{4}$ **61.** $\frac{xy^3\sqrt{3}}{2}$ **63.** $\frac{3x^3\sqrt{3y}}{4}$
65. a. $m = \sqrt{a \cdot b}$ **b.** $m = 4$ **67. a.** It takes the object 2 sec to reach the ground. **b.** No; $\sqrt{\frac{40}{5}} = \sqrt{8} = 2\sqrt{2}$, which is not equal to $2 \cdot 2$. **69.** The car was traveling at a speed of 60 mph at the time of the accident. **71.** The distance between the towns is $\sqrt{146}$ mi, or about 12 mi.

Practices: Section 8.2 *pp. 628–630*

1, *p. 628:* **a.** $6\sqrt{5}$ **b.** $11\sqrt{n}$ **c.** $11\sqrt{t^2 - 3}$
d. Cannot be combined because they are not like radicals
2, *p. 629:* **a.** $12\sqrt{2}$ **b.** $-6\sqrt{3}$ **c.** $-9\sqrt{t}$
d. $12b^2\sqrt{a}$ **3,** *p. 630:* The length of the front yard is $20\sqrt{2}$ m, or approximately 28 m.

Exercises 8.2, *p. 631*

1. $8\sqrt{7}$ **3.** $-5\sqrt{2}$ **5.** Cannot be combined
7. $-13\sqrt{11}$ **9.** $9t\sqrt{3}$ **11.** $23\sqrt{x}$ **13.** $5\sqrt{x + 1}$
15. $-2\sqrt{2}$ **17.** $11\sqrt{2}$ **19.** $3\sqrt{3}$ **21.** $26\sqrt{3}$
23. $11\sqrt{2} - 6\sqrt{3}$ **25.** $14\sqrt{y}$ **27.** $(3 - 4x)\sqrt{x}$
29. $14\sqrt{p}$
31. $(-5x^2y^2 + x^3y)\sqrt{2x}$ or $(x^3y - 5x^2y^2)\sqrt{2x}$
33. a. Each missing side measures $\sqrt{61}$ units.
b. The perimeter of the triangle is $10 + 2\sqrt{61}$ units.
35. a. $3\sqrt{10}$ in. and $2\sqrt{10}$ in. **b.** The larger tile is $\sqrt{10}$ in. longer. **37.** The manufacturer will charge $90\sqrt{10}$ more dollars for 4000 machine parts than for 1000 machine parts.

Practices: Section 8.3 *pp. 635–644*

1, *p. 635:* **a.** 5 **b.** $2y^3$ **c.** $t + 1$ **2,** *p. 635:* **a.** $\sqrt{70}$
b. $-108\sqrt{2}$ **c.** $4y^3$ **3,** *p. 636:* **a.** $9\sqrt{2} - 4\sqrt{3}$
b. $\sqrt{ab} + 3\sqrt{a}$ **4,** *p. 636:* **a.** $2 + 2\sqrt{3}$
b. $3x + 4\sqrt{x} - 4$ **5,** *p. 637:* **a.** -2 **b.** $p - q$
6, *p. 638:* **a.** $2 + 2b\sqrt{2} + b^2$ or $b^2 + 2b\sqrt{2} + 2$
b. $x - 12\sqrt{x} + 36$ **7,** *p. 638:* It takes Mercury about 93 twenty-four-hr days to revolve around the Sun.
8, *p. 639:* **a.** $\sqrt{7}$ **b.** $2x^2$ **c.** $\frac{1}{20y^2}$ **9,** *p. 639:* **a.** $\frac{m^2\sqrt{m}}{n^2}$
b. $\frac{y^3}{5x}$ **c.** $\frac{a\sqrt{5}}{3}$ **10,** *p. 640:* **a.** $\frac{\sqrt{2}}{2}$ **b.** $\frac{\sqrt{5s}}{s}$ **c.** $\frac{7r^2\sqrt{3}}{6}$
11, *p. 640:* **a.** $\frac{\sqrt{6}}{6}$ **b.** $\frac{\sqrt{5n}}{10}$ **12,** *p. 642:* **a.** $\frac{\sqrt{15} - \sqrt{3}}{3}$
b. $\frac{\sqrt{bc} + 2\sqrt{b}}{b}$ **13,** *p. 643:* **a.** $\frac{24 + 8\sqrt{2}}{7}$ **b.** $\frac{a\sqrt{b} - a\sqrt{5}}{b - 5}$
14, *p. 644:* $\frac{295\sqrt{2}}{6}$ beats per min, or approximately 70 beats per min

Exercises 8.3, *p. 645*

1. 21 **3.** $3n$ **5.** $16x - 16$ **7.** $3\sqrt{6}$ **9.** $-70\sqrt{2}$

11. $4x^2$ **13.** $r\sqrt{15}$ **15.** $10\sqrt{xy}$ **17.** $3 - \sqrt{3}$

19. $x - 7\sqrt{x}$ **21.** $4\sqrt{ab} + \sqrt{a}$ **23.** $11 + 5\sqrt{5}$

25. $118 - 11\sqrt{3}$ **27.** $3n + 14\sqrt{n} - 5$ **29.** 33 **31.** 13

33. $x - 4$ **35.** $a - b$ **37.** $3x - y$ **39.** $2 - 2x\sqrt{2} + x^2$

41. $x - 2\sqrt{x} + 1$ **43.** $\sqrt{5}$ **45.** $\frac{1}{5}$ **47.** $2a$ **49.** $\frac{4}{3y^2}$

51. $\frac{a^2}{b^3}$ **53.** $\frac{4x^6}{y^4}$ **55.** $\frac{x^5\sqrt{5}}{6}$ **57.** $\frac{2\sqrt{3}}{3}$ **59.** $\frac{\sqrt{5y}}{y}$

61. $\frac{\sqrt{22}}{11}$ **63.** $\frac{x\sqrt{5}}{5}$ **65.** $\frac{\sqrt{2t}}{10}$ **67.** $\frac{\sqrt{2a}}{2}$ **69.** $\frac{\sqrt{15} + 2\sqrt{3}}{3}$

71. $\frac{\sqrt{mn} - \sqrt{m}}{m}$ **73.** $\frac{12 - 3\sqrt{6}}{2}$ **75.** $4 + \sqrt{5}$

77. $2\sqrt{5} + 2\sqrt{3}$ **79.** $\frac{a\sqrt{b} + a\sqrt{3}}{b - 3}$ **81.** 72 square

centimeters **83.** The distance from $(0, 0)$ to $(3, 5)$ is $\sqrt{34}$,

and the distance from $(0, 0)$ to $(6, 10)$ is $2\sqrt{34}$.

85. It will take the hailstone $\frac{5\sqrt{5}}{2}$ sec, or about 5.6 sec to

drop 500 ft. **87.** $\frac{\sqrt{\pi h V}}{\pi h}$

Practices: Section 8.4 *pp. 651–655*

1, *p. 651:* 16 **2,** *p. 652:* No solution **3,** *p. 652:* 9

4, *p. 653:* 2, 3 **5,** *p. 653:* 4, 5 **6,** *p. 654:* A radius of

1000 ft will permit a maximum safe speed of 50 mph.

7, *p. 655:* $\frac{2}{3}d^2 = h$ or $h = \frac{2}{3}d^2$

Exercises 8.4, *p. 656*

1. 9 **3.** 32 **5.** No solution **7.** 64 **9.** 6 **11.** 3 **13.** 2

15. 3 **17.** No solution **19.** 5 **21.** 0 **23.** -2 **25.** 8

27. No solution **29.** $-1, 2$ **31.** 8, 17 **33.** No solution

35. 3 **37.** Its power is 2500 watts. **39.** A mass of $\frac{8}{\pi^2}$ g

will produce a period of 2 sec. **41.** $p = \frac{f^2}{14,400}$

Review Exercises: Chapter 8, *p. 661*

1. -7 **2.** 6 **3.** $7x$ **4.** $2\sqrt{7}$ **5.** $-9\sqrt{2}$ **6.** $4x\sqrt{2x}$

7. $\frac{3}{5}$ **8.** $-\frac{\sqrt{3t}}{4}$ **9.** $\frac{12}{x^{50}}$ **10.** $10a^2b\sqrt{ab}$ **11.** $3\sqrt{5}$

12. $8\sqrt{n}$ **13.** $x\sqrt{3}$ **14.** $-7\sqrt{3}$ **15.** $5x\sqrt{x}$

16. $7\sqrt{2a}$ **17.** $\sqrt{15}$ **18.** $4n$ **19.** $5ab^3\sqrt{2a}$

20. $x - 4\sqrt{x}$ **21.** 6 **22.** $2y - \sqrt{y} - 3$

23. $y + 10\sqrt{y} + 25$ **24.** 3 **25.** $\frac{1}{2}$ **26.** 4 **27.** $2a\sqrt{3a}$

28. $\frac{2\sqrt{11}}{11}$ **29.** $\frac{\sqrt{2x}}{2}$ **30.** 9 **31.** $\frac{5\sqrt{7} + 5}{3}$ **32.** 64 **33.** $\frac{15}{2}$

34. 5 **35.** 8 **36.** The area of the city block is 5000 sq ft.

37. You can see approximately 2 mi. **38.** No; an 8-in.

screwdriver will not fit diagonally in the box. **39.** 64 sq m

40. $r = \frac{\sqrt{S\pi}}{2\pi}$ **41. a.** $D = \frac{2\pi r}{2\sqrt{\pi(\pi r^2)}} = \frac{2\pi r}{2\pi r} = 1$

b. $D = \frac{L\sqrt{\pi A}}{2\pi A}$ **c.** $A = \frac{L^2}{4\pi(1.58)^2}$ **42.** $\frac{\sqrt{15V}}{15}$

Posttest: Chapter 8, *p. 664*

1. 12 **2.** $-9\sqrt{2}$ **3.** $4x\sqrt{2xy}$ **4.** $\frac{\sqrt{5n}}{4}$ **5.** $3\sqrt{x}$

6. $-15\sqrt{2}$ **7.** $10t\sqrt{t}$ **8.** $2\sqrt{6}$ **9.** $5x^2y\sqrt{x}$ **10.** 5

11. $5y - \sqrt{y}$ **12.** $19 + 8\sqrt{3}$ **13.** $\frac{\sqrt{10p}}{5}$ **14.** $2x\sqrt{6x}$

15. $\sqrt{2} - 3\sqrt{5}$ **16.** 7 **17.** 2 **18.** The windchill tem-

perature is 28°F. **19.** The length of the ladder is $6\sqrt{17}$ft.

20. The length of the rectangle is 16 in.

Cumulative Review: Chapter 8, *p. 666*

1. $\frac{2}{3}$ **2.**

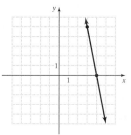

Slope: -5

3. The system has one solution. **4.** $16x^3 - 4x^2 - 12x + 3$

5. $(y - 4)(y - 8)$ **6.** $\frac{10c + 6}{(c - 2)(c + 1)} = \frac{2(5c + 3)}{(c - 2)(c + 1)}$ **7.** -2

8. The speed is 343 meters per second when the tempera-

ture is 20°C. **9.** The balance of payments (in billions of

dollars) can be modeled by the polynomial $-2x^2 - 11x -$

87. **10.** The distance from the camp to the waterfall is

$100\sqrt{514}$ m, or approximately 2267 m.

Chapter 9

Pretest: Chapter 9, *p. 670*

1. $3\sqrt{2}, -3\sqrt{2}$ **2.** $r = \frac{1}{2}\sqrt{\frac{A}{\pi}} = \frac{\sqrt{A\pi}}{2\pi}$ **3.** 36

4. $2 + \sqrt{2}, 2 - \sqrt{2}$ **5.** $\frac{1 + \sqrt{11}}{2}, \frac{1 - \sqrt{11}}{2}$ **6.** 11, 1

7. $-3, -4$ **8.** $3 + \sqrt{5}, 3 - \sqrt{5}$ **9.** $\sqrt{3}, -\sqrt{3}$

10. $\frac{5 + 3\sqrt{5}}{5}, \frac{5 - 3\sqrt{5}}{5}$ **11.** $-2 + 3\sqrt{2}, -2 - 3\sqrt{2}$

12.

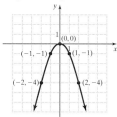

13. vertex: $(3, -2)$; axis of symmetry: $x = 3$

14.

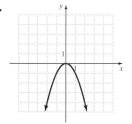

15.

16.

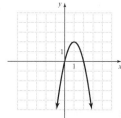

17. a. $v = \sqrt{2as}$ **b.** The velocity of the car is approxi-

mately 17 m per sec. **18.** 3-in. by 3-in. squares should be

cut from the corners to meet the specifications. **19.** The

speed of the plane in still air is 150 mph.

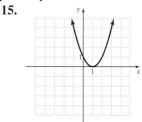

20. a.

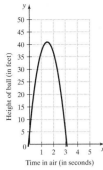

Height of ball (in feet) — y-axis, Time in air (in seconds) — x-axis

b. The ball reaches a maximum height of 41 ft.

Practices: Section 9.1 *pp. 672–676*

1, *p. 672:* **a.** $10, -10$ **b.** $3\sqrt{2}, -3\sqrt{2}$ **c.** $\frac{5}{9}, -\frac{5}{9}$

2, *p. 673:* **a.** $1, -5$ **b.** $4 + \sqrt{5}, 4 - \sqrt{5}$

c. $\frac{1 + 3\sqrt{6}}{4}, \frac{1 - 3\sqrt{6}}{4}$ **3,** *p. 674:* $-4 + \sqrt{2}, -4 - \sqrt{2}$

4, *p. 675:* **a.** $c = \sqrt{\frac{E}{m}} = \frac{\sqrt{Em}}{m}$ **b.** $a = \sqrt{c^2 - b^2}$

5, *p. 675:* **a.** $t = \frac{\sqrt{d}}{4}$ **b.** It takes the object 5 sec to fall 400 ft. **6,** *p. 676:* **a.** $d = 4 + \sqrt{B}$ **b.** 8 in.

Exercises 9.1, *p. 677*

1. $3, -3$ **3.** $\sqrt{2}, -\sqrt{2}$ **5.** $\frac{1}{2}, -\frac{1}{2}$ **7.** $2, -2$
9. $\sqrt{7}, -\sqrt{7}$ **11.** $2\sqrt{3}, -2\sqrt{3}$ **13.** $4\sqrt{5}, -4\sqrt{5}$
15. $\sqrt{6}, -\sqrt{6}$ **17.** $\sqrt{17}, -\sqrt{17}$ **19.** $\frac{3}{2}, -\frac{3}{2}$
21. $\frac{\sqrt{3}}{2}, -\frac{\sqrt{3}}{2}$ **23.** $1, -5$ **25.** $14, 0$
27. $-6 + \sqrt{5}, -6 - \sqrt{5}$ **29.** $\frac{17}{4}, \frac{23}{4}$ **31.** $7, 1$
33. $5 + \sqrt{3}, 5 - \sqrt{3}$ **35.** $-1 + 2\sqrt{2}, -1 - 2\sqrt{2}$
37. $\frac{1}{3}, -1$ **39.** $\frac{-5 + \sqrt{3}}{4}, \frac{-5 - \sqrt{3}}{4}$ **41.** $\frac{7 + 2\sqrt{5}}{2}, \frac{7 - 2\sqrt{5}}{2}$
43. $10 + 2\sqrt{10}, 10 - 2\sqrt{10}$ **45.** No solution
47. $-8 + \sqrt{5}, -8 - \sqrt{5}$ **49.** $3 + 2\sqrt{6}, 3 - 2\sqrt{6}$
51. $\sqrt{5}, -\sqrt{5}$ **53.** $x = \pm\sqrt{\frac{b}{a}}$ **55.** $v = \pm\frac{2\pi}{\sqrt{Kr}}$
57. $y = \pm\frac{5\sqrt{x^2 - 16}}{4}$ **59.** They can hear each other for 4 min. **61. a.** $t = \sqrt{\frac{2s}{a}}$ **b.** 2 sec **63.** $y = \pm\sqrt{r^2 - x^2}$
65. $d = 45\sqrt{\frac{2}{l}}$

Practices: Section 9.2 *pp. 682–687*

1, *p. 683:* **a.** 36 **b.** $\frac{25}{4}$ **2,** *p. 684:* **a.** $3, -7$
b. $\frac{-7 + \sqrt{29}}{2}, \frac{-7 - \sqrt{29}}{2}$ **3,** *p. 685:* **a.** $4 + 2\sqrt{5}, 4 - 2\sqrt{5}$
b. $\frac{1 + \sqrt{2}}{2}, \frac{1 - \sqrt{2}}{2}$ **4,** *p. 686:* $\frac{4}{3}, -\frac{1}{3}$ **5,** *p. 686:* **a.** The length of the table is $2w - 1$. **b.** The length is 8 ft and the width is 4.5 ft.

Exercises 9.2, *p. 688*

1. 9 **3.** 25 **5.** $\frac{25}{4}$ **7.** $\frac{1}{4}$ **9.** $0, -4$
11. $5 + 2\sqrt{6}, 5 - 2\sqrt{6}$ **13.** $1, -15$
15. $3 + \sqrt{13}, 3 - \sqrt{13}$ **17.** No real solution
19. $\frac{1 + \sqrt{13}}{2}, \frac{1 - \sqrt{13}}{2}$ **21.** $2, -6$

23. $-1 + \frac{\sqrt{66}}{6}, -1 - \frac{\sqrt{66}}{6}$ **25.** $\frac{5 + 3\sqrt{2}}{2}, \frac{5 - 3\sqrt{2}}{2}$
27. $\frac{3 + \sqrt{73}}{8}, \frac{3 - \sqrt{73}}{8}$ **29.** $1 + \sqrt{5}, 1 - \sqrt{5}$

31. There are 51 insects after 3 days. **33. a.** The fireworks will be 16 ft above the ground 1 sec after being shot into the air. **b.** They will be 8 ft above the ground in approximately 0.3 sec and again in 1.7 sec. **35.** One friend was 6 mi from the party and the other was 8 mi from the party. **37.** It would take the faster machine about 7 min to do the job alone.

Practices: Section 9.3 *pp. 692–697*

1, *p. 693:* **a.** $1, 0$ **b.** No real solution **2,** *p. 695:*

a. $\frac{4 + \sqrt{31}}{5}, \frac{4 - \sqrt{31}}{5}$ **b.** $\frac{-3 + \sqrt{93}}{6}, \frac{-3 - \sqrt{93}}{6}$ **3,** *p. 696:* 2.5, -0.5 **4,** *p. 696:* Working alone, it takes one pump about 4.4 hr and the other about 9.4 hr to empty the tank.

Exercises 9.3, *p. 698*

	Standard Form	$a =$	$b =$	$c =$
1.	$2x^2 = 9x - 1 = 0$	2	9	-1
3.	$-x^2 + 3x - 8 = 0$	-1	3	-8
5.	$x^2 - x + 8 = 0$	1	-1	8
7.	$\frac{1}{3}y^2 - \frac{1}{2}y + \frac{1}{4} = 0$	$\frac{1}{3}$	$-\frac{1}{2}$	$\frac{1}{4}$
9.	$6x^2 - 7x - 155 = 0$	6	-7	-15

11. $1, -3$ **13.** No real solution **15.** $-1, 7$
17. $2 + \sqrt{5}, 2 - \sqrt{5}$ **19.** $1, \frac{1}{3}$ **21.** $\frac{3 + \sqrt{5}}{4}, \frac{3 - \sqrt{5}}{4}$
23. $6, -\frac{5}{2}$ **25.** $-1, -2$ **27.** $-1, -3$ **29.** $0, \frac{2}{3}$
31. $-1, \frac{1}{4}$ **33.** $\frac{7 + \sqrt{29}}{2}, \frac{7 - \sqrt{29}}{2}$ **35.** $\frac{1 + 7\sqrt{5}}{2}, \frac{1 - 7\sqrt{5}}{2}$
37. No real solution **39.** $\frac{3 + \sqrt{3}}{2}, \frac{3 - \sqrt{3}}{2}$ **41.** n is 13.
43. Working alone, it takes the lab coordinator about 91 min to set up the lab and it takes the lab technician about 71 min to set up the lab. **45.** The speed of the car was approximately 27 mph. **47.** The value of the index was approximately 1000 in 1998.

Practices: Section 9.4 *pp. 702–707*

1, *p. 703:*

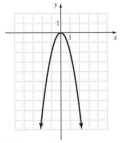

2, p. 704:

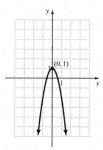

3, p. 705: a.

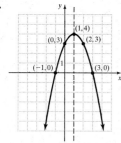

b. The graph of the parabola opens downward since $a = -1$ is negative. The curve turns at the point $(1, 4)$, the highest point of the graph. The equation of the axis of symmetry is $x = 1$. **4, p. 707:**

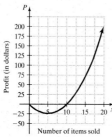

Selling 5 items results in the most money lost ($25).

Exercises 9.4, p. 708

1.

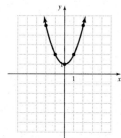

3.

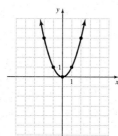

5.

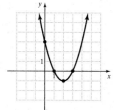

7. Axis of symmetry: $x = 0$; vertex: $(0, 0)$ **9.** Axis of symmetry: $x = 2$; vertex: $(2, 1)$

11.

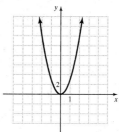

13.

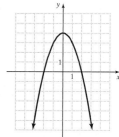

15.

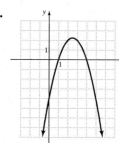

17.

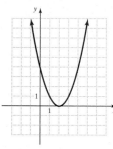

19.

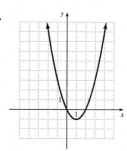

21.

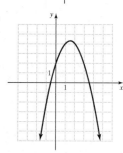

23.

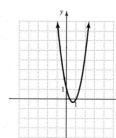

25.

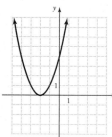

27.

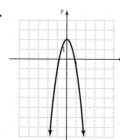

29.

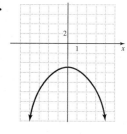

31. a. The perimeter of the rectangle is 80 and the length is x. The width is found by solving $2x + 2w = 80$. So the width is $40 - x$. The area then is length times width, which is $x(40 - x)$ sq ft. **b.**

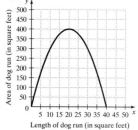

c. The area is a maximum (400 sq ft) when the length is 20 ft.   **33. a.**

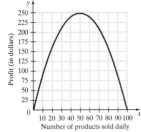

b. The company must sell 50 products each day to maximize the profit.

c. The height of the graph increases when 0 to 50 products are sold but then decreases for sales of more than 50 products.   **35. a.** $R = x\left(100 - \frac{1}{4}x\right) = 100x - \frac{1}{4}x^2$

b.

x	0	100	200	300	400
R	0	7500	10,000	7500	0

c.

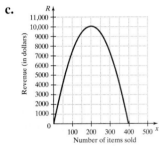

c. The store should sell 200 items to maximize the revenue.

d. The maximum revenue is $10,000.

Review Exercises: Chapter 9, p. 721

1. $2\sqrt{6}, -2\sqrt{6}$ **2.** $\sqrt{3}, -\sqrt{3}$ **3.** No real solution

4. $\frac{5 + 3\sqrt{2}}{2}, \frac{5 - 3\sqrt{2}}{2}$ **5.** $r = \sqrt{\frac{A}{\pi}}$

6. $c = \sqrt{\frac{E}{m}}$ **7.** 25   **8.** $\frac{49}{4}$ **9.** $9, -3$ **10.** $1, -4$

11. $-2 + \sqrt{6}, -2 - \sqrt{6}$ **12.** $\frac{1 + \sqrt{2}}{2}, \frac{1 - \sqrt{2}}{2}$

13. $1 + \sqrt{2}, 1 - \sqrt{2}$ **14.** $-4 + \sqrt{15}, -4 - \sqrt{15}$

15. $\frac{-1 + \sqrt{41}}{4}, \frac{-1 - \sqrt{41}}{4}$ **16.** No real solution   **17.** $-5, 0$

18. $\sqrt{6}, -\sqrt{6}$ **19.**

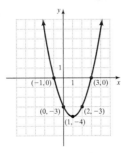

20.

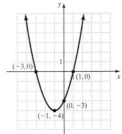

21. Axis of symmetry: $x = -2$; vertex: $(-2, -4)$

22. Axis of symmetry: $x = -1$; vertex: $(-1, 4)$

23.   **24.**

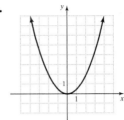 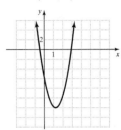

25.   **26.**

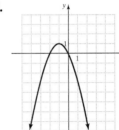 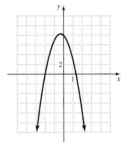

27. The radius of the sphere is approximately 7.0 in.

28. The company had sold either 40 rugs or 50 rugs since the profit is $2000 for both.   **29.** The banner is approximately 2.2 ft by 9.3 ft.   **30.** The building has 7 sides.

31. a.

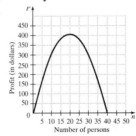

b. The profit per person if 16 people go is $384.   **c.** Either 13 people or 27 people went to the Bahamas since the profit is $351 for both.   **d.** The maximum profit per person that the agency can make is $400 (when 20 people go to the Bahamas).   **32. a.**

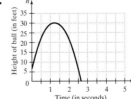

b. The ball reaches its maximum height in $\frac{5}{4}$, or 1.25 sec.

c. The maximum height of the ball is 31 ft.   **33.** Working alone, it would take the experienced Web designer 4 days to develop the Web site and it would take the inexperienced designer 12 days to develop the Web site.   **34.** Her average speed driving to work is approximately 36 mph.

Posttest: Chapter 9, *p. 725*

1. $-1 + 2\sqrt{2}, -1 - 2\sqrt{2}$ **2.** $r = \sqrt{\frac{3V}{\pi h}}$ **3.** $\frac{1}{4}$

4. $\frac{3 + \sqrt{13}}{2}, \frac{3 - \sqrt{13}}{2}$ **5.** $\frac{-3 + \sqrt{41}}{4}, \frac{-3 - \sqrt{41}}{4}$

6. $2\sqrt{3}, -2\sqrt{3}$ **7.** $4, -10$ **8.** $\frac{27}{5}, \frac{13}{5}$ **9.** $\frac{2 + \sqrt{7}}{2}, \frac{2 - \sqrt{7}}{2}$

10. $\frac{-4 + 2\sqrt{7}}{3}, \frac{-4 - 2\sqrt{7}}{3}$ **11.** $4 + \sqrt{15}, 4 - \sqrt{15}$

12.

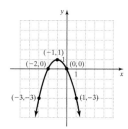

13. Vertex: $\left(-\frac{3}{2}, \frac{7}{4}\right)$; axis of symmetry $x = -\frac{3}{2}$

14.   **15.**

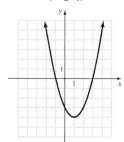   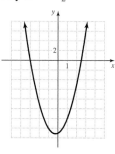

16.

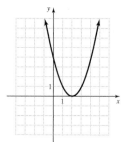

17. a. $t = \frac{\sqrt{l}}{0.9}$ **b.** The period of the pendulum is approximately 2 sec.   **c.** The period of the pendulum is approximately 10. 5 sec.   **18.** The width of the garden is about 2.2 yd and the length is about 10.6 yd.   **19.** $x = 5$ in.

20. a.

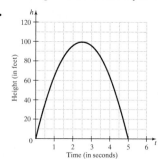

b. The object reaches a maximum height of 100 ft (when $t = 2.5$ sec)

Cumulative Review: Chapter 9, *p. 728*

1. -8 **2.** $-72x - 110$ **3.** $18n^2 + 3n - 10$

4. $3cd(2c + d)(c + d)$ **5.** $\frac{2x^2}{3(y - 2)}$ **6.** $-3, 2$

7. a.

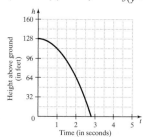

b. The sandbag has fallen 16 ft. At $t = 0$, the sandbag is at a height of 128 ft above the ground and at 1 sec the sandbag has fallen to a height of 112 ft above the ground. So it has fallen a total of $(128 - 112)$ ft, or 16 ft.

8. a. $n = \frac{5}{6}t + 2$ **b.**

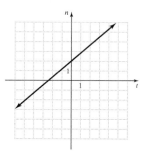

c. The slope of the graph, $\frac{5}{6}$, represents the rate of increase in the number of employees (5 employees every 6 months). In the equation it is the coefficient of t.   **9.** For $x = 0$, the number of bacteria is 400; for $x = 1$, the number of bacteria is 1200; for $x = 2$, the number of bacteria is 3600.

10. $xy\sqrt{y}$

Appendix A.3

Practices: *pp. 735–736*

1, *p. 735*: a. The binomial is a difference of cubes.   **b.** The binomial is a sum of cubes.   **c.** The binomial is a sum of cubes.   **d.** The binomial is a difference of cubes.

2, *p. 736*: a. $(r + s)(r^2 - rs + s^2)$

b. $(y - 4)(y^2 + 4y + 16)$

3, *p. 736*: a. $(5 - x)(15 + 5x + x^2)$

b. $5(n - 2)(n^2 + 2n + 4)$ **c.** $2n(1 + 3n)(1 - 3n + 9n^2)$

Exercises A.3, *p. 738*

1. $(y - 1)(y^2 - y + 1)$ **2.** $(t - 2)(t^2 + 2t + 4)$

3. $(p + q)(p^2 - pq + q^2)$ **4.** Cannot be factored.

5. $(x + y^2)(x^2 - xy^2 + y^4)$ **6.** $(a - b)(a^2 + ab + b^2)$

7. $(n + 2)(n^2 - 2n + 4)$ **8.** $(x + 3)(x^2 - 3x + 9)$

9. Cannot be factored.   **10.** $(2 - x^2)(4 + 2x^2 + x^4)$

11. $(3n + 1)(9n^2 - 3n + 1)$ **12.** Cannot be factored.

13. $5(x - 1)(x^2 - x + 1)$ **14.** $3(x - 2)(x^2 + 2x + 4)$

15. $2(p + 3)(p^2 - 3p + 9)$ **16.** $2n^3(4 + n)(16 - 4n + n^2)$

17. $x^3(x - 5)(x^2 + 5x + 25)$ **18.** $x^3(2 + x)(4 - 2x + x^2)$

Glossary

The numbers in brackets following each glossary term represent the section in which that term is discussed.

absolute value [1.1] The distance between a number and zero on the number line.

addition property of equality [2.1] A property which allows us to add any real number to each side of an equation, resulting in an equivalent equation.

additive identity property [1.2] A property which states that the sum of a number and 0 is that number.

additive inverse property [1.2] A property which states that the sum of a number and its opposite is 0.

associative property of addition [1.2] A property which states that when adding three numbers, re-grouping the addends does not affect the sum.

associative property of multiplication [1.4] A property which states that when multiplying three numbers, regrouping the factors does not affect the product.

axis of symmetry [9.4] The vertical line that passes through the vertex of a parabola.

base (exponent) [1.6] The number that is a repeated factor when written with an exponent.

binomial [5.3] A polynomial with two terms.

break-even point [4.1] The point at which the income for a business equals its expenses.

coefficient [1.8, 5.3] The constant factor of a term.

common factor [6.1] For two or more integers, an integer that is a factor of each integer.

common multiple [R.2] A number that is a multiple of two or more numbers is called a common multiple.

commutative property of addition [1.2] A property which allows us to add two numbers in any order getting the same sum.

commutative property of multiplication [1.4] A property which states that when we multiply two numbers in either order, we get the same product.

completing the square [9.2] A method for solving quadratic equations that involves taking square roots and factoring perfect square trinomials.

complex rational expression (complex algebraic fraction) [7.4] A rational expression that contains a rational expression in its numerator, denominator, or both.

composite number [R.2] A whole number that has more than two factors.

conjugate of $a + b$ [8.3] $a - b$.

constant term [5.3] In a polynomial, the term of degree 0.

coordinate plane [3.1] The flat surface on which we draw graphs.

decimal [R.4] A number written with three parts: a whole number, the decimal point, and a fraction whose denominator is a power of 10.

decimal place [R.4] The place to the right of the decimal point.

degree of a monomial [5.3] The power of the variable in the monomial.

degree of a polynomial [5.3] The highest degree of its terms.

demand curve [4.1] A curve which illustrates that when the price of an item increases, the quantity of items sold declines. It is commonly approximated by a straight line with a negative slope.

denominator [R.3] The number below the fraction line that stands for the number of parts into which the whole is divided.

difference of squares [6.4] An expression in the form $a^2 - b^2$, which can be factored as $(a + b)(a - b)$.

distributive property [1.8] A property which states that multiplying a factor by the sum of two numbers gives us the same result as multiplying the factor by each of the two numbers and then adding.

elimination (or addition) method [4.3] A method used to solve a system of equations that is based on the property of equality which states: If $a = b$ and $c = d$, then $a + c = b + d$.

equation [2.1] A mathematical statement that two expressions are equal.

equilibrium [4.1] The point of intersection of the supply curve and the demand curve where all items produced are sold and all customers are satisfied.

equivalent equations [2.1] Equations that have the same solution.

equivalent fractions [R.3] Fractions that represent the same value.

exponent (or power) [R.1, 1.6] A number that indicates how many times the base is used as a factor.

exponential form [1.6] A shorthand way of representing a repeated multiplication of the same factor.

extraneous solution [7.5, 8.4] A number that we find in solving an equation that is not a solution to the equation.

factored completely [6.2] Expressed as the product of a monomial and one or more prime polynomials.

factoring by grouping [6.1] A method of factoring a polynomial that has four terms by grouping pairs of terms in such a way that a common binomial factor can be found.

factors [R.2] In a multiplication problem, the numbers that are multiplied.

FOIL method [5.5] A method for multiplying two binomials. Multiply First terms, Outside terms, Inside terms, and Last terms, then combine like terms.

formula [1.7] An equation that provides a symbolic description of a real-world situation.

fraction [R.3] A part of a whole or the quotient of two whole numbers.

fraction line (or fraction bar) [R.3] The symbol that separates the numerator from the denominator, and stands for the phrase "out of" or "divided by."

graph [3.3] All points whose coordinates satisfy the given equation.

graphing method [4.1] A method of solving a linear system of equations in which we graph the equations that make up the system. Any point of intersection is a solution to the system.

greatest common factor (GCF) [6.1] The greatest integer that is a factor of each integer.

greatest common factor (GCF) of two or more monomials [6.1] The product of the greatest common factor of the coefficients and the highest powers of the variable factors common to all of the monomials.

improper fraction [R.3] A fraction whose numerator is larger than or equal to its denominator.

inequality [2.6] Any mathematical statement containing the symbol $<$, $\leq$, $>$, $\geq$, or $\neq$.

inequality symbols [1.1] The symbols $\neq$, $<$, $\leq$, $>$, and $\geq$, which are used to compare numbers.

integers [1.1] The numbers ....-4, -3, -2, -1, 0, $+1$, $+2$, $+3$, $+4$, ... continuing indefinitely in both directions.

irrational numbers [1.1] Real numbers that cannot be written as the quotient of two integers.

leading coefficient [5.3] The coefficient of the leading term in a polynomial.

leading term [5.3] The term in a polynomial with the highest degree.

least common denominator (LCD) [R.3] For any set of fractions, the least common multiple of the denominators.

least common multiple (LCM) [R.2] For two or more numbers, the smallest nonzero number that is a multiple of each number.

like fractions [R.3] Fractions which have the same denominator.

like radicals [8.2] Radical expressions that have the same radicand.

like terms [1.8] Terms that have the same variables with the same exponents.

linear equation in one variable [2.1] An equation that can be written in the form $ax + b = c$, where a, b and c are real numbers and $a \neq 0$.

linear equation in two variables [3.3] An equation that can be written in the general form $Ax + By = C$, where A, B and C are constants and A and B are not both 0.

linear inequality in two variables [3.5] An inequality that can be written in the form $Ax + By < C$, where A, B and C are constants and A and B are not both 0. The inequality symbol can be $<$, $>$, $\leq$, or $\geq$.

literal equation [2.4] An equation involving two or more variables.

mixed number [R.3] Consists of a whole number and a proper fraction.

monomial [5.3] An expression that is the product of a real number and variables raised to nonnegative integer powers.

multiples [R.2] For a number, the products of that number and the whole numbers.

multiplication property of equality [2.2] A property which states that if we multiply each side of an equation by any real number, then we get an equivalent equation.

multiplication property of zero [1.4] A property which states that the product of any number and 0 is 0.

multiplicative inverse property [1.5] A property which says that the product of a number and its multiplicative inverse is 1.

natural numbers [1.1] The numbers 1, 2, 3, 4, 5, 6, ….

negative number [1.1] A number to the left of 0 on a number line.

negative slope [3.2] On a graph, the slope of a line that falls to the right.

numerator [R.3] The number above the fraction line in a fraction that tells us how many parts of the whole the fraction contains.

opposites [1.1] Two real numbers that are the same distance from 0 on the number line but on opposite sides of 0.

ordered pair [3.1] A pair of numbers that represents a point in the coordinate plane.

order of operations [R.1] A rule we agree to follow when a mathematical expression involves more than one mathematical operation.

origin [1.1, 3.1] On the number line, the point at 0; in the coordinate plane, the point where the axes intersect, (0, 0).

parabola [9.4] The U-shaped graph of the equation of the form $y = ax^2 + bx + c$ which opens either upward or downward depending on the value of a.

parallel lines [3.2] Two lines whose slopes are equal.

percent [R.5] A ratio or fraction with denominator 100. A number written with the % sign means "divided by 100."

percent decrease [2.5] A percent if the quantity is decreasing.

percent increase [2.5] A percent if the quantity is increasing.

perfect square [8.1] A whole number equal to the square of another whole number.

perfect square trinomial [6.4] A trinomial that can be factored as the square of a binomial.

perpendicular lines [3.2] Two nonvertical lines, the product of whose slopes is -1.

point-slope form [3.4] The form of a linear equation written as $y - y_1 = m(x - x_1)$, where x_1, y_1 and m are constants, m is the slope, and (x_1, y_1) is a point that lies on the graph of the equation.

polynomial [5.3] An algebraic expression with one or more monomials added or subtracted.

positive number [1.1] A number to the right of 0 on a number line.

positive slope [3.2] On a graph, the slope of a line that rises to the right.

prime factorization [R.2] A whole number written as a product of its prime factors.

prime number [R.2] A whole number that has exactly two factors, itself and 1.

prime polynomials [6.2] Polynomials that are not factorable.

principle square root [8.1] The square root of a number that is nonnegative.

proper fraction [R.3] A fraction whose numerator is smaller than its denominator.

proportion [7.6] A statement that two ratios (or rates) are equal.

Pythagorean theorem [6.5] A theorem which states that for every right triangle, the sum of the squares of the legs equals the square of the hypotenuse: $a^2 + b^2 = c^2$.

quadrant [3.1] One of four regions of a coordinate plane separated by axes.

quadratic equation (second-degree equation) [6.5] An equation that can be written in the form $ax^2 + bx + c = 0$, where a, b, and c are real numbers and $a \neq 0$.

quadratic formula [9.3] A formula which states that if $ax^2 + bx + c = 0$, where a, b and c are real numbers and $a \neq 0$, then $x = (-b \pm \sqrt{b^2 - 4ac})/2a$.

radical equation [8.4] An equation in which a variable appears in one or more radicands.

radical expressions [8.1] Algebraic expressions that involve square roots.

radical sign [8.1] The symbol, $\sqrt{}$, that stands for the principle square root of a number.

radicand [8.1] The number under the radical sign.

rate of change [3.2] Slope that indicates how fast the graph of a line is changing and if it increases or decreases.

ratio [7.6] A comparison of two numbers expressed as a quotient.

rational equation (fractional equation) [7.5] An equation that contains one or more rational expressions.

rational expression [7.1] An algebraic expression that can be written as the quotient of two polynomials, P and Q, where $Q \neq 0$.

rational numbers [1.1] Numbers that can be written in the form a/b, where a and b are integers and $b \neq 0$.

rationalize the denominator [8.3] Rewrite an expression in an equivalent form that contains no radical in its denominator.

real numbers [1.1] Numbers that can be represented as points on a number line.

reciprocal [R.3] The fraction found by switching the position of the numerator and the denominator.

reduced to lowest terms [R.3] A fraction for which the only common factor of its numerator and its denominator is 1.

regression line [3.1] A straight line that is closest to passing through the points on a graph.

scientific notation [5.2] A way of writing numbers in the form $a \times 10^n$, where n is an integer and a is greater than or equal to 1 but less than 10.

second-degree equation (quadratic equation) [6.5] An equation that can be written in the form $ax^2 + bx + c = 0$, where a, b, and c are real numbers and $a \neq 0$.

similar triangles [7.6] Triangles that have the same shape but not necessarily the same size.

simplest form [R.3] For a fraction or rational expression, written so that the only common factor of its numerator and its denominator is 1.

slope [3.2] The ratio of the change in y-values to the change in x-values along a line. The slope m of a line passing through the points (x_1, y_1) and (x_2, y_2) is defined to be $m = (y_2 - y_1) / (x_2 - x_1)$ where $x_1 \neq x_2$.

slope-intercept form [3.4] For a linear equation, written in the form $y = mx + b$, where m and b are constants, m is the slope, and $(0, b)$ is the y-intercept of the graph of the equation.

solution of an equation in one variable [2.1] A value of the variable that makes the equation a true statement.

solution of an equation in two variables [3.3] An ordered pair of numbers that when substituted for the variables makes the equation true.

solution of an inequality [2.6] Any value of the variable that makes the inequality true.

solution of a system of equations [4.1] An ordered pair of numbers that satisfies both equations in the system.

solution to an inequality in two variables [3.5] An ordered pair of numbers that when substituted for the variables makes the inequality a true statement.

solve an inequality [2.6] To find all its solutions.

square root [8.1] For a nonnegative real number, a, a number that when squared is a.

square root property of equality [9.1] A property which says that if p is a positive number and $x^2 = p$, then $x = \pm \sqrt{p}$.

substitution method [4.2] A method for solving a system of equations in which one linear equation is solved for one of the variables and then the result is substituted into the other equation.

supply curve [4.1] A curve which illustrates that when the selling price increases, wholesalers are inclined to make more goods available to retailers. It is approximated by a straight line with positive slope.

system of equations [4.1] Two or more equations considered simultaneously.

term [1.6] A number, a variable, or the product or quotient of numbers and variables.

trinomial [5.3] A polynomial with three terms.

unit fraction [7.3] A fraction whose numerator is 1.

unlike fractions [R.3] Fractions which have different denominators.

unlike terms [1.8] Terms that do not have the same variables with the same powers.

vertex [9.4] The highest or lowest point of a parabola.

whole numbers [1.1] The numbers 0, 1, 2, 3, 4, 5, ...

x-axis [3.1] The horizontal number line in the coordinate plane.

x-intercept [3.3] For a line, the point where the graph crosses the x-axis.

y-axis [3.1] The vertical number line in the coordinate plane.

y-intercept [3.3] For a line, the point where the graph crosses the y-axis.

zero-product property [6.5] A property which states that if the product of two factors is 0, then either one or both of the factors must be 0.

Index

Index of Applications

Video Index